GO!

with Microsoft®

Excel 2016
Comprehensive

Shelley Gaskin and Alicia Vargas

Boston   Columbus   Indianapolis   New York   San Francisco
Amsterdam   Cape Town   Dubai   London   Madrid   Milan   Munich   Paris   Montréal   Toronto
Delhi   Mexico City   São Paulo   Sydney   Hong Kong   Seoul   Singapore   Taipei   Tokyo

Vice President, Career Skills: Andrew Gilfillan
Executive Editor: Jenifer Niles
Project Manager: Holly Haydash
Program Manager: Emily Biberger
Team Lead, Project Management: Laura Burgess
Development Editor: Ginny Munroe
Editorial Assistant: Michael Campbell
Director of Product Marketing: Maggie Waples
Director of Field Marketing: Leigh Ann Sims
Product Marketing Manager: Kaylee Carlson
Field Marketing Managers: Molly Schmidt and Joanna Conley
Marketing Coordinator: Susan Osterlitz
Operations Specialist: Maura Zaldivar-Garcia
Senior Art Director: Diane Ernsberger
Interior and Cover Design: Carie Keller/Cenveo
Project Manager, Permissions: Karen Sanatar
Cover Photos: GaudiLab, Rawpixel.com, Pressmaster, Eugenio Marongiu, Boggy, Gajus, Rocketclips, Inc

Senior Art Director: Diane Ernsberger
Associate Director of Design: Blair Brown
Vice President, Product Strategy: Jason Fournier
Director of Media Development: Blaine Christine
Senior Product Strategy Manager: Eric Hakanson
Product Team Lead, IT: Zachary Alexander
Course Producer, IT: Amanda Losonsky
Digital Project Manager, MyITLab: Becca Lowe
Media Project Manager, Production: John Cassar
Full-Service Project Management: Lumina Datamatics, Inc.
Composition: Lumina Datamatics, Inc.
Printer/Binder: LSC Communications/Menasha
Cover Printer: Phoenix Color
Efficacy Curriculum Manager: Jessica Sieminski
Text Font: Times LT Pro

Credits and acknowledgments borrowed from other sources and reproduced, with permission, in this textbook appear on the appropriate page within text. Microsoft and/or its respective suppliers make no representations about the suitability of the information contained in the documents and related graphics published as part of the services for any purpose. All such documents and related graphics are provided "as is" without warranty of any kind.

Microsoft and/or its respective suppliers hereby disclaim all warranties and conditions with regard to this information, including all warranties and conditions of merchantability, whether express, implied or statutory, fitness for a particular purpose, title and non-infringement. In no event shall Microsoft and/or its respective suppliers be liable for any special, indirect or consequential damages or any damages whatsoever resulting from loss of use, data or profits, whether in an action of contract, negligence or other tortious action, arising out of or in connection with the use or performance of information available from the services.

The documents and related graphics contained herein could include technical inaccuracies or typographical errors. Changes are periodically added to the information herein. Microsoft and/or its respective suppliers may make improvements and/or changes in the product(s) and/or the program(s) described herein at any time. Partial screen shots may be viewed in full within the software version specified.

Microsoft® and Windows® are registered trademarks of the Microsoft Corporation in the U.S.A. and other countries. This book is not sponsored or endorsed by or affiliated with the Microsoft Corporation.

Library of Congress Cataloging-in-Publication Data

Library of Congress Control Number: 2016932298

6 18

ISBN 10:   0-13-444392-6

ISBN 13: 978-0-13-444392-8

Brief Contents

Table of Contents

Chapter 8 Using the Data Analysis, Solver, and Scenario Features, and Building Complex Formulas 489

Chapter 9 Using Macros and Visual Basic for Applications 547

About the Authors

Shelley Gaskin, Series Editor, is a professor in the Business and Computer Technology Division at Pasadena City College in Pasadena, California. She holds a bachelor's degree in Business Administration from Robert Morris College (Pennsylvania), a master's degree in Business from Northern Illinois University, and a doctorate in Adult and Community Education from Ball State University (Indiana). Before joining Pasadena City College, she spent 12 years in the computer industry, where she was a systems analyst, sales representative, and director of Customer Education with Unisys Corporation. She also worked for Ernst & Young on the development of large systems applications for their clients. She has written and developed training materials for custom systems applications in both the public and private sector, and has also written and edited numerous computer application textbooks.

This book is dedicated to my students, who inspire me every day.

Alicia Vargas is a faculty member in Business Information Technology at Pasadena City College. She holds a master's and a bachelor's degree in business education from California State University, Los Angeles, and has authored several textbooks and training manuals on Microsoft Word, Microsoft Excel, and Microsoft PowerPoint.

This book is dedicated with all my love to my husband Vic, who makes everything possible; and to my children Victor, Phil, and Emmy, who are an unending source of inspiration and who make everything worthwhile.

GO! with Office 2016

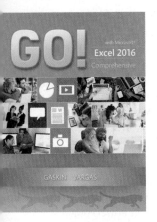

GO! with Office 2016 is the right approach to learning for today's fast-moving, mobile environment. The GO! Series focuses on the job and *success* skills students need to succeed in the workforce. Using job-related projects that put Microsoft Office into context, students learn the *how* and *why* at the moment they need to know, and because the GO! Series uses Microsoft procedural syntax, students never get lost in the instruction. For Office 2016, the hallmark GO! *guided practice-to-skill mastery pathway* is better than ever. Not only do students have multiple opportunities to work live in Microsoft Office to practice and apply the skills they have learned, but also, the *instructional* projects are now Grader projects, so students can work live in Office and receive auto-graded feedback as they learn!

By combining these new instructional Grader projects with the variety of existing Grader projects and the high-fidelity simulations that match the text, students have an effective pathway for learning, practicing, and assessing their abilities. After completing the instructional projects, students are ready to apply the skills with a wide variety of progressively challenging projects that require them to solve problems, think critically, and create projects on their own. The new *GO! with Google* projects also enable students to apply what they have learned in a different environment, and the integrated MOS objectives make this the one resource needed to learn Office, gain critical productivity skills, and prepare to get MOS certified!

What's New

Coverage of new features of Office 2016 ensures that students are learning the skills they need to work in today's job market.

NEW MyITLab 2016 Grader Projects In addition to the homework and assessment Graders already available, the A and B *instructional* projects are now Graders, enabling students to *learn by doing* live in the application *and* receive the instant feedback they need to ensure understanding.

MyITLab HTML 5 Training & Assessment Simulations for Office 2016 These simulations are rewritten by the authors to match the pedagogical approach of the textbook projects and to provide a direct one-to-one learning experience.

NEW Google Projects For each A and B instructional project in Chapters 1–3, students construct a parallel project using Google productivity tools. This gives students the opportunity to think critically and apply what they are learning about Microsoft Office to *other* productivity tools, which is an essential job skill.

NEW MOS Preparation MOS objectives are integrated into the text for easy review and reference for students who are preparing for a MOS certification exam. A MOS appendix is also included to provide a comprehensive list of the exam objectives.

NEW Lessons on the GO! How do you teach software that is constantly updated and getting new features all the time? This new project type will cover newer Microsoft apps such as Sway and MIX and things yet to come! These lessons are found in MyITLab and the Instructor Resource Center, and come with instructional content, student data files, solutions files, and rubrics for grading.

GO! To Work Page Here, students can review a summary of the chapter items focused on employability, including a MOS Objective summary, Build Your ePortfolio guidelines, and the GO! For Job Success soft skills videos or discussions.

Application Capstone Projects [MyITLab grader] Capstone projects for each application provide a variety of opportunities for students to ensure they have reached proficiency.

FOUR Types of Videos Students enjoy video learning, and these videos help students learn and gain skills and insight needed to succeed in the workforce.

- *(NEW) GO! Walk Thru:* Give students a quick 30-second preview of what they will do and create—from beginning to end—by completing each of the A and B Instructional Projects. These videos increase the student's confidence by letting the student see the entire project built quickly.
- *GO! Learn How (formerly Student Training):* Students learn visually by viewing these instructor-led videos that are broken down by Objective for direct guidance. This is the personal instruction students need—especially outside of the classroom—to answer the *How do I?* questions.
- *GO! to Work:* These videos provide short interviews with real business information workers showing how they use Office in the workplace.
- *GO! for Job Success:* These videos or discussions relate to the projects in the chapter and cover important career topics such as *Dressing for Success*, *Time Management*, and *Making Ethical Choices*.

Expanded Project Summary chart This easy-to-use guide outlines all the instructional and end-of-chapter projects by category, including Instruction, Review, Mastery and Transfer of Learning, and Critical Thinking.

In-text boxed content for easy navigation *Another Way*, *Notes*, *More Knowledge*, *Alerts*, and *By Touch* instructions are included in line with the instruction—not in the margins—so students won't miss this important information and will learn it in context with what is on their screen.

MyITLab 2016 for GO!

Let MyITLab do the work by giving students instantaneous feedback and saving hours of grading with GO!'s extensive Grader Project options. And the HTML5 Training and Assessment simulations provide a high-fidelity environment that provide step-by-step summary of student actions and include just-in-time learning aids to assist students: Read, Watch, Practice.

All other end-of-chapter projects, C, D, H, I, J, K, L, M, N, and O, have grading rubrics and solution files for easy hand grading. These are all Content-based, Outcomes-based, Problem-Solving, and Critical Thinking projects that enable you to add a variety of assessments—including authentic assessments—to evaluate a student's proficiency with the application.

IT Innovation Station

Stay current with Office and Windows updates and important Microsoft and office productivity news and trends with help from your Pearson authors! Now that Microsoft Office is in the cloud, automatic updates occur regularly. These can affect how you to teach your course and the resources you are using. To keep you and your students completely up to date on the changes occurring in Office 2016 and Windows 10, we are launching the *IT Innovation Station*. This website will contain monthly updates from our product team and our author-instructors with tips for understanding updates, utilizing new capabilities, implementing new instructional techniques, and optimizing your Office use.

Why the GO! Approach Helps Students Succeed

GO! Provides Personalized Learning

MyITLab from Pearson is an online homework, training, and assessment system that will improve student results by helping students master skills and concepts through immediate feedback and a robust set of tools that allows instructors to easily gauge and address the performance of individuals and classrooms.

MyITLab learning experiences engage students using both realistic, high-fidelity simulations of Microsoft Office as well as auto-graded, live-in-the-application assignments, so they can understand concepts more thoroughly. With the ability to approach projects and problems as they would in real life—coupled with tutorials that adapt based on performance—students quickly complete skills they know and get help when and where they need it.

For educators, MyITLab establishes a reliable learning environment backed by the Pearson Education 24/7, 99.97 percent uptime service level agreement, and that includes the tools educators need to track and support both individual and class-wide student progress.

GO! Engages Students by Combining a Project-Based Approach with the Teachable Moment

GO!'s project-based approach clusters the learning objectives around the projects rather than around the software features. This tested pedagogical approach teaches students to solve real problems as they practice and learn the features.

GO! instruction is organized around student learning outcomes with numbered objectives and two instructional projects per chapter. Students can engage in a wide variety of end-of-chapter projects where they apply what they have learned in outcomes-based, problem-solving, and critical thinking projects—many of which require students to create the project from scratch.

GO! instruction is based on the teachable moment where students learn important concepts at the exact moment they are practicing the skill. The explanations and concepts are woven into the steps—not presented as paragraphs of text at the beginning of the project before students have even seen the software in action.

Each Project Opening Page clearly outlines Project Activities (what the student will do in this project), Project Files (what starting files are needed and how the student will save the files), and Project Results (what the student's finished project will look like). Additionally, to support this page, the GO! Walk Thru video gives students a 30-second overview of how the project will progress and what they will create.

GO! Demonstrates Excellence in Instructional Design

Student Learning Outcomes and Objectives are clearly defined so students understand what they will learn and what they will be able to do when they finish the chapter.

Clear Instruction provided through project steps written following Microsoft® Procedural Syntax to guide students where to go *and then* what to do, so they never get lost!

Teachable moment approach has students learn important concepts when they need to as they work through the instructional projects. No long paragraphs of text.

Clean Design presents textbook pages that are clean and uncluttered, with screenshots that validate the student's actions and that engage visual learners.

Sequential Pagination displays the pages sequentially numbered, like every other textbook a student uses, instead of using letters or abbreviations. Student don't spend time learning a new numbering approach.

Important information is boxed within the text so that students won't miss or skip the Another Way, By Touch, Note, Alert, or More Knowledge details so there are no distracting and "busy-looking" marginal notes.

Color-Coded Steps guide students through the projects with colors coded by project.

End-of-Project Icon helps students know when they have completed the project, which is especially useful in self-paced or online environments. These icons give students a clearly identifiable end point for each project.

GO! Learn How Videos provide step-by-step visual instruction for the A and B instructional projects—delivered by a real instructor! These videos provide the assistance and personal learning students may need when working on their own.

GO! Delivers Easy Course Implementation

The *GO!* series' one-of-a-kind instructional system provides you with everything you need to prepare for class, teach the material, and assess your students.

Prepare

- **Office 2013 to 2016 Transition Guide** provides an easy-to-use reference for updating your course for Office 2016 using GO!
- **Annotated Instructor Tabs** provide clear guidance on how to implement your course.
- **MyITLab Implementation Guide** is provided for course planning and learning outcome alignment.
- **Syllabus templates** outline various plans for covering the content in an 8-, 12-, or 16-week course.
- **List of Chapter Outcomes and Objectives** is provided for course planning and learning outcome alignment.
- **Student Assignment Tracker** for students to track their own work.
- **Assignment Planning Guide** Description of the *GO!* assignments with recommendations based on class size, delivery method, and student needs.
- **Solution Files** Examples of homework submissions to serve as examples for students.
- **Online Study Guide for Students** Interactive objective-style questions based on chapter content.

Teach

- **The Annotated Instructors Edition** includes the entire student text, spiral-bound and wrapped with teaching notes and suggestions for how to implement your course.
- **Scripted Lectures** present a detailed guide for delivering live in-class demonstrations of the A and B Instructional Projects.
- **PowerPoint Presentations** provide a visual walk-through of the chapter with suggested lecture notes included.
- **Audio PowerPoint Presentations** provide a visual walk-through of the chapter with the lecture notes read out loud.
- **Walk Thru Videos** provide a quick 30-second preview of what the student will do and create—from beginning to end—by completing each of the A and B Instructional projects. These videos increase the student's confidence by letting the student see the entire project built quickly.

Assess

- **A scoring checklist, task-specific rubric, or analytic rubric** accompanies every assignment.
- **Prepared Exams** provide cumulative exams for each project, chapter, and application that are easy to score using the provided scoring checklist and point suggestions for each task.
- **Solution Files** are provided in three formats: native file, PDF, and annotated PDF.
- **Rubrics** provide guidelines for grading open-ended projects.
- **Testbank questions** are available for you to create your own objective-based quizzes for review.

Grader Projects

- **Projects A & B** (Guided Instruction)
- **Project E Homework** (Formative) and Assesment (Summative) (Cover Objectives in Project A)
- **Project F Homework** (Formative) and Assesment (Summative) (Cover Objectives in Project B)
- **Project G Homework** (Formative) and Assesment (Summative) (Cover Objectives in Projects A and B)
- **Application Capstone Homework** (Formative review of core objectives covered in application)
- **Application Capstone Exam** (Summative review of core objectives covered in application—generates badge with 90 percent or higher)

GO! Series Hallmarks

Teach the Course You Want in Less Time

A Microsoft® Office textbook designed for student success!

- **Project-Based** – Students learn by creating projects that they will use in the real world.

- **Microsoft Procedural Syntax** – Steps are written to put students in the right place at the right time.

- **Teachable Moment** – Expository text is woven into the steps—at the moment students need to know it—not chunked together in a block of text that will go unread.

- **Sequential Pagination** – Students have actual page numbers instead of confusing letters and abbreviations.

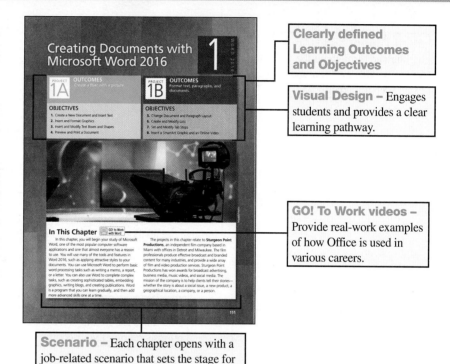

Clearly defined Learning Outcomes and Objectives

Visual Design – Engages students and provides a clear learning pathway.

GO! To Work videos – Provide real-work examples of how Office is used in various careers.

Application Introductions – Provide an overview of the application to prepare students for the upcoming chapters.

Scenario – Each chapter opens with a job-related scenario that sets the stage for the projects the student will create.

Project Activities – A project summary stated clearly and quickly.

Project Files – Clearly shows students which files are needed for the project and the names they will use to save their documents.

Build from Scratch icons – Indicate which projects students build from scratch.

NEW GO! Walk Thru videos – Give students a 30-second overview of what they will create in the project.

Simulation Training and Assessment – Give your students the most realistic Office 2016 experience with realistic, high-fidelity simulations.

NEW MyITLab Grader projects for Instructional A & B projects – Allow students to work live in the application to learn by doing.

Project Results – Shows students what successful completion looks like.

In-text Features

Another Way, Notes, More Knowledge, Alerts, and By Touch Instructions

Color Coding – Each chapter has two instructional projects, which is less overwhelming for students than one large chapter project. The projects are differentiated by different colored numbering and headings.

MOS Objectives – Are highlighted throughout the text to provide a review and exam prep reference.

Microsoft Procedural Syntax – Steps are written to put the student at the right place at the right time.

Teachable Moment – Expository text is woven into the steps—at the moment students need to know it—not chunked together in a block of text that will go unread.

Intext Callouts – Ensure that students will read this important material—Another Way, Notes, More Knowledge, Alerts, and By Touch instructions.

Sequential Pagination – Students are given actual page numbers to navigate through the textbook instead of confusing letters and abbreviations.

End-of-Chapter

MOS Skills Summary – List all the MOS objectives covered in the chapter.

Build Your ePortfolio – Provides guidelines for creating an effective representation of your course work.

GO! For Job Success – Soft skills, videos, and discussions to prepare students with the soft skills needed for today's work environment.

Review and Assessment Chart – Provides an easy-to-use guide to all the instructional and end-of-chapter projects by category from Mastery and Transfer of Knowledge to Critical Thinking.

End-of-Chapter Glossary – Gives students an easy way to review key terms.

End-of-Chapter

Objective List – Every end-of-chapter project includes a listing of covered Objectives from Projects A and B.

Grader Projects – In addition to the two Grader Projects for the instructional portion of the chapter (Projects A and B), each chapter has six MyITLab Grader projects within the end-of-chapter material—three homework and three assessment—clearly indicated by the MyITLab logo.

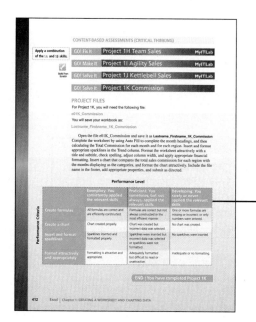

Task-Specific Rubric – A matrix specific to the GO! Solve It projects that states the criteria and standards for grading these defined-solution projects.

End-of-Chapter

Outcomes-Based Assessments – Assessments with open-ended solutions.

Outcomes-Based Assessments –
Assessments with open-ended solutions.

Outcomes Rubric – A standards-based analytic rubric specific to the GO! Think projects that states the criteria and standards for grading these open-ended assessments. For these authentic assessments, an analytic rubric enables the instructor to judge and the student to self assess.

Sample Solution – Outcomes-based assessments include a sample solution so the instructor can compare student work with an example of expert work.

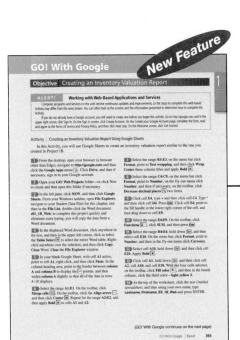

Google Projects for each A & B instructional project in Chapters 1–3 – Provide students the opportunity to think critically and apply what they are learning about Microsoft Office to other productivity tools—an essential job skill.

Student Materials

Student Data Files – All student data files are available in MyITLab for Office 2016 or at www.pearsonhighered.com/go

FOUR Types of Videos help students learn and gain skills and insight needed to succeed in the workforce.

- *(NEW) GO! Walk Thru* is a brief overview of the A & B instructional projects to give students the context of what they will be doing in the projects

- *GO! Learn How (formerly Student Training)* instructor-led videos are broken down by Objective for direct guidance; this personal instruction answers the "how-do-I" questions students ask.

- *GO! to Work* videos provide short interviews with workers showing how they use Office in the workplace.

- *GO! for Job Success* videos or discussions relate to the projects in the chapter and cover important career topics such as *Dressing for Success*, *Time Management*, and *Making Ethical Choices*.

Matching and multiple choice questions provide a variety of review options for content in each chapter.

MOS Objective quiz provides a quick assessment of student understanding of the MOS objectives covered in the chapter. Helpful for courses focused on the pathway to MOS certification.

Available in MyITLab for Office 2016.

GO! with MyITLab
Gives you a completely integrated solution

Instruction ▪ Training ▪ Assessment

All of the content in the book and MyITLab is written by the authors, who are instructors, so the instruction works seamlessly with the simulation trainings and grader projects—true 1:1. eText, Training & Assessment Simulations, and Grader Projects.

Instructor Resources

All Instructor Resources found in MyITLab or at pearsonhighered.com/go

Annotated Instructor Edition – This instructor tool includes a full copy of the student textbook and a guide to implementing your course depending on the emphasis you want to place on digital engagement. Also included are teaching tips, discussion topics, and other useful pieces for teaching each chapter.

Assignment Sheets – Lists all the assignments for the chapter. Just add the course information, due dates, and points. Providing these to students ensures they will know what is due and when.

Scripted Lectures – A script to guide your classroom lecture of each instructional project.

Annotated Solution Files – Coupled with the scorecards, these create a grading and scoring system that makes grading easy and efficient.

PowerPoint Lectures – PowerPoint presentations for each chapter.

Audio PowerPoints – Audio versions of the PowerPoint presentations for each chapter.

Scoring Rubrics – Can be used either by students to check their work or by you as a quick check-off for the items that need to be corrected.

Syllabus Templates – For 8-week, 12-week, and 16-week courses.

Test Bank – Includes a variety of test questions for each chapter.

Instruction

Instruction: General

Syllabi templates demonstrate different approaches for covering the content in an 8-, 12-, or 16-week course.

Application Intro Videos provide a quick overview of what the application is and its primary function.

GO! to Work Videos put each chapter into context as related to how people use productivity software in their daily lives and work.

GO! For Success videos and discussions provide real-life scenarios exploring the essential soft skills needed to succeed in the workplace and professional settings.

Instruction: Hands-On *using one or more of the following:*

- **Interactive eText** allows students to read the narrative and instruction and also link directly to the various types of videos included.
- **(NEW) Walk Thru Videos** provide a quick 30-second overview of what students will do in the A & B instructional projects.
- **Scripted Lectures** are a detailed guide through the A & B projects from the book for you to use for in-class demonstration.
- **GO! Learn How** (previously Student Training) videos are instructor-led videos that provide guided instruction through each Objective and the related Activities.
- **PowerPoint Presentations** provide a visual walk-through of the chapter with suggested lecture notes included.
- **Audio PowerPoint Presentations** provide the visual walk-through of chapters with the lecture notes read aloud.
- **(NEW) A & B Instruction Projects** assigned to students. Students can complete the Instructional Projects 1A and 1B and submit for instructor review or manual grading. They can also submit as a MyITLab Grader project, which allows the students to work live in the application starting with files downloaded from MyITLab and then submitted for automatic grading and feedback.
- **(NEW) MOS Objectives** are covered throughout the chapter and are indicated with the **MOS** icon. Instructors use these to point students to content they would encounter on a MOS exam. If a course is focused on MOS preparation, this content would be emphasized in the instruction.

Practice

MyITLab Skill-based Training Simulation provides students with hands-on practice applying the skills they have learned in a simulated environment where they have access to Learning Aids to assist if needed (READ, WATCH, PRACTICE). All of the student's keystrokes are recorded so that instructors can review and provide support to the students. Instructor can set the number of times the students can complete the simulation.

MyITLab Homework Grader Projects (E, F, or G) provide students with live-in-the-application practice with the skills they learned in Projects A and B. These projects provide students with detailed reports showing them where they made errors and also provide "live comments" explaining the details.

Student Assignment Tracker for students to track their work.

Review

GO! Online activities (multiple choice and matching activities) provide objective-based quizzing to allow students to review how they are doing.

Testbank questions are available for instructors to create their own quizzes for review or assessment.

End-of-chapter online projects H–O provide Content-based, Outcome-based, and Critical Thinking projects that you can assign for additional review, practice, or assessments. These are graded manually by the instructor using the provided Solution Files and Grading Scorecards or Rubrics.

MOS Quizzes provide an objective-based quiz to review the MOS objective-related content covered in the chapter. Provides students with review to help if they plan to take a MOS Certification exam.

Assessment

MyITLab Skill-based Exam Simulation provides students with an assessment of their knowledge and ability to apply the skills they have learned. In the Simulated Exams, students do not have access to the Learning Aids. All of the student's keystrokes are recorded so that instructors can review and provide support to the students. Instructors can set the number of times the students can complete the simulation exam.

MyITLab Assessment Grader Projects (E, F, or G) provide students with live-in-the-application testing of the skills they learned in Projects A and B. These projects provide students with detailed reports showing the student where they made errors and also provides "live comments" explaining the details.

Prepared Exams are additional projects created specifically for use as exams that the instructor will grade manually. They are available by Project, Chapter, and Unit.

Pre-built Chapter quizzes provide objective-based quizzing to allow students to review how they are doing.

Testbank questions are available for instructors to create their own quizzes for review or assessment.

Reviewers Of The GO! Series

Abul Sheikh	Abraham Baldwin Agricultural College	Kenneth A. Hyatt	Lonestar College - Kingwood
John Percy	Atlantic Cape Community College	Glenn Gray	Lonestar College North Harris
Janette Hicks	Binghamton University	Gene Carbonaro	Long Beach City College
Shannon Ogden	Black River Technical College	Betty Pearman	Los Medanos College
Karen May	Blinn College	Diane Kosharek	Madison College
Susan Fry	Boise State University	Peter Meggison	Massasoit Community College
Chigurupati Rani	Borough of Manhattan Community College / CUNY	George Gabb	Miami Dade College
Ellen Glazer	Broward College	Lennie Alice Cooper	Miami Dade College
Kate LeGrand	Broward College	Richard Mabjish	Miami Dade College
Mike Puopolo	Bunker Hill Community College	Victor Giol	Miami Dade College
Nicole Lytle-Kosola	California State University, San Bernardino	John Meir	Midlands Technical College
Nisheeth Agrawal	Calhoun Community College	Greg Pauley	Moberly Area Community College
Pedro Diaz-Gomez	Cameron	Catherine Glod	Mohawk Valley Community College
Linda Friedel	Central Arizona College	Robert Huyck	Mohawk Valley Community College
Gregg Smith	Central Community College	Kevin Engellant	Montana Western
Norm Cregger	Central Michigan University	Philip Lee	Nashville State Community College
Lisa LaCaria	Central Piedmont Community College	Ruth Neal	Navarro College
Steve Siedschlag	Chaffey College	Sharron Jordan	Navarro College
Terri Helfand	Chaffey College	Richard Dale	New Mexico State University
Susan Mills	Chambersburg	Lori Townsend	Niagara County Community College
Mandy Reininger	Chemeketa Community College	Judson Curry	North Park University
Connie Crossley	Cincinnati State Technical and Community College	Mary Zegarski	Northampton Community College
Marjorie Deutsch	City University of New York - Queensborough Community College	Neal Stenlund	Northern Virginia Community Colege
		Michael Goeken	Northwest Vista College
Mary Ann Zlotow	College of Dupage	Mary Beth Tarver	Northwestern State University
Christine Bohnsak	College of Lake County	Amy Rutledge	Oakland University
Gertrude Brier	College of Staten Island	Marcia Braddock	Okefenokee Technical College
Sharon Brown	College of The Albemarle	Richard Stocke	Oklahoma State University - OKC
Terry Rigsby	Columbia College	Jane Stam	Onondaga Community College
Vicki Brooks	Columbia College	Mike Michaelson	Palomar College
Donald Hames	Delgado Community College	Kungwen (Dave) Chu	Purdue University Calumet
Kristen King	Eastern Kentucky University	Wendy Ford	CUNY - Queensborough CC
Kathie Richer	Edmonds Community College	Lewis Hall	Riverside City College
Gary Smith	Elmhurst College	Karen Acree	San Juan College
Wendi Kappersw	Embry-Riddle Aeronautical University	Tim Ellis	Schoolcraft College
Nancy Woolridge	Fullerton College	Dan Combellick	Scottsdale Community College
Abigail Miller	Gateway Community & Technical College	Pat Serrano	Scottsdale Community College
Deep Ramanayake	Gateway Community & Technical College	Rose Hendrickson	Sheridan College
Gwen White	Gateway Community & Technical College	Kit Carson	South Georgia College
Debbie Glinert	Gloria K School	Rebecca Futch	South Georgia State College
Dana Smith	Golf Academy of America	Brad Hagy	Southern Illinois University Carbondale
Mary Locke	Greenville Technical College	Mimi Spain	Southern Maine Community College
Diane Marie Roselli	Harrisburg Area Community College	David Parker	Southern Oregon University
Linda Arnold	Harrisburg Area Community College - Lebanon	Madeline Baugher	Southwestern Oklahoma State University
Daniel Schoedel	Harrisburg Area Community College - York Campus	Brian Holbert	St. Johns River State College
Ken Mayer	Heald College	Bunny Howard	St. Johns River State College
Xiaodong Qiao	Heald College	Stephanie Cook	State College of Florida
Donna Lamprecht	Hopkinsville Community College	Sharon Wavle	Tompkins Cortland Community College
Kristen Lancaster	Hopkinsville Community College	George Fiori	Tri-County Technical College
Johnny Hurley	Iowa Lakes Community College	Steve St. John	Tulsa Community College
Linda Halverson	Iowa Lakes Community College	Karen Thessing	University of Central Arkansas
Sarah Kilgo	Isothermal Community College	Richard McMahon	University of Houston-Downtown
Chris DeGeare	Jefferson College	Shohreh Hashemi	University of Houston-Downtown
David McNair	Jefferson College	Donna Petty	Wallace Community College
Diane Santurri	Johnson & Wales	Julia Bell	Walters State Community College
Roland Sparks	Johnson & Wales University	Ruby Kowaney	West Los Angeles College
Ram Raghuraman	Joliet Junior College	Casey Thompson	Wiregrass Georgia Technical College
Eduardo Suniga	Lansing Community College	DeAnnia Clements	Wiregrass Georgia Technical College

Introduction to Microsoft Office 2016 Features

PROJECT 1A	OUTCOMES
	Create, save, and print a Microsoft Office 2016 document.

PROJECT 1B	OUTCOMES
	Perform commands, apply formatting, and install apps for Office in Microsoft Office 2016

OBJECTIVES

1. Explore Microsoft Office 2016
2. Enter, Edit, and Check the Spelling of Text in an Office 2016 Program
3. Perform Commands from a Dialog Box
4. Create a Folder and Name and Save a File
5. Insert a Footer, Add Document Properties, Print a File, and Close a Desktop App

OBJECTIVES

6. Open an Existing File and Save it with a New Name
7. Sign in to Office and Explore Options for a Microsoft Office Desktop App
8. Perform Commands from the Ribbon and Quick Access Toolbar
9. Apply Formatting in Office Programs and Inspect Documents
10. Compress Files and Get Help with Office
11. Install Apps for Office and Create a Microsoft Account

Imagewell10/Fotolia

In This Chapter   GO! to Work with Office Features

In this chapter, you will practice using features in Microsoft Office 2016 that work similarly across Word, Excel, Access, and PowerPoint. These features include managing files, performing commands, adding document properties, signing in to Office, applying formatting to text, and searching for Office commands quickly. You will also practice installing apps from the Office Store and setting up a free Microsoft account so that you can use OneDrive.

The projects in this chapter relate to **Skyline Metro Grill**, which is a chain of 25 casual, full-service restaurants based in Boston. The Skyline Metro Grill owners are planning an aggressive expansion program. To expand by 15 additional restaurants in Chicago, San Francisco, and Los Angeles by 2020, the company must attract new investors, develop new menus, develop new marketing strategies, and recruit new employees, all while adhering to the company's quality guidelines and maintaining its reputation for excellent service. To succeed, the company plans to build on its past success and maintain its quality elements.

PROJECT
1A

Note Form

MyITLab
Project 1A Grader

PROJECT ACTIVITIES

In Activities 1.01 through 1.08, you will create a note form using Microsoft Word 2016, save it in a folder that you create by using File Explorer, and then print the note form or submit it electronically as directed by your instructor. Your completed note form will look similar to Figure 1.1.

PROJECT FILES

MyITLab grader

If your instructor wants you to submit Project 1A in the MyITLab Grader system, log in to MyITLab, locate Grader Project1A, and then download the files for this project.

For Project 1A, you will need the following file:
New blank Word document

You will save your file as:
Lastname_Firstname_1A_Note_Form

Please always review the downloaded Grader instructions before beginning.

PROJECT RESULTS

Build From Scratch

GO!
Walk Thru
Project 1A

Skyline Metro Grill, Chef's Notes
Executive Chef, Sarah Jackson

Lastname_Firstname_1A_Note_Form

Word 2016, Windows 10, Microsoft Corporation

FIGURE 1.1 Project 1A Note Form

NOTE	If You Are Using a Touchscreen
	Tap an item to click it.
	Press and hold for a few seconds to right-click; release when the information or commands display.
	Touch the screen with two or more fingers and then pinch together to zoom out or stretch your fingers apart to zoom in.
	Slide your finger on the screen to scroll—slide left to scroll right and slide right to scroll left.
	Slide to rearrange—similar to dragging with a mouse.
	Swipe to select—slide an item a short distance with a quick movement—to select an item and bring up commands, if any.

Objective 1 Explore Microsoft Office 2016

NOTE   **Creating a Microsoft Account**

Use a free Microsoft account to sign in to Office 2016 so that you can work on different PCs and use your OneDrive. If you already sign in to a Windows PC, tablet, or phone, or you sign in to Xbox Live, Outlook.com, or OneDrive, use that account to sign in to Office. To create a Microsoft account, you can use *any* email address as the user name for your new Microsoft account—including addresses from Outlook.com, Yahoo! or Gmail.

GO! Learn How
Video OF1.1

The term *desktop application* or *desktop app* refers to a computer program that is installed on your PC and that requires a computer operating system such as Microsoft Windows. The programs in Microsoft Office 2016 are considered to be desktop apps. A desktop app typically has hundreds of features and takes time to learn.

An *app* refers to a self-contained program usually designed for a single purpose and that runs on smartphones and other mobile devices—for example, looking at sports scores or booking a flight on a particular airline. Microsoft's Windows 10 operating system supports both desktop apps that run only on PCs and *Windows apps* that run on all Windows device families—including PCs, Windows phones, Windows tablets, and the Xbox gaming system.

ALERT!   **Is Your Screen More Colorful and a Different Size Than the Figures in This Textbook?**

Your installation of Microsoft Office 2016 may use the default Colorful theme, where the ribbon in each application is a vibrant color and the ribbon tabs display with white text. In this textbook, figures shown use the White theme, but you can be assured that all the commands are the same. You can keep your Colorful theme, or if you prefer, you can change your theme to White to match the figures here. To do so, open any application and display a new document. On the ribbon, click the File tab, and then on the left, click Options. With General selected on the left, under Personalize your copy of Microsoft Office, click the Office Theme arrow, and then click White.

Additionally, the figures in this book were captured using a screen resolution of 1280 x 768. If that is not your screen resolution, your screen will closely resemble, but not match, the figures shown. To view or change your screen's resolution on a Windows 10 PC, on the desktop, right-click in a blank area, click Display settings, and then on the right, click Advanced display settings. On a Windows 7 PC, right-click on the desktop, and then click Screen resolution.

> **ALERT!**   **To submit as an autograded project, log into MyITLab, download the files for this project, and then begin with those files instead of a new blank document.**

1   On the computer you are using, start Microsoft Word 2016, and then compare your screen with Figure 1.2.

Depending on which operating system you are using and how your computer is set up, you might start Word from the taskbar in Windows 7, Windows 8, or Windows 10, or from the Start screen in Windows 8, or from the Start menu in Windows 10. On an Apple Mac computer, the program will display in the dock.

Documents that you have recently opened, if any, display on the left. On the right, you can select either a blank document or a *template*—a preformatted document that you can use as a starting point and then change to suit your needs.

FIGURE 1.2

2   Click **Blank document**. Compare your screen with Figure 1.3, and then take a moment to study the description of these screen elements in the table in Figure 1.4.

> **NOTE**   Displaying the Full Ribbon
>
> If your full ribbon does not display, click any tab, and then at the right end of the ribbon, click ⊞ to pin the ribbon to keep it open while you work.

FIGURE 1.3

SCREEN ELEMENT	DESCRIPTION
File tab	Displays Microsoft Office Backstage view, which is a centralized space for all of your file management tasks such as opening, saving, printing, publishing, or sharing a file—all the things you can do *with* a file.
Group names	Indicate the name of the groups of related commands on the displayed tab.
Quick Access Toolbar	Displays buttons to perform frequently used commands and resources with a single click. The default commands include Save, Undo, and Redo. You can add and delete buttons to customize the Quick Access Toolbar for your convenience.
Ribbon	Displays a group of task-oriented tabs that contain the commands, styles, and resources you need to work in an Office 2016 desktop app. The look of your ribbon depends on your screen resolution. A high resolution will display more individual items and button names on the ribbon.
Ribbon Display Options	Displays three ways you can display the ribbon: Auto-hide Ribbon, Show Tabs, or Show Tabs and Commands.
Ribbon tabs	Display the names of the task-oriented tabs relevant to the open program.
Share button	Opens the Share pane from which you can save your file to the cloud—your OneDrive—and then share it with others so you can collaborate.
Signed-in user	Identifies the signed-in user.
Status bar	Displays file information on the left; on the right displays buttons for Read Mode, Print Layout, and Web Layout views; on the far right displays Zoom controls.
Tell Me box	Provides a search feature for Microsoft Office commands that you activate by typing what you are looking for in the Tell Me box; as you type, every keystroke refines the results so that you can click the command as soon as it displays.
Title bar	Displays the name of the file and the name of the program; the window control buttons are grouped on the right side of the title bar.
Window control buttons	Displays buttons for commands to change the Ribbon Display Options, Minimize, Restore Down, or Close the window.

FIGURE 1.4

GO! Learn How
Video OF1.2

All of the programs in Office 2016 require some typed text. Your keyboard is still the primary method of entering information into your computer. Techniques to enter text and to *edit*—make changes to—text are similar across all of the Office 2016 programs.

1.4.6

Activity 1.02 | Entering and Editing Text in an Office 2016 Program

1 On the ribbon, on the **Home tab**, in the **Paragraph group**, if necessary, click **Show/Hide** ¶ so that it is active—shaded. If necessary, on the **View tab**, in the **Show group**, select the **Ruler** check box so that rulers display below the ribbon and on the left side of your window, and then redisplay the **Home tab**.

The *insertion point*—a blinking vertical line that indicates where text or graphics will be inserted—displays. In Office 2016 programs, the mouse *pointer*—any symbol that displays on your screen in response to moving your mouse device—displays in different shapes depending on the task you are performing and the area of the screen to which you are pointing.

When you press Enter, Spacebar, or Tab on your keyboard, characters display to represent these keystrokes. These screen characters do not print, and are referred to as *formatting marks* or *nonprinting characters*.

> **NOTE** | Activating Show/Hide in Word Documents
>
> When Show/Hide is active—the button is shaded—formatting marks display. Because formatting marks guide your eye in a document—like a map and road signs guide you along a highway—these marks will display throughout this instruction. Many expert Word users keep these marks displayed while creating documents.

2 Type **Skyline Grille Info** and notice how the insertion point moves to the right as you type. Point slightly to the right of the letter *e* in *Grille* and click one time to place the insertion point there. Compare your screen with Figure 1.5.

A *paragraph symbol* (¶) indicates the end of a paragraph and displays each time you press Enter. This is a type of formatting mark and does not print.

Word 2016, Windows 10, Microsoft Corporation

FIGURE 1.5

3 On your keyboard, locate and then press the Backspace key to delete the letter *e*.

Pressing Backspace removes a character to the left of the insertion point.

4 Press → one time to place the insertion point to the left of the *I* in *Info*. Type **Chef's** and then press Spacebar one time.

By *default*, when you type text in an Office program, existing text moves to the right to make space for new typing. Default refers to the current selection or setting that is automatically used by a program unless you specify otherwise.

5 Press [Del] four times to delete *Info* and then type **Notes**

Pressing [Del] removes a character to the right of the insertion point.

6 With your insertion point blinking after the word *Notes*, on your keyboard, hold down the [Ctrl] key. While holding down [Ctrl], press [←] three times to move the insertion point to the beginning of the word *Grill*. Release [Ctrl].

This is a **keyboard shortcut**—a key or combination of keys that performs a task that would otherwise require a mouse. This keyboard shortcut moves the insertion point to the beginning of the previous word.

A keyboard shortcut is indicated as [Ctrl] + [←] (or some other combination of keys) to indicate that you hold down the first key while pressing the second key. A keyboard shortcut can also include three keys, in which case you hold down the first two and then press the third. For example, [Ctrl] + [Shift] + [←] selects one word to the left.

7 With the insertion point blinking at the beginning of the word *Grill*, type **Metro** and press [Spacebar].

8 Press [Ctrl] + [End] to place the insertion point after the letter *s* in *Notes*, and then press [Enter] one time. With the insertion point blinking, type the following and include the spelling error: **Exective Chef, Madison Dunham**

9 With your mouse, point slightly to the left of the *M* in *Madison*, hold down the left mouse button, and then **drag**—hold down the left mouse button while moving your mouse—to the right to select the text *Madison Dunham* but not the paragraph mark following it, and then release the mouse button. Compare your screen with Figure 1.6.

The **mini toolbar** displays commands that are commonly used with the selected object, which places common commands close to your pointer. When you move the pointer away from the mini toolbar, it fades from view.

Selecting refers to highlighting—by dragging or clicking with your mouse—areas of text or data or graphics so that the selection can be edited, formatted, copied, or moved. The action of dragging includes releasing the left mouse button at the end of the area you want to select.

The Office programs recognize a selected area as one unit to which you can make changes. Selecting text may require some practice. If you are not satisfied with your result, click anywhere outside of the selection, and then begin again.

BY TOUCH   Double-tap on *Madison* to display the gripper—a small circle that acts as a handle—directly below the word. This establishes the start gripper. If necessary, with your finger, drag the gripper to the beginning of the word. Then drag the gripper to the end of *Dunham* to select the text and display the end gripper.

FIGURE 1.6

10 With the text *Madison Dunham* selected, type **Sarah Jackson**

In any Windows-based program, such as the Microsoft Office 2016 programs, selected text is deleted and then replaced when you begin to type new text. You will save time by developing good techniques for selecting and then editing or replacing selected text, which is easier than pressing the Del key numerous times to delete text.

Activity 1.03 | Checking Spelling

Office 2016 has a dictionary of words against which all entered text is checked. In Word and PowerPoint, words that are not in the dictionary display a wavy red line, indicating a possible misspelled word, a proper name, or an unusual word—none of which are in the Office 2016 dictionary.

In Excel and Access, you can initiate a check of the spelling, but red underlines do not display.

1 Notice that the misspelled word *Exective* displays with a wavy red underline.

2 Point to *Exective* and then **right-click**—click your right mouse button one time.

A ***shortcut menu*** displays, which displays commands and options relevant to the selected text or object. These are ***context-sensitive commands*** because they relate to the item you right-clicked. These shortcut menus are also referred to as ***context menus***. Here, the shortcut menu displays commands related to the misspelled word.

↻ BY TOUCH Tap and hold a moment—when a square displays around the misspelled word, release your finger to display the shortcut menu.

3 Press Esc to cancel the shortcut menu, and then in the lower left corner of your screen, on the status bar, click the ***Proofing*** icon [img], which displays an *X* because some errors are detected. Compare your screen with Figure 1.7.

The Spelling pane displays on the right. Here you have many more options for checking spelling than you have on the shortcut menu. The suggested correct word, *Executive*, is highlighted.

You can click the speaker icon to hear the pronunciation of the selected word. If you have not already installed a dictionary, you can click *Get a Dictionary*—if you are signed in to Office with a Microsoft account—to find and install one from the online Office store; or if you have a dictionary app installed, it will display here and you can search it for more information.

In the Spelling pane, you can ignore the word one time or in all occurrences, change the word to the suggested word, select a different suggestion, or add a word to the dictionary against which Word checks.

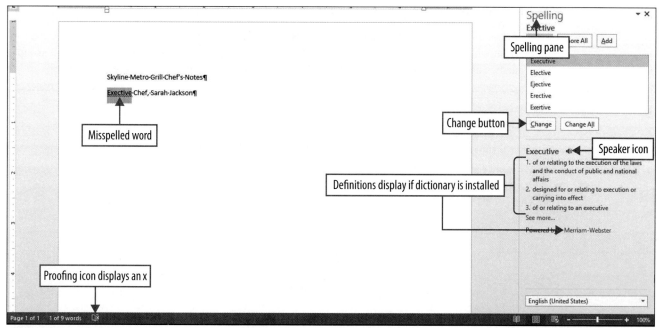

Misspelled word

Spelling pane

Change button

Speaker icon

Definitions display if dictionary is installed

Proofing icon displays an x

FIGURE 1.7

Word 2016, Windows 10, Microsoft Corporation

ANOTHER WAY   Press F7 to display the Spelling pane; or, on the Review tab, in the Proofing group, click Spelling & Grammar.

> 4 In the *Spelling* pane, click **Change** to change the spelling to *Executive*. In the message box that displays, click **OK**.

Objective 3 Perform Commands from a Dialog Box

GO! Learn How
Video OF1.3

In a dialog box, you make decisions about an individual object or topic. In some dialog boxes, you can make multiple decisions in one place.

Activity 1.04 | Performing Commands from a Dialog Box

MOS

1.3.6

> 1 On the ribbon, click the **Design tab**, and then in the **Page Background group**, click **Page Color**.

> 2 At the bottom of the menu, notice the command *Fill Effects* followed by an **ellipsis** (...). Compare your screen with Figure 1.8.

An *ellipsis* is a set of three dots indicating incompleteness. An ellipsis following a command name indicates that a dialog box will display when you click the command.

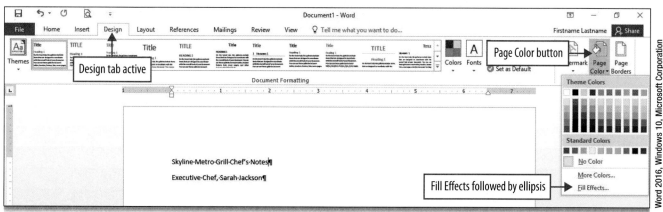

Design tab active

Page Color button

Fill Effects followed by ellipsis

FIGURE 1.08

Word 2016, Windows 10, Microsoft Corporation

3 Click **Fill Effects** to display the **Fill Effects** dialog box. Compare your screen with Figure 1.9.

Fill is the inside color of a page or object. Here, the dialog box displays a set of tabs across the top from which you can display different sets of options. Some dialog boxes display the option group names on the left. The Gradient tab is active. In a *gradient fill*, one color fades into another.

FIGURE 1.9

4 Under **Colors**, click the **One color** option button.

The dialog box displays settings related to the One color option. An *option button* is a round button that enables you to make one choice among two or more options.

5 Click the **Color 5 arrow**—the arrow under the text *Color 5*—and then in the third column, point to the second color to display the ScreenTip *Light Gray-25%, Background 2, Darker 10%*.

When you click an arrow in a dialog box, additional options display. A *ScreenTip* displays useful information about mouse actions, such as pointing to screen elements or dragging.

6 Click **Gray-25%, Background 2, Darker 10%**, and then notice that the fill color displays in the **Color 1** box. In the **Dark Light** bar, click the **Light arrow** as many times as necessary until the scroll box is all the way to the right. Under **Shading styles**, click the **Diagonal down** option button. Under **Variants**, click the **upper right variant**. Compare your screen with Figure 1.10.

This dialog box is a good example of the many different elements you may encounter in a dialog box. Here you have option buttons, an arrow that displays a menu, a slider bar, and graphic options that you can select.

⟳ BY TOUCH
In a dialog box, you can tap option buttons and other commands just as you would click them with a mouse. When you tap an arrow to display a color palette, a larger palette displays than if you used your mouse. This makes it easier to select colors in a dialog box.

FIGURE 1.10

7 At the bottom of the dialog box, click **OK**, and notice the subtle page color.

> In Word, the gray shading page color will not print—even on a color printer—unless you set specific options to do so. However, a subtle background page color is effective if people will be reading the document on a screen. Microsoft's research indicates that two-thirds of people who open Word documents on a screen never print them; they only read them.

MOS

2.2.6

Activity 1.05 │ Using Undo and Applying a Built-In Style to Text

1 Point to the *S* in *Skyline*, and then drag down and to the right to select both paragraphs of text and include the paragraph marks. On the mini toolbar, click **Styles**, and then *point to* but do not click **Title**. Compare your screen with Figure 1.11.

> A *style* is a group of *formatting* commands, such as font, font size, font color, paragraph alignment, and line spacing that can be applied to a paragraph with one command. Formatting is the process of establishing the overall appearance of text, graphics, and pages in an Office file— for example, in a Word document.

> *Live Preview* is a technology that shows the result of applying an editing or formatting change as you point to possible results—before you actually apply it.

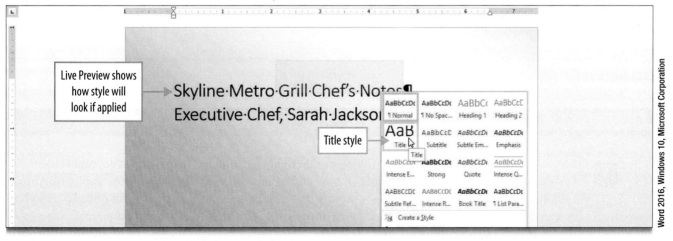

FIGURE 1.11

2 In the **Styles** gallery, click **Title**.

> A *gallery* is an Office feature that displays a list of potential results.

3 On the ribbon, on the **Home tab**, in the **Paragraph group**, click **Center** ☰ to center the two paragraphs.

Alignment refers to the placement of paragraph text relative to the left and right margins. *Center alignment* refers to text that is centered horizontally between the left and right margins. You can also align text at the left margin, which is the default alignment for text in Word, or at the right.

↻ ANOTHER WAY   Press Ctrl + E as the keyboard shortcut for the Center command.

4 With the two paragraphs still selected, on the **Home tab**, in the **Font group**, click **Text Effects and Typography** Ⓐ ▾ to display a gallery.

5 In the second row, click the first effect—**Gradient Fill – Gray**. Click anywhere to *deselect*—cancel the selection—the text and notice the text effect.

6 Because this effect might be difficult to read, in the upper left corner of your screen, on the *Quick Access Toolbar*, click **Undo** ↺.

The *Undo* command reverses your last action.

↻ ANOTHER WAY   Press Ctrl + Z as the keyboard shortcut for the Undo command.

7 With all of the text still selected, display the **Text Effects and Typography** Ⓐ ▾ gallery again, and then in the second row, click the second effect—**Gradient Fill – Blue, Accent 1, Reflection**. Click anywhere to deselect the text and notice the text effect. Compare your screen with Figure 1.12.

As you progress in your study of Microsoft Office, you will practice using many dialog boxes and commands to apply interesting effects such as this to your Word documents, Excel worksheets, Access database objects, and PowerPoint slides.

FIGURE 1.12

Objective 4   Create a Folder and Name and Save a File

GO! Learn How
Video OF1.5

A *location* is any disk drive, folder, or other place in which you can store files and folders. Where you store your files depends on how and where you use your data. For example, for your college classes, you might decide to store your work on a removable USB flash drive so that you can carry your files to different locations and access your files on different computers.

If you do most of your work on a single computer, for example, your home desktop system or your laptop computer that you take with you to school or work, then you can store your files in one of the folders—Documents, Music, Pictures, or Videos—on your hard drive provided by your Windows operating system.

The best place to store files if you want them to be available anytime, anywhere, from almost any device is on your **OneDrive**, which is Microsoft's free **cloud storage** for anyone with a free Microsoft account. Cloud storage refers to online storage of data so that you can access your data from different places and devices. **Cloud computing** refers to applications and services that are accessed over the Internet, rather than accessing applications installed on your local computer.

If you have an **Office 365** account—one of the versions of Microsoft Office to which you subscribe for an annual fee—your storage capacity on OneDrive is a terabyte or more, which is more than most individuals would ever require.

Because many people now have multiple computing devices—desktop, laptop, tablet, smartphone—it is common to store data *in the cloud* so that it is always available. **Synchronization**, also called **syncing**—pronounced SINK-ing—is the process of updating computer files that are in two or more locations according to specific rules. So if you create and save a Word document on your OneDrive using your laptop, you can open and edit that document on your tablet in OneDrive. When you close the document again, the file is properly updated to reflect your changes. Your OneDrive account will guide you in setting options for syncing files to your specifications.

You need not be connected to the Internet to access documents stored on OneDrive because an up-to-date version of your content is synched to your local system and available on OneDrive. You must, however, be connected to the Internet for the syncing to occur. Saving to OneDrive will keep the local copy on your computer and the copy in the cloud synchronized for as long as you need it. You can open and edit Office files by using Office apps available on a variety of device platforms, including iOS, Android, and Windows.

The Windows operating system helps you to create and maintain a logical folder structure, so always take the time to name your files and folders consistently.

Activity 1.06 | Creating a Folder and Naming and Saving a File

A Word document is an example of a file. In this Activity, you will create a folder in the storage location you have chosen to use for your files and then save your file. This example will use the Documents folder on the PC at which you are working. If you prefer to store on your OneDrive or on a USB flash drive, you can use similar steps.

1 Decide where you are going to store your files for this Project.

As the first step in saving a file, determine where you want to save the file, and if necessary, insert a storage device.

2 At the top of your screen, in the title bar, notice that *Document1 – Word* displays.

The Blank option on the opening screen of an Office 2016 program displays a new unsaved file with a default name— *Document1, Presentation1*, and so on. As you create your file, your work is temporarily stored in the computer's memory until you initiate a Save command, at which time you must choose a file name and a location in which to save your file.

3 In the upper left corner of your screen, click the **File tab** to display **Backstage** view. Compare your screen with Figure 1.13.

Backstage view is a centralized space that groups commands related to *file* management; that is why the tab is labeled *File*. File management commands include opening, saving, printing, publishing, or sharing a file. The *Backstage tabs*—Info, New, Open, Save, Save As, Print, Share, Export, and Close—display along the left side. The tabs group file-related tasks together.

Here, the *Info tab* displays information—*info*—about the current file, and file management commands display under Info. For example, if you click the Protect Document button, a list of options that you can set for this file that relate to who can open or edit the document displays.

On the right, you can also examine the *document properties*. Document properties, also known as *metadata*, are details about a file that describe or identify it, such as the title, author name, subject, and keywords that identify the document's topic or contents. To close Backstage view and return to the document, you can click ⊙ in the upper left corner or press Esc.

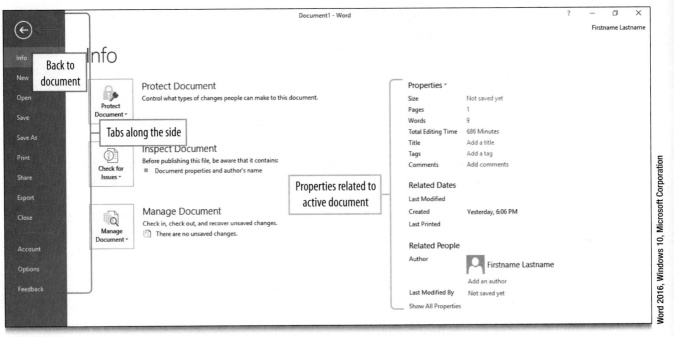

FIGURE 1.13

> **4** On the left, click **Save As**, and notice that the default location for storing Office files is your **OneDrive**—if you are signed in. Compare your screen with Figure 1.14.
>
> When you are saving something for the first time, for example, a new Word document, the Save and Save As commands are identical. That is, the Save As commands will display if you click Save or if you click Save As.

FIGURE 1.14

NOTE   Saving After Your File Is Named

After you name and save a file, the Save command on the Quick Access Toolbar saves any changes you make to the file without displaying Backstage view. The Save As command enables you to name and save a *new* file based on the current one—in a location that you choose. After you name and save the new document, the original document closes, and the new document—based on the original one—displays.

5 To store your Word file in the **Documents** folder on your PC, click **Browse** to display the **Save As** dialog box. On the left, in the **navigation pane**, scroll down; if necessary click > to expand This PC, and then click **Documents**, or navigate to your USB flash drive or other location. In a college lab, your work may be lost if you store in the Documents folder. Compare your screen with Figure 1.15.

In the Save As dialog box, you must indicate the name you want for the file and the location where you want to save the file. When working with your own data, it is good practice to pause at this point and determine the logical name and location for your file.

In the Save As dialog box, a *toolbar* displays, which is a row, column, or block of buttons or icons, that displays across the top of a window and that contains commands for tasks you perform with a single click.

FIGURE 1.15

6 On the toolbar, click **New folder**.

In the file list, Windows creates a new folder, and the text *New folder* is selected.

7 Type **Office Features Chapter 1** and press Enter. Compare your screen with Figure 1.16.

In Windows-based programs, the Enter key confirms an action.

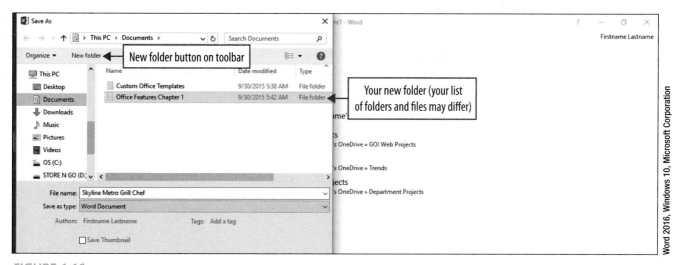

FIGURE 1.16

> **8** In the **file list**, double-click the name of your new folder to open it and display its name in the **address bar**.

> **9** In the lower portion of the dialog box, click in the **File name** box to select the existing text. Notice that as the suggested file name, Office inserts the text at the beginning of the document.

> **10** On your keyboard, locate the [-] key, to the right of zero on the number row. Notice that the [Shift] of this key produces the underscore character. With the text still selected and using your own name, type **Lastname_Firstname_1A_Note_Form** Compare your screen with Figure 1.17.

> You can use spaces in file names, however, some people prefer not to use spaces. Some programs, especially when transferring files over the Internet, may insert the extra characters %20 in place of a space. In general, however, unless you encounter a problem, it is OK to use spaces. In this instruction, underscores are used instead of spaces in file names.

FIGURE 1.17

> **11** In the lower right corner, click **Save** or press [Enter]. Compare your screen with Figure 1.18.

> The Word window redisplays and your new file name displays in the title bar, indicating that the file has been saved to the location that you have specified.

FIGURE 1.18

> **12** In the first paragraph, click to place the insertion point after the word *Grill* and type **,** (a comma). In the upper left corner of your screen, on the **Quick Access Toolbar**, click **Save** 🖫.

> After a document is named and saved in a location, you can save any changes you have made since the last Save operation by using the Save command on the Quick Access Toolbar. When working on a document, it is good practice to save your changes from time to time.

Objective 5 Insert a Footer, Add Document Properties, Print a File, and Close a Desktop App

GO! Learn How
Video OF1.5

MOS
1.3.4, 1.4.5

For most of your files, especially in a workplace setting, it is useful to add identifying information to help in finding files later. You might also want to print your file on paper or create an electronic printout. The process of printing a file is similar in all of the Office applications.

Activity 1.07 | Inserting a Footer, Inserting Document Info, and Adding Document Properties

> **NOTE** What Does Your Instructor Require for Submission? A Paper Printout, an Image That Looks Like a Printed Document, or Your Word File?
>
> In this Activity, you can produce a paper printout or an electronic image of your document that looks like a printed document. Or, your instructor may want only your completed Word file.

1 On the ribbon, click the **Insert tab**, and then in the **Header & Footer group**, click **Footer**.

2 At the bottom of the list, click **Edit Footer**. On the ribbon, notice that the **Header & Footer Tools** display.

The *Header & Footer Tools Design* tab displays on the ribbon. The ribbon adapts to your work and will display additional tabs like this one—referred to as **contextual tabs**—when you need them.

A **footer** is a reserved area for text or graphics that displays at the bottom of each page in a document. Likewise, a **header** is a reserved area for text or graphics that displays at the top of each page in a document. When the footer (or header) area is active, the document area is dimmed, indicating it is unavailable.

3 On the ribbon, under **Header & Footer Tools**, on the **Design tab**, in the **Insert group**, click **Document Info**, and then click **File Name** to insert the name of your file in the footer, which is a common business practice. Compare your screen with Figure 1.19.

Ribbon commands that display ▼ will, when clicked, display a list of options for the command.

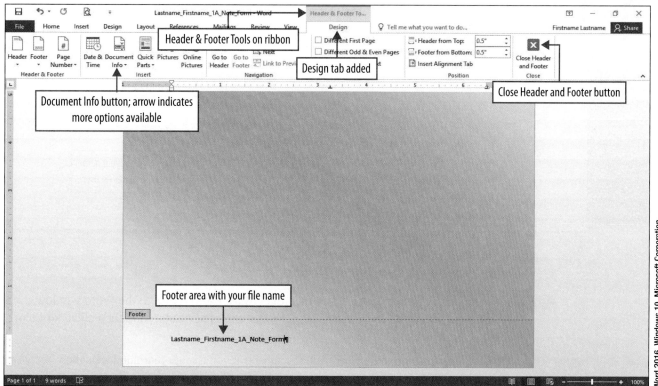

FIGURE 1.19

Word 2016, Windows 10, Microsoft Corporation

> **4** At the right end of the ribbon, click **Close Header and Footer**.

ANOTHER WAY   Double-click anywhere in the dimmed document to close the footer.

> **5** Click the **File tab** to display **Backstage** view. On the right, at the bottom of the **Properties** list, click **Show All Properties**.

ANOTHER WAY   Click the arrow to the right of Properties, and then click Advanced Properties to show and edit properties at the top of your document window.

> **6** On the list of **Properties**, click to the right of *Tags* to display an empty box, and then type **chef, notes, form**
>
> *Tags*, also referred to as ***keywords***, are custom file properties in the form of words that you associate with a document to give an indication of the document's content. Adding tags to your documents makes it easier to search for and locate files in File Explorer, on your OneDrive, and in systems such as Microsoft ***SharePoint*** document libraries. SharePoint is collaboration software with which people in an organization can set up team sites to share information, manage documents, and publish reports for others to see.

BY TOUCH   Tap to the right of Tags to display the Tags box and the onscreen keyboard.

> **7** Click to the right of *Subject* to display an empty box, and then type your course name and section #; for example, *CIS 10, #5543*.

> **8** Under **Related People**, be sure that your name displays as the author. If necessary, right-click the author name, click Edit Property, type your name, click outside of the Edit person dialog box, and then click OK. Compare your screen with Figure 1.20.

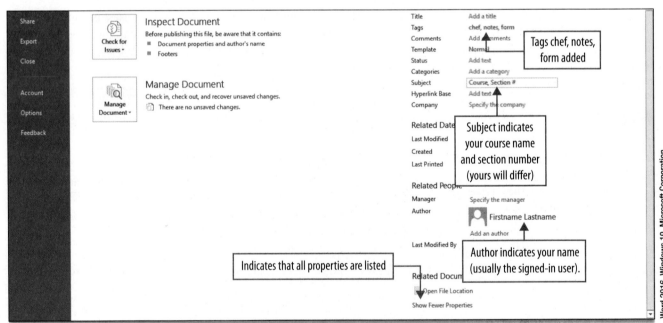

FIGURE 1.20

Activity 1.08 | Printing a File and Closing a Desktop App

> **1** In **Backstage** view, in the upper left corner, click **Back** ⬅ to return to the Word window. On the **Design tab**, in the **Page Background group**, click **Page Color**, and then click **No Color** to remove the fill effects.
>
> It's easy to remove formatting from your documents if you change your mind about how you want your document to look.

2 Click the **File tab** to return to **Backstage** view, on the left click **Print**, and then compare your screen with Figure 1.21.

Here you can select any printer connected to your system and adjust the settings related to how you want to print. On the right, the *Print Preview* displays, which is a view of a document as it will appear on paper when you print it.

At the bottom of the Print Preview area, in the center, the number of pages and page navigation arrows with which you can move among the pages in Print Preview display. On the right, the Zoom slider enables you to shrink or enlarge the Print Preview. *Zoom* is the action of increasing or decreasing the viewing area of the screen.

 ANOTHER WAY   From the document screen, press Ctrl + P or Ctrl + F2 to display Print in Backstage view.

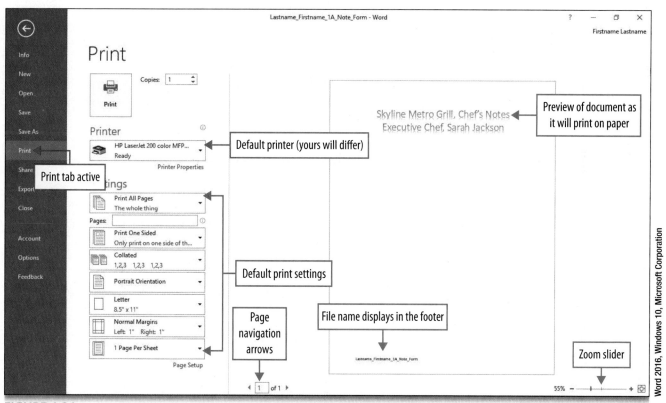

FIGURE 1.21

3 To create an electronic image of your document that looks like a printed document, skip this step and continue to Step 4. To print your document on paper using the default printer on your system, in the upper left portion of the screen, click **Print**.

The document will print on your default printer; if you do not have a color printer, the blue text will print in shades of gray. Backstage view closes and your file redisplays in the Word window.

4 To create an electronic image of your document that looks like a printed document, in **Backstage** view, on the left click **Export**. On the right, click the **Create PDF/XPS** button to display the **Publish as PDF or XPS** dialog box.

PDF stands for *Portable Document Format*, which is a technology that creates an image that preserves the look of your file. This is a popular format for sending documents electronically, because the document will display on most computers.

XPS stands for *XML Paper Specification*—a Microsoft file format that also creates an image of your document and that opens in the XPS viewer.

> **5** On the left in the **navigation pane**, if necessary expand > This PC, and then navigate to your **Office Features Chapter 1** folder in your **Documents** folder—or in whatever location you have created your Office Features Chapter 1 folder. Compare your screen with Figure 1.22.

Publish as PDF or XPS dialog box

Path to your Office Features Chapter 1 folder

Save as type indicates PDF

Word 2016, Windows 10, Microsoft Corporation

FIGURE 1.22

> **6** In the lower right corner of the dialog box, click **Publish**; if a program installed on your computer displays your PDF, in the upper right corner, click Close ☒. If your PDF displays in Microsoft Edge (on a Windows 10 computer), in the upper right corner click Close ☒. Notice that your document redisplays in Word.

⟳ ANOTHER WAY In Backstage view, click Save As, navigate to the location of your Chapter folder, click the Save as type arrow, on the list click PDF, and then click Save.

> **7** Click the **File tab** to redisplay **Backstage** view. On the left, click **Close**, click **Save** to save the changes you have made, and then compare your screen with Figure 1.23.

Word window with all documents closed

Close button

Word 2016, Windows 10, Microsoft Corporation

FIGURE 1.23

> **8** In the upper right corner of the Word window, click **Close** ☒. If directed by your instructor to do so, submit your paper printout, your electronic image of your document that looks like a printed document, or your original Word file.

END | You have completed Project 1A

PROJECT ACTIVITIES

In Activities 1.09 through 1.24, you will open, edit, and then compress a Word file. You will also use the Tell Me help feature and install an app for Office. Your completed document will look similar to Figure 1.24.

PROJECT FILES

If your instructor wants you to submit Project 1B in the MyITLab Grader system, log in to MyITLab, locate Grader Project1B, and then download the files for this project.

For Project 1B, you will need the following file:
of01B_Rehearsal_Dinner

You will save your file as:
Lastname_Firstname_1B_Rehearsal_Dinner

PROJECT RESULTS

Please always review the downloaded Grader instructions before beginning.

Skyline Metro Grill

TO: Sarah Jackson, Executive Chef

FROM: Laura Mabry Hernandez, General Manager

DATE: February 17, 2019

SUBJECT: Wedding Rehearsal Dinners

In the spring and summer months, wedding rehearsal dinners provide a new marketing opportunity for Skyline Metro Grill at all of our locations. A rehearsal dinner is an informal meal following a wedding rehearsal at which the bride and groom typically thank those that have helped them make their wedding a special event.

Our smaller private dining rooms with sweeping city views are an ideal location for a rehearsal dinner. At each of our locations, I have directed the Sales and Marketing Coordinator to partner with local wedding planners to promote Skyline Metro Grill as a relaxed yet sophisticated venue for rehearsal dinners. The typical rehearsal dinner includes the wedding party, the immediate family of the bride and groom, and out-of-town guests.

Please develop six menus—in varying price ranges—to present to local wedding planners so that they can easily promote Skyline Metro Grill to couples who are planning a rehearsal dinner. In addition to a traditional dinner, we should also include options for a buffet-style dinner and a family-style dinner.

This marketing effort will require extensive communication with our Sales and Marketing Coordinators and with local wedding planners. Let's meet to discuss the details and the marketing challenges, and to create a promotional piece that begins something like this:

Skyline Metro Grill for Your Rehearsal Dinner

Lastname_Firstname_1B_Rehearsal_Dinner

Word 2016, Windows 10, Microsoft Corporation

FIGURE 1.24 Project 1B Memo

Objective 6 Open an Existing File and Save It with a New Name

GO! Learn How
Video OF1.6

In any Office program, you can display the ***Open dialog box***, from which you can navigate to and then open an existing file that was created in that same program.

The Open dialog box, along with the Save and Save As dialog boxes, is a common dialog box. These dialog boxes, which are provided by the Windows programming interface, display in all Office programs in the same manner. So the Open, Save, and Save As dialog boxes will all look and perform the same regardless of the Office program in which you are working.

ALERT! **To Complete This Project, You Will Need the Student Data Files That Accompany This Chapter**

To complete this project, you will need the Student Data Files that accompany this chapter. Possibly your instructor has provided these to you already; for example, in the learning management system used by your college. Alternatively, to download the files, go to **www.pearsonhighered.com/go** On the left, narrow your choice by selecting the appropriate topic, and then on the right, locate and click the image of this book. In the window that displays, click Download Data Files, and then click the chapter name. Using the commands for your browser, store the zipped file in your storage location, and then use the Extract tools in File Explorer to extract the zipped folder. Instructions for extracting can be found in the Getting Started with Windows 10 chapter.

Activity 1.09 | Opening an Existing File and Saving It with a New Name

In this Activity, you will display the Open dialog box, open an existing Word document, and then save it in your storage location with a new name.

ALERT! **To submit as an autograded project, log into MyITLab, download the files for this project, and begin with those files instead of the student data file.**

---

1 Be sure you have saved the folder **of01_student_data_files** for this chapter in your storage location; you can download this folder from **www.pearsonhighered.com/go** or it may have been provided to you by your instructor.

2 Start Word, and then on Word's opening screen, on the left, click **Open Other Documents**. Under **Open**, click **Browse**.

3 In the **Open** dialog box, on the left in the **navigation pane**, navigate to the location where you stored the **of01_student_data_files** folder for this chapter, and then in the **file list**, double-click the folder name **of01_student_data_files** to open the folder.

4 In the **file list**, double-click the file **of01B_Rehearsal_Dinner** to open it in Word. If **PROTECTED VIEW** displays at the top of your screen, in the center click **Enable Editing**.

In Office 2016, a file will open in ***Protected View*** if the file appears to be from a potentially risky location, such as the Internet. Protected View is a security feature in Office 2016 that protects your computer from malicious files by opening them in a restricted environment until you enable them. ***Trusted Documents*** is another security feature that remembers which files you have already enabled.

You might encounter these security features if you open a file from an email or download files from the Internet; for example, from your college's learning management system or from the Pearson website. So long as you trust the source of the file, click Enable Editing or Enable Content—depending on the type of file you receive—and then go ahead and work with the file.

5 With the document displayed in the Word window, be sure that **Show/Hide** is active; if necessary, on the Home tab, in the Paragraph group, click Show/Hide to activate it; on the View tab, be sure that Rulers are active. Compare your screen with Figure 1.25.

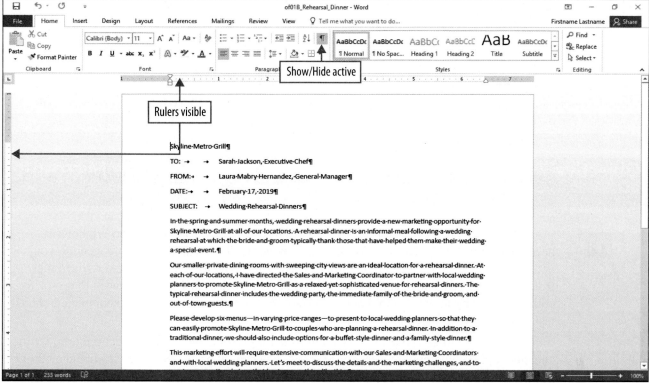

FIGURE 1.25

Word 2016, Windows 10, Microsoft Corporation

6 ▶ Click the **File tab** to display **Backstage** view, and then on the left, click **Save As**. Under **Save As**, click **Browse**.

7 ▶ In the **Save As** dialog box, use the **navigation pane** to navigate to and open the **Office Features Chapter 1** folder that you created to store your work from this chapter.

In Backstage view, on the right, you might also see your Office Features Chapter 1 folder listed, and if so, you can open it directly from there. The common dialog boxes Open, Save, and Save As remember your recently used locations and display them in Backstage view.

🔄 ANOTHER WAY From the Word window, press F12 to display the Save As dialog box.

8 ▶ Click in the **File name** box to select the existing text, and then, using your own name, type **Lastname_Firstname_1B_Rehearsal_Dinner** Compare your screen with Figure 1.26.

FIGURE 1.26

Word 2016, Windows 10, Microsoft Corporation

9 ▸ Click **Save** or press Enter; notice that your new file name displays in the title bar.

The original document closes, and your new document, based on the original, displays with the new name in the title bar.

Objective 7   Sign In to Office and Explore Options for a Microsoft Office Desktop App

GO! Learn How
Video OF1.7

If you sign in to a computer using Windows 8 or Windows 10—there is no Windows 9, because Microsoft skipped from Windows 8 to Windows 10—with a Microsoft account, you may notice that you are also signed in to Office. This enables you to save files to and retrieve files from your OneDrive and to *collaborate* with others on Office files when you want to do so. To collaborate means to work with others as a team in an intellectual endeavor to complete a shared task or to achieve a shared goal.

Within each Office application, an *Options dialog box* enables you to select program settings and other options and preferences. For example, you can set preferences for viewing and editing files.

Activity 1.10 | Signing In to Office and Viewing Application Options

1 ▸ In the upper right corner of your screen, if you are signed in with a Microsoft account, click your name, and then compare your screen with Figure 1.27.

Here you can change your photo, go to About me to edit your profile, examine your Account settings, or switch accounts to sign in with a different Microsoft account.

ALERT!   **Not Signed In to Office or Have Not Yet Created a Microsoft Account?**

In the upper right corner, click Sign in, and then enter your Microsoft account. If you have not created a free Microsoft account, click Sign in, type any email address that you currently use, click Next, and then click Sign up now. If you are working in a college lab, this process may vary.

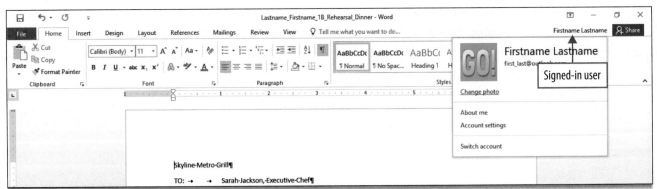

FIGURE 1.27

2 ▸ Click the **File tab** to display **Backstage** view. On the left, click **Options**.

3 In the **Word Options** dialog box, on the left, click **Display**, and then on the right, locate the information under **Always show these formatting marks on the screen**.

The Word Options dialog box—or the similar Options dialog box in any of the Office applications—controls nearly every aspect of the application. Next to many of the items, you will see small *i* icons, which when you point to them display a ScreenTip.

If you click each of the categories on the left side of the dialog box, you will see that the scope of each application is quite large and that you have a great deal of control over how the application behaves. For example, you can customize the tab names and group names in the ribbon.

If you are not sure what a setting or option does, in the upper right corner of the title bar, click the Help button—the question mark icon.

4 Under **Always show these formatting marks on the screen**, be sure the last check box, **Show all formatting marks**, is selected—select it if necessary. Compare your screen with Figure 1.28.

FIGURE 1.28

5 In the lower right corner of the dialog box, click **OK**.

Objective 8 — Perform Commands from the Ribbon and Quick Access Toolbar

GO! Learn How
Video OF1.8

The ribbon that displays across the top of the program window groups commands in the way that you would most logically use them. The ribbon in each Office program is slightly different, but all contain the same three elements: *tabs*, *groups*, and *commands*.

Tabs display across the top of the ribbon, and each tab relates to a type of activity; for example, laying out a page. Groups are sets of related commands for specific tasks. Commands—instructions to computer programs—are arranged in groups and might display as a button, a menu, or a box in which you type information.

You can also minimize the ribbon so only the tab names display, which is useful when working on a smaller screen such as a tablet computer where you want to maximize your screen viewing area.

MOS
1.4.3

Activity 1.11 | Performing Commands from and Customizing the Quick Access Toolbar

1 ▶ Take a moment to examine the document on your screen. If necessary, on the ribbon, click the View tab, and then in the Show group, click to place a check mark in the Ruler check box. Compare your screen with Figure 1.29.

This document is a memo from the General Manager to the Executive Chef regarding a new restaurant promotion for wedding rehearsal dinners.

When working in Word, display the rulers so that you can see how margin settings affect your document and how text and objects align. Additionally, if you set a tab stop or an indent, its location is visible on the ruler.

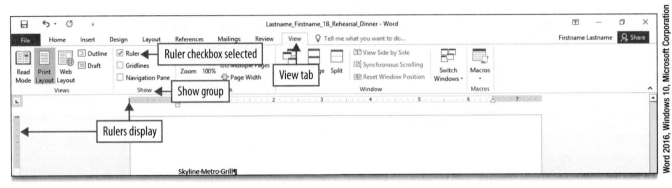

FIGURE 1.29

2 ▶ In the upper left corner of your screen, above the ribbon, locate the **Quick Access Toolbar**.

Recall that the Quick Access Toolbar contains commands that you use frequently. By default, only the commands Save, Undo, and Redo display, but you can add and delete commands to suit your needs. Possibly the computer at which you are working already has additional commands added to the Quick Access Toolbar.

3 ▶ At the end of the **Quick Access Toolbar**, click the **Customize Quick Access Toolbar** button ⊡, and then compare your screen with Figure 1.30.

A list of commands that Office users commonly add to their Quick Access Toolbar displays, including New, Open, Email, Quick Print, and Print Preview and Print. Commands already on the Quick Access Toolbar display a check mark. Commands that you add to the Quick Access Toolbar are always just one click away.

Here you can also display the More Commands dialog box, from which you can select any command from any tab to add to the Quick Access Toolbar.

 BY TOUCH   Tap once on Quick Access Toolbar commands.

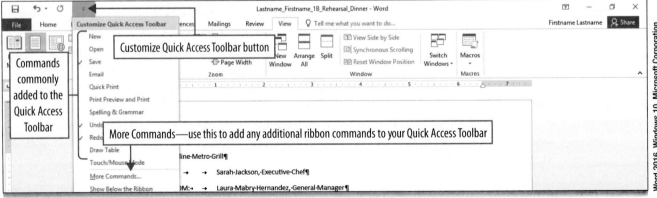

FIGURE 1.30

4 On the list, click **Print Preview and Print**, and then notice that the icon is added to the **Quick Access Toolbar**. Compare your screen with Figure 1.31.

The icon that represents the Print Preview command displays on the Quick Access Toolbar. Because this is a command that you will use frequently while building Office documents, you might decide to have this command remain on your Quick Access Toolbar.

 ANOTHER WAY   Right-click any command on the ribbon, and then on the shortcut menu, click Add to Quick Access Toolbar.

FIGURE 1.31   Word 2016, Windows 10, Microsoft Corporation

MOS

Activity 1.12 | Performing Commands from the Ribbon

5.2.5

1 In the first line of the document, if necessary, click to the left of the *S* in *Skyline* to position the insertion point there, and then press `Enter` one time to insert a blank paragraph. Press `↑` one time to position the insertion point in the new blank paragraph. Compare your screen with Figure 1.32.

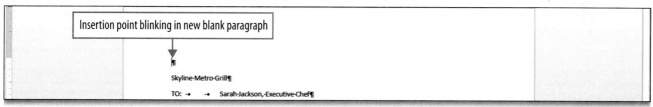

FIGURE 1.32   Word 2016, Windows 10, Microsoft Corporation

2 On the ribbon, click the **Insert tab**. In the **Illustrations group**, *point* to **Online Pictures** to display its ScreenTip.

Many buttons on the ribbon have this type of *enhanced ScreenTip*, which displays useful descriptive information about the command.

3 Click **Online Pictures**, and then compare your screen with Figure 1.33.

In the Insert Pictures dialog box, you can search for online pictures using Bing Image Search, and, if you are signed in with your Microsoft account, you can also find images on your OneDrive by clicking Browse. At the bottom, you can click a logo to download pictures from your Facebook and other types of accounts if you have them.

FIGURE 1.33

4 With the insertion point positioned in the **Bing Image Search** box, type **salad** and press Enter. Point to any of the results, and notice that keywords display. Compare your screen with Figure 1.34.

You can use various keywords to find images that are appropriate for your documents. The results shown indicate the images are licensed under **Creative Commons**, which, according to **www.creativecommons.org** is "a nonprofit organization that enables the sharing and use of creativity and knowledge through free legal tools."

Creative Commons helps people share and use their photographs, but does not allow companies to sell them. For your college assignments, you can use these images so long as you are not profiting by selling the photographs.

To find out more about Creative Commons, go to **https://creativecommons.org/about** and watch the video.

FIGURE 1.34

5 Locate an attractive picture of a salad on a plate or in a bowl that has a horizontal orientation—the picture is wider than it is tall—and then click that picture to select it. In the lower right corner, click **Insert**. In the upper right corner of the picture, point to the **Layout Options** button to display its ScreenTip, and then compare your screen with Figure 1.35.

Layout Options enable you to choose how the *object*—in this instance an inserted picture—interacts with the surrounding text. An object is a picture or other graphic such as a chart or table that you can select and then move and resize.

When a picture is selected, the Picture Tools become available on the ribbon. Additionally, *sizing handles*—small circles or squares that indicate an object is selected—surround the selected picture.

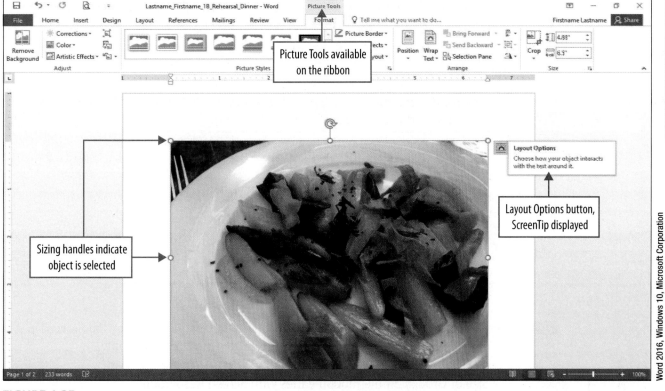

Within the image, labeled callouts read:
- Picture Tools available on the ribbon
- Sizing handles indicate object is selected
- Layout Options button, ScreenTip displayed
- Layout Options — Choose how your object interacts with the text around it.

Word 2016, Windows 10, Microsoft Corporation

FIGURE 1.35

6 With the image selected, click **Layout Options** 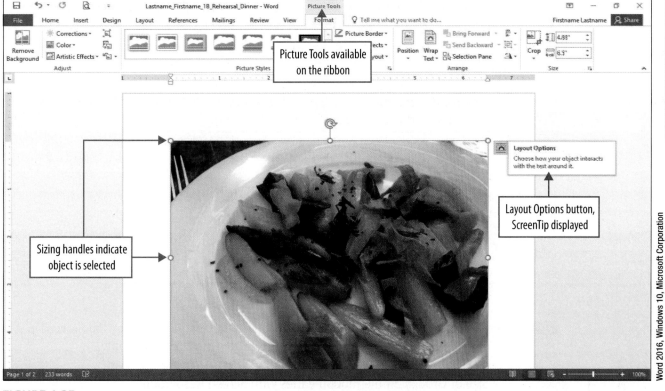, and then under **With Text Wrapping**, in the second row, click the first layout—**Top and Bottom**.

7 On the ribbon, with the **Picture Tools Format tab** active, at the right, in the **Size group**, click in the **Shape Height** box to select the existing text. Type **2** and press Enter.

8 Point to the image to display the pointer, hold down the left mouse button to display a green line at the left margin, and then drag the image to the right and slightly upward until a green line displays in the center of the image and at the top of the image, as shown in Figure 1.36, and then release the left mouse button. If you are not satisfied with your result, on the Quick Access Toolbar, click Undo and begin again.

Alignment guides are green lines that display to help you align objects with margins or at the center of a page.

Inserted pictures anchor—attach to—the paragraph at the insertion point location—as indicated by an anchor symbol.

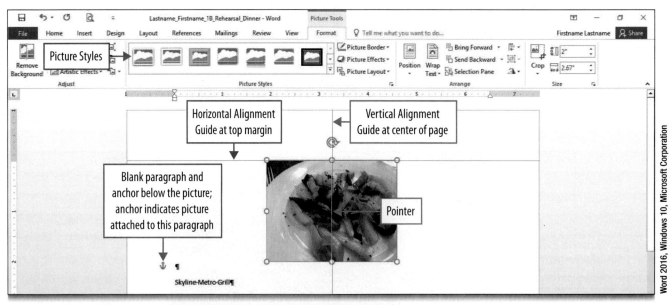

Labels in figure:
- Picture Styles
- Horizontal Alignment Guide at top margin
- Vertical Alignment Guide at center of page
- Blank paragraph and anchor below the picture; anchor indicates picture attached to this paragraph
- Pointer
- Skyline-Metro-Grill¶

Word 2016, Windows 10, Microsoft Corporation

FIGURE 1.36

9 ▶ On the ribbon, in the **Picture Styles group**, point to the first style to display the ScreenTip *Simple Frame, White*, and notice that the image displays with a white frame.

> **NOTE**   The Size of Groups on the Ribbon Varies with Screen Resolution
>
> Your monitor's screen resolution might be set higher than the resolution used to capture the figures shown here. At a higher resolution, the ribbon expands some groups to show more commands than are available with a single click, such as those in the Picture Styles group. Or, the group expands to add descriptive text to some buttons, such as those in the Arrange group. Regardless of your screen resolution, all Office commands are available to you. In higher resolutions, you will have a more robust view of the ribbon commands.

10 ▶ Watch the image as you point to the second picture style, and then to the third, and then to the fourth.

Recall that Live Preview shows the result of applying an editing or formatting change as you point to possible results—*before* you actually apply it.

11 ▶ In the **Picture Styles group**, click the second style—**Beveled Matte, White**—and then click anywhere outside of the image to deselect it. Notice that the Picture Tools no longer display on the ribbon. Compare your screen with Figure 1.37.

Contextual tabs on the ribbon display only when you need them.

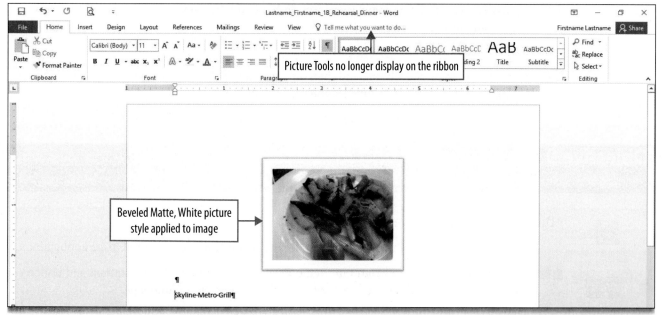

FIGURE 1.37

Word 2016, Windows 10, Microsoft Corporation

12 On the **Quick Access Toolbar**, click **Save** 🖫 to save the changes you have made.

Activity 1.13 | Minimizing the Ribbon and Using the Keyboard to Control the Ribbon

Instead of a mouse, some individuals prefer to navigate the ribbon by using keys on the keyboard.

1 On your keyboard, press Alt, and then on the ribbon, notice that small labels display on the tabs. Press N to activate the commands on the **Insert tab**, and then compare your screen with Figure 1.38.

Each label represents a *KeyTip*—an indication of the key that you can press to activate the command. For example, on the Insert tab, you can press F to open the Online Pictures dialog box.

FIGURE 1.38

Word 2016, Windows 10, Microsoft Corporation

2 Press Esc to redisplay the KeyTips for the tabs. Then, press Alt or Esc again to turn off keyboard control of the ribbon.

3 Point to any tab on the ribbon and right-click to display a shortcut menu.

Here you can choose to display the Quick Access Toolbar below the ribbon or collapse the ribbon to maximize screen space. You can also customize the ribbon by adding, removing, renaming, or reordering tabs, groups, and commands, although this is not recommended until you become an expert Word user.

4 Click **Collapse the Ribbon**. Notice that only the ribbon tabs display. Click the **Home tab** to display the commands. Click anywhere in the document, and notice that the ribbon goes back to the collapsed display.

5 Right-click any ribbon tab, and then click **Collapse the Ribbon** again to remove the check mark from this command.

> Most expert Office users prefer the full ribbon display.

6 Point to any tab on the ribbon, and then on your mouse device, roll the mouse wheel. Notice that different tabs become active as you roll the mouse wheel.

> You can make a tab active by using this technique, instead of clicking the tab.

Objective 9 | Apply Formatting in Office Programs and Inspect Documents

GO! Learn How
Video OF1.9

1.4.2

Activity 1.14 | Changing Page Orientation and Zoom Level

In this Activity, you will practice common formatting techniques used in Office applications.

1 On the ribbon, click the **Layout tab**. In the **Page Setup group**, click **Orientation**, and notice that two orientations display—*Portrait* and *Landscape*. Click **Landscape**.

> In *portrait orientation*, the paper is taller than it is wide. In *landscape orientation*, the paper is wider than it is tall.

2 In the lower right corner of the screen, locate the **Zoom slider**.

> Recall that to zoom means to increase or decrease the viewing area. You can zoom in to look closely at a section of a document, and then zoom out to see an entire page on the screen. You can also zoom to view multiple pages on the screen.

3 Drag the **Zoom slider** to the left until you have zoomed to approximately *60%*. Compare your screen with Figure 1.39.

FIGURE 1.39

🔄 **BY TOUCH**   Drag the Zoom slider with your finger.

4 Use the technique you just practiced to change the **Orientation** back to **Portrait**.

The default orientation in Word is Portrait, which is commonly used for business documents such as letters and memos.

5 In the lower right corner, click the **Zoom In** button **+** as many times as necessary to return to the **100%** zoom setting.

Use the zoom feature to adjust the view of your document for editing and for your viewing comfort.

 ANOTHER WAY You can also control Zoom from the ribbon. On the View tab, in the Zoom group, you can control the Zoom level and also zoom to view multiple pages.

6 On the **Quick Access Toolbar**, click **Save** 💾.

More **Knowledge** | **Zooming to Page Width**

Some Office users prefer **Page Width**, which zooms the document so that the width of the page matches the width of the window. Find this command on the View tab, in the Zoom group.

Activity 1.15 | Formatting Text by Using Fonts, Alignment, Font Colors, and Font Styles

1 If necessary, on the right edge of your screen, drag the vertical scroll box to the top of the scroll bar. To the left of *Skyline Metro Grill*, point in the margin area to display the ⟋ pointer and click one time to select the entire paragraph. Compare your screen with Figure 1.40.

Use this technique to select complete paragraphs from the margin area—drag downward to select multiple-line paragraphs—which is faster and more efficient than dragging through text.

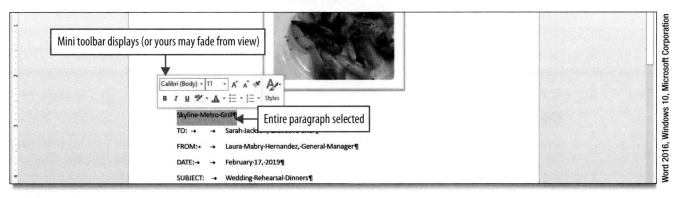

Mini toolbar displays (or yours may fade from view)

Entire paragraph selected

FIGURE 1.40

Word 2016, Windows 10, Microsoft Corporation

2 On the ribbon, click the **Home tab**, and then in the **Paragraph group**, click **Center** ▤ to center the paragraph.

3 On the **Home tab**, in the **Font group**, click the **Font button arrow** `Calibri (Body) ▾`. On the alphabetical list of font names, scroll down and then locate and *point to* **Cambria**.

A *font* is a set of characters with the same design and shape. The default font in a Word document is Calibri, which is a *sans serif font*—a font design with no lines or extensions on the ends of characters.

The Cambria font is a *serif font*—a font design that includes small line extensions on the ends of the letters to guide the eye in reading from left to right.

The list of fonts displays as a gallery showing potential results. For example, in the Font gallery, you can point to see the actual design and format of each font as it would look if applied to text.

4 Point to several other fonts and observe the effect on the selected text. Then, scroll back to the top of the **Font** gallery. Under **Theme Fonts**, click **Calibri Light**.

> A *theme* is a predesigned combination of colors, fonts, line, and fill effects that look good together and is applied to an entire document by a single selection. A theme combines two sets of fonts—one for text and one for headings. In the default Office theme, Calibri Light is the suggested font for headings.

5 With the paragraph *Skyline Metro Grill* still selected, on the **Home tab**, in the **Font group**, click the **Font Size button arrow** [11 ▾], point to **36**, and then notice how Live Preview displays the text in the font size to which you are pointing. Compare your screen with Figure 1.41.

FIGURE 1.41

6 On the list of font sizes, click **20**.

> Fonts are measured in *points*, with one point equal to 1/72 of an inch. A higher point size indicates a larger font size. Headings and titles are often formatted by using a larger font size. The word *point* is abbreviated as *pt*.

7 With *Skyline Metro Grill* still selected, on the **Home tab**, in the **Font group**, click the **Font Color button arrow** [A ▾]. Under **Theme Colors**, in the last column, click the last color—**Green, Accent 6, Darker 50%**. Click anywhere to deselect the text.

8 To the left of *TO:*, point in the left margin area to display the [⬧] pointer, hold down the left mouse button, drag down to select the four memo headings, and then release your mouse button. Compare your screen with Figure 1.42.

> Use this technique to select complete paragraphs from the margin area—drag downward to select multiple paragraphs—which is faster and more efficient than dragging through text.

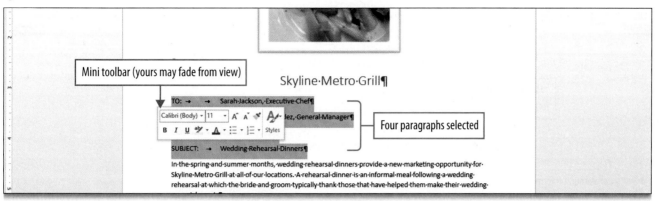

Mini toolbar (yours may fade from view)

Skyline·Metro·Grill¶

Four paragraphs selected

FIGURE 1.42

Word 2016, Windows 10, Microsoft Corporation

9 With the four paragraphs selected, on the mini toolbar, click the **Font Color** button [A⌄], and notice that the text color of the four paragraphs changes.

> The font color button retains its most recently used color—Green, Accent 6, Darker 50%. As you progress in your study of Microsoft Office, you will use other commands that behave in this manner; that is, they retain their most recently used format. This is commonly referred to as *MRU*—most recently used.

> Recall that the mini toolbar places commands that are commonly used for the selected text or object close by so that you reduce the distance that you must move your mouse to access a command. If you are using a touch screen device, most commands that you need are close and easy to touch.

10 On the right edge of your screen, if necessary drag the vertical scroll box down slightly to position more of the text on the screen. Click anywhere in the paragraph that begins *In the spring*, and then ***triple-click***—click the left mouse button three times—to select the entire paragraph. If the entire paragraph is not selected, click in the paragraph and begin again.

11 With the entire paragraph selected, on the mini toolbar, locate and then click the **Font Color button arrow** [A⌄], and then under **Theme Colors**, in the sixth column, click the last color—**Orange, Accent 2, Darker 50%**.

12 In the memo headings, select the guide word **TO:** and then on the mini toolbar, click **Bold** [B] and **Italic** [I].

> ***Font styles*** include bold, italic, and underline. Font styles emphasize text and are a visual cue to draw the reader's eye to important text.

13 On the mini toolbar, click **Italic** [I] again to turn off the Italic formatting.

> A ***toggle button*** is a button that can be turned on by clicking it once, and then turned off by clicking it again.

MOS

2.2.2

Activity 1.16 | Using Format Painter

Use the Format Painter to copy the formatting of specific text or of a paragraph and then apply it in other locations in your document.

1 With TO: still selected, on the mini toolbar, click **Format Painter** . Then, move your mouse under the word *Sarah*, and notice the [≜I] mouse pointer. Compare your screen with Figure 1.43.

> The pointer takes the shape of a paintbrush, and contains the formatting information from the paragraph where the insertion point is positioned. Information about the Format Painter and how to turn it off displays in the status bar.

FIGURE 1.43

2 With the ⊿I pointer, drag to select the guide word **FROM:** and notice that Bold formatting is applied. Then, point to the selected text *FROM:* and on the mini toolbar, *double-click* **Format Painter** ⟡.

3 Select the guide word **DATE:** to copy the Bold formatting, and notice that the pointer retains the ⊿I shape.

> When you *double-click* the Format Painter button, the Format Painter feature remains active until you either click the Format Painter button again, or press [Esc] to cancel it—as indicated on the status bar.

4 With **Format Painter** still active, select the guide word **SUBJECT:**, and then on the ribbon, on the **Home tab**, in the **Clipboard group**, notice that **Format Painter** ⟡ is selected, indicating that it is active. Compare your screen with Figure 1.44.

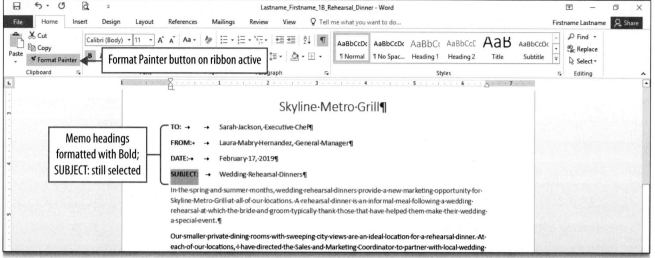

FIGURE 1.44

Word 2016, Windows 10, Microsoft Corporation

5 On the ribbon, click **Format Painter** to turn the command off.

⟳ ANOTHER WAY   Press Esc to turn off Format Painter.

6 In the paragraph that begins *In the spring*, triple-click again to select the entire paragraph. On the mini toolbar, click **Bold** B and **Italic** I. Click anywhere to deselect.

7 On the **Quick Access Toolbar**, click **Save** to save the changes you have made to your document.

MOS
2.1.2

Activity 1.17 | Using Keyboard Shortcuts and Using the Clipboard to Copy, Cut, and Paste

The *Clipboard* is a temporary storage area that holds text or graphics that you select and then cut or copy. When you *copy* text or graphics, a copy is placed on the Clipboard and the original text or graphic remains in place. When you *cut* text or graphics, a copy is placed on the Clipboard, and the original text or graphic is removed—cut—from the document.

After copying or cutting, the contents of the Clipboard are available for you to *paste*—insert—in a new location in the current document, or into another Office file.

1 On your keyboard, hold down Ctrl and press Home to move to the beginning of your document, and then take a moment to study the table in Figure 1.45, which describes similar keyboard shortcuts with which you can navigate quickly in a document.

TO MOVE	PRESS
To the beginning of a document	Ctrl + Home
To the end of a document	Ctrl + End
To the beginning of a line	Home
To the end of a line	End
To the beginning of the previous word	Ctrl + ←
To the beginning of the next word	Ctrl + →
To the beginning of the current word (if insertion point is in the middle of a word)	Ctrl + ←
To the beginning of the previous paragraph	Ctrl + ↑
To the beginning of the next paragraph	Ctrl + ↓
To the beginning of the current paragraph (if insertion point is in the middle of a paragraph)	Ctrl + ↑
Up one screen	PgUp
Down one screen	PgDn

Word 2016, Windows 10, Microsoft Corporation

FIGURE 1.45

2 To the left of *Skyline Metro Grill*, point in the left margin area to display the ⟍ pointer, and then click one time to select the entire paragraph. On the **Home tab**, in the **Clipboard group**, click **Copy** 🗎.

Because anything that you select and then copy—or cut—is placed on the Clipboard, the Copy command and the Cut command display in the Clipboard group of commands on the ribbon. There is no visible indication that your copied selection has been placed on the Clipboard.

⟳ ANOTHER WAY Right-click the selection, and then click Copy on the shortcut menu; or, use the keyboard shortcut Ctrl + C.

3 On the **Home tab**, in the **Clipboard group**, to the right of the group name *Clipboard*, click the **Dialog Box Launcher** button 🗗, and then compare your screen with Figure 1.46.

The Clipboard pane displays with your copied text. In any ribbon group, the ***Dialog Box Launcher*** displays either a dialog box or a pane related to the group of commands. It is not necessary to display the Clipboard in this manner, although sometimes it is useful to do so.

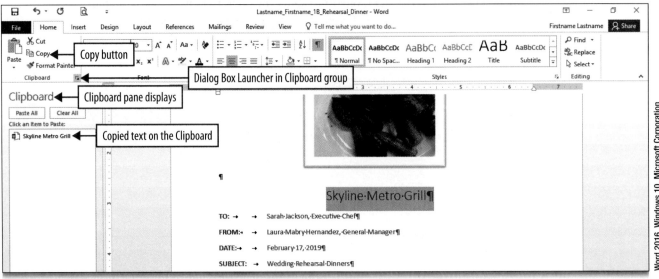

Word 2016, Windows 10, Microsoft Corporation

FIGURE 1.46

4 ▶ In the upper right corner of the **Clipboard** pane, click **Close** ☒.

5 ▶ Press Ctrl + End to move to the end of your document. Press Enter one time to create a new blank paragraph. On the **Home tab**, in the **Clipboard group**, point to **Paste**, and then click the *upper* portion of this split button.

The Paste command pastes the most recently copied item on the Clipboard at the insertion point location. If you click the lower portion of the Paste button, a gallery of Paste Options displays. A *split button* is divided into two parts; clicking the main part of the button performs a command, and clicking the arrow displays a list or gallery with choices.

🔄 **ANOTHER WAY**   Right-click, on the shortcut menu under Paste Options, click the desired option button; or, press Ctrl + V.

6 ▶ Below the pasted text, click **Paste Options** 🖺 as shown in Figure 1.47.

Here you can view and apply various formatting options for pasting your copied or cut text. Typically you will click Paste on the ribbon and paste the item in its original format. If you want some other format for the pasted item, you can choose another format from the ***Paste Options gallery***.

The Paste Options gallery provides a Live Preview of the various options for changing the format of the pasted item with a single click. The Paste Options gallery is available in three places: on the ribbon by clicking the lower portion of the Paste button—the Paste button arrow; from the Paste Options button that displays below the pasted item following the paste operation; or on the shortcut menu if you right-click the pasted item.

FIGURE 1.47

7 ▶ In the **Paste Options** gallery, *point* to each option to see the Live Preview of the format that would be applied if you clicked the button.

The contents of the Paste Options gallery are contextual; that is, they change based on what you copied and where you are pasting.

8 ▶ Press [Esc] to close the gallery; the button will remain displayed until you take some other screen action.

9 ▶ On your keyboard, press [Ctrl] + [Home] to move to the top of the document, and then click the **salad image** one time to select it. While pointing to the selected image, right-click, and then on the shortcut menu, click **Cut**.

Recall that the Cut command cuts—removes—the selection from the document and places it on the Clipboard.

🔄 ANOTHER WAY   On the Home tab, in the Clipboard group, click the Cut button; or use the keyboard shortcut [Ctrl] + [X].

10 ▶ Press [Del] one time to remove the blank paragraph from the top of the document, and then press [Ctrl] + [End] to move to the end of the document.

11 ▶ With the insertion point blinking in the blank paragraph at the end of the document, right-click, and notice that the **Paste Options** gallery displays on the shortcut menu. Compare your screen with Figure 1.48.

FIGURE 1.48

12 ▶ On the shortcut menu, under **Paste Options**, click the first button—**Keep Source Formatting**.

13 ▶ Point to the picture to display the 📍 pointer, and then drag to the right until the center green **Alignment Guide** displays and the blank paragraph is above the picture, as shown in Figure 1.49. Release the left mouse button.

🔄 BY TOUCH   Drag the picture with your finger to display the Alignment Guide.

FIGURE 1.49

 Activity 1.18 | Changing Text to WordArt and Adding Alternative Text for Accessibility

2.2.7, 5.2.8

1 Above the picture, click to position the insertion point at the end of the word *Grill*, press [Spacebar] one time, and then type **for Your Rehearsal Dinner**

2 Select the text *Skyline Metro Grill for Your Rehearsal Dinner*, and then on the **Insert tab**, in the **Text group**, click **Insert WordArt** 4 ▾ .

> *WordArt* is an Office feature available in Word, Excel, and PowerPoint that enables you to change normal text into decorative stylized text.

3 In the displayed gallery, use the ScreenTips to locate and then click **Fill - Gold, Accent 4, Soft Bevel**.

4 With the WordArt surrounded with a solid line, on the **Home tab**, in the **Font group**, change the font size to **16**.

5 Point to the solid line surrounding the WordArt to display the 🖫 pointer, and then drag the WordArt slightly to the right until the green center alignment guides display, as shown in Figure 1.50, and then release the mouse button to center the WordArt above your picture. Click outside of the WordArt to deselect.

FIGURE 1.50

6 Point to the picture of the salad and right-click. On the shortcut menu, click **Format Picture**.

7 In the **Format Picture** pane that displays on the right, under **Format Picture**, click **Layout & Properties** 🖼, and then click **Alt Text**.

Alternative text helps people using a *screen reader*, which is software that enables visually impaired users to read text on a computer screen to understand the content of pictures. *Alt text* is the term commonly used for this feature.

8 As the Title, type **Salad** and as the Description, type **Picture of salad on a plate**

Anyone viewing the document with a screen reader will see the alternative text displayed instead of the picture.

9 **Close** ☒ the **Format Picture** pane.

10 On the **Insert tab**, in the **Header & Footer group**, click **Footer**. At the bottom of the list, click **Edit Footer**, and then with the **Header & Footer Tools Design tab** active, in the **Insert group**, click **Document Info**. Click **File Name** to add the file name to the footer.

11 On the right end of the ribbon, click **Close Header and Footer**.

12 On the **Quick Access Toolbar**, point to the **Print Preview and Print icon** 🔍 you placed there, right-click, and then click **Remove from Quick Access Toolbar**.

If you are working on your own computer and you want to do so, you can leave the icon on the toolbar; in a college lab, you should return the software to its original settings.

13 Click **Save** 🖫 and then click the **File tab** to display **Backstage** view. With the **Info tab** active, in the lower right corner, click **Show All Properties**. As **Tags**, type **weddings, rehearsal dinners, marketing**

14 As the **Subject**, type your course name and number—for example, *CIS 10, #5543*. Under **Related People**, be sure your name displays as the author (edit it if necessary), and then on the left, click **Print** to display the Print Preview. Compare your screen with Figure 1.51.

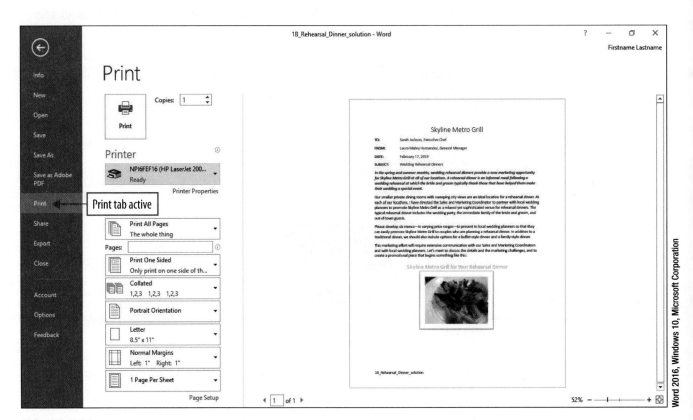

FIGURE 1.51

15 On the left side of **Backstage** view, click **Save**. In the upper right corner of the Word window, click **Close** ⊠. If a message indicates *Do you want to keep the last item you copied?* click **No**.

This message displays if you have copied some type of image to the Clipboard. If you click Yes, the items on the Clipboard will remain for you to use in another program or document.

16 As directed by your instructor, create and submit a paper printout or an electronic image of your document that looks like a printed document; or, submit your completed Word file. If necessary, refer to Activity 1.08 in Project 1A.

1.5.4, 1.5.5, 1.5.6

Activity 1.19 | Inspecting a Document

Word, Excel, and PowerPoint all have the same commands to inspect a file before sharing it.

1 If necessary, open your **Lastname_Firstname_1B_Rehearsal_Dinner** document.

2 Click the **File tab**, on the left, if necessary, click **Info**, and then on the right, click **Check for Issues**.

3 On the list, click **Inspect Document**.

The *Inspect Document* command searches your document for hidden data or personal information that you might not want to share publicly. This information could reveal company details that should not be shared.

4 In the lower right corner of the **Document Inspector** dialog box, click **Inspect**.

The Document Inspector runs and lists information that was found and that you could choose to remove.

5 Click **Close**, click **Check for Issues** again, and then click **Check Accessibility**.

The *Check Accessibility* command checks the document for content that people with disabilities might find difficult to read. The Accessibility Checker pane displays on the right and lists two objects that might require attention: a text box (your WordArt) and your picture.

6 Close ⊠ the **Accessibility Checker** pane, and then click the **File tab**.

7 Click **Check for Issues**, and then click **Check Compatibility**.

The *Check Compatibility* command checks for features in your document that may not be supported by earlier versions of the Office program. This is only a concern if you are sharing documents with individuals with older software.

8 Click **OK**. Leave your Word document displayed for the next Activity.

1.2.3

Activity 1.20 | Inserting a Bookmark

A *bookmark* identifies a word, section, or place in your document so that you can find it quickly without scrolling. This is especially useful in a long document.

1 In the paragraph that begins *Please develop*, select the text *six menus*.

2 On the **Insert tab**, in the **Links group**, click **Bookmark**.

3 In the Bookmark name box, type **menus** and then click **Add**.

4 Press Ctrl + Home to move to the top of your document.

5 Press Ctrl + G, which is the keyboard shortcut for the Go To command.

6 Under **Go to what**, click **Bookmark**, and then with menus selected, click **Go To**. **Close** the **Find and Replace** dialog box, and notice that your bookmarked text is selected for you.

7 Close ⊠ Word, and then click **Save**. Close any open windows.

GO! Learn How
Video OF1.10

A *compressed file* is a file that has been reduced in size. Compressed files take up less storage space and can be transferred to other computers faster than uncompressed files. You can also combine a group of files into one compressed folder, which makes it easier to share a group of files.

Within each Office program, you will see the *Tell Me* feature at the right end of the ribbon tabs, which is a search feature for Microsoft Office commands that you activate by typing what you are looking for in the Tell Me box.

Another method to get help with an Office command is to point to the command on the ribbon, and then at the bottom of the displayed ScreenTip, click Tell me more, which will display step-by-step assistance.

Activity 1.21 | Compressing Files

In this Activity, you will combine the two files you created in this chapter into one compressed file.

1 On the Windows taskbar, click **File Explorer** ▢. On the left, in the **navigation pane**, navigate to your storage location, and then open your **Office Features Chapter 1** folder. If you have been using this folder, in might appear under Quick access. Compare your screen with Figure 1.52.

FIGURE 1.52

2 In the **file list**, click your **Lastname_Firstname_1A_Note_Form** Word file one time to select it. Then, hold down Ctrl, and click your **Lastname_Firstname_1B_Rehearsal_Dinner** file to select both files in the list.

> In any Windows-based program, holding down Ctrl while selecting enables you to select multiple items.

3 On the **File Explorer** ribbon, click **Share**, and then in the **Send group**, click **Zip**. Compare your screen with Figure 1.53.

> Windows creates a compressed folder containing a *copy* of each of the selected files. The folder name is selected—highlighted in blue—so that you can rename it. The default folder name is usually the name of the first file in the group that you select.

🔁 BY TOUCH   Tap the ribbon commands.

FIGURE 1.53

Word 2016, Windows 10, Microsoft Corporation

ANOTHER WAY Point to the selected files in the File List, right-click, point to Send to, and then click Compressed (zipped) folder.

4 With the folder name selected—highlighted in blue—using your own name, type **Lastname_Firstname_Office_Features_Chapter_1** and press [Enter].

The compressed folder is ready to attach to an email or share in some other format.

5 In the upper right corner of the folder window, click **Close** [×].

Activity 1.22 | Using Microsoft Office Tell Me and Tell Me More to Get Help

In this Activity, you will use Tell Me to find information about formatting currency in Excel.

1 Start Excel and open a **Blank workbook**. With cell **A1** active, type **456789** and press [Enter]. Click cell **A1** again to make it the active cell.

2 At the top of the screen, click in the **Tell me what you want to do** box, and then type **format as currency** In the displayed list, point to **Accounting Number Formats**, and then click **$ English (United States)**.

As you type, every keystroke refines the results so that you can click the command as soon as it displays. This feature helps you apply the command immediately; it does not explain how to locate the command.

3 On the **Home tab**, in the **Alignment group**, *point to* **Merge & Center**, and then at the bottom of the displayed ScreenTip, click **Tell me more**. At the right edge of the displayed **Excel 2016 Help** window, use the scroll bar to scroll about halfway down the window, and then compare your screen with Figure 1.54.

The *Tell me more* feature opens the Office online Help system with explanations about how to perform the task.

FIGURE 1.54

4 If you want to do so, at the top of the **Excel Help** window, click Print 🖨 to print a copy of this information for your reference.

5 In the upper right corner of the Help window, click **Close** ☒.

6 Leave Excel open for the next Activity.

Objective 11 Install Apps for Office and Create a Microsoft Account

GO! Learn How
Video OF1.11

Apps for Office are a collection of downloadable apps that enable you to create and view information within your familiar Office programs. Apps for Office combine cloud services and web technologies within the user interface of Office. Some of these apps are developed by Microsoft, but many more are developed by specialists in different fields. As new apps are developed, they will be available from the online ***Office Store***—a public marketplace that Microsoft hosts and regulates on Office.com.

A ***task pane app*** works side-by-side with an Office document by displaying a separate pane on the right side of the window. For example, a task pane app can look up and retrieve product information from a web service based on the product name or part number selected in the document.

A ***content app*** integrates web-based features as content within the body of a document. For example, in Excel, you can use an app to look up and gather search results for a new apartment by placing the information in an Excel worksheet, and then use maps to determine the distance of each apartment to work and to family members. ***Mail apps*** display next to an Outlook item. For example, a mail app could detect a purchase order number in an email message and then display information about the order or the customer.

Activity 1.23 | Installing Apps for Office

1 With cell **A1** active, on your keyboard, press Delete to clear the cell. On the Excel ribbon, click the **Insert tab**. In the **Add-ins group**, click **Store**.

2 In the **Office Add-ins** dialog box, in the upper right, click in the **Search the Office Store** box, type **bing maps** and then press Enter.

3 Click the **Bing logo**, and then in the lower right corner, click **Trust It**.

4 If necessary, click Update. On the Welcome message, click **Insert Sample Data**.

Here, the Bing map displays information related to the sample data—this is a *content app*. Each city in the sample data displays a small pie chart that represents the two sets of data—revenue and expenses. Compare your screen with Figure 1.55.

This is just one example of many apps downloadable from the Office Store.

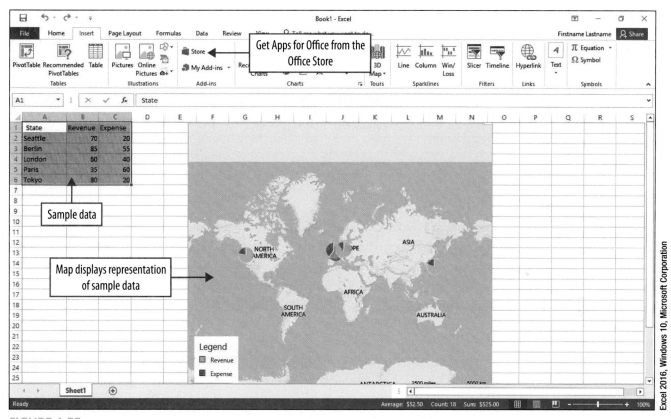

FIGURE 1.55

5 In the upper right corner of your screen, **Close** ☒ Excel without saving.

Activity 1.24 | Creating a Microsoft Account

ALERT! **This is an optional activity.**

You will find both Windows and Office to be much more useful if you sign in with a Microsoft account. If you already have an email account from **msn.com**, **hotmail.com**, **live.com**, or **outlook.com**, then you already have a Microsoft account. If you do not, you can create a free Microsoft account by following the steps in this activity.

In Windows 8 and Windows 10, you can use a Microsoft account to sign in to *any* Windows PC. Signing in with a Microsoft account is recommended because you can:

- Download Windows apps from the Windows Store.
- Get your online content—email, social network updates, updated news—automatically displayed in an app when you sign in.
- Synch settings online to make every Windows computer you use look and feel the same.
- Sign in to Office so that you can store documents on your OneDrive.

1 Use an Internet search engine to search for **create a microsoft account** or go to **signup.live.com** and at the bottom click **Sign up now**. You will see a screen similar to Figure 1.56. Complete the form to create your account.

You can use any email address that you currently have for your Microsoft account. Or, on this screen, you can create a new outlook.com account.

■■ Microsoft

Create an account ◄— Create a Microsoft account (your screen may vary)

You can use any email address as the user name for your new Microsoft account, including addresses from Outlook.com, Yahoo! or Gmail. If you already sign in to a Windows PC, tablet, or phone, Xbox Live, Outlook.com, or OneDrive, use that account to sign in.

First name   **Last name**

Your name will appear to your friends, co-workers, family, and others in the Microsoft services you use.

User name

someone@example.com

Get a new email address

Password

8-character minimum; case sensitive

Reenter password

Word 2016, Windows 10, Microsoft Corporation

FIGURE 1.56

END | You have completed Project 1B

GO! To Work

Andres Rodriguez/Fotolia; FotolEdhar/Fotolia; Andrey Popov/Fotolia; Shutterstock

MICROSOFT OFFICE SPECIALIST (MOS) SKILLS IN THIS CHAPTER

PROJECT 1A	PROJECT 1B
1.1.1 Create a blank document	**1.2.3** Create bookmarks
1.3.4 Insert headers and footers	**1.4.2** Customize views by using zoom settings
1.3.6 Format page background elements	**1.4.3** Customize the Quick Access toolbar
1.4.5 Add document properties	**1.5.4** Inspect a document for hidden properties or personal information
1.4.6 Show or hide formatting symbols	**1.5.5** Inspect a document for accessibility issues
2.2.6 Apply built-in styles to text	**1.5.6** Inspect a document for compatibility issues
	2.1.2 Cut, copy, and paste text
	2.2.2 Apply formatting by using Format Painter
	2.2.7 Change text to WordArt
	5.2.5 Apply a picture style
	5.2.8 Add alternative text to objects for accessibility

BUILD YOUR E-PORTFOLIO

An E-Portfolio is a collection of evidence, stored electronically, that showcases what you have accomplished while completing your education. Collecting and then sharing your work products with potential employers reflects your academic and career goals. Your completed documents from the following projects are good examples to show what you have learned: 1A and 1B.

END OF CHAPTER

SUMMARY

Many Office features and commands, such as accessing the Open and Save As dialog boxes, performing commands from the ribbon and from dialog boxes, and using the Clipboard are the same in all Office desktop apps.

A desktop app is installed on your computer and requires a computer operating system such as Microsoft Windows or Apple's Mac OS-X to run. The programs in Microsoft Office 2016 are considered to be desktop apps.

An app refers to a self-contained program usually designed for a single purpose and that runs on smartphones and other mobile devices—for example, looking at sports scores or booking a flight on a particular airline.

Within an Office app, you can add Apps for Office from the Office Store, which combine cloud services and web technologies within the Office user interface. Apps can be task pane apps, content apps, or mail apps.

GO! LEARN IT ONLINE

Review the concepts, key terms, and MOS skills in this chapter by completing these online challenges, which you can find at **MyITLab**.

Matching and Multiple Choice: Answer matching and multiple-choice questions to test what you learned in this chapter.

Lessons on the GO!: Learn how to use all the new apps and features as they are introduced by Microsoft.

MOS Prep Quiz: Answer questions to review the MOS skills that you practiced in this chapter.

GLOSSARY

GLOSSARY OF CHAPTER KEY TERMS

Alignment The placement of text or objects relative to the left and right margins.

Alignment guides Green lines that display when you move an object to assist in alignment.

Alt text Another name for alternative text.

Alternative text Text added to a picture or object that helps people using a screen reader understand what the object is.

App A self-contained program usually designed for a single purpose and that runs on smartphones and other mobile devices.

Apps for Office A collection of downloadable apps that enable you to create and view information within Office programs, and that combine cloud services and web technologies within the user interface of Office.

Backstage tabs The area along the left side of Backstage view with tabs to display screens with related groups of commands.

Backstage view A centralized space for file management tasks; for example, opening, saving, printing, publishing, or sharing a file. A navigation pane displays along the left side with tabs that group file-related tasks together.

Bookmark A command that identifies a word, section, or place in a document so that you can find it quickly without scrolling.

Center alignment The alignment of text or objects that is centered horizontally between the left and right margin.

Clipboard A temporary storage area that holds text or graphics that you select and then cut or copy.

Check Accessibility A command that checks the document for content that people with disabilities might find difficult to read.

Check Compatibility A command that searches your document for features that may not be supported by older versions of Office.

Cloud computing Applications and services that are accessed over the Internet, rather than accessing applications that are installed on your local computer.

Cloud storage Online storage of data so that you can access your data from different places and devices.

Collaborate To work with others as a team in an intellectual endeavor to complete a shared task or to achieve a shared goal.

Commands Instructions to a computer program that cause an action to be carried out.

Compressed file A file that has been reduced in size and thus takes up less storage space and can be transferred to other computers quickly.

Content app An app for Office that integrates web-based features as content within the body of a document.

Context menus Menus that display commands and options relevant to the selected text or object; also called *shortcut menus*.

Context-sensitive commands Commands that display on a shortcut menu that relate to the object or text that you right-clicked.

Contextual tabs Tabs that are added to the ribbon automatically when a specific object, such as a picture, is selected, and that contain commands relevant to the selected object.

Copy A command that duplicates a selection and places it on the Clipboard.

Creative Commons A nonprofit organization that enables sharing and use of images and knowledge through free legal tools.

Cut A command that removes a selection and places it on the Clipboard.

Default The term that refers to the current selection or setting that is automatically used by a computer program unless you specify otherwise.

Deselect The action of canceling the selection of an object or block of text by clicking outside of the selection.

Desktop app A computer program that is installed on your PC and requires a computer operating system such as Microsoft Windows; also known as a *desktop application*.

Desktop application A computer program that is installed on your PC and requires a computer operating

system such as Microsoft Windows; also known as a *desktop app*.

Dialog Box Launcher A small icon that displays to the right of some group names on the ribbon and that opens a related dialog box or pane providing additional options and commands related to that group.

Document properties Details about a file that describe or identify it, including the title, author name, subject, and keywords that identify the document's topic or contents; also known as *metadata*.

Drag The action of holding down the left mouse button while moving your mouse.

Edit The process of making changes to text or graphics in an Office file.

Ellipsis A set of three dots indicating incompleteness; an ellipsis following a command name indicates that a dialog box will display if you click the command.

Enhanced ScreenTip A ScreenTip that displays more descriptive text than a normal ScreenTip.

Fill The inside color of an object.

Font A set of characters with the same design and shape.

Font styles Formatting emphasis such as bold, italic, and underline.

Footer A reserved area for text or graphics that displays at the bottom of each page in a document.

Formatting The process of establishing the overall appearance of text, graphics, and pages in an Office file— for example, in a Word document.

Formatting marks Characters that display on the screen, but do not print, indicating where the Enter key, the Spacebar, and the Tab key were pressed; also called *nonprinting characters*.

Gallery An Office feature that displays a list of potential results instead of just the command name.

Gradient fill A fill effect in which one color fades into another.

Groups On the Office ribbon, the sets of related commands that you might need for a specific type of task.

Header A reserved area for text or graphics that displays at the top of each page in a document.

Info tab The tab in Backstage view that displays information about the current file.

Inspect Document A command that searches your document for hidden data or personal information that you might not want to share publicly.

Insertion point A blinking vertical line that indicates where text or graphics will be inserted.

Keyboard shortcut A combination of two or more keyboard keys, used to perform a task that would otherwise require a mouse.

KeyTip The letter that displays on a command in the ribbon and that indicates the key you can press to activate the command when keyboard control of the Ribbon is activated.

Keywords Custom file properties in the form of words that you associate with a document to give an indication of the document's content; used to help find and organize files. Also called *tags*.

Landscape orientation A page orientation in which the paper is wider than it is tall.

Layout Options A button that displays when an object is selected and that has commands to choose how the object interacts with surrounding text.

Live Preview A technology that shows the result of applying an editing or formatting change as you point to possible results—*before* you actually apply it.

Location Any disk drive, folder, or other place in which you can store files and folders.

Mail app An app for Office that displays next to an Outlook item.

Metadata Details about a file that describe or identify it, including the title, author name, subject, and keywords that identify the document's topic or contents; also known as *document properties*.

Mini toolbar A small toolbar containing frequently used formatting commands that displays as a result of selecting text or objects.

MRU Acronym for *most recently used*, which refers to the state of some commands that retain the characteristic most recently applied; for example, the Font Color button retains the most recently used color until a new color is chosen.

Nonprinting characters Characters that display on the screen, but do not

print, indicating where the Enter key, the Spacebar, and the Tab key were pressed; also called *formatting marks*.

Object A text box, picture, table, or shape that you can select and then move and resize.

Office 365 A version of Microsoft Office to which you subscribe for an annual fee.

Office Store A public marketplace that Microsoft hosts and regulates on Office.com.

OneDrive Microsoft's free cloud storage for anyone with a free Microsoft account.

Open dialog box A dialog box from which you can navigate to, and then open on your screen, an existing file that was created in that same program.

Option button In a dialog box, a round button that enables you to make one choice among two or more options.

Options dialog box A dialog box within each Office application where you can select program settings and other options and preferences.

Page Width A view that zooms the document so that the width of the page matches the width of the window. Find this command on the View tab, in the Zoom group.

Paragraph symbol The symbol ¶ that represents the end of a paragraph.

Paste The action of placing text or objects that have been copied or cut from one location to another location.

Paste Options gallery A gallery of buttons that provides a Live Preview of all the Paste options available in the current context.

PDF The acronym for *Portable Document Format*, which is a file format that creates an image that preserves the look of your file, but that cannot be easily changed; a popular format for sending documents electronically, because the document will display on most computers.

Pointer Any symbol that displays on your screen in response to moving your mouse.

Points A measurement of the size of a font; there are 72 points in an inch.

Portable Document Format A file format that creates an image that preserves the look of your file, but that cannot be easily changed; a popular format for sending documents electronically, because the document

will display on most computers; also called a *PDF*.

Portrait orientation A page orientation in which the paper is taller than it is wide.

Print Preview A view of a document as it will appear when you print it.

Protected View A security feature in Office 2016 that protects your computer from malicious files by opening them in a restricted environment until you enable them; you might encounter this feature if you open a file from an e-mail or download files from the Internet.

pt The abbreviation for *point*; for example, when referring to a font size.

Quick Access Toolbar In an Office program window, the small row of buttons in the upper left corner of the screen from which you can perform frequently used commands.

Read-only A property assigned to a file that prevents the file from being modified or deleted; it indicates that you cannot save any changes to the displayed document unless you first save it with a new name.

Right-click The action of clicking the right mouse button one time.

Sans serif font A font design with no lines or extensions on the ends of characters.

Screen reader Software that enables visually impaired users to read text on a computer screen to understand the content of pictures.

ScreenTip A small box that that displays useful information when you perform various mouse actions such as pointing to screen elements or dragging.

Selecting Highlighting, by dragging with your mouse, areas of text or data or graphics, so that the selection can be edited, formatted, copied, or moved.

Serif font A font design that includes small line extensions on the ends of the letters to guide the eye in reading from left to right.

Share button Opens the Share pane from which you can save your file to the cloud—your OneDrive—and then share it with others so you can collaborate.

SharePoint Collaboration software with which people in an organization can set up team sites to share information, manage documents, and publish reports for others to see.

Shortcut menu A menu that displays commands and options relevant to the selected text or object; also called a *context menu*.

Sizing handles Small squares or circles that indicate a picture or object is selected.

Split button A button divided into two parts and in which clicking the main part of the button performs a command and clicking the arrow opens a menu with choices.

Status bar The area along the lower edge of an Office program window that displays file information on the left and buttons to control how the window looks on the right.

Style A group of formatting commands, such as font, font size, font color, paragraph alignment, and line spacing that can be applied to a paragraph with one command.

Synchronization The process of updating computer files that are in two or more locations according to specific rules—also called *syncing*.

Syncing The process of updating computer files that are in two or more locations according to specific rules—also called *synchronization*.

Tabs (ribbon) On the Office ribbon, the name of each task-oriented activity area.

Tags Custom file properties in the form of words that you associate with a document to give an indication of the document's content; used to help find and organize files. Also called *keywords*.

Task pane app An app for Office that works side-by-side with an Office document by displaying a separate pane on the right side of the window.

Tell Me A search feature for Microsoft Office commands that you activate by typing what you are looking for in the Tell Me box.

Tell me more A prompt within a ScreenTip that opens the Office online Help system with explanations about how to perform the command referenced in the ScreenTip.

Template A preformatted document that you can use as a starting point and then change to suit your needs.

Theme A predesigned combination of colors, fonts, and effects that looks good together and is applied to an entire document by a single selection.

Title bar The bar at the top edge of the program window that indicates the name of the current file and the program name.

Toggle button A button that can be turned on by clicking it once, and then turned off by clicking it again.

Toolbar In a folder window, a row of buttons with which you can perform common tasks, such as changing the view of your files and folders.

Triple-click The action of clicking the left mouse button three times in rapid succession.

Trusted Documents A security feature in Office that remembers which files you have already enabled; you might encounter this feature if you open a file from an e-mail or download files from the Internet.

Windows apps An app that runs on all Windows device families—including PCs, Windows phones, Windows tablets, and the Xbox gaming system.

WordArt An Office feature in Word, Excel, and PowerPoint that enables you to change normal text into decorative stylized text.

XML Paper Specification A Microsoft file format that creates an image of your document and that opens in the XPS viewer.

XPS The acronym for XML Paper Specification—a Microsoft file format that creates an image of your document and that opens in the XPS viewer.

Zoom The action of increasing or decreasing the size of the viewing area on the screen.

Introducing Microsoft Excel 2016

E Excel 2016

Georgejmclittle/Fotolia

Excel 2016: Introduction

Quantitative information! Defined as a type of information that can be counted or that communicates the quantity of something, quantitative information can be either easy or hard to understand—depending on how it is presented. According to Stephen Few, in his book *Show Me the Numbers*: "Quantitative information forms the core of what businesses must know to operate effectively."

Excel 2016 is a tool to communicate quantitative business information effectively. Sometimes you need to communicate quantitative relationships. For example, the number of units sold per geographic region shows a relationship of sales to geography. Sometimes you need to summarize numbers. A list of every student enrolled at your college with his or her major indicated is not as informative as a summary of the total number of students in each major. In business, the most common quantitative information is some measure of money—costs, sales, payroll, expenses—and so on.

Rather than just a tool for making calculations, Excel is now a tool for you to communicate and collaborate with others. When you want to communicate visually with tables and graphs, Excel 2016 has many features to help you do so. If you engage in Business Intelligence activities, you will find rich tools for forecasting and analysis. Excel is the world's most widely used and familiar data analysis tool.

Creating a Worksheet and Charting Data

1

PROJECT 1A

OUTCOMES
Create a sales report with an embedded column chart and sparklines.

OBJECTIVES

1. Create, Save, and Navigate an Excel Workbook
2. Enter Data in a Worksheet
3. Construct and Copy Formulas and Use the SUM Function
4. Format Cells with Merge & Center, Cell Styles, and Themes
5. Chart Data to Create a Column Chart and Insert Sparklines
6. Print a Worksheet, Display Formulas, and Close Excel

PROJECT 1B

OUTCOMES
Calculate the value of an inventory.

OBJECTIVES

7. Check Spelling in a Worksheet
8. Enter Data by Range
9. Construct Formulas for Mathematical Operations
10. Edit Values in a Worksheet
11. Format a Worksheet

Lee Torrens/Shutterstock

In This Chapter

GO! to Work with Excel

In this chapter, you will use Microsoft Excel 2016 to create and analyze data organized into columns and rows. After entering data in a worksheet, you can perform complex calculations, analyze the data to make logical decisions, and create attractive charts that help readers visualize your data in a way they can understand and that is meaningful. In this chapter, you will create and modify Excel workbooks. You will practice the basics of worksheet design, create a footer, enter and edit data in a worksheet, and chart data. You will save, preview, and print workbooks, and you will construct formulas for mathematical operations.

The projects in this chapter relate to **Pro Fit Marietta**, a distributor of fitness equipment and apparel to private gyms, personal trainers, health clubs, corporate wellness centers, hotels, college athletic facilities, physical therapy practices, and multi-unit residential properties. The company's mission is to find, test, and distribute the highest-quality fitness products in the world to its customers for the benefit of consumers. Their popular blog provides useful tips on how to use the latest workout and fitness equipment. The company is located in Marietta, Georgia, which is metropolitan Atlanta's largest suburb.

Sales Report with Embedded Column Chart and Sparklines

PROJECT ACTIVITIES

In Activities 1.01 through 1.17, you will create an Excel worksheet for Michelle Barry, the President of Pro Fit Marietta. The worksheet displays the second quarter sales of cardio equipment for the current year and includes a chart to visually represent the data. Your completed worksheet will look similar to Figure 1.1.

Please always review the downloaded Grader instructions before beginning.

PROJECT FILES

MyITLab grader

If your instructor wants you to submit Project 1A in the MyITLab Grader system, log in to MyITLab, locate Grader Project 1A, and then download the files for this project.

For Project 1A, you will need the following file:

New blank Excel workbook

You will save your workbook as:

Lastname_Firstname_1A_Quarterly_Sales

Lastname_Firstname_1A_Quarterly_Sales_ formulas (if your instructor requires)

PROJECT RESULTS

Build From Scratch

GO! Walk Thru Project 1A

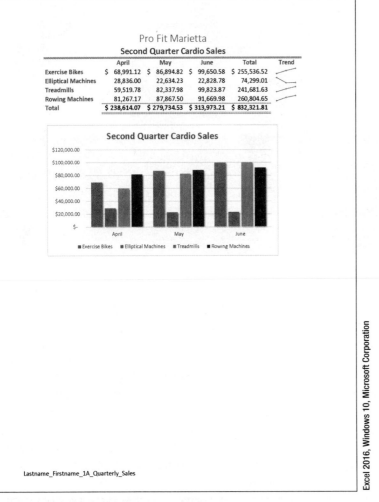

Excel 2016, Windows 10, Microsoft Corporation

FIGURE 1.1 Project 1A Quarterly Sales

NOTE	If You Are Using a Touchscreen
👆	Tap an item to click it.
👆	Press and hold for a few seconds to right-click; release when the information or commands display.
👆	Touch the screen with two or more fingers and then pinch together to zoom out or stretch your fingers apart to zoom in.
👆	Slide your finger on the screen to scroll—slide left to scroll right and slide right to scroll left.
👆	Slide to rearrange—similar to dragging with a mouse.
👆	Swipe to select—slide an item a short distance with a quick movement—to select an item and bring up commands, if any.

Objective 1 Create, Save, and Navigate an Excel Workbook

GO! Learn How
Video E1-1

On startup, Excel displays a new blank *workbook*—the Excel document that stores your data—which contains one or more pages called a *worksheet*. A worksheet—or *spreadsheet*—is stored in a workbook, and is formatted as a pattern of uniformly spaced horizontal rows and vertical columns. The intersection of a column and a row forms a box referred to as a *cell*.

1.1.1

Activity 1.01 | Starting Excel, Navigating Excel, and Naming and Saving a Workbook

ALERT!	To submit as an autograded project, log into MyITLab, download the files for this project, and begin with those files instead of a new blank workbook.

1 Start Excel, and on the opening screen, click **Blank workbook**. In the lower right corner of the window, on the status bar, if necessary, click the Normal button 🔲, and then to the right, locate the zoom—magnification—level.

Your zoom level should be 100%, although some figures in this textbook may be shown at a higher zoom level. The *Normal view* maximizes the number of cells visible on your screen and keeps the column letters and row numbers closer to the cells.

🔄 BY TOUCH   On Excel's opening screen, tap Blank workbook.

2 On the ribbon, click the **File tab**, on the left click **Save As**, under **Save As**, click **Browse** to display the **Save As** dialog box, and then navigate to the location where you will store your workbooks for this chapter.

3 In your storage location, create a new folder named **Excel Chapter 1** and then open the new folder to display its folder window. In the **File name** box, notice that *Book1* displays as the default file name.

4 In the **File name** box, click **Book1** to select it, and then using your own name, type **Lastname_Firstname_1A_Quarterly_Sales** being sure to include the underscore (_) instead of spaces between words.

5 Click **Save**. Compare your screen with Figure 1.2, and then take a moment to study the parts of the Excel window described in the table in Figure 1.3.

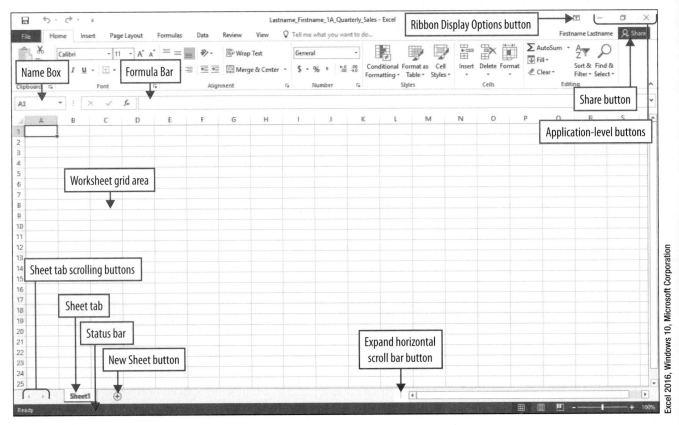

FIGURE 1.2

PARTS OF THE EXCEL WINDOW	
SCREEN PART	**DESCRIPTION**
Horizontal scroll bar button	Increases or decreases the width of the horizontal scroll bar by sliding left or right.
Formula Bar	Displays the value or formula contained in the active cell; also permits entry or editing.
Sheet tab	Identifies the worksheet in the workbook.
New sheet button	Inserts an additional worksheet.
Name Box	Displays the name of the selected cell, table, chart, or object.
Share button	Opens the Share pane from which you can save your file to the cloud—your OneDrive—and then share it with others so you can collaborate.
Sheet tab scrolling buttons	Display sheet tabs that are not in view when there are numerous sheet tabs.
Status bar	Displays the current cell mode, page number, worksheet information, view and zoom buttons, and for numerical data, common calculations such as Sum and Average.
Application-level buttons	Minimize, close, or restore the previous size of the displayed workbook window.
Ribbon Display Options button	Displays various ways you can display the ribbon—the default is Show Tabs and Commands.
Worksheet grid area	Displays the columns and rows that intersect to form the worksheet's cells.

FIGURE 1.3

6 ▶ Take a moment to study Figure 1.4 and the table in Figure 1.5 to become familiar with the Excel worksheet window.

FIGURE 1.4

Excel 2016, Windows 10, Microsoft Corporation

PARTS OF THE EXCEL WORKSHEET WINDOW	
WORKBOOK WINDOW ELEMENT	**DESCRIPTION**
Excel pointer	Displays the location of the pointer.
Expand Formula Bar button	Increases the height of the Formula Bar to display lengthy cell content.
Lettered column headings	Indicate the column letter.
Numbered row headings	Indicate the row number.
Select All box	Selects all the cells in a worksheet.

FIGURE 1.5

7 In the lower right corner of the screen, in the horizontal scroll bar, click the **right scroll arrow** one time to shift **column A** out of view.

> A *column* is a vertical group of cells in a worksheet. Beginning with the first letter of the alphabet, A, a unique letter identifies each column—this is called the *column heading*. Clicking one of the horizontal scroll bar arrows shifts the window either left or right one column at a time.

8 Point to the **right scroll arrow**, and then hold down the left mouse button until the columns begin to scroll rapidly to the right; release the mouse button when you begin to see pairs of letters as the column headings.

🔄 **BY TOUCH**   Anywhere on the worksheet, slide your finger to the left to view columns to the right.

9 Slowly drag the horizontal scroll box to the left, and notice that just above the scroll box, ScreenTips with the column letters display as you drag. Drag the horizontal scroll box left or right—or click the left or right scroll arrow—as necessary to position **column Z** near the center of your screen.

> Column headings after column Z use two letters starting with AA, AB, and so on through ZZ. After that, columns begin with three letters beginning with AAA. This pattern provides 16,384 columns. The last column is XFD.

10 In the vertical scroll bar, click the **down scroll arrow** one time to move **Row 1** out of view.

> A *row* is a horizontal group of cells. Beginning with number 1, a unique number identifies each row—this is the *row heading*, located at the left side of the worksheet. A single worksheet can have 1,048,576 rows of data.

11 Use the skills you just practiced to scroll horizontally to display **column A**, and if necessary, **row 1**.

12 Click **Save** 🔲.

GO! Learn How
Video E1-2

Cell content, which is anything you type in a cell, can be one of two things: either a ***constant value***—referred to simply as a ***value***—or a ***formula***. A formula is an equation that performs mathematical calculations on values in your worksheet. The most commonly used values are ***text values*** and ***number values***, but a value can also include a date or a time of day. A text value is also referred to as a ***label***.

Activity 1.02 | Entering Text, Using AutoComplete, and Using the Name Box to Select a Cell

A text value usually provides information about number values in other worksheet cells. For example, a title such as Second Quarter Cardio Sales gives the reader an indication that the data in the worksheet relates to information about sales of cardio equipment during the three-month period April through June.

1 Point to and then click the cell at the intersection of **column A** and **row 1** to make it the ***active cell***—the cell is outlined and ready to accept data.

The intersecting column letter and row number form the ***cell reference***—also called the ***cell address***. When a cell is active, its column letter and row number are highlighted. The cell reference of the selected cell, *A1*, displays in the Name Box.

2 With cell **A1** as the active cell, type the worksheet title **Pro Fit Marietta** and then press Enter. Compare your screen with Figure 1.6.

Text or numbers in a cell are referred to as ***data***. You must confirm the data you type in a cell by pressing Enter or by some other keyboard movement, such as pressing Tab or an arrow key. Pressing Enter moves the active cell to the cell below.

Excel 2016, Windows 10, Microsoft Corporation

FIGURE 1.6

3 In cell **A1**, notice that the text does not fit; the text extends into cell **B1** to the right.

If text is too long for a cell and cells to the right are empty, the text will display. If the cells to the right contain other data, only the text that will fit in the cell displays.

4 In cell **A2**, type the worksheet subtitle **Second Quarter Cardio Sales** and then press Enter. Compare your screen with Figure 1.7.

FIGURE 1.7

Excel 2016, Windows 10, Microsoft Corporation

5 Above **column A**, click in the **Name Box** to select the cell reference *A3*. Type **a4** and then press Enter to make cell **A4** the active cell. In cell **A4**, type **Exercise Bikes** to form the first row title, and then press Enter.

> The text characters that you typed align at the left edge of the cell—referred to as *left alignment*—and cell A5 becomes the active cell. Left alignment is the default for text values. You can type a cell address in the Name Box and press Enter to move to a specific cell quickly.

6 In cell **A5**, type **E** and notice the text from the previous cell displays.

> If the first characters you type in a cell match an existing entry in the column, Excel fills in the remaining characters for you. This feature, called *AutoComplete*, assists only with alphabetic values.

7 Continue typing the remainder of the row title **lliptical Machines** and press Enter.

> The AutoComplete suggestion is removed when the entry you are typing differs from the previous value.

8 In cell **A6**, type **Treadmills** and press Enter. In cell **A7**, type **Rowing Machines** and press Enter. In cell **A8**, type **Total** and press Enter. On the Quick Access Toolbar, click **Save** 🔲.

ANOTHER WAY Use the keyboard shortcut Ctrl + S to save changes to your workbook.

Activity 1.03 | Using Auto Fill and Keyboard Shortcuts

MOS
2.1.4

1 Click cell **B3**. Type **A** and notice that when you begin to type in a cell, on the **Formula Bar**, the **Cancel** and **Enter** buttons become active, as shown in Figure 1.8.

FIGURE 1.8

Excel 2016, Windows 10, Microsoft Corporation

2 Continue to type **pril** and then on the **Formula Bar**, notice that values you type in a cell also display there. Then, on the **Formula Bar**, click **Enter** ☑ to confirm the entry and keep cell **B3** active.

3 With cell **B3** active, locate the small square in the lower right corner of the selected cell.

> You can drag this *fill handle*—the small square in the lower right corner of a selected cell—to adjacent cells to fill the cells with values based on the first cell.

4 Point to the **fill handle** until the ➕ pointer displays, hold down the left mouse button, drag to the right to cell **D3**, and as you drag, notice the ScreenTips *May* and *June*. Release the mouse button.

5 Under the text that you just filled, click the **Auto Fill Options** button ⊞ that displays, and then compare your screen with Figure 1.9.

> *Auto Fill* generates and extends a *series* of values into adjacent cells based on the value of other cells. A series is a group of things that come one after another in succession; for example, *April*, *May*, *June*.
>
> The Auto Fill Options button displays options to fill the data; options vary depending on the content and program from which you are filling, and the format of the data you are filling.
>
> *Fill Series* is selected, indicating the action that was taken. Because the options are related to the current task, the button is referred to as being *context sensitive*.

FIGURE 1.9

Excel 2016, Windows 10, Microsoft Corporation

6 Click in any cell to cancel the display of the list.

> The list no longer displays; the button will display until you perform some other screen action.

7 Press Ctrl + Home, which is the keyboard shortcut to make cell **A1** active.

8 On the Quick Access Toolbar, click **Save** 🖫 to save the changes you have made to your workbook.

9 Take a moment to study the table in Figure 1.10 to become familiar with keyboard shortcuts with which you can navigate the Excel worksheet.

KEYBOARD SHORTCUTS TO NAVIGATE THE EXCEL WORKSHEET	
TO MOVE THE LOCATION OF THE ACTIVE CELL:	**PRESS:**
Up, down, right, or left one cell	⬆️ ⬇️ ➡️ ⬅️
Down one cell	Enter
Up one cell	Shift + Enter
Up one full screen	PageUp
Down one full screen	PageDown
To column A of the current row	Home
To the last cell in the last column of the active area (the rectangle formed by all the rows and columns in a worksheet that contain entries)	Ctrl + End
To cell A1	Ctrl + Home
Right one cell	Tab
Left one cell	Shift + Tab
To the cell one worksheet window to the right	Alt + PageDown
To the cell one worksheet window to the left	Alt + PageUp
To the cell containing specific content that you enter in the Find and Replace dialog box	Shift + F5
To the cell that corresponds with the cell reference you enter in the Go To dialog box	F5

Excel 2016, Windows 10, Microsoft Corporation

FIGURE 1.10

Activity 1.04 | Aligning Text and Adjusting the Size of Columns

5.1.4

1 In the **column heading area**, point to the vertical line between **column A** and **column B** to display the ➕ pointer, press and hold down the left mouse button, and then compare your screen with Figure 1.11.

A ScreenTip displays information about the width of the column. The default width of a column is 64 *pixels*. A pixel, short for *picture element*, is a point of light measured in dots per square inch. Sixty-four pixels equal 8.43 characters, which is the average number of characters that will fit in a cell using the default font. The default font in Excel is Calibri and the default font size is 11.

Excel 2016, Windows 10, Microsoft Corporation

FIGURE 1.11

2 Drag to the right, and when the number of pixels indicated in the ScreenTip reaches **120 pixels**, release the mouse button. If you are not satisfied with your result, click Undo 🔄 on the Quick Access Toolbar and begin again.

This width accommodates the longest row title in cells A4 through A8—*Elliptical Machines*. The worksheet subtitle in cell A2 spans more than one column and still does not fit in column A.

3 Point to cell **B3** and then drag across to select cells **B3**, **C3**, and **D3**. Compare your screen with Figure 1.12; if you are not satisfied with your result, click anywhere and begin again.

The three cells, B3 through D3, are selected and form a *range*—two or more cells on a worksheet that are adjacent (next to each other) or nonadjacent (not next to each other). This range of cells is referred to as *B3:D3*. When you see a colon (:) between two cell references, the range includes all the cells between the two cell references.

A range of cells you select this way is indicated by a dark border, and Excel treats the range as a single unit so you can make the same changes to more than one cell at a time. The selected cells in the range are highlighted except for the first cell in the range, which displays in the Name Box.

When you select a range of data, the *Quick Analysis tool* displays in the lower right corner of the selected range, with which you can analyze your data by using Excel tools such as charts, color-coding, and formulas.

FIGURE 1.12

🔄 **BY TOUCH** To select a range, tap a cell to display a circular gripper in the upper left and lower right corners of the cell, and then drag one of the grippers as necessary to select the desired range.

4 With the range **B3:D3** selected, point anywhere over the selected range, right-click, and then on the mini toolbar, click **Center** ≡. On the Quick Access Toolbar, click **Save** 🖫.

The column titles *April*, *May*, *June* align in the center of each cell.

Activity 1.05 | Entering Numbers

To type number values, use either the number keys across the top of your keyboard or the numeric keypad if you have one—laptop computers might not have a numeric keypad.

1 Under *April*, click cell **B4**, type **68991.12** and then on the **Formula Bar**, click **Enter** ✓ to maintain cell **B4** as the active cell. Compare your screen with Figure 1.13.

By default, *number* values align at the right edge of the cell. The default *number format*—a specific way in which Excel displays numbers—is the *general format*. In the default general format, whatever you type in the cell will display, with the exception of trailing zeros to the right of a decimal point. For example, in the number 237.50 the *0* following the *5* is a trailing zero and would not display.

Data that displays in a cell is the *displayed value*. Data that displays in the Formula Bar is the *underlying value*. The number of digits or characters that display in a cell—the displayed value—depends on the width of the column. Calculations on numbers will always be based on the underlying value, not the displayed value.

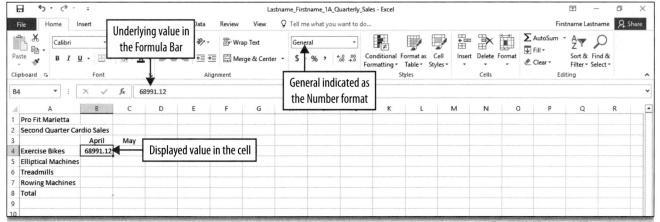

FIGURE 1.13

Excel 2016, Windows 10, Microsoft Corporation

2 Press Tab to make cell **C4** active. Type **86894.82** and then press Tab to move to cell **D4**. Type **99650.58** and then press Enter to move to cell **B5** in the next row. Then, by using the same technique, enter the remaining sales numbers as shown:

	APRIL	MAY	JUNE
Elliptical Machines	28836	22634.23	22828.78
Treadmills	59519.78	82337.98	99823.87
Rowing Machines	81267.17	87867.50	91669.98

3 Compare the numbers you entered with Figure 1.14, and then **Save** 💾 your workbook.

In the default General format, trailing zeros to the right of a decimal point will not display. For example, when you type *87867.50*, the cell displays 87867.5 instead.

FIGURE 1.14

Excel 2016, Windows 10, Microsoft Corporation

Objective 3 Construct and Copy Formulas and Use the SUM Function

GO! Learn How
Video E1-3

A cell contains either a constant value (text or numbers) or a formula. A formula is an equation that performs mathematical calculations on values in other cells, and then places the result in the cell containing the formula. You can create formulas or use a ***function***—a prewritten formula that looks at one or more values, performs an operation, and then returns a value.

In this Activity, you will practice three different ways to sum a group of numbers in Excel.

4.1.2

1 Click cell **B8** to make it the active cell and type **=**

The equal sign (=) displays in the cell with the insertion point blinking, ready to accept more data.

All formulas begin with the = sign, which signals Excel to begin a calculation. The Formula Bar displays the = sign, and the Formula Bar Cancel and Enter buttons display.

2 At the insertion point, type **b4** and then compare your screen with Figure 1.15.

A list of Excel functions that begin with the letter *B* may briefly display—as you progress in your study of Excel, you will use functions of this type. A blue border with small corner boxes surrounds cell B4, which indicates that the cell is part of an active formula. The color used in the box matches the color of the cell reference in the formula.

Excel 2016, Windows 10, Microsoft Corporation

FIGURE 1.15

3 At the insertion point, type **+** and then type **b5**

A border of another color surrounds cell B5, and the color matches the color of the cell reference in the active formula. When typing cell references, it is not necessary to use uppercase letters.

4 At the insertion point, type **+b6+b7** and then press Enter.

The result of the formula calculation—*238614.1*—displays in the cell. Recall that in the default General format, trailing zeros do not display.

5 Click cell **B8** again, look at the **Formula Bar**, and then compare your screen with Figure 1.16.

The formula adds the values in cells B4 through B7, and the result displays in cell B8. In this manner, you can construct a formula by typing. Although cell B8 displays the *result* of the formula, the formula itself displays in the Formula Bar. This is referred to as the ***underlying formula***.

Always view the Formula Bar to be sure of the exact content of a cell—*a displayed number may actually be a formula.*

Excel 2016, Windows 10, Microsoft Corporation

FIGURE 1.16

6 Click cell **C8** and type **=** to signal the beginning of a formula. Then, point to cell **C4** and click one time.

> The reference to the cell C4 is added to the active formula. A moving border surrounds the referenced cell, and the border color and the color of the cell reference in the formula are color coded to match.

7 At the insertion point, type **+** and then click cell **C5**. Repeat this process to complete the formula to add cells **C6** and **C7**, and then press **Enter**.

> The result of the formula calculation—*279734.5*—displays in the cell. This method of constructing a formula is the ***point and click method***.

8 Click cell **D8**. On the **Home tab**, in the **Editing group**, click **AutoSum**, and then compare your screen with Figure 1.17.

> SUM is an Excel function—a prewritten formula. A moving border surrounds the range D4:D7 and =*SUM(D4:D7)* displays in cell D8.

> The = sign signals the beginning of a formula, *SUM* indicates the type of calculation that will take place (addition), and *(D4:D7)* indicates the range of cells on which the sum calculation will be performed. A ScreenTip provides additional information about the action.

FIGURE 1.17

ANOTHER WAY Use the keyboard shortcut **Alt** + **=**; or, on the Formulas tab, in the Function Library group, click the AutoSum button.

---

9 Look at the **Formula Bar**, and notice that the formula also displays there. Then, look again at the cells surrounded by the moving border.

> When you activate the ***Sum function***, Excel first looks *above* the active cell for a range of cells to sum. If no range is above the active cell, Excel will look to the *left* for a range of cells to sum. If the proposed range is not what you want to calculate, you can select a different group of cells.

10 Press **Enter** to construct a formula by using the prewritten SUM function.

> Your total is *313973.2*. Because the Sum function is frequently used, it has its own button in the Editing group on the Home tab of the ribbon. A larger version of the button also displays on the Formulas tab in the Function Library group. This button is also referred to as ***AutoSum***.

11 Notice that the totals in the range **B8:D8** display only one decimal place. Click **Save** 🖫.

> Number values that are too long to fit in the cell do *not* spill over into the unoccupied cell to the right in the same manner as text values. Rather, Excel rounds the number to fit the space.

> ***Rounding*** is a procedure that determines which digit at the right of the number will be the last digit displayed and then increases it by one if the next digit to its right is 5, 6, 7, 8, or 9.

Activity 1.07 | Copying a Formula by Using the Fill Handle

You have practiced three ways to create a formula—by typing, by using the point-and-click technique, and by using a Function button from the ribbon. You can also copy formulas. When you copy a formula from one cell to another, Excel adjusts the cell references to fit the new location of the formula.

> **1** Click cell **E3**, type **Total** and then press Enter.

The text in cell E3 is centered because the centered format continues from the adjacent cell.

> **2** With cell **E4** as the active cell, hold down Alt, and then press =. Compare your screen with Figure 1.18.

Alt + = is the keyboard shortcut for the SUM function. Recall that Excel first looks above the selected cell for a proposed range of cells to sum, and if no data is detected, Excel looks to the left and proposes a range of cells to sum.

FIGURE 1.18

> **3** On the **Formula Bar**, click **Enter** ✓ to display the result and keep cell **E4** active.

The total dollar amount of *Exercise Bikes* sold in the quarter is *255536.5*. In cells E5:E8, you can see that you need a formula similar to the one in E4, but formulas that refer to the cells in row 5, row 6, and so on.

> **4** With cell **E4** active, point to the fill handle in the lower right corner of the cell until the + pointer displays. Then, drag down through cell **E8**; if you are not satisfied with your result, on the Quick Access Toolbar, click Undo ↺ and begin again. Compare your screen with Figure 1.19.

FIGURE 1.19

Excel 2016, Windows 10, Microsoft Corporation

5 Click cell **E5**, look at the **Formula Bar**, and notice the formula *=SUM(B5:D5)*. Click cell **E6**, look at the **Formula Bar**, and then notice the formula *=SUM(B6:D6)*.

In each row, Excel copied the formula but adjusted the cell references *relative to* the row number. This is called a *relative cell reference*—a cell reference based on the relative position of the cell that contains the formula and the cells referred to in the formula.

The calculation is the same, but it is performed on the cells in that particular row. Use this method to insert numerous formulas into spreadsheets quickly.

6 Click cell **F3**, type **Trend** and then press [Enter]. **Save** 🔲 your workbook.

Objective 4 Format Cells with Merge & Center, Cell Styles, and Themes

GO! Learn How
Video E1-4

Format—change the appearance of—cells to make your worksheet attractive and easy to read.

Activity 1.08 | Using Merge & Center and Applying Cell Styles

2.2.1, 2.2.7

1 Select the range **A1:F1**, and then in the **Alignment group**, click **Merge & Center**. Then, select the range **A2:F2** and click **Merge & Center**.

The *Merge & Center* command joins selected cells into one larger cell and centers the contents in the merged cell; individual cells in the range B1:F1 and B2:F2 can no longer be selected—they are merged into cell A1 and A2, respectively.

🔄 **ANOTHER WAY** Select the range, right-click over the selection, and then on the mini toolbar, click the Merge & Center command.

2 Click cell **A1**. In the **Styles group**, click **Cell Styles**, and then compare your screen with Figure 1.20.

A *cell style* is a defined set of formatting characteristics, such as font, font size, font color, cell borders, and cell shading.

FIGURE 1.20

3 In the displayed gallery, under **Titles and Headings**, click **Title** and notice that the row height adjusts to accommodate the larger font size.

4 Click cell **A2**, display the **Cell Styles** gallery, and then under **Titles and Headings**, click **Heading 1**.

Use cell styles to maintain a consistent look in a worksheet and across worksheets in a workbook.

5 Select the horizontal range **B3:F3**, hold down Ctrl, and then select the vertical range **A4:A8** to select the column titles and the row titles. Release Ctrl.

Use this technique to select two or more ranges that are nonadjacent—not next to each other.

6 With the two ranges selected, display the **Cell Styles** gallery, click **Heading 4** to apply this cell style to the column titles and row titles, and then **Save** 🖫 your workbook.

Activity 1.09 | Formatting Financial Numbers

MOS

2.2.5

1 Select the range **B4:E4**, hold down Ctrl, and then select the range **B8:E8**. Release Ctrl.

This range is referred to as *b4:e4,b8:e8* with a comma separating the references to the two nonadjacent ranges.

🔄 **ANOTHER WAY**   In the Name Box type b4:e4,b8:e8 and then press Enter.

2 With the two ranges selected, on the **Home tab**, in the **Number group**, click **Accounting Number Format** $ ▾. Compare your screen with Figure 1.21.

The *Accounting Number Format* applies a thousand comma separator where appropriate, inserts a fixed U.S. dollar sign aligned at the left edge of the cell, applies two decimal places, and leaves a small amount of space at the right edge of the cell to accommodate a parenthesis when negative numbers are present. Excel widens the columns to accommodate the formatted numbers.

At the bottom of your screen, in the status bar, Excel displays the results for some common calculations that might be made on the range; for example, the Average of the numbers selected and the Count—the number of items selected.

FIGURE 1.21

🔄 **ANOTHER WAY**   Display the Cell Styles gallery, and under Number Format, click Currency.

3 Select the range **B5:E7**, and then in the **Number group**, click **Comma Style** ▯.

The ***Comma Style*** inserts a thousand comma separator where appropriate and applies two decimal places. Comma Style also leaves space at the right to accommodate a parenthesis when negative numbers are present.

When preparing worksheets with financial information, the first row of dollar amounts and the total row of dollar amounts are formatted in the ***Accounting Number Format***; that is, with thousand comma separators, dollar signs, two decimal places, and space at the right to accommodate a parenthesis for negative numbers, if any. Rows that are *not* the first row or the total row should be formatted with the Comma Style.

4 Select the range **B8:E8**. In the **Styles group**, display the **Cell Styles** gallery, and then under **Titles and Headings**, click **Total**. Click any blank cell to cancel the selection, and then compare your screen with Figure 1.22.

This is a common way to apply borders to financial information. The single border indicates that calculations were performed on the numbers above, and the double border indicates that the information is complete. Sometimes financial documents do not display values with cents; rather, the values are rounded up. You can do this by selecting the cells, and then clicking the Decrease Decimal button two times.

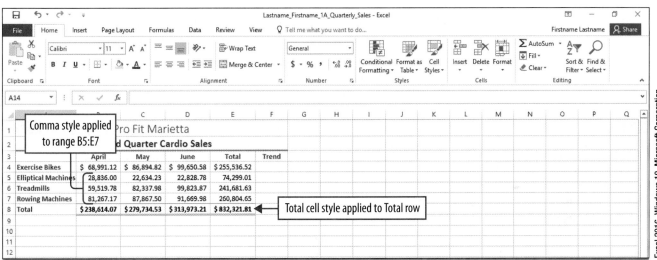

FIGURE 1.22

Activity 1.10 │ Changing the Workbook Theme

1.3.6

A ***theme*** is a predefined set of colors, fonts, lines, and fill effects that coordinate for an attractive look.

1 Click the **Page Layout tab**, and then in the **Themes group**, click **Themes**.

2 Click the **Retrospect** theme, and notice that the cell styles change to match the new theme. Click **Save** ▯.

More Knowledge	**Formatting a Cell's Font, Style, Size, or Color with Individual Commands**

Instead of using Cell Styles, you could use a combination of individual commands to format a cell. For example, on the Home tab, in the Font group, you can change a cell's font by clicking the Font arrow and selecting a different font. You can change the font size by clicking the Font Size arrow and selecting a size. From the same group, you can apply various styles to the cell—such as Bold or Italic or Underline. To change a cell's font color, in the Font Group, click the Font Color arrow and select a different color.

GO! Learn How
Video E1-5

A *chart* is a graphic representation of data in a worksheet. Data in a chart is easier to understand than a table of numbers. *Sparklines* are tiny charts embedded in a cell that give a visual trend summary alongside your data. A sparkline makes a pattern more obvious to the eye.

Activity 1.11 | Charting Data and Using Recommended Charts to Select and Insert a Column Chart

5.1.1, 5.1.3

Recommended Charts is an Excel feature that displays a customized set of charts that, according to Excel's calculations, will best fit your data based on the range of data that you select. In this Activity, you will create a *column chart* showing the monthly sales of cardio equipment by category during the second quarter. A column chart is useful for illustrating comparisons among related numbers. The chart will enable the company president, Michelle Barry, to see a pattern of overall monthly sales.

1 Select the range **A3:D7**.

> When charting data, typically you should *not* include totals—include only the data you want to compare.

2 With the data that you want to compare selected, click the **Insert tab**, and then in the **Charts group**, click **Recommended Charts**. Compare your screen with Figure 1.23.

> The Insert Chart dialog box displays a list of recommended charts on the left and a preview of the first chart, which is selected, on the right. The second tab of the Insert Chart dialog box includes all chart types—even those that are not recommended by Excel for this type of data.

> By using different *chart types*, you can display data in a way that is meaningful to the reader—common examples are column charts, pie charts, and line charts.

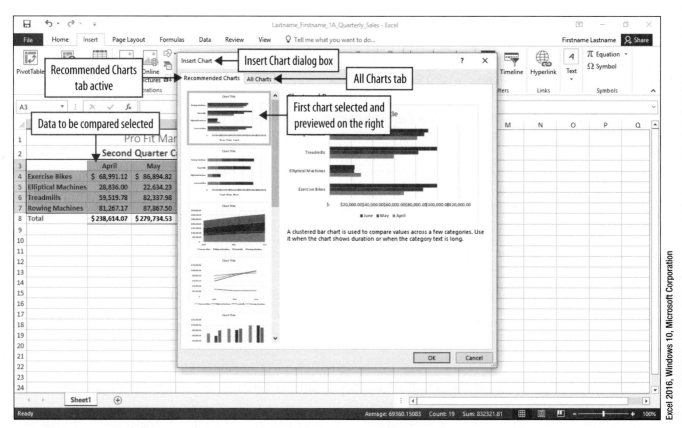

FIGURE 1.23

3 In the **Insert Chart** dialog box, use the scroll bar to scroll down about one-third of the way, and then click the second Clustered Column chart. Compare your screen with Figure 1.24.

Here, *each type of cardio equipment* displays its *sales for each month*. A clustered column chart is useful to compare values across a few categories, especially if the order of categories is not important.

FIGURE 1.24

4 ▸ In the **Insert Chart** dialog box, click the chart directly above the selected chart—the first clustered column chart. Compare your screen with Figure 1.25.

In this clustered column chart, *each month* displays its *sales for each type of cardio equipment*. When constructing a chart, you can switch the row and column data in this manner to display the data in a way that is most useful to the reader. Here, the president of Pro Fit Marietta wants to compare sales of each type of equipment by month to detect patterns.

The comparison of data—either by month or by type of equipment—depends on the type of analysis you want to perform. You can select either chart, or, after your chart is complete, you can use the ***Switch/Row Column*** command on the ribbon to swap the data over the axis; that is, data being charted on the vertical axis will move to the horizontal axis and vice versa.

FIGURE 1.25

> **5** In the lower right corner of the **Insert Chart** dialog box, click **OK** to insert the selected chart into the worksheet. Compare your screen with Figure 1.26.

> Your selected column chart displays in the worksheet, and the charted data is bordered by colored lines. Because the chart object is selected—surrounded by a border and displaying sizing handles—contextual tools named *Chart Tools* display and add contextual tabs next to the standard tabs on the ribbon.

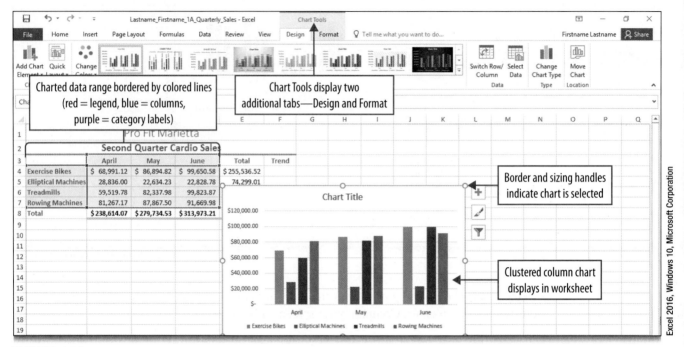

FIGURE 1.26

Activity 1.12 | Using the Chart Tools to Apply Chart Styles

5.2.2, 5.2.3

> **1** On the ribbon, locate the contextual tabs under **Chart Tools—Design** and **Format**.

> When a chart is selected, Chart Tools become available and these two tabs provide commands for working with the chart.

> Based on the data you selected in your worksheet and the chart you selected in the Insert Chart dialog box, Excel constructs a column chart and adds *category labels*—the labels that display along the bottom of the chart to identify the category of data. This area is referred to as the *category axis* or the *x-axis*.

> Depending on which arrangement of row and column data you select in the Insert Chart dialog box, Excel arranges either the row titles or the column titles as the category names. Here, based on your selection, the column titles that form the category labels are bordered in purple, indicating the cells that contain the category names.

> On the left side of the chart, Excel includes a numerical scale on which the charted data is based; this is the *value axis* or the *y-axis*. Along the lower edge of the chart, a *legend*, which is a chart element that identifies the patterns or colors that are assigned to the categories in the chart, displays. Here, the row titles are bordered in red, indicating the cells containing the legend text.

> **2** To the right of the chart, notice the three buttons, and then point to each button to display its ScreenTip, as shown in Figure 1.27.

> The *Chart Elements button* enables you to add, remove, or change chart elements such as the title, legend, gridlines, and data labels.

> The *Chart Styles button* enables you to set a style and color scheme for your chart.

> The *Chart Filters button* enables you to change which data displays in the chart—for example, to see only the data for *May* and *June* or only the data for *Treadmills* and *Rowing Machines*.

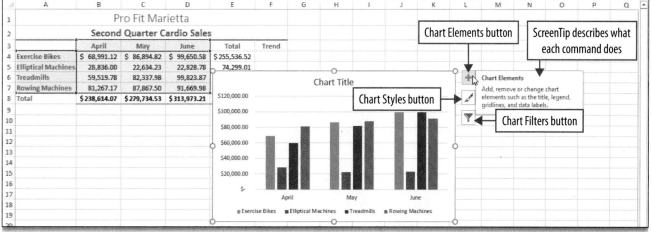

FIGURE 1.27

Excel 2016, Windows 10, Microsoft Corporation

3 In the worksheet data, locate the group of cells bordered in blue.

Each of the twelve cells bordered in blue is referred to as a ***data point***—a value that originates in a worksheet cell. Each data point is represented in the chart by a ***data marker***—a column, bar, area, dot, pie slice, or other symbol in a chart that represents a single data point.

Related data points form a ***data series***; for example, there is a data series for *April*, for *May*, and for *June*. Each data series has a unique color or pattern represented in the chart legend.

4 On the **Design tab**, in the **Chart Layouts group**, click **Quick Layout**, and then compare your screen with Figure 1.28.

In the Quick Layout gallery, you can change the overall layout of the chart by selecting a predesigned ***chart layout***—a combination of chart elements, which can include a title, legend, labels for the columns, and the table of charted cells.

FIGURE 1.28

Excel 2016, Windows 10, Microsoft Corporation

5 *Point* to several different layouts to see how Live Preview displays the effect on your chart, and then click the **Quick Layout** button again without changing the layout.

6 In the chart, click anywhere in the text *Chart Title* to select the title box, watch the **Formula Bar** as you begin to type **Second** and notice that AutoComplete fills in the subtitle for you. Press Enter at any point to insert the worksheet subtitle as the chart title.

7 Click in a white area just slightly *inside* the chart border to deselect the chart title but keep the chart selected. To the right of the chart, click **Chart Styles** ✎, and then at the top of the **Chart Styles** gallery, be sure that **Style** is selected. Compare your screen with Figure 1.29.

The ***Chart Styles gallery*** displays an array of predefined ***chart styles***—the overall visual look of the chart in terms of its colors, backgrounds, and graphic effects such as flat or shaded columns. You can also select Chart Styles from the Chart Styles group on the ribbon, but having the gallery closer to the chart makes it easier to use a touch gesture on a touch device to format a chart.

FIGURE 1.29

8 On the right side of the **Style** gallery, scroll down about halfway, and then by using the ScreenTips as your guide, locate and click **Style 6**.

This style uses a white background, formats the columns with theme colors, and applies a slight shadowed effect to the columns. With this clear visual representation of the data, the president can see the sales of all product categories in each month, and can see that the sale of exercise bikes and treadmills has risen markedly during the quarter.

9 At the top of the gallery, click **Color**. Under **Colorful**, point to the third row of colors to display the ScreenTip *Color 3*, and then click to apply the **Color 3** variation of the theme colors.

10 Point to the top border of the chart to display the ⌖ pointer, and then drag the upper left corner of the chart just inside the upper left corner of cell **A10**, approximately as shown in Figure 1.30.

FIGURE 1.30

11 ▶ Click any cell to deselect the chart, and notice that the chart buttons no longer display to the right of the chart and the Chart Tools no longer display on the ribbon. Click **Save** 🖫.

Contextual tabs display when an object is selected and then are removed from view when the object is deselected.

Activity 1.13 │ Creating and Formatting Sparklines

By creating sparklines, you provide a context for your numbers. Your readers will be able to see the relationship between a sparkline and its underlying data quickly.

1 ▶ Select the range **B4:D7**, which represents the monthly sales figures for each product and for each month. Click the **Insert tab**, and then in the **Sparklines group**, click **Line**. In the displayed **Create Sparklines** dialog box, notice that the selected range *B4:D7* displays.

2 ▶ With the insertion point blinking in the **Location Range** box, type **f4:f7** which is the range of cells where you want the sparklines to display. Compare your screen with Figure 1.31.

FIGURE 1.31

🔄 **ANOTHER WAY** In the worksheet, select the range F4:F7 to insert it into the Location Range box.

3 ▶ Click **OK** to insert the sparklines in the range **F4:F7**, and then on the **Design tab**, in the **Show group**, click the **Markers** check box to select it.

Alongside each row of data, the sparkline provides a quick visual trend summary for sales of each cardio item over the three-month period. For example, you can see instantly that of the four items, only Elliptical Machines had declining sales for the period.

4 ▸ On the **Design tab**, in the **Style group**, click **More** ⊡. In the second row, click the fourth style—**Sparkline Style Accent 4, Darker 25%**. Press Ctrl + Home to deselect the range and make cell **A1** the active range. Click **Save** 🔲, and then compare your screen with Figure 1.32.

> Use markers, colors, and styles in this manner to further enhance your sparklines.

FIGURE 1.32

Objective 6 | Print a Worksheet, Display Formulas, and Close Excel

GO! Learn How
Video E1-6

Use the *Show Formulas* command to display the formula in each cell instead of the resulting value. Use the commands on the Page Layout tab to prepare for printing.

Activity 1.14 | Creating a Footer and Centering a Worksheet

MOS
1.3.8, 1.3.4

For each Excel project in this textbook, you will create a footer containing the file name, which includes your name and the project name. You will also center the data horizontally on the page to create an attractive result if your worksheet is printed.

1 ▸ If necessary, click cell **A1** to deselect the chart. Click the **Page Layout tab**, and then in the **Page Setup group**, click **Margins**. At the bottom of the **Margins** gallery, click **Custom Margins**, to display the **Page Setup** dialog box. Compare your screen with Figure 1.33.

FIGURE 1.33

> **2** On the **Margins tab**, under **Center on page**, select the **Horizontally** check box.

This action will center the data and chart horizontally on the page, as shown in the Preview area.

> **3** In the **Page Setup** dialog box, click the **Header/Footer tab**, and then in the center of the dialog box, click **Custom Footer**. In the **Footer** dialog box, with your insertion point blinking in the **Left section**, on the row of buttons, click **Insert File Name** 🔳. Compare your screen with Figure 1.34.

&[File] displays in the Left section. Here you can type or insert information from the row of buttons into the left, middle, or right section of the footer. The Custom Header button displays a similar screen to enter information in the header of the worksheet.

FIGURE 1.34

> **4** Click **OK** two times.

The vertical dotted line between columns indicates that as currently arranged, only the columns to the left of the dotted line will print on the first page. The exact position of the vertical line may depend on your default printer setting.

🔄 ANOTHER WAY Deselect the chart. On the Insert tab, in the Text group, click Header & Footer to display Page Layout view. Click in the left section of the displayed footer, and then in the Header & Footer Elements group, click File Name. Click any cell in the workbook to deselect the footer area, and then on the status bar, click the Normal button to return to Normal view.

Activity 1.15 │ Adding Document Properties and Printing a Workbook

> **1** In the upper left corner of your screen, click the **File tab** to display **Backstage** view. In the lower right corner, click **Show All Properties**.

> **2** As the **Tags**, type **cardio sales** In the **Subject** box, type your course name and section number. Be sure your name displays in the **Author** box and edit if necessary.

> **3** On the left, click **Print** to view the **Print Preview**. Compare your screen with Figure 1.35.

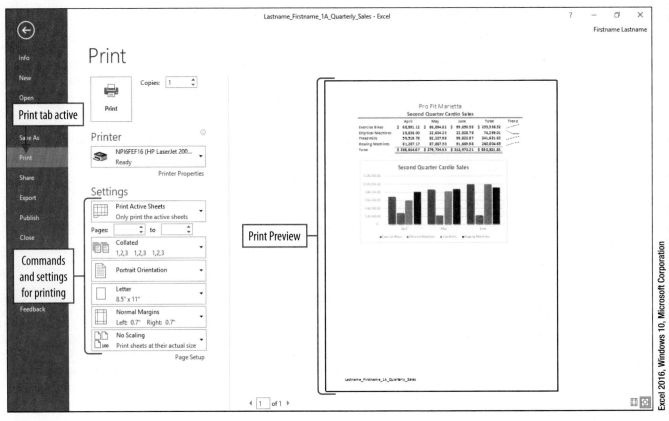

FIGURE 1.35

> 4 ▸ Note any adjustments that need to be made, and then on the left, click **Save** to save and return to the workbook.

NOTE | **What Does Your Instructor Require for Submission? A Paper Printout, an Image That Looks Like a Printed Document, or Your Excel File?**

You can produce a paper printout of your worksheet or an electronic image of your worksheet that looks like a printed document. Or, your instructor may want only your completed Excel file.

> 5 ▸ If you are directed to print on paper, be sure that a printer is available to your system. Press Ctrl + F2, which is the keyboard shortcut to display the **Print Preview**, and then under **Print**, click the **Print** button.

> 6 ▸ If you are directed to create an electronic image of your worksheet that looks like a printed document, click the **File tab**, on the left click **Export**, and then on the right, click **Create PDF/XPS**. In the **Publish as PDF or XPS** dialog box, navigate to your storage location, in the **Save as type** box, be sure **PDF** is indicated, and then click **Publish** to create the PDF file.

Activity 1.16 | Printing a Section of the Worksheet

1.5.1

From Backstage view, you can print only the portion of the worksheet that you select, and there are times you might want to do this.

> 1 ▸ Select the range **A2:F5** to select only the subtitle and the data for *Exercise Bikes* and *Elliptical Machines* and the column titles

2 Press `Ctrl` + `F2`, which is the keyboard shortcut to display **Print Preview**, and then under **Settings**, click the first arrow, which currently displays *Print Active Sheets*. On the list that displays, click **Print Selection**, and then compare your screen with Figure 1.36.

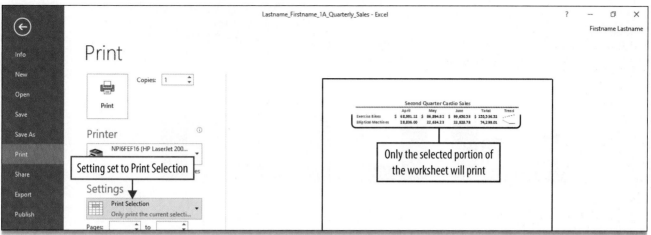

FIGURE 1.36

3 If directed by your instructor, print the selection on paper; otherwise, in the upper left corner, click **Back** to return to your workbook.

4 Press `Ctrl` + `Home`, and then click **Save**.

Activity 1.17 | Changing Page Orientation and Displaying, Printing, and Hiding Formulas

1.4.8, 1.5.4

When you type a formula in a cell, the cell displays the *results* of the formula calculation. Recall that this value is called the displayed value. You can view and print the underlying formulas in the cells. When you do so, a formula often takes more horizontal space to display than the result of the calculation.

1 If necessary, redisplay your worksheet. Because you will make some temporary changes to your workbook, on the Quick Access Toolbar, click **Save** to be sure your work is saved up to this point.

2 On the **Formulas tab**, in the **Formula Auditing group**, click **Show Formulas**.

🔄 **ANOTHER WAY**   Hold down `Ctrl`, and then press `~` (usually located below `Esc`).

3 In the **column heading area**, point to the **column A** heading to display the ⬇ pointer, hold down the left mouse button, and then drag to the right to select columns **A:F**. Compare your screen with Figure 1.37.

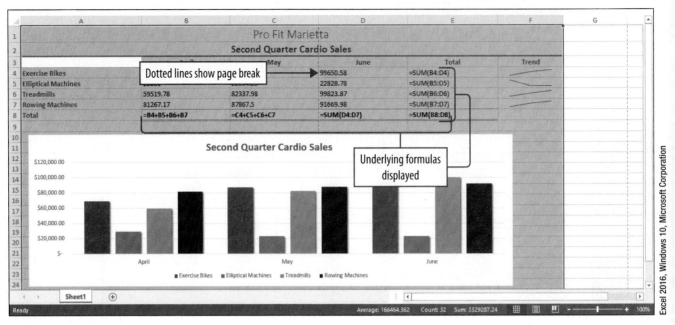

FIGURE 1.37

> **NOTE** Turning the Display of Formulas On and Off
>
> The Show Formulas button is a toggle button. Clicking it once turns the display of formulas on—the button will be shaded. Clicking the button again turns the display of formulas off.

4 ▶ Point to the column heading boundary between any two of the selected columns to display the ⊞ pointer, and then double-click to AutoFit the selected columns.

AutoFit adjusts the width of a column to fit the cell content of the *widest* cell in the column.

🔄 **ANOTHER WAY** With the columns selected, on the Home tab, in the Cells group, click Format, and then click AutoFit Column Width.

5 ▶ On the **Page Layout tab**, in the **Page Setup group**, click **Orientation**, and then click **Landscape**. In the **Scale to Fit** group, click the **Width arrow**, and then click **1 page** to scale the data to fit onto one page.

Scaling shrinks the width or height of the printed worksheet to fit a maximum number of pages and is convenient for printing formulas. Although it is not always the case, formulas frequently take up more space than the actual data.

🔄 **ANOTHER WAY** In the Scale to Fit group, click the Dialog Box Launcher button to display the Page tab of the Page Setup dialog box. Then, under Scaling, click the Fit to option button.

6 ▶ In the **Page Setup group**, click **Margins**, click **Custom Margins**, and then on the **Margins tab**, under **Center on page**, be sure the **Horizontally** check box is selected—select it if necessary.

7 ▶ Click **OK** to close the dialog box. Check to be sure your chart is centered below the data and the left and right edges are slightly inside column A and column F—use the 📐 pointer to drag a chart edge and then deselect the chart if necessary.

8 Click any cell so that the chart is not selected, and then press Ctrl + F2 to display the **Print Preview**. Under **Settings**, if necessary switch back to the option to **Print Active Sheets**. If directed to do so by your instructor, print on paper; or, to save the workbook in this format, click Save As and name the worksheet **Lastname_Firstname_1A_Quarterly_Sales_formulas**

> If you save the workbook with this new name, your original workbook is automatically saved and closed.

9 If you did not save your formulas worksheet, on the left, click **Close**, and when prompted, click **Don't Save** so that you do *not* save the changes you made—displaying formulas, changing column widths and orientation, and scaling—to print your formulas.

10 In the upper right corner of your screen, click **Close** ☒ to close Excel.

END | You have completed Project 1A

GO! With Google

> **ALERT!**   **Working with Web-Based Applications and Services**
>
> Computer programs and services on the web receive continuous updates and improvements, so the steps to complete this web-based Activity may differ from the ones shown. You can often look at the screens and the information presented to determine how to complete the Activity.
>
> If you do not already have a Google account, you will need to create one before you begin this activity. Go to http://google.com and in the upper right corner, click Sign In. On the Sign In screen, click Create Account. On the Create your Google Account page, complete the form, read and agree to the Terms of Service and Privacy Policy, and then click Next step. On the Welcome screen, click Get Started.

Activity | **Creating a Sales Report with an Embedded Column Chart Using Google Sheets**

In this Activity, you will use Google Sheets to create a sales report and chart similar to the one you created in Project 1A.

1 From the desktop, open your browser, (use a browser other than Edge), navigate to **http://google.com** and then click the **Google Apps** menu ▦. Click **Drive**, and then if necessary, sign in to your Google account.

2 Open your **GO! Web Projects** folder—or click NEW to create and then open this folder if necessary.

3 In the left pane, click **NEW**, and then click **Google Sheets**. From your Windows taskbar, open **File Explorer**, navigate to your Student Data Files for this chapter, and then in the **File List**, double-click to open **e01_1A_Web**.

4 In the displayed Excel worksheet, select the range **A1:E8**, right-click over the selection, click **Copy**, and then **Close** Excel. **Close** the **File Explorer** window.

5 In your blank Google Sheet, with cell **A1** active, point to cell **A1**, right-click, and then click **Paste**; by copying and pasting the data, you can create this project more quickly without having to do extra typing. In the column heading area, point to the border between **column A** and **column B** to display the ⟷ pointer, and then widen **column A** slightly so that all of the data in rows 4–8 displays.

6 Select the range **A1:E1**. On the toolbar, click **Merge cells** ⊞. On the toolbar, click the **Align arrow** ▾, and then click **Center** ≡. Repeat for the range **A2:E2**, and then apply **Bold** to cells **A1** and **A2**.

7 Select the range with the month names, center them, and apply **Bold**. Apply **Bold** to the totals in the range **B8:E8**.

8 Select the range **A3:D7** (the data without the totals and without the titles). On the menu bar, click **Insert**, and

then click **Chart**. In the **Chart Editor** dialog box, notice the three tabs.

9 In the **Chart Editor** window, with the first chart type selected, click the **Chart types tab**, and then select the **Switch rows/columns** check box.

10 Click the **Customization tab**. In the **Title** box, replace the existing text with **Second Quarter Cardio Sales**

11 Click the **Legend arrow**, and then click **None**. Click the **Background arrow**, and then in the fourth column, click the third color—**light yellow 3**.

12 In the lower left corner, click **Insert**. Point anywhere inside the selected chart, hold down the left mouse button to display the ✋ pointer, and then drag the chart slightly below the data. Then using the corner sizing handles resize and reposition the chart attractively below the data.

13 At the top of the worksheet, click the text *Untitled spreadsheet*, and then using your own name, type **Lastname_Firstname_EX_1A_Web** and press ENTER.

14 If you are instructed to submit your file to your instructor, you can either share the file through Google Drive, or create a PDF or Excel file. Click the File menu, point to Download as, and click the format you want. The file will download to your default download folder as determined by your browser settings. Ask your instructor in what format he or she would like to receive your file.

15 **Close** the browser tab—a new Google Sheet always opens in a new window in your browser; your work is automatically saved. Notice that your new Google Sheet displays in the file list on your Google Drive. Sign out of your Google account.

Inventory Valuation

PROJECT ACTIVITIES

In Activities 1.18 through 1.27 you will create a workbook for Josh Feingold, Operations Manager, which calculates the retail value of an inventory of plyometric training products. Your completed worksheet will look similar to Figure 1.38.

Please always review the downloaded Grader instructions before beginning.

PROJECT FILES

If your instructor wants you to submit Project 1B in the MyITLab Grader system, log in to MyITLab, locate Grader Project 1B, and then download the files for this project.

For Project 1B, you will need the following file:
New blank Excel workbook

You will save your workbook as:
Lastname_Firstname_1B_Plyo_Products

PROJECT RESULTS

From atch

hru
1B

Pro Fit Marietta
Plyometric Products Inventory Valuation

As of September 30					
	Warehouse Location	Quantity in Stock	Retail Price	Total Retail Value	Percent of Total Retail Value
Power Hurdle	Atlanta	125	$ 32.95	$ 4,118.75	1.41%
Speed Hurdle	Atlanta	995	59.95	59,650.25	20.37%
Stackable Steps	Marietta	450	251.59	113,215.50	38.65%
Pro Jump Rope	Marietta	1,105	49.95	55,194.75	18.84%
Plyometric Box Set	Marietta	255	158.05	40,302.75	13.76%
Plyometric Mat	Atlanta	215	94.99	20,422.85	6.97%
Total Retail Value for All Products				$ 292,904.85	

Lastname_Firstname_1B_Plyo_Products

Excel 2016, Windows 10, Microsoft Corporation

FIGURE 1.38 Project 1B Plyo Products

Objective 7 | Check Spelling in a Worksheet

GO! Learn How
Video E1-7

In Excel, the spelling checker performs similarly to the other Microsoft Office programs.

Activity 1.18 | Checking Spelling in a Worksheet

> **ALERT!** To submit as an autograded project, log into MyITLab, download the files for this project, and begin with those files instead of a new blank workbook.

1 Start Excel and display a new blank workbook. In cell **A1**, type **Pro Fit Marietta** and press Enter. In cell **A2**, type **Plyometric Products Inventory** and press Enter.

2 Click the **File tab**, on the left click **Save As**, under **Save As**, click **Browse** to display the **Save As** dialog box, and then navigate to your **Excel Chapter 1** folder. As the **File name**, using your own name, type **Lastname_Firstname_1B_Plyo_Products** and then click **Save**.

3 Press Tab to move to cell **B3**, type **Quantity** and press Tab. In cell **C3**, type **Average Cost** and press Tab. In cell **D3**, type **Retail Price** and press Tab.

4 Click cell **C3**, and then look at the **Formula Bar**. Notice that in the cell, the displayed value is cut off; however, in the **Formula Bar**, the entire text value—the underlying value—displays. Compare your screen with Figure 1.39.

> Text that is too long to fit in a cell extends into cells on the right only if they are empty. If the cell to the right contains data, the text in the cell to the left is truncated—cut off. The entire value continues to exist, but it is not completely visible.

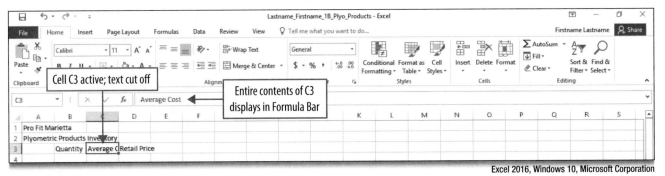

Excel 2016, Windows 10, Microsoft Corporation

FIGURE 1.39

5 Click cell **E3**, type **Total Retail Value** and press Tab. In cell **F3**, type **Percent of Total Retail Value** and press Enter.

6 Click cell **A4**. *Without* correcting the spelling error, type **Powr Hurdle** Press Enter. In the range **A5:A10**, type the remaining row titles shown below. Then compare your screen with Figure 1.40.

Speed Hurdle
Stackable Steps
Pro Jump Rope
Plyometric Box Set
Plyometric Mat
Total Retail Value for All Products

FIGURE 1.40

Excel 2016, Windows 10, Microsoft Corporation

7 In the **column heading area**, point to the right boundary of **column A** to display the ➕ pointer, and then drag to the right to widen **column A** to **215** pixels.

8 Select the range **A1:F1**, **Merge & Center** the text, and then from the **Cell Styles** gallery, apply the **Title** style.

9 Select the range **A2:F2**, **Merge & Center** the text, and then from the **Cell Styles** gallery, apply the **Heading 1** style. Press Ctrl + Home to move to the top of your worksheet.

10 With cell **A1** as the active cell, click the **Review tab**, and then in the **Proofing group**, click **Spelling**. Compare your screen with Figure 1.41.

FIGURE 1.41

Excel 2016, Windows 10, Microsoft Corporation

ANOTHER WAY Press F7, which is the keyboard shortcut for the Spelling command.

11 In the **Spelling** dialog box, under **Not in Dictionary**, notice the word *Powr*.

The spelling tool does not have this word in its dictionary. Under *Suggestions*, Excel provides a list of suggested spellings.

12 Under **Suggestions**, click **Power**, and then click **Change**.

Powr, a typing error, is changed to *Power*. A message box displays *The spelling check is complete for the entire sheet*—unless you have additional unrecognized words. Because the spelling check begins its checking process starting with the currently selected cell, it is good practice to return to cell A1 before starting the Spelling command.

13 Correct any other errors you may have made. When the message displays, *Spell check complete. You're good to go!*, click **OK**. Save 🖫 your workbook.

Objective 8 | Enter Data by Range

GO! Learn How
Video E1-8

You can enter data by first selecting a range of cells. This is a time-saving technique, especially if you use the numeric keypad to enter the numbers.

Activity 1.19 | Entering Data by Range

1 Select the range **B4:D9**, type **125** and then press Enter.

The value displays in cell B4, and cell B5 becomes the active cell.

2 With cell **B5** active in the range, and pressing Enter after each entry, type the following, and then compare your screen with Figure 1.42:

1125
450
1105
255
215

After you enter the last value and press Enter, the active cell moves to the top of the next column within the selected range. Although it is not required to enter data in this manner, you can see that selecting the range before you enter data saves time because it confines the movement of the active cell to the selected range. When you select a range of data, the Quick Analysis button displays.

FIGURE 1.42

Excel 2016, Windows 10, Microsoft Corporation

3 With the selected range still active, from the following table, beginning in cell **C4** and pressing Enter after each entry, enter the data for the **Average Cost** column and then the **Retail Price** column. If you prefer, deselect the range to enter the values—typing in a selected range is optional.

AVERAGE COST	RETAIL PRICE
15.50	32.95
29.55	59.95
125.95	251.59
18.75	49.95
85.25	159.05
49.95	94.99

Recall that the default number format for cells is the *General* number format, in which numbers display exactly as you type them and trailing zeros do not display, even if you type them.

4 Click any blank cell, and then compare your screen with Figure 1.43. Correct any errors you may have made while entering data, and then click **Save** 🗄.

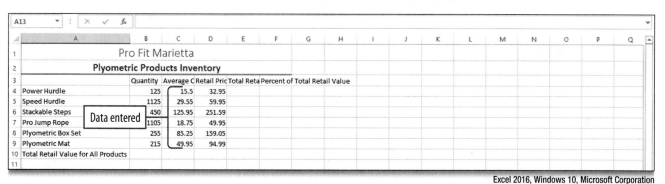

Excel 2016, Windows 10, Microsoft Corporation

FIGURE 1.43

Objective 9 Construct Formulas for Mathematical Operations

GO! Learn How
Video E1-9

Operators are symbols with which you can specify the type of calculation you want to perform in a formula.

Activity 1.20 │ Using Arithmetic Operators

1 Click cell **E4**, type **=b4*d4** and notice that the two cells are outlined as part of an active formula. Then press Enter.

The *Total Retail Value* of all *Power Hurdle* items in inventory—*4118.75*—equals the *Quantity* (125) times the *Retail Price* (selling price) of 32.95. In Excel, the asterisk (*) indicates multiplication.

2 Take a moment to study the symbols you will use to perform basic mathematical operations in Excel as shown in the table in Figure 1.44, which are referred to as *arithmetic operators*.

SYMBOLS USED IN EXCEL FOR ARITHMETIC OPERATORS	
OPERATOR SYMBOL	**OPERATION**
+	Addition
–	Subtraction (also negation)
*	Multiplication
/	Division
%	Percent
^	Exponentiation

FIGURE 1.44

3 Click cell **E4**.

You can see that in cells E5:E9 you need a formula similar to the one in E4, but one that refers to the cells in row 5, row 6, and so forth. Recall that you can copy formulas and the cell references will change *relative to* the row number.

4 With cell **E4** selected, position your pointer over the fill handle in the lower right corner of the cell until the ⊞ pointer displays. Then, drag down through cell **E9** to copy the formula.

5 Select the range **B4:B9**, and then on the **Home tab**, in the **Number group**, click **Comma Style** [,]. In the **Number group**, click **Decrease Decimal** [.00→.0] two times to remove the decimal places from these values.

Comma Style formats a number with two decimal places; because these are whole numbers referring to quantities, no decimal places are necessary.

ANOTHER WAY Select the range, display the Cell Styles gallery, and then under Number Format, click Comma [0].

6 Select the range **E4:E9**, and then at the bottom of your screen, in the status bar, notice the displayed values for **Average**, **Count**, and **Sum**—*50158.89167, 6* and *300953.35*.

When you select a range of numerical data, Excel's *AutoCalculate* feature displays three calculations in the status bar by default—Average, Count, and Sum. Here, Excel indicates that if you averaged the selected values, the result would be *50158.89167*, there are *6* cells in the selection that contain values, and that if you added the values the result would be *300953.35*.

You can display three additional calculations to this area by right-clicking the status bar and selecting them—Numerical Count, Minimum, and Maximum.

Activity 1.21 | Using the Quick Analysis Tool

5.1.4

Recall that the Quick Analysis button displays when you select a range of data. Quick Analysis is convenient because it keeps common commands close to your mouse pointer and also displays commands in a format that is easy to touch with your finger if you are using a touchscreen device.

1 Be sure the range **E4:E9** is still selected. In the lower right corner of the selected range, click **Quick Analysis** [▦], and then in the displayed gallery, click **Totals**. *Point to*, but do not click, the first **Sum** button, which shows blue cells at the bottom. Compare your screen with Figure 1.45.

Here, the shaded cells on the button indicate what will be summed and where the result will display, and a preview of the result displays in the cell bordered with a gray shadow.

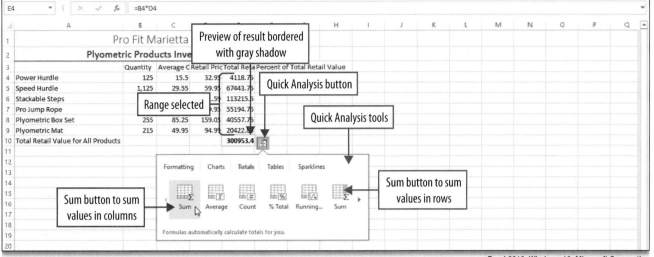

FIGURE 1.45

Excel 2016, Windows 10, Microsoft Corporation

2 ▶ Click the first **Sum** button to display the column total *300953.4* formatted in Bold.

Sums calculated using the Quick Analysis tool are formatted in Bold.

3 ▶ Select the range **C5:E9** and apply the **Comma Style** [⟩]; notice that Excel widens the columns to accommodate the data.

4 ▶ Select the range **C4:E4**, hold down Ctrl, and then click cell **E10**. Release Ctrl, and then apply the **Accounting Number Format** [$ ·]. Notice that Excel widens the columns as necessary.

5 ▶ Click cell **E10**, and then from the **Cell Styles** gallery, apply the **Total** style. Click any blank cell, **Save** [⊟] your workbook, and then compare your screen with Figure 1.46.

FIGURE 1.46

Excel 2016, Windows 10, Microsoft Corporation

Activity 1.22 │ Copying Formulas Containing Absolute Cell References

4.1.1

In a formula, a relative cell reference refers to a cell by its position *relative to* the cell that contains the formula. An ***absolute cell reference***, on the other hand, refers to a cell by its *fixed* position in the worksheet, for example, the total in cell E10.

A relative cell reference automatically adjusts when a formula is copied. In some calculations, you do *not* want the cell reference to adjust; rather, you want the cell reference to remain the same when the formula is copied.

1 ▶ Click cell **F4**, type **=** and then click cell **E4**. Type **/** and then click cell **E10**.

The formula *=E4/E10* indicates that the value in cell E4 will be *divided* by the value in cell E10. Why? Because Mr. Feingold wants to know the percentage by which each product's Total Retail Value makes up the Total Retail Value for All Products.

Arithmetically, the percentage is computed by dividing the *Total Retail Value* for each product by the *Total Retail Value for All Products*. The result will be a percentage expressed as a decimal.

2 Press Enter. Click cell **F4** and notice that the formula displays in the **Formula Bar**. Then, point to cell **F4** and double-click.

The formula, with the two referenced cells displayed in color and bordered with the same color, displays in the cell. This feature, called the *range finder*, is useful for verifying formulas because it visually indicates which workbook cells are included in a formula calculation.

3 Press Enter to redisplay the result of the calculation in the cell, and notice that .013686, which is approximately 1% of the total retail value of the inventory, is made up of Power Hurdles.

4 Click cell **F4** again, and then drag the fill handle down through cell **F9**. Compare your screen with Figure 1.47.

Each cell displays an error message—*#DIV/0!* and a green triangle in the upper left corner of each cell indicates that Excel detects an error.

Like a grammar checker, Excel uses rules to check for formula errors and flags errors in this manner. Additionally, the Auto Fill Options button displays, from which you can select formatting options for the copied cells.

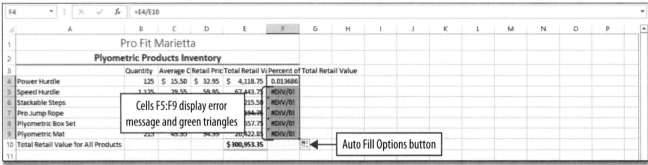

FIGURE 1.47

5 Click cell **F5**, and then to the left of the cell, point to the **Error Checking** button ◆ to display its ScreenTip—*The formula or function used is dividing by zero or empty cells.*

In this manner, Excel suggests the cause of an error.

6 Look at the **Formula Bar** and examine the formula.

The formula is =E5/E11. The cell reference to E5 is correct, but the cell reference following the division operator (/) is *E11*, and E11 is an *empty* cell.

7 Click cell **F6**, point to the **Error Checking** button ◆, and in the **Formula Bar** examine the formula.

Because the cell references are relative, Excel builds the formulas by increasing the row number for each equation. But in this calculation, the divisor must always be the value in cell E10—the *Total Retail Value for All Products*.

8 Point to cell **F4**, and then double-click to place the insertion point within the cell.

9 Within the cell, use the arrow keys as necessary to position the insertion point to the left of *E10*, and then press F4. Compare your screen with Figure 1.48.

Dollar signs ($) display, which changes the reference to cell E10 to an absolute cell reference. The use of the dollar sign to denote an absolute reference is not related in any way to whether or not the values you are working with are currency values. It is simply the symbol that Excel uses to denote an absolute cell reference.

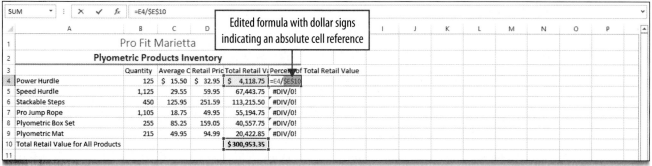

FIGURE 1.48

Excel 2016, Windows 10, Microsoft Corporation

🔄 **ANOTHER WAY**   Edit the formula so that it indicates =*E4/$E$10*.

10 On the **Formula Bar**, click **Enter** ✓ so that **F4** remains the active cell. Then, drag the fill handle to copy the new formula down through cell **F9**. Compare your screen with Figure 1.49.

FIGURE 1.49

Excel 2016, Windows 10, Microsoft Corporation

11 Click cell **F5**, examine the formula in the **Formula Bar**, and then examine the formulas for cells **F6, F7, F8**, and **F9**.

For each formula, the cell reference for the *Total Retail Value* of each product changed relative to its row; however, the value used as the divisor—*Total Retail Value for All Products* in cell E10—remained absolute. You can see that by using either relative or absolute cell references, it is easy to duplicate formulas without typing them.

12 Save 💾 your workbook.

More Knowledge   **Calculate a Percentage if You Know the Total and the Amount**

Using the equation *amount/total = percentage*, you can calculate the percentage by which a part makes up a total—with the percentage formatted as a decimal. For example, if on a test you score 42 points correctly out of 50, your percentage of correct answers is 42/50 = 0.84 or 84%.

Objective 10   Edit Values in a Worksheet

GO! Learn How
Video E1-10

Excel performs calculations on numbers; that is why you use Excel. If you make changes to the numbers, Excel automatically *re*-calculates the results. This is one of the most powerful and valuable features of Excel.

Activity 1.23 | Editing Values in a Worksheet

You can edit text and number values directly within a cell or in the Formula Bar.

1 In cell **E10**, notice the column total *$300,953.35*. Click cell **B5**. To change its value, type **995** and watch cell E5 as you press Enter.

> Excel formulas *recalculate* if you change the value in a cell that is referenced in a formula. It is not necessary to delete the old value in a cell; selecting the cell and typing a new value replaces the old value with your new typing.

> The *Total Retail Value* of all *Speed Hurdle* items recalculates to *59,650.25* and the total in cell E10 recalculates to *$293,159.85*. Additionally, all of the percentages in column F recalculate.

2 Point to cell **D8**, and then double-click to place the insertion point within the cell. Use the arrow keys to move the insertion point to the left or right of *9*, and use either Del or Backspace to delete *9* and then type **8** so that the new Retail Price is *158.05*.

3 Watch cell **E8** and **E10** as you press Enter, and then notice the recalculation of the formulas in those two cells.

> Excel recalculates the value in cell E8 to *40,302.75* and the value in cell E10 to *$292,904.85*. Additionally, all of the percentages in column F recalculate because the *Total Retail Value for All Products* recalculated.

4 Point to cell **A2** so that the ⊕ pointer is positioned slightly to the right of the word *Inventory*, and then double-click to place the insertion point in the cell. Edit the text to add the word **Valuation** pressing Spacebar as necessary, and then press Enter.

5 Click cell **B3**, and then in the **Formula Bar**, click to place the insertion point after the letter *y*. Press Spacebar one time, type **in Stock** and then on the **Formula Bar**, click **Enter** ✔. Click **Save** 🖫, and then compare your screen with Figure 1.50.

> Recall that if text is too long to fit in the cell and the cell to the right contains data, the text is truncated—cut off—but the entire value still exists as the underlying value.

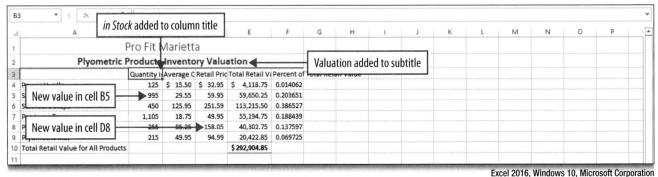

Excel 2016, Windows 10, Microsoft Corporation

FIGURE 1.50

Activity 1.24 | Formatting Cells with the Percent Style

[MOS] 2.2.5

A percentage is part of a whole expressed in hundredths. For example, 75 cents is the same as 75 percent of one dollar. The Percent Style button formats the selected cell as a percentage rounded to the nearest hundredth.

1 Click cell **F4**, and then in the **Number group**, click **Percent Style** %.

> Your result is *1%*, which is *0.014062* rounded to the nearest hundredth and expressed as a percentage. Percent Style displays the value of a cell as a percentage.

2 Select the range **F4:F9**, right-click over the selection, and then on the mini toolbar, click **Percent Style** %, click **Increase Decimal** ⬓ two times, and then click **Center** ≡.

> Percent Style may not offer a percentage precise enough to analyze important financial information—adding additional decimal places to a percentage makes data more precise.

3 Click any cell to cancel the selection, **Save** 🔲 your workbook, and then compare your screen with Figure 1.51.

	A	B	C	D	E	F	G
1	Pro Fit Marietta						
2	Plyometric Products Inventory Valuation						
3		Quantity in	Average C	Retail Pric	Total Retail Va	Percent of Total Retail Value	
4	Power Hurdle	125	$ 15.50	$ 32.95	$ 4,118.75	1.41%	
5	Speed Hurdle	995	29.55	59.95	59,650.25	20.37%	
6	Stackable Steps	450		Percentages formatted	.50	38.65%	
7	Pro Jump Rope	1,105			.75	18.84%	
8	Plyometric Box Set	255	85.25	158.05	40,302.75	13.76%	
9	Plyometric Mat	215	49.95	94.99	20,422.85	6.97%	
10	Total Retail Value for All Products				$292,904.85		
11							

Excel 2016, Windows 10, Microsoft Corporation

FIGURE 1.51

Objective 11   Format a Worksheet

GO! Learn How
Video E1-11

Formatting refers to the process of specifying the appearance of cells and the overall layout of your worksheet. Formatting is accomplished through various commands on the ribbon, for example, applying Cell Styles, and also from commands on shortcut menus, using keyboard shortcuts, and in the Format Cells dialog box.

Activity 1.25 │ Inserting and Deleting Rows and Columns

MOS
1.3.5

1 In the **row heading area** on the left side of your screen, point to the row heading for **row 3** to display the ➡ pointer, and then right-click to simultaneously select the row and display a shortcut menu.

2 On the shortcut menu, click **Insert** to insert a new **row 3** above the selected row.

The rows below the new row 3 move down one row, and the Insert Options button displays. By default, the new row uses the formatting of the row *above*.

🔄 **ANOTHER WAY**   Select the row, on the Home tab, in the Cells group, click the Insert button arrow, and then click Insert Sheet Rows. Or, select the row and click the Insert button—the default setting of the button inserts a new sheet row above the selected row.

3 Click cell **E11**. On the **Formula Bar**, notice that the range changed to sum the new range **E5:E10**. Compare your screen with Figure 1.52.

If you move formulas by inserting additional rows or columns in your worksheet, Excel automatically adjusts the formulas. Excel adjusted all of the formulas in the worksheet that were affected by inserting this new row.

E11	▼	:	×	✓	*fx*	=SUM(E5:E10)	◄──	Formula Bar displays the formula in E11					

	A	B	C	D	E	F	...	J	K	L	M	N	O	P
	Insert Options button	Pro Fit Marietta												
2	Plyometric Products Inventory Valuation													
3							New row 3 inserted							
4			Quantity in	Average C	Retail Pric	Total Retail Va	Percent of Total Retail Value							
5	Power Hurdle	125	$ 15.50	$ 32.95	$ 4,118.75	1.41%								
6	Speed Hurdle	995	29.55	59.95	59,650.25	20.37%								
7	Stackable Steps	450	125.95	251.59	113,215.50	38.65%								
8	Pro Jump Rope	1,105	18.75	49.95	55,194.75	18.84%								
9	Plyometric Box Set	255	85.25	158.05	40,302.75	13.76%								
10	Plyometric Mat	215	49.95	94.99	20,422.85	6.97%								
11	Total Retail Value for All Products				$292,904.85									
12														

Excel 2016, Windows 10, Microsoft Corporation

FIGURE 1.52

4 Click cell **A3**, type **As of September 30** and then on the **Formula Bar**, click **Enter** ☑ to maintain **A3** as the active cell. **Merge & Center** the text across the range **A3:F3**, and then apply the **Heading 2** cell style.

5 In the **column heading area**, point to **column B** to display the ⬇ pointer, right-click, and then click **Insert**.

> A column is inserted to the left of column B. By default, the new column uses the formatting of the column to the *left*.

🔄 **ANOTHER WAY** Select the column, on the Home tab, in the Cells group, click the Insert button arrow, and then click Insert Sheet Columns. Or, select the column and click the Insert button—the default setting of the button inserts a new sheet column to the right of the selected column.

6 Click cell **B4**, type **Warehouse Location** and then press Enter.

7 In cell **B5**, type **Atlanta** and then type **Atlanta** again in cells **B6** and **B10**. Use AutoComplete to speed your typing by pressing Enter as soon as the AutoComplete suggestion displays. In cells **B7**, **B8**, and **B9**, type **Marietta**

8 In the **column heading area**, point to **column D**, right-click, and then click **Delete**.

> The remaining columns shift to the left, and Excel adjusts all the formulas in the worksheet accordingly. You can use a similar technique to delete a row in a worksheet.

9 Compare your screen with Figure 1.53, and then **Save** 🖫 your workbook.

Excel 2016, Windows 10, Microsoft Corporation

FIGURE 1.53

Activity 1.26 | Adjusting Column Widths and Wrapping Text

Use the Wrap Text command to display the contents of a cell on multiple lines.

MOS
1.3.7, 2.2.4

1 In the **column heading area**, point to the **column B** heading to display the ⬇ pointer, and then drag to the right to select **columns B:F**.

2 With the columns selected, in the **column heading area**, point to the right boundary of any of the selected columns to display the ✛ pointer, and then drag to set the width to **95 pixels**.

> Use this technique to format multiple columns or rows simultaneously.

3 Select the range **B4:F4** that comprises the column headings, and then on the **Home tab**, in the **Alignment group**, click **Wrap Text** 📑. Notice that the row height adjusts to display the titles on multiple lines.

4 With the range **B4:F4** still selected, in the **Alignment group**, click **Center** ☰ and **Middle Align** ☰. With the range **B4:F4** still selected, apply the **Heading 4** cell style.

> The Middle Align command aligns text so that it is centered between the top and bottom of the cell.

5 Select the range **B5:B10**, right-click, and then on the mini toolbar, click **Center** ▤ . Click cell **A11**, and then from the **Cell Styles** gallery, under **Themed Cell Styles**, click **40% - Accent1**. **Save** ▤ your workbook.

Activity 1.27 | Changing Theme Colors

You can change only the theme *colors* of a workbook—without changing the theme fonts or effects.

1 On the **Page Layout tab**, in the **Themes group**, click **Colors**, and then click **Green** to change the Theme Color. Click any blank cell, and then compare your screen with Figure 1.54.

	A	B	C	D	E	F	G	H	I	J	K	L	M	N
1		Pro Fit Marietta												
2		Plyometric Products Inventory Valuation												
3		As of September 30												
4			Warehouse Location	Quantity in Stock	Retail Price	Total Retail Value	Percent of Total Retail Value							
5	Power Hurdle		Atlanta	125	$ 32.95	$ 4,118.75	1.41%							
6	Speed Hurdle		Atlanta	995	59.95	59,650.25	20.37%							
7	Stackable Steps		Marietta	450	251.59	113,215.50	38.65%							
8	Pro Jump Rope		Marietta	1,105	49.95	55,194.75	18.84%							
9	Plyometric Box Set		Marietta	255	158.05	40,302.75	13.76%							
10	Plyometric Mat		Atlanta	215	94.99	20,422.85	6.97%							
11	Total Retail Value for All Products					$ 292,904.85								
12														

Theme colors changed to Green

FIGURE 1.54

Excel 2016, Windows 10, Microsoft Corporation

2 On the **Page Layout tab**, in the **Page Setup group**, click **Margins**, and then click **Custom Margins**.

3 In the **Page Setup** dialog box, on the **Margins tab**, under **Center on page**, select the **Horizontally** check box.

This action will center the data horizontally on the page, as shown in the Preview area.

4 Click the **Header/Footer tab**, and then in the center of the dialog box, click **Custom Footer**. In the **Footer** dialog box, with your insertion point blinking in the **Left section**, on the row of buttons, click **Insert File Name** 🔳 .

&[File] displays in the Left section. Here you can type or insert information from the row of buttons into the left, middle, or right section of the footer. The Custom Header button displays a similar screen to enter information in the header of the worksheet.

5 Click **OK** two times.

6 Click the **File tab** to display Backstage view, and then in the lower right corner, click **Show All Properties**.

7 As the **Tags**, type **plyo products, inventory** and as the **Subject**, type your course name and section number. Be sure your name displays in the **Author** box, or edit it if necessary.

8 On the left, click **Print** to view the **Print Preview**. At the bottom of the **Print Preview**, click **Next Page** ▶ , and notice that as currently formatted, the worksheet occupies two pages.

9 Under **Settings**, click **Portrait Orientation**, and then click **Landscape Orientation**. Compare your screen with Figure 1.55.

You can change the orientation on the Page Layout tab, or here, in Print Preview. Because it is in the Print Preview that you will often see adjustments that need to be made, commonly used settings display on the Print tab in Backstage view.

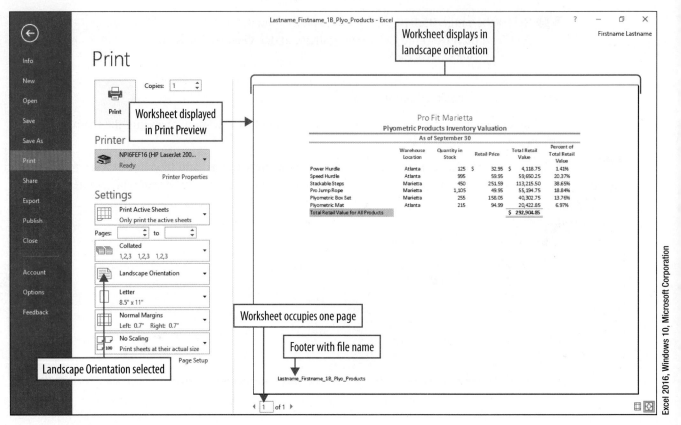

FIGURE 1.55

10 On the left, click **Save**. By using the techniques you practiced in Project 1A and as directed by your instructor, print, create a PDF image that looks like a printed document, or submit your completed Excel file. If required by your instructor, print or create an electronic version of your worksheet with formulas displayed.

11 In **Backstage** view, click **Close** to close your workbook, and then **Close** ☒ Excel.

END | You have completed Project 1B

GO! With Google

Objective   Creating an Inventory Valuation Report

> **ALERT!**   **Working with Web-Based Applications and Services**
>
> Computer programs and services on the web receive continuous updates and improvements, so the steps to complete this web-based Activity may differ from the ones shown. You can often look at the screens and the information presented to determine how to complete the Activity.
>
> If you do not already have a Google account, you will need to create one before you begin this activity. Go to http://google.com and in the upper right corner, click Sign In. On the Sign In screen, click Create Account. On the Create your Google Account page, complete the form, read and agree to the Terms of Service and Privacy Policy, and then click Next step. On the Welcome screen, click Get Started.

Activity | Creating an Inventory Valuation Report Using Google Sheets

In this Activity, you will use Google Sheets to create an inventory valuation report similar to the one you created in Project 1B.

1 From the desktop, open your browser (a browser other than Edge), navigate to **http://google.com** and then click the **Google Apps** menu ⊞. Click **Drive**, and then if necessary, sign in to your Google account.

2 Open your **GO! Web Projects** folder—or click New to create and then open this folder if necessary.

3 In the left pane, click **NEW**, and then click **Google Sheets**. From your Windows taskbar, open **File Explorer**, navigate to your Student Data Files for this chapter, and then in the **File List**, double-click the Word document **e01_1B_Web**; to complete this project quickly and eliminate extra typing, you will copy the data from a Word document.

4 In the displayed Word document, click anywhere in the text, and then in the upper left corner, click to select the **Table Select** ⊞ to select the entire Word table. Right-click anywhere over the selection, and then click **Copy**. **Close** Word. **Close** the **File Explorer** window.

5 In your blank Google Sheet, with cell **A1** active, point to cell **A1**, right-click, and then click **Paste**. In the column heading area, point to the border between **column A** and **column B** to display the ↔ pointer, and then widen **column A** slightly so that all of the data in rows 4–10 displays.

6 Select the range **A1:E1**. On the toolbar, click **Merge cells** ⊞. On the toolbar, click the **Align arrow** ▾, and then click **Center** ≡. Repeat for the range **A2:E2**, and then apply **Bold** B to cells **A1** and **A2**.

7 Select the range **B3:E3**, on the menu bar click **Format**, point to **Text wrapping**, and then click **Wrap**. **Center** these column titles and apply **Bold** B.

8 Select the range **C4:C9**, on the menu bar click **Format**, point to **Number**, on the fly-out menu click **Number**, and then if necessary, on the toolbar, click **Decrease decimal places** ▾ two times.

9 Click cell **E4**, type = and then click cell **C4**. Type * and then click cell **D4**. Press Enter. Click cell **E4**, point to the fill handle in the lower right corner of the cell, and then drag down to cell **E9**.

10 Select the range **E4:E9**. On the toolbar, click **Functions** Σ ▾, click **SUM**, and then press Enter.

11 Select the range **D4:E4**, hold down Ctrl, and then select cell **E10**. On the menu bar, click **Format**, point to **Number**, and then in the fly-out menu click **Currency**.

12 Select cell **A10**, hold down Ctrl, and then click cell **E10**. Apply **Bold** B.

13 Click cell **A1**, hold down Ctrl, and then click cell **A2**, cell **A10**, and cell **E10**. With the four cells selected, on the toolbar, click **Fill color** ▾, and then in the fourth column, click the third color—**light yellow 3**.

14 At the top of the worksheet, click the text *Untitled spreadsheet*, and then using your own name, type **Lastname_Firstname_EX_1B_Web** and press ENTER.

(GO! With Google continues on the next page)

GO! With Google

15 If you are instructed to submit your file to your instructor, you can either share the file through Google Drive, or create a PDF or Excel file as described in the Note box below. Ask your instructor in what format he or she would like to receive your file.

16 **Close** the browser tab—a new Google Sheet always opens in a new window in your browser; your work is automatically saved. Notice that your new Google Sheet displays in the file list on your Google Drive. Sign out of your Google account.

NOTE   Downloading Google Files

You can download your file in several formats, including PDF or PowerPoint. Click the File menu, point to Download as, and click the format directed by your instructor. The file will download to your default download folder as determined by your browser settings.

Lastname_Firstname_EX_1B_Web

File Edit View Insert Format Data Tools Add-ons Help

$ % .0 .00 123 ▾ Arial ▾ 10 ▾ **B** *I* S A ▾

	A	B	C	D	E
1			Pro Fit Marietta		
2			Plyometric Products Inventory Valuation		
3		Warehouse Location	Quantity In Stock	Retail Price	Total Retail Value
4	Power Hurdle	Atlanta	125	$32.95	$4,118.75
5	Speed Hurdle	Atlanta	995	59.95	59650.25
6	Stackable Steps	Marietta	450	251.59	113215.5
7	Pro Jump Rope	Marietta	1,105	49.95	55194.75
8	Plyometric Box Set	Marietta	255	158.05	40302.75
9	Plyometric Mat	Atlanta	215	94.99	20422.85
10	Total Retail Value for All Products				$292,904.85
11					

FIGURE A

GO! To Work

Andres Rodriguez/Fotolia; FotolEdhar/Fotolia; Andrey Popov/Fotolia; Shutterstock

MICROSOFT OFFICE SPECIALIST (MOS) SKILLS IN THIS CHAPTER

PROJECT 1A	PROJECT 1B
1.1.1 Create a workbook	**1.3.5** Insert and delete columns or rows
1.3.4 Modify page setup	**1.3.7** Adjust row height and column width
1.3.6 Change workbook themes	**2.2.5** Apply number formats
1.3.8 Insert headers and footers	**2.2.6** Apply cell formats
1.4.6 Modify document properties	**4.1.1** Insert references
1.4.8 Display formulas	**5.1.4** Analyze data by using Quick Analysis
1.5.1 Set a print area	
1.5.3 Print all or part of a workbook	
1.5.4 Set print scaling	
2.1.4 Fill cells by using Auto Fill	
2.2.1 Merge cells	
2.2.5 Apply number formats	
2.2.7 Apply cell styles	
2.3.1 Insert sparklines	
5.1.1 Create a new chart	
5.1.3 Switch between rows and columns in source data	
5.2.2 Add and modify chart elements	
5.2.3 Apply chart layouts and styles	

BUILD YOUR E-PORTFOLIO

An E-Portfolio is a collection of evidence, stored electronically, that showcases what you have accomplished while completing your education. Collecting and then sharing your work products with potential employers reflects your academic and career goals. Your completed documents from the following projects are good examples to show what you have learned: 1G, 1K, and 1L.

GO! FOR JOB SUCCESS
Video: Customer Service
Your instructor may assign this video to your class, and then ask you to think about, or discuss with your classmates, these questions:

FotolEdhar/Fotolia

If you were interviewing people for your company, what would you look for in terms of their dress and personal presentation?

What might you want to change about your personal dress for work or for an interview?

Do you feel that it's right to "judge a book by its cover"? Why or why not?

END OF CHAPTER

SUMMARY

In Excel, you work with worksheets that are contained in a workbook. A worksheet is formatted as a pattern of uniformly spaced horizontal rows and vertical columns, the intersection of which forms a cell.

A cell can contain a constant value—referred to as a value—or a formula, which is an equation that performs mathematical calculations on the values in your worksheet. Common values are text and numbers.

You can insert sparklines in an Excel worksheet, which are tiny charts embedded in a cell that give a visual trend summary alongside your data. A sparkline makes a pattern more obvious to the eye.

Charts provide a graphic representation of data in a worksheet. Use the Recommended Charts feature to display customized charts that, according to Excel's calculations, will best represent your data.

GO! LEARN IT ONLINE

Review the concepts, key terms, and MOS skills in this chapter by completing these online challenges, which you can find at MyITLab.

Matching and Multiple Choice: Answer matching and multiple choice questions to test what you learned in this chapter.

Lessons on the GO!: Learn how to use all the new apps and features as they are introduced by Microsoft.

MOS Prep Quiz: Answer questions to review the MOS skills that you practiced in this chapter.

GO! COLLABORATIVE TEAM PROJECT (Available in MyITLab and Instructor Resource Center)

If your instructor assigns this project to your class, you can expect to work with one or more of your classmates—either in person or by using Internet tools—to create work products similar to those that you created in this chapter. A team is a group of workers who work together to solve a problem, make a decision, or create a work product. Collaboration is when you work together with others as a team in an intellectual endeavor to complete a shared task or achieve a shared goal.

PROJECT GUIDE FOR EXCEL CHAPTER 1

Your instructor will assign Projects from this list to ensure your learning and assess your knowledge.

	PROJECT GUIDE FOR EXCEL CHAPTER 1		
Project	Apply Skills from These Chapter Objectives	Project Type	Project Location
1A MyITLab	Objectives 1–6 from Project 1A	**1A Instructional Project (Grader Project)** Guided instruction to learn the skills in Project 1A.	In text
1B MyITLab	Objectives 7–11 from Project 1B	**1B Instructional Project (Grader Project)** Guided instruction to learn the skills in Project 1B.	In text
1C	Objectives 1–6 from Project 1A	**1C Skills Review (Scorecard Grading)** A guided review of the skills from Project 1A.	In text
1D	Objectives 7–11 from Project 1B	**1D Skills Review (Scorecard Grading)** A guided review of the skills from Project 1B.	In text
1E MyITLab	Objectives 1–6 from Project 1A	**1E Mastery (Grader Project) Mastery and Transfer of Learning** A demonstration of your mastery of the skills in Project 1A with extensive decision making.	In text
1F MyITLab	Objectives 7–11 from Project 1B	**1F Mastery (Grader Project) Mastery and Transfer of Learning** A demonstration of your mastery of the skills in Project 1B with extensive decision making.	In text
1G MyITLab	Objectives 1–11 from Projects 1A and 1B	**1G Mastery (Grader Project) Mastery and Transfer of Learning** A demonstration of your mastery of the skills in Projects 1A and 1B with extensive decision making.	In text
1H	Combination of Objectives from Projects 1A and 1B	**1H GO! Fix It (Scorecard Grading) Critical Thinking** A demonstration of your mastery of the skills in Projects 1A and 1B by creating a correct result from a document that contains errors you must find.	Instructor Resource Center (IRC)
1I	Combination of Objectives from Projects 1A and 1B	**1I GO! Make It (Scorecard Grading) Critical Thinking** A demonstration of your mastery of the skills in Projects 1A and 1B by creating a result from a supplied picture.	IRC
1J	Combination of Objectives from Projects 1A and 1B	**1J GO! Solve It (Rubric Grading) Critical Thinking** A demonstration of your mastery of the skills in Projects 1A and 1B, your decision-making skills, and your critical-thinking skills. A task-specific rubric helps you self-assess your result.	IRC
1K	Combination of Objectives from Projects 1A and 1B	**1K GO! Solve It (Rubric Grading) Critical Thinking** A demonstration of your mastery of the skills in Projects 1A and 1B, your decision-making skills, and your critical-thinking skills. A task-specific rubric helps you self-assess your result.	In text
1L	Combination of Objectives from Projects 1A and 1B	**1L GO! Think (Rubric Grading) Critical Thinking** A demonstration of your understanding of the chapter concepts applied in a manner that you would outside of college. An analytic rubric helps you and your instructor grade the quality of your work by comparing it to the work an expert in the discipline would create.	In text
1M	Combination of Objectives from Projects 1A and 1B	**1M GO! Think (Rubric Grading) Critical Thinking** A demonstration of your understanding of the chapter concepts applied in a manner that you would outside of college. An analytic rubric helps you and your instructor grade the quality of your work by comparing it to the work an expert in the discipline would create.	IRC
1N	Combination of Objectives from Projects 1A and 1B	**1N You and GO! (Rubric Grading) Critical Thinking** A demonstration of your understanding of the chapter concepts applied in a manner that you would in a personal situation. An analytic rubric helps you and your instructor grade the quality of your work.	IRC
1O	Combination of Objectives from Projects 1A and 1B	**1O Cumulative Group Project for Excel Chapter 1** A demonstration of your understanding of concepts and your ability to work collaboratively in a group role-playing assessment, requiring both collaboration and self-management.	IRC

GLOSSARY

GLOSSARY OF CHAPTER KEY TERMS

Absolute cell reference A cell reference that refers to cells by their fixed position in a worksheet; an absolute cell reference remains the same when the formula is copied.

Accounting Number Format The Excel number format that applies a thousand comma separator where appropriate, inserts a fixed U.S. dollar sign aligned at the left edge of the cell, applies two decimal places, and leaves a small amount of space at the right edge of the cell to accommodate a parenthesis for negative numbers.

Active cell The cell, surrounded by a border, ready to receive data or be affected by the next Excel command.

Arithmetic operators The symbols +, −, *, /, %, and ^ used to denote addition, subtraction (or negation), multiplication, division, percentage, and exponentiation in an Excel formula.

Auto Fill An Excel feature that generates and extends values into adjacent cells based on the values of selected cells.

AutoCalculate A feature that displays three calculations in the status bar by default—Average, Count, and Sum—when you select a range of numerical data.

AutoComplete A feature that speeds your typing and lessens the likelihood of errors; if the first few characters you type in a cell match an existing entry in the column, Excel fills in the remaining characters for you.

AutoFit An Excel feature that adjusts the width of a column to fit the cell content of the widest cell in the column.

AutoSum A button that provides quick access to the SUM function.

Category axis The area along the bottom of a chart that identifies the categories of data; also referred to as the x-axis.

Category labels The labels that display along the bottom of a chart to identify the categories of data; Excel uses the row titles as the category names.

Cell The intersection of a column and a row.

Cell address Another name for a cell reference.

Cell content Anything typed into a cell.

Cell reference The identification of a specific cell by its intersecting column letter and row number.

Cell style A defined set of formatting characteristics, such as font, font size, font color, cell borders, and cell shading.

Chart The graphic representation of data in a worksheet; data presented as a chart is usually easier to understand than a table of numbers.

Chart Elements button A button that enables you to add, remove, or change chart elements such as the title, legend, gridlines, and data labels.

Chart Filters button A button that enables you to change which data displays in the chart.

Chart layout The combination of chart elements that can be displayed in a chart such as a title, legend, labels for the columns, and the table of charted cells.

Chart style The overall visual look of a chart in terms of its graphic effects, colors, and backgrounds; for example, you can have flat or beveled columns, colors that are solid or transparent, and backgrounds that are dark or light.

Chart Styles button A button that enables you to set a style and color scheme for your chart.

Chart Styles gallery A group of predesigned chart styles that you can apply to an Excel chart.

Chart types Various chart formats used in a way that is meaningful to the reader; common examples are column charts, pie charts, and line charts.

Column A vertical group of cells in a worksheet.

Column chart A chart in which the data is arranged in columns and that is useful for showing data changes over a period of time or for illustrating comparisons among items.

Column heading The letter that displays at the top of a vertical group of cells in a worksheet; beginning with the first letter of the alphabet, a unique letter or combination of letters identifies each column.

Comma Style The Excel number format that inserts thousand comma separators where appropriate and applies two decimal places; Comma Style also leaves space at the right to accommodate a parenthesis when negative numbers are present.

Constant value Numbers, text, dates, or times of day that you type into a cell.

Context sensitive A command associated with the currently selected or active object; often activated by right-clicking a screen item.

Data Text or numbers in a cell.

Data marker A column, bar, area, dot, pie slice, or other symbol in a chart that represents a single data point; related data points form a data series.

Data point A value that originates in a worksheet cell and that is represented in a chart by a data marker.

Data series Related data points represented by data markers; each data series has a unique color or pattern represented in the chart legend.

Displayed value The data that displays in a cell.

Excel pointer An Excel window element with which you can display the location of the pointer.

Expand Formula Bar button An Excel window element with which you can increase the height of the Formula Bar to display lengthy cell content.

Expand horizontal scroll bar button An Excel window element with which you can increase the width of the horizontal scroll bar.

Fill handle The small square in the lower right corner of a selected cell.

Format Changing the appearance of cells and worksheet elements to make a worksheet attractive and easy to read.

Formula An equation that performs mathematical calculations on values in a worksheet.

Formula Bar An element in the Excel window that displays the value or formula contained in the active cell; here you can also enter or edit values or formulas.

Function A predefined formula—a formula that Excel has already built for you—that performs calculations by using specific values in a particular order.

General format The default format that Excel applies to numbers; this format has no specific characteristics—whatever you type in the cell will display, with the exception that trailing zeros to the right of a decimal point will not display.

Label Another name for a text value, and which usually provides information about number values.

Left alignment The cell format in which characters align at the left edge of the cell; this is the default for text entries and is an example of formatting information stored in a cell.

Legend A chart element that identifies the patterns or colors that are assigned to the categories in the chart.

Lettered column headings The area along the top edge of a worksheet that identifies each column with a unique letter or combination of letters.

Merge & Center A command that joins selected cells in an Excel worksheet into one larger cell and centers the contents in the merged cell.

Name Box An element of the Excel window that displays the name of the selected cell, table, chart, or object.

Normal view A screen view that maximizes the number of cells visible on your screen and keeps the column letters and row numbers close to the columns and rows.

Number format A specific way in which Excel displays numbers in a cell.

Number values Constant values consisting of only numbers.

Numbered row headings The area along the left edge of a worksheet that identifies each row with a unique number.

Operators The symbols with which you can specify the type of calculation you want to perform in an Excel formula.

Picture element A point of light measured in dots per square inch on a screen; 64 pixels equals 8.43 characters, which is the average number of characters that will fit in a cell in an Excel worksheet using the default font.

Pixel The abbreviated name for a picture element.

Point and click method The technique of constructing a formula by pointing to and then clicking cells; this method

is convenient when the referenced cells are not adjacent to one another.

Quick Analysis Tool A tool that displays in the lower right corner of a selected range, with which you can analyze your data by using Excel tools such as charts, color-coding, and formulas.

Range Two or more selected cells on a worksheet that are adjacent or nonadjacent; because the range is treated as a single unit, you can make the same changes or combination of changes to more than one cell at a time.

Range finder An Excel feature that outlines cells in color to indicate which cells are used in a formula; useful for verifying which cells are referenced in a formula.

Recommended Charts An Excel feature that displays a customized set of charts that, according to Excel's calculations, will best fit your data based on the range of data that you select.

Relative cell reference In a formula, the address of a cell based on the relative positions of the cell that contains the formula and the cell referred to in the formula.

Rounding A procedure in which you determine which digit at the right of the number will be the last digit displayed and then increase it by one if the next digit to its right is 5, 6, 7, 8, or 9.

Row A horizontal group of cells in a worksheet.

Row heading The numbers along the left side of an Excel worksheet that designate the row numbers.

Scaling The process of shrinking the width and/or height of printed output to fit a maximum number of pages.

Select All box A box in the upper left corner of the worksheet grid that, when clicked, selects all the cells in a worksheet.

Series A group of things that come one after another in succession; for example, January, February, March, and so on.

Sheet tab scrolling buttons Buttons to the left of the sheet tabs used to display Excel sheet tabs that are not in view; used when there are more sheet tabs than will display in the space provided.

Sheet tabs The labels along the lower border of the Excel window that identify each worksheet.

Show Formulas A command that displays the formula in each cell instead of the resulting value.

Sparkline A tiny chart in the background of a cell that gives a visual trend summary alongside your data; makes a pattern more obvious.

Spreadsheet Another name for a worksheet.

Status bar The area along the lower edge of the Excel window that displays, on the left side, the current cell mode, page number, and worksheet information; on the right side, when numerical data is selected, common calculations such as Sum and Average display.

SUM function A predefined formula that adds all the numbers in a selected range of cells.

Switch Row/Column A charting command to swap the data over the axis—data being charted on the vertical axis will move to the horizontal axis and vice versa.

Text values Constant values consisting of only text, and which usually provide information about number values; also referred to as labels.

Theme A predefined set of colors, fonts, lines, and fill effects that coordinate with each other.

Underlying formula The formula entered in a cell and visible only on the Formula Bar.

Underlying value The data that displays in the Formula Bar.

Value Another name for a constant value.

Value axis A numerical scale on the left side of a chart that shows the range of numbers for the data points; also referred to as the Y-axis.

Workbook An Excel file that contains one or more worksheets.

Worksheet The primary document that you use in Excel to work with and store data, and which is formatted as a pattern of uniformly spaced horizontal and vertical lines.

Worksheet grid area A part of the Excel window that displays the columns and rows that intersect to form the worksheet's cells.

X-axis Another name for the horizontal (category) axis.

Y-axis Another name for the vertical (value) axis.

1 Create, Save, and Navigate an Excel Workbook

2 Enter Data in a Worksheet

3 Construct and Copy Formulas and Use the SUM Function

4 Format Cells with Merge & Center, Cell Styles, and Themes

5 Chart Data to Create a Column Chart and Insert Sparklines

6 Print a Worksheet, Display Formulas, and Close Excel

Build From Scratch

Skills Review | Project 1C Step Sales

In the following Skills Review, you will create a new Excel worksheet with a chart that summarizes the first quarter sales of fitness equipment for step training. Your completed worksheet will look similar to Figure 1.56.

PROJECT FILES

For Project 1C, you will need the following file:

New blank Excel workbook

You will save your workbook as:

Lastname_Firstname_1C_Step_Sales

PROJECT RESULTS

Lastname_Firstname_1C_Step_Sales

FIGURE 1.56

(Project 1C Step Sales continues on the next page)

Excel 2016, Windows 10, Microsoft Corporation

1 Start Excel and open a new blank workbook. Click the **File tab** to display **Backstage** view, click **Save As**, and then navigate to your **Excel Chapter 1** folder. In the **File name** box, using your own name, type **Lastname_Firstname_1C_Step_Sales** and then press Enter.

a. With cell **A1** as the active cell, type the worksheet title **Pro Fit Marietta** and then press Enter. In cell **A2**, type the worksheet subtitle **First Quarter Step Sales** and then press Enter.

b. Click in cell **A4**, type **Basic Step Box** and then press Enter. In cell **A5**, type **Step Storage Box** and then press Enter. In cell **A6**, type **Stackable Steps** and then press Enter. In cell **A7**, type **Step Mats** and then press Enter. In cell **A8**, type **Total** and then press Enter.

c. Click cell **B3**. Type **January** and then in the **Formula Bar**, click **Enter** to keep cell **B3** the active cell. With **B3** as the active cell, point to the fill handle in the lower right corner of the selected cell, drag to the right to cell **D3**, and then release the mouse button to enter the text *February* and *March*.

d. Press Ctrl + Home to make cell **A1** the active cell. In the **column heading area**, point to the vertical line between **column A** and **column B** to display the ┿ pointer, hold down the left mouse button, and drag to the right to increase the column width to **130 pixels**.

e. Point to cell **B3**, and then drag across to select cells **B3** and **C3** and **D3**. With the range **B3:D3** selected, point anywhere over the selected range, right-click, and then on the mini toolbar, click **Center**.

f. Click cell **B4**, type **75826.99** and press Tab to make cell **C4** active. Enter the remaining values, as shown in **Table 1**, pressing Tab to move across the rows and Enter to move down the columns.

TABLE 1

	January	February	March
Basic Step Box	75826.99	81657.32	72431.22
Step Storage Box	85245.90	92618.95	88337.68
Stackable Steps	68751.64	71997.48	78951.23
Step Mats	63255.10	58742.67	67995.20

2 Click cell **B8** to make it the active cell and type **=**

a. At the insertion point, type **b4** and then type **+** Type **b5** and then type **+b6+b7** Press Enter. Your result is *293079.6*.

b. Click in cell **C8**. Type **=** and then click cell **C4**. Type **+** and then click cell **C5**. Repeat this process to complete the formula to add cells **C6** and **C7** to the formula, and then press Enter. Your result is *305016.4*.

c. Click cell **D8**. On the **Home tab**, in the **Editing group**, click **AutoSum**, and then press Enter to construct a formula by using the SUM function. Your result is *307715.3*.

d. In cell **E3** type **Total** and press Enter. With cell **E4** as the active cell, hold down Alt, and then press =. On the **Formula Bar**, click **Enter** to display the result and keep cell **E4** active.

e. With cell **E4** active, point to the fill handle in the lower right corner of the cell. Drag down through cell **E8**, and then release the mouse button to copy the formula with relative cell references down to sum each row.

3 Click cell **F3**. Type **Trend** and then press Enter.

a. Select the range **A1:F1**, and then on the **Home tab**, in the **Alignment group**, click **Merge & Center**. Select the range **A2:F2** and **Merge & Center** the selection.

b. Click cell **A1**. In the **Styles group**, click **Cell Styles**. Under **Titles and Headings**, click **Title**. Click cell **A2**, display the **Cell Styles** gallery, and then click **Heading 1**.

c. Select the range **B3:F3**, hold down Ctrl, and then select the range **A4:A8**. From the **Cell Styles** gallery, click **Heading 4** to apply this cell style to the column and row titles.

d. Select the range **B4:E4**, hold down Ctrl, and then select the range **B8:E8**. On the **Home tab**, in the **Number group**, click **Accounting Number Format**. Select the range **B5:E7**, and then in the **Number group**, click **Comma Style**. Select the range **B8:E8**. From the **Styles group**, display the **Cell Styles** gallery, and then under **Titles and Headings**, click **Total**.

e. On the ribbon, click the **Page Layout tab**, and then in the **Themes group**, click **Themes** to display the **Themes** gallery. Click the **Basis** theme. (This theme widens the columns slightly). On the Quick Access Toolbar, click **Save**.

(Project 1C Step Sales continues on the next page)

4 Select the range **A3:D7**, which includes the row titles, the column titles, and the data without the totals. Click the **Insert tab**, and then in the **Charts group**, click **Recommended Charts**. In the **Insert Chart** dialog box, scroll down and click the fifth recommended chart—a **Clustered Column** chart in which *each month* displays its *sales for each type of step training equipment*. Click **OK**.

a. In the chart, click anywhere in the text *Chart Title* to select the text box. Watch the **Formula Bar** as you type **First** and then let AutoComplete complete the title by pressing Enter.

b. Click in a white area just slightly *inside* the chart border to deselect the chart title but keep the chart selected. To the right of the chart, click the second button—the **Chart Styles** button.

Be sure the **Style** tab is selected. Use the scroll bar to scroll down, and then by using the ScreenTips, locate and click **Style 6**.

c. At the top of the gallery, click **COLOR**. Under **Colorful**, point to the fourth row of colors to display the ScreenTip *Color 4*, and then click to apply the **Color 4** variation of the theme colors.

d. Point to the top border of the chart to display the pointer, and then drag the upper left corner of the chart just to the center of cell **A10** to visually center it below the data.

5 Select the range **B4:D7**. Click the **Insert tab**, and then in the **Sparklines group**, click **Line**. In the **Create Sparklines** dialog box, in the **Location Range** box, type **f4:f7** and then click **OK** to insert the sparklines.

a. On the **Design tab**, in the **Show group**, select the **Markers** check box to display markers in the sparklines.

b. On the **Design tab**, in the **Style group**, click **More** and then in the second row, click the fourth style—**Sparkline Style Accent 4, Darker 25%**.

6 Click cell **A1** to deselect the chart. Click the **Page Layout tab**, and then in the **Page Setup group**, click **Margins**. Click **Custom Margins**. In the **Page Setup** dialog box, on the **Margins tab**, under **Center on page**, select the **Horizontally** check box.

a. Click the **Header/Footer tab**, and then click **Custom Footer**. With your insertion point in the **Left section**, click **Insert File Name**. Click **OK** two times.

b. Click the **File tab** to display **Backstage** view. In the lower right corner, click **Show All Properties**. As the **Tags**, type **step sales, 1st quarter** In the **Subject** box, type your course name and section number. Be sure your name displays as the author—edit if necessary.

c. On the left, click **Save**.

d. By using the techniques you practiced in Project 1A and as directed by your instructor, print, create a PDF image that looks like a printed document, or submit your completed Excel file. If required by your instructor, print or create an electronic version of your worksheet with formulas displayed. In the upper right corner of your Excel window, click Close.

END | You have completed Project 1C

Skills Review Project 1D Band and Tubing Inventory

In the following Skills Review, you will create a worksheet that summarizes the inventory of band and tubing exercise equipment. Your completed worksheet will look similar to Figure 1.57.

PROJECT FILES

For Project 1D, you will need the following file:

New blank Excel workbook

You will save your workbook as:

Lastname_Firstname_1D_Band_Inventory

Build From Scratch

PROJECT RESULTS

Pro Fit Marietta
Band and Tubing Inventory
As of June 30

	Material	Quantity in Stock	Retail Price	Total Retail Value	Percent of Total Retail Value
Super Strength Bands	Latex	225 $	48.98 $	11,020.50	25.16%
Medium Tubing	Rubber	198	27.95	5,534.10	12.64%
Resistance Band, Average	Latex	165	42.95	7,086.75	16.18%
Mini Bands, Medium	Latex	245	25.95	6,357.75	14.52%
Mini Bands, Heavy	Rubber	175	32.95	5,766.25	13.17%
Heavy Tubing	Latex	187	42.95	8,031.65	18.34%
Total Retail Value for All Products				$ 43,797.00	

Lastname_Firstname_1D_Band_Inventory

FIGURE 1.57

Excel 2016, Windows 10, Microsoft Corporation

(Project 1D Band and Tubing Inventory continues on the next page)

1 Start Excel and display a new blank workbook. **Save** the workbook in your **Excel Chapter 1** folder as **Lastname_Firstname_1D_Band_Inventory** In cell **A1** type **Pro Fit Marietta** and in cell **A2** type **Band and Tubing Inventory**

a. Click cell **B3**, type **Quantity in Stock** and press `Tab`. In cell **C3** type **Average Cost** and press `Tab`. In cell **D3**, type **Retail Price** and press `Tab`. In cell **E3**, type **Total Retail Value** and press `Tab`. In cell **F3** type **Percent of Total Retail Value** and press `Enter`.

b. Click cell **A4**, type **Super Strength Bands** and press `Enter`. In the range **A5:A10**, type the remaining row titles as shown below, including any misspelled words.

Medium Tubing

Resistnce Band, Average

Mini Bands, Medium

Mini Bands, Heavy

Heavy Tubing

Total Retail Value for All Products

c. Press `Ctrl` + `Home` to move to the top of your worksheet. On the **Review tab**, in the **Proofing group**, click **Spelling**. Correct *Resistnce* to **Resistance** and any other spelling errors you may have made, and then when the message displays, *Spell check complete. You're good to go!* click **OK**.

d. In the **column heading area**, point to the right boundary of **column A** to display the ✛ pointer, and then drag to the right to widen **column A** to **225** pixels.

e. In the **column heading area**, point to the **column B** heading to display the ⬇ pointer, and then drag to the right to select **columns B:F**. With the columns selected, in the **column heading area**, point to the right boundary of any of the selected columns, and then drag to the right to set the width to **100 pixels**.

f. Select the range **A1:F1**. On the **Home tab**, in the **Alignment group**, click **Merge & Center**, and then in the **Cell Styles** gallery, apply the **Title** style. Select the range **A2:F2**. **Merge & Center** the text across the selection, and then in the **Cell Styles** gallery, apply the **Heading 1** style.

2 On the **Page Layout tab**, in the **Themes group**, change the **Colors** to **Blue Green**. Select the empty range

B4:D9. With cell **B4** active in the range, type **225** and then press `Enter`.

a. With cell **B5** active in the range, and pressing `Enter` after each entry, type the following data in the *Quantity in Stock* column:

198
265
245
175
187

b. With the selected range still active, from the following table, beginning in cell **C4** and pressing `Enter` after each entry, enter the following data for the **Average Cost** column and then the **Retail Price** column. If you prefer, type without selecting the range first; recall that this is optional.

Average Cost	Retail Price
22.75	48.98
15.95	27.95
26.90	42.95
12.95	25.95
18.75	32.95
26.90	42.95

3 In cell **E4**, type **=b4*d4** and then press `Enter` to construct a formula that calculates the *Total Retail Value* of the *Super Strength Bands* (Quantity in Stock X Retail Price).

a. Click cell **E4**, position your pointer over the fill handle, and then drag down through cell **E9** to copy the formula with relative cell references.

b. Select the range **B4:B9**, and then on the **Home tab**, in the **Number group**, click **Comma Style**. Then, in the **Number group**, click **Decrease Decimal** two times to remove the decimal places from these non-currency values.

c. To calculate the *Total Retail Value for All Products*, select the range **E4:E9**, and then in the lower right corner of the selected range, click the **Quick Analysis** button 📊.

(Project 1D Band and Tubing Inventory continues on the next page)

d. In the gallery, click **Totals**, and then click the *first* **Sum** button, which visually indicates that the column will be summed with a result at the bottom of the column.

e. Select the range **C5:E9** and apply the **Comma Style**. Select the range **C4:E4**, hold down Ctrl, and then click cell **E10**. With the nonadjacent cells selected, apply the **Accounting Number Format**. Click cell **E10**, and then from the **Cell Styles** gallery, apply the **Total** style.

f. Click cell **F4**, type **=** and then click cell **E4**. Type **/** and then click cell **E10**. Press F4 to make the reference to cell *E10* absolute, and then on the **Formula Bar**, click **Enter** so that cell **F4** remains the active cell. Drag the fill handle to copy the formula down through cell **F9**.

g. Point to cell **B6**, and then double-click to place the insertion point within the cell. Use the arrow keys to move the insertion point to the left or right of *2*, and use either Delete or Backspace to delete *2*, and then type **1** and press Enter so that the new *Quantity in Stock* is *165*. Notice the recalculations in the worksheet.

4 Select the range **F4:F9**, right-click over the selection, and then on the mini toolbar, click **Percent Style**. Click **Increase Decimal** two times, and then **Center** the selection.

a. In the **row heading area** on the left side of your screen, point to **row 3** to display the ➡ pointer, and then right-click to simultaneously select the row and display a shortcut menu. On the shortcut menu, click **Insert** to insert a new **row 3**.

b. Click cell **A3**, type **As of June 30** and then on the **Formula Bar**, click **Enter** to keep cell **A3** as the active cell. **Merge & Center** the text across the range **A3:F3**, and then apply the **Heading 2** cell style.

5 In the **column heading area**, point to **column B**. When the ⬇ pointer displays, right-click, and then click **Insert** to insert a new column.

a. Click cell **B4**, type **Material** and then press Enter. In cell **B5**, type **Latex** and then press Enter. In cell **B6**, type **Rubber** and then press Enter.

b. Using AutoComplete to speed your typing by pressing Enter as soon as the AutoComplete suggestion displays, in cells **B7**, **B8**, and **B10** type **Latex** and in cell **B9** type **Rubber**

c. In the **column heading area**, point to the right boundary of **column B**, and then drag to the left and set the width to **90 pixels**. In the **column heading area**, point to **column D**, right-click, and then click **Delete**.

d. Select the column titles in the range **B4:F4**, and then on the **Home tab**, in the **Alignment group**, click **Wrap Text**, **Center**, and **Middle Align**. With the range still selected, apply the **Heading 4** cell style.

e. Click cell **A11**, and then in the **Cell Styles** gallery, under **Themed Cell Styles**, click **40% - Accent1**.

6 Click the **Page Layout tab**, and then in the **Page Setup group**, click **Margins**. Click **Custom Margins**. In the **Page Setup** dialog box, on the **Margins tab**, under **Center on page**, select the **Horizontally** check box.

a. Click the **Header/Footer tab**, and then click **Custom Footer**. With your insertion point in the **Left section**, click **Insert File Name**. Click **OK** two times.

b. In the **Page Setup group**, click **Orientation**, and then click **Landscape**.

c. Click the **File tab** to display **Backstage** view. In the lower right corner, click **Show All Properties**. As the **Tags**, type **bands, tubing, inventory** In the **Subject** box, type your course name and section number. Be sure your name displays as the author—edit if necessary.

d. On the left, click **Save**.

e. By using the techniques you practiced in Project 1A and as directed by your instructor, print, create a PDF image that looks like a printed document, or submit your completed Excel file. If required by your instructor, print or create an electronic version of your worksheet with formulas displayed. In the upper right corner of your Excel window, click Close.

End | You have completed Project 1D

MyITLab® grader

Mastering Excel | Project 1E Gym Sales

In the following Mastering Excel project, you will create a worksheet comparing the sales of different types of home gym equipment sold in the second quarter. Your completed worksheet will look similar to Figure 1.58.

Apply 1A skills from these Objectives:

1 Create, Save, and Navigate an Excel Workbook

2 Enter Data in a Worksheet

3 Construct and Copy Formulas and Use the SUM Function

4 Format Cells with Merge & Center, Cell Styles, and Themes

5 Chart Data to Create a Column Chart and Insert Sparklines

6 Print a Worksheet, Display Formulas, and Close Excel

PROJECT FILES

For Project 1E, you will need the following file:

e01_1E_Gym_Sales

You will save your workbook as:

Lastname_Firstname_1E_Gym_Sales

PROJECT RESULTS

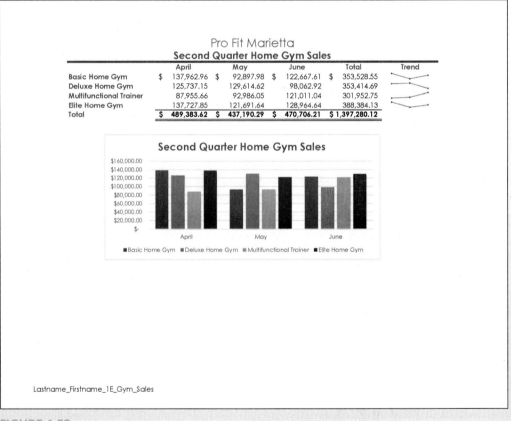

FIGURE 1.58

(Project 1E Gym Sales continues on the next page)

Mastering Excel   Project 1E Gym Sales (continued)

1 Start Excel, and then on the opening screen, in the lower left, click **Open Other Workbooks**. Click **Browse**, and then navigate to your student data files for this chapter. Open the file **e01_1E_Gym_Sales**. Click the **File tab**, on the left click **Save As**, and then click **Browse**. In the **Save As** dialog box, navigate to your **Excel Chapter 1** folder, and then using your own name, save the file as **Lastname_Firstname_1E_Gym_Sales**

2 Change the theme to **Wisp**.

3 In cell **B3**, use the fill handle to fill the months *May* and *June* in the range **C3:D3**.

4 **Merge & Center** the title across the range **A1:F1**, and then apply the **Title** cell style. **Merge & Center** the subtitle across the range **A2:F2**, and then apply the **Heading 1** cell style. **Center** the column titles in the range **B3:F3**.

5 Widen **column A** to **180 pixels**, and then widen columns **B:F** to **115 pixels**. In the range **B7:D7**, enter the monthly sales figures for the Elite Home Gym as shown in the table below:

	April	May	June
Elite Home Gym	137727.85	121691.64	128964.64

6 In cell **B8**, on the **Home tab**, use the **AutoSum** command to sum the April sales. Copy the resulting formula across to cells **C8:D8** to sum the May monthly sales and the June monthly sales. In cell **E4**, use the **AutoSum** button to sum the *Basic Home Gym* sales. Copy the formula down to cells **E4:E8**.

7 Apply the **Heading 4** cell style to the row titles and the column titles. Apply the **Total** cell style to the totals in the range **B8:E8**.

8 Apply the **Accounting Number Format** to the first row of sales figures and to the total row. Apply the **Comma Style** to the remaining sales figures.

9 To compare the monthly sales of each product visually, select the range that represents the sales figures for the three months, including the month names and the product names—do not include any totals in the range. With this data selected, use the **Recommended Charts** command to insert a **Clustered Column** chart with the month names displayed on the category axis and the product names displayed in the legend.

10 Move the chart so that its upper left corner is positioned in the center of cell **A10**. Then drag the center right sizing handle to the right until the right edge of the chart aligns with the right edge of **column E**; this will display the legend on one row and, after you add the sparklines, center the chart below the data.

11 Apply **Chart Style 6** and **Color 2** under **Colorful**. Change the **Chart Title** to **Second Quarter Home Gym Sales**

12 In the range **F4:F7**, insert **Line** sparklines that compare the monthly data. Do not include the totals. Show the sparkline **Markers** and apply **Sparkline Style Accent 2, Darker 50%** in the first row, the second style.

13 Center the worksheet **Horizontally** on the page, and then insert a **Footer** with the **File Name** in the **left section**.

14 Change the **Orientation** to **Landscape**. Display the document properties, and then as the **Tags** type **home gym, sales** As the **Subject**, type your course name and section number. Be sure your name displays as the **Author**. Check your worksheet by previewing it in **Print Preview**, and then make any necessary corrections.

15 **Save** your workbook. By using the techniques you practiced in Project 1A and as directed by your instructor, print, create a PDF image that looks like a printed document, or submit your completed Excel file. If required by your instructor, print or create an electronic version of your worksheet with formulas displayed. In the upper right corner of your Excel window, click **Close**.

END | You have completed Project 1E

Mastering Excel Project 1F Balance Sales

In the following Mastering Excel project, you will create a worksheet that summarizes the sales of balance and stabilization equipment that Pro Fit Marietta is marketing. Your completed worksheet will look similar to Figure 1.59.

Apply 1B skills from these Objectives:

7 Check Spelling in a Worksheet

8 Enter Data by Range

9 Construct Formulas for Mathematical Operations

10 Edit Values in a Worksheet

11 Format a Worksheet

PROJECT FILES

For Project 1F, you will need the following file:

e01_1F_Balance_Sales

You will save your workbook as:

Lastname_Firstname_1F_Balance_Sales

PROJECT RESULTS

Pro Fit Marietta
Balance and Stabilization Sales
Month Ending March 31

	Quantity Sold	Retail Price	Total Sales	Percent of Total Sales
Balance Pillow	275	$ 22.95	$ 6,311.25	5.43%
Slide Board	382	75.50	28,841.00	24.82%
Foam Roller	251	39.50	9,914.50	8.53%
Rebounder	162	139.95	22,671.90	19.51%
Stability Ball	380	51.50	19,570.00	16.84%
Balance Board	206	84.95	17,499.70	15.06%
Balance Pad	150	75.99	11,398.50	9.81%
Total Sales for All Products			$ 116,206.85	

Lastname_Firstname_1F_Balance_Sales

Excel 2016, Windows 10, Microsoft Corporation

FIGURE 1.59

(Project 1F Balance Sales continues on the next page)

Mastering Excel Project 1F Balance Sales (continued)

1 Start Excel, and then on the opening screen, in the lower left, click **Open Other Workbooks**. Click **Browse**, and then navigate to your student data files for this chapter. Open the file **e01_1F_Balance_Sales**. Click the **File tab**, on the left click **Save As**, and then click **Browse**. In the **Save As** dialog box, navigate to your **Excel Chapter 1** folder, and then using your own name, save the file as **Lastname_Firstname_1F_Balance_Sales**

2 **Merge & Center** the title and the subtitle across **columns A:F**. Apply the **Title** and **Heading 1** cell styles respectively.

3 Make cell **A1** the active cell, and then check spelling in your worksheet. Correct *Silde* to **Slide**. Widen **column A** to **180 pixels** and **columns B:F** to **95 pixels**.

4 In cell **E4**, construct a formula to calculate the *Total Sales* of the *Balance Pillow* by multiplying the *Quantity Sold* times the *Retail Price*. Copy the formula down for the remaining products.

5 Select the range **E4:E10**, and then use the **Quick Analysis** tool to **Sum** the *Total Sales for All Products*, which will be formatted in Bold. To the total in cell **E11**, apply the **Total** cell style.

6 Using absolute cell references as necessary so that you can copy the formula, in cell **F4**, construct a formula to calculate the *Percent of Total Sales* for the first product. Copy the formula down for the remaining products.

7 To the computed percentages, apply **Percent Style** with two decimal places, and then **Center** the percentages.

8 Apply the **Comma Style** with no decimal places to the *Quantity Sold* figures. To cells **D4**, **E4**, and **E11** apply the **Accounting Number Format**.

9 To the range **D5:E10**, apply the **Comma Style**.

10 Change the *Retail Price* of the *Slide Board* to **75.50** and the *Quantity Sold* of the *Balance Pad* to **150**

11 Delete **column B**.

12 Insert a new **row 3**. In cell **A3**, type **Month Ending March 31** and then **Merge & Center** the text across the range **A3:E3**. Apply the **Heading 2** cell style.

13 To cell **A12**, apply the **20%-Accent1** cell style.

14 Select the four column titles, apply **Wrap Text**, **Middle Align**, and **Center** formatting, and then apply the **Heading 3** cell style.

15 Center the worksheet **Horizontally** on the page, and then insert a **Footer** with the **File Name** in the **left section**.

16 Display the document properties, and then as the **Tags**, type **balance, stability, sales** In the **Subject** box, add your course name and section number. Be sure your name displays as the Author.

17 **Save** your workbook. By using the techniques you practiced in Project 1A and as directed by your instructor, print, create a PDF image that looks like a printed document, or submit your completed Excel file. If required by your instructor, print or create an electronic version of your worksheet with formulas displayed. In the upper right corner of your Excel Window, click **Close**.

END | You have completed Project 1F

MyITLab®
grader

Mastering Excel Project 1G Regional Sales

In the following Mastering Excel project, you will create a new worksheet that compares annual sales by region. Your completed worksheet will look similar to Figure 1.60.

Apply a combination of 1A and 1B skills:

1 Create, Save, and Navigate an Excel Workbook

2 Enter Data in a Worksheet

3 Construct and Copy Formulas and Use the SUM Function

4 Format Cells with Merge & Center, Cell Styles, and Themes

5 Chart Data to Create a Column Chart and Insert Sparklines

6 Print a Worksheet, Display Formulas, and Close Excel

7 Check Spelling in a Worksheet

8 Enter Data by Range

9 Construct Formulas for Mathematical Operations

10 Edit Values in a Worksheet

11 Format a Worksheet

PROJECT FILES

For Project 1G, you will need the following file:

e01_1G_Regional_Sales

You will save your workbook as

Lastname_Firstname_1G_Regional_Sales

PROJECT RESULTS

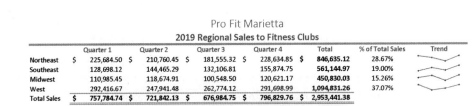

Pro Fit Marietta
2019 Regional Sales to Fitness Clubs

	Quarter 1	Quarter 2	Quarter 3	Quarter 4	Total	% of Total Sales	Trend
Northeast	$ 225,684.50	$ 210,760.45	$ 181,555.32	$ 228,634.85	$ 846,635.12	28.67%	
Southeast	128,698.12	144,465.29	132,106.81	155,874.75	561,144.97	19.00%	
Midwest	110,985.45	118,674.91	100,548.50	120,621.17	450,830.03	15.26%	
West	292,416.67	247,941.48	262,774.12	291,698.99	1,094,831.26	37.07%	
Total Sales	$ 757,784.74	$ 721,842.13	$ 676,984.75	$ 796,829.76	$ 2,953,441.38		

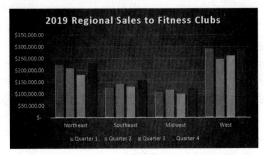

Lastname_Firstname_1G_Regional_Sales

FIGURE 1.60

(Project 1G Regional Sales continues on the next page)

1 Start Excel, and then on the opening screen, in the lower left, click **Open Other Workbooks**. Click **Browse**, and then navigate to your student data files for this chapter. Open the file **e01_1G_Regional_Sales**. Click the **File tab**, on the left click **Save As**, and then click **Browse**. In the **Save As** dialog box, navigate to your **Excel Chapter 1** folder, and then using your own name, save the file as **Lastname_Firstname_1G_Regional_Sales**

2 Change the **Theme** to **Retrospect**. Set the width of **column A** to **80 pixels** and the width of columns **B:H** to **110 pixels**.

3 **Merge & Center** the title across the range **A1:H1**, and then apply the **Title** cell style. **Merge & Center** the subtitle across the range **A2:H2**, and then apply the **Heading 1** cell style.

4 Select the seven column titles, apply **Center** formatting, and then apply the **Heading 4** cell style.

5 By using the **Quick Analysis** tool, **Sum** the *Quarter 1* sales, and then copy the formula across for the remaining Quarters; the Quick Analysis tool formats totals in Bold.

6 Select the *Northeast* sales for the four quarters, and then display the **Quick Analysis** gallery for **Totals**. Click the second **Sum** option—the sixth item in the gallery—which displays the column selection in yellow. Copy the formula down through cell **F7**; recall that the Quick Analysis tool formats sums in Bold.

7 Apply the **Accounting Number Format** to the first row of sales figures and to the total row. Apply the **Comma Style** to the remaining sales figures. Format the totals in **row 7** with the **Total** cell style.

8 **Insert** a new **row 6** with the row title **Midwest** and the following sales figures for each quarter: **110985.45** and **118674.91** and **100548.50** and **120621.17** Copy the formula in cell **F5** down to cell **F6** to sum the new row.

9 Using absolute cell references as necessary so that you can copy the formula, in cell **G4** construct a formula to calculate the *Percent of Total Sales* for the first region. Copy the formula down for the remaining regions.

10 To the computed percentages, apply **Percent Style** with two decimal places, and then **Center** the percentages.

11 Insert **Line** sparklines in the range **H4:H7** that compare the quarterly data. Do not include the totals. Show the sparkline **Markers** and apply the second style in the second row—**Sparkline Style Accent 2, Darker 25%**.

12 **Save** your workbook. To compare the quarterly sales of each region visually, select the range that represents the sales figures for the four quarters, including the quarter names and each region—do not include any totals in the range. With this data selected, by using the **Recommended Charts** command, insert a **Clustered Column** with the regions as the category axis and the Quarters as the legend.

13 Apply **Chart Style 8** and **Color 3** under **Colorful**. Position the chart so that its upper right corner aligns with the upper right corner of cell **F10**.

14 Change the **Chart Title** to **2019 Regional Sales to Fitness Clubs**

15 Deselect the chart. Change the page **Orientation** to **Landscape**, center the worksheet **Horizontally** on the page, and then insert a footer with the file name in the left section.

16 Show the document properties. As the **Tags**, type **fitness clubs, sales** In the **Subject** box, type your course name and section number. Be sure your name displays as the Author.

17 **Save** your workbook. By using the techniques you practiced in Project 1A and as directed by your instructor, print, create a PDF image that looks like a printed document, or submit your completed Excel file. If required by your instructor, print or create an electronic version of your worksheet with formulas displayed. In the upper right corner of your Excel Window, click **Close**.

END | You have completed Project 1G

Apply a combination of the 1A and 1B skills.	**GO! Fix It**	**Project 1H Team Sales** MyITLab
Build From Scratch	**GO! Make It**	**Project 1I Agility Sales** MyITLab
	GO! Solve It	**Project 1J Kettlebell Sales** MyITLab
	GO! Solve It	**Project 1K Commission**

PROJECT FILES

For Project 1K, you will need the following file:

e01K_Commission

You will save your workbook as:

Lastname_Firstname_1K_Commission

Open the file e01K_Commission and save it as **Lastname_Firstname_1K_Commission** Complete the worksheet by using Auto Fill to complete the month headings, and then calculating the Total Commission for each month and for each region. Insert and format appropriate sparklines in the Trend column. Format the worksheet attractively with a title and subtitle, check spelling, adjust column width, and apply appropriate financial formatting. Insert a chart that compares the total sales commission for each region with the months displaying as the categories, and format the chart attractively. Include the file name in the footer, add appropriate properties, and submit as directed.

Performance Level

Performance Criteria	Exemplary: You consistently applied the relevant skills	Proficient: You sometimes, but not always, applied the relevant skills	Developing: You rarely or never applied the relevant skills
Create formulas	All formulas are correct and are efficiently constructed.	Formulas are correct but not always constructed in the most efficient manner.	One or more formulas are missing or incorrect; or only numbers were entered.
Create a chart	Chart created properly.	Chart was created but incorrect data was selected.	No chart was created.
Insert and format sparklines	Sparklines inserted and formatted properly.	Sparklines were inserted but incorrect data was selected or sparklines were not formatted.	No sparklines were inserted.
Format attractively and appropriately	Formatting is attractive and appropriate.	Adequately formatted but difficult to read or unattractive.	Inadequate or no formatting.

END | You have completed Project 1K

RUBRIC

The following outcomes-based assessments are *open-ended assessments*. That is, there is no specific correct result; your result will depend on your approach to the information provided. Make *Professional Quality* your goal. Use the following scoring rubric to guide you in *how* to approach the problem and then to evaluate *how well* your approach solves the problem.

The *criteria*—Software Mastery, Content, Format and Layout, and Process—represent the knowledge and skills you have gained that you can apply to solving the problem. The *levels of performance*—Professional Quality, Approaching Professional Quality, or Needs Quality Improvements—help you and your instructor evaluate your result.

	Your completed project is of Professional Quality if you:	Your completed project is Approaching Professional Quality if you:	Your completed project Needs Quality Improvements if you:
1-Software Mastery	Choose and apply the most appropriate skills, tools, and features and identify efficient methods to solve the problem.	Choose and apply some appropriate skills, tools, and features, but not in the most efficient manner.	Choose inappropriate skills, tools, or features, or are inefficient in solving the problem.
2-Content	Construct a solution that is clear and well organized, contains content that is accurate, appropriate to the audience and purpose, and is complete. Provide a solution that contains no errors of spelling, grammar, or style.	Construct a solution in which some components are unclear, poorly organized, inconsistent, or incomplete. Misjudge the needs of the audience. Have some errors in spelling, grammar, or style, but the errors do not detract from comprehension.	Construct a solution that is unclear, incomplete, or poorly organized, contains some inaccurate or inappropriate content, and contains many errors of spelling, grammar, or style. Do not solve the problem.
3-Format and Layout	Format and arrange all elements to communicate information and ideas, clarify function, illustrate relationships, and indicate relative importance.	Apply appropriate format and layout features to some elements, but not others. Overuse features, causing minor distraction.	Apply format and layout that does not communicate information or ideas clearly. Do not use format and layout features to clarify function, illustrate relationships, or indicate relative importance. Use available features excessively, causing distraction.
4-Process	Use an organized approach that integrates planning, development, self-assessment, revision, and reflection.	Demonstrate an organized approach in some areas, but not others; or, use an insufficient process of organization throughout.	Do not use an organized approach to solve the problem.

Apply a combination of the 1A and 1B skills.

GO! Think   Project 1L Video Sales

PROJECT FILES

Build From Scratch

For Project 1L, you will need the following file:

New blank Excel workbook

You will save your workbook as:

Lastname_Firstname_1L_Video_Sales

Michelle Barry, President of Pro Fit Marietta, needs a worksheet that summarizes the following data regarding the first quarter sales of training videos. Michelle would like the worksheet to include a calculation of the total sales for each type of video and a total of the sales of all of the videos. She would also like to know each type of video's percentage of total sales.

	Number Sold	Price
Pilates	156	29.99
Step	392	14.99
Weight Training	147	54.99
Kickboxing	282	29.99
Yoga	165	34.99

Create a worksheet that provides Michelle with the information needed. Include appropriate worksheet, column, and row titles. Using the formatting skills that you practiced in this chapter, format the worksheet in a manner that is professional and easy to read and understand. Insert a footer with the file name and add appropriate document properties. Save the file as **Lastname_Firstname_1L_Video_Sales** and print or submit as directed by your instructor.

END | You have completed Project 1L

Build From Scratch

GO! Think   Project 1M Expenses   MyITLab

You and GO!   Project 1N Personal Expenses   MyITLab

Build From Scratch

GO! Collaborative Team Project   Project 1O Bell Orchid Hotels   MyITLab

Using Functions, Creating Tables, and Managing Large Workbooks

2

PROJECT 2A

OUTCOMES
Analyze inventory by applying statistical and logical calculations to data and by sorting and filtering data.

OBJECTIVES

1. Use Flash Fill and the SUM, AVERAGE, MEDIAN, MIN, and MAX Functions
2. Move Data, Resolve Error Messages, and Rotate Text
3. Use COUNTIF and IF Functions and Apply Conditional Formatting
4. Use Date & Time Functions and Freeze Panes
5. Create, Sort, and Filter an Excel Table
6. View, Format, and Print a Large Worksheet

PROJECT 2B

OUTCOMES
Summarize the data on multiple worksheets.

OBJECTIVES

7. Navigate a Workbook and Rename Worksheets
8. Enter Dates, Clear Contents, and Clear Formats
9. Copy and Paste by Using the Paste Options Gallery
10. Edit and Format Multiple Worksheets at the Same Time
11. Create a Summary Sheet with Column Sparklines
12. Format and Print Multiple Worksheets in a Workbook

Jbd30/Shutterstock

In This Chapter

GO! to Work with Excel

In this chapter, you will use the Statistical functions to calculate the average of a group of numbers and perform other summary calculations. You will also use Logical and Date & Time functions. Excel's statistical functions are useful for common calculations that you probably encounter frequently. You will also use Excel's Flash Fill feature to automatically fill in values, use the counting functions, and apply different types of conditional formatting to make data easy to visualize. You will create a table to organize related information and analyze the table's information by sorting and filtering. You will summarize a workbook that contains multiple worksheets.

The projects in this chapter relate to **Rosedale Landscape and Garden**, which grows and sells trees and plants suitable for all areas of North America. Throughout its 75-year history, the company has introduced many new plants for the enjoyment of home gardeners. The company has nurseries and stores in the major metropolitan areas in the United States and Canada. In addition to high-quality plants and trees, Rosedale sells garden tools and outdoor furniture. Rosedale also offers professional landscape design and installation for both commercial and residential clients. The company headquarters is in Pasadena, California.

MyITLab
Project 2A Training
Project 2A Grader

PROJECT 2A Inventory Status Report

PROJECT ACTIVITIES

In Activities 2.01 through 2.20, you will edit a worksheet for Holman Hill, President of Rosedale Landscape and Garden, detailing the current inventory of trees at the Pasadena nursery. Your completed worksheet will look similar to Figure 2.1.

Please always review the downloaded Grader instructions before beginning.

PROJECT FILES

If your instructor wants you to submit Project 2A in the MyITLab Grader system, log in to MyITLab, locate Grader Project 2A, and then download the files for this project.

For Project 2A, you will need the following file:

e02A_Tree_Inventory

You will save your workbook as:

Lastname_Firstname_2A_Tree_Inventory

PROJECT RESULTS

GO!
Walk Thru
Project 2A

Quantity in Stock	Item #	Tree Name	Retail Price	Light	Landscape Use	Category	Stock Level
93	38700	Pacific Fire	103.75	Full Shade	Erosion Control	Oak	OK
45	38744	Cheals Weeping	104.99	Partial Shade	Erosion Control	Cherry	Order
58	39704	Embers	105.99	Partial Sun	Erosion Control	Oak	Order
90	42599	Beurre	109.98	Partial Sun	Border	Pear	OK
350	43153	Bradford	104.99	Full Shade	Border	Pear	OK

10/2/2015 15:32

Pasadena Tree Nursery
As of December 31

Tree Statistics

Total Items in Stock	3,022
Average Price	$ 107.89
Median Price	$ 107.99
Lowest Price	$ 102.99
Highest Price	$ 117.98

Oak Trees   13
Maple Trees   6 (571 total items in stock)

Quantity in Stock	Item #	Tree Name	Retail Price	Light	Landscape Use	Category	Stock Level
78	13129	Golden Oak	108.99	Partial Sun	Erosion Control	Oak	OK
35	13358	Columnar English	106.95	Full Shade	Border	Oak	Order
60	15688	Coral Bark	106.25	Partial Shade	Erosion Control	Oak	Order
20	16555	Crimson King	105.50	Full Shade	Border	Oak	Order
75	21683	Japanese Blooming	103.99	Partial Shade	Erosion Control	Cherry	OK
60	22189	Crimson Queen	109.95	Filtered Sun	Erosion Control	Oak	Order
68	23677	Black Japanese	107.99	Partial Sun	Border	Maple	OK
71	23688	Artist Flowering	109.95	Partial Sun	Erosion Control	Pear	Order
159	24896	Bing Small Sweet	105.99	Partial Shade	Border	Cherry	OK
60	25678	Bartlett	109.75	Partial Sun	Erosion Control	Pear	Order
179	25844	Bloodgood	110.99	Partial Shade	Border	Maple	OK
90	26787	Sentry	108.50	Partial Sun	Border	Oak	OK
81	32544	Burgundy Bell	110.95	Partial Sun	Border	Maple	OK
81	34266	Lace Maple	109.99	Partial Sun	Border	Maple	OK
113	34793	Emerald Elf	103.98	Full Shade	Erosion Control	Oak	OK
191	34878	Ginger Pear	107.78	Partial Sun	Border	Pear	OK
102	34982	Fernleaf	105.99	Partial Shade	Border	Oak	OK
170	35677	Flamingo	109.99	Partial Sun	Border	Oak	OK
170	35690	Bing Sweet	107.99	Partial Shade	Border	Cherry	OK
70	35988	Butterfly Japanese	111.75	Partial Sun	Border	Maple	Order
92	36820	Ever Red	110.95	Partial Sun	Border	Maple	OK
173	37803	Osakazuki	103.88	Full Shade	Erosion Control	Oak	OK
113	37845	Anna	117.98	Partial Sun	Woodland Garden	Magnolia	OK
75	38675	Palo Alto	102.99	Partial Shade	Erosion Control	Oak	OK

Lastname_Firstname_2A_Tree_Inventory

Excel 2016, Windows 10, Microsoft Corporation

FIGURE 2.1

124   Excel | Chapter 2: USING FUNCTIONS, CREATING TABLES, AND MANAGING LARGE WORKBOOKS

GO! Learn How
Video E2-1

Flash Fill recognizes a pattern in your data, and then automatically fills in values when you enter examples of the output that you want. Use Flash Fill to split data into two or more cells or to combine data from two cells.

A ***function*** is the name given to a predefined formula—a formula that Excel has already built for you—that performs calculations by using specific values that you insert in a particular order or structure. ***Statistical functions***, which include the AVERAGE, MEDIAN, MIN, and MAX functions, are useful to analyze a group of measurements.

Activity 2.01 | Using Flash Fill

> **ALERT!** **To submit as an autograded project, log into MyITLab and download the files for this project, and begin with those files instead of e02A_Tree_Inventory.**

1 Start Excel, and then in the lower left corner of Excel's opening screen, click **Open Other Workbooks**.

2 Click **Browse**. Navigate to the student files that accompany this chapter, and then locate and open **e02A_Tree_Inventory**. Press F12 to display the **Save As** dialog box, and then navigate to the location where you are storing your projects for this chapter.

3 Create a new folder named **Excel Chapter 2** and then open the new folder. In the **File name** box, type **Lastname_Firstname_2A_Tree_Inventory** and then click **Save** or press Enter.

4 Scroll down. Notice that the worksheet contains data related to types of trees in inventory, including information about the *Quantity in Stock*, *Item #/Category*, *Tree Name*, *Retail Price*, *Light*, and *Landscape Use*.

5 In the **column heading area**, point to **column C** to display the ⬇ pointer, and then drag to the right to select **columns C:D**. On the **Home tab**, in the **Cells group**, click the **Insert button arrow**, and then click **Insert Sheet Columns**.

New columns for C and D display and the remaining columns move to the right.

🔄 **ANOTHER WAY** Select the columns, right-click anywhere over the selected columns, and then on the shortcut menu, click Insert.

6 Click cell **C11**, type **13129** and then on the **Formula Bar**, click **Enter** ✓ to confirm the entry and keep **C11** as the active cell.

7 On the **Home tab**, in the **Editing group**, click **Fill**, and then click **Flash Fill**. Compare your screen with Figure 2.2.

Use this technique to split a column of data based on what you type. Flash Fill looks to the left and sees the pattern you have established, and then fills the remaining cells in the column with only the Item #. The Flash Fill Options button displays.

FIGURE 2.2

8 ▶ Near the lower right corner of cell **C11**, click the **Flash Fill Options** button, and notice that here you can *Undo Flash Fill*, *Accept suggestions*, or *Select all 28 changed cells*, for example, to apply specific formatting. Click the button again to close it.

> If Excel is not sure what pattern to use, it suggests a pattern by filling with pale gray characters, and then you can use the Accept suggestions command to accept or start again.

9 ▶ Click cell **D11**, type **Oak** and then on the **Formula Bar**, click ✔ to confirm the entry and keep **D11** as the active cell. Press Ctrl + E, which is the keyboard shortcut for Flash Fill.

> Flash Fill extracts the text from the *Item#/Category* column and also inserts *Category* as the column name. Now that *Item #* and *Category* are in two separate columns, the data can be sorted and filtered by both Item # and Category.

10 ▶ Select **column B**, and then in the **Cells group**, click the **Delete button arrow**. Click **Delete Sheet Columns**. On the Quick Access Toolbar, click **Save** 🔲.

ANOTHER WAY Select the column, right-click anywhere over the selected column, and then on the shortcut menu, click Delete.

Activity 2.02 | Moving a Column

1 ▶ In cell **B10**, type **Item #** and then press Enter. Select **column C**, and then on the **Home tab**, in the **Clipboard group**, click **Cut** ✂. Click cell **H1**, and then in the **Clipboard group**, click the upper portion of the **Paste** button.

ANOTHER WAY Press Ctrl + X to cut and Ctrl + V to paste.

2 ▶ Select and then delete **column C**. Select **columns A:G**. In the **Cells group**, click **Format**, and then click **AutoFit Column Width**.

ANOTHER WAY Select the columns, in the column heading area point to any of the selected column borders to display the ⟷ pointer, and then double-click to AutoFit the columns.

3 ▶ **Merge & Center** cell **A1** across the range **A1:H1**, and then apply the **Title** cell style. **Merge & Center** cell **A2** across the range **A2:H2**, and then apply the **Heading 1** cell style. Compare your screen with Figure 2.3. **Save** 🔲 your workbook.

FIGURE 2.3

Excel 2016, Windows 10, Microsoft Corporation

Activity 2.03 | Using the SUM and AVERAGE Functions

4.1.2, 4.1.5

In this Activity, you will use the SUM and AVERAGE functions to gather information about the product inventory.

> **1** Click cell **B4**. Click the **Formulas tab**, and then in the **Function Library group**, click the upper portion of the **AutoSum** button. Compare your screen with Figure 2.4.

The **SUM function** is a predefined formula that adds all the numbers in a selected range of cells. Because it is frequently used, there are several ways to insert the function. For example, you can insert the function from the Home tab's Editing group, or by using the keyboard shortcut Alt + =, or from the Function Library group on the Formulas tab, or from the Math & Trig button in that group.

FIGURE 2.4

Excel 2016, Windows 10, Microsoft Corporation

2 With the insertion point blinking in the function, type the cell range **a11:a39** to sum all the values in the *Quantity in Stock* column, and then press ⏎; your result is *3022*.

3 Click cell **B4**, look at the **Formula Bar**, and then compare your screen with Figure 2.5.

SUM is the name of the function. The values in parentheses are the ***arguments***—the values that an Excel function uses to perform calculations or operations. In this instance, the argument consists of the values in the range A11:A39.

FIGURE 2.5

4 Click cell **B5**. In the **Function Library group**, click **More Functions**, point to **Statistical**, point to **AVERAGE**, and notice the ScreenTip. Compare your screen with Figure 2.6.

The ScreenTip describes how the AVERAGE function will compute the calculation.

FIGURE 2.6

5 Click **AVERAGE**, and then if necessary, drag the title bar of the Function Arguments dialog box down and to the right so you can view the Formula Bar and cell B5.

The ***AVERAGE function*** adds a group of values, and then divides the result by the number of values in the group. In the cell, the Formula Bar, and the dialog box, Excel proposes to average the value in cell B4. Recall that Excel functions will propose a range if there is data above or to the left of a selected cell.

6 In the **Function Arguments** dialog box, notice that *B4* is highlighted. Press ⟨Del⟩ to delete the existing text, type **d11:d39** and then compare your screen with Figure 2.7.

Because you want to average the Retail Price values in the range D11:D39—and not cell B4—you must edit the proposed range.

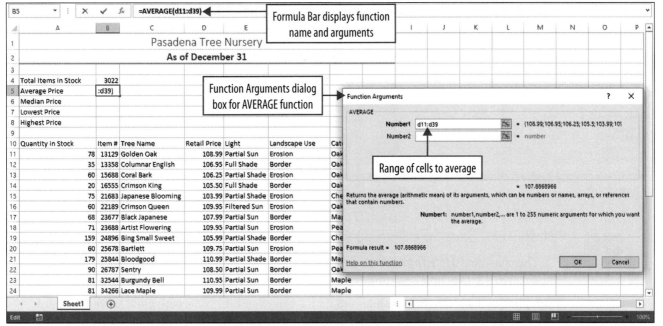

FIGURE 2.7

7 In the **Function Arguments** dialog box, click **OK**, and then click **Save** 🖫.

The result indicates that the average Retail Price of all products is *107.89*.

Activity 2.04 | Using the MEDIAN Function

The **MEDIAN function** is a statistical function that describes a group of data—it is commonly used to describe the price of houses in a particular geographical area. The MEDIAN function finds the middle value that has as many values above it in the group as are below it. It differs from AVERAGE in that the result is not affected as much by a single value that is greatly different from the others.

1 Click cell **B6**. In the **Function Library group**, click **More Functions**, display the list of **Statistical** functions, scroll down as necessary, and then click **MEDIAN**.

2 Press ⌦ to delete the text in the **Number1** box. Type **d11:d39** and then compare your screen with Figure 2.8.

When indicating which cells you want to use in the function's calculation—known as *defining the arguments*—you can either select the values with your mouse or type the range of values, whichever you prefer.

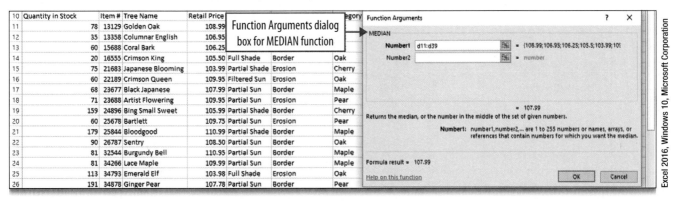

FIGURE 2.8

3 Click **OK** to display *107.99* in cell **B6**. Click **Save** and compare your screen with Figure 2.9.

In the range of prices, 107.99 is the middle value. Half of all trees in inventory are priced *above* 107.99 and half are priced *below* 107.99.

FIGURE 2.9

Excel 2016, Windows 10, Microsoft Corporation

MOS

4.1.3

Activity 2.05 | Using the MIN and MAX Functions

The statistical *MIN function* determines the smallest value in a selected range of values. The statistical *MAX function* determines the largest value in a selected range of values.

1 Click cell **B7**. On the **Formulas tab**, in the **Function Library group**, click **More Functions**, display the list of **Statistical** functions, scroll as necessary, and then click **MIN**.

2 Press Del, and then in the **Number1** box, type **d11:d39** Click **OK**.

The lowest Retail Price is *102.99*.

3 Click cell **B8**, and then by using a similar technique, insert the **MAX** function to determine the highest **Retail Price**, and then check to see that your result is *117.98*.

4 Press Ctrl + Home. Point to cell **B4**, right-click, and then on the mini toolbar, click **Comma Style** ▾ one time and **Decrease Decimal** .00→ two times.

5 Select the range **B5:B8**, apply the **Accounting Number Format** $ ▾, click **Save** 🖫, and then compare your screen with Figure 2.10.

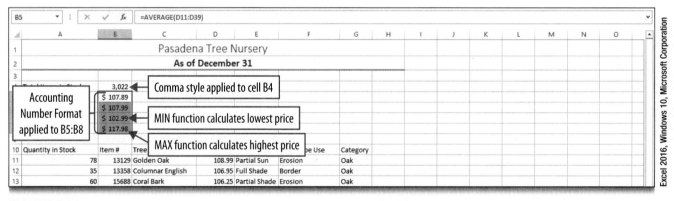

Excel 2016, Windows 10, Microsoft Corporation

FIGURE 2.10

GO! Learn How
Video E2-2

When you move a formula, the cell references within the formula do not change, no matter what type of cell reference you use.

If you move cells into a column that is not wide enough to display number values, Excel will display a message so that you can adjust as necessary.

You can reposition data within a cell at an angle by rotating the text.

Activity 2.06 | Moving Data and Resolving a # # # # # Error Message

1 Select **column E** and set the width to **50 pixels**. Select the range **A4:B8**. Point to the right edge of the selected range to display the pointer, and then compare your screen with Figure 2.11.

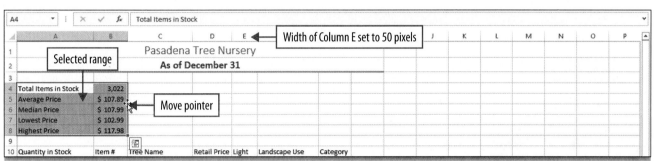

FIGURE 2.11

Excel 2016, Windows 10, Microsoft Corporation

2 Drag the selected range to the right until the ScreenTip displays *D4:E8*, release the mouse button, and then notice that a series of # symbols displays in **column E**. Point to any of the cells that display # symbols, and then compare your screen with Figure 2.12.

Using this technique, cell contents can be moved from one location to another; this is referred to as *drag and drop*.

If a cell width is too narrow to display the entire number, Excel displays the ##### message, because displaying only a portion of a number would be misleading. The underlying values remain unchanged and are displayed in the Formula Bar for the selected cell. An underlying value also displays in the ScreenTip if you point to a cell containing # symbols.

FIGURE 2.12

Excel 2016, Windows 10, Microsoft Corporation

3 Select **columns D:E**, and then in the **column heading area**, point to the right boundary of **column E** to display the pointer. Double-click to AutoFit the column to accommodate the widest entry.

4 Select the range **D4:E8**. On the **Home tab**, in the **Styles group**, display the **Cell Styles** gallery. Under **Themed Cell Styles**, click **20%-Accent1**. Click **Save**.

Activity 2.07 | Rotating Text

1▶ In cell **C6**, type **Tree Statistics** and then press Enter.

2▶ Select cell **C6**. On the **Home tab**, in the **Font group**, change the **Font Size** 11 ▾ to **14**, and then apply **Bold** B and **Italic** I. Click the **Font Color arrow** A ▾, and then in the fifth column, click the first color—**Blue, Accent 1**.

3▶ In the **Alignment group**, apply **Align Right** ≡.

4▶ Select the range **C4:C8**, right-click over the selection, and then on the shortcut menu, click **Format Cells**. In the **Format Cells** dialog box, click the **Alignment tab**. Under **Text control**, select the **Merge cells** check box.

5▶ Under **Orientation**, click in the **Degrees** box to select the value, type **30** and then compare your screen with Figure 2.13.

🔄 **ANOTHER WAY**   In the upper right portion of the dialog box, under Orientation, point to the red diamond, and then drag the diamond upward until the Degrees box indicates 30.

FIGURE 2.13

Excel 2016, Windows 10, Microsoft Corporation

6▶ In the lower right corner of the **Format Cells** dialog box, click **OK**. Press Ctrl + Home, **Save** 🖫 your workbook, and then compare your screen with Figure 2.14.

FIGURE 2.14

Excel 2016, Windows 10, Microsoft Corporation

7▶ In the **row heading area**, point to **row 9** and right-click to select the row and display the shortcut menu. Click **Insert**, and then press F4 two times to repeat the last action and insert two additional blank rows.

> F4 is useful to repeat commands in Microsoft Office programs. Most commands can be repeated in this manner.

> **8** From the **row heading area**, select **rows 9:11**. On the **Home tab**, in the **Editing group**, click **Clear** ⬚ and then click **Clear Formats** to remove the blue accent color in columns D and E from the new rows. Click **Save** 🖫.

When you insert rows or columns, formatting from adjacent rows or columns repeats in the new cells.

> **9** Click cell **E4**, look at the **Formula Bar**, and then notice that the arguments of the **SUM** function adjusted and refer to the appropriate cells in rows 14:42.

The referenced range updates to *A14:A42* after you insert the three new rows. In this manner, Excel adjusts the cell references in a formula relative to their new locations.

Objective 3 Use COUNTIF and IF Functions and Apply Conditional Formatting

GO! Learn How
Video E2-3

Recall that statistical functions analyze a group of measurements. Another group of Excel functions, referred to as *logical functions*, test for specific conditions. Logical functions typically use conditional tests to determine whether specified conditions—called *criteria*—are true or false.

Activity 2.08 | Using the COUNTIF Function

4.1.4, 4.2.4

The *COUNT function* counts the number of cells in a range that contain numbers. The *COUNTIF function* is a statistical function that counts the number of cells within a range that meet the given condition—the criteria that you provide. The COUNTIF function has two arguments—the range of cells to check and the criteria.

The trees of Rosedale Landscape and Garden will be featured on an upcoming segment of a TV gardening show. In this Activity, you will use the COUNTIF function to determine the number of *Oak* trees currently available in inventory that can be featured in the TV show.

> **1** In cell **A10**, type **Oak Trees** and then press Tab.

> **2** With cell **B10** as the active cell, on the **Formulas tab**, in the **Function Library group**, click **More Functions**, and then display the list of **Statistical** functions. Click **COUNTIF**.

Recall that the COUNTIF function counts the number of cells within a range that meet the given condition.

> **3** In the **Range** box, type **g14:g42** Click in the **Criteria** box, type **Oak** and then compare your screen with Figure 2.15.

FIGURE 2.15

4 In the lower right corner of the **Function Arguments** dialog box, click **OK**.

There are *13* different *Oak* trees available to feature on the TV show.

5 On the **Home tab**, in the **Alignment group**, click **Align Left** ☰ to place the result closer to the row title. **Save** 🖫 your workbook.

Activity 2.09 | Using the IF Function

A *logical test* is any value or expression that you can evaluate as being true or false. The *IF function* uses a logical test to check whether a condition is met, and then returns one value if true, and another value if false.

For example, *C14=228* is an expression that can be evaluated as true or false. If the value in cell C14 is equal to 228, the expression is true. If the value in cell C14 is not 228, the expression is false.

In this Activity, you will use the IF function to evaluate the inventory levels and determine if more products should be ordered.

1 Click cell **H13**, type **Stock Level** and then press (Enter).

2 In cell **H14**, on the **Formulas tab**, in the **Function Library group**, click **Logical**, and then in the list, click **IF**. Drag the title bar of the **Function Arguments** dialog box up or down to view **row 14** on your screen.

3 With the insertion point in the **Logical_test** box, type **a14<75**

This logical test will look at the value in cell A14, which is *78*, and then determine if the number is less than 75. The expression *<75* includes the *comparison operator*, which means *less than*. Comparison operators compare values.

4 Examine the table in Figure 2.16 for a list of comparison operator symbols and their definitions.

COMPARISON OPERATORS	
COMPARISON OPERATORS	**SYMBOL DEFINITION**
=	Equal to
>	Greater than
<	Less than
>=	Greater than or equal to
<=	Less than or equal to
<>	Not equal to

FIGURE 2.16

5 Press (Tab) to move the insertion point to the **Value_if_true** box, and then type **Order**

If the result of the logical test is true—the Quantity in Stock is less than 75—cell H14 will display the text *Order* indicating that additional trees must be ordered.

6 Press (Tab) to move to the **Value_if_false** box, type **OK** and then compare your screen with Figure 2.17.

If the result of the logical test is false—the Quantity in Stock is *not* less than 75—then Excel will display *OK* in the cell.

FIGURE 2.17

Excel 2016, Windows 10, Microsoft Corporation

7 Click **OK** to display the result *OK* in cell **H14**.

8 Using the fill handle, copy the function in cell **H14** down through cell **H42**. Then scroll as necessary to view cell **A18**, which contains the value *75*. Look at cell **H18** and notice that the **Stock Level** is indicated as *OK*. **Save** 🖫 your workbook. Compare your screen with Figure 2.18.

> The comparison operator indicated <75 (less than 75) and therefore a value of *exactly* 75 is indicated as OK.

FIGURE 2.18

Excel 2016, Windows 10, Microsoft Corporation

Activity 2.10 │ Applying Conditional Formatting by Using Highlight Cells Rules and Data Bars

2.3.4

A ***conditional format*** changes the appearance of a cell based on a condition—a criteria. If the condition is true, the cell is formatted based on that condition; if the condition is false, the cell is *not* formatted. In this Activity, you will use conditional formatting as another way to draw attention to the Stock Level of trees.

1 Be sure the range **H14:H42** is selected. On the **Home tab**, in the **Styles group**, click **Conditional Formatting**. In the list, point to **Highlight Cells Rules**, and then click **Text That Contains**.

2 In the **Text That Contains** dialog box, with the insertion point blinking in the first box, type **Order** and notice that in the selected range, the text *Order* displays with the default format— Light Red Fill with Dark Red Text.

3 In the second box, click the **arrow**, and then in the list, click **Custom Format**.

> Here, in the Format Cells dialog box, you can select any combination of formats to apply to the cell if the condition is true. The custom format you specify will be applied to any cell in the selected range if it contains the text *Order*.

4 On the **Font tab**, under **Font style**, click **Bold Italic**. Click the **Color arrow**, and then under **Theme Colors**, in the last column, click the first color—**Green, Accent 6**. Click **OK**. Compare your screen with Figure 2.19.

In the range, if the cell meets the condition of containing *Order*, the font color will change to Bold Italic, Green, Accent 6.

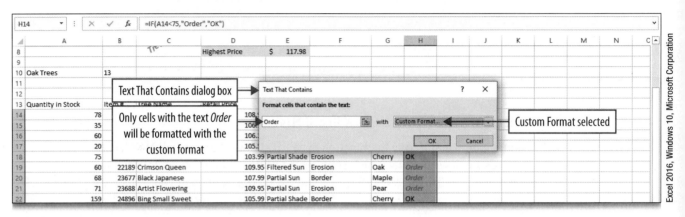

FIGURE 2.19

5 In the **Text That Contains** dialog box, click **OK**.

6 Select the range **A14:A42**. In the **Styles group**, click **Conditional Formatting**. Point to **Data Bars**, and then under **Gradient Fill**, click **Orange Data Bar**. Click anywhere to cancel the selection, click **Save** 🖫, and then compare your screen with Figure 2.20.

A *data bar* provides a visual cue to the reader about the value of a cell relative to other cells. The length of the data bar represents the value in the cell. A longer bar represents a higher value and a shorter bar represents a lower value. Data bars are useful for identifying higher and lower numbers quickly within a large group of data, such as very high or very low levels of inventory.

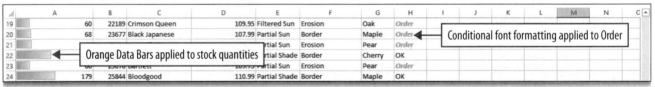

FIGURE 2.20

Excel 2016, Windows 10, Microsoft Corporation

1.2.1 and 2.1.1

Activity 2.11 | Using Find and Replace

The *Find and Replace* feature searches the cells in a worksheet—or in a selected range—for matches, and then replaces each match with a replacement value of your choice.

Comments from customers on the company's blog indicate that using the term *Erosion Control* would be clearer than *Erosion* when describing the best landscape use for specific trees. Therefore, all products of this type will be relabeled accordingly. In this Activity, you will replace all occurrences of *Erosion* with *Erosion Control*.

1 Select the range **F14:F42**. On the **Home tab**, in the **Editing group**, click **Find & Select**, and then click **Replace**.

Restrict the find and replace operation to a specific range in this manner, especially if there is a possibility that the name occurs elsewhere.

2 Type **Erosion** to fill in the **Find what** box. In the **Replace with** box, type **Erosion Control** and then compare your screen with Figure 2.21.

FIGURE 2.21

Excel 2016, Windows 10, Microsoft Corporation

3 Click **Replace All**. In the message box, notice that 13 replacements were made, and then click **OK**. In the lower right corner of the **Find and Replace** dialog box, click **Close**. Click **Save** 🖫.

Objective 4 | Use Date & Time Functions and Freeze Panes

GO! Learn How
Video E2-4

Excel can obtain the date and time from your computer's calendar and clock and display this information on your worksheet.

By freezing or splitting panes, you can view two areas of a worksheet and lock rows and columns in one area. When you freeze panes, you select the specific rows or columns that you want to remain visible when scrolling in your worksheet.

Activity 2.12 | Using the NOW Function to Display a System Date

3.3.1

The **NOW function** retrieves the date and time from your computer's calendar and clock and inserts the information into the selected cell. The result is formatted as a date and time.

1 To the left of the **Formula Bar**, click in the **Name Box**, type **a44** and then press [Enter]. Notice that cell A44 is the active cell.

2 With cell **A44** as the active cell, on the **Formulas tab**, in the **Function Library group**, click **Date & Time**. In the list of functions, click **NOW**. Compare your screen with Figure 2.22.

FIGURE 2.22

Excel 2016, Windows 10, Microsoft Corporation

3 Read the description in the **Function Arguments** dialog box, and notice that this result is *Volatile*.

The Function Arguments dialog box displays a message indicating that this function does not require an argument. It also states that this function is ***volatile***, meaning the date and time will not remain as entered, but rather the date and time will automatically update each time you open this workbook.

4 In the **Function Arguments** dialog box, click **OK** to close the dialog box to display the current date and time in cell **A44**. **Save** 🖫 your workbook.

More **Knowledge** | **NOW Function Recalculates Each Time a Workbook Opens**

The NOW function updates each time the workbook is opened. With the workbook open, you can force the NOW function to update by pressing F9, for example, to update the time.

Activity 2.13 │ Freezing and Unfreezing Panes

In a large worksheet, if you scroll down more than 25 rows or scroll beyond column O (the exact row number and column letter varies, depending on your screen size and screen resolution), you will no longer see the top rows or first column of your worksheet where identifying information about the data is usually placed. You will find it easier to work with your data if you can always view the identifying row or column titles.

The *Freeze Panes* command enables you to select one or more rows or columns and then freeze (lock) them into place. The locked rows and columns become separate panes. A *pane* is a portion of a worksheet window bounded by and separated from other portions by vertical or horizontal bars.

1 Press Ctrl + Home to make cell **A1** the active cell. Scroll down until **row 21** displays at the top of your Excel window, and notice that all of the identifying information in the column titles is out of view.

2 Press Ctrl + Home again, and then from the **row heading area**, select **row 14**. Click the **View tab**, and then in the **Window group**, click **Freeze Panes**. In the list, click **Freeze Panes**. Click any cell to deselect the row, and then notice that a line displays along the upper border of **row 14**.

By selecting row 14, the rows above—rows 1–13—are frozen in place and will not move as you scroll down.

3 Watch the row numbers below **row 13**, and then begin to scroll down to bring **row 21** into view again. Notice that rows 1:13 are frozen in place. Compare your screen with Figure 2.23.

The remaining rows of data continue to scroll. Use this feature when you have long or wide worksheets.

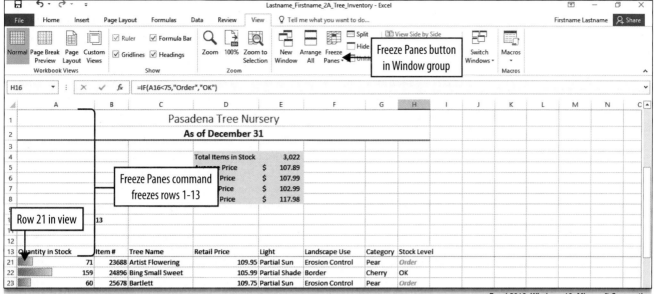

FIGURE 2.23

Excel 2016, Windows 10, Microsoft Corporation

4 In the **Window group**, click **Freeze Panes**, and then click **Unfreeze Panes** to unlock all rows and columns. **Save** 🖫 your workbook.

More **Knowledge** | **Freeze Columns or Freeze Both Rows and Columns**

You can freeze columns that you want to remain in view on the left. Select the column to the right of the column(s) that you want to remain in view while scrolling to the right, and then click the Freeze Panes command. You can also use the command to freeze both rows and columns; click a *cell* to freeze the rows *above* the cell and the columns to the *left* of the cell.

Objective 5 | Create, Sort, and Filter an Excel Table

GO! Learn How
Video E2-5

To analyze a group of related data, you can convert a range of cells to an ***Excel table***. An Excel table is a series of rows and columns that contains related data that is managed independently from the data in other rows and columns in the worksheet.

MOS
3.1.1, 3.2.1

Activity 2.14 | Creating an Excel Table and Applying a Table Style

1 Be sure that you have applied the Unfreeze Panes command—no rows on your worksheet are locked. Click any cell in the data below row 13. Click the **Insert tab**. In the **Tables group**, click **Table**. In the **Create Table** dialog box, if necessary, click to select the My table has headers check box, and then compare your screen with Figure 2.24.

The column titles in row 13 will form the table headers. By clicking in a range of contiguous data, Excel will suggest the range as the data for the table. You can adjust the range if necessary.

FIGURE 2.24

ANOTHER WAY   Select the range of cells that make up the table, including the header row, and then click the Table button.

> **2** Click **OK**. With the range still selected, on the ribbon notice that the **Table Tools** are active.

> **3** On the **Design tab**, in the **Table Styles group**, click **More**, and then under **Light**, locate and click **Table Style Light 16**.

> **4** Press Ctrl + Home. Click **Save**, and then compare your screen with Figure 2.25.

> Sorting and filtering arrows display in the table's header row.

FIGURE 2.25

Activity 2.15 | Sorting an Excel Table

3.3.2, 3.3.3

You can *sort* tables—arrange all the data in a specific order—in ascending or descending order.

> **1** In the header row of the table, click the **Retail Price arrow**, and then on the menu, click **Sort Smallest to Largest**. Next to the arrow, notice the small **up arrow** indicating an ascending (smallest to largest) sort.

> This action sorts the rows in the table from the lowest retail price to highest retail price.

> **2** In the table's header row, click the **Category arrow**, and then click **Sort Z to A**.

> This action sorts the rows in the table in reverse alphabetic order by Category name, and the small arrow points downward, indicating a descending (Z to A) sort. The Retail Price continues to be sorted from smallest to largest within each category.

3 ▸ Click the **Category arrow**, and then sort from **A to Z**. Next to the arrow, notice the small **up arrow** indicating an ascending (A to Z) sort.

This action sorts the rows in the table alphabetically by Category, and within a Category sorts the rows from smallest to largest by Retail Price.

4 ▸ In the table header row, click the **Item # arrow**, and then click **Sort Smallest to Largest**, which will apply an ascending sort to the data using the *Item #* column.

Activity 2.16 | Filtering an Excel Table and Displaying a Total Row

You can *filter* tables—display only a portion of the data based on matching a specific value—to show only the data that meets the criteria that you specify.

1 ▸ Click the **Category arrow**. On the menu, click the (**Select All**) check box to clear all the check boxes. Click to select only the **Maple** check box, and then click **OK**. Compare your screen with Figure 2.26.

Only the rows containing *Maple* in the Category column display—the remaining rows are hidden from view. A small funnel—the filter icon—indicates that a filter is applied to the data in the table. Additionally, the row numbers display in blue to indicate that some rows are hidden from view. A filter hides entire rows in the worksheet.

FIGURE 2.26

Excel 2016, Windows 10, Microsoft Corporation

2 ▸ Point to the right of *Category*, and notice that *Equals "Maple"* displays to indicate the filter criteria.

3 ▸ Click any cell in the table so that the table is selected. Click the **Design tab**, and then in the **Table Style Options group**, select the **Total Row** check box.

Total displays in cell A43. In cell H43, the number 6 indicates that six rows currently display.

4 ▸ Click cell **A43**, click the **arrow** that displays to the right of cell **A43**, and then in the list, click **Sum**.

Excel sums only the visible rows in Column A, and indicates that 571 products in the Maple category are in stock. In this manner, you can use an Excel table to quickly find information about a group of data.

5 ▸ Click cell **A11**, type **Maple Trees** and press ⎢Tab⎟. In cell **B11**, type **6 (571 total items in stock)** and then press ⎢Enter⎟.

6 ▸ In the table header row, click the **Category arrow**, and then on the menu, click **Clear Filter From "Category"**.

All the rows in the table redisplay.

7 ▸ Click the **Landscape Use arrow**, click the (**Select All**) check box to clear all the check boxes, and then click to select the **Erosion Control** check box. Click **OK**.

8 ▶ Click the **Category arrow**, click the **(Select All)** check box to clear all the check boxes, and then click the **Oak** check box. Click **OK**, **Save** 🖫 your workbook, and then compare your screen with Figure 2.27.

By applying multiple filters, you can determine quickly that eight tree names identified with a *Landscape Use* of *Erosion Control* are in the *Oak* tree category with a total of 710 such trees in stock.

FIGURE 2.27

More **Knowledge**	**Band Rows and Columns in a Table**

You can band rows to format even rows differently from odd rows, making them easier to read. To band rows or columns, on the Design tab, in the Table Style Options group, select the Banded Rows or Banded Columns check box.

Activity 2.17 | Clearing Filters

When you are finished answering questions about the data in a table, you can clear the filters and remove the total row.

1 ▶ Click the **Category arrow**, and then click **Clear Filter From "Category"**. Use the same technique to remove the filter from the **Landscape Use** column.

2 ▶ Click anywhere in the table to activate the table and display the **Table Tools** on the ribbon. Click the **Design tab**, and then in the **Table Style Options group**, click the **Total Row** check box to clear the check mark and remove the Total row from the table.

3 ▶ Click **Save** 🖫, and then compare your screen with Figure 2.28.

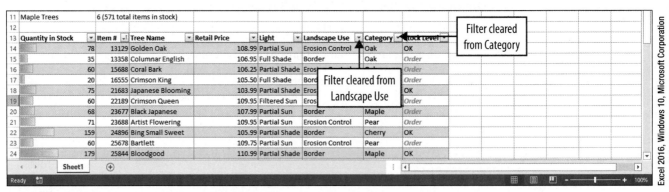

FIGURE 2.28

More **Knowledge**	**Converting a Table to a Range**

When you are finished answering questions about the data in a table by sorting, filtering, and totalling, you can convert the table into a normal range. Doing so is useful if you want to use the Table feature only to apply an attractive Table Style to a range of cells. For example, you can insert a table, apply a Table Style, and then convert the table to a normal range of data but keep the formatting. To convert a table to a range, on the Design tab, in the Tools group, click Convert to Range. In the message box, click Yes. Or, with any table cell selected, right-click, point to Table, and then click Convert to Range.

GO! Learn How
Video E2-6

You can magnify or shrink the view of a worksheet on your screen to either zoom in to view specific data or zoom out to see the entire worksheet. You can also split a worksheet window into panes to view different parts of a worksheet at the same time.

A worksheet might be too wide, too long—or both—to print on a single page. Use Excel's *Print Titles* and *Scale to Fit* commands to create pages that are attractive and easy to read.

The Print Titles command enables you to specify rows and columns to repeat on each printed page. Scale to Fit commands enable you to stretch or shrink the width, height, or both, of printed output to fit a maximum number of pages.

1.4.7

Activity 2.18 | Modifying and Shrinking the Worksheet View

1 Press Ctrl + Home to display the top of your worksheet. On the **View tab**, in the **Zoom group**, click **Zoom**.

2 In the **Zoom** dialog box, click the **75%** option button, and then click **OK**. Notice that by zooming out in this manner, you can see additional rows of your worksheet on the screen.

3 In the lower right corner of your worksheet, in the status bar, click **Zoom In** ➕ until the worksheet redisplays at 100%.

Activity 2.19 | Splitting a Worksheet Window into Panes

1.4.5

The *Split* command splits the window into multiple resizable panes that contain views of your worksheet. This is useful to view multiple distant parts of your worksheet at one time.

1 Click cell **F9**. On the **View tab**, in the **Window group**, click **Split**.

> Horizontal and vertical split bars display. You can drag the split bars to view any four portions of the worksheet. On the right, separate vertical scroll bars display for the upper and lower panes and at the bottom, separate horizontal scroll bars display for the left and right panes.

2 Drag the lower vertical scroll box down to the bottom of the scroll bar to view **row 43**. Compare your screen with Figure 2.29.

> Here it could be useful to isolate the Tree Statistics at the top and then scroll to the bottom to browse the inventory items.

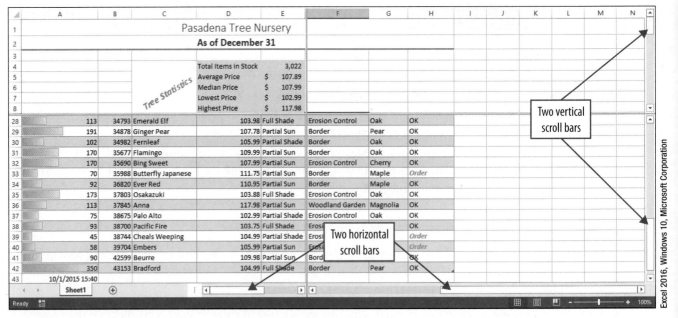

FIGURE 2.29

---

3 Click **Split** again to remove the split bars.

4 Press Ctrl + Home to display the top of your worksheet. On the **Page Layout tab**, in the **Themes group**, click **Themes**, and then click **Slice**.

5 Select the range **A13:H13**. On the **Home tab**, from the **Styles group**, apply the **Heading 4** cell style, and then apply **Center** ☰. Click cell **A1**.

Activity 2.20 | Printing Titles and Scaling to Fit

1.5.4, 1.5.5

1 Click the **Page Layout tab**, and then in the **Page Setup group**, click **Margins**. At the bottom of the gallery, click **Custom Margins** to display the **Page Setup** dialog box. Under **Center on page**, select the **Horizontally** check box.

2 Click the **Header/Footer tab**, and then in the center of the dialog box, click **Custom Footer**. In the **Footer** dialog box, with your insertion point blinking in the **Left section**, on the row of buttons, click **Insert File Name** 🔳. Click **OK** two times.

3 In the **Page Setup group**, click **Orientation**, and then click **Landscape**.

The dotted line indicates that as currently formatted, column H will not fit on the page.

4 Press Ctrl + F2 to display the **Print Preview**. At the bottom of the **Print Preview**, click **Next Page** ▶.

As currently formatted, the worksheet will print on four pages, and the columns will span multiple pages. Additionally, after Page 1, no column titles are visible to identify the data in the columns.

5 Click **Next Page** ▶ two times to display **Page 4**, and notice that one column moves to an additional page.

6 In the upper left corner of **Backstage** view, click **Back** ⊙ to return to the worksheet. In the **Page Setup group**, click **Print Titles**. Under **Print titles**, click in the **Rows to repeat at top** box, and then at the right, click **Collapse Dialog** 🔝.

7 From the **row heading area**, select **row 13**, and then in the **Page Setup – rows to repeat at top:** dialog box, click **Expand Dialog** 🔲. Click **OK** to print the column titles in row 13 at the top of every page.

You can collapse and then expand dialog boxes on your screen to enable a better view of your data.

8 Press Ctrl + F2 to display the **Print Preview** again. At the bottom of the **Settings group**, click the **No Scaling arrow**, and then on the displayed list, point to **Fit All Columns on One Page**. Compare your screen with Figure 2.30.

This action will shrink the width of the printed output to fit all the columns on one page. You can make adjustments like this on the Page Layout tab, or here, in the Print Preview.

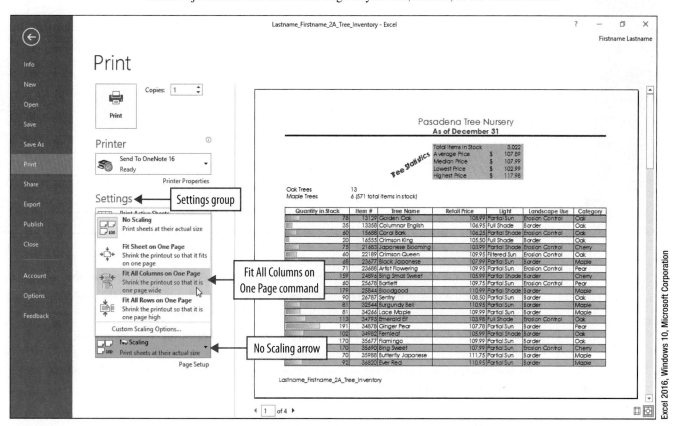

FIGURE 2.30

9 Click **Fit All Columns on One Page**. Notice in the **Print Preview** that all the columns display on one page.

ANOTHER WAY   With the worksheet displayed, on the Page Layout tab, in the Scale to Fit group, click the Width button arrow, and then click 1 page.

10 At the bottom of the **Print Preview**, click **Next Page** ▶ one time. Notice that the output will now print on two pages and that the column titles display at the top of **Page 2**. Compare your screen with Figure 2.31.

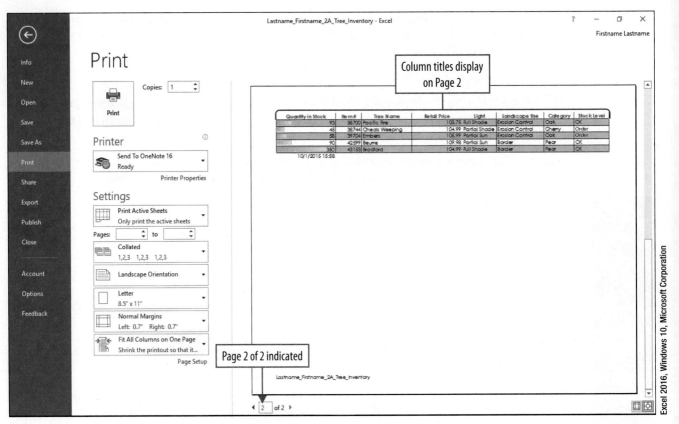

FIGURE 2.31

11 ▶ On the left, click **Info**, and then click **Show All Properties**. As the **Tags**, type **tree inventory, Pasadena** and as the **Subject**, type your course name and section number. Be sure your name displays as the Author; edit if necessary. On the left, click **Save**.

12 ▶ If directed by your instructor to do so, submit your paper printout, your electronic image of your document that looks like a printed document, or your original Excel file. If required by your instructor, print or create an electronic version of your worksheet with formulas displayed. In the upper right corner of the Excel window, click **Close** ☒.

More Knowledge | **Scaling for Data That Is Slightly Larger Than the Printed Page**

If your data is just a little too large to fit on a printed page, you can scale the worksheet to make it fit. Scaling reduces both the width and height of the printed data to a percentage of its original size or by the number of pages that you specify. On the Page Layout tab, in the Scale to Fit group, click the Scale arrows to select a percentage.

END | You have completed Project 2A

GO! With Google

Objective | Summarize an Inventory List

ALERT! **Working with Web-Based Applications and Services**

Computer programs and services on the web receive continuous updates and improvements, so the steps to complete this web-based activity may differ from the ones shown. You can often look at the screens and the information presented to determine how to complete the activity.

If you do not already have a Google account, you will need to create one before you begin this activity. Go to http://google.com and, in the upper right corner, click Sign In. On the Sign In screen, click Create Account. On the Create your Google Account page, complete the form, read and agree to the Terms of Service and Privacy Policy, and then click Next step. On the Welcome screen, click Get Started.

Activity | Create SUM, AVERAGE, COUNTIF, and IF functions

1 From the desktop, open your browser, navigate to **http://google.com**, and then click the **Google Apps** menu ⊞. Click **Drive** ☁, and then if necessary, sign in to your Google account.

2 Open your **GO! Web Projects** folder—or click New to create and then open this folder if necessary. In the left pane, click **NEW**, and then click **File upload**. Navigate to your student data files, click **e02_2A_Web**, and then click **Open**.

3 Right-click the file you uploaded, point to **Open with**, and then click **Google Sheets**.

4 Select the range **A1:H1**. Click **Merge cells** ⊞. Click **Format**, point to **Align**, and then click **Center**. With **A1** selected, click **Paint format** 🖌, and then click cell **A2**.

5 Select **A1:A2**, and then click the **Font size** arrow ▾. Click **18**.

6 Click cell **B4**. On the ribbon, click **Functions** Σ ▾, and then click **SUM**. Within the formula's parentheses, type **a11:a33** and press Enter for a result of *2311*. Click **B4**, and then on the ribbon, click **More formats** 123 ▾. Click **Number**, and then click **Decrease decimal places** ▾ two times.

7 Click cell **B5**, click **Functions** Σ ▾, and then click **AVERAGE**. Within the parentheses, type **d11:d33** and press Enter. Click **B5**, and then on the ribbon, click **Format as currency** $.

8 Click cell **B7**. Type **=countif(g11:g33,"Oak")** and then press Enter to create a function that counts the number of Oak trees in the category column.

9 Click cell **H11**. Type **=if(a11<75,"Order","OK")** and then press Enter. Click cell **H11**, and then drag the fill handle down through cell **H33**.

10 With the range **H11:H33** selected, click **Format**, and then click **Conditional formatting**. On the right side of the window, in the **Apply to range** box, make sure that **H11:H33** displays. Under **Format cells if…**, click the displayed box, and then click **Text contains**. Click in the **Value or formula** box, and then type **Order** Under **Formatting style,** click **Bold**. Click **Done** to apply the default green background conditional format and bold to all cells containing the word *Order*. Click cell **A1** and compare your screen with Figure A.

11 Submit your file as directed by your instructor. Sign out of your Google account and close your browser.

1			Austin Tree Nursery					
2			As of March 30					
3								
4	Total Items in Stock	2,311						
5	Average Price	$108.52						
6								
7	Oak Trees:	10						
8								
9								
10	Quantity in Stock	Item #	Tree Name	Retail Price	Light	Landscape Use	Category	Stock Level
11	78	13129	Golden Oak	108.99	Partial Sun	Erosion	Oak	OK
12	35	13358	Columnar English	106.95	Full Shade	Border	Oak	Order
13	60	15688	Coral Bark	106.25	Partial Shade	Erosion	Oak	Order
14	20	16555	Crimson King	105.5	Full Shade	Border	Oak	Order
15	75	21683	Japanese Blooming	103.99	Partial Shade	Erosion	Cherry	OK
16	60	22189	Crimson Queen	109.95	Filtered Sun	Erosion	Oak	Order

FIGURE A

Weekly Sales Summary

PROJECT ACTIVITIES

In Activities 2.21 through 2.35, you will edit an existing workbook for the Sales Director, Mariam Daly. The workbook summarizes the online and in-store sales of products during a one-week period in April. The worksheets of your completed workbook will look similar to Figure 2.32.

PROJECT FILES

 MyITLab
grader

If your instructor wants you to submit Project 2B in the MyITLab Grader system, log in to MyITLab, locate Grader Project 2B, and then download the files for this project.

For Project 2B, you will need the following file:
e02B_Weekly_Sales

You will save your workbook as:
Lastname_Firstname_2B_Weekly_Sales

Please always review the downloaded Grader instructions before beginning.

PROJECT RESULTS

GO!
Walk Thru
Project 2B

FIGURE 2.32 Project 2B Weekly Sales

GO! Learn How
Video E2-7

Use multiple worksheets in a workbook to organize data in a logical arrangement. When you have more than one worksheet in a workbook, you can **navigate** (move) among worksheets by clicking the **sheet tabs**. Sheet tabs identify each worksheet in a workbook and display along the lower left edge of the workbook window. When you have more worksheets in the workbook than can display in the sheet tab area, use the sheet tab scrolling buttons to move sheet tabs into and out of view.

Activity 2.21 | Navigating Among Worksheets, Renaming Worksheets, and Changing the Tab Color
              of Worksheets

ALERT!   To submit as an autograded project, log into MyITLab and download
             the files for this project, and begin with those files instead of
             e02B_Weekly_Sales.

MOS
1.3.1, 1.3.2

Excel names the first worksheet in a workbook *Sheet1* and each additional worksheet that you add in order—*Sheet2*, *Sheet3*, and so on. Most Excel users rename their worksheets with meaningful names. In this Activity, you will navigate among worksheets, rename worksheets, and change the tab color of sheet tabs.

1 Start Excel. In the lower left corner of Excel's opening screen, click **Open Other Workbooks**, and then click **Browse**.

ANOTHER WAY   Press Ctrl + F12 to display the Open dialog box.

2 Navigate to the student files that accompany this chapter, and then open **e02B_Weekly_Sales**. Press F12 to display the **Save As** dialog box, and then navigate to your **Excel Chapter 2** folder. In the **File name** box, using your own name, type **Lastname_Firstname_2B_Weekly_Sales** and then click **Save** or press Enter.

In this workbook, two worksheets display, into which some data has already been entered. For example, on the first worksheet, the days of the week and sales data for the one-week period displays.

3 Along the bottom of the Excel window, point to and then click the **Sheet2 tab**.

The second worksheet in the workbook displays and becomes the active worksheet. *Sheet2* displays in bold.

4 In cell **A1**, notice the text *In-Store*—this worksheet will contain data for in-store sales.

5 Click the **Sheet1 tab**. Then, point to the **Sheet1 tab**, and double-click to select the sheet tab name. Type **Online Sales** and press Enter.

The first worksheet becomes the active worksheet, and the sheet tab displays *Online Sales*.

6 Point to the **Online Sales sheet tab** and right-click. Point to **Tab Color**, and then in the next to last column, point to the first color—**Blue, Accent 5**. Compare your screen with Figure 2.33.

ANOTHER WAY   On the Home tab, in the Cells group, click the Format button, and then on the displayed list, point to Tab Color.

First sheet tab displays Online Sales

Tab color changed to Blue, Accent 5

FIGURE 2.33

7 Click **Blue, Accent 5** to change the tab color.

8 Point to the **Sheet2 tab**, right-click, and then from the shortcut menu, click **Rename**. Type **In-Store Sales** and press Enter.

You can either double-click the sheet name or use the shortcut menu to rename a sheet tab.

9 Point to the **In-Store Sales sheet tab** and right-click. Point to **Tab Color**, and then in the last column, click the first color—**Green, Accent 6**. **Save** 💾 your workbook.

More Knowledge   **Copying a Worksheet**

To copy a worksheet to the same workbook, right-click the sheet tab, on the shortcut menu click Move or Copy, click the sheet before which you want to insert the copied sheet, select the Create a copy check box, and then click OK. To copy to a different, opened workbook, in the Move or Copy dialog box, click the To book arrow, and then select the workbook into which you want to insert the copy.

Objective 8   Enter Dates, Clear Contents, and Clear Formats

GO! Learn How
Video E2-8

Dates represent a type of value that you can enter in a cell. When you enter a date, Excel assigns a serial value—a number—to the date. This makes it possible to treat dates like other numbers. For example, if two cells contain dates, you can find the number of days between the two dates by subtracting the older date from the more recent date.

Activity 2.22 | Entering and Formatting Dates

In this Activity, you will examine the various ways that Excel can format dates in a cell. Date values entered in any of the following formats will be recognized by Excel as a date:

VALUE TYPED	EXAMPLE
m/d/yy	7/4/2016
d-mmm	4-Jul
d-mmm-yy	4-Jul-16
mmm-yy	Jul-16

On your keyboard, ⊟ (the hyphen key) and ⟋ (the forward slash key) function identically in any of these formats and can be used interchangeably. You can abbreviate the month name to three characters or spell it out. You can enter the year as two digits, four digits, or even leave it off. When left off, the current year is assumed but does not display in the cell.

A two-digit year value of 30 through 99 is interpreted by the Windows operating system as the four-digit years of 1930 through 1999. All other two-digit year values are assumed to be in the 21st century. If you always type year values as four digits, even though only two digits may display in the cell, you can be sure that Excel interprets the year value as you intended. Examples are shown in Figure 2.34.

HOW EXCEL INTERPRETS DATES	
DATE TYPED AS:	**COMPLETED BY EXCEL AS:**
7/4/15	7/4/2015
7/4/98	7/4/1998
7/4	4-Jul (current year assumed)
7-4	4-Jul (current year assumed)
July 4	4-Jul (current year assumed)
Jul 4	4-Jul (current year assumed)
Jul/4	4-Jul (current year assumed)
Jul-4	4-Jul (current year assumed)
July 4, 1998	4-Jul-98
July 2012	Jul-12 (first day of month assumed)
July 1998	Jul-98 (first day of month assumed)

FIGURE 2.34

1 Click the **Online Sales sheet tab** to make it active. Click cell **A16** and notice that the cell displays *6/3*. In the **Formula Bar**, notice that the full date of June 3, 2016, displays in the format *6/3/2016*.

2 With cell **A16** selected, on the **Home tab**, in the **Number group**, click the **Number Format arrow**. At the bottom, click **More Number Formats** to display the **Number tab** of the **Format Cells** dialog box.

Under Category, *Date* is selected, and under Type, *3/14* is selected. Cell A16 uses this format type; that is, only the month and day display in the cell.

3 In the displayed dialog box, under **Type**, click several other date types and watch the **Sample** area to see how applying the selected date format will format your cell. When you are finished, click the **3/14/12** type, and then compare your screen with Figure 2.35.

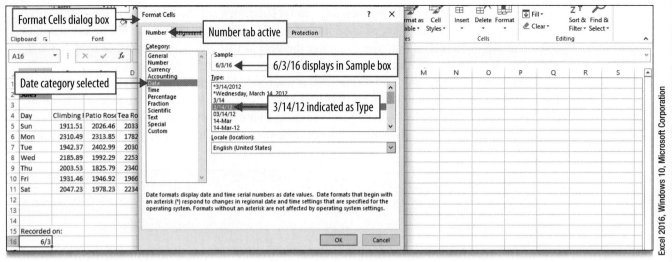

Format Cells dialog box

Number tab active

Date category selected

6/3/16 displays in Sample box

3/14/12 indicated as Type

Format Cells

Number | Alignment | Protection

Category:
General
Number
Currency
Accounting
Date
Time
Percentage
Fraction
Scientific
Text
Special
Custom

Sample
6/3/16

Type:
*3/14/2012
*Wednesday, March 14, 2012
3/14
3/14/12
03/14/12
14-Mar
14-Mar-12

Locale (location):
English (United States)

Date formats display date and time serial numbers as date values. Date formats that begin with an asterisk (*) respond to changes in regional date and time settings that are specified for the operating system. Formats without an asterisk are not affected by operating system settings.

OK | Cancel

FIGURE 2.35

4 At the bottom of the dialog box, click **OK**. Click cell **A19**, type **6-7-16** and then press Enter.

Cell A19 has no special date formatting applied, and displays in the default date format *6/7/2016*.

ALERT!   **The Date Does Not Display as 6/7/2016?**

Settings in your Windows operating system determine the default format for dates. If your result is different, it is likely that the formatting of the default date was adjusted on the computer at which you are working.

---

5 Click cell **A19** again. Hold down Ctrl and press ; (semicolon). Press Enter to confirm the entry.

Excel enters the current date, obtained from your computer's internal calendar, in the selected cell using the default date format. Ctrl + ; is a quick method to enter the current date.

6 Click cell **A19** again, type **6/7/16** and then press Enter.

Because the year *16* is less than 30, Excel assumes a 21st century date and changes *16* to *2016* to complete the four-digit year. Typing *98* would result in *1998*. For two-digit years that you type that are between 30 and 99, Excel assumes a 20th century date.

7 Click cell **A16**, and then on the **Home tab**, in the **Clipboard group**, click **Format Painter**. Click cell **A19**, and notice that the date format from cell A16 is copied to cell A19. **Save** your workbook.

Activity 2.23 | Clearing Cell Contents and Formats

A cell has *contents*—a value or a formula—and a cell may also have one or more *formats* applied, for example, bold and italic font styles, fill color, font color, and so on. You can choose to clear—delete—the *contents* of a cell, the *formatting* of a cell, or both.

Clearing the contents of a cell deletes the value or formula typed there, but it does *not* clear formatting applied to a cell. In this Activity, you will clear the contents of a cell and then clear the formatting of a cell that contains a date to see its underlying content.

1 In the **Online Sales** worksheet, click cell **A1**. In the **Editing group**, click **Clear**, and then click **Clear Contents**. Notice that the text is cleared, but the green formatting remains.

2 Click cell **A2**, and then press Delete.

You can use either of these two methods to delete the *contents* of a cell. Deleting the contents does not, however, delete the formatting of the cell; you can see that the green fill color format applied to the two cells still displays.

3 In cell **A1**, type **Online Sales** and then on the **Formula Bar**, click **Enter** ☑ so that cell **A1** remains the active cell.

In addition to the green fill color, the bold italic text formatting remains with the cell.

4 In the **Editing group**, click **Clear** ⬚, and then click **Clear Formats**.

Clearing the formats deletes formatting from the cell—the green fill color and the bold and italic font styles—but does not delete the cell's contents.

5 Use the same technique to clear the green fill color from cell **A2**. Click cell **A16**, click **Clear** ⬚, and then click **Clear Formats**. In the **Number group**, notice that *General* displays as the number format of the cell.

The box in the Number group indicates the current Number format of the selected cell. Clearing the date formatting from the cell displays the date's serial number. The date, June 3, 2016, is stored as a serial number that indicates the number of days since January 1, 1900. This date is the 42,524th day since the reference date of January 1, 1900.

6 On the Quick Access Toolbar, click **Undo** ↺ to restore the date format. **Save** 🖫 your workbook, and then compare your screen with Figure 2.36.

FIGURE 2.36

More Knowledge   **Clearing an Entire Worksheet**

To clear an entire worksheet, in the upper left corner of the worksheet, click the Select All button, and then on the Home tab, in the Editing group, click Clear, and then click Clear All.

Data in cells can be copied to other cells in the same worksheet, to other sheets in the same workbook, or to sheets in another workbook. The action of placing cell contents that have been copied or moved to the Clipboard into another location is called **paste**.

Activity 2.24 | Copying and Pasting by Using the Paste Options Gallery

2.1.2, 2.1.3

Recall that the Clipboard is a temporary storage area maintained by your Windows operating system. When you select one or more cells, and then perform the Copy command or the Cut command, the selected data is placed on the Clipboard. From the Clipboard storage area, the data is available for pasting into other cells, other worksheets, other workbooks, and even into other Office programs. When you paste, the **Paste Options gallery** displays, which includes Live Preview to preview the Paste formatting that you want.

1 With the **Online Sales** worksheet active, select the range **A4:A19**.

A range of cells identical to this one is required for the *In-Store Sales* worksheet.

2 Right-click over the selection, and then click **Copy** to place a copy of the cells on the Clipboard. The copied cells may display a moving border.

> **ANOTHER WAY** Use the keyboard shortcut for Copy, which is Ctrl + C; or click the Copy button in the Clipboard group on the Home tab.

3 At the bottom of the workbook window, click the **In-Store Sales sheet tab** to make it the active worksheet. Point to cell **A4**, right-click, and then on the shortcut menu, under **Paste Options**, *point* to the first button—**Paste**. Compare your screen with Figure 2.37.

Live Preview displays how the copied cells will be placed in the worksheet if you click the Paste button. In this manner, you can experiment with different paste options, and then be sure you are selecting the paste operation that you want. When pasting a range of cells, you need only point to or select the cell in the upper left corner of the *paste area*—the target destination for data that has been cut or copied using the Clipboard.

> **ANOTHER WAY** Use the keyboard shortcut for Paste, which is Ctrl + V; or click the Paste button in the Clipboard group on the Home tab.

Excel 2016, Windows 10, Microsoft Corporation

FIGURE 2.37

4 Click the first button, **Paste**. In the status bar, notice the message that displays, indicating that your selected range remains available on the Office Clipboard.

5 Display the **Online Sales** worksheet. Press Esc to cancel the moving border. **Save** your workbook.

The status bar no longer displays the message.

GO! Learn How
Video E2-10

You can enter or edit data on several worksheets at the same time by selecting and grouping multiple worksheets. Data that you enter or edit on the active sheet is reflected in all selected sheets. If the sheet tab displays with a solid background color, you know the sheet is not selected.

Activity 2.25 | Grouping Worksheets for Editing

In this Activity, you will group the two worksheets, and then format both worksheets at the same time.

1 With the **Online Sales** sheet active, press Ctrl + Home to make cell **A1** the active cell. Point to the **Online Sales sheet tab**, right-click, and then click **Select All Sheets**.

2 At the top of your screen, notice that *[Group]* displays in the title bar. Compare your screen with Figure 2.38.

Both worksheets are selected, as indicated by *[Group]* in the title bar and the sheet tab names underlined. Data that you enter or edit on the active sheet will also be entered or edited in the same manner on all the selected sheets in the same cells.

FIGURE 2.38

3 Select **columns A:G**, and then set their width to **85 pixels**.

4 Click cell **A2**, type **Week of May 24** and then on the **Formula Bar**, click **Enter** ✓ to keep cell **A2** as the active cell. **Merge & Center** the text across the range **A2:G2**, and then apply the **Heading 1** cell style.

5 Click cell **E4**, type **Total Rose Sales** and then press Tab. In cell **F4**, type **Rose Supply Sales** and then press Tab. In cell **G4**, type **Total Sales** and then press Enter.

6 Select the range **A4:G4**, and then apply the **Heading 3** cell style. In the **Alignment group**, click **Center** 🔲, **Middle Align** 🔲, and **Wrap Text**. **Save** 🔲 your workbook.

7 Display the **In-Store Sales** worksheet to cancel the grouping, and then compare your screen with Figure 2.39.

> As soon as you select a single sheet, the grouping of the sheets is cancelled and *[Group]* no longer displays in the title bar. Because the sheets were grouped, the same new text and formatting were applied to both sheets. In this manner, you can make the same changes to all the sheets in a workbook at one time.

ANOTHER WAY Right-click any sheet tab, and then click Ungroup Sheets.

FIGURE 2.39

More **Knowledge** **Hide Worksheets**

You can hide any worksheet in a workbook to remove it from view using this technique:
Select the sheet tabs of the worksheets you want to hide, right-click any of the selected sheet tabs, and then click Hide.

Activity 2.26 | Formatting and Constructing Formulas on Grouped Worksheets

Recall that formulas are equations that perform calculations on values in your worksheet and that a formula starts with an equal sign (=). Operators are the symbols with which you specify the type of calculation that you want to perform on the elements of a formula. In this Activity, you will enter sales figures for Rose Supply items from both Online and In-Store sales, and then calculate the total sales.

1 Display the **Online Sales** worksheet. Verify that the sheets are not grouped—*[Group]* does *not* display in the title bar.

2 ▶ Click cell **A1**, replace *Online Sales* by typing **Rose Plants and Rose Supplies: Weekly Online Sales** and then on the **Formula Bar**, click **Enter** ☑ to keep cell **A1** as the active cell. **Merge & Center** the text across the range **A1:G1**, and then apply the **Title** cell style.

3 ▶ In the column titled *Rose Supply Sales*, click cell **F5**. In the range **F5:F11**, type the following data for Rose Supply Sales, and then compare your screen with Figure 2.40.

ROSE SUPPLY SALES	
Sun	1926.49
Mon	1526.03
Tue	1853.82
Wed	1922.36
Thu	1973.73
Fri	2121.47
Sat	2025.55

	A	B	C	D	E	F	G		M	N	O	P	Q
1		Rose Plants and Rose Supplies: Weekly Online Sales						Worksheet title entered and formatted for Online Sales sheet					
2			Week of May 24										
3													
4	Day	Climbing Roses	Patio Roses	Tea Roses	Total Rose Sales	Rose Supply Sales	Total Sales						
5	Sun	1911.51	2026.46	2033.47		1926.49							
6	Mon	2310.49	2313.85	1782.64		1526.03		Rose Supply Sales data entered					
7	Tue	1942.37	2402.99	2030.08		1853.82							
8	Wed	2185.89	1992.29	2253.98		1922.36							
9	Thu	2003.53	1825.79	2340.34		1973.73							
10	Fri	1931.46	1946.92	1966.92		2121.47							
11	Sat	2047.23	1978.23	2234.12		2025.55							
12													
13													
14													
15	Recorded on:												
16	6/3/16												
17													
18	Reviewed on:												
19	6/7/16												

Excel 2016, Windows 10, Microsoft Corporation

FIGURE 2.40

4 ▶ Display the **In-Store Sales** sheet. In cell **A1**, replace *In-Store* by typing **Rose Plants and Rose Supplies: Weekly In-Store Sales** and then on the **Formula Bar**, click **Enter** ☑ to keep cell **A1** as the active cell. **Merge & Center** the text across the range **A1:G1**, and then apply the **Title** cell style.

5 ▶ In the column titled *Rose Supply Sales*, click cell **F5**. In the range **F5:F11**, type the following data for Rose Supply Sales, and then compare your screen with Figure 2.41.

ROSE SUPPLY SALES	
Sun	1626.59
Mon	1483.69
Tue	1693.82
Wed	1778.94
Thu	1416.37
Fri	1645.24
Sat	1493.47

FIGURE 2.41

6 ▸ Save 🖫 your workbook. Right-click the **Online Sales sheet tab**, and then click **Select All Sheets**.

The first worksheet becomes the active sheet, and the worksheets are grouped. *[Group]* displays in the title bar, and the sheet tabs are underlined, indicating they are selected as part of the group. Recall that when grouped, any action that you perform on the active worksheet is *also* performed on any other selected worksheets.

7 ▸ With the sheets *grouped* and the **Online Sales** sheet active, click cell **E5**. On the **Home tab**, in the **Editing group**, click **AutoSum**. Compare your screen with Figure 2.42.

Recall that when you enter the SUM function, Excel looks first above and then left for a proposed range of cells to sum.

FIGURE 2.42

8 ▸ Press Enter to display Total Rose Sales for Sunday, which is *5971.44*.

9 ▸ Click cell **E5**, and then drag the fill handle down to copy the formula through cell **E11**.

10 ▸ Click cell **G5**, type = click cell **E5**, type + click cell **F5**, and then compare your screen with Figure 2.43.

Using the point-and-click technique to construct this formula is only one of several techniques you can use. Alternatively, you could use any other method to enter the SUM function to add the values in these two cells.

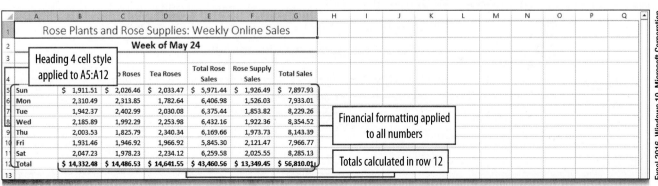

Excel 2016, Windows 10, Microsoft Corporation

FIGURE 2.43

The spreadsheet in Figure 2.43 shows:

	Day	Climbing Roses	Patio Roses	Tea Roses	Total Rose Sales	Rose Supply Sales	Total Sales
5	Sun	1911.51	2026.46	2033.47	5971.44	1926.49	=E5+F5
6	Mon	2310.49	2313.85	1782.64	6406.98	1526.03	
7	Tue	1942.37	2402.99	2030.08	6375.44	1853.82	
8	Wed	2185.89	1992.29	2253.98	6432.16	1922.36	
9	Thu	2003.53	1825.79	2340.34	6169.66	1973.73	
10	Fri	1931.46	1946.92	1966.92	5845.3	2121.47	
11	Sat	2047.23	1978.23	2234.12	6259.58	2025.55	

11 Press Enter to display the result *7897.93*, and then copy the formula down through cell **G11**. **Save** 🖫 your workbook.

Activity 2.27 | Determining Multiple Totals at the Same Time

You can select a contiguous range of cells adjacent to rows or columns of numbers and then click the AutoSum button—or use Alt + = —to enter the SUM function for each row or column.

1 With the two worksheets still grouped, in cell **A12**, type **Total** and then select the range **B5:G12**, which is all of the sales data and the empty cells at the bottom of each column of sales data.

2 With the range **B5:G12** selected, hold down Alt and press = to enter the **SUM** function in each empty cell. Click **Save** 🖫.

> Selecting a range in this manner and then clicking the AutoSum button, or entering the SUM function with the keyboard shortcut Alt + = , places the SUM function in the empty cells at the bottom of each column.

Activity 2.28 | Formatting Grouped Worksheets

1 With the two worksheets still grouped, select the range **A5:A12**, and then apply the **Heading 4** cell style.

2 To apply financial formatting to the worksheets, select the range **B5:G5**, hold down Ctrl, and then select the range **B12:G12**. With the nonadjacent ranges selected, apply the **Accounting Number Format** $ · .

3 Select the range **B6:G11** and apply **Comma Style** ₃. Select the range **B12:G12** and apply the **Total** cell style. Press Ctrl + Home to move to the top of the worksheet; compare your screen with Figure 2.44.

FIGURE 2.44

Excel 2016, Windows 10, Microsoft Corporation

Activity 2.29 | Ungrouping Worksheets

1 ▶ Right-click the **Online Sales sheet**. On the shortcut menu, click **Ungroup Sheets** to cancel the grouping.

2 ▶ Click the **In-Store Sales sheet**. Click **Save** 🖫, and then compare your screen with Figure 2.45.

With your worksheets grouped, the calculations and formatting on the first worksheet were also added on the second worksheet.

			Roses	Tea Roses	Total Rose Sales	Rose Supply Sales	Total Sales	
1	Rose Plants and Rose Supplies: Weekly In-Store Sales							
2	Week of May 24							
3								
4								Heading 4 cell style applied to A5:A12
5	Sun		,681.92	$ 1,594.22	$ 4,769.35	$ 1,626.59	$ 6,395.94	
6	Mon		1,689.37	1,552.58	1,624.44	4,866.39	1,483.69	6,350.08
7	Tue		1,271.12	1,709.58	1,386.26	4,366.96	1,693.82	6,060.78
8	Wed		1,192.61	1,584.02	1,596.72	4,373.35	1,778.94	6,152.29
9	Thu		1,558.58	1,526.63	1,735.51	4,820.72	1,416.37	6,237.09
10	Fri		1,483.62	1,486.91	1,656.56	4,627.09	1,645.24	6,272.33
11	Sat		1,605.58	1,783.64	1,526.23	4,915.45	1,493.47	6,408.92
12	Total		$ 10,294.09	$ 11,325.28	$ 11,119.94	$ 32,739.31	$ 11,138.12	$ 43,877.43
13								
14								

Financial formatting applied to all numbers

Totals calculated in row 12

Excel 2016, Windows 10, Microsoft Corporation

FIGURE 2.45

Objective 11 Create a Summary Sheet with Column Sparklines

GO! Learn How
Video E2-11

A **summary sheet** is a worksheet where totals from other worksheets are displayed and summarized. Recall that sparklines are tiny charts within a single cell that show a data trend.

Activity 2.30 | Inserting a Worksheet

MOS
1.1.3

1 ▶ To the right of the **In-Store Sales** sheet tab, click **New sheet** ⊕.

2 ▶ Rename the new worksheet tab **Summary** and change its **Tab Color** to **Gold, Accent 4**—in the eighth column, the first color.

3 ▶ Widen **columns A:E** to **110** pixels. In cell **A1**, type **Sales of Rose Plants and Rose Supplies** and then **Merge & Center** the title across the range **A1:E1**. Apply the **Title** cell style.

4 ▶ In cell **A2**, type **Week of May 24** and then **Merge & Center** across **A2:E2**; apply the **Heading 1** cell style.

5 ▶ Leave **row 3** blank. To form column titles, in cell **B4**, type **Roses/Rose Supplies** and press ⇥ Tab. In cell **C4**, type **Rose Sales** and press ⇥ Tab. In cell **D4**, type **Rose Supply Sales** and press ⇥ Tab. In cell **E4**, type **Total Sales** and press ↵ Enter.

6 ▶ Select the range **B4:E4**. Apply the **Heading 3** cell style. In the **Alignment group**, click **Center** ☰, **Middle Align** ☰, and **Wrap Text**.

7 ▶ To form row titles, in cell **A5**, type **Online Sales** In cell **A6**, type **In-Store Sales**

8 ▶ **Save** 🖫, and then compare your screen with Figure 2.46.

FIGURE 2.46

Excel 2016, Windows 10, Microsoft Corporation

4.1.1

Activity 2.31 | Constructing Formulas that Refer to Cells in Another Worksheet

In this Activity, you will construct formulas in the Summary worksheet to display the total sales for both online sales and in-store sales that will update the Summary worksheet whenever changes are made to the other worksheet totals.

1 Click cell **C5**. Type **=** and then click the **Online Sales sheet tab**. On the **Online Sales** worksheet, click cell **E12**, and then press Enter to redisplay the **Summary** worksheet and insert the total **Rose Sales** amount of *$43,460.56*.

2 Click cell **C5** to select it again. Look at the **Formula Bar**, and notice that instead of a value, the cell contains a formula that is equal to the value in another cell in another worksheet. Compare your screen with Figure 2.47.

> The value in this cell is equal to the value in cell E12 of the *Online Sales* worksheet. The Accounting Number Format applied to the referenced cell is carried over. By using a formula of this type, changes in cell E12 on the *Online Sales* worksheet will be automatically updated in this *Summary* worksheet.

FIGURE 2.47

Excel 2016, Windows 10, Microsoft Corporation

3 Click cell **D5**. Type **=** and then click the **Online Sales sheet tab**. Click cell **F12**, and then press Enter to redisplay the **Summary** worksheet and insert the total **Rose Supply Sales** amount of *$13,349.45*.

4 By using the techniques you just practiced, in cells **C6** and **D6** insert the total **Rose Sales** and **Rose Supply Sales** data from the **In-Store Sales** worksheet. Click **Save** 🖫, and then compare your screen with Figure 2.48.

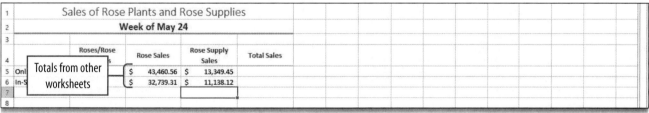

FIGURE 2.48

Excel 2016, Windows 10, Microsoft Corporation

Activity 2.32 | Changing Values in a Detail Worksheet to Update a Summary Worksheet

The formulas in cells C5:D6 display the totals from the other two worksheets. Changes made to any of the other two worksheets—sometimes referred to as *detail sheets* because the details of the information are contained there—that affect their totals will display on this Summary worksheet. In this manner, the Summary worksheet accurately displays the current totals from the other worksheets.

1 In cell **A7**, type **Total** Select the range **C5:E6**, and then on the **Home tab**, in the **Editing group**, click **AutoSum** to total the two rows.

> This technique is similar to selecting the empty cells at the bottom of columns and then inserting the SUM function for each column. Alternatively, you could use any other method to sum the rows. Recall that cell formatting carries over to adjacent cells unless two cells are left blank.

2 Select the range **C5:E7**, and then click **AutoSum** to total the three columns. Compare your screen with Figure 2.49.

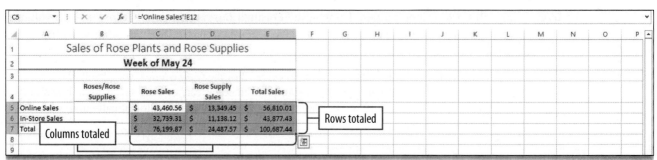

FIGURE 2.49

Excel 2016, Windows 10, Microsoft Corporation

3 Notice that in cell C6, Rose Sales for In-Store Sales is $32,739.31, and in cell C7, the total is $76,199.87. Display the **In-Store Sales** worksheet, click cell **B8**, type **1410.88** and then press Enter. Notice that the formulas in the worksheet recalculate.

4 Display the **Summary** worksheet, and notice that in the **Rose Sales** column, both the total for the *In-Store Sales* and the *Total* were recalculated.

> In this manner, a Summary sheet recalculates any changes made in the other worksheets.

5 On the **Summary** worksheet, select the range **C6:E6** and change the format to **Comma Style**. Select the range **C7:E7**, and then apply the **Total** cell style. Select the range **A5:A7** and apply the **Heading 4** cell style. **Save** your workbook. Click cell **A1**, and then compare your screen with Figure 2.50.

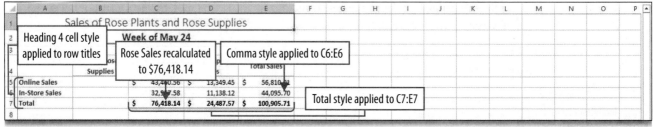

FIGURE 2.50

Excel 2016, Windows 10, Microsoft Corporation

2.3.1

Activity 2.33 | Inserting Column Sparklines

In this Activity, you will insert column sparklines to visualize the ratio of Rose sales to Rose Supply sales for both Online and In-Store.

1 On the **Summary** worksheet, click cell **B5**. On the **Insert tab**, in the **Sparklines group**, click **Column**. In the **Create Sparklines** dialog box, with the insertion point blinking in the **Data Range** box, type **c5:d5** and then compare your screen with Figure 2.51.

FIGURE 2.51   Excel 2016, Windows 10, Microsoft Corporation

> **2** Click **OK**. Click cell **B6**, and then **Insert** a **Column Sparkline** for the range **c6:d6**

> **3** With cell **B6** selected, on the **Design tab**, in the **Style group**, click **More** ⏷, and then click
> **Sparkline Style Accent 4, (no dark or light)**—in the third row, the fourth style. Press
> Ctrl + Home, click **Save** 💾, and then compare your screen with Figure 2.52.

>> You can see, at a glance, that for both Online and In-Store sales, Rose sales are greater than Rose
>> Supply sales.

FIGURE 2.52   Excel 2016, Windows 10, Microsoft Corporation

Objective 12   Format and Print Multiple Worksheets in a Workbook

GO! Learn How
Video E2-12

Each worksheet within a workbook can have different formatting, for example, different
headers or footers. If all the worksheets in the workbook will have the same header or footer, you
can select all the worksheets and apply formatting common to all of the worksheets; for example,
you can set the same footer in all of the worksheets.

1.1.4, 1.3.3

Activity 2.34 | Moving a Worksheet, Repeating Footers, and Formatting Multiple Worksheets in a Workbook

In this Activity, you will move the Summary sheet to become the first worksheet in the
workbook. Then you will format and prepare your workbook for printing. The three worksheets
containing data can be formatted simultaneously.

> **1** Point to the **Summary sheet tab**, hold down the left mouse button to display a small black
> triangle—a caret—and then notice that a small paper icon attaches to the mouse pointer.

> **2** Drag to the left until the caret and mouse pointer are to the left of the **Online Sales sheet tab**,
> as shown in Figure 2.53, and then release the left mouse button.

>> Use this technique to rearrange the order of worksheets within a workbook.

FIGURE 2.53   Excel 2016, Windows 10, Microsoft Corporation

3 Be sure the **Summary** worksheet is the active sheet, point to its sheet tab, right-click, and then click **Select All Sheets** to display *[Group]* in the title bar.

4 Click the **Page Layout tab**. In the **Page Setup group**, click **Margins**, and then at the bottom of the gallery, click **Custom Margins** to display the **Page Setup** dialog box.

5 In the **Page Setup** dialog box, on the **Margins tab**, under **Center on page**, select the **Horizontally** check box.

6 Click the **Header/Footer tab**, and then in the center of the dialog box, click **Custom Footer**. In the **Footer** dialog box, with your insertion point blinking in the **Left section**, on the row of buttons, click **Insert File Name** .

7 Click **OK** two times.

The dotted line indicates the page break as currently formatted.

8 Press Ctrl + Home; verify that *[Group]* still displays in the title bar.

By selecting all sheets, you can apply the same formatting to all the worksheets at the same time, for example, to repeat headers or footers.

9 Click the **File tab** to display **Backstage** view, and then click **Show All Properties**. As the **Tags**, type **weekly sales** and in the **Subject** box, type your course name and section number. Be sure your name displays as the **Author**; edit if necessary.

10 On the left, click **Print** to display the **Print Preview**, and then compare your screen with Figure 2.54.

By grouping, you can view all sheets in Print Preview. If you do not see *1 of 3* at the bottom of the Preview, redisplay the workbook, select all the sheets again, and then redisplay Print Preview.

FIGURE 2.54

11 At the bottom of the **Print Preview**, click **Next Page** ▶ as necessary and take a moment to view each page of your workbook.

1.5.3

Activity 2.35 | Printing All or Individual Worksheets in a Workbook

1 In **Backstage** view, click **Save** to save your workbook before printing. In the displayed workbook, right-click the **Summary sheet tab**, and then click **Ungroup Sheets**.

2 Press Ctrl + F2 to display **Print Preview**, and then at the bottom of the window, notice that *1 of 1* is indicated.

Because the worksheets are no longer grouped, only the active sheet is available for printing.

3 On the left, under **Settings**, click **Print Active Sheets**, and then click **Print Entire Workbook**.

At the bottom of the window, *1 of 3* is indicated. You can use this command to print an entire workbook.

4 If directed by your instructor to do so, submit your paper printout, your electronic image of your document that looks like a printed document, or your original Excel file. If required by your instructor, print or create an electronic version of your worksheet with formulas displayed. In the upper right corner of the Excel window, click **Close** ☒.

END | You have completed Project 2B

GO! With Google

> **ALERT!** | **Working with Web-Based Applications and Services**
>
> Computer programs and services on the web receive continuous updates and improvements, so the steps to complete this web-based activity may differ from the ones shown. You can often look at the screens and the information presented to determine how to complete the activity.
>
> If you do not already have a Google account, you will need to create one before you begin this activity. Go to http://google.com and, in the upper right corner, click Sign In. On the Sign In screen, click Create Account. On the Create your Google Account page, complete the form, read and agree to the Terms of Service and Privacy Policy, and then click Next step. On the Welcome screen, click Get Started.

Activity | Calculating Weekly Sales with Google Sheets

1 From the desktop, open your browser, navigate to **http://google.com**, and then click the **Google Apps** menu ⊞. Click **Drive**, and then if necessary, sign in to your Google account.

2 Open your **GO! Web Projects** folder—or click New to create and then open this folder if necessary. In the left pane, click **NEW**, and then click **File upload**. Navigate to your student data files, click **e02_2B_Web**, and then click **Open**.

3 Right-click the file you uploaded, point to **Open with**, and then click **Google Sheets**.

4 Click cell **E5**. On the ribbon, click **Functions** Σ ▾, and then click **SUM**. Select **B5:D5** and then press Enter to total the rose sales for Sunday. Click cell **E5**, and then drag the fill handle down through cell **E11**. Select **E6:E11**, and then on the ribbon, click **More Formats** 123 ▾. Click **Number**.

5 Click cell **G5** and then enter a formula to add cells **E5** and **F5**. Fill the formula down through cell **G11**, and then format the range **G6:G11** with **Number** format.

6 Select the range **B5:B11**. Click **Functions** Σ ▾, click **SUM**, and then press Enter to sum the selected range and place the result in cell B12. With **B12** selected, fill the formula across to cell **G12**.

7 Click cell **H5**. To calculate the percent that the Sunday sales are of the total sales, type **=g5/g12** and then press F4 to make the cell reference to G12 absolute. Press Enter and then fill the formula down through cell **H11**. With the range **H5:H11** selected, click **Format as percent** % .

8 Click cell **A1** and then compare your screen with Figure A.

9 Submit your file as directed by your instructor. Sign out of your Google account and close your browser.

	A	B	C	D	E	F	G	H	I	J	K	L	M	N	O	P	Q
1		**Rose Plants and Rose Supplies: Austin Sales**															
2				**Week of May 24**													
3																	
4	Day	Climbing Roses	Patio Roses	Tea Roses	Total Rose Sales	Rose Supply Sales	Total Sales	Percent of Sales									
5	Sun	$911.51	$26.46	$33.47	$971.44	$1,926.49	$2,897.93	12.17%									
6	Mon	310.49	313.85	782.64	1,406.98	1,526.03	2,933.01	12.32%									
7	Tue	942.37	402.99	30.08	1,375.44	1,853.82	3,229.26	13.56%									
8	Wed	185.89	992.29	253.98	1,432.16	1,922.36	3,354.52	14.09%									
9	Thu	3.53	825.79	340.34	1,169.66	1,973.73	3,143.39	13.20%									
10	Fri	931.46	946.92	966.92	2,845.30	2,121.47	4,966.77	20.86%									
11	Sat	47.23	978.23	234.12	1,259.58	2,025.55	3,285.13	13.80%									
12	Total Sales	$3,332.48	$4,486.53	$2,641.55	$10,460.56	$13,349.45	$23,810.01										
13																	
14																	
15																	

FIGURE A

GO! To Work

Andres Rodriguez/Fotolia; FotolEdhar/Fotolia; Andrey Popov/Fotolia; Shutterstock

MICROSOFT OFFICE SPECIALIST (MOS) SKILLS IN THIS CHAPTER

PROJECT 2A	PROJECT 2B
1.2.1 Search for data within a workbook	**1.1.3** Add a worksheet to an existing workbook
1.4.5 Change window views	**1.1.4** Copy and move a worksheet
1.4.7 Change magnification by using zoom tools	**1.3.1** Change worksheet tab color
1.5.4 Set print scaling	**1.3.2** Rename a worksheet
1.5.5 Display repeating row and column titles on multipage worksheets	**1.3.3** Change worksheet order
2.1.1 Replace data	**1.5.3** Print all or part of a workbook
2.3.4 Apply conditional formatting	**2.1.2** Cut, copy, or paste data
3.1.1 Create an Excel table from a cell range	**2.1.3** Paste data by using special paste options
3.2.1 Apply styles to tables	**2.3.1** Insert sparklines
3.2.3 Insert total rows	**4.1.1** Insert references
3.3.1 Filter records	
3.3.2 Sort data by multiple columns	
3.3.3 Change sort order	
4.1.2 Perform calculations by using the SUM function	
4.1.3 Perform calculations by using MIN and MAX functions	
4.1.5 Perform calculations by using the AVERAGE function	
4.2.1 Perform logical operations by using the IF function	
4.2.4 Perform statistical operations by using the COUNTIF function	

BUILD YOUR E-PORTFOLIO

An E-Portfolio is a collection of evidence, stored electronically, that showcases what you have accomplished while completing your education. Collecting and then sharing your work products with potential employers reflects your academic and career goals. Your completed documents from the following projects are good examples to show what you have learned: 2G, 2K, and 2L.

GO! FOR JOB SUCCESS

Video: Customer Service

Your instructor may assign this video to your class, and then ask you to think about, or discuss with your classmates, these questions:

How could Lee have been more helpful to the customer?

What did the supervisor, Christine, do to calm the customer?

What might SunTel do on a company-wide basis to create a better customer service experience?

FotolEdhar/Fotolia

END OF CHAPTER

SUMMARY

Use Flash Fill to recognize a pattern in data and automatically fill in values when you enter examples of desired output. Flash Fill can split data from two or more cells or combine data from two cells.

Functions are formulas that Excel provides and that perform calculations by using specific values in a particular order or structure. Statistical functions are useful to analyze a group of measurements.

You can navigate among worksheets in a workbook by clicking the sheet tabs, which identify each worksheet in a workbook. Use multiple worksheets in a workbook to organize data in a logical arrangement.

Dates are a value you can enter in a cell to which Excel assigns a serial value—a number—so that you can treat dates like other numbers. For example, you can find the number of days between two dates.

GO! LEARN IT ONLINE

Review the concepts, key terms, and MOS skills in this chapter by completing these online challenges, which you can find at **MyITLab**.

Matching and Multiple Choice: Answer matching and multiple choice questions to test what you learned in this chapter.

Lessons on the GO!: Learn how to use all the new apps and features as they are introduced by Microsoft.

MOS Prep Quiz: Answer questions to review the MOS skills that you practiced in this chapter.

GO! COLLABORATIVE TEAM PROJECT (Available in **MyITLab** and Instructor Resource Center)

If your instructor assigns this project to your class, you can expect to work with one or more of your classmates—either in person or by using Internet tools—to create work products similar to those that you created in this chapter. A team is a group of workers who work together to solve a problem, make a decision, or create a work product. Collaboration is when you work together with others as a team in an intellectual endeavor to complete a shared task or achieve a shared goal.

PROJECT GUIDE FOR EXCEL CHAPTER 2

Your instructor will assign Projects from this list to ensure your learning and assess your knowledge.

	Project Guide for Excel Chapter 2		
Project	**Apply Skills from These Chapter Objectives**	**Project Type**	**Project Location**
2A MyITLab	Objectives 1–6 from Project 2A	**2A Instructional Project (Grader Project)** Guided instruction to learn the skills in Project 2A.	In MyITLab and in text
2B MyITLab	Objectives 7–12 from Project 2B	**2B Instructional Project (Grader Project)** Guided instruction to learn the skills in Project 2B.	In MyITLab and in text
2C	Objectives 1–6 from Project 2A	**2C Skills Review (Scorecard Grading)** A guided review of the skills from Project 2A.	In text
2D	Objectives 7–12 from Project 2B	**2D Skills Review (Scorecard Grading)** A guided review of the skills from Project 2B.	In text
2E MyITLab	Objectives 1–6 from Project 2A	**2E Mastery (Grader Project) Mastery and Transfer of Learning** A demonstration of your mastery of the skills in Project 2A with extensive decision making.	In MyITLab and in text
2F MyITLab	Objectives 7–12 from Project 2B	**2F Mastery (Grader Project) Mastery and Transfer of Learning** A demonstration of your mastery of the skills in Project 2B with extensive decision making.	In MyITLab and in text
2G MyITLab	Objectives 1–12 from Projects 2A and 2B	**2G Mastery (Grader Project) Mastery and Transfer of Learning** A demonstration of your mastery of the skills in Projects 2A and 2B with extensive decision making.	In MyITLab and in text
2H	Combination of Objectives from Projects 2A and 2B	**2H GO! Fix It (Scorecard Grading) Critical Thinking** A demonstration of your mastery of the skills in Projects 2A and 2B by creating a correct result from a document that contains errors you must find.	Instructor Resource Center (IRC) and MyITLab
2I	Combination of Objectives from Projects 2A and 2B	**2I GO! Make It (Scorecard Grading) Critical Thinking** A demonstration of your mastery of the skills in Projects 2A and 2B by creating a result from a supplied picture.	IRC and MyITLab
2J	Combination of Objectives from Projects 2A and 2B	**2J GO! Solve It (Rubric Grading) Critical Thinking** A demonstration of your mastery of the skills in Projects 2A and 2B, your decision-making skills, and your critical-thinking skills. A task-specific rubric helps you self-assess your result.	IRC and MyITLab
2K	Combination of Objectives from Projects 2A and 2B	**2K GO! Solve It (Rubric Grading) Critical Thinking** A demonstration of your mastery of the skills in Projects 2A and 2B, your decision-making skills, and your critical-thinking skills. A task-specific rubric helps you self-assess your result.	In text
2L	Combination of Objectives from Projects 2A and 2B	**2L GO! Think (Rubric Grading) Critical Thinking** A demonstration of your understanding of the chapter concepts applied in a manner that you would outside of college. An analytic rubric helps you and your instructor grade the quality of your work by comparing it to the work an expert in the discipline would create.	In text
2M	Combination of Objectives from Projects 2A and 2B	**2M GO! Think (Rubric Grading) Critical Thinking** A demonstration of your understanding of the chapter concepts applied in a manner that you would outside of college. An analytic rubric helps you and your instructor grade the quality of your work by comparing it to the work an expert in the discipline would create.	IRC and MyITLab
2N	Combination of Objectives from Projects 2A and 2B	**2N You and GO! (Rubric Grading) Critical Thinking** A demonstration of your understanding of the chapter concepts applied in a manner that you would in a personal situation. An analytic rubric helps you and your instructor grade the quality of your work.	IRC and MyITLab
2O	Combination of Objectives from Projects 2A and 2B	**2O Collaborative Team Project for EXCEL Chapter 2 Critical Thinking** A demonstration of your understanding of concepts and your ability to work collaboratively in a group role-playing assessment, requiring both collaboration and self-management.	IRC and MyITLab

GLOSSARY

GLOSSARY OF CHAPTER KEY TERMS

Arguments The values that an Excel function uses to perform calculations or operations.

AVERAGE function An Excel function that adds a group of values, and then divides the result by the number of values in the group.

Comparison operators Symbols that evaluate each value to determine if it is the same (=), greater than (>), less than (<), or in between a range of values as specified by the criteria.

Conditional format A format that changes the appearance of a cell—for example, by adding cell shading or font color—based on a condition; if the condition is true, the cell is formatted based on that condition, and if the condition is false, the cell is *not* formatted.

COUNT function A statistical function that counts the number of cells in a range that contains numbers.

COUNTIF function A statistical function that counts the number of cells within a range that meet the given condition and that has two arguments—the range of cells to check and the criteria.

Criteria Conditions that you specify in a logical function.

Data bar A cell format consisting of a shaded bar that provides a visual cue to the reader about the value of a cell relative to other cells; the length of the bar represents the value in the cell—a longer bar represents a higher value and a shorter bar represents a lower value.

Detail sheet The worksheets that contain the details of the information summarized on a summary sheet.

Drag and drop The action of moving a selection by dragging it to a new location.

Excel table A series of rows and columns that contains related data that is managed independently from the data in other rows and columns in the worksheet.

Filter The process of displaying only a portion of the data based on matching a specific value to show only the data that meets the criteria that you specify.

Find and Replace A command that searches the cells in a worksheet—or in a selected range—for matches and then replaces each match with a replacement value of your choice.

Flash Fill Recognizes a pattern in your data, and then automatically fills in values when you enter examples of the output that you want. Use it to split data from two or more cells or to combine data from two cells.

Freeze Panes A command that enables you to select one or more rows or columns and freeze (lock) them into place; the locked rows and columns become separate panes.

Function A predefined formula—a formula that Excel has already built for you—that performs calculations by using specific values in a particular order or structure.

IF function A function that uses a logical test to check whether a condition is met, and then returns one value if true, and another value if false.

Logical functions A group of functions that test for specific conditions and that typically use conditional tests to determine whether specified conditions are true or false.

Logical test Any value or expression that can be evaluated as being true or false.

MAX function An Excel function that determines the largest value in a selected range of values.

MEDIAN function An Excel function that finds the middle value that has as many values above it in the group as are below it; it differs from AVERAGE in that the result is not affected as much by a single value that is greatly different from the others.

MIN function An Excel function that determines the smallest value in a selected range of values.

Navigate The process of moving within a worksheet or workbook.

NOW function An Excel function that retrieves the date and time from your computer's calendar and clock and inserts the information into the selected cell.

Pane A portion of a worksheet window bounded by and separated from other portions by vertical and horizontal bars.

Paste The action of placing cell contents that have been copied or moved to the Clipboard into another location.

Paste area The target destination for data that has been cut or copied using the Office Clipboard.

Paste Options gallery A gallery of buttons that provides a Live Preview of all the Paste options available in the current context.

Print Titles An Excel command that enables you to specify rows and columns to repeat on each printed page.

Scale to Fit Excel commands that enable you to stretch or shrink the width, height, or both, of printed output to fit a maximum number of pages.

Sheet tabs The labels along the lower border of the workbook window that identify each worksheet.

Sort The process of arranging data in a specific order based on the value in each field.

Split Splits the window into multiple resizable panes that contain views of your worksheet. This is useful to view multiple distant parts of your worksheet at one time.

Statistical functions Excel functions, including the AVERAGE, MEDIAN, MIN, and MAX functions, which are useful to analyze a group of measurements.

SUM function A predefined formula that adds all the numbers in a selected range of cells.

Summary sheet A worksheet where totals from other worksheets are displayed and summarized.

Volatile A term used to describe an Excel function that is subject to change each time the workbook is reopened; for example, the NOW function updates itself to the current date and time each time the workbook is opened.

Apply 2A skills from these Objectives:

1 Use Flash Fill and the SUM, AVERAGE, MEDIAN, MIN, and MAX Functions

2 Move Data, Resolve Error Messages, and Rotate Text

3 Use COUNTIF and IF Functions and Apply Conditional Formatting

4 Use Date & Time Functions and Freeze Panes

5 Create, Sort, and Filter an Excel Table

6 View, Format, and Print a Large Worksheet

Skills Review Project 2C Roses

In the following Skills Review, you will edit a worksheet detailing the current inventory of roses at the Pasadena nursery. Your completed workbook will look similar to Figure 2.55.

PROJECT FILES

For Project 2C, you will need the following file:

e02C_Roses

You will save your workbook as:

Lastname_Firstname_2C_Roses

PROJECT RESULTS

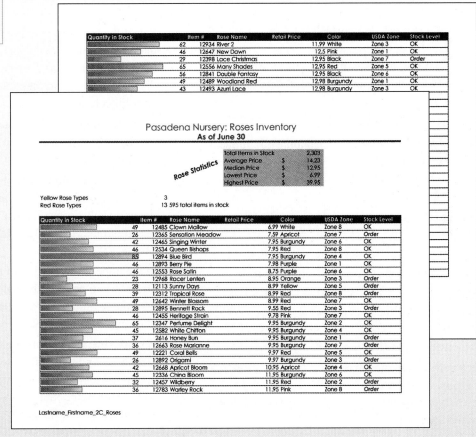

FIGURE 2.55

Excel 2016, Windows 10, Microsoft Corporation

(Project 2C Roses continues on the next page)

1 Start Excel. From your student files, locate and open **e02C_Roses**. **Save** the file in your **Excel Chapter 2** folder as **Lastname_Firstname_2C_Roses**

a. In the **column heading area**, point to **column C** to display the ⬇ pointer, and then drag to the right to select **columns C:D**. On the **Home tab**, in the **Cells group**, click the **Insert button arrow**, and then click **Insert Sheet Columns**.

b. Click cell **C14**, type **12113** and then on the **Formula Bar**, click **Enter** to confirm the entry and keep cell **C14** as the active cell. On the **Home tab**, in the **Editing group**, click **Fill**, and then click **Flash Fill**.

c. Click cell **D14**, type **Zone 5** On the **Formula Bar**, click **Enter** to confirm the entry and keep the cell active. Press ⌃Ctrl + Ⓔ, which is the keyboard shortcut for Flash Fill.

d. Select **column B**, and then in the **Cells group**, click the **Delete button arrow**. Click **Delete Sheet Columns**.

2 In cell **B13** type **Item #** and press ⏎Enter.

a. Select **column C**, and then on the **Home tab**, in the **Clipboard group**, click **Cut**. Click cell **G1**, and then in the **Clipboard group**, click the upper portion of the **Paste** button.

b. Select and then delete **column C**. In cell **F13** type **USDA Zone** and in cell **G13** type **Stock Level**

c. Select columns **A:G**. In the **Cells group**, click **Format**, and then click **AutoFit Column Width**.

d. Press ⌃Ctrl + ⌂Home. **Merge & Center** cell **A1** across the range **A1:G1**, and then apply the **Title** cell style. **Merge & Center** cell **A2** across the range **A2:G2**, and then apply the **Heading 1** cell style. Click **Save**.

3 Click cell **B4**. On the **Formulas tab**, in the **Function Library group**, click **AutoSum**, and then within the parentheses, type **a14:a68** which is the range containing the quantities for each item.

a. Click cell **B5**. On the **Formulas tab**, in the **Function Library group**, click **More Functions**. Point to **Statistical**, click **AVERAGE**, and then in the **Number1** box, type **d14:d68** which is the range containing the *Retail Price* for each item. Click **OK**.

b. Click cell **B6**. In the **Function Library group**, click **More Functions**, point to **Statistical**, and then click **MEDIAN**. In the **Function Arguments** dialog box,

to the right of the **Number1** box, click **Collapse Dialog**, and then select the range **D14:D68**. Click **Expand Dialog**, and then click **OK**. Recall that you can select or type a range and that you can collapse the dialog box to make it easier to view your selection.

c. Click cell **B7**, and then by typing or selecting, insert the **MIN** function to determine the lowest **Retail Price**. Click cell **B8**, and then insert the **MAX** function to determine the highest **Retail Price**.

4 Select cell **B4**. On the **Home tab**, apply **Comma Style**, and then click **Decrease Decimal** two times. Select the range **B5:B8**, and then apply the **Accounting Number Format**.

a. Select the range **A4:B8**. Point to the right edge of the selected range to display the ⟨k⟩ pointer. Drag the selected range to the right until the ScreenTip displays *D4:E8*, and then release the mouse button. AutoFit **column D**.

b. With the range **D4:E8** selected, on the **Home tab**, in the **Styles group**, display the **Cell Styles** gallery, and then apply **20% - Accent1**.

c. In cell **C6**, type **Rose Statistics** Select the range **C4:C8**, right-click over the selection, and then click **Format Cells**. In the **Format Cells** dialog box, click the **Alignment tab**. Under **Text control**, select the **Merge cells** check box.

d. In the upper right portion of the dialog box, under **Orientation**, point to the **red diamond**, and then drag the diamond upward until the **Degrees** box indicates *20*. Click **OK**.

e. With the merged cell still selected, change the **Font Size** to **14**, and then apply **Bold** and **Italic**. Click the **Font Color button arrow**, and then in the fifth column, click the first color—**Blue, Accent 1**. Apply **Middle Align** and **Center** to the cell.

5 Click cell **B10**. On the **Formulas tab**, in the **Function Library group**, click **More Functions**, and then display the list of **Statistical** functions. Click **COUNTIF**.

a. As the range, type **e14:e68** which is the range with the color of each item. Click in the **Criteria** box, type **Yellow** and then click **OK** to calculate the number of yellow rose types.

(Project 2C Roses continues on the next page)

b. Click cell **G14**. On the **Formulas tab**, in the **Function Library group**, click **Logical**, and then on the list, click **IF**. If necessary, drag the title bar of the **Function Arguments** dialog box up or down so that you can view **row 14** on your screen.

c. With the insertion point in the **Logical_test** box, click cell **A14**, and then type **<40** Press [Tab] to move the insertion point to the **Value_if_true** box, and then type **Order** Press [Tab] to move the insertion point to the **Value_if_false** box, type **OK** and then click **OK**. Using the fill handle, copy the function in cell **G14** down through cell **G68**.

6 With the range **G14:G68** selected, on the **Home tab**, in the **Styles group**, click **Conditional Formatting**. In the list, point to **Highlight Cells Rules**, and then click **Text that Contains**.

a. In the **Text That Contains** dialog box, with the insertion point blinking in the first box, type **Order** and then in the second box, click the **arrow**. On the list, click **Custom Format**.

b. In the **Format Cells** dialog box, on the **Font tab**, under **Font style**, click **Bold Italic**. Click the **Color arrow**, and then under **Theme Colors**, in the fourth column, click the first color—**Blue-Gray, Text 2**. Click **OK** two times to apply the font color, bold, and italic to the cells that contain the word *Order*.

c. Select the range **A14:A68**. In the **Styles group**, click **Conditional Formatting**. In the list, point to **Data Bars**, and then under **Gradient Fill**, click **Red Data Bar**. Click anywhere to cancel the selection.

d. Select the range **E14:E68**. On the **Home tab**, in the **Editing group**, click **Find & Select**, and then click **Replace**. In the **Find and Replace** dialog box, in the **Find what** box, type **Deep Burgundy** and then in the **Replace with** box type **Burgundy** Click **Replace All** and then click **OK**. In the lower right corner of the **Find and Replace** dialog box, click **Close**.

e. Scroll down as necessary, and then click cell **A70**. Type **Edited by Maria Rios** and then press [Enter]. With cell **A71** as the active cell, on the **Formulas tab**, in the **Function Library group**, click **Date & Time**. In the list of functions, click **NOW**, and then click **OK** to enter the current date and time. **Save** your workbook.

7 Click any cell in the data below row 13. Click the **Insert tab**, and then in the **Tables group**, click **Table**. In the **Create Table** dialog box, be sure the **My table has headers** check box is selected, and then click **OK**. On the **Design tab**, in the **Table Styles group**, click **More** [▾] and then under **Light**, locate and click **Table Style Light 9**.

a. In the header row of the table, click the **Retail Price arrow**, and then from the menu, click **Sort Smallest to Largest**. Click the **Color arrow**. On the menu, click the **(Select All)** check box to clear all the check boxes. Scroll as necessary and then select only the **Red** check box. Click **OK**.

b. Click anywhere in the table. On the **Design tab**, in the **Table Style Options group**, select the **Total Row** check box. Click cell **A69**, click the arrow that displays to the right of cell **A69**, and then click **Sum**. In cell **B11**, type the result **13** and then press [Tab]. In cell **C11**, type **595 total items in stock** and then press [Enter].

c. In the header row of the table, click the **Color arrow** and then click **Clear Filter From "Color"** to redisplay all of the data. Click anywhere in the table. Click the **Design tab**, in the **Table Style Options group**, clear the **Total Row** check box.

8 On the **Page Layout tab**, in the **Themes group**, click **Themes** and then click the **Ion** theme. Change the **Orientation** to **Landscape**.

a. In the **Page Setup group**, click **Margins**, and then click **Custom Margins** to display the **Page Setup** dialog box.

b. On the **Margins tab**, under **Center on page**, select the **Horizontally** check box. On the **Header/Footer tab**, display the **Custom Footer**, and then in the **Left section**, insert the file name. Click **OK** two times.

c. In the **Page Setup** group, click **Print Titles** to redisplay the **Page Setup** dialog box. Under **Print titles**, click in the **Rows to repeat at top** box, and then at the right, click **Collapse Dialog**. From the **row heading area**, select **row 13**, and then click **Expand Dialog**. Click **OK** to print the column titles in row 13 at the top of every page.

d. Press [Ctrl] + [F2] to display the **Print Preview**. At the bottom of the **Settings group**, click **No Scaling**, and then on the displayed list, click **Fit All Columns on One Page**.

(Project 2C Roses continues on the next page)

e. On the left, click **Info**, and then in the lower right corner, click **Show All Properties**. As the **Tags**, type **inventory, Pasadena, roses** In the **Subject** box, type your course name and section number. Be sure your name displays as the author.

9 **Save** your workbook. If directed by your instructor to do so, submit your paper printout, your electronic image of your document that looks like a printed document, or your original Excel file. If required by your instructor, print or create an electronic version of your worksheet with formulas displayed. In the upper right corner of the Excel window, click **Close**.

END | You have completed Project 2C

Apply 2B skills from these Objectives:

7 Navigate a Workbook and Rename Worksheets

8 Enter Dates, Clear Contents, and Clear Formats

9 Copy and Paste by Using the Paste Options Gallery

10 Edit and Format Multiple Worksheets at the Same Time

11 Create a Summary Sheet with Column Sparklines

12 Format and Print Multiple Worksheets in a Workbook

Skills Review Project 2D Canada

In the following Skills Review, you will edit a workbook that summarizes sales in the Eastern and Western region of Canada. Your completed workbook will look similar to Figure 2.56.

PROJECT FILES

For Project 2D, you will need the following file:

e02D_Canada

You will save your workbook as:

Lastname_Firstname_2D_Canada

PROJECT RESULTS

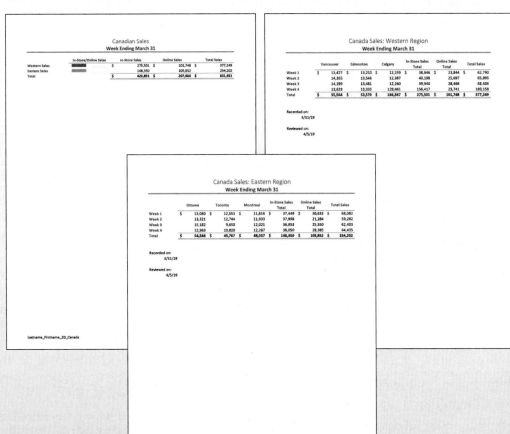

FIGURE 2.56

(Project 2D Canada continues on the next page)

1 ▶ Start Excel. From your student files, open **e02D_Canada**. **Save** the file in your **Excel Chapter 2** folder as **Lastname_Firstname_2D_Canada**

a. Point to the **Sheet1 tab**, and then double-click to select the sheet tab name. Type **Western Sales** and then press Enter.

b. Point to the **Sheet2 tab**, right-click, and then from the shortcut menu, click **Rename**. Type **Eastern Sales** and press Enter.

c. Point to the **Western Sales sheet tab** and right-click. On the shortcut menu, point to **Tab Color**, and then in the last column, click the first color—**Green, Accent 6**. Change the **Tab Color** of the **Eastern Sales sheet tab** to **Blue, Accent 5**.

d. Click the **Western Sales sheet tab**, and then click cell **A13**. On the **Home tab**, in the **Number group**, click the **Number Format arrow**. At the bottom of the list, click **More Number Formats** to display the **Number tab** of the **Format Cells** dialog box. Click the **3/14/12** type, and then click **OK**.

e. Click cell **A16**, type **4/5/19** and then press Enter. Click cell **A13**, and then on the **Home tab**, in the **Clipboard group**, click **Format Painter**. Click cell **A16** to copy the date format from cell **A13** to cell **A16**.

f. Click cell **A1**. In the **Editing group**, click **Clear**, and then click **Clear Formats**.

g. Select the range **A5:A16**. On the **Home tab**, in the **Clipboard group**, click **Copy**. At the bottom of the workbook window, click the **Eastern Sales sheet tab** to make it the active worksheet. Right-click cell **A5**, and then under **Paste Options**, click the first button—**Paste**. Display the **Western Sales** sheet. Press Esc to cancel the moving border.

2 ▶ With the **Western Sales** sheet active, make cell **A1** the active cell. Point to the sheet tab, right-click, and then on the shortcut menu, click **Select All Sheets**. Verify that *[Group]* displays in the title bar.

a. **Merge & Center** the text in cell **A1** across the range **A1:G1**, and then apply the **Title** cell style. Select **columns A:G**, and then set their widths to **100 pixels**.

b. Click cell **A2**, type **Week Ending March 31** and then on the **Formula Bar**, click the **Enter** button to keep cell **A2** as the active cell. **Merge & Center** the text across the range **A2:G2**, and then apply the **Heading 1** cell style.

c. Select the range **B4:G4**, and then apply the **Heading 3** cell style. In the **Alignment group**, click **Center**, **Middle Align**, and **Wrap Text**.

d. With the sheets still grouped and the **Western Sales** sheet active, click cell **E5**. On the **Home tab**, in the **Editing group**, click the **AutoSum** button, and then press Enter. Click cell **E5**, and then drag the fill handle down to copy the formula through cell **E8**.

e. Click cell **G5**, type **=** click cell **E5**, type **+** click cell **F5**, and then press Enter. Copy the formula down through cell **G8**. In cell **A9**, type **Total** Select the range **B5:G9**, and then hold down Alt and press = to enter the SUM function for all the columns. Select the range **A5:A9**, and then apply the **Heading 4** cell style.

f. Select the range **B5:G5**, hold down Ctrl, and then select the range **B9:G9**. Apply the **Accounting Number Format** and decrease the decimal places to zero. Select the range **B6:G8**, and then apply **Comma Style** with zero decimal places. Select the range **B9:G9**, and then apply the **Total** cell style.

3 ▶ Click the **Eastern Sales sheet tab** to cancel the grouping and display the second worksheet.

a. To the right of the **Eastern Sales sheet tab**, click the **New sheet** button. **Rename** the new worksheet tab **Summary** and then change the **Tab Color** to **Gold, Accent 4**.

b. Widen **columns A:E** to **150** pixels. In cell **A1**, type **Canadian Sales** and then **Merge & Center** the title across the range **A1:E1**. Apply the **Title** cell style. In cell **A2**, type **Week Ending March 31** and then **Merge & Center** the text across the range **A2:E2**. Apply the **Heading 1** cell style. In cell **A5**, type **Western Sales** and in cell **A6**, type **Eastern Sales**

c. In cell **B4**, type **In-Store/Online Sales** and in cell **C4**, type **In-Store Sales** In cell **D4**, type **Online Sales** and in cell **E4**, type **Total Sales** Select the range **B4:E4**, apply the **Heading 3** cell style, and then **Center** these column titles.

d. Click cell **C5**. Type **=** and then click the **Western Sales sheet tab**. In the **Western Sales** worksheet, click cell **E9**, and then press Enter. Click cell **D5**. Type **=** and then click the **Western Sales sheet tab**. Click cell **F9**, and then press Enter.

(Project 2D Canada continues on the next page)

e. By using the same technique, in cells **C6** and **D6**, insert the total **In-Store Sales** and **Online Sales** data from the **Eastern Sales** worksheet.

f. Select the range **C5:E6**, and then click **AutoSum** to total the two rows. In cell **A7**, type **Total** and then in **C7** sum the range **C5:C6**. Fill the formula across to **D7:E7**.

g. Select the nonadjacent ranges **C5:E5** and **C7:E7**, and then apply **Accounting Number Format** with zero decimal places. Select the range **C6:E6**, and then apply **Comma Style** with zero decimal places. Select the range **C7:E7**, and then apply the **Total** cell style. Select the range **A5:A7** and apply the **Heading 4** cell style.

h. Click cell **B5**. On the **Insert tab**, in the **Sparklines group**, click **Column**. In the **Create Sparklines** dialog box, with the insertion point blinking in the **Data Range** box, select the range **C5:D5** and then click **OK**.

i. Click cell **B6**, and then insert a **Column Sparkline** for the range **C6:D6**. With the **Eastern Sales** sparkline selected, in the **Style group**, apply the second style in the third row—**Sparkline Style Accent 2, (no dark or light)**.

4 Point to the **Summary sheet tab**, hold down the left mouse button to display a small black triangle, drag to the left until the triangle and mouse pointer are to the left of the **Western Sales sheet tab**, and then release the left mouse button to move the sheet to the first position in the workbook.

a. Be sure the **Summary** worksheet is the active sheet. Point to the **Summary sheet tab**, right-click, and then click **Select All Sheets** to display [*Group*] in the title bar. Press Ctrl + Home to move to cell A1. On the **Page Layout tab**, in the **Page Setup group**, click **Margins**, and then click **Custom Margins** to display the **Page Setup** dialog box. On the **Margins tab**, center the worksheets **Horizontally**. On the **Header/Footer tab**, insert the file name in the **left section** of the footer.

b. Display the **Print Preview** of the worksheets. Under **Settings**, click **No Scaling**, and then click **Fit All Columns on One Page**. Use the **Next** button to view all three worksheets.

c. On the left, click **Info**, and then in the lower right corner of the screen, click **Show All Properties**. As the **Tags**, type **Canada, sales** In the **Subject** box, type your course name and section number. Be sure your name displays as the author.

d. **Save** your workbook. If directed by your instructor to do so, submit your paper printout, your electronic image of your document that looks like a printed document, or your original Excel file. If required by your instructor, print or create an electronic version of your worksheet with formulas displayed. In the upper right corner of the Excel window, click **Close**.

END | You have completed Project 2D

Mastering Excel Project 2E Plants

In the following project, you will edit a worksheet detailing the current inventory of plants at the Pasadena facility. Your completed worksheet will look similar to Figure 2.57.

PROJECT FILES

For Project 2E, you will need the following file:

e02E_Plants

You will save your workbook as:

Lastname_Firstname_2E_Plants

PROJECT RESULTS

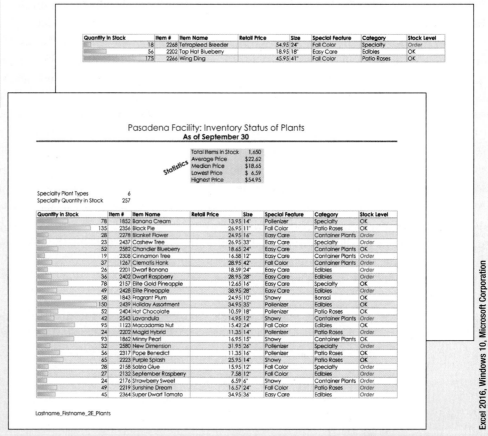

FIGURE 2.57

(Project 2E Plants continues on the next page)

Mastering Excel   Project 2E Plants (continued)

1 Start Excel. From your student files, locate and open **e02E_Plants**, and then **Save** the file in your **Excel Chapter 2** folder as **Lastname_Firstname_2E_Plants**

2 To the right of **column B**, insert two new columns to create **new blank columns C and D**. By using **Flash Fill** in the two new columns, split the data in **column B** into a column for *Item #* in **column C** and *Category* in **column D**. As necessary, type **Item #** as the column title in **column C** and **Category** as the column title in **column D**. Delete **column B**.

3 By using the **Cut** and **Paste** commands, cut **column C**—*Category*—and paste it to **column H**, and then delete the empty **column C**. Apply **AutoFit** to **columns A:G**.

4 In cell **B4**, insert a function to calculate the **Total Items in Stock** by summing the **Quantity in Stock** data, and then apply **Comma Style** with zero decimal places to the result.

5 In each cell in the range **B5:B8**, insert functions to calculate the Average, Median, Lowest, and Highest retail prices, and then apply the **Accounting Number Format** to each result.

6 Move the range **A4:B8** to the range **D4:E8**, apply the **40% - Accent4** cell style to the range, and then select **columns D:E** and **AutoFit**.

7 In cell **C6**, type **Statistics** and then select the range **C4:C8**. In the **Format Cells** dialog box, merge the selected cells, and change the text **Orientation** to **25 Degrees**. Format the cell with **Bold**, a **Font Size** of **14 pt**, and then change the **Font Color** to **Blue-Gray, Text 2**. Apply **Middle Align** and **Align Right**.

8 In the **Category** column, **Replace All** occurrences of **Vine Roses** with **Patio Roses**

9 In cell **B10**, use the **COUNTIF** function to count the number of **Specialty** plant types in the **Category** column.

10 In cell **H13**, type **Stock Level** In cell **H14**, enter an **IF** function to determine the items that must be ordered.

If the **Quantity in Stock** is less than **50** the **Value_if_true** is **Order** Otherwise the **Value_if_false** is **OK** Fill the formula down through cell **H42**.

11 Apply **Conditional Formatting** to the **Stock Level** column so that cells that contain the text *Order* are formatted with **Bold Italic** and with a **Color** of **Green, Accent 6**. Apply conditional formatting to the **Quantity in Stock** column by applying a **Gradient Fill Green Data Bar**.

12 Format the range **A13:H42** as a **Table** with headers, and apply the style **Table Style Light 20**. Sort the table from **A to Z** by **Item Name**, and then filter on the **Category** column to display the **Specialty** types.

13 Display a **Total Row** in the table, and then in cell **A43**, **Sum** the **Quantity in Stock** for the **Specialty** items. Type the result in cell **B11**. Click in the table, and then on the **Design tab**, remove the total row from the table. Clear the **Category** filter.

14 **Merge & Center** the title and subtitle across **columns A:H**, and apply **Title** and **Heading 1** styles, respectively. Change the theme to **Mesh**, and then select and **AutoFit** all the columns.

15 Set the orientation to **Landscape**. In the **Page Setup** dialog box, center the worksheet **Horizontally**, insert a custom footer in the **left section** with the file name, and set **row 13** to repeat at the top of each page. Display the **Print Preview**. Apply the **Fit All Columns on One Page** setting.

16 As the **Tags**, type **plants inventory, Pasadena** As the **Subject**, type your course name and section number. Be sure your name displays as the **Author**.

17 **Save** your workbook. If directed by your instructor to do so, submit your paper printout, your electronic image of your document that looks like a printed document, or your original Excel file. If required by your instructor, print or create an electronic version of your worksheet with formulas displayed. In the upper right corner of the Excel window, click **Close**.

> **END | You have completed Project 2E**

Mastering Excel Project 2F Bonus

In the following project, you will edit a workbook that summarizes the compensation for the commercial salespersons who qualified for bonuses in the Western and Eastern Canadian regions. Your completed worksheets will look similar to Figure 2.58.

PROJECT FILES

For Project 2F, you will need the following file:

e02F_Bonus

You will save your workbook as:

Lastname_Firstname_2F_Bonus

PROJECT RESULTS

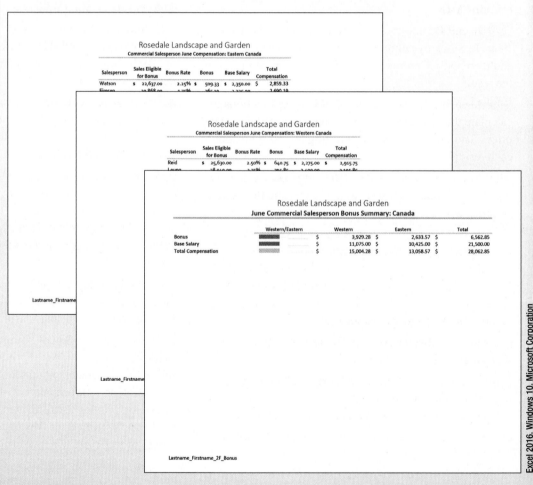

FIGURE 2.58

(Project 2F Bonus continues on the next page)

Mastering Excel   Project 2F Bonus (continued)

1 Start Excel. From your student files, open **e02F_Bonus**, and then save the file in your **Excel Chapter 2** folder as **Lastname_Firstname_2F_Bonus**

2 Rename **Sheet1** as **Western** and change the **Tab Color** to **Brown, Accent 2**. Rename **Sheet2** as **Eastern** and change the **Tab Color** to **Orange, Accent 1**.

3 Click the **Western sheet tab** to make it the active sheet, and then group the worksheets. In cell **A1**, type **Rosedale Landscape and Garden** and then **Merge & Center** the text across the range **A1:F1**. Apply the **Title** cell style. **Merge & Center** the text in cell **A2** across the range **A2:F2**, and then apply the **Heading 3** cell style.

4 With the sheets still grouped, in cell **D5** calculate the **Bonus** for *Reid* by multiplying the **Sales Eligible for Bonus** by the **Bonus Rate**. **Copy** the formula down through cell **D8**.

5 In cell **F5**, calculate **Total Compensation** by summing the **Bonus** and **Base Salary** for *Reid*. Copy the formula down through the cell **F8**.

6 In **row 9**, sum the columns for **Sales Eligible for Bonus**, **Bonus**, **Base Salary**, and **Total Compensation**. Apply the **Accounting Number Format** with two decimal places to the appropriate cells in **row 5** and **row 9** (do not include the percentages).

7 Apply the **Comma Style** with two decimal places to the appropriate cells in **rows 6:8** (do not include the percentages). Apply the **Total** cell style to the appropriate cells in the Total row.

8 Click the Eastern sheet tab to ungroup the sheets, and then insert a new worksheet. Change the sheet name to **Summary** and then change the **Tab Color** to **Brown, Text 2**. Widen **column A** to 210 pixels, widen **columns B:E** to 155 pixels.

9 Move the **Summary** sheet so that it is the first sheet in the workbook. In cell **A1** of the **Summary** sheet, type **Rosedale Landscape and Garden** and then **Merge & Center** the title across the range **A1:E1**. Apply the **Title** cell style. In cell **A2**, type **June Commercial Salesperson Bonus Summary: Canada** and then **Merge & Center** the text across the range **A2:E2**. Apply the **Heading 1** cell style.

10 In the range **A5:A7**, type the following row titles and then apply the **Heading 4** cell style:

Bonus

Base Salary

Total Compensation

11 In the range **B4:E4**, type the following column titles, and then **Center** and apply the **Heading 3** cell style.

Western/Eastern

Western

Eastern

Total

12 In cell **C5**, enter a formula that references cell **D9** in the **Western** worksheet so that the total bonus amount for the Western region displays in cell **C5**. Create similar formulas to enter the total **Base Salary** for the Western region in cell **C6**. Using the same technique, enter formulas in the range **D5:D6** so that the **Eastern** totals display.

13 Sum the **Bonus** and **Base Salary** rows, and then calculate **Total Compensation** for the **Western**, **Eastern**, and **Total** columns.

14 In cell **B5**, insert a **Column Sparkline** for the range **C5:D5**. In cells **B6** and **B7**, insert **Column** sparklines for the appropriate ranges to compare Western totals with Eastern totals.

15 To the sparkline in cell **B5**, apply the second style in the third row—**Sparkline Style Accent 2**, (**no dark or light**). To the sparkline in cell **B6**, apply the first style in the fifth row—**Sparkline Style Dark #1**. To the sparkline in cell **B7**, apply the first style in the fourth row—**Sparkline Style Accent 1, Lighter 40%**.

16 **Group** the three worksheets, and then center the worksheets **Horizontally** on the page, and insert a **Custom Footer** in the **left section** with the file name. Change the **Orientation** to **Landscape**.

17 As the **Tags**, type **June, bonus, compensation** As the **Subject**, type your course name and section number. Be sure your name displays as the **Author** and then **Save**. If directed by your instructor to do so, submit your paper printout, your electronic image of your document that looks like a printed document, or your original Excel file. If required by your instructor, print or create an electronic version of your worksheet with formulas displayed. In the upper right corner of the Excel window, click **Close**.

END | You have completed Project 2F

Mastering Excel   Project 2G Inventory

In the following project, you will edit a worksheet that summarizes the inventory of bulbs and trees at the Pasadena facility. Your completed workbook will look similar to Figure 2.59.

PROJECT FILES

For Project 2G, you will need the following file:

e02G_Inventory

You will save your workbook as:

Lastname_Firstname_2G_Inventory

PROJECT RESULTS

FIGURE 2.59

(Project 2G Inventory continues on the next page)

1 Start Excel. From your student files, open **e02G_Inventory**. Save the file in your **Excel Chapter 2** folder as **Lastname_Firstname_2G_Inventory**

2 Change the **Theme** to **Slice**. Rename **Sheet1** as **Bulbs** and **Sheet2** as **Trees** and then make the **Bulbs sheet** the active sheet.

3 To the right of **column B**, insert two new columns to create **new blank columns C and D**. By using **Flash Fill** in the two new columns, split the data in **column B** into a column for *Item #* in **column C** and *Category* in **column D**. Type **Item #** as the column title in **column C** and **Category** as the column title in **column D**.

4 Delete **column B**. By using the **Cut** and **Paste** commands, cut **column C**—*Category*—and paste it to **column G**, and then delete the empty **column C**. Apply **AutoFit** to **columns A:F**.

5 Display the **Trees** worksheet, and then repeat Steps 3 and 4 on this worksheet.

6 Group the worksheets and then make the following calculations:

- In cell **B4**, enter a function to sum the **Quantity in Stock** data, and then apply **Comma Style** with zero decimal places to the result.
- In cells **B5:B8**, enter formulas to calculate the Average, Median, Lowest, and Highest retail prices, and then apply the **Accounting Number Format**.

7 Ungroup the worksheets. In each of the two worksheets, make the following calculations *without* grouping the sheets:

- In cell **B10**, enter a COUNTIF function to determine how many different types of **Tulips** are in stock on the **Bulbs** sheet and how many different types of **Evergreens** are in stock on the **Trees** worksheet.
- In cell **G14**, type **Stock Level** In cell **G15**, enter an **IF** function to determine the items that must be ordered. If the **Quantity in Stock** is less than **75** the **Value_if_true** is **Order** Otherwise the **Value_if_false** is **OK** Fill the formula down through all the rows.
- Apply **Conditional Formatting** to the **Stock Level** column so that cells that contain the text *Order* are formatted with **Bold Italic** with a **Font Color** of **Dark Blue, Text 2**. Apply **Gradient Fill Blue Data Bars** to the **Quantity in Stock** column.

8 In the **Bulbs** sheet, format the range **A14:G42** as a table with headers and apply **Table Style Light 20**. Insert a **Total Row**, filter by **Category** for **Tulips**, and then **Sum** the **Quantity in Stock** column. Record the result in cell **B11**.

9 Select the table, clear the filter, **Sort** the table on the **Item #** column from **Smallest to Largest**, and then remove the **Total Row**. On the **Page Layout tab**, set **Print Titles** so that **row 14** repeats at the top of each page.

10 In the **Trees** sheet, format the range **A14:G42** as a table with headers and apply **Table Style Light 19**. Insert a **Total Row**, filter by **Category** for **Evergreens**, and then **Sum** the **Quantity in Stock** column. Record the result in cell **B11**.

11 Select the table, clear the filter, **Sort** the table on the **Item #** column from **Smallest to Largest**, and then remove the **Total Row**. On the **Page Layout tab**, set **Print Titles** so that **row 14** repeats at the top of each page, and then **Save** your workbook.

12 **Group** the two worksheets. **Merge & Center** the title in cell **A1** across the range **A1:G1** and apply the **Title** cell style. **Merge & Center** the subtitle in cell **A2** across the range **A2:G2** and apply the **Heading 1** cell style. **AutoFit** Column A. **Center** the worksheets **Horizontally**, change the **Orientation** to **Landscape**, display the **Print Preview**, and then change the **Settings** to **Fit All Columns on One Page**.

13 In **Backstage** view, on the left click **Save**, and then ungroup the sheets. Make the **Trees** sheet the active sheet, and then insert a new worksheet. Change the sheet name to **Summary** and then widen **columns A:D** to **170** pixels. Move the **Summary** sheet so that it is the first sheet in the workbook.

14 In cell **A1**, type **Pasadena Inventory Summary** and then **Merge & Center** the title across the range **A1:D1**. Apply the **Title** cell style. In cell **A2**, type **As of December 31** and then **Merge & Center** the text across the range **A2:D2**. Apply the **Heading 1** cell style.

15 On the **Bulbs sheet**, **Copy** the range **A4:A8**. Display the **Summary sheet** and **Paste** the selection to cell **A5**. Apply the **Heading 4** cell style to the selection.

16 In the **Summary sheet**, in cell **B4**, type **Bulbs** In cell **C4** type **Trees** In cell **D4** type **Bulbs/Trees** and then **Center** the column titles. Apply the **Heading 3** cell style.

(Project 2G Inventory continues on the next page)

17 In cell **B5**, enter a formula that references cell **B4** in the **Bulbs sheet** so that the **Bulbs Total Items in Stock** displays in **B5**. Create similar formulas to enter the **Average Price**, **Median Price**, **Lowest Price**, and **Highest Price** from the **Bulbs sheet** into the **Summary** sheet in the range **B6:B9**.

18 Enter formulas in the range **C5:C9** that reference the appropriate cells in the **Trees** worksheet.

19 In cells **D5**, **D6**, **D7**, **D8**, and **D9**, insert **Column** sparklines using the values in the *Bulbs* and *Trees* columns. Format each sparkline using the first five Sparkline styles in the first row.

20 To the range **B5:C5**, apply **Comma Style** with zero decimal places, and to the range **B6:C9**, apply

Accounting Number Format. Center the **Summary** worksheet **Horizontally** and change the **Orientation** to **Landscape**. **Group** the worksheets and insert a footer in the left section with the **File Name**.

21 As the **Tags**, type **Pasadena inventory** As the **Subject**, type your course name and section number. Be sure your name displays as the **Author**.

22 In **Backstage** view, on the left click **Save**. If directed by your instructor to do so, submit your paper printout, your electronic image of your document that looks like a printed document, or your original Excel file. If required by your instructor, print or create an electronic version of your worksheet with formulas displayed. In the upper right corner of the Excel window, click **Close**.

END | You have completed Project 2G

Apply a combination of the 2A and 2B skills.	GO! Fix It	Project 2H Planters	MyITLab
	GO! Make It	Project 2I Salary	MyITLab
	GO! Solve It	Project 2J Sod	MyITLab
	GO! Solve It	Project 2K Products	MyITLab

PROJECT FILES

For Project 2K, you will need the following file:

e02K_Products

You will save your workbook as:

Lastname_Firstname_2K_Products

From your student data files, open the file e02K_Products and save it as **Lastname_Firstname_2K_Products** This workbook contains two worksheets: one for U.S. sales data by product and one for Canadian sales data by product. Complete the two worksheets by calculating totals by product and by month. Then calculate the Percent of Total for each product, using absolute cell references as necessary. Format the worksheet, percentages, and values appropriately. Insert a new worksheet that summarizes the monthly totals for the United States and Canada. Enter the months as the column titles and the countries as the row titles. Include a Product Total column and a column for sparklines comparing the months. Format the Summary worksheet appropriately, including a title and subtitle. Include the file name in the footer, add appropriate document properties, and submit as directed.

Performance Level

	Exemplary: You consistently applied the relevant skills.	Proficient: You sometimes, but not always, applied the relevant skills.	Developing: You rarely or never applied the relevant skills.
Create formulas	All formulas are correct and are efficiently constructed.	Formulas are correct but not always constructed in the most efficient manner.	One or more formulas are missing or incorrect; or only numbers were entered.
Create Summary worksheet	Summary worksheet created properly.	Summary worksheet was created but some elements were incorrect.	No Summary worksheet was created.
Format appropriately	Formatting is appropriate.	Not all worksheets were appropriately formatted.	No formatting was applied.

Performance Criteria (left margin label)

END | You have completed Project 2K

OUTCOMES-BASED ASSESSMENTS

RUBRIC

The following outcomes-based assessments are open-ended assessments. That is, there is no specific correct result; your result will depend on your approach to the information provided. Make Professional Quality your goal. Use the following scoring rubric to guide you in how to approach the problem and then to evaluate how well your approach solves the problem.

The *criteria*—Software Mastery, Content, Format and Layout, and Process—represent the knowledge and skills you have gained that you can apply to solving the problem. The *levels of performance*—Professional Quality, Approaching Professional Quality, or Needs Quality Improvements—help you and your instructor evaluate your result.

	Your completed project is of Professional Quality if you:	Your completed project is Approaching Professional Quality if you:	Your completed project Needs Quality Improvements if you:
1-Software Mastery	Choose and apply the most appropriate skills, tools, and features and identify efficient methods to solve the problem.	Choose and apply some appropriate skills, tools, and features, but not in the most efficient manner.	Choose inappropriate skills, tools, or features, or are inefficient in solving the problem.
2-Content	Construct a solution that is clear and well organized, contains content that is accurate, appropriate to the audience and purpose, and is complete. Provide a solution that contains no errors in spelling, grammar, or style.	Construct a solution in which some components are unclear, poorly organized, inconsistent, or incomplete. Misjudge the needs of the audience. Have some errors in spelling, grammar, or style, but the errors do not detract from comprehension.	Construct a solution that is unclear, incomplete, or poorly organized; contains some inaccurate or inappropriate content; and contains many errors in spelling, grammar, or style. Do not solve the problem.
3-Format & Layout	Format and arrange all elements to communicate information and ideas, clarify function, illustrate relationships, and indicate relative importance.	Apply appropriate format and layout features to some elements, but not others. Overuse features, causing minor distraction.	Apply format and layout that does not communicate information or ideas clearly. Do not use format and layout features to clarify function, illustrate relationships, or indicate relative importance. Use available features excessively, causing distraction.
4-Process	Use an organized approach that integrates planning, development, self-assessment, revision, and reflection.	Demonstrate an organized approach in some areas, but not others; or, use an insufficient process of organization throughout.	Do not use an organized approach to solve the problem.

| Apply a combination of the 2A and 2B skills. | **GO! Think** | **Project 2L Palms** |

PROJECT FILES

For Project 2L, you will need the following file:

e02L_Palms

You will save your workbook as:

Lastname_Firstname_2L_Palms

Melanie Castillo, Product Manager for Rosedale Landscape and Garden, has requested a worksheet that summarizes the current palm tree inventory data. Melanie would like the worksheet to include the total Quantity in Stock and Number of Items for each of the four categories of palm trees, and she would like the items to be sorted from lowest to highest retail price. She would also like a separate column for Item # and for Category.

Edit the file e02L_Palms to provide Melanie with the information requested, and use the Table feature to find the data requested. Format the worksheet titles and data and include an appropriately formatted table so that the worksheet is professional and easy to read and understand. Insert a footer with the file name and add appropriate document properties. Save the file as **Lastname_Firstname_2L_Palms** and print or submit as directed by your instructor.

END | You have completed Project 2L

| **GO! Think** | **Project 2M Contracts** | **MyITLab** |

Build from Scratch

| **You and GO!** | **Project 2N Annual Expenses** | **MyITLab** |

Build from Scratch

| **GO! Collaborative Team Project** | **Project 2O Bell Orchid Hotels** | **MyITLab** |

Analyzing Data with Pie Charts, Line Charts, and What-If Analysis Tools

3

EXCEL 2016

PROJECT **3A**

OUTCOMES
Present fund data in a pie chart.

PROJECT **3B**

OUTCOMES
Make projections using what-if analysis and present projections in a line chart.

OBJECTIVES

1. Chart Data with a Pie Chart
2. Format a Pie Chart
3. Edit a Workbook and Update a Chart
4. Use Goal Seek to Perform What-If Analysis

OBJECTIVES

5. Design a Worksheet for What-If Analysis
6. Answer What-If Questions by Changing Values in a Worksheet
7. Chart Data with a Line Chart

EuToch/Fotolia

In This Chapter

GO! to Work with Excel

In this chapter, you will work with two different types of commonly used charts that make it easy to visualize data. You will create a pie chart in a separate chart sheet to show how the parts of a fund contribute to a total fund. Pie charts are one type of chart you can use to show part-to-whole relationships. You will also practice using parentheses in a formula, calculate the percentage rate of an increase, answer what-if questions, and then chart data in a line chart to show the flow of data over time. In this chapter, you will also practice formatting the axes in a line chart.

The projects in this chapter relate to the city of **Pacifica Bay**, a coastal city south of San Francisco. The city's access to major transportation provides both residents and businesses an opportunity to compete in the global marketplace. The city's mission is to create a more beautiful and more economically viable community for its residents. Each year the city welcomes a large number of tourists who enjoy exploring the rocky coastline and seeing the famous landmarks in San Francisco. The city encourages best environmental practices and partners with cities in other countries to promote sound government at the local level.

PROJECT

3A

Enterprise Fund Pie Chart

MyITLab
Project 3A Training
Project 3A Grader

PROJECT ACTIVITIES

In Activities 3.01 through 3.12, you will edit a worksheet for Michael Larsen, City Manager, that reports the adjusted figures for Enterprise Fund Expenditures for the next fiscal year, and then present the data in a pie chart. Your completed worksheets will look similar to Figure 3.1.

 PROJECT FILES

MyITLab
grader

If your instructor wants you to submit Project 3A in the MyITLab Grader system, log in to MyITLab, locate Grader Project 3A, and then download the files for this project.

Please always review the downloaded Grade instructions before beginning.

For Project 3A, you will need the following file: You will save your workbook as:

e03A_Enterprise_Fund   Lastname_Firstname_3A_Enterprise_Fund

 PROJECT RESULTS

GO!
Walk Thru
Project 3A

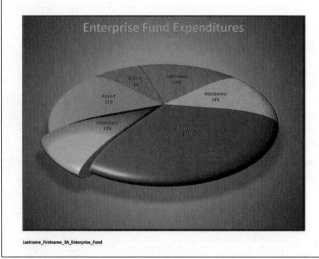

Lastname_Firstname_3A_Enterprise_Fund

Pacifica Bay
Enterprise Fund Expenditures
Recommended Adjustments

	Originally Proposed	Adjusted	% of Total Fund Expenditures
Airport	$ 17,610,810	$ 18,121,067	18.12%
Parking	6,824,865	7,897,526	7.90%
Solid Waste	18,695,222	17,845,287	17.85%
Wastewater	12,657,765	13,985,695	13.99%
Water Usage	30,457,903	32,356,236	32.36%
Waterfront	10,976,843	9,794,189	9.79%
Total	$ 97,223,408	$ 100,000,000	

Lastname_Firstname_3A_Enterprise_Fund

Excel 2016, Windows 10, Microsoft Corporation

FIGURE 3.1 Project 3A Enterprise Fund Pie Chart

A *pie chart* shows the relationship of each part to a whole. The size of each pie slice is equal to its value compared to the total value of all the slices. A pie chart displays data that is arranged in a single column or single row, and shows the size of items in a single data series proportional to the sum of the items. Whereas a column or bar chart can have two or more data series in the chart, a pie chart can have only one data series.

Consider using a pie chart when you have only one data series to plot, you do not have more than seven categories, and the categories represent parts of a total value.

Activity 3.01 | Calculating Values for a Pie Chart

> **ALERT!**   **To submit as an autograded project, log into MyITLab and download the files for this project, and begin with those files instead of e03A_Enterprise_Fund.**

A *fund* is a sum of money set aside for a specific purpose. In a municipal government like the city of Pacifica Bay, the *general fund* is money set aside for the normal operating activities of the city, such as police, fire, and administering the everyday functions of the city.

Municipal governments also commonly establish an *enterprise fund* to report income and expenditures related to municipal services for which a fee is charged in exchange for goods or services. For example, Pacifica Bay receives income from airport landing fees, parking fees, water usage fees, and rental fees along public beaches, but there are costs—expenditures—related to building and maintaining these facilities and services from which income is received.

1 Start Excel. From the student files that accompany this chapter, open **e03A_Enterprise_Fund**. Display the **Save As** dialog box, and then navigate to the location where you are storing projects for this chapter. Create and open a new folder named **Excel Chapter 3**. In the **File name** box, type **Lastname_Firstname_3A_Enterprise_Fund** and then click **Save** or press Enter.

> The worksheet indicates the originally proposed and adjusted expenditures from the Enterprise Fund for the next fiscal year.

2 Click cell **D5**, and then type = to begin a formula.

3 Click cell **C5**, which is the first value that is part of the total adjusted Fund Expenditures, to insert it into the formula. Type **/** to indicate division, and then click cell **C11**, which is the total adjusted expenditures.

> Recall that to determine the percentage by which a value makes up a total, you must divide the value by the total. The result will be a percentage expressed as a decimal.

4 Press F4 to make the reference to the value in cell **C11** absolute, which will enable you to copy the formula. Compare your screen with Figure 3.2.

> Recall that an *absolute cell reference* refers to a cell by its fixed position in the worksheet—the cell reference will not change when you copy the formula. The reference to cell C5 is a *relative cell reference*, because when you copy the formula, you want the reference to change *relative* to its row. In the formula, the dollar signs display to indicate that a cell reference is absolute.

FIGURE 3.2

> 5 On the **Formula Bar**, click **Enter** ☑ to confirm the entry and to keep cell **D5** the active cell.

> 6 Copy the formula down through cell **D10**, and then compare your screen with Figure 3.3.

FIGURE 3.3

> 7 With the range **D5:D10** still selected, right-click over the selection, and then on the mini toolbar, click **Percent Style** 🔳 and **Center** 🔳. Click cell **A1** to cancel the selection, and then **Save** 🔳 your workbook. Compare your screen with Figure 3.4.

	Pacifica Bay			
	Enterprise Fund Expenditures			
	Recommended Adjustments			
		Originally Proposed	Adjusted	% of Total Fund Expenditures
5 Airport	$	17,610,810	$ 17,456,056	17%
6 Parking		6,824,865	7,897,526	8%
7 Solid Waste		18,695,222	17,845,287	18%
8 Wastewater		12,657,765	13,985,695	14%
9 Water Usage		30,457,903	32,356,236	32%
10 Waterfront		10,976,843	10,945,369	11%
11 Total	$	97,223,408	$ 100,486,169	

Percent of Total for each item calculated, expressed as percentages

Excel 2016, Windows 10, Microsoft Corporation

FIGURE 3.4

5.1.1, 5.2.4

1 Select the range **A5:A10**, hold down Ctrl, and then select the range **C5:C10** to select the nonadjacent ranges with the item names and the adjusted expenditure for each item.

To create a pie chart, you must select two ranges. One range contains the labels for each slice of the pie chart, and the other range contains the values that add up to a total. The two ranges must have the same number of cells and the range with the values should *not* include the cell with the total.

The item names (Airport, Parking, and so on) are the category names and will identify the slices of the pie chart. Each adjusted expenditure is a *data point*—a value that originates in a worksheet cell and that is represented in a chart by a *data marker*. In a pie chart, each pie slice is a data marker. Together, the data points form the *data series*—related data points represented by data markers— and determine the size of each pie slice.

2 With the nonadjacent ranges selected, click the **Insert tab**, and then in the **Charts group**, click **Insert Pie or Doughnut Chart** ⬤▾. Under **3-D Pie**, click the chart **3-D Pie** to create the chart on your worksheet and to display the Chart Tools contextual tabs on the ribbon.

3 On the **Design tab**, at the right end of the ribbon in the **Location group**, click **Move Chart**. In the **Move Chart** dialog box, click the **New sheet** option button.

4 In the **New sheet** box, replace the highlighted text *Chart1* by typing **Expenditures Chart** and then click **OK** to display the chart on a separate worksheet in your workbook. Compare your screen with Figure 3.5.

The pie chart displays on a separate new sheet in your workbook, and a *legend* identifies the pie slices. Recall that a legend is a chart element that identifies the patterns or colors assigned to the categories in the chart.

A *chart sheet* is a workbook sheet that contains only a chart; it is useful when you want to view a chart separately from the worksheet data. The sheet tab indicates *Expenditures Chart*.

FIGURE 3.5

Activity 3.03 | Formatting a Chart Title by Applying a WordArt Style and Changing Font Size

1 Click the text **Chart Title** to surround it with selection handles, and then watch the **Formula Bar** as you type **Enterprise Fund Expenditures** Press [Enter] to create the new chart title in the box.

2 Click the **Format tab**, and then in the **WordArt Styles group**, click **More** ⊡. In the first row, click the last style—**Fill – Gold, Accent 4, Soft Bevel**.

3 With the [I] pointer, drag to select the chart title text, and then on the mini toolbar, change the **Font Size** to **32**. Click the edge of the chart to deselect the title, and then compare your screen with Figure 3.6.

Chart Title text typed, WordArt Style applied, Font Size 32 → Enterprise Fund Expenditures

Excel 2016, Windows 10, Microsoft Corporation

FIGURE 3.6

4 **Save** 💾 your workbook.

Activity 3.04 | Formatting Chart Elements by Removing a Legend and Adding and Formatting Data Labels

In your worksheet, for each budget item, you calculated the percent of the total in column D. These percentages can also be calculated by the Chart feature and added to the pie slices as labels.

1 If necessary, click the edge of the chart to display the three chart buttons on the right, and then click **Chart Elements** ⊞. Compare your screen with Figure 3.7.

Use the Chart Elements button to add, remove, or change chart elements such as the chart title, the legend, and the data labels.

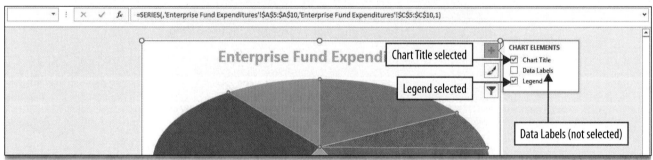

=SERIES(,'Enterprise Fund Expenditures'!$A$5:$A$10,'Enterprise Fund Expenditures'!$C$5:$C$10,1)

Enterprise Fund Expendi — Chart Title selected

CHART ELEMENTS
☑ Chart Title
☐ Data Labels
☑ Legend

Legend selected

Data Labels (not selected)

Excel 2016, Windows 10, Microsoft Corporation

FIGURE 3.7

2 Click the **Legend** check box to deselect it and remove the legend from the bottom of the chart.

3 *Point* to **Data Labels**, and then click the ▶ **arrow** to display a menu. At the bottom of the menu, click **More Options** to display the **Format Data Labels** pane on the right.

The Format Data Labels pane displays and data labels representing the values display on each pie slice.

4 In the **Format Data Labels** pane, under **Label Options**, click as necessary to select the **Category Name** and **Percentage** check boxes. Click to *clear* any other check boxes in this group. Under **Label Position**, click the **Center** option button. Compare your screen with Figure 3.8.

All of the data labels are selected and display both the category name and the percentage. In the worksheet, you calculated the percent of the total in column D. Here, the percentage will be calculated by the Chart feature and added to the chart as a label.

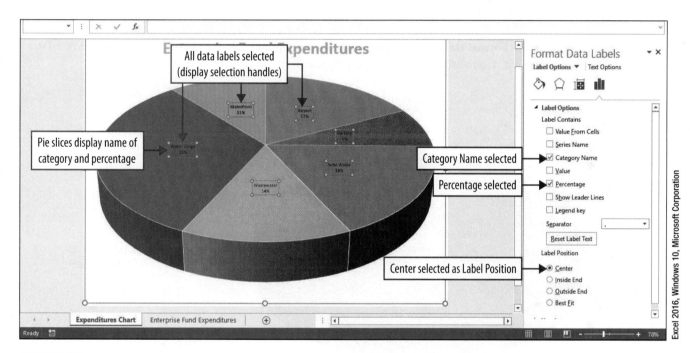

FIGURE 3.8

5 Point to any of the selected data labels, right-click to display a shortcut menu, and then click **Font** to display the **Font** dialog box.

6 On the **Font tab**, click the **Font style arrow**, and then click **Bold Italic**. In the **Size** box, drag to select **9** and type **11** Compare your screen with Figure 3.9.

FIGURE 3.9

7 Click **OK** to close the dialog box and apply the formatting to the data labels. In the upper right corner of the **Format Data Labels** pane, click **Close** ⊠. **Save** 🖫 your workbook.

Activity 3.05 | Formatting a Data Series with 3-D Effects

3-D, which is short for *three-dimensional*, refers to an image that appears to have all three spatial dimensions—length, width, and depth.

1 In any pie slice, point anywhere outside of the selected label, and then double-click to display the **Format Data Series** pane on the right.

🔄**ANOTHER WAY**   Right-click outside the label of any pie slice, and then click Format Data Series to display the Format Data Series pane. Or, on the Format tab, in the Current Selection group, click the Chart Elements arrow, click Series 1, and then click Format Selection.

2 In the **Format Data Series** pane, under **Series Options**, click **Effects** ⬠, and then click **3-D Format**. Compare your screen with Figure 3.10.

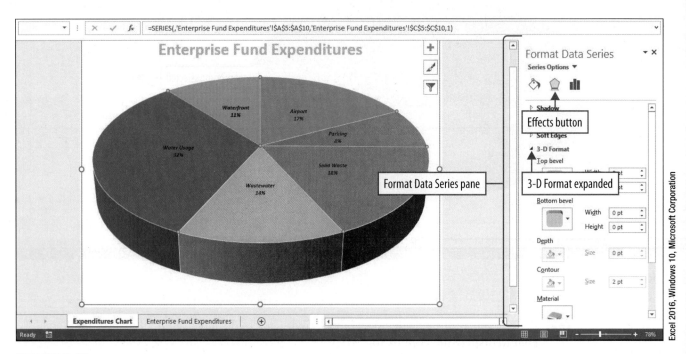

FIGURE 3.10

3 Click the **Top bevel arrow**, and then in the gallery, under **Bevel**, click the first bevel—**Circle**—as shown in Figure 3.11.

Bevel is a shape effect that uses shading and shadows to make the edges of a shape appear to be curved or angled.

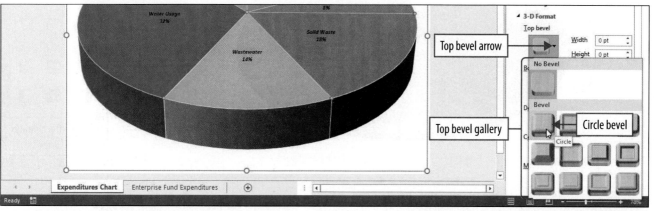

FIGURE 3.11

> **4** Under **Top bevel**, in the **Width** box, select the existing text and type **512** Change the **Height** to **512** and then press Enter.

> **5** Under **Bottom bevel**, use the technique you just practiced to apply a **Circle** bevel with **Width** of **512** and **Height** of **512** Compare your screen with Figure 3.12.

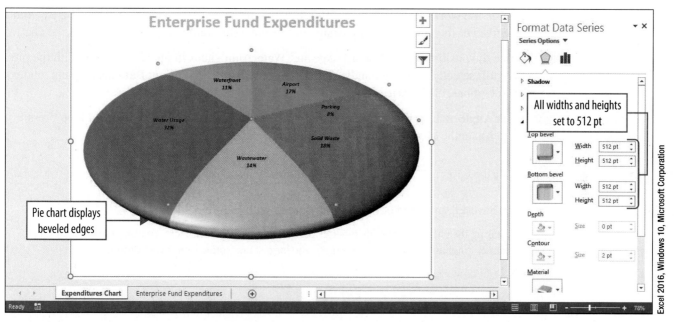

FIGURE 3.12

> **6** In the **Format Data Series** pane, scroll down as necessary, and then click the **Material arrow**. Under **Standard**, click the third material—**Plastic**.

> **7** **Save** your workbook.

Activity 3.06 | Formatting a Data Series with a Shadow Effect

> **1** In the **Format Data Series** pane, scroll back to the top of the pane, and then click **Shadow** to expand the options for this effect.

> **2** Under **Shadow**, click the **Presets arrow**, use the scroll bar to move to the bottom of the gallery, and then under **Perspective**, in the first row, point to the third effect to display the ScreenTip *Below*. Compare your screen with Figure 3.13.

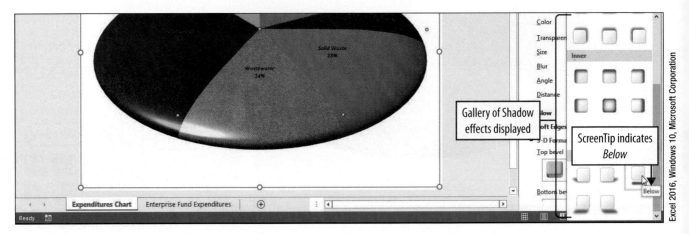

Gallery of Shadow effects displayed

ScreenTip indicates *Below*

Excel 2016, Windows 10, Microsoft Corporation

FIGURE 3.13

> **3** Click **Below** to apply the shadow to the chart. **Save** 🖫 your workbook.

Activity 3.07 | Rotating a Pie Chart by Changing the Angle of the First Slice

The order in which the data series in pie charts are plotted in Excel is determined by the order of the data on the worksheet. To gain a different view of the chart, you can rotate the chart within the 360 degrees of the circle of the pie shape to present a different visual perspective of the chart.

> **1** Notice the position of the **Water Usage** and **Waterfront** slices in the chart. Then, with the pie chart still selected—sizing handles surround the pie—in the **Format Data Series** pane, under **Series Options**, click **Series Options** 📊.

> **2** Under **Angle of first slice**, in the box to the right, drag to select **0°**, type **250** and then press ⏎ to rotate the chart 250 degrees to the right.

🔄 **ANOTHER WAY**   Drag the slider to 250°, or click the spin box up arrow as many times as necessary.

> **3** Click **Save** 🖫, and then compare your screen with Figure 3.14.

> Rotating the chart can provide a better perspective to the chart. Here, rotating the chart in this manner emphasizes that Water Usage is the largest enterprise fund expenditure.

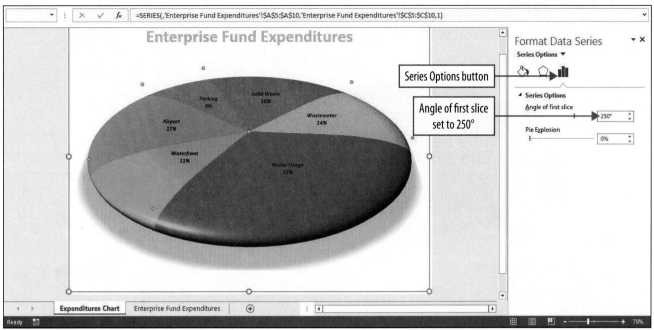

FIGURE 3.14

Activity 3.08 │ Exploding and Coloring a Pie Slice

You can pull out—***explode***—one or more slices of a pie chart to emphasize a specific slice or slices.

1 In the **Format Data Series** pane, under **Series Options**, notice the slider and box for *Pie Explosion*.

When all the pie slices are selected, as they currently are, you can use this command to explode *all* of the pie pieces away from the center by varying degrees to emphasize all the individual slices of the pie chart. An exploded pie chart visualizes the contribution of each value to the total, while at the same time emphasizing individual values.

2 On the pie chart, click the **Waterfront** slice to select only that slice, and then on the right, notice that the **Format Data Point** pane displays.

Excel adjusts the pane, depending on what you have selected, so that the commands you need are available.

3 In the **Format Data Point** pane, in the **Point Explosion** box, select the existing text, type **10%** and then press Enter.

4 With the **Waterfront** slice still selected, in the **Format Data Point** pane, under **Series Options**, click **Fill & Line** ◇, and then click **Fill** to expand its options.

5 Click the **Gradient fill** option button, click the **Preset gradients arrow**, and then in the fourth row, click the last gradient—**Bottom Spotlight – Accent 6**. Click **Save** 🖫, and then compare your screen with Figure 3.15.

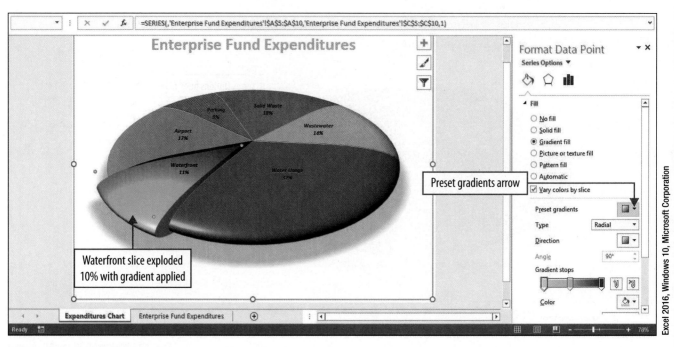

FIGURE 3.15

Activity 3.09 │ Formatting the Chart Area

The entire chart and all of its elements comprise the ***chart area***.

1 Point to the white area just inside the border of the chart to display the ScreenTip *Chart Area*. Click one time, and notice that on the right, the **Format Chart Area** pane displays.

2 Under **Chart Options**, click **Fill & Line** 🖌, and be sure the **Fill** options are still displayed.

3 Click the **Gradient fill** option button, click the **Preset gradients arrow**, and then in the fourth row, click the first gradient—**Bottom Spotlight – Accent 1**.

4 In the **Format Chart Area** pane, click **Fill** to collapse the options, and then click **Border** to expand its options.

5 Under **Border**, click **Solid line**, click the **Color arrow** to display the Outline colors, and then in the fourth column, click the first color—**Blue – Gray, Text 2**. In the **Width** box, drag to select the existing width, and then type **5**

6 **Close** ☒ the **Format Chart Area** pane, and then click outside of the Chart Area to deselect the chart. Click **Save** 💾, and then compare your screen with Figure 3.16.

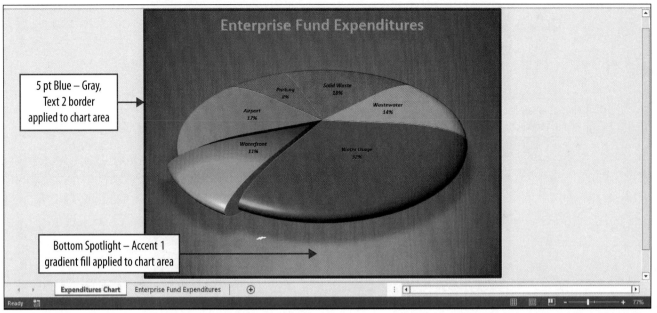

5 pt Blue – Gray, Text 2 border applied to chart area

Bottom Spotlight – Accent 1 gradient fill applied to chart area

FIGURE 3.16

Objective 3 Edit a Workbook and Update a Chart

Activity 3.10 | Editing a Workbook and Updating a Chart

GO! Learn How
Video E3-3

If you edit the data in your worksheet, the chart data markers—in this instance, the pie slices—will adjust automatically to accurately represent the new values.

1 On the pie chart, notice that *Airport* represents 17% of the total projected expenses.

2 In the sheet tab area at the bottom of the workbook, click the **Enterprise Fund Expenditures tab** to redisplay the worksheet.

3 Click cell **C5**, type **18,121,067** and then press Enter. Notice that the Accounting Number Format is retained in the cell.

ANOTHER WAY Double-click the cell to position the insertion point in the cell and edit.

4 Notice that the total in cell **C11** recalculated to *$101,151,180* and the percentages in **column D** also recalculated.

5 Display the **Expenditures Chart** sheet. Notice that the pie slices adjust to show the recalculation—*Airport* is now *18%* of the adjusted expenditures. Click **Save** 🖫, and then compare your screen with Figure 3.17.

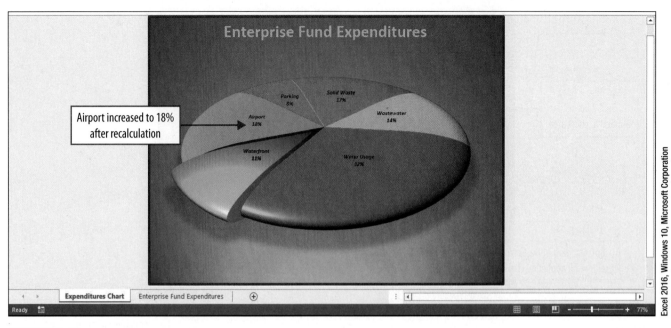

FIGURE 3.17

Objective 4 | Use Goal Seek to Perform What-If Analysis

GO! Learn How
Video E3-4

Expert 3.4.2

Activity 3.11 | Using Goal Seek to Perform What-If Analysis

The process of changing the values in cells to see how those changes affect the outcome of formulas in your worksheet is referred to as *what-if analysis*. One what-if analysis tool in Excel is *Goal Seek*, which finds the input needed in one cell to arrive at the desired result in another cell.

1 Click the **Enterprise Fund Expenditures sheet tab** to redisplay the worksheet.

2 Select the range **D5:D10**, and then increase the number of decimal places to two. Compare your screen with Figure 3.18.

FIGURE 3.18

3 ▶ Click cell **C11**. On the **Data tab**, in the **Forecast group**, click **What-If Analysis**, and then click **Goal Seek**.

4 ▶ In the **Goal Seek** dialog box, notice that the active cell, **C11**, is indicated in the **Set cell** box. Press Tab to move to the **To value** box, and then type **100,000,000**

C11 is the cell in which you want to set a specific value; $100,000,000 is the total expenditures budgeted for the Enterprise Fund. The Set cell box contains the formula that calculates the information you seek.

5 ▶ Press Tab to move the insertion point to the **By changing cell** box, and then click cell **C10**. Compare your screen with Figure 3.19.

Cell C10 contains the value that Excel changes to reach the goal. In the Goal Seek dialog box, Excel formats this cell as an absolute cell reference.

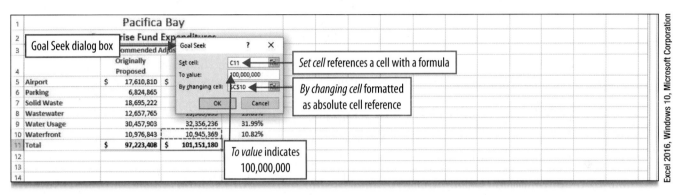

FIGURE 3.19

6 ▶ Click **OK**. In the displayed **Goal Seek Status** dialog box, click **OK**.

7 ▶ Press Ctrl + Home, click **Save** 🖫, and then compare your screen with Figure 3.20.

Excel calculates that the city must budget for *$9,794,189* in Waterfront expenditures in order to maintain a total Enterprise Fund Expenditure budget of $100,000,000.

	A	B	C	D	% of Total Fund Expenditures
1	Pacifica Bay				
2	Enterprise Fund Expenditures				
3	Recommended Adjustments				
4		Originally Proposed	Adjusted		% of Total Fund Expenditures
5	Airport	$ 17,610,810	$ 18,121,067		18.12%
6	Parking	6,824,865	7,897,526		7.90%
7	Solid Waste	18,695,222	17,845,287		17.85%
8	Wastewater	12,657,765	13,985,695		13.99%
9	Water Usage	30,457,903	32,356,236		32.36%
10	Waterfront	10,976,843	9,794,189		9.79%
11	Total	$ 97,223,408	$ 100,000,000		

Goal of $100,000,000   Waterfront changed to 9,794,189

FIGURE 3.20

Activity 3.12 | Preparing and Printing a Workbook with a Chart Sheet

1 ▶ Click the **Page Layout tab**. In the **Page Setup group**, click the Dialog Box Launcher ▫.

2 ▶ In the **Page Setup** dialog box, on the **Margins tab**, under **Center on page**, select the **Horizontally** check box.

3 Click the **Header/Footer tab**, and then in the center of the dialog box, click **Custom Footer**. In the **Footer** dialog box, with the insertion point blinking in the **Left section**, on the row of buttons, click **Insert File Name** 📄. Click **OK** two times.

> The dotted line indicates the page break as currently formatted.

4 Display the **Expenditures Chart**, which must have its footer formatted separately. In the **Page Setup group**, click the **Dialog Box Launcher** 🗗.

> Chart sheets are automatically centered on the page.

5 Click the **Header/Footer tab**, and then in the center of the dialog box, click **Custom Footer**. In the **Footer** dialog box, with the insertion point blinking in the **Left section**, on the row of buttons, click **Insert File Name** 📄. Click **OK** two times.

6 Right-click the **Expenditures Chart sheet tab**, and then click **Select All Sheets**. Verify that *[Group]* displays in the title bar.

> Recall that by selecting all sheets, you can view all of the workbook pages in Print Preview.

7 Press Ctrl + F2 to display the **Print Preview**. Examine the first page, and then at the bottom of the **Print Preview**, click **Next Page** ▶ to view the second page of your workbook.

NOTE	Printing a Chart Sheet Uses More Toner

Printing a chart that displays on a chart sheet will use more toner or ink than a small chart that is part of a worksheet. If you are printing your work, check with your instructor to verify whether or not you should print the chart sheet.

8 Click **Info**, and then click **Show All Properties**. As the **Tags**, type **enterprise fund, expenditures** As the **Subject**, type your course name and section number. Be sure your name displays as the **Author**. **Save** 💾 the workbook.

9 If directed by your instructor to do so, submit your paper printout, your electronic image of your document that looks like a printed document, or your original Excel file. If required by your instructor, print or create an electronic version of your worksheet with formulas displayed. In the upper right corner of the Excel window, click **Close** ✕.

> END | You have completed Project 3A

Go! With Google

> **ALERT!** **Working with Web-Based Applications and Services**
>
> Computer programs and services on the web receive continuous updates and improvements, so the steps to complete this web-based activity may differ from the ones shown. You can often look at the screens and the information presented to determine how to complete the activity.
>
> If you do not already have a Google account, you will need to create one before you begin this Activity. Go to http://google.com and, in the upper right corner, click Sign In. On the Sign In screen, click Create Account. On the Create your Google Account page, complete the form, read and agree to the Terms of Service and Privacy Policy, and then click Next step. On the Welcome screen, click Get Started.

Activity | Create a Pie Chart

1 From the desktop, open your browser, navigate to **http://google.com**, and then click the **Google Apps** menu ⊞. Click **Drive**, and then if necessary, sign in to your Google account.

2 Open your **GO! Web Projects** folder—or click New to create and then open this folder if necessary. In the left pane, click **NEW**, and then click **File upload**. Navigate to your student data files, click **e03_3A_Web**, and then click **Open**.

3 Right-click the file you uploaded, point to **Open with**, and then click **Google Sheets**.

4 Click cell **D5**. Type = and then click cell **C5**. Type / and then click **C11** and press ⌗F4⌗ to make the cell reference absolute. Press Enter to create a formula to calculate % of Total Fund Expenditures.

5 Click cell **D5**, and then apply percent formatting. Fill the formula down through cell **D10**. Click **Format**, point to **Align**, and then click **Center**.

6 Select the range **A5:A10**, hold down ⌗Ctrl⌗, and then select **C5:C10**. Click **Insert**, and then click **Chart**. To the right of the chart gallery, point to the vertical scroll bar

and drag down to display the Pie charts. Click the third chart—**3D pie chart**, and then click **Insert**.

7 Point to the chart and then drag down and to the left to position the pie chart under the worksheet data so that its left edge aligns with the left edge of cell **A13**. Click the **Chart title** to display a box in which you can type the chart title. Type **Enterprise Fund Expenditures** and then press Enter. In the chart title ribbon, click the **Font Size arrow**, and then click **20**. Click anywhere in the chart outside of the title so that the title is not selected.

8 In the upper right corner of the chart area, click the **down-pointing triangle**, and then click **Advanced edit**. Under **Legend**, click **Right**, and then in the list, click **Labeled**. To the right of **Background**, click the **Background color arrow**, and then in the seventh column, click the third color—**light cornflower blue 3**. Click **Update** to apply the formatting changes and close the **Chart Editor**.

9 Click cell **A1** and then scroll down to view the entire chart. Compare your screen with Figure A.

10 Submit your file as directed by your instructor. Sign out of your Google account and close your browser.

FIGURE A

Tourism Spending Projection with Line Chart

PROJECT ACTIVITIES

In Activities 3.13 through 3.20, you will assist Michael Larsen, City Manager, in creating a worksheet to estimate future tourism spending based on two possible growth rates. You will also create a line chart to display past visitor spending. Your resulting worksheet and chart will look similar to Figure 3.21.

PROJECT FILES

MyITLab
grader

If your instructor wants you to submit Project 3B in the MyITLab Grader system, log in to MyITLab, locate Grader Project 3B, and then download the files for this project.

For Project 3B, you will need the following files:
e03B_Tourism
e03B_Surfers

You will save your workbook as:
Lastname_Firstname_3B_Tourism

Please always review the downloaded Grader instructions before beginning.

PROJECT RESULTS

GO!
Walk Thru
Project 3B

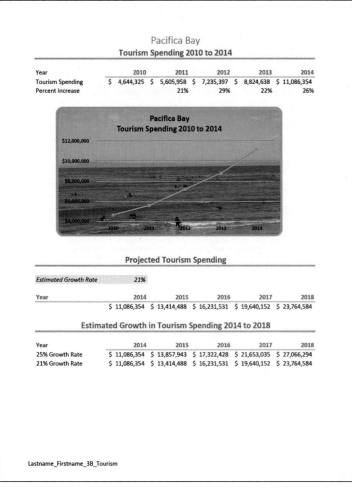

FIGURE 3.21 Project 3B Tourism Spending Projection with Line Chart

GO! Learn How
Video E3-5

If you change the value in a cell referenced in a formula, Excel automatically recalculates the result of the formula. This means that you can change cell values to see what would happen if you tried different values. Recall that this process of changing the values in cells to see how those changes affect the outcome of formulas in your worksheet is referred to as what-if analysis.

Activity 3.13 | Using Parentheses in a Formula to Calculate a Percentage Rate of Increase

ALERT! | **To submit as an autograded project, log into MyITLab and download the files for this project, and begin with those files instead of e03B_Tourism.**

Mr. Larsen has the city's tourism spending figures for the recent 5-year period. In each year, tourism spending has increased. In this Activity, you will construct a formula to calculate the *percentage rate of increase*—the percent by which one number increases over another number—for each year since 2010. From this information, future tourism spending growth can be estimated.

Excel follows a set of mathematical rules called the *order of operations*, which has four basic parts:

- Expressions within parentheses are processed first.
- Exponentiation, if present, is performed before multiplication and division.
- Multiplication and division are performed before addition and subtraction.
- Consecutive operators with the same level of precedence are calculated from left to right.

1 Start Excel. From your student data files, open **e03B_Tourism**. **Save** the file in your **Excel Chapter 3** folder as **Lastname_Firstname_3B_Tourism**

2 In cell **B4**, type **2010** and then press Tab. In cell **C4**, type **2011** and then press Tab. Select the range **B4:C4**, and then drag the fill handle to the right through cell **F4** to extend the series to *2014*. Compare your screen with Figure 3.22.

By establishing a pattern of 1-year intervals with the first two cells, you can use the fill handle to continue the series. The AutoFill feature will do this for any pattern that you establish with two or more cells.

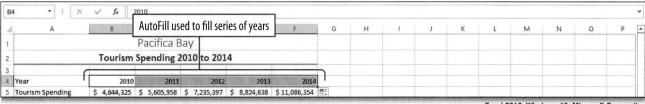

FIGURE 3.22

Excel 2016, Windows 10, Microsoft Corporation

3 Click cell **C6**. Being sure to include the parentheses, type **=(c5-b5)/b5** and then on the **Formula Bar**, click **Enter** ✓ to keep cell **C6** active. Notice that your result displays as *$0.21* because Excel retains the Accounting Number Format of the cells referenced in the formula.

As you type, a list of Excel functions that begin with the letters *C* and *B* may briefly display. This is **Formula AutoComplete**, an Excel feature which, after typing an = (equal sign) and the beginning letter or letters of a function name, displays a list of function names that match the typed letter(s). In this instance, the letters represent cell references, *not* the beginning of a function name.

4 With cell **C6** selected, apply **Percent Style** %, and then compare your screen with Figure 3.23.

Excel 2016, Windows 10, Microsoft Corporation

FIGURE 3.23

5 With cell **C6** selected, drag the fill handle to the right to copy the formula through cell **F6**.

Because this formula uses relative cell references—that is, for each year, the formula is the same but the values used are relative to the formula's location—you can copy the formula in this manner. For example, the result for 2012 uses the 2011 value as the base, the result for 2013 uses the 2012 value as the base, and the result for 2014 uses the 2013 value as the base.

6 Click cell **C6** and look at the **Formula Bar**.

The mathematical formula *rate = amount of increase/base* is used to calculate the percentage rate of tourism spending increase from 2010 to 2011. The formula is applied as follows:

First, determine the *amount of increase* by subtracting the *base*—the starting point represented by the 2010 tourism spending—from the 2011 tourism spending. Therefore, the *amount of increase* = \$5,605,958 − \$4,644,325 or \$961,633. Between 2010 and 2011, tourism spending increased by \$961,633. In the formula, this calculation is represented by *C5-B5*.

Second, calculate the *rate*—what the amount of increase (\$961,633) represents as a percentage of the base (2010's tourism spending of \$4,644,325). Determine this by dividing the amount of increase (\$961,633) by the base (\$4,644,325). Therefore, \$961,633 divided by \$4,644,325 is equal to *0.207055492* or, when formatted as a percent and rounded up, 21%.

7 In the **Formula Bar**, locate the parentheses enclosing *C5-B5*.

Recall that Excel follows a set of mathematical rules called the order of operations, in which expressions within parentheses are processed first, multiplication and division are performed before addition and subtraction, and consecutive operators with the same level of precedence are calculated from left to right.

8 **Save** 🖫 your workbook, and then compare your screen with Figure 3.24.

C6		✕	✓	*fₓ*	=(C5-B5)/B5												
	A	B		C	D	E		F	G	H	I	J	K	L	M	N	O	P
1				Pacifica Bay													
2			Tourism Spending 2010 to 2014														
3																	
4	Year		2010	2011	2012	2013		2014									
5	Tourism Spending	\$ 4,644,325	\$ 5,605,958	\$ 7,235,397	\$ 8,824,638	\$ 11,086,354											
6	Percent Increase		21%	29%	22%	26%			Formula filled across row								
7																	
8	Projected Tourism Spending																

Excel 2016, Windows 10, Microsoft Corporation

FIGURE 3.24

Activity 3.14 | Using Format Painter

In this Activity, you will use Format Painter to copy formatting.

2.2.3

1 Point to cell **A2**, right-click, on the mini toolbar, click **Format Painter** ✎, and then click cell **A8** to copy the format.

> The format of cell A2 is *painted*—applied to—cell A8, including the merging and centering of the text across the range A8:F8.

↻ **ANOTHER WAY**   On the Home tab, in the Clipboard group, click the Format Painter button.

2 Point to cell **F5**, right-click, and then click **Copy**. Point to cell **B13**, right-click, and then on the shortcut menu, under **Paste Options**, click **Paste** 📋. Compare your screen with Figure 3.25, and then **Save** 💾 your workbook.

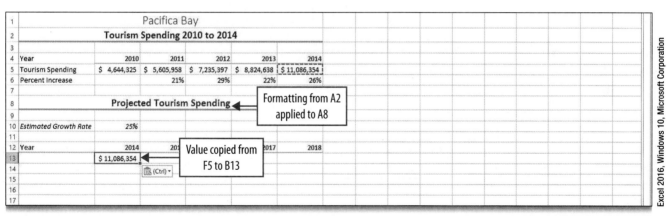

FIGURE 3.25

Activity 3.15 | Calculating a Value After an Increase

A growth in tourism spending means that the city can plan for additional revenues and also plan more hotel and conference space to accommodate the increasing number of visitors. Therefore, city planners in Pacifica Bay want to estimate how much tourism spending will increase in the future. The calculations you made in the previous Activity show that tourism spending has increased at varying rates during each year from 2010 to 2014, ranging from a low of 21% to a high of 29% per year.

Economic data suggests that future growth will trend close to that of the recent past. To plan for the future, Mr. Larsen wants to prepare a forecast of tourism spending based on the percentage increase halfway between the high of 29% and the low of 21%; that is, for 25%. In this Activity, you will calculate the tourism spending that would result from a 25% increase.

1 Click cell **C13**. Type **=b13*(100%+b10)** and then on the **Formula Bar**, click **Enter** ☑ to display a result of *13857942.5*.

2 Point to cell **B13**, right-click, click **Format Painter** 🖌, and then click cell **C13** to copy the format. Compare your screen with Figure 3.26.

This formula calculates what tourism spending will be in the year 2015 assuming an increase of 25% over 2014's tourism spending. Use the mathematical formula *value after increase = base × percent for new value* to calculate a value after an increase as follows:

First, establish the *percent for new value*. The **percent for new value = base percent + percent of increase**. The *base percent* of 100% represents the base tourism spending and the *percent of increase*—in this instance, 25%. Therefore, the tourism spending will equal 100% of the base year plus 25% of the base year. This can be expressed as 125% or 1.25. In this formula, you will use 100% + the rate in cell B10, which is 25%, to equal 125%.

Second, enter a reference to the cell that contains the *base*—the tourism spending in 2014. The base value resides in cell B13—*$11,086,354*.

Third, calculate the *value after increase*. Because in each future year the increase will be based on 25%—an absolute value located in cell B10—this cell reference can be formatted as absolute by typing dollar signs.

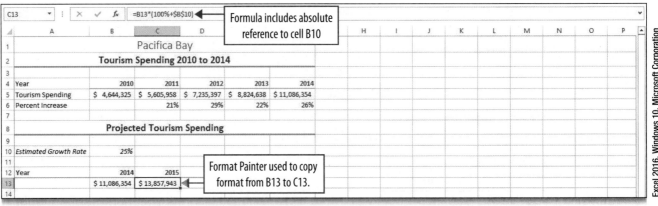

FIGURE 3.26

3 With cell **C13** as the active cell, drag the fill handle to copy the formula to the range **D13:F13**. Click an empty cell to cancel the selection, click **Save** 💾 and then compare your screen with Figure 3.27.

The formula in cell C13 uses a relative cell address—B13—for the *base*; the tourism spending in the previous year is used in each of the formulas in cells D13:F13 as the *base* value. Because the reference to the *percent of increase* in cell B10 is an absolute reference, each *value after increase* is calculated with the value from cell B10.

The tourism spending projected for 2015—*$13,857,943*—is an increase of 25% over the spending in 2014. The projected spending in 2016—*$17,322,428*—is an increase of 25% over the spending in 2015, and so on.

| F21 | ▾ | : | × | ✓ | fx | | | | | | | | | | | | |

◢			C	D	E	F	G	H	I	J	K	L	M	N	O	P	
1	*Projection calculated using a 25% growth rate*		Pacifica Bay														
2			Tourism Spending 2010 to 2014														
3																	
4	Year		2010	2011	2012	2013	2014										
5	Tourism Spending		$ 4,644,325	$ 5,605,958	$ 7,235,397	$ 8,824,638	$ 11,086,354										
6	Percent Increase			21%	29%	22%	26%										
7																	
8			**Projected Tourism Spending**														
9																	
10	*Estimated Growth Rate*	▶	25%														
11																	
12	Year		2014	2015	2016	2017	2018										
13			$ 11,086,354	$ 13,857,943	$ 17,322,428	$ 21,653,035	$ 27,066,294		*Each value represents a 25% increase over the previous base year*								
14																	
15																	

FIGURE 3.27

More Knowledge   **Percent Increase or Decrease**

The basic formula for calculating an increase or decrease can be done in two parts. First determine the percent by which the base value will be increased or decreased, and then add or subtract the results to the base. The formula can be simplified by using (1+amount of increase) or (1−amount of decrease), where 1, rather than 100%, represents the whole. Therefore, the formula used in Step 1 of Activity 3.15 could also be written =b13*(1+b10), or =(b13*b10)+b13.

Objective 6 Answer What-If Questions by Changing Values in a Worksheet

GO! Learn How
Video E3-6

If a formula depends on the value in a cell, you can see what effect it will have if you change the value in that cell. Then, you can copy the value computed by the formula and paste it into another part of the worksheet where you can compare it to other values.

Activity 3.16 | Answering What-If Questions and Using Paste Special

MOS
2.1.3

A growth rate of 25% in tourism spending in each year will result in tourism spending of approximately $27 million by 2018. The city planners will likely ask: *What if* tourism spending grows at the lowest rate of 21%?

Because the formulas are constructed to use the growth rate displayed in cell B10, Mr. Larsen can answer that question quickly by entering a different percentage into that cell. To keep the results of the new calculation so it can be compared, you will paste the results of the what-if question into another area of the worksheet.

1 Leave **row 14** blank, and then click cell **A15**. Type **Estimated Growth in Tourism Spending 2014 to 2018** and then press Enter. Use **Format Painter** ✱ to copy the format from cell **A8** to cell **A15**.

2 Select the range **A10:B10**, right-click to display the mini toolbar, click the **Fill Color button arrow** ◇ ▾ , and then under **Theme Colors**, in the first column, click the third color—**White, Background 1, Darker 15%**.

3 Leave **row 16** blank, and then in the range **A17:A19**, type the following row titles:

Year

25% Growth Rate

21% Growth Rate

4 Select the range **B12:F12**, right-click over the selection, and then on the shortcut menu, click **Copy**.

5 Point to cell **B17**, right-click, and then on the shortcut menu, under **Paste Options**, click **Paste** .

Recall that when pasting a group of copied cells to a target range, you need only point to or select the first cell of the range.

6 Select and **Copy** the range **B13:F13**, and then **Paste** it beginning in cell **B18**.

7 Click cell **C18**. On the **Formula Bar**, notice that the *formula* was pasted into the cell, as shown in Figure 3.28.

This is *not* the desired result. The actual *calculated values*—not the formulas—are needed in the range.

FIGURE 3.28

8 On the Quick Access Toolbar, click **Undo** . With the range **B13:F13** still copied to the Clipboard—as indicated by the message in the status bar and the moving border—point to cell **B18**, and then right-click to display the shortcut menu.

9 Under **Paste Options**, point to **Paste Special** to display another gallery, and then under **Paste Values**, point to **Values & Number Formatting** to display the ScreenTip as shown in Figure 3.29.

The ScreenTip *Values & Number Formatting (A)* indicates that you can paste the calculated values that result from the calculation of formulas along with the formatting applied to the copied cells. *(A)* is the keyboard shortcut for this command.

FIGURE 3.29

10 Click **Values & Number Formatting** 🔲, click cell **C18** and notice on the **Formula Bar** that the cell contains a *value*, not a formula. Press Esc to cancel the moving border. Compare your screen with Figure 3.30.

The calculated estimates based on a 25% growth rate are pasted along with their formatting.

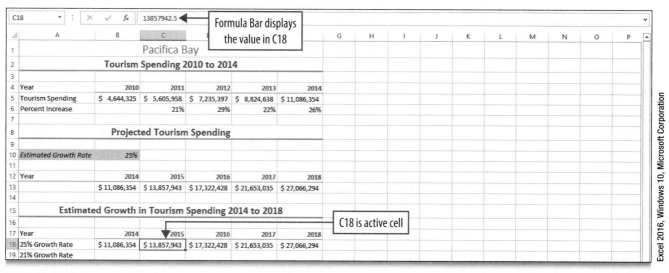

FIGURE 3.30

11 Click cell **B10**. Type **21** and then watch the values in **C13:F13** *recalculate* as, on the **Formula Bar**, you click **Enter** ✓.

The value *21%* is the lowest percent increase for the past 5-year period.

12 Select and **Copy** the new values in the range **B13:F13**. Point to cell **B19**, right-click, and then on the shortcut menu, point to **Paste Special**. Under **Paste Values**, click **Values & Number Formatting** 🔲.

13 Press Esc to cancel the moving border, click cell **A1**, click **Save** 💾, and then compare your screen with Figure 3.31.

With this information, Mr. Larsen can answer what-if questions about the projected increase in tourism spending based on the rates of increase over the past five years.

	A	B	C	D	E	F				
8		Projected Tourism Spending								
9										
10	*Estimated Growth Rate*	21%								
11										
12	Year	2014	2015	2016	2017	2018				
13		$ 11,086,354	$ 13,414,488	$ 16,231,531	$ 19,640,152	$ 23,764,584				
14										
15		Estimated Growth in Tourism Spending 2014 to 2018								
16										
17	Year	2014	2015	2016	2017	2018				
18	25% Growth Rate	$ 11,086,354	$ 13,857,943	$ 17,322,428	$ 21,653,035	$ 27,066,294				
19	21% Growth Rate	$ 11,086,354	$ 13,414,488	$ 16,231,531	$ 19,640,152	$ 23,764,584				
20										

Values copied for each what-if question

Excel 2016, Windows 10, Microsoft Corporation

FIGURE 3.31

Objective 7 | Chart Data with a Line Chart

GO! Learn How
Video E3-7

A *line chart* displays trends over time. Time is displayed along the bottom axis and the data point values connect with a line. The curve and direction of the line make trends obvious to the reader.

The columns in a column chart and the pie slices in a pie chart emphasize the distinct values of each data point. A line chart, on the other hand, emphasizes the flow from one data point value to the next.

Activity 3.17 | Inserting Multiple Rows and Creating a Line Chart

MOS
1.3.5, 5.1.1

So that City Council members can see how tourism spending has increased over a 5-year period, in this Activity, you will chart the actual tourism spending from 2010 to 2014 in a line chart.

1 Click the **Page Layout tab**. In the **Themes group**, click **Colors**, and then change the **Theme Colors** to **Orange**.

2 In the **row header area**, point to **row 8** to display the ➡ pointer, and then drag down to select **rows 8:24**. Right-click over the selection, and then click **Insert** to insert the same number of blank rows as you selected. Compare your screen with Figure 3.32.

Use this technique to insert multiple rows quickly.

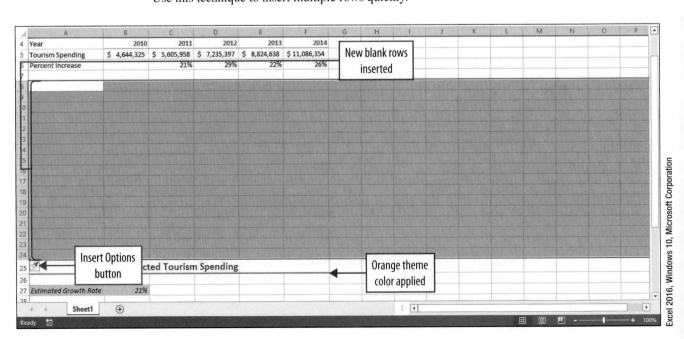

FIGURE 3.32

3 Near **row 25**, click **Insert Options** ⌧, and then click the **Clear Formatting** option button to clear any formatting from these rows.

> You will use this blank area to position your line chart.

4 Press `Ctrl` + `Home` to deselect the rows and move to the top of your worksheet. Select the range **A5:F5**. On the **Insert tab**, in the **Charts group**, click **Insert Line or Area Chart** 📈 ▾.

5 In the gallery of line charts, under **2-D Line**, point to the fourth chart type to display the ScreenTip *Line with Markers*. Compare your screen with Figure 3.33.

FIGURE 3.33

6 Click the **Line with Markers** chart type to create the chart in the worksheet.

7 Point to the border of the chart to display the 🡒 pointer, and then drag the chart so that its upper left corner is positioned in cell **A8**, aligned approximately under the *t* in the word *Percent* above.

> Excel uses the label in cell A5—*Tourism Spending*—as the suggested chart title.

8 Point to the **Chart Title** *Tourism Spending* and right-click. On the shortcut menu, click **Edit Text** to place the insertion point at the beginning of the title. Type **Pacifica Bay** and press `Enter`. Press `End` to move to the end of *Spending*, press `Spacebar`, and then type **2010 to 2014**

9 Click the dashed border surrounding the **Chart Title** so that it is a solid line, indicating the entire title is selected. Right-click over the title, and then click **Font**. In the **Font** dialog box, click the **Font style arrow**, and then click **Bold**. Click the **Font color arrow**, and then in the second column, click the first color—**Black, Text 1**. Click **OK**.

10 On the right side of the chart, click **Chart Elements** ➕, and then compare your screen with Figure 3.34.

> Three of the available chart elements are included for this chart by default—the axes, the chart title, and the gridlines.

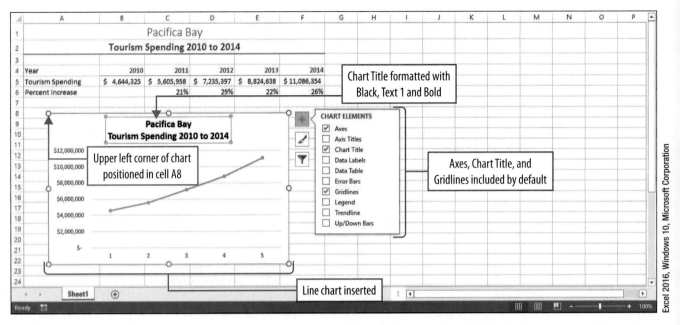

FIGURE 3.34

Activity 3.18 | Formatting Axes in a Line Chart

An **axis** is a line that serves as a frame of reference for measurement; it borders the chart **plot area**. The plot area is the area bounded by the axes, including all the data series. In a line chart, the area along the bottom of a chart that identifies the categories of data is referred to as the **category axis** or the **x-axis**. The area along the left side of a chart that shows the range of numbers for the data points is referred to as the **value axis** or the **y-axis**.

In this Activity, you will change the category axis to include the years 2010 to 2014 and adjust the numeric scale of the value axis.

1 Be sure the chart is still selected. At the bottom of the chart, point to any of the numbers *1* through *5* to display the ScreenTip *Horizontal (Category) Axis*, and then right-click. On the shortcut menu, click **Select Data**.

ANOTHER WAY   Click the Design tab, and then in the Data group, click Select Data.

2 On the right side of the **Select Data Source** dialog box, under **Horizontal (Category) Axis Labels**, locate **Edit**, as shown in Figure 3.35.

Here you can change the labels on the category axis to the years that are represented in the chart.

FIGURE 3.35

3 In the right column, click **Edit**. If necessary, drag the title bar of the Axis Labels dialog box to the right of the chart so that it is not blocking your view of the data. Select the years in the range **B4:F4**. Compare your screen with Figure 3.36.

FIGURE 3.36

4 In the **Axis Labels** dialog box, click **OK**, and notice that in the right column of the **Select Data Source** dialog box, the years display as the category labels. Click **OK** to close the **Select Data Source** dialog box. Compare your screen with Figure 3.37.

FIGURE 3.37

5 With the **Horizontal (Category) Axis** still selected, click the **Chart Elements** button ➕, point to **Axes**, click the ▶ arrow, and then click **More Options** to display the **Format Axis** pane.

6 Under **Axis Options**, click **Fill & Line** ◇, if necessary click Line to expand the options. Click the **No line** option button and then **Close** ✕ the **Format Axis** pane.

7 On the chart, notice that the orange line—the data series—does not display in the lower portion of the chart. On the left side of the chart, point to any of the dollar values to display the ScreenTip *Vertical (Value) Axis*, and then right-click. On the shortcut menu, click **Format Axis** to display the **Format Axis** pane on the right. Compare your screen with Figure 3.38.

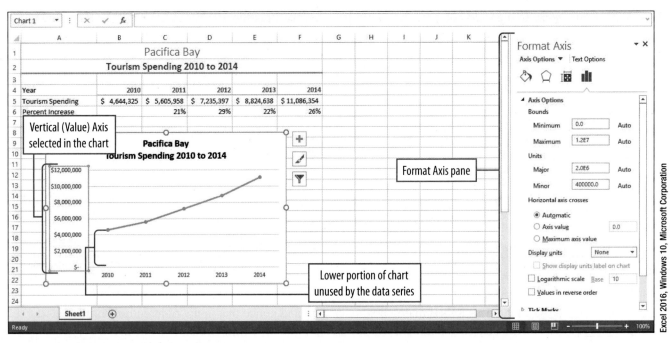

FIGURE 3.38

🔄 **ANOTHER WAY**   On the Format tab, in the Current Selection group, click the Chart Elements arrow, click Vertical (Value) Axis, and then click Format Selection. Or, click the Chart Elements button, point to Axes, click the arrow, click More Options, and then in the Format Axis pane, click the Axis Options arrow. On the displayed list, click Vertical (Value) Axis.

8 In the **Format Axis** pane, under **Bounds**, click in the **Minimum** box, and then select the existing text **0.0**. Type **4000000** and then press Enter.

Because none of the spending figures are under $4,000,000, changing the Minimum number to $4,000,000 will enable the data series to occupy more of the plot area.

9 Under **Units**, in the **Major** box, select the text **1.0E6**, type **2000000** and press Enter. Click **Save** 💾, and then compare your screen with Figure 3.39.

The *Major unit* value determines the spacing between the gridlines in the plot area. By default, Excel started the values at zero and increased in increments of $2,000,000. By setting the Minimum value on the value axis to $4,000,000, the Major unit is changed to 1.0E6—$1,000,000. Changing the Minimum value to $4,000,000 and setting the Major unit back to $2,000,000 displays a clearer and more pronounced trend in tourism spending.

Numbers that display E + a number are expressed by Excel in the Scientific format, which displays a number in exponential notation.

FIGURE 3.39

Activity 3.19 | Formatting the Chart Area in a Line Chart

An Excel chart has two background elements—the plot area and the chart area—which by default display a single fill color. To add visual appeal to a chart, you can insert a graphic image as the background.

1 Near the top of the **Format Axis** pane, click the **Axis Options arrow**, and then click **Chart Area** to display the **Format Chart Area** pane. Click **Fill & Line** ⬨.

> When formatting chart elements, Excel provides multiple ways to display the panes that you need. You can right-click the area you want to format and choose a command on the shortcut menu. You can use an existing pane to move to a different pane. And you can use the Format tab on the ribbon to navigate among various chart elements in the Current Selection group. Use whatever method is easiest for you.

🔄 **ANOTHER WAY** On the Format tab, in the Current Selection group, click the Chart Elements arrow, click Chart Area, and then click Format Selection. Or, right-click slightly inside the chart to display the shortcut menu, and then click Format Chart Area.

2 In the **Format Chart Area** pane, click **Fill** to expand the options, and then click the **Picture or texture fill** option button.

> A default texture displays in the chart area.

3 In the **Format Chart Area** pane, under **Insert picture from**, click **File**. In the **Insert Picture** dialog box, navigate to the student data files that accompany this textbook, and then click **e03B_Surfers**. Click **Insert**. Compare your screen with Figure 3.40.

FIGURE 3.40

4 In the **Format Chart Area** pane, click **Fill** to collapse the options, and then if necessary, click Border to expand the options. Click the **Solid line** option button, click the **Color arrow**, and then under **Theme Colors**, in the fifth column, notice that the first color—**Orange, Accent 1**—is already selected by default.

5 Click the **Color arrow** again to accept the default color and close the color palette.

6 Set the **Width** to **4 pt** either by selecting the existing text in the Width box and typing or by clicking the up spin box arrow as necessary.

7 Use the scroll bar on the right side of the Format Chart Area pane if necessary to scroll to the bottom of the pane, and then select the **Rounded corners** check box. On the Quick Access Toolbar, click **Save**, and then compare your screen with Figure 3.41.

FIGURE 3.41

Activity 3.20 | Formatting the Plot Area Gridlines and Axis Fonts in a Line Chart

5.2.2

1 To the right of the chart, if necessary click Chart Elements ⊞ to display the list of elements. Point to **Gridlines**, click the **arrow**, and then click **More Options** to display the **Format Major Gridlines** pane. Compare your screen with Figure 3.42.

FIGURE 3.42

2 Click the **Solid line** option button. Click the **Color arrow**, and be sure that **Orange, Accent 1**—in the fifth column, the first color—is selected.

3 Set the **Width** to **1 pt**.

4 In the chart, point to any of the dollar values on the **Vertical (Value) Axis**, right-click, and then click **Font**.

5 In the **Font** dialog box, change the **Font style** to **Bold**, and then change the **Font color** to **Black, Text 1**—in the second column, the first color. Click **OK**.

6 Use the same technique to format the font of the **Horizontal (Category) Axis** to **Bold** with **Black, Text 1**.

7 **Close** ⊠ the **Format Axis** pane. Click cell **A1** to deselect the chart. Click **Save** 🖫, and then compare your screen with Figure 3.43.

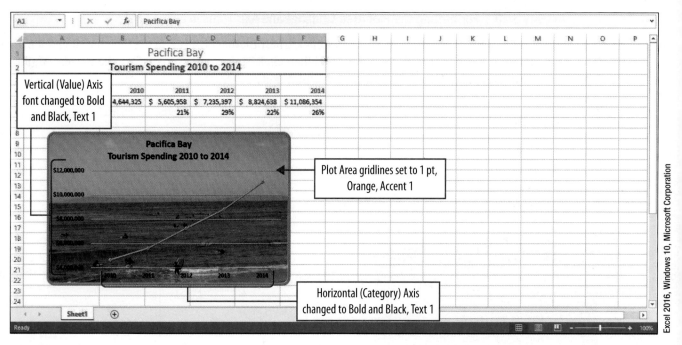

FIGURE 3.43

8 ▶ Click the **Page Layout tab**. In the **Page Setup group**, click **Margins**, and then click **Custom Margins**. In the **Page Setup** dialog box, on the **Margins tab**, under **Center on page**, select the **Horizontally** check box.

9 ▶ Click the **Header/Footer tab**, and then in the center of the dialog box, click **Custom Footer**. In the **Footer** dialog box, with your insertion point blinking in the **Left section**, on the row of buttons, click **Insert File Name** 🗐.

10 ▶ Click **OK** two times. Click the **File tab**, and then click **Show All Properties**. As the **Tags**, type **tourism spending** and as the **Subject**, type your course name and section number. Be sure your name displays as the **Author**.

11 ▶ On the left, click **Print** to display the **Print Preview**, and then compare your screen with Figure 3.44. If necessary, return to the worksheet and make any corrections.

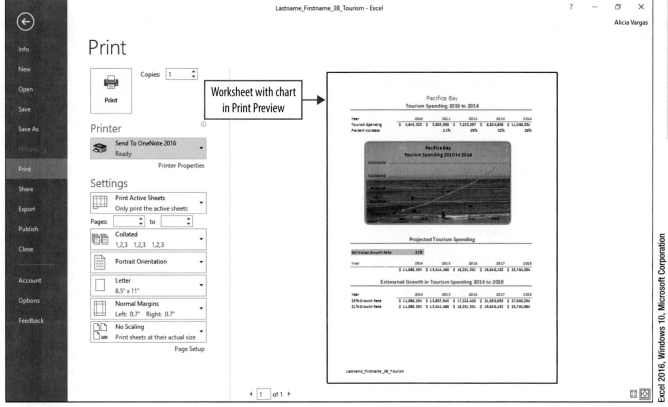

FIGURE 3.44

12 On the left, click **Save** to redisplay the workbook.

13 If directed by your instructor to do so, submit your paper printout, your electronic image of your document that looks like a printed document, or your original Excel file. If required by your instructor, print or create an electronic version of your worksheet with formulas displayed. In the upper right corner of the Excel window, click **Close** ☒.

More **Knowledge**   **Resizing a Chart**

To resize a chart, on the Chart Tools Format tab, in the Size group, type the dimensions in the Shape Height or Shape Width box. Or:

• To change the width of a chart, drag a left or right sizing handle.
• To change the height of a chart, drag a top or bottom sizing handle.
• To size a chart proportionately, hold down Shift and drag a corner sizing handle.

END | You have completed Project 3B

GO! With Google

> **ALERT!** | **Working with Web-Based Applications and Services**
>
> Computer programs and services on the web receive continuous updates and improvements, so the steps to complete this web-based activity may differ from the ones shown. You can often look at the screens and the information presented to determine how to complete the activity.
>
> If you do not already have a Google account, you will need to create one before you begin this Activity. Go to http://google.com and, in the upper right corner, click Sign In. On the Sign In screen, click Create Account. On the Create your Google Account page, complete the form, read and agree to the Terms of Service and Privacy Policy, and then click Next step. On the Welcome screen, click Get Started.

Activity | Create a Line Chart

1 From the desktop, open your browser, navigate to **http://google.com**, and then click the **Google Apps** menu . Click **Drive** , and then if necessary, sign in to your Google account.

2 Open your **GO! Web Projects** folder—or click New to create and then open this folder if necessary. In the left pane, click **NEW**, and then click **File upload**. Navigate to your student data files, click **e03_3B_Web**, and then click **Open**.

3 Right-click the file you uploaded, point to **Open with**, and then click **Google Sheets**.

4 Drag to select the years and values in the range **A4:F5**, and then on the menu bar, click **Insert**. On the menu, click **Chart**. With the **Recommendations** tab selected, click the **Line chart**, and then click **Insert**.

5 Point to the chart, and then drag down and to the left to position the chart so that its upper left corner is aligned with the upper left corner of cell **A21**.

6 In the upper right corner of the chart area, click the **down-pointing triangle**, and then click **Advanced edit**. Under **Title**, select the existing text. Type **Tourism Spending 2010 to 2014** and then press Enter.

7 Under **Legend**, click **Right**, and then click **None**. In the **Chart Editor**, to the right of the chart options, drag the vertical scroll bar down to display the **Axis** options. To the right of **Axis**, click **Horizontal**, and then click **Left vertical**. Click in the **Min** box, type **3000000** and then press Enter.

8 In the **Chart Editor**, scroll down to display all of the **Series** options. Click the **Point size arrow**, and then click **7px**. In the **Chart Editor**, click **Update**, and then compare your screen with Figure A.

9 Submit your file as directed by your instructor. Sign out of your Google account and close your browser.

FIGURE A

GO! To Work

MICROSOFT OFFICE SPECIALIST (MOS) SKILLS IN THIS CHAPTER	
PROJECT 3A	**PROJECT 3B**
5.1.1 Create a new chart	**1.3.5** Insert or delete columns or rows
5.2.2 Add and modify chart elements	**2.1.3** Paste data by using special paste options
5.2.4 Move charts to a chart sheet	**2.2.3** Format cells by using Format Painter

BUILD YOUR E-PORTFOLIO

An E-Portfolio is a collection of evidence, stored electronically, that showcases what you have accomplished while completing your education. Collecting and then sharing your work products with potential employers reflects your academic and career goals. Your completed documents from the following projects are good examples to show what you have learned: 3G, 3K, and 3L.

GO! FOR JOB SUCCESS

Video: Planning and Managing Your Career

Your instructor may assign this video to your class, and then ask you to think about, or discuss with your classmates, these questions:

FotolEdhar/Fotolia

When did you start career planning and what were the main steps you took to plan your career?

What have been your best sources for networking?

What advice would you give to others about how to stay employable throughout your career?

END OF CHAPTER

SUMMARY

Use pie charts when you want to show the relationship of each part to a whole. Consider using a pie chart when you have only one data series to plot and you do not have more than seven categories.

To create a pie chart, you must select two ranges. One range contains the labels for each pie slice; the other contains the values that add up to a total. Both ranges must have the same number of cells.

In formulas, Excel follows rules called the order of operations; expressions within parentheses are processed first, and multiplication and division are performed before addition and subtraction.

Use a line chart when you want to show trends over time. Time displays along the bottom axis and the data point values connect with a line. The curve and direction of the line make trends obvious.

GO! LEARN IT ONLINE

Review the concepts, key terms, and MOS skills in this chapter by completing these online challenges, which you can find at **MyITLab**.

Matching and Multiple Choice: Answer matching and multiple-choice questions to test what you learned in this chapter.

Lesson on the GO! Learn how to use all the new apps and features as they are introduced by Microsoft.

MOS Prep Quiz: Answer questions to review the MOS skills that you practiced in this chapter.

GO! COLLABORATIVE TEAM PROJECT (Available in MyITLab and Instructor Resource Center)

If your instructor assigns this project to your class, you can expect to work with one or more of your classmates—either in person or by using Internet tools—to create work products similar to those that you created in this chapter. A team is a group of workers who work together to solve a problem, make a decision, or create a work product. Collaboration is when you work together with others as a team in an intellectual endeavor to complete a shared task or achieve a shared goal.

PROJECT GUIDE FOR EXCEL CHAPTER 3

Your instructor will assign Projects from this list to ensure your learning and assess your knowledge.

		PROJECT GUIDE FOR EXCEL CHAPTER 3	
Project	Apply Skills from These Chapter Objectives	Project Type	Project Location
3A **MyITLab**	Objectives 1–4 from Project 3A	**3A Instructional Project (Grader Project)** Guided instruction to learn the skills in Project 3A.	In MyITLab and in text
3B **MyITLab**	Objectives 5–7 from Project 3B	**3B Instructional Project (Grader Project)** Guided instruction to learn the skills in Project 3B.	In MyITLab and in text
3C	Objectives 1–4 from Project 3A	**3C Skills Review (Scorecard Grading)** A guided review of the skills from Project 3A.	In text
3D	Objectives 5–7 from Project 3B	**3D Skills Review (Scorecard Grading)** A guided review of the skills from Project 3B.	In text
3E **MyITLab**	Objectives 1–4 from Project 3A	**3E Mastery (Grader Project)** **Mastery and Transfer of Learning** A demonstration of your mastery of the skills in Project 3A with extensive decision making.	In MyITLab and in text
3F **MyITLab**	Objectives 5–7 from Project 3B	**3F Mastery (Grader Project)** **Mastery and Transfer of Learning** A demonstration of your mastery of the skills in Project 3B with extensive decision making.	In MyITLab and in text
3G **MyITLab**	Objectives 1–7 from Projects 3A and 3B	**3G Mastery (Grader Project)** **Mastery and Transfer of Learning** A demonstration of your mastery of the skills in Projects 3A and 3B with extensive decision making.	In MyITLab and in text
3H	Combination of Objectives from Projects 3A and 3B	**3H GO! Fix It (Scorecard Grading)** **Critical Thinking** A demonstration of your mastery of the skills in Projects 3A and 3B by creating a correct result from a document that contains errors you must find.	Instructor Resource Center (IRC) and MyITLab
3I	Combination of Objectives from Projects 3A and 3B	**3I GO! Make It (Scorecard Grading)** **Critical Thinking** A demonstration of your mastery of the skills in Projects 3A and 3B by creating a result from a supplied picture.	IRC and MyITLab
3J	Combination of Objectives from Projects 3A and 3B	**3J GO! Solve It (Rubric Grading)** **Critical Thinking** A demonstration of your mastery of the skills in Projects 3A and 3B, your decision-making skills, and your critical-thinking skills. A task-specific rubric helps you self-assess your result.	IRC and MyITLab
3K	Combination of Objectives from Projects 3A and 3B	**3K GO! Solve It (Rubric Grading)** **Critical Thinking** A demonstration of your mastery of the skills in Projects 3A and 3B, your decision-making skills, and your critical-thinking skills. A task-specific rubric helps you self-assess your result.	In text
3L	Combination of Objectives from Projects 3A and 3B	**3L GO! Think (Rubric Grading)** **Critical Thinking** A demonstration of your understanding of the chapter concepts applied in a manner that you would outside of college. An analytic rubric helps you and your instructor grade the quality of your work by comparing it to the work an expert in the discipline would create.	In text
3M	Combination of Objectives from Projects 3A and 3B	**3M GO! Think (Rubric Grading)** **Critical Thinking** A demonstration of your understanding of the chapter concepts applied in a manner that you would outside of college. An analytic rubric helps you and your instructor grade the quality of your work by comparing it to the work an expert in the discipline would create.	IRC and MyITLab
3N	Combination of Objectives from Projects 3A and 3B	**3N You and GO! (Rubric Grading)** **Critical Thinking** A demonstration of your understanding of the chapter concepts applied in a manner that you would in a personal situation. An analytic rubric helps you and your instructor grade the quality of your work.	IRC and MyITLab
3O	Combination of Objectives from Projects 3A and 3B	**3O Collaborative Team Project for EXCEL Chapter 2 Critical Thinking** A demonstration of your understanding of concepts and your ability to work collaboratively in a group role-playing assessment, requiring both collaboration and self-management.	IRC and MyITLab
Capstone Project for EXCEL Chapters 1–3	Combination of Objectives from Chapters 1–3	A demonstration of your mastery of the skills in Chapters 1–3 with extensive decision making. **(Grader Project)**	IRC and MyITLab

GLOSSARY

GLOSSARY OF CHAPTER KEY TERMS

3-D The shortened term for *three-dimensional*, which refers to an image that appears to have all three spatial dimensions—length, width, and depth.

Absolute cell reference A cell reference that refers to cells by their fixed position in a worksheet; an absolute cell reference remains the same when the formula is copied.

Axis A line that serves as a frame of reference for measurement and which borders the chart plot area.

Base The starting point when you divide the amount of increase by it to calculate the rate of increase.

Bevel A shape effect that uses shading and shadows to make the edges of a shape appear to be curved or angled.

Category axis The area along the bottom of a chart that identifies the categories of data; also referred to as the x-axis.

Chart area The entire chart and all of its elements.

Chart sheet A workbook sheet that contains only a chart.

Data marker A column, bar, area, dot, pie slice, or other symbol in a chart that represents a single data point; related data points form a data series.

Data point A value that originates in a worksheet cell and that is represented in a chart by a data marker.

Data series Related data points represented by data markers; each data series has a unique color or pattern represented in the chart legend.

Enterprise fund A municipal government fund that reports income and expenditures related to municipal services for which a fee is charged in exchange for goods or services.

Explode The action of pulling out one or more pie slices from a pie chart for emphasis.

Formula AutoComplete An Excel feature which, after typing an = (equal sign) and the beginning letter or letters of a function name, displays a list of function names that match the typed letter(s).

Fund A sum of money set aside for a specific purpose.

General fund The term used to describe money set aside for the normal operating activities of a government entity such as a city.

Goal Seek A what-if analysis tool that finds the input needed in one cell to arrive at the desired result in another cell.

Legend A chart element that identifies the patterns or colors that are assigned to the categories in the chart.

Line chart A chart type that displays trends over time; time displays along the bottom axis and the data point values are connected with a line.

Major unit The value in a chart's value axis that determines the spacing between tick marks and between the gridlines in the plot area.

Order of operations The mathematical rules for performing multiple calculations within a formula.

Percent for new value = base percent + percent of increase The formula for calculating a percentage by which a value increases by adding the base percentage—usually 100%—to the percent increase.

Percentage rate of increase The percent by which one number increases over another number.

Pie chart A chart that shows the relationship of each part to a whole.

Plot area The area bounded by the axes of a chart, including all the data series.

Rate = amount of increase/base The mathematical formula to calculate a rate of increase.

Relative cell reference In a formula, the address of a cell based on the relative positions of the cell that contains the formula and the cell referred to in the formula.

Value after increase = base x percent for new value The formula for calculating the value after an increase by multiplying the original value—the base—by the percent for new value (see the *Percent for new value* formula).

Value axis A numerical scale on the left side of a chart that shows the range of numbers for the data points; also referred to as the y-axis.

What-if analysis The process of changing the values in cells to see how those changes affect the outcome of formulas in a worksheet.

x-axis Another name for the category axis.

y-axis Another name for the value axis.

Apply 3A skills from these Objectives:

1 Chart Data with a Pie Chart

2 Format a Pie Chart

3 Edit a Workbook and Update a Chart

4 Use Goal Seek to Perform What-If Analysis

Skills Review | Project 3C Parks

In the following Skills Review, you will edit a worksheet for Jerry Silva, City Parks Manager, which details the revenue generated from city parks and structures. Your completed worksheets will look similar to Figure 3.45.

PROJECT FILES

For Project 3C, you will need the following file:

e03C_Parks

You will save your workbook as:

Lastname_Firstname_3C_Parks

PROJECT RESULTS

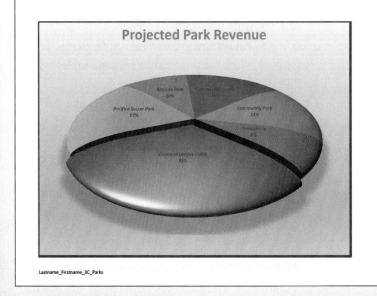

City of Pacifica Bay
Fee and Rental Revenue from City Parks
Projection for Next Fiscal Year Budget

	Current Year Revenue	Projected Revenue for Next Fiscal Year	% of Total Projected Budget
Community Park	$ 2,510,980	$ 2,536,529	14%
Grand Park	1,245,730	1,395,218	8%
Diamond League Fields	3,385,050	5,896,360	33%
Pacifica Soccer Park	2,231,050	3,423,515	19%
Bayside Park	1,907,890	1,812,297	10%
Community Center	2,582,340	2,736,081	15%
Total	$ 13,863,040	$ 17,800,000	

Lastname_Firstname_3C_Parks

FIGURE 3.45

(Project 3C Parks continues on the next page)

1 Start Excel. From your student data files, open the file **e03C_Parks**. Save the file in your **Excel Chapter 3** folder as **Lastname_Firstname_3C_Parks**

a. Click cell **D5**, and then type **=** to begin a formula. Click cell **C5**, type **/** and then click cell **C11**. Press F4 to make the reference to the value in cell **C11** absolute. On the **Formula Bar**, click **Enter**, and then fill the formula down through cell **D10**.

b. With the range **D5:D10** selected, right-click over the selection, and then on the mini toolbar, click **Percent Style** and **Center**.

2 Select the nonadjacent ranges **A5:A10** and **C5:C10** to select the park names and the projected revenue. Click the **Insert tab**, and then in the **Charts group**, click **Insert Pie or Doughnut Chart**. Under **3-D Pie**, click the chart type **3-D Pie**.

a. On the **Design tab**, in the **Location group**, click **Move Chart**. In the **Move Chart** dialog box, click the **New sheet** option button. In the **New sheet** box, replace the highlighted text *Chart1* by typing **Projected Park Revenue Chart** and then click **OK**.

b. Click the text *Chart Title*. Type **Projected Park Revenue** and then press Enter to create the new chart title.

c. With the title selected, on the **Format tab**, in the **WordArt Styles group**, click **More** to display the gallery. In the second row, select the fifth style— **Fill – Olive Green, Accent 3, Sharp Bevel**. Drag to select the chart title text, and then on the mini toolbar, change the **Font Size** to **32**.

d. Click in a white area of the chart to deselect the chart title. Click **Chart Elements**, and then click the **Legend** check box to remove the legend.

e. In the list of **Chart Elements**, point to **Data Labels**, click the **arrow** that displays, and then click **More Options**. In the **Format Data Labels** pane on the right, under **Label Options**, select the **Category Name** and **Percentage** check boxes, and *clear* all other check boxes. Under **Label Position**, click **Center**.

f. Point to any of the selected labels, right-click to display a shortcut menu, and then click **Font**. In the **Font** dialog box, on the **Font tab**, change the **Font style** to **Bold Italic** and change the **Size** to **11** Click **OK**.

3 In any pie slice, point anywhere outside the selected label, and then double-click to display the **Format Data Series** pane. Under **Series Options**, click **Effects**, and then click **3-D Format**.

a. Click the **Top bevel arrow**, and then under **Bevel**, click the first button—**Circle**. Apply the **Circle** bevel to the **Bottom bevel**.

b. Set the **Width** and **Height** of both the **Top bevel** and the **Bottom bevel** to **512 pt**

c. Scroll down, click the **Material arrow**, and then under **Standard**, click the third material—**Plastic**.

d. Scroll to the top of the **Format Data Series** pane, click **Shadow**, and then click the **Presets arrow**. Scroll down, and then under **Perspective**, in the first row, click the third effect—**Below**.

e. In the **Format Data Series** pane, under **Series Options**, click the third button—**Series Options**. Set the **Angle of first slice** to **50**

f. On the pie chart, click the **Diamond League Fields** slice to select only that slice, and then in the **Format Data Point** pane, set the **Point Explosion** to **10%**

g. With the **Diamond League Fields** slice still selected, in the **Format Data Point** pane, under **Series Options**, click **Fill & Line**, and then click **Fill** to expand the options.

h. Click the **Gradient fill** option button, click the **Preset gradients arrow**, and then in the fourth row, click the third gradient—**Bottom Spotlight – Accent 3**.

4 Point to the white area just inside the border of the chart to display the ScreenTip *Chart Area*, and then click one time to display the **Format Chart Area** pane.

a. Under **Chart Options**, click **Fill & Line**, and be sure the **Fill** options are still displayed.

b. Click the **Gradient fill** option button, click the **Preset gradients arrow**, and then in the first row, click the fifth gradient—**Light Gradient – Accent 5**.

c. In the **Format Chart Area** pane, click **Fill** to collapse the options, and then click **Border** to expand the options.

d. Click the **Solid line** option button, click the **Color arrow**, and then in the fifth column, click the last color—**Ice Blue, Accent 1, Darker 50%**. Set the **Width** of the border to **5 pt** Close the pane, and then **Save** your workbook.

(Project 3C Parks continues on the next page)

5 ▶ In the sheet tab area at the bottom of the workbook, click the **Sheet1 tab**.

a. Click cell **C11**. On the **Data tab**, in the **Forecast group**, click **What-If Analysis**, and then click **Goal Seek**. In the **Goal Seek** dialog box, press `Tab` to move to the **To value** box, and then type **17,800,000**

b. Press `Tab` to move the insertion point to the **By changing cell** box, and then click cell **C10**. Click **OK**. In the displayed **Goal Seek Status** dialog box, click **OK** to set the total projected revenue to $17,800,000 by changing the projected revenue for the Community Center.

6 ▶ With your worksheet displayed, in the sheet tab area, double-click *Sheet1* to select the text, and then type **Projected Park Revenue Data** and press `Enter`.

a. Click the **Page Layout tab**. In the **Page Setup Group**, click **Margins**, click **Custom Margins**, and then in the **Page Setup** dialog box, on the **Margins tab**, under **Center on page**, select the **Horizontally** check box.

b. Click the **Header/Footer tab**, click **Custom Footer**, and then with your insertion point in the **Left**

section, on the row of buttons, click **Insert File Name**. Click **OK** two times.

c. Display the **Projected Park Revenue Chart**, and then display the **Page Setup** dialog box.

d. Click the **Header/Footer tab**, click **Custom Footer**, and then in the **Left section**, click the **Insert File Name** button. Click **OK** two times.

e. Click the **File tab**, and then click **Show All Properties**. As the **Tags**, type **park revenue** As the **Subject**, type your course name and section number. Be sure your name displays as the **Author**.

f. **Save** your workbook. If directed by your instructor to do so, submit your paper printout, your electronic image of your document that looks like a printed document, or your original Excel file. If required by your instructor, print or create an electronic version of your worksheet with formulas displayed. In the upper right corner of the Excel window, click **Close**.

END | You have completed Project 3C

Skills Review Project 3D Housing Permits

In the following Skills Review, you will edit a worksheet that forecasts the revenue from new housing permits that the City of Pacifica Bay expects to collect in the five-year period 2014–2018. Your completed worksheet will look similar to Figure 3.46.

PROJECT FILES

For Project 3D, you will need the following files:

e03D_Housing_Permits
e03D_Housing

You will save your workbook as:

Lastname_Firstname_3D_Housing_Permits

PROJECT RESULTS

Pacifica Bay
Housing Permit Revenue Forecast

	2010	2011	2012	2013	2014
Permit Revenue	$ 1,945,923	$ 2,025,684	$ 2,115,783	$ 2,234,897	$ 2,397,445
Projected Increase		4%	4%	6%	7%

Projected Future Housing Permit Revenue

Forecasted Increase	**8%**				
Year	**2014**	**2015**	**2016**	**2017**	**2018**
Projected Permit Revenue	$ 2,397,445	$ 2,589,241	$ 2,796,380	$ 3,020,090	$ 3,261,697

Forecasted Revenue Estimates 2014 to 2018

Year	**2014**	**2015**	**2016**	**2017**	**2018**
7% Increase	$ 2,397,445	$ 2,565,266	$ 2,744,835	$ 2,936,973	$ 3,142,561
8% Increase	$ 2,397,445	$ 2,589,241	$ 2,796,380	$ 3,020,090	$ 3,261,697

Lastname_Firstname_3D_Housing_Permits

Excel 2016, Windows 10, Microsoft Corporation

FIGURE 3.46

(Project 3D Housing Permits continues on the next page)

1 Start Excel. From your student data files, open **e03D_Housing_Permits**. Using your own name, save the file in your **Excel Chapter 3** folder as **Lastname_Firstname_3D_Housing_Permits**

a. In cell **B4**, type **2010** and then press Tab. In cell **C4**, type **2011** and then press Enter.

b. Use the fill handle to fill the remaining years through **column F** so that the last year that displays is 2014.

2 Click cell **C6**. Being sure to include the parentheses, type **=(c5-b5)/b5** and then press Enter. Select cell **C6**, and then apply **Percent Style**.

a. With cell **C6** selected, drag the fill handle to the right through cell **F6**.

b. In cell **A8**, type **Projected Future Housing Permit Revenue** and then press Enter. Point to cell **A2**, right-click, on the mini toolbar, click **Format Painter**, and then click cell **A8**. In cell **A10**, type **Forecasted Increase** and then click cell **A12**. Type **Year**

c. In cell **A13**, type **Projected Permit Revenue** and then in cell **B12**, type **2014** and press Tab. In cell **C12**, type **2015** and then press Tab. Select the range **B12:C12**, and then drag the fill handle through cell **F12** to extend the pattern of years to *2018*. Apply **Bold** to the selection.

d. Right-click cell **F5**, and then click **Copy**. Right-click over cell **B13**, and then click **Paste**.

e. In cell **B10**, type **7%** which is the percent of increase from 2013 to 2014. Select the range **A10:B10**, and then from the mini toolbar, apply **Bold** and **Italic**.

3 Click cell **C13**. Type **=b13*(100%+b10)** and then on the **Formula Bar**, click **Enter** to keep the cell active. With cell **C13** as the active cell, drag the fill handle to copy the formula to the range **D13:F13**.

a. Point to cell **B13**, right-click, click **Format Painter**, and then select the range **C13:F13**.

b. Click cell **A15**. Type **Forecasted Revenue Estimates 2014 to 2018** and then press Enter. Use **Format Painter** to copy the format from cell **A8** to cell **A15**.

c. In the range **A17:A19**, type the following row titles:

Year

7% Increase

8% Increase

4 Select the range **B12:F12**, right-click over the selection, and then on the shortcut menu, click **Copy**. **Paste** the selection to the range **B17:F17**.

a. Select the range **B13:F13**, right-click over the selection, and then on the shortcut menu, click **Copy**. Point to cell **B18**, right-click, and then from the shortcut menu, point to **Paste Special**. Under **Paste Values**, click the second button—**Values & Number Formatting**. Press Esc to cancel the moving border.

b. Click cell **B10**. Type **8** and then press Enter. Copy the new values in the range **B13:F13**. Point to cell **B19**, right-click, and then point to **Paste Special**. Under **Paste Values**, click **Values & Number Formatting**. **Save** your workbook.

5 In the **row header area**, point to **row 8** to display the pointer, and then drag down to select **rows 8:24**. Right-click over the selection, and then click **Insert** to insert the same number of blank rows as you selected. Under the selection area near cell **A25**, click **Insert Options**, and then click the **Clear Formatting** option button to clear any formatting from these rows.

a. On the **Page Layout tab**, in the **Themes group**, click the **Colors arrow**, and then click **Yellow**. Select the range **A5:F5**. On the **Insert tab**, in the **Charts group**, click **Insert Line or Area Chart**. In the displayed gallery of line charts, click the **Line with Markers** chart type to create the chart.

b. Point to the border of the chart to display the [pointer icon] pointer, and then drag the chart so that its upper left corner is positioned in cell **A9**, aligned approximately under the *c* in the word *Projected* above.

c. Point to the Chart Title *Permit Revenue* and right-click. On the shortcut menu, click **Edit Text**. Type **Pacifica Bay Housing** and then press Spacebar. Press End and then press Enter to create a second line. Type **2010 to 2014**

d. Click the dashed border around the chart title to change it to a solid border, right-click over the title, and then on the shortcut menu, click **Font**. In the **Font** dialog box, change the **Font style** to **Bold**, change the **Size** to **16**, and change the **Font color** to **White, Background 1, Darker 5%**—in the first column, the second color. Click **OK**.

(Project 3D Housing Permits continues on the next page)

6 At the bottom of the chart, point to any of the numbers *1* through *5*, and then right-click. On the shortcut menu, click **Select Data**. On the right side of the **Select Data Source** dialog box, click **Edit**. In the worksheet, select the years in the range **B4:F4**, and then click **OK** two times to enter the years as the category labels.

a. With the **Horizontal (Category) Axis** still selected, click **Chart Elements**, point to **Axes**, click the **arrow**, and then click **More Options**. In the **Format Axis** pane, under **Axis Options**, click **Fill & Line**. If necessary, click Line to expand the options. Click the **No line** option button, and then **close** the **Format Axis** pane.

b. On the left side of the chart, point to any of the dollar values, right-click, and then click **Format Axis**. In the **Format Axis** pane, under **Bounds**, select the text in the **Minimum** box, and then type **1900000**

c. Under **Units**, in the **Major** box, select the existing text, and then type **50000**

d. Near the top of the **Format Axis** pane, click the **Axis Options arrow**, and then click **Chart Area** to display the **Format Chart Area** pane. Click **Fill & Line**.

e. In the **Format Chart Area** pane, click **Fill** to expand the options, and then click the **Picture or texture fill** option button. Under **Insert picture from**, click **File**. In the **Insert Picture** dialog box, navigate to the student data files, and then click **e03D_Housing**. Click **Insert**.

f. In the **Format Chart Area** pane, click **Fill** to collapse the options, and then if necessary click Border to expand the Border section. Click the **Solid line** option button, click the **Color arrow**, and then under **Theme Colors**, in the fifth column, click the first color—**Gold, Accent 1**. Set the **Width** to **4 pt** Scroll to the bottom of the pane, and then select the **Rounded corners** check box.

7 To the right of the chart, click **Chart Elements**, point to **Gridlines**, click the **arrow**, and then click **More Options** to display the **Format Major Gridlines** pane.

a. Under **Line**, click the **Solid line** option button. Click the **Color arrow**, and be sure that **Gold, Accent 1** is the selected color. Set the **Width** to **1 pt**

b. In the chart, point to any of the dollar values on the **Vertical (Value) Axis**, right-click, and then click **Font**. In the **Font** dialog box, change the **Font style** to **Bold**, and then change the **Font color** to **White, Background 1**—in the first column, the first color. Click **OK**.

c. By using the same technique, format the **Font** of the **Horizontal (Category) Axis** to **Bold** with **White, Background 1** as the font color.

d. **Close** the **Format Axis** pane, and then click cell **A1** to deselect the chart. Click the **Page Layout tab**. In the **Page Setup group**, click **Margins**, and then click **Custom Margins**. On the **Margins tab**, select the **Horizontally** check box. Click the **Header/Footer tab**, click **Custom Footer**, and then in the **Left section**, insert the file name. Click **OK** two times.

e. Click the **File tab**, and then click **Show All Properties**. As the **Tags**, type **housing permit revenue** In the **Subject** box, type your course name and section number. Be sure your name displays as the **Author**.

f. **Save** your workbook. If directed by your instructor to do so, submit your paper printout, your electronic image of your document that looks like a printed document, or your original Excel file. If required by your instructor, print or create an electronic version of your worksheet with formulas displayed. In the upper right corner of the Excel window, click **Close**.

END | You have completed Project 3D

Mastering Excel | Project 3E Revenue

In the following project, you will edit a worksheet that summarizes the revenue budget for the City of Pacifica Bay. Your completed worksheets will look similar to Figure 3.47.

Apply 3A skills from these Objectives:

1 Chart Data with a Pie Chart

2 Format a Pie Chart

3 Edit a Workbook and Update a Chart

4 Use Goal Seek to Perform What-If Analysis

PROJECT FILES

For Project 3E, you will need the following file:

e03E_Revenue

You will save your workbook as:

Lastname_Firstname_3E_Revenue

PROJECT RESULTS

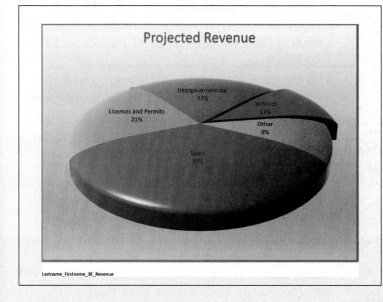

FIGURE 3.47

(Project 3E Revenue continues on the next page)

1 Start Excel. From your student data files, locate and open **e03E_Revenue**. **Save** the file in your **Excel Chapter 3** folder as **Lastname_Firstname_3E_Revenue**

2 In cell **D5**, construct a formula to calculate the **% of Total Projected Revenue** from **Taxes** by dividing the **Projected Revenue for Next Fiscal Year** for **Taxes** by the **Total Projected Revenue for Next Fiscal Year**. Use absolute cell references as necessary, format the result in **Percent Style**, and **Center** the percentage. Fill the formula down through cell **D9**.

3 Select the nonadjacent ranges **A5:A9** and **C5:C9** as the data for a pie chart, and then insert a **3-D Pie** chart. Move the chart to a **New sheet** named **Projected Revenue Chart**

4 As the text for the **Chart Title** element, type **Projected Revenue** Format the **Chart Title** using the **WordArt Style Fill – Aqua, Accent 1, Shadow**—in the first row, the second style and a **Font Size** of **32**.

5 Remove the **Legend** chart element, and then add the **Data Labels** chart element formatted so that only the **Category Name** and **Percentage** display positioned in the **Center**. Format the data labels with a **Font style** of **Bold** and a **Font Size** of **14**.

6 Format the **Data Series** using a **3-D Format** effect. Change the **Top bevel** and **Bottom bevel** to **Art Deco**. Set the **Top bevel Width** and **Height** to **350 pt** and then set the **Bottom bevel Width** and **Height** to **0 pt** Change the **Material** to the second **Special Effect—Soft Edge**.

7 Display the **Series Options**, and then set the **Angle of first slice** to **115** so that the **Taxes** slice is in the front of the pie.

8 Select the **Services** slice, and then explode the slice **10%**. Change the **Fill Color** of the **Services** slice to a **Solid fill** using **Gray-50%, Accent 4**—in the eighth column, the first color.

9 Format the **Chart Area** by applying a **Gradient fill** using the **Preset gradients Light Gradient – Accent 4**. Format the **Border** of the **Chart Area** by applying a **Solid line** border using **Gray-50%, Accent 4** and a **5 pt Width**. Close any panes that are open on the right.

10 Display the **Page Setup** dialog box, and then for this chart sheet, insert a **Custom Footer** in the **left section** with the file name.

11 Display the **Revenue Sources sheet**. Click cell **C10**, and then use **Goal Seek** to determine the projected amount of Other revenue in cell **C9** if the value in **C10** is **150,125,000**

12 Display the **Page Setup** dialog box, center the worksheet **Horizontally**, and then insert a custom footer in the **left section** with the file name.

13 Show all the properties, and then as the **Tags**, type **revenue sources** As the **Subject**, type your course name and section number. Be sure your name displays as the **Author**. **Save** your workbook. If directed by your instructor to do so, submit your paper printout, your electronic image of your document that looks like a printed document, or your original Excel file. If required by your instructor, print or create an electronic version of your worksheet with formulas displayed. In the upper right corner of the Excel window, click **Close**.

END | You have completed Project 3E

Mastering Excel **Project 3F Streets**

Apply 3B skills from these Objectives:

5 Design a Worksheet for What-If Analysis

6 Answer What-If Questions by Changing Values in a Worksheet

7 Chart Data with a Line Chart

In the following project, you will edit a worksheet that the City of Pacifica Bay Facilities Director will use to prepare a five-year forecast of the costs associated with street maintenance. Your completed worksheet will look similar to Figure 3.48.

PROJECT FILES

For Project 3F, you will need the following file:

New blank Excel workbook

You will save your workbook as:

Lastname_Firstname_3F_Streets

Build from Scratch

PROJECT RESULTS

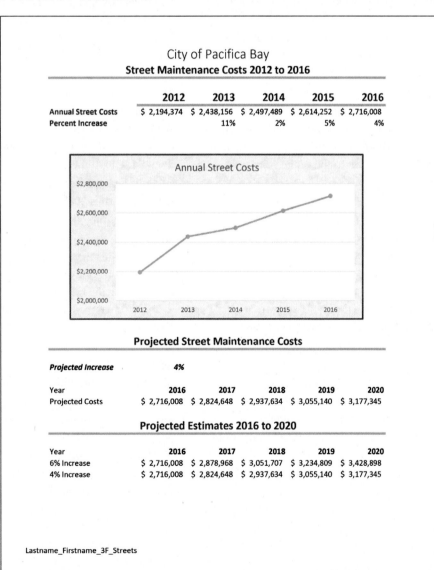

FIGURE 3.48

(Project 3F Streets continues on the next page)

Mastering Excel | **Project 3F Streets** (continued)

1 Start Excel and display a new **Blank workbook**. **Save** the file in your **Excel Chapter 3** folder as **Lastname_Firstname_3F_Streets**

2 Change the **Theme Colors** to **Paper**. In cell **A1**, type the title **City of Pacifica Bay** and then **Merge & Center** the title across **columns A:F**. Apply the **Title** cell style.

3 In cell **A2** type the subtitle **Street Maintenance Costs 2012 to 2016** and then **Merge & Center** the subtitle across **columns A:F**. Apply the **Heading 1** cell style.

4 In the range **B4:F4**, fill the year range with the values 2012 through 2016. In cell **A5** type **Annual Street Costs** and in cell **A6** type **Percent Increase**

5 Change the width of **column A** to **145 pixels**, and then change the width of **columns B:F** to **82 pixels**. In the range **B5:F5** type **2194374** and **2438156** and **2497489** and **2614252** and **2716008**

6 Select **B5:F5**, display the **Cell Styles** gallery, and then apply the **Currency [0]** cell style to the values in **B5:F5**. Apply the **Heading 1** cell style to the years, and apply the **Heading 4** cell style to the range **A5:A6**.

7 In cell **C6**, construct a formula to calculate the percent of increase in annual street maintenance costs from 2012 to 2013. Format the result with the **Percent Style** and then fill the formula through cell **F6** to calculate the percent of increase in each year.

8 In cell **A8**, type **Projected Street Maintenance Costs** and then use **Format Painter** to copy the formatting from cell **A2** to cell **A8**. In cell **A10**, type **Projected Increase** and then in cell **A12**, type **Year**

9 In cell **A13**, type **Projected Costs** and then in the range **B12:F12**, use the fill handle to enter the years 2016 through 2020. Apply **Bold** to the years. **Copy** the value in cell **F5** to cell **B13**. In cell **B10**, type **6%** which is the projected increase estimated by the City financial analysts. To the range **A10:B10**, apply **Bold** and **Italic**.

10 In cell **C13**, construct a formula to calculate the annual projected street maintenance costs for the year 2017 after the projected increase of 6% is applied. Fill the formula through cell **F13**, and then use **Format Painter** to copy the formatting from cell **B13** to the range **C13:F13**.

11 In cell **A15**, type **Projected Estimates 2016 to 2020** and then use **Format Painter** to copy the format from cell **A8** to cell **A15**. In cells **A17:A19**, type the following row titles:

> **Year**
>
> **6% Increase**
>
> **4% Increase**

12 **Copy** the range **B12:F12**, and then **Paste** the selection to **B17:F17**. Copy the range **B13:F13** and then paste the **Values & Number Formatting** to the range **B18:F18**. Complete the Projected Estimates section of the worksheet by changing the *Projected Increase* in **B10** to **4%** and then copying and pasting the **Values & Number Formatting** to the appropriate range in the worksheet. **Save** your workbook.

13 Select **rows 8:24**, and then **Insert** the same number of blank rows as you selected. **Clear Formatting** from the inserted rows. By using the data in **A4:F5**, insert a **Line with Markers** chart in the worksheet. Move the chart so that its upper left corner is positioned in cell **A9** and visually centered under the data above.

14 Format the **Bounds** of the **Vertical (Value) Axis** so that the **Minimum** is **2000000** and the **Major unit** is **200000**

15 Format the **Fill** of the **Chart Area** with a **Texture fill** by applying the **Parchment** texture—in the third row, the fifth texture. Format the **Chart Area** with a **Border** by applying a **Solid line** using **Olive Green, Accent 1, Darker 50%**—in the fifth column, the last color. Change the **Width** of the border to **2 pt**. Format the **Plot Area** with a **Solid fill** using **White, Background 1**—in the first column, the first color.

16 Click cell **A1** to deselect the chart. Center the worksheet **Horizontally**, and then insert a **Custom Footer** in the **left section** with the file name.

17 Show all the properties, and then as the **Tags**, type **street maintenance costs** As the **Subject**, type your course name and section number. Be sure your name displays as the **Author**. **Save** your workbook. If directed by your instructor to do so, submit your paper printout, your electronic image of your document that looks like a printed document, or your original Excel file. If required by your instructor, print or create an electronic version of your worksheet with formulas displayed. In the upper right corner of the Excel window, click **Close**.

END | You have completed Project 3F

Mastering Excel | Project 3G Expenses

In the following project, you will you will edit a workbook for Jennifer Carson, City Finance Manager. Your completed worksheets will look similar to Figure 3.49.

Apply a combination of 3A and 3B skills:

1 Chart Data with a Pie Chart

2 Format a Pie Chart

3 Edit a Workbook and Update a Chart

4 Use Goal Seek to Perform What-If Analysis

5 Design a Worksheet for What-If Analysis

6 Answer What-If Questions by Changing Values in a Worksheet

7 Chart Data with a Line Chart

PROJECT FILES

For Project 3G, you will need the following file:

e03G_Expenses

You will save your workbook as

Lastname_Firstname_3G_Expenses

PROJECT RESULTS

FIGURE 3.49

Excel 2016, Windows 10, Microsoft Corporation

(Project 3G Expenses continues on the next page)

1 Start Excel. From your student data files, open **e03G_Expenses**. **Save** the file in your **Excel Chapter 3** folder as **Lastname_Firstname_3G_Expenses**

2 In the **Expenses** worksheet, calculate row totals for each Expense item in the range **F5:F9**. Calculate column totals for each quarter and for the Annual Total in the range **B10:F10**. Be sure that **F6:F9** are formatted with **Comma Style** and zero decimal places.

3 In cell **G5**, construct a formula to calculate the **Percent of Total** by dividing the **Annual Total** for **Salaries and Benefits** by the **Annual Total** for all quarters. Use absolute cell references as necessary, format the result in **Percent Style**, and then **Center**. Fill the formula down through cell **G9**.

4 Use a **3-D Pie** chart to chart the **Annual Total** for each item. Move the chart to a **New sheet**; name the sheet **Annual Expenses Chart**

5 As the text for the **Chart Title** element, type **Summary of Annual Expenses** Format the **Chart Title** using **WordArt Style Fill - Blue, Accent 1, Shadow**—in the first row, the second style and a **Font Size** of **28**.

6 Remove the **Legend** from the chart, and then add **Data Labels** formatted so that only the **Category Name** and **Percentage** display positioned in the **Center**. Format the data labels by applying a **Font style** of **Bold** and **Italic** and a **Font Size** of **12**.

7 Format the **Data Series** using a **3-D Format** effect. Change the **Top bevel** and **Bottom bevel** to **Circle**. Set the **Top bevel Width** and **Height** to **50 pt** and then set the **Bottom bevel Width** and **Height** to **256 pt** Change the **Material** to the fourth **Standard Effect—Metal**.

8 Display the **Series Options**, and then set the **Angle of first slice** to **125** so that the **Salaries and Benefits** slice is in the front of the pie. Select the **Salaries and Benefits** slice, and then explode the slice **10%**. Change the **Fill Color** of the **Salaries and Benefits** slice to a **Solid fill** using **Green, Accent 6, Lighter 40%**—in the last column, the fourth color.

9 Format the **Chart Area** by applying a **Gradient fill** using the **Preset gradients Light Gradient – Accent 4**. Format the **Border** of the **Chart Area** by adding a **Solid line** border using **Gold, Accent 4** and a **5 pt Width**.

10 Display the **Page Setup** dialog box, and then for this chart sheet, insert a **Custom Footer** in the **left section** with the file name. **Save** your workbook.

11 Display the **Expenses** worksheet, and then by using the Quarter names and the Totals by Quarter, insert a **Line with Markers** chart in the worksheet. Do *not* include the Annual Total. Move the chart so that its upper left corner is positioned slightly inside the upper left corner of cell **A12**, and then drag the center-right sizing handle so that the chart extends to slightly inside the right border of **column G**. As the **Chart Title**, type **City of Pacifica Bay Annual Expense Summary**

12 Format the **Bounds** of the **Vertical (Value) Axis** so that the **Minimum** is **2100000** and the **Major unit** is **50000** Format the **Fill** of the **Chart Area** with a **Gradient fill** by applying the **Preset gradient Light Gradient - Accent 3**—in the first row, the third gradient. Format the **Plot Area** with a **Solid fill** using **White, Background 1**—in the first column, the first color. Close any panes on the right, click cell **A1** to deselect the chart, and then **Save** your workbook.

13 **Copy** the **Annual Total** in cell **F10** and then use **Paste Special** to paste **Values & Number Formatting** in cell **B35**. In cell **C35**, construct a formula to calculate the **Projected Expenses** after the forecasted increase of **3.5%** in cell **B31** is applied. Fill the formula through cell **F35**, and then use **Format Painter** to copy the formatting from cell **B35** to the range **C35:F35**.

14 Change the **Orientation** of this worksheet to **Landscape**, and then use the **Scale to Fit** options to fit the **Height** to **1 page**. In the **Page Setup** dialog box, center this worksheet **Horizontally**, and insert a **Custom Footer** in the **left section** with the file name. **Save** your workbook.

15 Show all the properties, and then as the **Tags**, type **annual expense summary** As the **Subject**, type your course name and section number. Be sure your name displays as the **Author**. **Save** your workbook. If directed by your instructor to do so, submit your paper printout, your electronic image of your document that looks like a printed document, or your original Excel file. If required by your instructor, print or create an electronic version of your worksheet with formulas displayed. In the upper right corner of the Excel window, click **Close**.

END | You have completed Project 3G

GO! Fix It	Project 3H Schools	MyITLab

GO! Make It	Project 3I Tax	MyITLab

GO! Solve It	Project 3J Staffing	MyITLab

GO! Solve It	Project 3K Water Usage	

Build from
Scratch

PROJECT FILES

For Project 3K, you will need the following file:

New blank Excel workbook

You will save your workbook as:

Lastname_Firstname_3K_Water_Usage

Pacifica Bay is a growing community and the City Council has requested an analysis of future resource needs. In this project, you will create a worksheet for the Department of Water and Power that illustrates residential water usage over a five-year period. Create a worksheet with the following data:

	2014	2015	2016	2017	2018
Water Use in Acre Feet	62518	65922	71864	76055	82542

Calculate the percent increase for the years 2015 to 2018. Below the Percent Increase, insert a line chart that illustrates the city's water usage from 2014 to 2018. Format the chart and worksheet attractively with a title and subtitle, and apply appropriate formatting. Include the file name in the footer and enter appropriate document properties. Save the workbook as **Lastname_Firstname_3K_Water_Usage** and submit as directed.

Performance Level

	Exemplary: You consistently applied the relevant skills	Proficient: You sometimes, but not always, applied the relevant skills	Developing: You rarely or never applied the relevant skills
Create formulas	All formulas are correct and are efficiently constructed.	Formulas are correct but not always constructed in the most efficient manner.	One or more formulas are missing or incorrect or only numbers were entered.
Insert and format line chart	Line chart created correctly and is attractively formatted.	Line chart was created but the data was incorrect or the chart was not appropriately formatted.	No line chart was created.
Format attractively and appropriately	Formatting is attractive and appropriate.	Adequately formatted but difficult to read or unattractive.	Inadequate or no formatting.

Performance Criteria

END | You have completed Project 3K

RUBRIC

The following outcomes-based assessments are open-ended assessments. That is, there is no specific correct result; your result will depend on your approach to the information provided. Make Professional Quality your goal. Use the following scoring rubric to guide you in how to approach the problem and then to evaluate how well your approach solves the problem.

The *criteria*—Software Mastery, Content, Format and Layout, and Process—represent the knowledge and skills you have gained that you can apply to solving the problem. The *levels of performance*—Professional Quality, Approaching Professional Quality, or Needs Quality Improvements—help you and your instructor evaluate your result.

	Your completed project is of Professional Quality if you:	Your completed project is Approaching Professional Quality if you:	Your completed project Needs Quality Improvements if you:
1-Software Mastery	Choose and apply the most appropriate skills, tools, and features and identify efficient methods to solve the problem.	Choose and apply some appropriate skills, tools, and features, but not in the most efficient manner.	Choose inappropriate skills, tools, or features, or are inefficient in solving the problem.
2-Content	Construct a solution that is clear and well organized, contains content that is accurate, appropriate to the audience and purpose, and is complete. Provide a solution that contains no errors in spelling, grammar, or style.	Construct a solution in which some components are unclear, poorly organized, inconsistent, or incomplete. Misjudge the needs of the audience. Have some errors in spelling, grammar, or style, but the errors do not detract from comprehension.	Construct a solution that is unclear, incomplete, or poorly organized; contains some inaccurate or inappropriate content; and contains many errors in spelling, grammar, or style. Do not solve the problem.
3-Format & Layout	Format and arrange all elements to communicate information and ideas, clarify function, illustrate relationships, and indicate relative importance.	Apply appropriate format and layout features to some elements, but not others. Overuse features, causing minor distraction.	Apply format and layout that does not communicate information or ideas clearly. Do not use format and layout features to clarify function, illustrate relationships, or indicate relative importance. Use available features excessively, causing distraction.
4-Process	Use an organized approach that integrates planning, development, self-assessment, revision, and reflection.	Demonstrate an organized approach in some areas, but not others; or, use an insufficient process of organization throughout.	Do not use an organized approach to solve the problem.

<table>
<tr><td>Apply a combination of the 3A and 3B skills.</td><td>GO! Think   Project 3L Employment</td></tr>
</table>

PROJECT FILES

Build from Scratch

For Project 3L, you will need the following file:

New blank Excel workbook

You will save your workbook as:

Lastname_Firstname_3L_Employment

Sandy Ingram, the Director of the Employment Development Department for the city of Pacifica Bay, has requested an analysis of employment sectors in the city. Employment data for the previous two years is listed below:

Job Sector	2015 Employment	2016 Employment
Government	1,795	1,524
Healthcare	2,832	2,952
Retail	2,524	2,480
Food Service	3,961	3,753
Industrial	1,477	1,595
Professional	2,515	2,802

Create a workbook to provide Sandy with the employment information for each sector and the total employment for each year. Insert a column to calculate the percent change from 2015 to 2016. Note that some of the results will be negative numbers. Format the percentages with two decimal places. Insert a pie chart in its own sheet that illustrates the 2016 employment figures, and format the chart attractively. Format the worksheet so that it is professional and easy to read and understand. Insert a footer with the file name and add appropriate document properties. Save the file as **Lastname_Firstname_3L_Employment** and print or submit as directed by your instructor.

> **END | You have completed Project 3L**

Build From Scratch

GO! Think   **Project 3M Population**   **MyITLab**

Build From Scratch

You and GO!   **Project 3N Expense Analysis**   **MyITLab**

Build From Scratch

GO! Collaborative Team Project   **Project 3O Bell Orchid Hotels**   **MyITLab**

Use Financial and Lookup Functions, Define Names, Validate Data, and Audit Worksheets

4

OUTCOMES
Calculate loan options and create a loan amortization schedule.

OUTCOMES
Automate workbooks to look up information automatically and to validate data. Audit workbook formulas to locate and correct errors.

OBJECTIVES

1. Use Financial Functions
2. Use Goal Seek
3. Create a Data Table
4. Use Defined Names in a Formula

OBJECTIVES

5. Use Lookup Functions
6. Validate Data
7. Audit Worksheet Formulas
8. Use the Watch Window to Monitor Cell Values

Anna Issakova/Fotolia

In This Chapter

GO! to Work with Excel

In this chapter, you will use Financial functions and What-If Analysis tools to make your worksheets more valuable for analyzing data and making financial decisions. In addition, you will define names and use them in a formula. You will use the Lookup functions to locate information that is needed in a form and create a validation list to ensure that only accurate data is entered. In this chapter, you will also use Excel's auditing features to help you understand the construction of formulas in a worksheet and to locate and correct any errors. For example, by tracing relationships you will be able to test your formulas for accuracy.

The projects in this chapter relate to **Jesse Jewelers**, a Toronto-based retailer of jewelry and accessories for men and women. Jesse sells unique and beautiful items at a great price. Products include necklaces, bracelets, key chains, business cases, jewelry boxes, handmade bags, and personalized items. Founded in 2005 by two college friends, this growing company has several retail locations and an online store. The company distributes its products to department and specialty stores throughout the United States and Canada. Jesse Jewelers provides exceptional customer service from a well-trained staff of product experts.

PROJECT 4A Amortization Schedule and Merchandise Costs

MyITLab
Project 4A Training
Project 4A Grader

PROJECT ACTIVITIES

In Activities 4.01 through 4.09, you will create a worksheet for Alaina Dubois, International Sales Director for Jesse Jewelers, that details the loan information to purchase furniture and fixtures for a new store in Houston. You will also define names for ranges of cells in a workbook containing quarterly and annual merchandise costs for the new store. Your completed worksheets will look similar to Figure 4.1.

Please always review the downloaded Grader instructions before beginning.

PROJECT FILES

MyITLab grader — If your instructor wants you to submit Project 4A in the MyITLab Grader system, log in to MyITLab, locate Grader Project 4A, and then download the files for this project.

For Project 4A, you will need the following file:
e04A_Loan_and_Costs

You will save your workbook as:
Lastname_Firstname_4A_Loan_and_Costs

PROJECT RESULTS

GO!
Walk Thru
Project 4A

Excel 2016, Windows 10, Microsoft Corporation

FIGURE 4.1 Project 4A Amortization Schedule and Merchandise Costs

NOTE	If You Are Using a Touchscreen
	Tap an item to click it.
	Press and hold for a few seconds to right-click; release when the information or commands displays.
	Touch the screen with two or more fingers and then pinch together to zoom out or stretch your fingers apart to zoom in.
	Slide your finger on the screen to scroll—slide left to scroll right and slide right to scroll left.
	Slide to rearrange—similar to dragging with a mouse.
	Swipe to select—slide an item a short distance with a quick movement—to select an item and bring up commands, if any.

Objective 1 Use Financial Functions

GO! Learn How
Video E4-1

Financial functions are prebuilt formulas that make common business calculations such as calculating a loan payment on a vehicle or calculating how much to save each month to buy something. Financial functions commonly involve a period of time such as months or years.

When you borrow money from a bank or other lender, the amount charged to you for your use of the borrowed money is called *interest*. Loans are typically made for a period of years, and the interest that must be paid is a percentage of the loan amount that is still owed. In Excel, this interest percentage is called the *rate*.

The initial amount of the loan is called the *Present value (Pv)*, which is the total amount that a series of future payments is worth now, and is also known as the *principal*. When you borrow money, the loan amount is the present value to the lender. The number of time periods—number of payments—is abbreviated *Nper*. The value at the end of the time periods is the *Future value (Fv)*—the cash balance you want to attain after the last payment is made. The future value is usually zero for loans, because you will have paid off the full amount at the end of the term.

Activity 4.01 | Inserting the PMT Financial Function

ALERT!
To submit as an autograded project, log into MyITLab, download the files for this project, and then begin with those files instead of e04A_Loan_and_Costs.

MOS
3.4.5 Expert

In this Activity, you will calculate the monthly payments that Jesse Jewelers must make to finance the purchase of the furniture and fixtures for a new store in Houston, the total cost of which is $300,000. You will calculate the monthly payments, including interest, for a three-year loan at an annual interest rate of 4.0%. To stay within Alaina's budget, the monthly payment must be approximately $8,000.

1 ▶ Start Excel, and then on Excel's opening screen, on the left, click **Open Other Workbooks**. Click **Browse**, and then from the student data files that accompany this chapter, open **e04A_Loan_and_Costs**. Display the **Save As** dialog box, navigate to the location where you will store your workbooks for this chapter, and then create a new folder named **Excel Chapter 4** Open the folder, and then **Save** the workbook as **Lastname_Firstname_4A_Loan_and_Costs** Compare your screen with Figure 4.2.

FIGURE 4.2

2 Be sure that the **Houston New Store Loan** worksheet is active, and then click cell **B5**. On the **Formulas tab**, in the **Function Library group**, click **Financial**. In the list, scroll down as necessary, and then click **PMT**.

> The Function Arguments dialog box displays. Recall that **arguments** are the values that an Excel function uses to perform calculations or operations.

3 If necessary, drag the Function Arguments dialog box to the right side of your screen so you can view columns A:B.

> The **PMT function** calculates the payment for a loan based on constant payments and at a constant interest rate.

4 With your insertion point positioned in the **Rate** box, type **b4/12** and then compare your screen with Figure 4.3.

> Excel will divide the annual interest rate of 4%, which is 0.04 in decimal notation, located in cell B4 by 12 (months), which will result in a *monthly* interest rate.

> When borrowing money, the interest rate and number of periods are quoted in years. The payments on a loan, however, are usually made monthly. Therefore, the number of periods, which is stated in years, and the *annual* interest rate must be changed to a monthly equivalent in order to calculate the monthly payment amount. You can see that calculations like these can be made as part of the argument in a function.

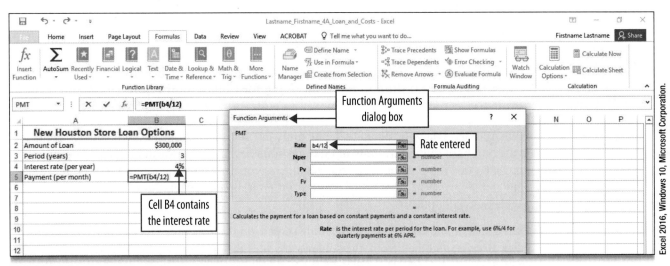

FIGURE 4.3

5 Press [Tab] to move the insertion point to the **Nper** box. In the lower portion of the dialog box, notice Excel points out that *Nper is the total number of payments for the loan* (number of periods).

248 **Excel** | Chapter 4: USE FINANCIAL AND LOOKUP FUNCTIONS, DEFINE NAMES

> 6 ▸ Type **b3*12** to have Excel convert the number of years in the loan in cell B3 (3 years) to the total number of months.

> Recall that the PMT function calculates a *monthly* payment. Therefore, all values in the function must be expressed in months. To complete the PMT function, you must determine the total number of loan payment periods (months), which is 3 years × 12 months per year, or 36 months.

> 7 ▸ Press [Tab] to move to the **Pv** box, and then type **b2** to indicate the cell that contains the amount of the loan.

> Pv represents the present value—the amount of the loan before any payments are made. In this instance, the Pv is $300,000.

> 8 ▸ In cell **B5** and on the **Formula Bar**, notice that the arguments that comprise the PMT function are separated by commas. Notice also, in the **Function Arguments** dialog box, that the value of each argument displays to the right of the argument box. Compare your screen with Figure 4.4.

N O T E   Optional Arguments

The PMT function has two arguments not indicated by bold; these are optional. The future value (Fv) argument assumes that the unpaid portion of the loan should be zero at the end of the last period. The *Type* argument indicates when the loan payment is due. If not specified, the *Type* argument assumes that the payment will be made at the end of each period. These default values are typical of most loans and may be left blank.

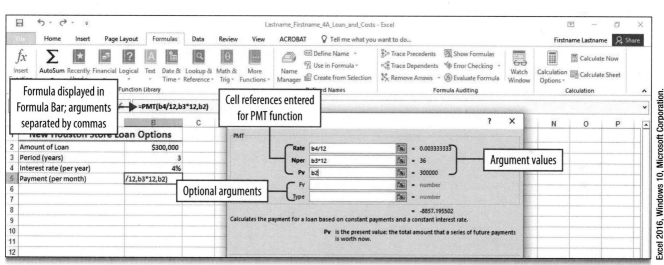

FIGURE 4.4

> 9 ▸ In the lower right corner of the **Function Arguments** dialog box, click **OK**.

> The monthly payment amount—($8,857.20)—displays in cell B5. The amount displays in red and in parentheses to show that it is a negative number, a number that will be paid out. This monthly payment of $8,857.20 is larger than the $8,000 per month that Alaina has budgeted for her payments.

> 10 ▸ Click in the **Formula Bar**, and then using the arrow keys on the keyboard, position the insertion point between the equal sign and *PMT*. Type – (minus sign) to insert a minus sign into the formula, and then press [Enter].

> By placing a minus sign in the formula, the monthly payment amount of $8,857.20 displays in cell B5 as a *positive* number, which is more familiar and simpler to work with.

> 11 ▸ **Save** 🖫 your workbook.

GO! Learn How
Video E4-2

What-If Analysis is a process of changing the values in cells to determine how those changes affect the outcome of formulas on the worksheet; for example, you might vary the interest rate to determine the amount of loan payments.

Goal Seek is part of a suite of data tools used for What-If Analysis. It is a method to find a specific value for a cell by adjusting the value of another cell. With Goal Seek, you can work backward from the desired outcome to find the number necessary to achieve your goal. If you have a result in mind, you can try different numbers in one of the cells used as an argument in the function until you get close to the result you want.

Activity 4.02 │ Using Goal Seek to Produce a Desired Result

3.4.3 Expert

Alaina knows that her budget cannot exceed $8,000 per month for the new store loan. The amount of $300,000 is necessary to purchase the furniture and fixtures to open the new store. Now she has two options: borrow less money and reduce the amount or quality of the furniture and fixtures in the store or extend the time to repay the loan. To find out how much she can borrow for three years to stay within the budget or how much to increase the repayment period, you will use the Goal Seek tool.

1️⃣ Click cell **B5**. On the **Data tab**, in the **Forecast group**, click **What-If Analysis**, and then on the list, click **Goal Seek**. In the **Goal Seek** dialog box, in the **Set cell** box, confirm that *B5* displays.

The cell address in this box is the cell that will display the desired result.

2️⃣ Press ⎇Tab. In the **To value** box, type the payment goal of **8000** and press ⎇Tab. In the **By changing cell** box, type **b2** which is the amount of the loan, and then compare your screen with Figure 4.5.

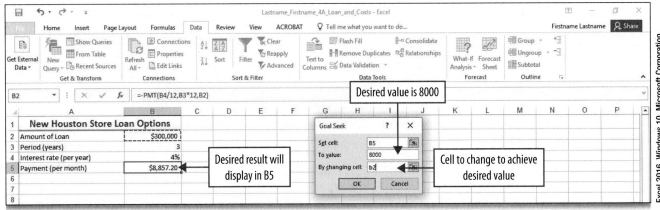

FIGURE 4.5

3️⃣ Click **OK**, and then in the **Goal Seek Status** dialog box, click **OK**.

Excel's calculations indicate that to achieve a monthly payment of $8,000.00 using a 3-year loan, Alaina can borrow only *$270,966*—not $300,000.

4️⃣ Click cell **A7**. Type **Option #1 Reduce Loan Amount** and then on the **Formula Bar**, click **Enter** ✓ to keep the cell active. Select the range **A7:B7**, and then from the **Home tab**, **Merge & Center** 🔲▾ this heading. Display the **Cell Styles** gallery, and then under **Titles and Headings**, click the **Heading 2** cell style.

5 Select the range **A2:B5**, right-click, and then click **Copy**. Point to cell **A8**, right-click, point to **Paste Special**, and then under **Paste Values**, click the **second** button—**Values & Number Formatting (A)** . Press Esc to cancel the moving border.

🔄 **ANOTHER WAY**   Click cell A8, right-click, and then click Paste Special. In the Paste Special dialog box, under Paste, click the Values and number formats option button, and then click OK.

6 **Save** 🖫 your workbook, and then compare your worksheet with Figure 4.6.

Recall that by using the Paste Special command, you can copy the *value* in a cell, rather than the formula, and the cell formats are retained—cell B5 contains the PMT function formula, and here you need only the value that *results* from that formula.

FIGURE 4.6

7 In cell **B2**, replace the existing value by typing **300000** and then press Enter to restore the original loan amount.

Activity 4.03 │ Using Goal Seek to Find an Increased Period

For Alaina's purchase of furniture and fixtures for the new store in Houston, an alternative to borrowing less money—which would mean buying fewer items or items of lesser quality—would be to increase the number of years of payments.

1 Be sure that you have restored cell A2 to $300,000, and then click cell **B5**. On the **Data tab**, in the **Forecast group**, click **What-If Analysis**, and then click **Goal Seek**.

2 In the **Set cell** box, confirm that *B5* displays. Press Tab. In the **To value** box, type **8000** and press Tab. In the **By changing cell** box, type **b3** which is the number of years for the loan. Compare your screen with Figure 4.7.

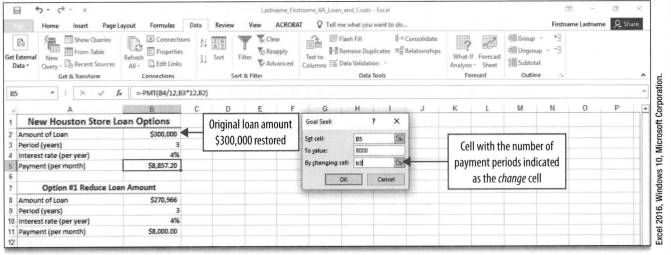

FIGURE 4.7

3 Click **OK** two times.

> Excel's calculations indicate that by making payments for 3.3 years—*3.343845511*—the monthly payment is the desired amount of $8,000.00.

4 Click cell **A13**. Type **Option #2 Increase Number of Years** and then press Enter. Right-click over cell **A7**, on the mini toolbar, click **Format Painter**, and then click cell **A13** to copy the format.

5 Select the range **A2:B5** and right-click, and then click **Copy**. Point to cell **A14**, right-click, point to **Paste Special**, and then under **Paste Values**, click the **second** button—**Values & Number Formatting (A)**. Press Esc to cancel the moving border.

BY TOUCH   Press and hold an item to display a shaded square and then release to right-click it.

6 Click cell **B15**, right-click to display the mini toolbar, and then click **Decrease Decimal** until the number of decimal places displayed is two. Click cell **B3**. Type **3** and then press Enter to restore the original value. **Save** your workbook, and then compare your screen with Figure 4.8.

FIGURE 4.8

GO! Learn How
Video E4-3

A **Data table** is a range of cells that shows how changing certain values in your formulas affects the results of those formulas. Data tables make it easy to calculate multiple versions in one operation, and then to view and compare the results of all the different variations.

For example, banks may offer loans at different rates for different periods of time, which require different payments. By using a data table, you can calculate the possible values for each argument.

A **one-variable data table** changes the value in only one cell. For example, use a one-variable data table if you want to see how different interest rates affect a monthly payment. A **two-variable data table** changes the values in two cells—for example, if you want to see how different interest rates *and* different payment periods will affect a monthly payment.

Activity 4.04 | Designing a Two-Variable Data Table

Recall that the PMT function has three required arguments: Present value (Pv), Rate, and Number of periods (Nper). Because Alaina would still like to borrow $300,000 and purchase the fixtures and furniture that she has selected for the new store, in this data table, the present value will *not* change. The two values that will change are the Rate and Number of periods. Possible periods will range from 24 months (2 years) to 60 months (5 years) and the rate will vary from 5% to 3%.

1 At the lower edge of the worksheet, click the **Payment Table sheet**.

2 In the range **B2:B4**, enter the following data:

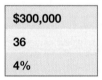

| $300,000 |
| 36 |
| 4% |

3 In cell **C7**, type **24** and then press `Tab`. Type **30** and then press `Tab`. Select the range **C7:D7**, point to the fill handle, and then drag to the right through cell **I7** to use Auto Fill to fill in a pattern of months from 24 to 60 in increments of six months.

Recall that the Auto Fill feature will duplicate a pattern of values that you set in the beginning cells.

4 In cell **B8**, type **5.000%** and then press `Enter`. In cell **B9**, type **4.875%** and then press `Enter`. Compare your screen with Figure 4.9.

Excel rounds both values to two decimal places.

FIGURE 4.9

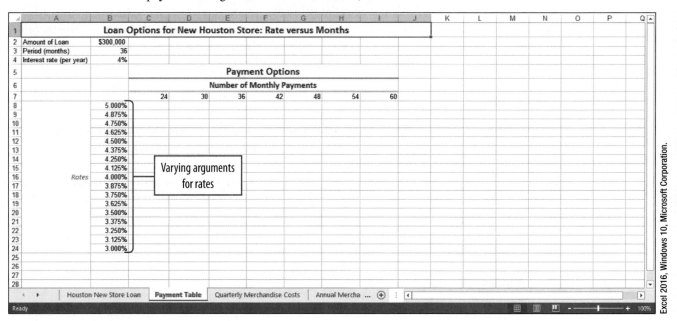

5 Select the range **B8:B9**. Point to the fill handle, and then drag down through cell **B24** to fill a pattern of interest rates in increments of 0.125 from 5.00% down to 3.00%.

6 Right-click anywhere over the selected range, and then on the mini toolbar, click **Increase Decimal** ⬚ one time. Press Ctrl + Home to make cell **A1** the active cell.

7 **Save** 🖫 your workbook, and then compare your screen with Figure 4.10.

> Row 7 represents the number of monthly payments, and the range B8:B24 in column B represents a range of possible annual interest rates. These two arguments will be used to calculate varying payment arrangements for a loan of $300,000.

FIGURE 4.10

Activity 4.05 | Using a Data Table to Calculate Options

Recall that a data table is a range of cells that shows how changing certain values in your formulas affects the results of those formulas.

In this Activity, you will create a table of payments for every combination of payment periods, which are represented by the column titles under *Number of Monthly Payments*, and interest rates, which are represented by the row titles to the right of *Rates*. From the resulting table, Alaina can find a combination of payment periods and interest rates that will enable her to go forward with her plan to borrow $300,000 to purchase furniture and fixtures.

1 In cell **B7**, type = and notice that in the upper left corner of your screen, in the **Name Box**, *PMT* displays indicating the most recently used function. Click in the **Name Box** to open the **Function Arguments** dialog box with the PMT function.

> You can use this technique to open the most recently used function.

> When creating a data table, you enter the PMT function in the upper left corner of your range of data, so that when the data table is completed, the months in row 7 and the rates in column B will be substituted into each cell's formula and will fill the table with the range of months and interest rate options.

2 In the **Rate** box, type **b4/12** to divide the interest rate per year shown in cell B4 by 12 and convert it to a monthly interest rate.

3 Press Tab to move the insertion point to the **Nper** box. Type **b3** which is the cell that contains the number of months, and then press Tab.

> The periods in cell B3 are already stated in months and do not need to be changed.

4 In the **Pv** box, type **-b2** to enter the amount of the loan as a negative number. Compare your dialog box with Figure 4.11.

FIGURE 4.11

5 Click **OK** to close the **Function Arguments** dialog box and display the result in cell **B7**.

The payment—*$8,857.20*—is calculated by using the values in cells B2, B3, and B4. This is the same payment that you calculated on the first worksheet. Now it displays as a positive number because you entered the loan amount in cell B2 as a negative number.

6 Select the range **B7:I24**, which encompasses all of the months and all of the rates. With the range **B7:I24** selected, on the **Data tab**, in the **Forecast group**, click **What-If Analysis**, and then click **Data Table**.

7 In the **Data Table** dialog box, in the **Row input cell** box, type **b3** and then press ⒯Ⓐ⒝. In the **Column input cell** box, type **b4** and then compare your screen with Figure 4.12.

The row of months will be substituted for the value in cell B3, and the column of interest rates will be substituted for the value in cell B4.

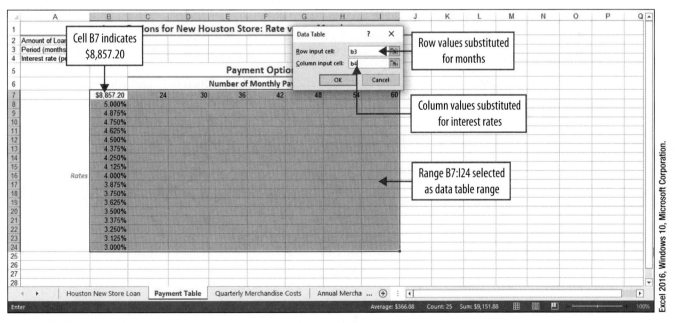

FIGURE 4.12

8 ▸ Click **OK**. Click cell **F8**, and then examine the formula in the **Formula Bar**. Compare your screen with Figure 4.13.

The table is filled with payment options that use the month and interest rate corresponding to the position in the table. So, if Alaina chooses a combination of 42 months at an interest rate of 5.000%, the monthly payment will be $7,800.91, which is slightly under the monthly payment she wanted. The data table is one of a group of Excel's What-If Analysis tools.

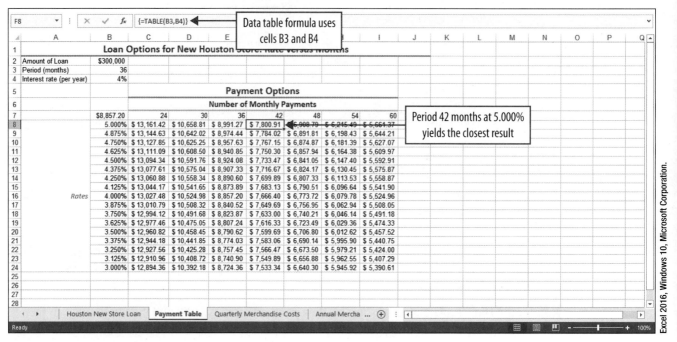

FIGURE 4.13

9 ▸ Select the range **F8:F19**. From the **Home tab**, display the **Cell Styles** gallery, and then under **Data and Model**, click the **Note** cell style to highlight the desired payment options.

10 ▸ Select the range **B8:B24**, hold down Ctrl, and then select the range **C7:I7**. Right-click over the selection, on the mini toolbar, click **Bold** **B** and then click **Center** ≡.

11 ▸ Click anywhere to deselect the range, click **Save** 🖫, and then compare your worksheet with Figure 4.14.

 BY TOUCH   Swipe to select the range B8:B24, hold it, and then select the range C7:I7.

By using a data table of payment options, you can see that Alaina can get a loan for at least 42 months (3.5 years) for any of the interest rates between 5.000% and 3.625% in order to purchase the furniture and fixtures she wants and still keep the monthly payment under $8,000.

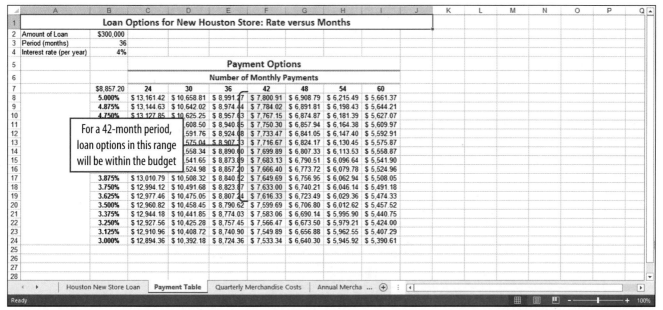

	Loan Options for New Houston Store: Rate versus Months								
Amount of Loan	$300,000								
Period (months)	36								
Interest rate (per year)	4%								
				Payment Options					
				Number of Monthly Payments					
	$8,857.20	24	30	36	42	48	54	60	
	5.000%	$ 13,161.42	$ 10,658.81	$ 8,991.27	$ 7,800.91	$ 6,908.79	$ 6,215.49	$ 5,661.37	
	4.875%	$ 13,144.63	$ 10,642.02	$ 8,974.44	$ 7,784.02	$ 6,891.81	$ 6,198.43	$ 5,644.21	
	4.750%	$ 13,127.85	$ 10,625.25	$ 8,957.63	$ 7,767.15	$ 6,874.87	$ 6,181.39	$ 5,627.07	
				608.50	$ 8,940.85	$ 7,750.30	$ 6,857.94	$ 6,164.38	$ 5,609.97
				591.76	$ 8,924.08	$ 7,733.47	$ 6,841.05	$ 6,147.40	$ 5,592.91
				575.04	$ 8,907.33	$ 7,716.67	$ 6,824.17	$ 6,130.45	$ 5,575.87
				558.34	$ 8,890.60	$ 7,699.89	$ 6,807.33	$ 6,113.53	$ 5,558.87
				541.65	$ 8,873.89	$ 7,683.13	$ 6,790.51	$ 6,096.64	$ 5,541.90
				524.98	$ 8,857.20	$ 7,666.40	$ 6,773.72	$ 6,079.78	$ 5,524.96
	3.875%	$ 13,010.79	$ 10,508.32	$ 8,840.52	$ 7,649.69	$ 6,756.95	$ 6,062.94	$ 5,508.05	
	3.750%	$ 12,994.12	$ 10,491.68	$ 8,823.87	$ 7,633.00	$ 6,740.21	$ 6,046.14	$ 5,491.18	
	3.625%	$ 12,977.46	$ 10,475.05	$ 8,807.24	$ 7,616.33	$ 6,723.49	$ 6,029.36	$ 5,474.33	
	3.500%	$ 12,960.82	$ 10,458.45	$ 8,790.62	$ 7,599.69	$ 6,706.80	$ 6,012.62	$ 5,457.52	
	3.375%	$ 12,944.18	$ 10,441.85	$ 8,774.03	$ 7,583.06	$ 6,690.14	$ 5,995.90	$ 5,440.75	
	3.250%	$ 12,927.56	$ 10,425.28	$ 8,757.46	$ 7,566.47	$ 6,673.50	$ 5,979.21	$ 5,424.00	
	3.125%	$ 12,910.96	$ 10,408.72	$ 8,740.90	$ 7,549.89	$ 6,656.88	$ 5,962.55	$ 5,407.29	
	3.000%	$ 12,894.36	$ 10,392.18	$ 8,724.36	$ 7,533.34	$ 6,640.30	$ 5,945.92	$ 5,390.61	

For a 42-month period, loan options in this range will be within the budget

Houston New Store Loan | **Payment Table** | Quarterly Merchandise Costs | Annual Mercha ...

Excel 2016, Windows 10, Microsoft Corporation.

FIGURE 4.14

GO! Learn How
Video E4-4

A **name**, also referred to as a **defined name**, is a word or string of characters in Excel that represents a cell, a range of cells, a formula, or a constant value. A defined name that is distinctive and easy to remember typically defines the *purpose* of the selected cells. When creating a formula, the defined name may be used instead of the cell reference.

All names have a **scope**, which is the location within which the name is recognized without qualification. The name's scope usually refers either to a specific worksheet or to an entire workbook.

Activity 4.06 | Defining a Name

MOS
3.6.1 Expert
3.6.2 Expert

In this Activity, you will practice three ways to define a name for a cell or group of cells. After defining a name, you can use the name in a formula to refer to the cell or cells. Names make it easier for you and others to understand the meaning of formulas in a worksheet.

1 At the bottom of your workbook, click the **Quarterly Merchandise Costs** worksheet, and then compare your screen with Figure 4.15.

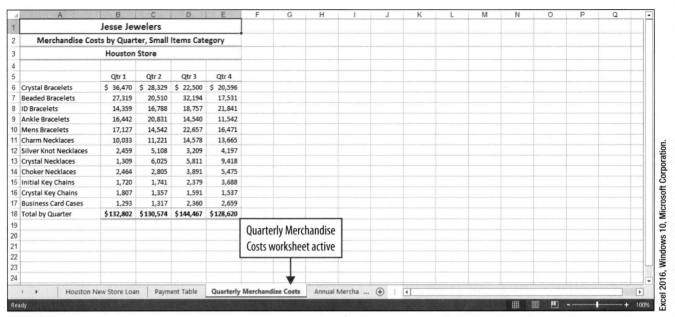

FIGURE 4.15

2 Select the range **B6:E10**. On the **Formulas tab**, in the **Defined Names group**, click **Define Name**. Compare your screen with Figure 4.16.

The New Name dialog box displays—some text may display in the Name Box as a suggested name for the range.

FIGURE 4.16

3 In the **New Name** dialog box, in the **Name** box, delete any existing text, and then type **Bracelet_Costs** as the name. Compare your screen with Figure 4.17.

Naming cells has no effect on the displayed or underlying values; it simply creates an easy-to-remember name that you can use when creating formulas that refers to this range of cells. A named range cannot contain spaces.

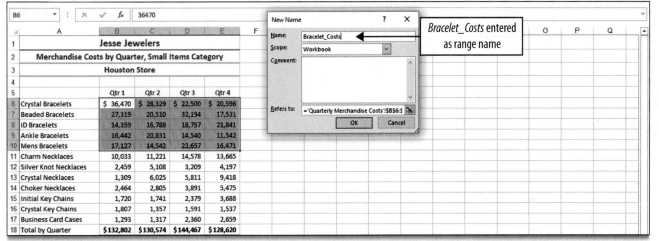

FIGURE 4.17

4 ▶ At the bottom of the dialog box, at the right edge of the **Refers to** box, point to and click **Collapse Dialog Box** 🔲. Compare your screen with Figure 4.18.

The dialog box collapses (shrinks) so that only the *Refers to* box is visible, and the selected range is surrounded by a moving border. When you define a name, the stored definition is an absolute cell reference and includes the worksheet name.

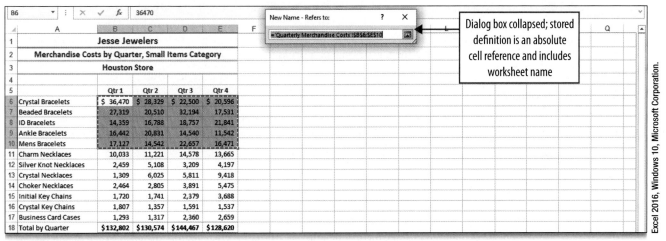

FIGURE 4.18

5 ▶ Click **Expand Dialog Box** 🔲 to redisplay the entire **New Name** dialog box, and then click **OK**.

6 ▶ Select the range **B11:E14**. In the upper left corner of the Excel window, to the left of the **Formula Bar**, click in the **Name Box**, and notice that the cell reference *B11* is highlighted in blue. Type **Necklace_Costs** and then compare your screen with Figure 4.19.

FIGURE 4.19

> 7 ▸ Press Enter, and then take a moment to study the rules for defining names, as described in the table in Figure 4.20.

RULES FOR DEFINING NAMES
The first character of the defined name must be a letter, an underscore (_), or a backslash (\).
After the first character, the remaining characters in the defined name can be letters, numbers, periods, and underscore characters.
Spaces are not valid in a defined name; use a period or the underscore character as a word separator, for example, 1st.Quarter or 1st_Qtr.
The single letter C or R in either uppercase or lowercase cannot be defined as a name, because these letters are used by Excel for selecting a row or column when you enter them in a Name or a Go To text box.
A defined name can be no longer than 255 characters; short, meaningful names are the most useful.
Defined names cannot be the same as a cell reference, for example M$10 or QTR1.
Defined names can contain uppercase and lowercase letters; however, Excel does not distinguish between them. So, for example, if you create the name Sales and then create another name SALES in the same workbook, Excel considers the names to be the same and prompts you for a unique name.

FIGURE 4.20

> 8 ▸ Click any cell to cancel the selection. Click the **Name Box arrow**, and then compare your screen with Figure 4.21.
>
>> Your two defined names display in alphabetical order. You can drag the edge of the Name Box to resize it.

FIGURE 4.21

> 9 ▸ From the list, click **Bracelet_Costs** and notice that Excel selects the range of values that comprise the cost of various Bracelet styles.
>
> 10 ▸ Click the **Name Box arrow** again, and then click **Necklace_Costs** to select the range of values that comprise the Necklace costs.

11 ▸ Select the range **B15:E16**. On the **Formulas tab**, in the **Defined Names group**, click **Name Manager**, and then notice that the two names that you have defined display in a list.

12 ▸ In the upper left corner of the **Name Manager** dialog box, click **New**. With *Initial_Key_Chains* selected, type **Key_Chain_Costs** and then click **OK**. Compare your screen with Figure 4.22.

FIGURE 4.22

13 ▸ **Close** the **Name Manager** dialog box and **Save** 🖫 your workbook.

This is another method to define a name—by creating a new name in the Name Manager dialog box. The Name Manager dialog box displays the three range names that you have created, in alphabetical order.

Activity 4.07 │ Inserting New Data into a Named Range

MOS
3.6.4 Expert

You can insert new data into the range of cells that a name represents. In this Activity, you will modify the range named *Necklace_Costs* to include new data.

1 ▸ On the left side of your window, point to the **row 15** heading and right-click to select the entire row and display a shortcut menu. On the menu, click **Insert** to insert a new blank row above.

A new row 15 is inserted, and the remaining rows move down one row. Recall that when new rows are inserted in this manner, Excel adjusts formulas accordingly.

2 ▸ In the upper left, above **column A**, to the left of the **Formula Bar**, click the **Name Box arrow**, and then click **Key_Chain_Costs**. Notice that Excel highlights the correct range of cells, adjusting for the newly inserted row.

If you insert rows, the defined name adjusts to the new cell addresses to represent the cells that were originally defined. Likewise, if you move the cells, the defined name goes with them to the new location.

3 ▸ In cell **A15**, type **Sweetheart Necklaces** and then press Tab. In cell **B15**, type **1166** and press Tab. In cell **C15**, type **1087** and press Tab. In cell **D15**, type **847** and press Tab. In cell **E15**, type **965** and press Enter.

The cells in the newly inserted row adopt the format from the cells above.

4 On the **Formulas tab**, in the **Defined Names group**, click **Name Manager**.

5 In the **Name Manager** dialog box, in the **Name** column, click **Necklace_Costs**. At the bottom of the dialog box, click in the **Refers to** box and edit the reference, changing **$E$14** to **$E$15** as shown in Figure 4.23.

This action will include the Sweetheart Necklaces values in the named range.

FIGURE 4.23

6 In the **Name Manager** dialog box, click **Close**, and then click **Yes** to save the changes you made to the name reference. In the upper left corner of the window, click the **Name Box arrow**, and then click the range name **Necklace_Costs**. Notice that the selected range now includes the new row 15. **Save** 🖫 your workbook.

NOTE	Changing a Defined Name

If you create a defined name and then decide to change it, you can use the Name Manager to edit the name. Display the Name Manager dialog box, select the defined name, and then at the top of the dialog box, click Edit. If the defined name is used in a formula, the new name is automatically changed in any affected formulas.

Activity 4.08 | **Creating a Defined Name by Using Row and Column Titles**

3.6.2 Expert

You can use the **Create from Selection** command to use existing row or column titles as the name for a range of cells.

1 Select the range **A18:E18**. On the **Formulas tab**, in the **Defined Names group**, click **Create from Selection**. Compare your screen with Figure 4.24.

The Create Names from Selection dialog box displays. A check mark displays in the *Left column* check box, which indicates that Excel will use the value of the cell in the leftmost column of the selection as the range name, unless you specify otherwise.

FIGURE 4.24

Excel 2016, Windows 10, Microsoft Corporation

2 In the **Create Names from Selection** dialog box, click **OK**, and then click anywhere to cancel the selection.

3 Click the **Name Box arrow**, and then click the name **Business_Card_Cases**, and notice that in the new range name, Excel inserts the underscores necessary to fill a blank space in the range name. Also notice that the actual range consists of only the numeric values, as shown in Figure 4.25. **Save** 🖫 your workbook.

This method is convenient for naming a range of cells without having to actually type a name—Excel uses the text of the first cell to the left of the selected range as the range name and then formats the name properly.

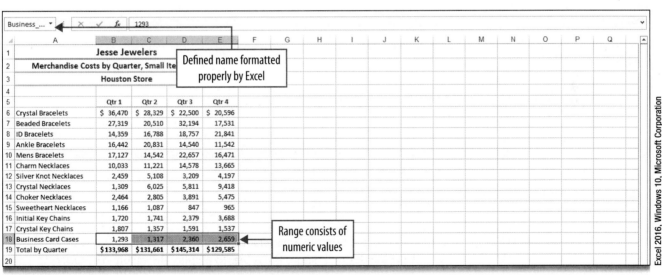

FIGURE 4.25

Excel 2016, Windows 10, Microsoft Corporation

NOTE Deleting a Defined Name

If you create a defined name and then decide that you no longer need it, you can delete the name and its accompanying range reference. Display the Name Manager dialog box, select the defined name, and then at the top of the dialog box, click Delete. Deleting a defined name does not modify the cell contents or formatting of the cells. Deleting a defined name does not delete any cells or any values. It deletes only the name that you have applied to a group of cells. However, any formula that contains the range name will display the #name? Error message, and will have to be adjusted manually.

MOS
3.6.4 Expert

The advantage to naming a range of cells is that you can use the name in a formula in other parts of your workbook. The defined name provides a logical reference to data. For example, referring to data as *Bracelet_Costs* is easier to understand than referring to data as *B6:E10*.

When you use a defined name in a formula, the result is the same as if you typed the cell references.

> **1** Display the **Annual Merchandise Costs** worksheet.

> **2** In cell **B5**, type **=sum(B** and then scroll to the bottom of the AutoComplete list. Compare your screen with Figure 4.26.

> The Formula AutoComplete list displays, containing all of Excel's built-in functions that begin with the letter B and any defined names in this workbook that begin with the letter B. To the left of your defined name *Bracelet_Costs*, a defined name icon ⌨ displays.

FIGURE 4.26

> **3** Double-click **Bracelet_Costs**, and then press Enter.

> Your result is *$411,346*—cell styles are already applied in the worksheet. Recall that SUM is a function—a formula already built by Excel—that adds all the cells in a selected range. Therefore, Excel sums all the cells in the range you defined as *Bracelet_Costs* on the first worksheet in the workbook, and then places the result in cell B5 of this worksheet.

♻ **ANOTHER WAY**   You can type the defined name in the formula.

> **4** In cell **B6**, type **=sum(N** and then on the **Formula AutoComplete** list, double-click **Necklace_Costs** to insert the defined name. Press Enter to display the result *105,733*.

> **5** In cell **B7**, type **=sum(** and then on the **Formulas tab**, in the **Defined Names group**, click **Use in Formula**. On the list, click **Key_Chain_Costs**, and then press Enter to display the total *15,820*.

> **6** In cell **B8**, use any of the techniques you just practiced to sum the cells containing the costs for **Business Card Cases** and to display a result of *7,629*. In cell **B9**, in the **Function Library group**, click **AutoSum** Σ AutoSum ▾ to sum **column B** and press Enter to display a result of *$540,528*. Compare your screen with Figure 4.27.

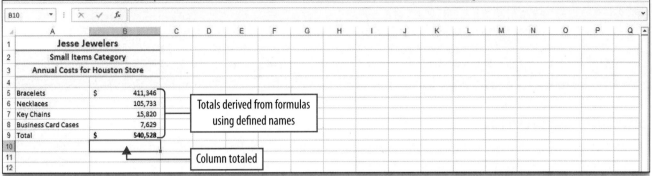

Excel 2016, Windows 10, Microsoft Corporation.

FIGURE 4.27

7 At the bottom of the workbook window, right-click the sheet tab name, and then click **Select All Sheets**.

8 With the four worksheets grouped, from the **Page Layout tab**, display the **Page Setup** dialog box, and then insert a **Custom Footer** in the **left section** that includes the file name. Center the worksheets **Horizontally** on the page.

9 Click the **Payment Table** worksheet, and then on the **Page Layout tab**, in the **Page Setup group**, change the **Orientation** to **Landscape**.

10 Click the **File tab** to display **Backstage** view. On the right, at the bottom of the **Properties** list, click **Show All Properties**. Under **Related People**, be sure that your name displays as the author. If necessary, right-click the author name, click **Edit Property**, type your name, and then click OK. In the **Subject** box, type your course name and section number, and in the **Tags** box, type **store loan, merchandise costs.**

11 On the left, click **Save** to return to your workbook. Point to any sheet tab and right-click, click **Select All Sheets** to group the worksheets, and then display the grouped worksheets in **Print Preview**. At the bottom of the Print Preview, scroll through the four worksheets to be sure each worksheet is formatted properly. In the upper left, click the **Back** arrow ⬅ to close the **Print Preview**, and then make any necessary corrections or adjustments.

🔁 **ANOTHER WAY**   On the File tab, click Print, and then under Settings, click the first arrow and click Print Entire Workbook.

12 If directed by your instructor to do so, submit a paper printout of each of the four worksheets, an electronic image of each of your four worksheets that looks like a printed document, or your original Excel file. If required by your instructor, print or create an electronic version of your worksheet with formulas displayed. In the upper right corner of the Excel window, click **Close** ☒.

> **END | You have completed Project 4A**

PROJECT
4B

Lookup Form and Revenue Report

MyITLab

Project 4B Training
Project 4B Grader

PROJECT ACTIVITIES

In Activities 4.10 through 4.18, you will assist Mike Connor, the Vice President of Marketing at Jesse Jewelers, by adding lookup functions to a phone order form so that an order taker can complete the form quickly. You will use the Formula Auditing features to review a revenue worksheet and to resolve the errors, and you will use the Watch Window to monitor changes in sales worksheets. Your completed worksheets will look similar to Figure 4.28.

Please always review the downloaded Grader instructions before beginning.

PROJECT FILES

MyITLab grader

If your instructor wants you to submit Project 4B in the MyITLab grader system, log in to MyITLab, locate Grader Project 4B, and then download the files for this project.

For Project 4B, you will need the following file:
e04B_Lookup_Revenue_Report

You will save your workbook as:
Lastname_Firstname_4B_Lookup_
Revenue_Report

PROJECT RESULTS

GO!
Walk Thru
Project 4B

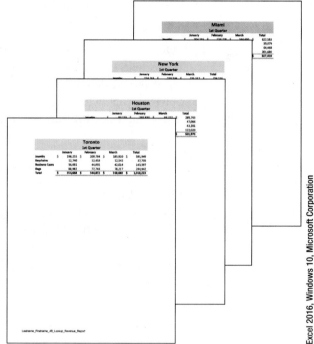

Excel 2016, Windows 10, Microsoft Corporation

FIGURE 4.28 Project 4B Lookup Form and Revenue Report

GO! Learn How
Video E4-5

Lookup functions look up a value in a defined range of cells located in another part of the workbook to find a corresponding value. For example, you can define a two-column range of cells containing names and phone numbers. Then, when you type a name in the cell referred to by the lookup formula, Excel fills in the phone number by looking it up in the defined range. In the lookup formula, the defined range is referred to as the *table array*.

The *VLOOKUP* function looks up values in a table array arranged as vertical columns. The function searches the first column of the table array for a corresponding value, and then returns a value from any cell on the same row. The *HLOOKUP* function looks up values in a table array arranged in horizontal rows. The function searches the top row of the table array for a corresponding value, and then returns a value from any cell in the same column.

There is one requirement for the lookup functions to work properly. The data in the table array, which can be numbers or text, must be sorted in ascending order. For the VLOOKUP function, the values must be sorted on the first column in ascending order. For the HLOOKUP function, the values must be sorted on the first row in ascending order.

Activity 4.10 | Defining a Range of Cells for a Lookup Function

ALERT! **To submit as an autograded project, log into MyITLab, download the files for this project, and then begin with those files instead of e04B_Lookup_Revenue_Report.**

MOS
3.2.1 Expert

The first step in using a lookup function is to define the range of cells that will serve as the table array. In the Jesse Jewelers Phone Order form, after an Item Number is entered on the form, Mr. Connors wants the description of the item to display automatically in the Description column. He also wants to automatically look up the Unit Price. To accomplish this, you will define a table array that includes the item number in one column and a description of the item in the second column.

1 Start Excel, on the left click **Open Other Workbooks**, and then from your student files, open the file **e04B_Lookup_Revenue_Report**. **Save** the file in your **Excel Chapter 4** folder as **Lastname_Firstname_4B_Lookup_Revenue_Report** and then compare your screen with Figure 4.29.

2 At the bottom of the screen, in the sheet tab row, be sure that the **Phone Order** worksheet is active.

When store managers call Jesse Jewelers headquarters to place an order, the order taker uses this type of worksheet to record the information.

FIGURE 4.29

3 Click the **Product Information sheet tab** to display the second worksheet.

The Product Information worksheet contains the Style Code, Description, and Unit Price of specific bracelets and necklaces.

4 On the **Product Information** worksheet, select the range **A4:C11**. On the **Data tab**, in the **Sort & Filter group**, click **Sort**. If necessary, drag the **Sort** dialog box to the right side of your screen so you can view **columns A:C**.

To use this list to look up information with the Excel VLOOKUP function, you must sort the list in ascending order by Style Code, which is the column that will be used to look up the matching information.

5 In the **Sort** dialog box, under **Column**, click the **Sort by arrow**. Notice that the selected range is now **A5:C11** and that the column titles in the range **A4:C4** display in the **Sort by** list. Compare your screen with Figure 4.30.

When the selected range includes a header row that should remain in place while the remaining rows are sorted, Excel usually recognizes those column headings, selects the *My data has headers* check box, and then displays the column headings in the Sort by list.

FIGURE 4.30

6 On the **Sort by** list, click **Style Code**, which is the first column heading and the column heading that Excel selects by default.

7 Under **Sort On**, verify that *Values* displays, and under **Order**, verify that *A to Z* displays.

Values indicates that the sort will be based on the values in the cells of the first column, rather than cell color or some other cell characteristic. *A to Z* indicates that the cells will be sorted in ascending order.

8 Click **OK** to sort the data by *Style Code* in ascending order.

Excel sorts the data alphabetically by Style Code; *B-DB* is first in the list and *N-CH* is last.

9 **Save** 🖫 your workbook.

Activity 4.11 │ Inserting the VLOOKUP Function

3.2.1 Expert

Recall that the VLOOKUP function looks up values in a range of cells arranged as vertical columns. The arguments for this function include *lookup_value*—the value to search in the first column of the table array, *table_array*—the range that contains the data, and *col_index_num*—the column number (1, 2, 3, 4, and so on) in the table array that contains the result you want to retrieve from the table, which in this instance is the Description.

1 Display the **Phone Order** worksheet. In cell **A9**, type **G-ID** and press Tab.

2 With cell **B9** as the active cell, on the **Formulas tab**, in the **Function Library group**, click **Lookup & Reference**, and then click **VLOOKUP**.

The Function Arguments dialog box for VLOOKUP displays.

3 With the insertion point in the **Lookup_value** box, click cell **A9** to look up the description of Item G-ID.

4 ▶ Click in the **Table_array** box, and then at the bottom of the workbook, click the **Product Information sheet tab**. On the **Product Information** worksheet, select the range **A4:C11**, and then press ⎗F4⎘.

This range (table array) includes the value that will be looked up—*G-ID* and the corresponding value to be displayed—*ID Bracelet*. By pressing ⎗F4⎘, the absolute cell reference is applied to the table array so that the formula can be copied to the remainder of the column in the Phone Order sheet.

5 ▶ Click in the **Col_index_num** box and type **2** Compare your screen with Figure 4.31.

The description for the selected item—the value to be looked up—is located in column 2 of the table array.

FIGURE 4.31

6 ▶ Click **OK**.

In the Phone Order form, the description for Item G-ID displays in cell B9.

7 ▶ If necessary, click cell **B9** so that it is the active cell. In the **Formula Bar**, notice that this cell contains the VLOOKUP formula. Point to the fill handle in the lower right corner of the cell, and then drag to fill the VLOOKUP formula down through cell **B18**. Compare your screen with Figure 4.32.

The *#N/A* error notation displays in the cells where you copied the formula. Excel displays this error when a function or formula exists in a cell but has no value available with which to perform a calculation; values have not yet been entered in column A in those rows.

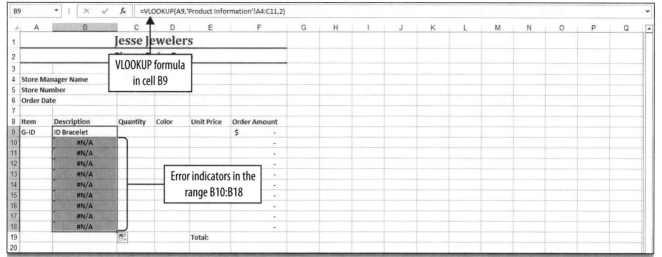

FIGURE 4.32

Excel 2016, Windows 10, Microsoft Corporation.

8 ▶ Click cell **C9**, type **12** as the quantity ordered and press Tab. In cell **D9**, type **Silver** and press Tab.

9 ▶ With cell **E9** as the active cell, on the **Formulas tab**, in the **Function Library group**, click **Lookup & Reference**, and then click **VLOOKUP**.

10 ▶ With the insertion point in the **Lookup_value** box, click cell **A9** to look up information for Item G-ID. Click in the **Table_array** box, display the **Product Information** sheet, and then select the range **A4:C11**. Press F4 to make the values in the range absolute.

11 ▶ In the **Col_index_num** box, type **3** to look up the price in the third column of the range, and then click **OK**.

The Unit Price for the ID Bracelet—*$17.00*—displays in cell E9.

12 ▶ Click cell **F9**, and notice in the **Formula Bar** that a formula to calculate the total for the item, Quantity times Unit Price, has already been entered in the worksheet; this formula has also been copied to the range F10:F18.

13 ▶ Click cell **E9**, and then copy the VLOOKUP formula down through cell **E18**. Compare your screen with Figure 4.33.

The *#N/A* error notation displays in the cells where you copied the formula, and also in cells F10:F18, because the formulas there have no values yet with which to perform a calculation—values have not yet been entered in column A in those rows.

FIGURE 4.33

Excel 2016, Windows 10, Microsoft Corporation.

14 ▶ Click cell **A10**, type **N-CB** and press ⑆Tab⑇ two times.

> Excel looks up the product description and the product price in the vertical table array on the Product Information sheet, and then displays the results in cells B10 and E10.

15 ▶ In cell **C10**, type **24** as the Quantity and press ⑆Tab⑇. Notice that Excel calculates the total for this item in cell **F10**—*432.00*.

16 ▶ In cell **D10**, type **White** and then press ⑆Enter⑇. Notice that after data is entered in the row, the error notations no longer display. **Save** 🖫 your workbook. Compare your screen with Figure 4.34.

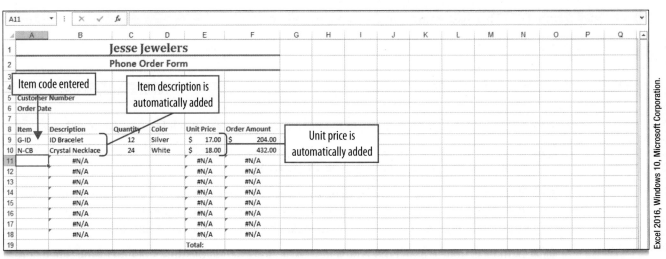

FIGURE 4.34

Objective 6 Validate Data

GO! Learn How
Video E4-6

Another technique to improve accuracy when completing a worksheet is ***data validation***—a technique in which you control the type of data or the values that are entered into a cell. This technique improves accuracy because it limits and controls the type of data an individual, such as an order taker, can enter into the form.

One way to control the type of data entered is to create a ***validation list***—a list of values that are acceptable for a group of cells. Only values on the list are valid; any value *not* on the list is considered invalid. For example, in the Phone Order sheet, it would be useful if in the Item column, only valid Style Codes could be entered.

Activity 4.12 | Creating a Validation List

3.5.3 Expert
2.1.3 Expert

A list of valid values must either be on the same worksheet as the destination cell, or if the list is in another worksheet, the cell range must be named. In this Activity, you will create a defined name for the Style Codes, and then create a validation list for column A of the Phone Order worksheet.

1 ▶ Display the **Product Information** worksheet. Select the range **A4:A11**. On the **Formulas tab**, in the **Defined Names group**, click **Create from Selection**.

> Recall that by using the Create from Selection command, you can automatically generate a name from the selected cells that uses the text in the top row or the leftmost column of a selection.

2 ▶ In the **Create Names from Selection** dialog box, be sure the **Top row** check box is selected, and then click **OK** to use *Style Code* as the range name.

3 In the **Defined Names group**, click **Name Manager**, and then notice that the new defined name is listed with the name *Style_Code*.

Style_Code displays as the defined name for the selected cells. Recall that Excel replaces spaces with an underscore when it creates a range name.

4 **Close** the **Name Manager** dialog box. Display the **Phone Order** sheet, and then select the range **A9:A18**.

Before you set the validation requirement, you must first select the cells that you want to restrict to only valid entries from the list.

5 On the **Data tab**, in the **Data Tools group**, click **Data Validation**. In the **Data Validation** dialog box, be sure the **Settings tab** is selected.

6 Under **Validation criteria**, click the **Allow arrow**, and then click **List**.

A Source box displays as the third box in the Data Validation dialog box. Here you select or type the source data.

7 Click to position the insertion point in the **Source** box, type **=Style_Code** and then compare your screen with Figure 4.35.

FIGURE 4.35

8 Click **OK**. Click cell **A11**, and notice that a list arrow displays at the right edge of the cell.

9 In cell **A11**, click the list arrow to display the list, and then compare your screen with Figure 4.36.

FIGURE 4.36

10 From the list, click **B-DB**.

The Style Code is selected from the list and the Item, Description, and Unit Price cells are filled in for row 11.

11 Press Tab two times, type **24** as the Quantity and press Tab, type **Multi** as the Color, and then press Enter to return to the beginning of the next row. Compare your screen with Figure 4.37.

You can see that when taking orders by phone, it will speed the process if all of the necessary information can be filled in automatically. Furthermore, accuracy will be improved if item codes are restricted to only valid data.

	A	B	C	D	E	F	G	H	I	J	K	L	M	N	O	P	Q
1		Jesse Jewelers															
2		Phone Order Form															
3																	
4	Customer Name																
5	Customer Number																
6	Order Date																
7																	
8	Item	Description	Quantity	Color	Unit Price	Order Amount											
9	G-ID	ID Bracelet	12	Silver	$ 17.00	$ 204.00											
10	N-CB	Crystal Necklace	24	White	$ 18.00	432.00											
11	B-DB	Beaded Bracelet	24	Multi	$ 15.50	372.00											
12		#N/A			#N/A	#N/A											
13		#N/A			#N/A	#N/A											
14		#N/A			#N/A	#N/A											
15		#N/A			#N/A	#N/A											

Order in row 11 completed using a validation list

Excel 2016, Windows 10, Microsoft Corporation.

FIGURE 4.37

12 With cell **A12** active, click the **list arrow**, and then click **F-SK**. As the **Quantity**, type **18** and as the **Color**, type **Antique** and then press Enter.

13 In cell **A13**, type **G-W** and press Tab.

An error message displays indicating that you entered a value that is not valid; that is, it is not on the validation list you created. If the order taker mistakenly types an invalid value into the cell, this message will display.

Restricting the values that an order taker can enter will greatly improve the accuracy of orders. Also, encouraging order takers to select from the list, rather than typing, will reduce the time it takes to fill in the order form.

14 In the error message, click **Cancel**. Click the **list arrow** again, click **H-CK,** and press Tab two times. As the **Quantity**, type **18** and for the **Color**, type **Ivory** and then press Enter.

15 Select the unused rows **14:18**, right-click over the selection, and then click **Delete**.

16 In cell **F14**, sum the **Order Amount** column, and apply the **Total** cell style.

17 Save 💾 your workbook.

More Knowledge **Creating Validation Messages**

In the Data Validation dialog box, you can use the Input Message tab to create a ScreenTip that will display when the cell is selected. The message can be an instruction that tells the user what to do. You can also use the Error Alert tab to create a customized warning message that displays if invalid data is entered in the cell.

GO! Learn How
Video E4-7

Auditing is the process of examining a worksheet for errors in *formulas*. Formulas are equations that perform calculations on values in your worksheet. A formula consists of a sequence of values, cell references, names, functions, or operators in a cell, which together produce a new value. Recall that a formula always begins with an equal sign.

Excel includes a group of *Formula Auditing* features, which consists of tools and commands accessible from the Formulas tab that help you to check your worksheet for errors. In complex worksheets, use these Formula Auditing features to show relationships between cells and formulas to ensure that formulas are logical and correct and also to resolve error messages. Although sometimes it is appropriate to hide the error message, at other times error notations can indicate a problem that should be corrected.

Activity 4.13 | Tracing Precedents

3.5.1 Expert

Precedent cells are cells that are referred to by a formula in another cell. The *Trace Precedents command* displays arrows that indicate what cells affect the values of the cell that is selected. By using the Trace Precedents command, you can see the relationships between formulas and cells. As an auditing tool, the process of tracing a formula is a way to ensure that you constructed the formula correctly.

1 Display the **Revenue** worksheet, and then compare your screen with Figure 4.38.

The worksheet details the revenue and expenses related to the Miami store over a six-month period. Several error notations are present (#VALUE!, #REF!, #DIV/0!), green triangles display in the top left corners of several cells indicating a potential error, and two columns are too narrow to fit the data, which Excel indicates by displaying pound signs—####.

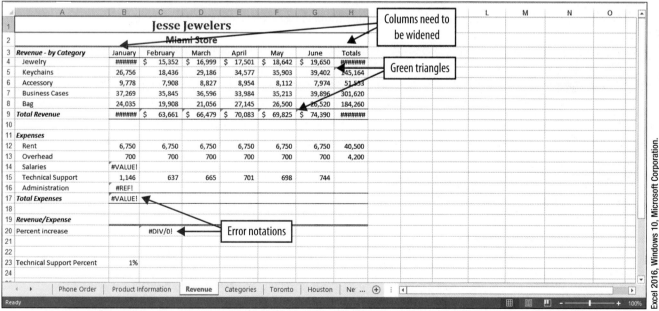

FIGURE 4.38

2 Display **Backstage** view, and then on the left, click **Options**. In the **Excel Options** dialog box, click **Formulas**. Under **Error checking rules**, point to the small information icon after the first Error checking rule to display the ScreenTip. Compare your screen with Figure 4.39.

Here you can control which error checking rules you want to activate, and you can get information about each of the rules by clicking the small blue information icon at the end of each rule. By default, all but the next to last rules are selected, and it is recommended that you maintain these default settings. This textbook assumes the default settings.

FIGURE 4.39

3 In the lower right corner of the dialog box, click **Cancel** to close the dialog box.

4 Take a moment to study the table in Figure 4.40, which details some common error values that might display on your worksheet.

An *error value* is the result of a formula that Excel cannot evaluate correctly.

MICROSOFT EXCEL ERROR VALUES		
ERROR VALUE	**MEANING**	**POSSIBLE CAUSE**
#####	Cannot see data.	The column is not wide enough to display the entire value.
#DIV/0!	Cannot divide by zero.	The divisor in a formula refers to a blank cell or a cell that contains zero.
#NAME?	Does not recognize a name you used in a formula.	A function or a named range may be misspelled or does not exist.
#VALUE!	Cannot use a text field in a formula.	A formula refers to a cell that contains a text value rather than a numeric value or a formula.
#REF!	Cannot locate the reference.	A cell that is referenced in a formula may have been deleted or moved.
#N/A	No value is available.	No information is available for the calculation you want to perform.
#NUM!	Invalid argument in a worksheet function.	An unacceptable argument may have been used in a function. Or, a formula result could be too large or too small.
#NULL!	No common cells.	A space was entered between two ranges in a formula to indicate an intersection, but the ranges have no common cells.

FIGURE 4.40

5 On your worksheet, in the **column heading area**, select **column B**, hold down Ctrl, and then select **column H**. Release Ctrl, point to the right edge of either of the selected column headings to display the ⊞ pointer, and then double-click to apply AutoFit.

AutoFit widens the columns to accommodate the longest values in each column; the ##### errors no longer display.

BY TOUCH Tap the column B heading and hold it, then tap column H. With both columns selected, double-tap the border to the right edge of either of the selected column headings to apply AutoFit.

6 Click cell **C9**, and then notice the **green triangle** in the upper left corner of the cell.

A green triangle in the upper left corner of a cell indicates that the formula in the cell is suspect for some reason. Typically, this is because the formula does not match the formula in the cells next to it or because it does not include all of the adjacent cells.

7 In cell **C9**, to the left of the cell, point to **Error Checking** ⚠, and then read the **ScreenTip** that displays. Compare your screen with Figure 4.41.

The ScreenTip indicates that adjacent cells containing numbers are not included in the formula. It is possible that the formula purposely consists of a group of cells that excludes some of the cells adjacent to it. However, because that is not as common as including *all* of the cells that are adjacent to one another, Excel flags this as a potential error.

FIGURE 4.41

8 On the **Formulas tab**, in the **Formula Auditing group**, click **Trace Precedents**. Notice that the range **C6:C8** is bordered in blue and a blue arrow points to cell **C9**.

Recall that precedent cells are cells that are referred to by a formula in another cell. Here, the precedent cells are bordered in blue. A blue arrow, called a *tracer arrow*, displays from C6:C8, pointing to the selected cell C9. A tracer arrow shows the relationship between the active cell and its related cells. Tracer arrows are blue when pointing from a cell that provides data to another cell.

Because this total should include *all* of the revenue categories for February, this is an error in the formula—the formula should include the range C4:C8. By tracing the precedents, you can see that two cells were mistakenly left out of the formula.

9 To the left of cell **C9**, click **Error Checking** ⚠ to display a list of error checking options. Compare your screen with Figure 4.42.

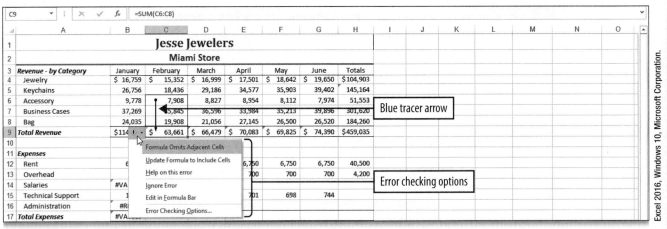

FIGURE 4.42

10 ▸ On the list, notice that Excel indicates the potential error highlighted—*Formula Omits Adjacent Cells*. Notice also that you can update the formula, seek help with the error, ignore the error, edit the formula in the Formula Bar, or display the Error Checking Options in the Excel Options dialog box. Click **Update Formula to Include Cells**, and then look at the formula in the **Formula Bar**.

As shown in the Formula Bar, the formula is updated to include the range C4:C8; the green triangle no longer displays in the cell.

11 ▸ Click cell **D9**, which also displays a green triangle, and then point to **Error Checking** ⬥ to display the **ScreenTip**.

The same error exists in cell D9—not all adjacent cells in the column were included in the formula. This error also exists in the range E9:G9. You can click in each cell and use the Error Checking button's options list to correct each formula, or you can use the fill handle to copy the corrected formula in cell C9 to the remaining cells.

12 ▸ Click cell **C9**, drag the fill handle to the right to copy the corrected formula to the range **D9:G9**, and then notice that all the green triangles are removed from the range.

13 ▸ Click cell **H5**, point to **Error Checking** ⬥, and read the **ScreenTip**.

The formula in this cell is not the same as the formula in the other cells in this area of the worksheet.

14 ▸ On the **Formulas tab**, in the **Formula Auditing group**, click **Trace Precedents**. Compare your screen with Figure 4.43.

A blue border surrounds the range B8:G8, and a blue tracer arrow displays from the cell B8 to cell H5. This indicates that the formula in cell H5 is summing the values in row 8 rather than the values in row 5.

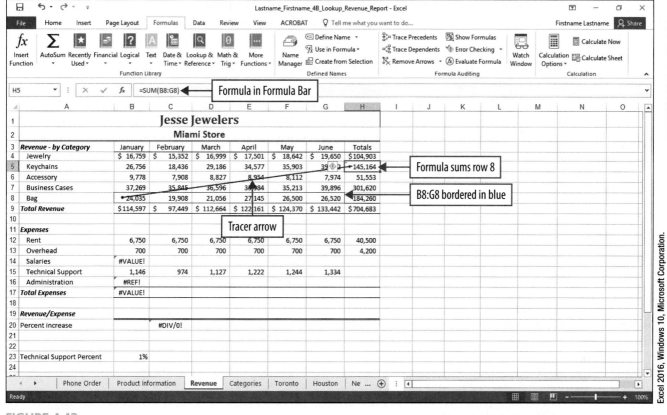

FIGURE 4.43

15 To the left of cell **H5**, click **Error Checking** ⊞ to display the list of error checking options, notice the explanation *Inconsistent Formula*, examine the formula in the Formula Bar, and then click **Copy Formula from Above**. If necessary, AutoFit **column H** to display the values correctly.

16 Look at the **Formula Bar** to verify that the formula is summing the numbers in **row 5**—the range **B5:G5**. With cell **H5** still selected, from the **Home tab**, display the **Cell Styles gallery**, and then, under **Number Format**, click the **Comma [0]** number format.

The blue tracer arrow no longer displays, the formula sums row 5, and the proper number format is applied.

17 Click cell **H4**. On the **Formulas tab**, in the **Formula Auditing group**, click **Trace Precedents**. Notice the tracer arrow indicates that the appropriate cells are included in the formula, as shown in Figure 4.44.

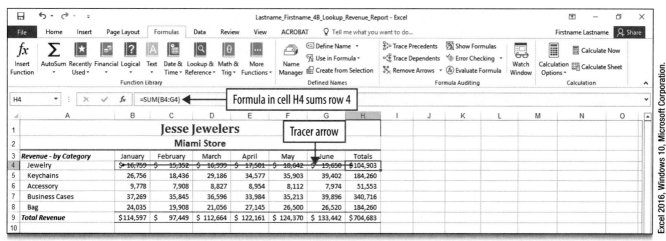

FIGURE 4.44

18 Click cell **H5**, click **Trace Precedents**, notice the **tracer arrow**, and then click cell **H6**. Click **Trace Precedents**, notice the tracer arrow, and verify that the correct cells are included in the formula.

19 Click cell **H7**, click **Trace Precedents**, and then click cell **H8**. Click **Trace Precedents**. Compare your screen with Figure 4.45.

Cells H7 and H8 display blue tracer arrows that are inconsistent with the other formulas in this column. However, green triangle indicators do not display in either of these cells. When auditing a worksheet, you cannot rely on the error notations and triangle indicators alone. To ensure the accuracy of a worksheet, you should use the tracer arrows to verify that all of the formulas are logical and correct.

⊿	A	B	C	D	E	F	G	H	I	J	K	L	M	N	O
1				**Jesse Jewelers**											
2				Miami Store											
3	*Revenue - by Category*	January	February	March	April	May	June	Totals							
4	Jewelry	$ 16,759	$ 15,352	$ 16,999	$ 17,501	$ 18,642	$ 19,650	$104,903		Inconsistent					
5	Keychains	26,750	18,490	29,186	34,577	35,909	39,402	184,260		tracer arrows					
6	Accessory	9,778	7,508	8,827	8,954	8,112	7,974	51,553							
7	Business Cases	37,269	35,845	36,596	33,984	35,213	39,896	240,716							
8	Bag	24,035	19,908	21,056	27,145	26,500	26,520	184,260							
9	*Total Revenue*	$114,597	$ 97,449	$ 112,664	$ 122,161	$ 124,370	$ 133,442	$704,683							
10															

FIGURE 4.45

20 In the **Formula Auditing group**, click **Remove Arrows**. Click cell **H6** and then use the fill handle to copy the correct formula down to cells **H7:H8**.

21 Save 🖫 your workbook.

Activity 4.14 | Tracing Dependents

3.5.1, Expert
3.5.4

Dependent cells are cells that contain formulas that refer to other cells—they depend on the values of other cells to display a result. The *Trace Dependents command* displays arrows that indicate what cells are affected by the value of the currently selected cell.

1 Click cell **B14**, which displays the error *#VALUE!*. To the left of the cell, point to **Error Checking** ⬦ and read the ScreenTip.

This formula contains a reference to a cell that is the wrong data type—a cell that does not contain a number.

2 In the **Formula Auditing group**, click **Trace Precedents**.

A blue tracer arrow indicates that cell B3 is included in the formula. Because cell B3 contains text—*January*—and not a number, no mathematical calculation is possible. The salaries should be calculated as 5 percent of *Total Revenue*, plus the constant amount of 36,000.

3 In the **Formula Auditing group**, click **Trace Dependents**. Compare your screen with Figure 4.46.

A red tracer arrow displays, showing that the formula in cell B17 depends on the result of the formula in cell B14. Tracer arrows are red if a cell contains an error value, such as #VALUE!.

FIGURE 4.46

4 To the left of cell **B14**, click **Error Checking** ⬦ and then click **Show Calculation Steps**.

> The Evaluate Formula dialog box displays and indicates the formula as =*"January"*0.05+36000*. January is not a number, nor is it a range name that refers to a group of numbers; so, it cannot be used in a mathematical formula. At the bottom of the dialog box, Excel indicates that the next evaluation will result in an error.

5 At the bottom of the dialog box, click **Evaluate**.

> The formula in the Evaluation box indicates *#Value!+36000*. You can use this box to evaluate each step of the formula. With complex formulas, this can be helpful in examining each piece of a formula to see where the error has occurred.

6 **Close** the **Evaluate Formula** dialog box. With cell **B14** still the active cell, click in the **Formula Bar** and edit the formula to change cell **B3** to **B9**, and then press Enter. If necessary, AutoFit **column B**.

> The error is removed and the result—41,730—displays in cell B14.

7 Click cell **B14**. Drag the fill handle to copy the corrected formula in cell **B14** across the row to cells **C14:G14**.

8 Click cell **B9**. In the **Formula Auditing group**, click **Trace Dependents**. Compare your screen with Figure 4.47.

> Each cell where an arrowhead displays indicates a dependent relationship.

FIGURE 4.47

9 In the **Formula Auditing group**, click **Remove Arrows**. **Save** 🖫 your workbook.

Activity 4.15 | Tracing Formula Errors

3.5.1 Expert

Another tool you can use to help locate and resolve an error is the ***Trace Error command***. Use this command to trace a selected error value such as #VALUE!, #REF!, #NAME?, or #DIV/0!.

1 Click cell **B16**, point to **Error Checking** ⚠ and read the ScreenTip.

The error message indicates that a cell that was referenced in the formula has been moved or deleted, or the function is causing an invalid reference error. In other words, Excel does not know where to look to get the value that should be used in the formula.

2 On the ribbon, on the **Formulas tab**, in the **Formula Auditing group**, click the **Error Checking arrow** to display a list, and then compare your screen with Figure 4.48.

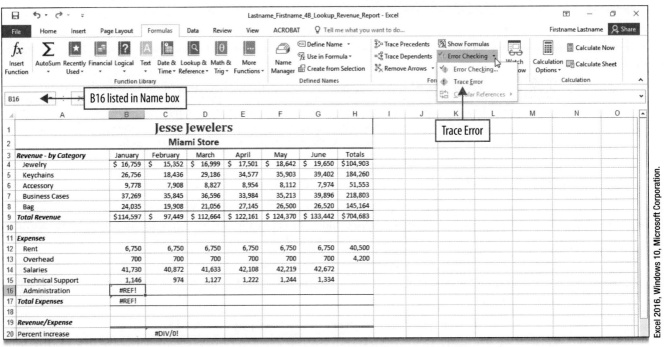

FIGURE 4.48

3 On the list, click **Trace Error**.

A precedent arrow is drawn from cell B9 to B16.

4 In the **Formula Auditing group**, click the **Error Checking arrow** again, and then click **Trace Error** again.

An arrow is drawn between cells B9 and B4 and the range B4:B8 is bordered in blue. The blue border indicates that this range is used in the formula in cell B9, which sums the values.

5 Click in cell **A24**. Type **Admin Percent** press Tab, type **2** and then press Enter.

The percent used to calculate administrative expenses was moved or deleted from the worksheet causing the #REF! error. You must re-enter the value so that it can be referenced in the formula in cell B16.

6 Click **B16**. Next to the cell, click **Error Checking** ⚠ to display the list of error checking options, and then click **Edit in Formula Bar**.

The insertion point displays in the Formula Bar so that you can edit the formula.

7 Delete **#REF!**. Type **b24** Press F4 to make the cell reference absolute, and then press Enter.

> The error notation in cell B16 is replaced with 2,292. The corrected formula needs to be copied across row 16, and the corrected formula also needs to use an absolute reference so that the 2% Admin Percent will be applied for each month.

8 Click cell **B16** and then drag the fill handle to copy the formula to the right to cells **C16:G16**.

9 **Save** 🖫 your workbook, press Ctrl + Home, and then compare your screen with Figure 4.49.

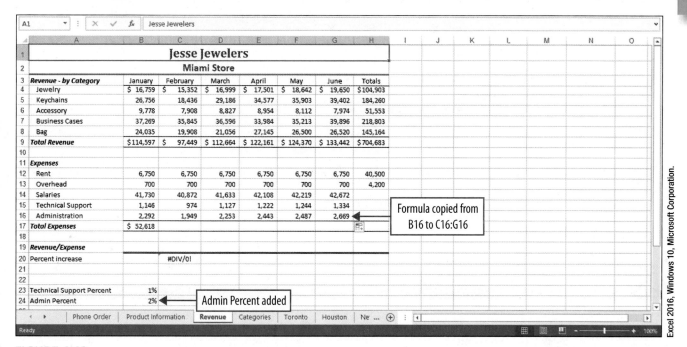

FIGURE 4.49

Activity 4.16 | Using Error Checking

The **Error Checking command** checks for common errors that occur in formulas. The behavior is similar to checking for spelling; that is, the command uses a set of rules to check for errors in formulas. The command opens the Error Checking dialog box, which provides an explanation about the error and enables you to move from one error to the next. Therefore, you can review all of the errors on a worksheet.

1 Be sure that cell **A1** is the active cell. In the **Formula Auditing group**, click the **Error Checking arrow**, and then click **Error Checking**.

> The Error Checking dialog box displays, and indicates the first error—in cell C20. Here the error notation *#DIV/0!* displays. The Error Checking dialog box provides an explanation of this error—a formula or function is trying to divide by zero or divide by an empty cell.

2 In the **Error Checking** dialog box, click **Show Calculation Steps**.

> The Evaluate Formula dialog box displays, and in the Evaluation box, *0/0* displays.

3 In the **Evaluate Formula** dialog box, click **Evaluate**.

> The Evaluation box displays the error *#DIV/0!* and the Evaluate button changes to Restart.

4 Click **Restart**.

> The formula *(C19-B19)/C19* displays; the first reference to C19 is underlined. The underline indicates that this is the part of the formula that is being evaluated. Each time you click the Evaluate button, it moves to the next cell reference or value in the formula.

5 In the **Evaluate Formula** dialog box, click **Step In**. Compare your screen with Figure 4.50.

A second box displays, which normally displays the value in the referenced cell. In this instance, the cell that is referenced is empty, as indicated in the message in the lower part of the dialog box. In a complex formula, this dialog box can help you examine and understand each part of the formula and identify exactly where the error is located.

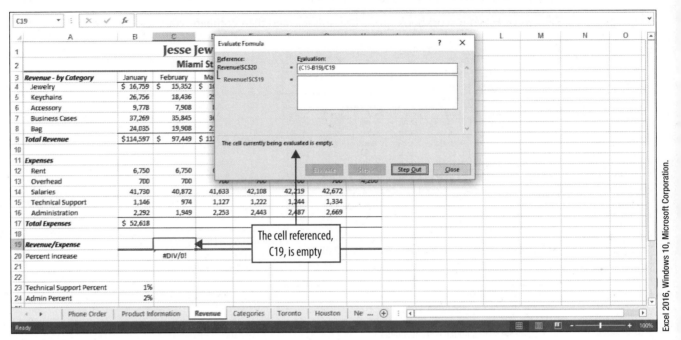

FIGURE 4.50

6 Click **Step Out**.

The cell evaluation box closes and the underline moves to the next cell in the formula—B19—which you can visually verify is empty by looking at the worksheet. To remove this error, you must complete the remainder of the worksheet.

7 **Close** the **Evaluate Formula** dialog box. In the **Error Checking** dialog box, click **Next**.

A message box displays stating that the error checking is complete for the entire sheet.

8 Click **OK**.

Both the message box and the Error Checking dialog box close.

9 Click cell **H13** and then use the fill handle to copy this formula down to cells **H14:H16**. Click cell **B17** and use the fill handle to copy this formula to the right into cells **C17:H17**. **AutoFit** any columns, if necessary, to display all of the data.

The formulas in the rows and columns are completed.

10 Click cell **B19** and type **=b9-b17** In the **Formula Bar**, click Enter ✓ to keep cell B19 active, and then copy the formula to the right into cells **C19:H19**.

The revenue/expense for each month is calculated. Notice that the *#DIV/0!* error in cell C20 is removed, but the formatting of the cell needs to be changed from dollars to percent.

11 Click cell **C20**, and then on the **Home tab**, in the **Number group**, click **Percent Style** %. Copy the formula to the right into cells **D20:G20**.

This formula calculates the percent change in revenue versus expenses, month to month.

12 Press Ctrl + Home. **Save** 💾 your workbook. Compare your screen with Figure 4.51.

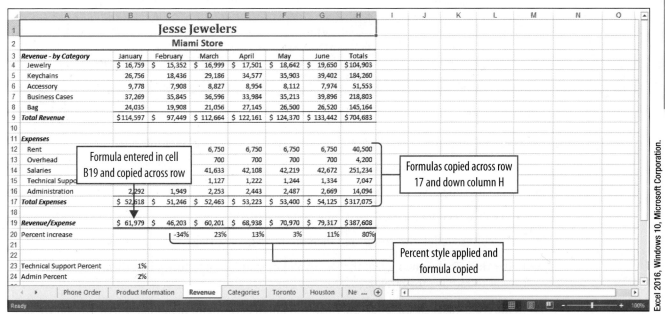

FIGURE 4.51

Activity 4.17 | Circling Invalid Data

MOS
3.5.3 Expert

If you use validation lists in a worksheet, you can apply data validation and instruct Excel to circle invalid data. In this manner you can verify that valid values—values from the list—have been entered on the worksheet.

1 At the bottom of the Excel window, click the **Categories sheet tab**.

> This worksheet lists the merchandise types included in each category; only merchandise types from these categories are valid.

2 In the upper left corner, click the **Name Box arrow**, and then click **Items**. Compare your screen with Figure 4.52.

> The named range in row 2 is highlighted.

FIGURE 4.52

3 Display the **Revenue** worksheet. On the **Data tab**, in the **Data Tools group**, click the **Data Validation arrow**, and then click **Circle Invalid Data**. Compare your screen with Figure 4.53.

> Red circles display around *Accessory* and *Bag*.

Project 4B: Lookup Form and Revenue Report | **Excel** **285**

Revenue - by Category	January	February	March	April	May	June	Totals
Jesse Jewelers							
Miami Store							
Jewelry	$ 16,759	15,352	16,999	$ 17,501	$ 18,642	$ 19,650	$104,903
Keychains	26,756			34,577	35,903	39,402	184,260
Accessory	3,778			8,954	8,112	7,974	51,553
Business Cases	37,269			33,984	35,213	39,896	218,803
Bag	24,035	19,908	21,056	27,145	26,500	26,520	145,164
Total Revenue	$114,597	$ 97,449	$ 112,664	$ 122,161	$ 124,370	$ 133,442	$704,683

Cells with invalid data circled

FIGURE 4.53

4 Click cell **A6** and click the arrow that displays at the right side of the cell.

The validation list displays.

5 On the list, click **Accessories**.

The item is corrected but the red circle is not removed.

6 Click cell **A8**, click the arrow, and then on the list, click **Bags**.

7 In the **Data Tools group**, click the **Data Validation arrow**, and then click **Clear Validation Circles** to remove the circles.

8 In the **Data Tools group**, click the **Data Validation arrow**, and then click **Circle Invalid Data**.

No circles are applied, which confirms that the data is now valid against the validation list.

9 **Save** 🖫 your workbook.

Objective 8 | Use the Watch Window to Monitor Cell Values

GO! Learn How
Video E4-8

You can monitor cells in one part of a workbook while working on another part of the workbook using the **Watch Window**—a window that displays the results of specified cells. You can monitor cells on other worksheets and see the results as soon as formulas are calculated or changes are made that affect the outcome of the watched cells. This feature is also useful on large worksheets for which the total rows and columns are not visible on the screen with the details.

Activity 4.18 | Using the Watch Window to Monitor Changes

MOS
3.5.2 Expert

Mike Connor's assistant is preparing the 1st Quarter sales worksheets using the Watch Window for sales totals for the four largest retail stores.

1 At the bottom of the Excel window, in the **sheet tab row**, click the **Toronto** worksheet.

2 Click cell **E8**. On the **Formulas tab**, in the **Formula Auditing group**, click **Watch Window**.

The Watch Window displays on your screen. As you create totals for the columns and rows on each worksheet in this Activity, you will be able to use the Watch Window to view the results for all the worksheets at once.

3 In the upper left corner of the **Watch Window**, click **Add Watch**. Point to the title bar of the **Add Watch** window, and then drag it below your data. Compare your screen with Figure 4.54.

The Add Watch dialog box displays the address for the selected cell—Toronto!$E$8

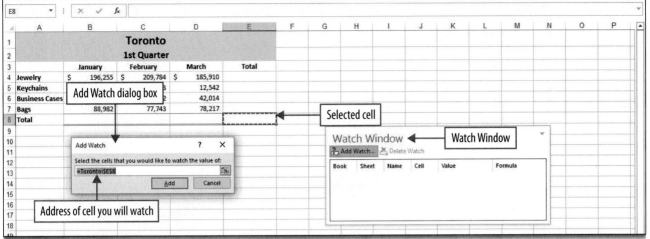

FIGURE 4.54

Excel 2016, Windows 10, Microsoft Corporation.

4 In the **Add Watch** dialog box, click **Add**.

Because there is no value or formula in the cell at this time, the Name, Value, and Formula columns in the Watch Window are empty.

5 Display the **Houston** worksheet and then click cell **E8**. In the **Watch Window**, click **Add Watch**, and then in the **Add Watch** dialog box, click **Add**. Compare your screen with Figure 4.55.

A second cell is added to the Watch Window.

FIGURE 4.55

6 Using the technique you just practiced, add cell **E8** from the **New York** sheet and from the **Miami** sheet to the **Watch Window**. Adjust the size of the Watch Window columns as necessary to view all four sheets. Compare your screen with Figure 4.56, and verify cell **E8** is listed for each of the four worksheets.

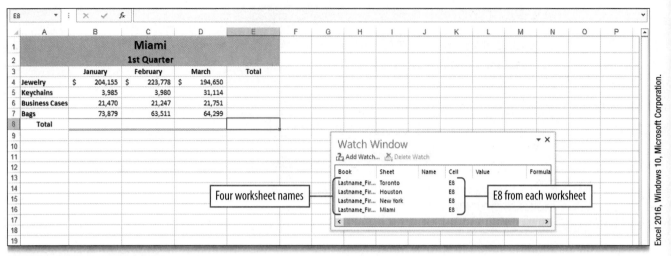

FIGURE 4.56

7 With the **Miami** worksheet active, hold down Shift, and then click the **Toronto sheet tab**.

The four store worksheets are selected and *[Group]* displays in the title bar.

8 In the **Miami** worksheet, select the range **B4:E8**.

This range includes the data and the empty row and column immediately adjacent to the data. Because the sheets are grouped, this action is taking place on all four worksheets.

9 On the **Formulas tab**, in the **Function Library group**, click the upper portion of **AutoSum** ∑ AutoSum ▾ . Select the range **B8:E8**, and then from the **Home tab**, display the **Cell Styles gallery**. At the bottom, click **Currency [0]**. Compare your screen with Figure 4.57.

The totals for the rows and columns in this worksheet, as well as in the other three worksheets, are calculated. The results display immediately in the Watch Window, indicating that calculations took place on all four sheets simultaneously.

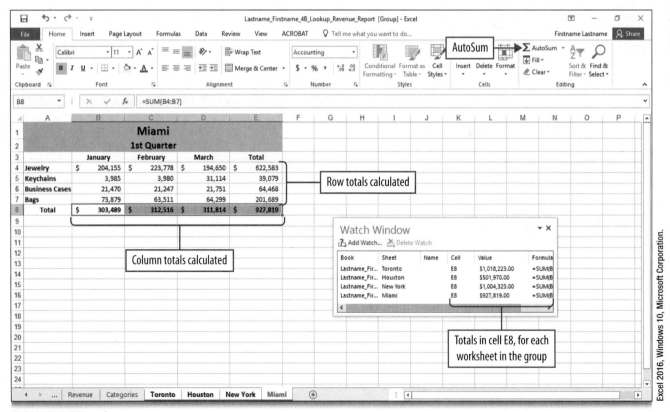

FIGURE 4.57

10 Close ☒ the **Watch Window**, and then **Save** 🖫 your workbook.

11 In the **sheet tab row**, right-click any sheet tab, and then click **Select All Sheets**.

12 On the **Page Layout tab**, in the **Page Setup group**, click the **Dialog Box Launcher** 🖙 to display the **Page Setup** dialog box.

13 Click the **Margins tab**, and then under **Center on page**, click **Horizontally**. Click the **Header/Footer tab**, click **Custom Footer**, and then in the **Left section**, insert the **File Name** 🖾. Click **OK** two times.

14 Right-click any sheet tab, and then click **Ungroup Sheets**. Click the **Revenue sheet tab**, hold down [Ctrl], and then click the **Categories sheet tab**.

15 With these two worksheets selected, on the **Page Layout tab**, in the **Page Setup group**, click **Orientation**, and then click **Landscape**.

16 **Ungroup** the sheets. Display **Backstage** view, click **Show All Properties**. On the list of **Properties**, in the **Tags** box, type **revenue by category and phone order form** In the **Subject** box, type your course name and section #. Under **Related People**, be sure that your name displays as the author. If necessary, right-click the author name, click **Edit Property**, type your name, click outside of the **Edit person** dialog box, and then click **OK**.

17 On the left, click **Print**. Under **Settings**, click the **Print Active Sheets arrow**, and then click **Print Entire Workbook**. At the bottom of the window, click **Next Page** ▸ to scroll through the worksheets.

18 On the left, click **Save** to save your workbook and redisplay the Excel window. If directed by your instructor to do so, submit a paper printout of the eight worksheets, an electronic image of each worksheet that looks like a printed document, or your original Excel file. If required by your instructor, print or create an electronic version of your worksheets with formulas displayed. In the upper right corner of the Excel window, click **Close** ☒.

> **END | You have completed Project 4B**

GO! To Work

Andrew Rodriguez / Fotolia; FotolEdhar / Fotolia; apops / Fotolia; Yuri Arcurs / Fotolia

MICROSOFT OFFICE SPECIALIST (MOS) SKILLS IN THIS CHAPTER	
PROJECT 4A	**PROJECT 4B**
3.4.3 Expert: Perform what-if analysis by using Goal Seek and Scenario Manager	2.1.3 Configure data validation
	3.2.1 Expert: Look up data by using the VLOOKUP function
3.4.5 Expert: Calculate data by using financial functions	3.5.1 Expert: Trace precedence and dependence
3.6.1 Expert: Name cells	3.5.2 Expert: Monitor cells by using the Watch Window
3.6.2 Expert: Name data ranges	3.5.3 Expert: Validate formulas by using error checking rules
3.6.4 Expert: Manage named ranges and objects	3.5.4 Expert: Evaluate formulas

BUILD YOUR E-PORTFOLIO

An E-Portfolio is a collection of evidence, stored electronically, that showcases what you have accomplished while completing your education. Collecting and then sharing your work products with potential employers reflects your academic and career goals. Your completed documents from the following projects are good examples to show what you have learned: 4G, 4K, and 4L.

GO! FOR JOB SUCCESS

Discussion: Mobile Devices

Your instructor may assign these questions to your class, and then ask you to think about them or discuss them with your classmates:

Mobile devices that can do more at low cost are popular for employers and employees. Employers who provide a smartphone or tablet to employees benefit by having employees available to handle customer or production issues quickly from any location. Employees like not being tied to a desk and a phone. A downside, however, is that many employees feel they have to be available 24 hours a day and are constantly tempted to check their work emails even when they are on personal time.

FotolEdhar / Fotolia

Do you think employers should expect employees to be available during non-work hours if they are issued an employer-paid mobile device?

What are two reasons an employee might prefer having mobile access to work rather than being at a desk in the office?

What are two strategies an employee can implement to avoid looking at work emails during non-work hours?

END OF CHAPTER

SUMMARY

The PMT function is used to calculate the payment for a loan. The PMT function has three required arguments: Rate (interest), Nper (number of payments), and Pv (present value), and two optional arguments.

Two of Excel's What-If Analysis tools are Goal Seek—used to find a specific value for a cell by adjusting the value of another cell; and Data Tables—which display the results of different inputs into a formula.

A defined name can represent a cell, range of cells, formula, or constant value and can be used in a formula. A Lookup function looks up data located in another part of a workbook to find a corresponding value.

Data validation is used to control the type of data or the values that are entered into a cell. Formula auditing improves the accuracy of data entry and checks a worksheet for various types of errors.

GO! LEARN IT ONLINE

Review the concepts, key terms, and MOS skills in this chapter by completing these online challenges, which you can find at **MyITLab**.

Matching and Multiple Choice: Answer matching and multiple choice questions to test what you learned in this chapter.

Lessons on the GO!: Learn how to use all the new apps and features as they are introduced by Microsoft.

MOS Prep Quiz: Answer questions to review the MOS skills that you practiced in this chapter.

Your instructor will assign Projects from this list to ensure your learning and assess your knowledge.

	PROJECT GUIDE FOR EXCEL CHAPTER 4		
Project	**Apply Skills from These Chapter Objectives**	**Project Type**	**Project Location**
4A MyITLab	Objectives 1–4 from Project 4A	**4A Instructional Project (Grader Project)** Guided instruction to learn the skills in Project 4A.	In MyITLab and in text
4B MyITLab	Objectives 5–8 from Project 4B	**4B Instructional Project (Grader Project)** Guided instruction to learn the skills in Project 4B.	In MyITLab and in text
4C	Objectives 1–4 from Project 4A	**4C Skills Review (Scorecard Grading)** A guided review of the skills from Project 4A.	In text
4D	Objectives 5–8 from Project 4B	**4D Skills Review (Scorecard Grading)** A guided review of the skills from Project 4B.	In text
4E MyITLab	Objectives 1–4 from Project 4A	**4E Mastery (Grader Project)** **Mastery and Transfer of Learning** A demonstration of your mastery of the skills in Project 4A with extensive decision-making.	In MyITLab and in text
4F MyITLab	Objectives 5–8 from Project 4B	**4F Mastery (Grader Project)** **Mastery and Transfer of Learning** A demonstration of your mastery of the skills in Project 4B with extensive decision-making.	In MyITLab and in text
4G MyITLab	Combination of Objectives from Projects 4A and 4B	**4G Mastery (Grader Project)** **Mastery and Transfer of Learning** A demonstration of your mastery of the skills in Projects 4A and 4B with extensive decision-making.	In MyITLab and in text
4H	Combination of Objectives from Projects 4A and 4B	**4H GO! Fix It (Scorecard Grading)** **Critical Thinking** A demonstration of your mastery of the skills in Projects 4A and 4B by creating a correct result from a document that contains errors you must find.	Instructor Resource Center (IRC) and MyITLab
4I	Combination of Objectives from Projects 4A and 4B	**4I GO! Make It (Scorecard Grading)** **Critical Thinking** A demonstration of your mastery of the skills in Projects 4A and 4B by creating a result from a supplied picture.	IRC and MyITLab
4J	Combination of Objectives from Projects 4A and 4B	**4J GO! Solve It (Rubric Grading)** **Critical Thinking** A demonstration of your mastery of the skills in Projects 4A and 4B, your decision-making skills, and your critical thinking skills. A task-specific rubric helps you self-assess your result.	IRC and MyITLab
4K	Combination of Objectives from Projects 4A and 4B	**4K GO! Solve It (Rubric Grading)** **Critical Thinking** A demonstration of your mastery of the skills in Projects 4A and 4B, your decision-making skills, and your critical thinking skills. A task-specific rubric helps you self-assess your result.	In text
4L	Combination of Objectives from Projects 4A and 4B	**4L GO! Think (Rubric Grading)** **Critical Thinking** A demonstration of your understanding of the Chapter concepts applied in a manner that you would outside of college. An analytic rubric helps you and your instructor grade the quality of your work by comparing it to the work an expert in the discipline would create.	In text
4M	Combination of Objectives from Projects 4A and 4B	**4M GO! Think (Rubric Grading)** **Critical Thinking** A demonstration of your understanding of the Chapter concepts applied in a manner that you would outside of college. An analytic rubric helps you and your instructor grade the quality of your work by comparing it to the work an expert in the discipline would create.	IRC and MyITLab
4N	Combination of Objectives from Projects 4A and 4B	**4N You and GO! (Rubric Grading)** **Critical Thinking** A demonstration of your understanding of the Chapter concepts applied in a manner that you would in a personal situation. An analytic rubric helps you and your instructor grade the quality of your work.	IRC and MyITLab

GLOSSARY

GLOSSARY OF CHAPTER KEY TERMS

Arguments The values that an Excel function uses to perform calculations or operations.

Auditing The process of examining a worksheet for errors in formulas.

Create from Selection A command by which you can name a cell range based on existing row or column titles.

Data table A range of cells that shows how changing certain values in your formulas affect the results of those formulas and that makes it easy to calculate multiple versions in one operation.

Data validation A technique by which you can control the type of data or the values that are entered into a cell by limiting the acceptable values to a defined list.

Defined name A word or string of characters in Excel that represents a cell, a range of cells, a formula, or a constant value; also referred to as simply a *name*.

Dependent cells Cells that contain formulas that refer to other cells.

Error Checking command A command that checks for common errors that occur in formulas.

Error value The result of a formula that Excel cannot evaluate correctly.

Financial functions Pre-built formulas that perform common business calculations such as calculating a loan payment on a vehicle or calculating how much to save each month to buy something; financial functions commonly involve a period of time such as months or years.

Formula Auditing Tools and commands accessible from the Formulas tab that help you check your worksheet for errors.

Formula An equation that performs mathematical calculations on values in a worksheet.

Future value (Fv) The value at the end of the time period in an Excel function; the cash balance you want to attain after the last payment is made—usually zero for loans.

Goal Seek One of Excel's What-If Analysis tools that provides a method to find a specific value for a cell by adjusting the value of one other cell—find the right input when you know the result you want.

HLOOKUP An Excel function that looks up values that are displayed horizontally in a row.

Interest The amount charged for the use of borrowed money.

Lookup functions A group of Excel functions that look up a value in a defined range of cells located in another part of the workbook to find a corresponding value.

Name A word or string of characters in Excel that represents a cell, a range of cells, a formula, or a constant value; also referred to as *a defined name*.

Nper The abbreviation for *number of time periods* in various Excel functions.

One-variable Data table A data table that changes the value in only one cell.

PMT function An Excel function that calculates the payment for a loan based on constant payments and a constant interest rate.

Precedent cells Cells that are referred to by a formula in another cell.

Present value (Pv) The total amount that a series of future payments is worth now; also known as the *principal*.

Principal The total amount that a series of future payments is worth now; also known as the *Present value (Pv)*.

Rate In the Excel PMT function, the term used to indicate the interest rate for a loan.

Scope The location within which a defined name is recognized without qualification—usually either to a specific worksheet or to the entire workbook.

Table array A defined range of cells, arranged in a column or a row, used in a VLOOKUP or HLOOKUP function.

Trace Dependents command A command that displays arrows that indicate what cells are affected by the value of the currently selected cell.

Trace Error command A tool that helps locate and resolve an error by tracing the selected error value.

Trace Precedents command A command that displays arrows to indicate what cells affect the value of the cell that is selected.

Tracer arrow An indicator that shows the relationship between the active cell and its related cell.

Two-variable Data table A data table that changes the values in two cells.

Type argument An optional argument in the PMT function that assumes that the payment will be made at the end of each time period.

Validation list A list of values that are acceptable for a group of cells; only values on the list are valid and any value *not* on the list is considered invalid.

VLOOKUP An Excel function that looks up values that are displayed vertically in a column.

Watch Window A window that displays the results of specified cells.

What-If Analysis The process of changing the values in cells to see how those changes affect the outcome of formulas in a worksheet.

Apply **4A skills** from these Objectives:

1 Use Financial Functions
2 Use Goal Seek
3 Create a Data Table
4 Use Defined Names in a Formula

Skills Review | Project 4C Auto Loan

In the following Skills Review, you will create a worksheet for Patricia Murphy, U.S. Sales Director, which details loan information for purchasing seven automobiles for Jesse Jewelers sales representatives. The monthly payment for the seven automobiles cannot exceed $3,500. You will also help Ms. Murphy calculate quarterly Store Supply costs using defined names. Your four completed worksheets will look similar to Figure 4.58.

PROJECT FILES

For Project 4C, you will need the following file:

e04C_Loan_Supply_Costs

You will save your workbook as:

Lastname_Firstname_4C_Loan_Supply_Costs

PROJECT RESULTS

FIGURE 4.58

(Project 4C Auto Loan continues on the next page)

Excel 2016, Windows 10, Microsoft Corporation

1 Start Excel. From your student files, open the file **e04C_Loan_Supply_Costs**, and then save the file in your Excel Chapter 4 folder as **Lastname_Firstname_4C_Loan_Supply_Costs**

a. In the **Auto Loan** worksheet, in the range **A2:B5**, enter the following row titles and data.

Amount of Loan	$135,000
Period (years)	3
Interest rate (per year)	4.75%
Payment (per month)	

b. Click cell **B5**. On the **Formulas tab**, in the **Function Library group**, click **Financial**, and then scroll down and click **PMT**. Drag the **Function Arguments** dialog box to the right side of your screen so you can view **columns A:B**.

c. In the **Rate** box, type **b4/12** to convert the annual interest rate to a monthly interest rate. Press Tab, and then in the **Nper** box, type **b3*12** to have Excel convert the number of years in the loan (3) to the total number of months. Press Tab, and then in the **Pv** box, type **b2** to enter the present value of the loan. Click **OK** to create the function. In the **Formula Bar**, between the equal sign and PMT, type – (minus sign) to insert a minus sign into the formula, and then press Enter to display the loan payment as a positive number.

2 Click cell **B5**. On the **Data tab**, in the **Forecast group**, click **What-If Analysis**, and then in the list, click **Goal Seek**. In the **Goal Seek** dialog box, in the **Set cell** box, confirm that B5 displays.

a. Press Tab. In the **To value** box, type the payment goal of **3500** and then press Tab. In the **By changing cell** box, type **b2** which is the amount of the loan. Click **OK** two times. For three years at 4.75%, Patricia can borrow only $117,218 if she maintains a monthly payment of $3,500.

b. Click cell **A7**. Type **Option #1 Reduce the Loan** and then on the **Formula Bar**, press Enter. **Merge & Center** the title across the range **A7:B7**, display the **Cell Styles** gallery, and then apply the **Heading 2** cell style.

c. Select the range **A2:B5**, right-click, and then click **Copy**. Point to cell **A8**, right-click, point to **Paste Special**, and then under **Paste Values**, click the second button—**Values & Number Formatting (A)**. Press Esc to cancel the moving border.

d. In cell **B2**, type **135000** and then press Enter to restore the original loan amount. Click cell **B5**. On the **Data tab**, in the **Forecast group**, click **What-If Analysis**, and then click **Goal Seek**.

e. In the **Set cell** box, confirm that **B5** displays. Press Tab. In the **To value** box, type **3500** Press Tab. In the **By changing cell** box, type **b3** which is the number of years for the loan. Click **OK** two times.

f. Click **A13**. Type **Option #2 Increase Years** and then press Enter. Use the **Format Painter** to copy the format from cell **A7** to cell **A13**. Select the range **A2:B5**, right-click, and then click **Copy**. Point to cell **A14**, right-click, point to **Paste Special**, and then under **Paste Values**, click the second button—**Values & Number Formatting (A)**. Press Esc to cancel the moving border.

g. Point to cell **B15**, right-click to display the mini toolbar, and then click **Decrease Decimal** until the number of decimal places is two. Click cell **B3**. Type **3** and then press Enter to restore the original value. Press Ctrl + Home to move to the top of the worksheet. **Save** your workbook.

3 To determine how variable interest rates and a varying number of payments affect the payment amount, Patricia will set up a two-variable data table. Click the **New sheet** button to create a new worksheet. Double-click the **Sheet1 tab**, rename it **Payment Table** and then press Enter. In cell **A1**, type **Loan Options for Auto Purchase: Rates versus Months** and then press Enter. **Merge & Center** this title across the range **A1:I1**, and then apply the **Title** cell style.

a. In the range **A2:B4**, enter the following row titles and data.

Amount of Loan	$135,000
Period (months)	36
Interest rate (per year)	4.75%

(Project 4C Auto Loan continues on the next page)

b. Change the width of **column A** to **20** (145 pixels). Click cell **C8**. Type **24** and then press Tab. Type **30** and then press Tab. Select the range **C8:D8**. Drag the fill handle to the right through cell **I8** to fill a pattern of months from 24 to 60 in increments of six months.

c. In cell **B9**, type **7.0%** and press Enter. Type **6.5%** and press Enter. Select the range **B9:B10**, and then drag the fill handle down through cell **B16** to fill a pattern of interest rates in increments of 0.5% from 7.00% down to 3.50%. If necessary, adjust to display two decimal places.

d. Click cell **C6**. Type **Payment Options** and then press Enter. **Merge & Center** this title across the range **C6:I6**. Apply the **Heading 1** cell style. Click cell **C7**. Type **Number of Monthly Payments** and then use the **Format Painter** to apply the format of cell **C6** to cell **C7**.

e. Click cell **A9**, type **Rates** and then press Enter. Select the range **A9:A16**. On the **Home tab**, in the **Alignment group**, click **Merge & Center**, click **Align Right**, and then click **Middle Align**. Apply the **Explanatory Text** cell style.

f. Click cell **B8**. On the **Formulas tab**, in the **Function Library group**, click **Financial**, and then click **PMT**. In the **Rate** box, type **b4/12** to divide the interest rate per year by 12 to convert it to a monthly interest rate. Press Tab, and then in the **Nper** box, type **b3** Press Tab. In the **Pv** box, type **-b2** and then click **OK**.

g. Select the range **B8:I16**. On the **Data tab**, in the **Forecast group**, click **What-If Analysis**, and then in the list, click **Data Table**. In the **Data Table** dialog box, in the **Row input cell** box, type **b3** and then press Tab. In the **Column input cell** box, type **b4** and then in the **Data Table** dialog box, click **OK** to create the data table. Click in any cell outside of the table to deselect.

h. Use the **Format Painter** to copy the format from cell **B8** to the range **C9:I16**. Select **columns C:I** and apply **Auto Fit**.

i. Select the range **F14:F16** and apply the **Note** cell style to highlight the desired payment option. Select the nonadjacent ranges **C8:I8** and **B9:B16**, apply

Bold and **Center**. On the **Page Layout tab**, set the orientation for this worksheet to **Landscape**.

j. Group the **Payment Table** worksheet and the **Auto Loan** worksheet. Click the **Insert tab**, from the **Page Setup** dialog box, insert a custom footer, and then in the left section, click **File Name**. Click **OK**, and then on the **Margins tab**, select the **Horizontally** check box. Click **OK**. Press Ctrl + Home to move to the top of the worksheet.

4 Display the **Quarterly Supply Costs** worksheet.

a. Select the range **B6:E18**, which includes the empty cells in **row 18**, and then click **AutoSum**. Click anywhere to cancel the selection. Select the range **B6:E6**, hold down Ctrl and select the range **B18:E18**, and then from the **Cell Styles** gallery, under **Number Format**, apply the **Currency [0]** cell style. Select the range **B7:E17**, display the **Cell Styles** gallery, and then under **Number Format**, click **Comma [0]**. Select the range **B18:E18**, and then apply the **Total** cell style.

b. Select the range **B6:E9**. On the **Formulas tab**, in the **Defined Names group**, click **Define Name**. With Revolving_Glass_Towers selected, type **Showcase_Costs** as the name. At the bottom of the dialog box, at the right edge of the **Refers to** box, point to and click **Collapse Dialog Box**. Change the range by selecting the range **B6:E10**.

c. Click **Expand Dialog Box** to redisplay the **New Name** dialog box, and then click **OK**. Select the range **B11:E14**. In the upper left corner of the Excel window, to the left of the **Formula Bar**, click in the **Name Box**. Type **Wrapping_Costs** and press Enter.

d. Select the range **B15:E16**. On the **Formulas tab**, in the **Defined Names group**, click **Name Manager**. In the upper left corner of the **Name Manager** dialog box, click **New**. With *Slant_Back_Counter_Racks* selected, type **Countertop_Costs** and then click **OK**. **Close** the **Name Manager** dialog box and **Save** your workbook.

e. On the left side of your window, in the **row heading area**, point to the **row 15** heading and right-click to select the entire row and display a shortcut menu. Click **Insert** to insert a new blank row above. Click cell **A15**, type **Ribbons and Bows**

(Project 4C Auto Loan continues on the next page)

and then press [Tab]. In cell **B15**, type **220** and press [Tab]. In cell **C15**, type **215** and press [Tab]. In cell **D15**, type **345** and press [Tab]. In cell **E15**, type **300** and press [Enter].

f. On the **Formulas tab**, from the **Defined Names group**, display the **Name Manager** dialog box. In the **Name Manager** dialog box, in the **Name** column, click **Wrapping_Costs**. At the bottom of the dialog box, click in the **Refers to** box and edit the reference, changing **$E$14** to **$E$15** to include the new row in the range. **Close** the **Name Manager** dialog box, and click **Yes** to save the changes you made to the name reference.

g. On the **Formulas tab**, from the **Defined Names group**, display the **Name Manager** dialog box. Click **Wrapping_Costs**, and then click **Edit**. In the **Edit Name** dialog box, with *Wrapping_Costs* selected, type **Packaging_Costs** Click **OK**, and then **Close** the **Name Manager** dialog box. In the upper left corner of the window, click the **Name Box arrow** and notice the modified range name, Packaging_Costs. Click any cell to close the list, and then **Save** your workbook.

h. Select the range **A18:E18**. On the **Formulas tab**, in the **Defined Names group**, click **Create from Selection**. In the **Create Names from Selection** dialog box, click **OK**, and then click anywhere to cancel the selection. Click the **Name Box arrow**, and then click the name **Tags_and_Labels**. Notice that in the new range name, Excel inserted the underscore necessary to fill a blank space in the range name.

5 Display the **Annual Supply Costs** worksheet.

a. In cell **B5**, type **=sum(S** Continue typing **howcase_Costs** and then press [Enter]. Your result is 50257. In cell **B6**, type **=sum(P** and then on the **Formula AutoComplete list**, double-click **Packaging_Costs** to insert the formula. Press [Enter] to display the result 13081.

b. In cell **B7**, type **=sum(** and then on the **Formulas tab**, in the **Defined Names group**, click **Use in Formula**. On the list, click **Countertop_Costs** and then press [Enter] to display the total 5372.

c. In cell **B8**, use any of the techniques you just practiced to sum the cells containing the costs for **Tags_and_Labels** and to display a result of 6922. Click cell **B9**, hold down [Alt] and press [=] to insert the SUM function, and then press [Enter] to display a total of *75632*.

d. Select the nonadjacent cells **B5** and **B9**, and then from the **Home tab**, display the **Cell Styles** gallery. Under **Number Format**, click the **Currency [0]** cell style. To the range **B6:B8**, apply the **Comma [0]** cell style. Click cell **B9** and apply the **Total** cell style.

6 Group the **Annual Supply Cost** worksheet and the **Quarterly Supply Costs** worksheets.

a. On the **Page Layout tab**, in the **Page Setup group**, click the **Dialog Box Launcher** 🔲 to display the **Page Setup** dialog box.

b. Click the **Margins tab**, and then under **Center on page**, click **Horizontally**. Click the **Header/Footer tab**, click **Custom Footer**, and then in the **Left section**, insert the **File Name** 🔲. Click **OK** two times.

c. Right-click the **Annual Supply Costs** sheet tab, and then click **Ungroup Sheets**. Click the **Payment Table sheet tab**, hold down [Ctrl] and then click the **Quarterly Supply Costs sheet tab**.

d. With these two worksheets selected, on the **Page Layout tab**, in the **Page Setup group**, click **Orientation**, and then click **Landscape**.

e. Click the **Auto Loan** sheet tab to ungroup the sheets. Display **Backstage** view, click **Show All Properties**. On the list of **Properties**, in the **Tags** box, type **auto loan, supply costs** In the **Subject** box, type your course name and section #. Under **Related People**,

(Project 4C Auto Loan continues on the next page)

be sure that your name displays as the author. If necessary, right-click the author name, click **Edit Property**, type your name, click outside of the **Edit person** dialog box, and then click **OK**.

f. On the left, click **Print**. Under **Settings**, click the **Print Active Sheets arrow**, and then click **Print Entire Workbook**. At the bottom of the window, click **Next Page** ▶ to scroll through the worksheets. On the left, click **Save**.

g. If directed by your instructor to do so, submit a paper printout of the four worksheets, an electronic image of each worksheet that looks like a printed document, or your original Excel file. If required by your instructor, print or create an electronic version of your worksheets with formulas displayed. In the upper right corner of the Excel window, click **Close**.

END | You have completed Project 4C

Skills Review Project 4D Quarterly Cost Report and Lookup Form

In the following Skills Review, you will assist Mike Connor, the Vice President of Marketing at Jesse Jewelers, by adding lookup functions to a Packing Slip form so that an order taker can complete the form quickly. You will use the Formula Auditing tools to review a revenue worksheet for the Houston store and you will use the Watch Window to edit the store's utility cost worksheets. Your completed workbooks will look similar to Figure 4.59.

PROJECT FILES

For Project 4D, you will need the following file:

e04D_Form_Cost_Report

You will save your workbook as:

Lastname_Firstname_4D_Form_Cost_Report

PROJECT RESULTS

FIGURE 4.59

Excel 2016, Windows 10, Microsoft Corporation

(Project 4D Quarterly Cost Report and Lookup Form continues on the next page)

1 Start Excel. From your student files, open the file **e04D_Form_Cost_Report**, and then save the file in your **Excel Chapter 4** folder as **Lastname_Firstname_4D_Form_Cost_Report**

a. Display the **Product Information** worksheet. Select the range **A4:C11**. On the **Data tab**, in the **Sort & Filter group**, click **Sort**. If necessary, drag the Sort dialog box to the right side of your screen so you can view **columns A:C**.

b. In the **Sort** dialog box, under **Column**, click the **Sort by arrow**. Notice that the selected range is now **A5:C11** and that the column titles in the range **A4:C4** display in the **Sort by** list. In the **Sort by** list, click **Style Code**. Under **Sort On**, verify that *Values* displays, and under **Order**, verify that *A to Z* displays. Click **OK** to sort the data by Style Code in ascending order. **Save** your workbook.

c. Display the **Packing Slip** worksheet. In cell **A9**, type **BC-MO** and press Tab. With cell **B9** as the active cell, on the **Formulas tab**, in the **Function Library group**, click **Lookup & Reference**, and then click **VLOOKUP**.

d. With the insertion point in the **Lookup_value** box, click cell **A9** to look up the description of Item BC-MO. Click in the **Table_array** box, and then at the bottom of the workbook, click the **Product Information sheet tab**. On the **Product Information** sheet, select the range **A4:C11**, and then press F4. Click in the **Col_index_num** box, type **2** and then click **OK**.

e. With cell **B9** as the active cell and containing the VLOOKUP formula, point to the fill handle in the lower right corner of the cell, and then drag to fill the VLOOKUP formula down through cell **B18**.

f. Click cell **C9**, type **12** as the quantity ordered, and then press Tab. In cell **D9**, type **Black** and press Tab. With cell **E9** as the active cell, on the **Formulas tab**, in the **Function Library group**, click **Lookup & Reference**, and then click **VLOOKUP**.

g. With the insertion point in the **Lookup_value** box, click cell **A9** to look up information for Item BC-MO. Click in the **Table_array** box, display the **Product Information** sheet, and then select the range **A4:C11**. Press F4 to make the values in the range absolute.

h. In the **Col_index_num** box, type **3** to look up the price in the third column of the range, and then click **OK**. The Unit Price for the Monogramed Business Card Case displays in cell **E9**. Fill the formula down through cell **E18**. Click cell **F9**, and notice that a formula to calculate the total for the item, Quantity times Unit Price, was already entered in the worksheet.

i. Click cell **E9**, and then copy the VLOOKUP formula down through cell **E18**.

j. Click cell **A10**, type **BC-CB** and press Tab two times. In cell **C10**, type **24** and press Tab. Notice that Excel calculates the total for this item in cell **F10**— 1,104.00. In cell **D10**, type **Pearl** and then press Enter. **Save** your workbook.

2 Display the **Product Information** sheet. Select the range **A4:A11**. On the **Formulas** tab, in the **Defined Names** group, click **Create from Selection**.

a. In the **Create Names from Selection** dialog box, be sure only the **Top row** check box is selected, and then click **OK**.

b. Display the **Packing Slip** worksheet, and then select the range **A9:A18**. On the **Data tab**, in the **Data Tools group**, click **Data Validation**. In the **Data Validation** dialog box, be sure the **Settings tab** is selected.

c. Under **Validation criteria**, click the **Allow arrow**, and then click **List**. Click to position the insertion point in the **Source** box, type **=Style_Code** and then click **OK**.

d. Click cell **A11**, and notice that a list arrow displays at the right edge of the cell. In cell **A11**, click the list arrow to display the list. In the list, click **KC-CB**. Press Tab two times, type **24** and press Tab, type **Blue** and then press Enter to return to the beginning of the next row.

e. With cell **A12** active, click the **list arrow**, and then click **KC-EN**. As the **Quantity**, type **18** and as the **Color**, type **Red** Press Enter. In cell **A13**, type **B-W** and press Tab. An error message displays indicating that you entered a value that is not valid; that is, it is not on the validation list you created. In the error message, click **Cancel**.

f. Select the unused **rows 13:18**, right-click over the selected rows, and then click **Delete**. In cell **F13**, **Sum** the order amounts and then apply the **Total** cell style. **Save** your workbook.

(Project 4D Quarterly Cost Report and Lookup Form continues on the next page)

Skills Review Project 4D Quarterly Cost Report and Lookup Form (continued)

3 ▸ Display the **Revenue** worksheet.

a. In the **column heading area**, select **column B**, hold down Ctrl, and then select **column H**. Point to the *right* edge of either of the selected column headings to display the pointer, and then double-click to AutoFit the columns.

b. Click cell **C9**. On the **Formulas tab**, in the **Formula Auditing group**, click **Trace Precedents**. To the left of the cell, click **Error Checking**, and then click **Update Formula to Include Cells**. Drag the fill handle to copy the corrected formula in cell **C9** to the range **D9:G9**.

c. Click cell **H5**, and then point to the **Error Checking** button to read the ScreenTip. On the **Formulas tab**, in the **Formula Auditing group**, click **Trace Precedents**. To the left of cell **H5**, click **Error Checking** to display the list of error checking options, click **Copy Formula from Above**, and then look at the **Formula Bar** to verify that the formula is summing the numbers in **row 5**. With cell **H5** still selected, from the **Home tab**, display the **Cell Styles gallery**, and then click the **Comma [0]** number format.

d. Click cell **H6**, on the **Formulas tab**, click **Trace Precedents**, and then verify that the row is correctly summed. Click cell **H7**, and then click **Trace Precedents**. Notice that the formula is not correct. Click cell **H8**, and then click **Trace Precedents**. Notice that the formula is not correct. In the **Formula Auditing group**, click **Remove Arrows**. Click cell **H6**, and then use the fill handle to copy the correct formula down to cells **H7:H8**.

4 ▸ Click cell **B14**, which displays the error *#VALUE!*. To the left of the cell, point to **Error Checking** and read the ScreenTip. In the **Formula Auditing group**, click **Trace Precedents**.

a. To the left of the cell, click **Error Checking**, and then on the list, click **Show Calculation Steps**. Notice that the formula is multiplying by a text value.

b. **Close** the **Evaluate Formula** dialog box. With cell **B14** still the active cell, click in the **Formula Bar**, and then edit the formula to change the reference to cell **B3** to **B9** and press Enter. Click cell **B14**, and then drag the fill handle to copy the corrected formula across the row to cells **C14:G14**.

5 ▸ Click cell **B16**, point to **Error Checking**, and read the ScreenTip. In the **Formula Auditing group**, click the **Error Checking arrow** to display a list. On the list, click **Trace Error**. In the **Formula Auditing group**, click the **Error Checking arrow**, and then click **Trace Error** again to view the precedent cells. Click in cell **A24**. Type **Admin Percent** and press Tab, and then type **2** to fill in the missing data.

a. Click **B16**. Remove the arrows. To the left of the cell, click **Error Checking** to display the list of error checking options, and then click **Edit in Formula Bar**. Delete *#REF!*. Type **b24** and press F4 to make the cell reference absolute. Press Enter. Click cell **B16**, and then use the fill handle to copy the formula to the right to cells **C16:G16**.

6 ▸ Click cell **A1**. In the **Formula Auditing group**, click the **Error Checking arrow**, and then click **Error Checking**—cell C20 is selected. In the **Error Checking** dialog box, click **Show Calculation Steps**; notice that the divisor is an empty cell. In the **Evaluate Formula** dialog box, click **Evaluate**. Click **Restart**.

a. In the **Evaluate Formula** dialog box, click **Step In** to examine the formula. Click **Step Out**. Close the **Evaluate Formula** dialog box.

b. In the **Error Checking** dialog box, click **Next**. Click **OK**. Click cell **H13**, and then use the fill handle to copy this formula down to cells **H14:H16**. Click cell **B17** and drag the fill handle to copy this formula to the right into cells **C17:H17**.

c. Click cell **B19** and type **=b9-b17** Press Enter, and then copy the formula to the right into cells **C19:H19**. Click cell **C20**, and then on the **Home tab**, in the **Number group**, click **Percent Style**. Copy the formula to the right into cells **D20:G20**. **Save** your workbook.

7 ▸ Display the **Categories** worksheet. To the left of the **Formula Bar**, click the **Name Box** arrow, and then click **Items**. Examine the selected range.

a. Redisplay the **Revenue** worksheet. On the **Data tab**, in the **Data Tools group**, click the **Data Validation arrow**, and then click **Circle Invalid Data**.

b. Click cell **A8**, and then click the arrow at the right side of the cell. From the list, click **Bags**. In the **Data Tools group**, click the **Data Validation arrow**, and then click **Clear Validation Circles**.

(Project 4D Quarterly Cost Report and Lookup Form continues on the next page)

8 ▸ Display the **Toronto** worksheet, and then click cell **E8**. On the **Formulas tab**, in the **Formula Auditing group**, click **Watch Window**. In the upper left corner of the **Watch Window**, click **Add Watch**. In the **Add Watch** dialog box, click **Add**.

a. Display the **Houston** worksheet, and using the same technique, add cell **E8** from the **Houston** worksheet. Repeat this for the **New York** worksheet and for the **Miami** worksheet. Adjust the size of the **Watch Window** and columns as necessary to view all four sheets, and verify that cell **E8** is listed for each of the four worksheets.

b. With the **Miami** worksheet active, hold down Shift and click the **Toronto** sheet tab to select all four worksheets. In the **Miami** worksheet, select the range **B4:E8**. On the **Formulas tab**, in the **Function Library group**, click **AutoSum**. **Close** the **Watch Window**. Select the range **E5:E7**, and then apply **Comma Style** with zero decimal places. Select cell **E4**, and then from the **Cell Styles** gallery, apply the **Currency [0]** format.

9 ▸ In the **sheet tab row**, right-click any sheet tab, and then click **Select All Sheets**.

a. On the **Page Layout tab**, in the **Page Setup group**, click the **Dialog Box Launcher** ⌐ to display the **Page Setup** dialog box.

b. Click the **Header/Footer tab**, click **Custom Footer**, and then in the **Left section**, insert the **File Name** 🗎. Click **OK** two times.

c. **Ungroup** the sheets. Display **Backstage** view, click **Show All Properties**. On the list of **Properties**, in the **Tags** box, type **order form, cost report** In the **Subject** box, type your course name and section #. Under **Related People**, be sure that your name displays as the author. If necessary, right-click the author name, click **Edit Property**, type your name, click outside of the **Edit person** dialog box, and then click **OK**.

d. On the left, click **Print**. Under **Settings**, click the **Print Active Sheets arrow**, and then click **Print Entire Workbook**. At the bottom of the window, click **Next Page** ▸ to scroll through the worksheets. On the left, click **Save**. Make any necessary adjustments to the Page Layout, and then **Save**.

e. If directed by your instructor to do so, submit a paper printout of the eight worksheets, an electronic image of each worksheet that looks like a printed document, or your original Excel file. If required by your instructor, print or create an electronic version of your worksheets with formulas displayed. In the upper right corner of the Excel window, click **Close**.

END | You have completed Project 4D

Mastering Excel | Project 4E Condo Loan and Quarterly Cost Report

Apply 4A skills from these Objectives:

1 Use Financial Functions

2 Use Goal Seek

3 Create a Data Table

4 Use Defined Names in a Formula

In the following Mastering Excel project, you will create a worksheet for Jacques Celestine, President of Jesse Jewelers, which analyzes loan options for a condo in Toronto that the company is considering purchasing. Jacques wants to provide a lodging facility for company visitors, but would like to keep the monthly loan payment below $6,250. You will also define names for ranges of cells in a worksheet containing quarterly Advertising costs. The worksheets of your workbook will look similar to Figure 4.60.

PROJECT FILES

For Project 4E, you will need the following file:

e04E_Condo_Loan_Advertising

You will save your workbook as:

Lastname_Firstname_4E_Condo_Loan_Advertising

PROJECT RESULTS

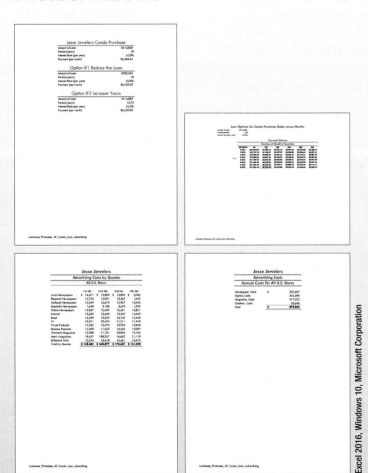

Excel 2016, Windows 10, Microsoft Corporation

FIGURE 4.60

(Project 4E Condo Loan and Quarterly Cost Report continues on the next page)

1 Start Excel. From your student data files, locate and open **e04E_Condo_Loan_Advertising**. **Save** the file in your **Excel Chapter 4** folder as **Lastname_Firstname_4E_Condo_Loan_Advertising**

2 Display the **Condo Purchase** worksheet. In cell **B5**, insert the **PMT** function using the data from the range **B2:B5**—be sure to divide the interest rate by **12** multiply the years by **12** and display the payment as a positive number. The result, $6,598.44, is larger than the maximum desired payment of $6,250.

3 Use **Goal Seek** to change the amount of the loan so that the payment is $6,250. Then, in cell **A7**, type **Option #1 Reduce the Loan** To cell **A1**, apply the **Title** cell style, and then **Copy** the format from cell **A1** to cell **A7**. **Copy** the range **A2:B5**, and then **Paste** the **Values & Number Formatting** to cell **A8**. In cell **B2**, type **615000** to restore the original loan amount.

4 Use **Goal Seek** to change the period of the loan (of the original data) so that the payment is $6,250. Then, in cell **A13**, type **Option #2 Increase Years** Format the cell the same as cell **A7**. **Copy** the range **A2:B5**, and then **Paste** the **Values & Number Formatting** to cell **A14**. Display the value in cell **B15** with two decimal places, and then in cell **B3**, type **10** to restore the original value. **Save** your workbook.

5 Display the **Payment Table** worksheet, in the range **A2:B4**, enter the following row titles and data.

Amount of Loan	$615,000
Period (months)	120
Interest rate (per year)	5.25%

6 In cell **C8**, type **60**—the number of months in a 5-year loan. In **D8**, type **120**—the number of months in a 10-year loan. Fill the series through cell **H8**. Apply **Bold** and **Center** to the range **C8:H8**.

7 Beginning in cell **B9**, enter varying interest rates in decrements of 0.5% beginning with **7.5%** and ending with **4.0%** If necessary, format all the interest rates with two decimal places, and then apply **Bold** and **Center** to the range **B9:B16**.

8 In cell **B8**, enter a **PMT** function using the information in cells **B2:B4**. Be sure that you convert the interest rate to a monthly rate and that the result displays as a positive number.

9 Create a **Data table** in the range **B8:H16** using the information in cells **B2:B4** in which the **Row input cell** is the **Period** and the **Column input cell** is the **Interest rate**. **Copy** the format from cell **B8** to the results in the data table. Format cell **D16** with the **Note** cell style as the payment option that is close to but less than $6,250 per month.

10 Display the **Advertising Costs by Quarter** worksheet, and then apply the **Currency [0]** cell style to the range **B6:E6** and to the range **B18:E18**. Apply the **Comma [0]** cell style to the range **B7:E17**, and then apply the **Total** cell style to the range **B18:E18**.

11 Name the following ranges: **B6:E10** **Newspaper_Costs B11:E14 Digital_Costs B15:E16 Magazine_Costs B17:E17 Billboard_Costs** Insert a new row **15**. In cell **A15**, type **Business Podcasts** In cell **B15**, type **12500** In cell **C15**, type **11525** In cell **D15**, type **14455** In cell **E15**, type **13009**

12 Display the **Name Manager**, click **Digital_Costs**, and then change cell **E14** to **E15**. Select the **Billboard_Costs** and then **Edit** the name to **Outdoor_Costs Save** your workbook.

13 Display the **Annual Advertising Costs** sheet. In cell **B5**, type **=sum(N** and sum the values using the appropriate range name in the displayed list of functions. Repeat for the other named ranges. From the **Formulas tab**, in the **Function Library group**, use **AutoSum** to sum all the costs. Apply **Currency [0]**, **Comma [0]**, and **Total** cell styles to the appropriate cells.

14 In the **sheet tab row**, right-click any sheet tab, and then click **Select All Sheets**. Display the **Page Setup** dialog box, click the **Margins tab**, and then under **Center on page**, click **Horizontally**. Click the **Header/Footer tab**, click **Custom Footer**, and then in the **Left section**, insert the **File Name**. Click **OK** two times. **Ungroup** the sheets, display the **Payment Table** sheet. Set the **Orientation** of this sheet to **Landscape** and set the **Scale** to **85%**.

(Project 4E Condo Loan and Quarterly Cost Report continues on the next page)

15 Display **Backstage** view, click **Show All Properties**. On the list of **Properties**, in the **Tags** box, type **payment table, advertising costs** In the **Subject** box, type your course name and section #. Under **Related People**, be sure that your name displays—edit if necessary. On the left, click **Print**. Under **Settings**, click the **Print Active Sheets arrow**, and then click **Print Entire Workbook**. At the bottom of the window, click **Next Page** ▶ to scroll through the worksheets. On the left, click **Save**.

16 If directed by your instructor to do so, submit a paper printout of the four worksheets, an electronic image of each worksheet that looks like a printed document, or your original Excel file. If required by your instructor, print or create an electronic version of your worksheets with formulas displayed. In the upper right corner of the Excel window, click **Close**.

> END | You have completed Project 4E

Mastering Excel | **Project 4F Lookup Form and Sales Revenue**

Apply 4B skills from these Objectives:

5 Use Lookup Functions

6 Validate Data

7 Audit Worksheet Formulas

8 Use the Watch Window to Monitor Cell Values

In the following Mastering Excel project, you will assist Mike Connor, the Vice President of Marketing at Jesse Jewelers, by adding lookup functions to an Advertising Order form so that an order taker can complete the form quickly. You will also use the Formula Auditing features and visual inspection to find and correct several types of errors. Your completed worksheets will look similar to Figure 4.61.

PROJECT FILES

For Project 4F, you will need the following file:

e04F_Ad_Form_NY_Revenue

You will save your workbooks as:

Lastname_Firstname_4F_Ad_Form_NY_Revenue

PROJECT RESULTS

FIGURE 4.61

Excel 2016, Windows 10, Microsoft Corporation

(Project 4F Lookup Form and Sales Revenue continues on the next page)

Mastering Excel Project 4F Lookup Form and Sales Revenue (continued)

1 Start Excel. From your student data files, open **e04F_Ad_Form_NY_Revenue**. Save the file in your **Excel Chapter 4** folder as **Lastname_Firstname_4F_Ad_Form_NY_Revenue** Display the second worksheet named **Advertising Rate Information** sheet. Select the range **A4:C11**, and then sort by **Code**. Name the range **A4:A11** by using the **Create from Selection** command and using the top row as the name.

2 Display the first worksheet named **Advertising Order Form** sheet. In the range **A9:A18**, create a data validation list using the defined name *Code*.

3 Click cell **A9**, click the **list arrow**, and then click **D-PH**. Click cell **B9** to make it the active cell, and then insert a **VLOOKUP** function that will look up the **Description** of the item in cell **A9** using the information in the **Advertising Rate Information** sheet as the table array. After selecting the table array, be sure to press F4 to make it an absolute reference. The Description to be looked up is in column 2 of the table array.

4 With cell **B9** as the active cell, fill the VLOOKUP formula through cell **B18**. In cell **C9**, type **4** as the Quantity ordered and in cell **D9**, type **Regional** In cell **E9**, insert a **VLOOKUP** function to look up **Unit Price** of the item in cell **A9** of the Advertising Order Form; the Unit Price is in column 3 of the table array. Copy the VLOOKUP formula down through cell **E18**. Add the following orders beginning in **row 10**:

ITEM	QUANTITY	TYPE
D-R	6	National
D-IN	15	Internet
B-BB	7	Billboard

5 Delete the unused rows. Sum the **Order Amount**, and then apply the **Total** cell style.

6 Display the **Sales Data** sheet. Click cell **I5**, which displays a green triangle indicating a potential error, and then on the **Formulas tab**, click **Trace Precedents**. To the left of the cell, click **Error Checking**, and then click

Edit in Formula Bar. Change *$B$14* to **$B$15** so that the formula is using the Growth Assumption for *Belts*, not for Key Chains, and then press Enter.

7 On the **Formulas tab**, in the **Formula Auditing group**, click **Error Checking** to begin checking for errors from this point in the worksheet. In cell **M6**, the flagged error, notice the formula is trying to divide by cell **L10**, which is empty. Click **Edit in Formula Bar**, change **10** to **9** and then in the **Error Checking** dialog box, click **Resume**.

8 In cell **F7**, examine the error information, and then click **Copy Formula from Above**. Examine the error in cell **J8**, and then click **Copy Formula from Left**. Click **OK**, and then use **Format Painter** to copy the format in cell **M5** to cell **M6**.

9 In the **sheet tab row**, right-click any sheet tab, and then click **Select All Sheets**. Display the **Page Setup** dialog box, click the **Margins tab**, and then under **Center on page**, click **Horizontally**. Click the **Header/Footer tab**, click **Custom Footer**, and then in the **Left section**, insert the **File Name**. Click **OK** two times. Ungroup the sheets, and then display the **Sales Data** sheet. For this sheet, set the **Orientation** to **Landscape**, and it in the **Scale to Fit** group, set the **Scale** to **88%**

10 Display **Backstage** view, click **Show All Properties**. On the list of **Properties**, in the **Tags** box, type **advertising costs, New York revenue** In the **Subject** box, type your course name and section number. Under **Related People**, be sure that your name displays. On the left, click **Print**. Under **Settings**, click the **Print Active Sheets arrow**, and then click **Print Entire Workbook**. At the bottom of the window, click **Next Page** ▶ to scroll through the worksheets. On the left, click **Save**.

11 If directed by your instructor to do so, submit a paper printout of the three worksheets, an electronic image of each worksheet that looks like a printed document, or your original Excel file. If required by your instructor, print or create an electronic version of your worksheets with formulas displayed. In the upper right corner of the Excel window, click **Close**.

END | You have completed Project 4F

4
EXCEL

Mastering Excel **Project 4G Warehouse Loan and Staff Lookup Form**

Apply 4A and 4B skills from these Objectives:

1 Use Financial Functions

2 Use Goal Seek

3 Create a Data Table

4 Use Defined Names in a Formula

5 Use Lookup Functions

6 Validate Data

7 Audit Worksheet Formulas

8 Use the Watch Window to Monitor Cell Values

In the following Mastering Excel project, you will create a worksheet for Jacques Celestine, President of Jesse Jewelers, which analyzes loan options for a warehouse that the company is considering purchasing. Jacques wants to establish an additional storage facility in the United States, but would like to keep the monthly loan payment below $10,000 using a 15-year loan. You will also assist Mike Connor, the Vice President of Marketing at Jesse Jewelers by adding lookup functions to a Staff Planning form so that a manager can complete the form quickly. You will also use Formula Auditing to check a worksheet for errors. Your completed worksheets will look similar to Figure 4.62.

PROJECT FILES

For Project 4G, you will need the following file:

e04G_Loan_Staff_Form

You will save your workbook as:

Lastname_Firstname_4G_Loan_Staff_Form

PROJECT RESULTS

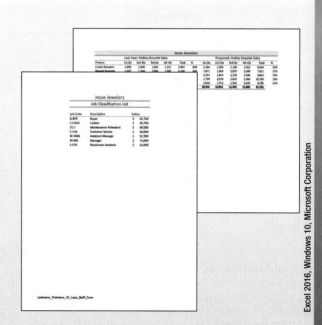

FIGURE 4.62

(Project 4G Warehouse Loan and Staff Lookup Form continues on the next page)

Mastering Excel Project 4G Warehouse Loan and Staff Lookup Form (continued)

1 Start Excel. From your student data files, open the file **e04G_Loan_Staff_Form**, and then save it in your **Excel Chapter 4** folder as **Lastname_Firstname_4G_Loan_Staff_Form**

2 Display the second worksheet named **Warehouse Payment Table**. In cell **B8**, enter a **PMT** function using cell **B4** divided by **12** as the rate, cell **B3** as the number of payment periods, and cell **B2** as the present value of the loan. Display the result as a positive number.

3 Create a two-variable data table in the range **B8:H16**. Set cell **B3** as the row input cell, and cell **B4** as the column input cell. From the **Cell Styles** gallery, apply the **Currency** cell style to the range **C9:H16**. Select the payment option closest to but less than $10,000 per month for a 120-month loan—cell **D16**—and format the option with the **Note** cell style. **Save** your workbook.

4 Display the fourth worksheet named **Job Information**, select the range **A4:C11**, and then sort the range by **Job Code** in ascending order. Create a range named **Job_Code** using the data in cells **A5:A11**.

5 Display the **Staffing Plan** worksheet, and then select the range **A9:A18**. Display the **Data Validation** dialog box, and validate from a **List** using the **Source =Job_Code**

6 Click cell **A9**, click the list arrow, and then click **M-MG**. Click cell **B9** to make it the active cell, and then insert a **VLOOKUP** function that will look up the Description of the Job Code in cell **A9** using the information in the **Job Information** worksheet as the table array. After selecting the table array, be sure to press F4 to make it an absolute cell reference. The Description to be looked up is in column 2 of the table array.

7 With cell **B9** as the active cell, copy the VLOOKUP formula down through cell **B18**. In cell **C9**, type **1** as the # of Positions and in cell **D9**, type **Management** as the Type.

8 In cell **E9**, insert the **VLOOKUP** function to look up the **Salary** of the Job Code in cell **A9** by using the information in the **Job Information** sheet as the table array; the Salary is in column 3 of the table array. Copy the VLOOKUP formula in cell **E9** down through cell **E18**.

9 Beginning in cell **A10**, add these staff positions:

ITEM	# OF POSITIONS	TYPE
C-CASH	3	Cashier
C-CSA	1	Customer Service
M-AMG	3	Management

10 Delete any unused rows between the last item and the Total row. Sum the **Budget Amount** column and apply the **Total** cell style. **Save** your workbook.

11 Display the **Bracelet Revenue** worksheet. Click cell **I5**, and then on the **Formulas tab**, click **Trace Precedents**. On the ribbon, in the **Formula Auditing group**, click **Error Checking**, and then click **Edit in Formula Bar**. Edit the formula so that the formula is using the Growth Assumption for *Beaded Bracelets*, not for *Crystal Bracelets*.

12 In the **Error Checking** dialog box, click **Resume**. In cell **M6**, notice the formula is trying to divide by cell **L10**, which is empty. Click **Edit in Formula Bar**, change **10** to **9** Ensure that the reference to L9 is an absolute reference, and then in the **Error Checking** dialog box, click **Resume**.

13 In cell **F7**, examine the error information, and then click **Copy Formula from Above**. Examine the error in cell **J8**, and then click **Copy Formula from Left**. Click **OK**. Use **Format Painter** to copy the format in cell **M5** to cell **M6**. **Save** your workbook.

14 In the **sheet tab row**, right-click any sheet tab, and then click **Select All Sheets**. Display the **Page Setup** dialog box, click the **Margins tab**, and then under **Center on page**, click **Horizontally**. Click the **Header/Footer tab**, click **Custom Footer**, and then in the **Left section**, insert the **File Name**. Click **OK** two times. Ungroup the sheets, and then for these three worksheets—**Warehouse Payment Table**, **Staffing Plan**, and **Bracelet Revenue**— set the **Orientation** to **Landscape**. Select only the **Bracelet Revenue** sheet, and on the **Page Layout tab**, set the **Scale** to **90%**.

15 Display **Backstage** view, click **Show All Properties**. On the list of **Properties**, in the **Tags** box, type **New York revenue** In the **Subject** box, type your course name and section number. Under **Related People**, be sure that your

(Project 4G Warehouse Loan and Staff Lookup Form continues on the next page)

name displays as the Author. On the left, click **Print**. Under **Settings**, click the **Print Active Sheets arrow**, and then click **Print Entire Workbook**. At the bottom of the window, click **Next Page** [▸] to scroll through the five worksheets. On the left, click **Save**.

16 If directed by your instructor to do so, submit a paper printout of the five worksheets, an electronic image of each worksheet that looks like a printed document, or your original Excel file. If required by your instructor, print or create an electronic version of your worksheets with formulas displayed. In the upper right corner of the Excel window, click **Close**.

END | You have completed Project 4G

Apply a combination of the **4A** and **4B** skills.	**GO! Fix It**	Project 4H Bag Costs by Quarter	**MyITLab**
	GO! Make It	Project 4I Arizona Store Loan	**MyITLab**
	GO! Solve It	Project 4J Store Furnishings	**MyITLab**
	GO! Solve It	Project 4K Order Form	

PROJECT FILES

For Project 4K, you will need the following file:

e04K_Order_Form

You will save your workbook as:

Lastname_Firstname_4K_Order_Form

Open the file **e04K_Order_Form** and save it as **Lastname_Firstname_4K_Order_Form**

Prepare the Product Information worksheet for a VLOOKUP function by sorting the items by Style Code, and then create a named range for the Style Code information. On the Order Form worksheet, using the named range, set data validation for the Item column. Insert the VLOOKUP function in column B and column E, referencing the appropriate data in the Product Information worksheet. Then enter the data below.

ITEM	DESCRIPTION	QUANTITY	COLOR
C-S		12	White
C-T		15	Natural
M-MC		25	Assorted
M-CF		50	Green

Delete the unused row. Construct formulas to total the order, and then apply appropriate financial formatting. On both sheets, include your file name in the footer, add appropriate properties, and then submit them as directed.

Performance Level

		Exemplary: You consistently applied the relevant skills	Proficient: You sometimes, but not always, applied the relevant skills	Developing: You rarely or never applied the relevant skills
Performance Criteria	Use Lookup Functions	The VLOOKUP function correctly looks up data on the validation list.	The VLOOKUP function looks up some but not all data on the validation list.	The VLOOKUP function does not look up any of the correct information.
	Validate Data	The Validation List is sorted correctly and used on the order form.	The Validation List was sorted, but not used on the order form.	The Validation List is not sorted and not used on the order form.
	Calculate and Format the Order Amount	The Order Amount and financial information is properly calculated and formatted.	Some, but not all, of the Order Amount and financial information is properly calculated and formatted.	Incorrect formulas and/or incorrect financial formatting were applied in most of the cells.

END | You have completed Project 4K

OUTCOMES-BASED ASSESSMENTS

RUBRIC

The following outcomes-based assessments are open-ended assessments. That is, there is no specific correct result; your result will depend on your approach to the information provided. Make Professional Quality your goal. Use the following scoring rubric to guide you in how to approach the problem and then to evaluate how well your approach solves the problem.

The criteria—Software Mastery, Content, Format and Layout, and Process—represent the knowledge and skills you have gained that you can apply to solving the problem. The levels of performance—Professional Quality, Approaching Professional Quality, or Needs Quality Improvements—help you and your instructor evaluate your result.

	Your completed project is of Professional Quality if you:	Your completed project is Approaching Professional Quality if you:	Your completed project Needs Quality Improvements if you:
1-Software Mastery	Choose and apply the most appropriate skills, tools, and features and identify efficient methods to solve the problem.	Choose and apply some appropriate skills, tools, and features, but not in the most efficient manner.	Choose inappropriate skills, tools, or features, or are inefficient in solving the problem.
2-Content	Construct a solution that is clear and well organized, contains content that is accurate, appropriate to the audience and purpose, and is complete. Provide a solution that contains no errors of spelling, grammar, or style.	Construct a solution in which some components are unclear, poorly organized, inconsistent, or incomplete. Misjudge the needs of the audience. Have some errors in spelling, grammar, or style, but the errors do not detract from comprehension.	Construct a solution that is unclear, incomplete, or poorly organized, contains some inaccurate or inappropriate content, and contains many errors of spelling, grammar, or style. Do not solve the problem.
3-Format and Layout	Format and arrange all elements to communicate information and ideas, clarify function, illustrate relationships, and indicate relative importance.	Apply appropriate format and layout features to some elements, but not others. Overuse features, causing minor distraction.	Apply format and layout that does not communicate information or ideas clearly. Do not use format and layout features to clarify function, illustrate relationships, or indicate relative importance. Use available features excessively, causing distraction.
4-Process	Use an organized approach that integrates planning, development, self-assessment, revision, and reflection.	Demonstrate an organized approach in some areas, but not others; or, use an insufficient process of organization throughout.	Do not use an organized approach to solve the problem.

Apply a combination of the 1A and 1B skills.

GO! Think | Project 4L Key Chains

PROJECT FILES

For Project 4L, you will need the following file:

e04L_Key_Chains

You will save your workbook as:

Lastname_Firstname_4L_Key_Chains

From your student files, open the file **e04L_Key_Chains**, and then save it in your chapter folder as **Lastname_Firstname_4L_Key_Chains** So that order takers do not have to type the Style Code, Description, and Unit Price in the Order Form worksheet, use the information on the Product Information sheet to create a validation list for the Item and then insert a VLOOKUP function in the Description and Unit Price columns. Then create an order for two of the Plush Animal Key Chains (K-S) and two of the Classic Key Chains (M-TF). Delete unused rows, create appropriate totals, apply financial formatting, and then save and submit it as directed.

END | You have completed Project 4L

Build from Scratch

GO! Think | Project 4M Delivery Van Purchase | MyITLab

Build from Scratch

You and GO! | Project 4N Vehicle Loan | MyITLab

Managing Large Workbooks and Using Advanced Sorting and Filtering

5

| PROJECT **5A** | **OUTCOMES**
Manage and format large workbooks and save workbooks to share with others. |

OBJECTIVES

1. Navigate and Manage Large Worksheets
2. Enhance Worksheets with Themes and Styles
3. Format a Worksheet to Share with Others
4. Save Excel Data in Other File Formats

| PROJECT **5B** | **OUTCOMES**
Analyze information in a database format using advanced sort, filter, subtotaling, and outlining. |

OBJECTIVES

5. Use Advanced Sort Techniques
6. Use Custom and Advanced Filters
7. Subtotal, Outline, and Group a List of Data

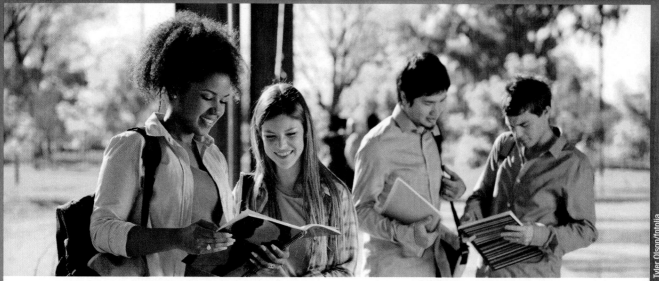

Tyler Olson/fotolia

In this chapter 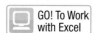 GO! To Work with Excel

In this chapter, you will navigate within a worksheet, insert a hyperlink in a worksheet, and save a worksheet as a webpage or other file format that you can share with others. You will practice applying and modifying themes, styles, lines, and borders to enhance the format of your worksheets. You will use Excel's advanced table features and database capabilities to organize data in a useful manner. You will use advanced sorting, sorting on multiple columns, and custom filtering to compare subsets of data. You will also limit data to display records that meet one or more specific conditions, add subtotals, and outline data.

The projects in this chapter relate to **Laurel College**. The college offers this diverse geographic area in Pennsylvania a wide range of academic and career programs, including associate degrees, certificate programs, and noncredit continuing education courses. Over 2,100 faculty and staff make student success a top priority. The college makes positive contributions to the community through cultural and athletic programs and partnerships with businesses and nonprofit organizations. The college also provides industry-specific training programs for local businesses through its Economic Development Center.

PROJECT

5A Class Schedule

MyITLab
Project 5A Training
Project 5A Grader

PROJECT ACTIVITIES

In Activities 5.01 through 5.13, you will assist Michael Schaeffler, Vice President of Instruction, in formatting and navigating a worksheet that lists the class schedule for the Business Office Systems and Computer Information Systems departments at Laurel College. You will also save Excel data in other file formats. The worksheets in your completed workbook will look similar to Figure 5.1.

Please always review the downloaded Grader instructions before beginning.

PROJECT FILES

MyITLab
grader

If your instructor wants you to submit Project 5A in the MyITLab Grader system, log in to MyITLab, locate Grader Project 5A, and then download the files for this project.

For Project 5A, you will need the following files:

e05A_Class_Schedule
e05A_Faculty_Contacts
e05A_Teaching_Requests

You will save your workbooks as:

Lastname_Firstname_5A_Class_Schedule
Lastname_Firstname_5A_Schedule_PDF (not shown)
Lastname_Firstname_5A_Schedule_CSV (not shown)
Lastname_Firstname_5A_Schedule_ Webpage (not shown)
5A_Faculty_Contacts_2015 (not shown)

GO!
Walk Thru
Project 5A

PROJECT RESULTS

Excel 2016, Windows 10, Microsoft Corporation

FIGURE 5.1 Project 5A Class Schedule

GO! Learn How
Video E5-1

Because you may not be able to view all the columns and rows of a large worksheet on your screen at one time, Excel provides features that help you control the screen display and navigate the worksheet so you can locate information quickly. For example, you can hide columns or use the *Freeze Panes* command, which sets the column and row titles so that they remain on the screen while you scroll. The locked rows and columns become separate *panes*—portions of a worksheet window bounded by and separated from other portions by vertical or horizontal lines.

You can also use the *Find* command to find and select specific text, formatting, or a type of information within the workbook quickly.

Activity 5.01 | Using the Go To Special Command

Use the *Go To Special* command to move to cells that have special characteristics, for example, to cells that are blank or to cells that contain constants as opposed to formulas.

1 Start Excel. Navigate to the student files that accompany this chapter, and then open **e05A_Class_Schedule**. Display the **Save As** dialog box, and then navigate to the location where you are storing projects for this chapter. Create a new folder named **Excel Chapter 5** and then open the folder. **Save** the file as **Lastname_Firstname_5A_Class_Schedule**

This worksheet lists the computer courses that are available for the upcoming semester in three college departments.

2 On the **Home tab,** in the **Editing group**, click **Find & Select**, and then click **Go To Special.** Compare your screen with Figure 5.2.

In the Go To Special dialog box, you can click an option button to move to cells that contain the special options listed.

FIGURE 5.2

3 In the first column, click **Blanks**, and then click **OK**.

The blank cell—J33—in the *active area* of the worksheet is located and selected. The active area is the area of the worksheet that contains data or has contained data—it does not include any empty cells that have not been used in this worksheet. Cell J33 is missing the time for a Linux/ UNIX Fundamentals class held on Wednesday.

4 Point to cell **J33** and right-click. On the mini toolbar, click the **Fill Color arrow** [⬧ ▾] and then under **Standard Colors**, click the fourth color—**Yellow**—to highlight the blank cell.

This missing information must be researched before a time can be entered, and the yellow fill color will help locate this cell later, when the correct time for the class is determined.

5 Save 🖫 your workbook and compare your screen with Figure 5.3.

	A	B	C	D	E	F	G	H	I	J	K	L	M	N	O	P	Q	R	S
24	Medical Office Procedures	BOS	75271	223	1	1	3	A	MW	1600 - 1755	TE282	Main	Thomas, Donnielle	24	11	No			
25	Integrated Office Applications	BOS	71575	225	1	1	3	A	MW	1500 - 1655	TE280	Main	McIntrye, Alice	24	12	Yes			
26	Intro to Computer Info Systems	CIS	70310	110	5	1	3	A	T	1900 - 2025	TE272	Main	Staff	24	3	No			
27	Intro to Computer Info Systems	CIS	70323	110	6	1	3	A	R	1730 - 1855	TE270	Main	Staff	24	5	No			
28	Intro to Computer Info Systems	CIS	70315	110	7	1	3	A	R	1900 - 2025	TE272	Main	Mandala, Elena	24	8	No			
29	Windows Operating System	CIS	73227	117	1	1	2	A	W	0900 - 1155	WC1	West	Williams, George	24	1	No			
30	Windows Operating System	CIS	70380	117	2	1	2	A	W	0930 - 1055	EC2	Valley	Randolph, Trudi	24	5	No			
31	Windows Operating System	CIS	70382	117	3	1	2	A	T	1730 - 2025	WC1	West	Randolph, Trudi	24	6	No			
32	Windows Operating System	CIS	70						T	1800 - 2055	NR230	Park	Staff	24	10	No			
33	Linux/UNIX Fundamentals	CIS	70		Blank cell with missing information highlighted				W		NR230	Park	Staff	24	9	No			
34	Linux/UNIX Fundamentals	CIS	70						T	1800 - 2055	TE170	Main	Staff	24	5	No			
35	Beginning Java Programming	CIS	75542	175	2	1	4	A	W	1400 - 1525	TE172	Main	Desprez, Joan	24	1	No			
36	Beginning Java Programming	CIS	75562	175	3	1	4	A	W	1230 - 1355	TE176	Main	Desprez, Joan	24	5	No			
37	Linux Installation and Config	CIS	74484	204	A1	2	3	A	R	1400 - 1525	TE270	Main	Desprez, Joan	24	8	Yes			
38	Linux System Administration	CIS	74501	206	H1	4	3	A	R	1230 - 1355	TE272	Main	Matthews, Christina	24	1	Yes			

Excel 2016, Windows 10, Microsoft Corporation

FIGURE 5.3

Activity 5.02 | Hiding Columns

In a large worksheet, you can hide columns that are not necessary for the immediate task, and then unhide them later. You can also hide columns or rows to control the data that will print or to remove confidential information from view—hidden data does not print. For example, to create a summary report, you can hide the columns between the row titles and the totals column, and the hidden columns would not display on the printed worksheet, resulting in a summary report.

1 Press [Ctrl] + [Home]. From the column heading area, select **columns E:G**.

2 Right-click over the selected columns, and then click **Hide**. Compare your screen with Figure 5.4.

Columns E, F, and G are hidden from view—the column headings skip from D to H. A dark line between columns D and H indicates that columns from this location are hidden from view. After you click in another cell, this line will not be visible; however, the column letters provide a visual indication that some columns are hidden from view.

	A	B	C	D	H	I	J	K	L	M	N	O	P	Q	R	S	T	U
1	Course Name	Dept	Section #	Course #	Status	Days	Time	Room	Campus	Instructor	Max	Enrolled	Pre-Req					
2	Beginning Keyboarding	BOS	75007	101A	A	F	0800 - 0855	TE276	Main	Carlton, Ellis	24	5	No					
3	Beginning Keyboarding	BOS	74432	101	A		0900 - 0955	TE282	Main	Thomas, Donnielle	24	6	No					
4	Intermediate Keyboarding	BOS		Columns E, F, and G are hidden from view			1600 - 1755	WC103	West	Staff	24	1	Yes					
5	Intermediate Keyboarding	BOS					1600 - 1755	EC101	Valley	Applebee, Luis	15	1	Yes					
6	Advanced Keyboarding	BOS					0800 - 0855	TE276	Main	Carlton, Ellis	24	5	Yes					
7	Advanced Keyboarding	BOS	74437	101C	A	T	0900 - 0955	TE282	Main	Thomas, Donnielle	24	6	Yes					
8	Document Formatting	BOS	74376	102	A	T	1000 - 1255	TE282	Main	Carlton, Ellis	24	21	No					
9	Document Formatting	BOS	76442	102	A	R	1800 - 2055	TE276	Main	Staff	24	11	No					
10	Office Administration I	BOS	70685	105	A	TR	1300 - 1455	TE276	Main	Thomas, Donnielle	24	22	No					
11	Intro to Medical Transcription	BOS	76563	112	A	M	1300 - 1455	TE282	Main	Thomas, Donnielle	24	16	No					

Excel 2016, Windows 10, Microsoft Corporation

FIGURE 5.4

Select the columns that you want to hide. On the Home tab, in the Cells group, click Format. Under Visibility, point to Hide & Unhide, and then click Hide Columns.

Drag to select the columns, tap and hold over the selected columns, and then click Hide.

3 Notice that the line between the **column D heading** and the **column H heading** is slightly wider, indicating hidden columns. Press Ctrl + Home, and then **Save** 🖫 your workbook.

More Knowledge **Unhiding Columns**

To unhide columns, select the columns on both sides of the hidden columns. Right-click over the selection, and then click Unhide.

Activity 5.03 │ Using the Go To Command

1.2.2

Use the *Go To* command to move to a specific cell or range of cells in a large worksheet.

1 On the **Home tab**, in the **Editing group**, click **Find & Select**, and then click **Go To**. In the **Go To** dialog box, with the insertion point blinking in the **Reference** box, type **m50** and then click **OK**.

2 With cell **M50** active, on the **Formulas tab**, in the **Functions Library group**, click **More Functions**, point to **Statistical**, scroll down the list, and then click **COUNTIF**. As the **Range**, type **m2:m49** and as the **Criteria**, type **Staff** to count the number of courses that are assigned to Staff and still need an instructor assignment. Click **OK**. Compare your screen with Figure 5.5.

Your result is 13, indicating that 13 courses still need an instructor assigned.

FIGURE 5.5

3 In cell **J50**, type **Unassigned classes** and press Enter.

4 Press Ctrl + Home, and then **Save** 🖫 your workbook.

If you need to refer to information in one workbook while you have another workbook open, you can arrange the window to display sheets from more than one workbook—instead of jumping back and forth between the two workbooks from the taskbar. This is accomplished by using the **Arrange All** command, which tiles all open Excel windows on the screen. Additionally, you can view separate parts of the *same* worksheet on your screen by using the **Split** command, which splits the window into multiple resizable panes to view distant parts of your worksheet at once.

1 Display the **Open** dialog box, and then from your student files, open the file **e05A_Teaching_Requests**.

The e05A_Teaching_Requests file opens, and your Lastname_Firstname_5A_Class_Schedule file is no longer visible on your screen. This worksheet contains a list of instructors who submitted requests for classes they would like to teach. You do not need to save this file; it is for reference only.

2 On the **View tab**, in the **Window group**, click **Switch Windows**, and then click your **Lastname_Firstname_5A_Class_Schedule** file to make it the active worksheet.

3 On the **View tab**, in the **Window group**, click **Arrange All**. Click **Horizontal** and then compare your screen with Figure 5.6.

Here, in the Arrange Windows dialog box, you can control how two or more worksheets from multiple open workbooks are arranged on the screen.

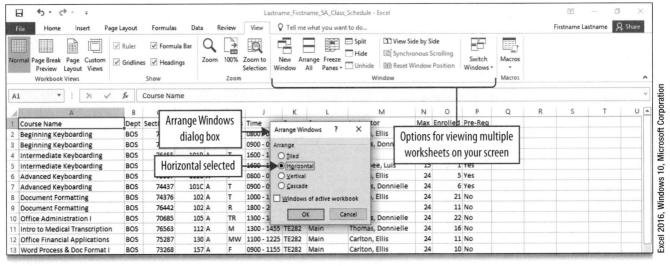

FIGURE 5.6

4 Click **OK**. Compare your screen with Figure 5.7.

The screen is split horizontally, and the e05A_Teaching_Requests worksheet displays below your Lastname_Firstname_5A_Class_Schedule worksheet. The active window title bar displays the file name in a darker shade of gray, and the row and column headings are shaded to indicate active cells. When multiple worksheets are open on the screen, only one is active at a time. To activate a worksheet, click anywhere on the worksheet or click the worksheet's title bar.

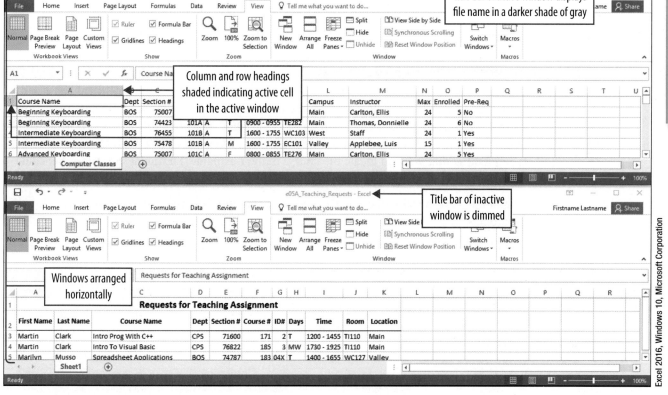

FIGURE 5.7

5 ▸ Press Ctrl + End to move to cell **P50**, which is now the end of the active area of the worksheet.

6 ▸ Click cell **A50**. On the **View tab**, in the **Window group**, click **Split** to split this upper window horizontally at row 50. Compare your screen with Figure 5.8.

> A light gray horizontal bar displays at the top of row 50, and two sets of vertical scroll bars display in the Lastname_Firstname_5A_Class_Schedule worksheet—one in each of the two worksheet panes displayed in this window. You can drag the horizontal bar up slightly to make the lower pane easier to see.

FIGURE 5.8

7 ▸ Click above the **split bar**, press Ctrl + Home and then click in any cell in **column C**. Press Ctrl + F to display the **Find tab** of the **Find and Replace** dialog box.

Column C lists the Section # for each class. This is a unique number that identifies each class.

🔄 **BY TOUCH**   On the Home tab, in the Editing group, tap Find.

8 ▸ Drag the title bar of the dialog box into the upper right area of your screen. Then, in the lower half of your screen, look at the first request in the **e05A_Teaching_Requests** worksheet, which is from *Martin Clark* to teach *Intro Prog With C++, Section # 71600*. In the **Find what** box, type **71600** so that you can locate the course in the **Lastname_Firstname_5A_Class_Schedule** worksheet.

9 ▸ Click **Find Next,** be sure that you can see the **Name Box**, and then compare your screen with Figure 5.9.

Section # 71600 is located and selected in cell C49 of the Class Schedule worksheet.

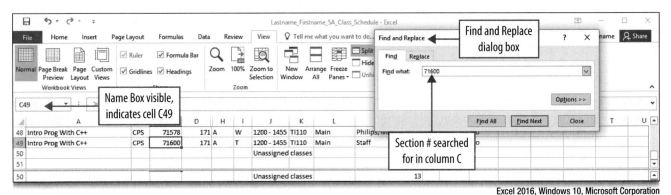

FIGURE 5.9

Excel 2016, Windows 10, Microsoft Corporation

10 ▸ In your **Lastname_Firstname_5A_Class_Schedule** worksheet, click in cell **M49**, type **Clark, Martin** to replace *Staff* and assign the class to Mr. Clark. Press Enter.

The class is assigned to Mr. Clark, and the number of unassigned classes, which you can view below the split bar, decreases by one, to 12. Use the Split command when you need to see two distant parts of the same worksheet simultaneously.

11 ▸ In the **Find and Replace** dialog box, click **Close**, and then compare your screen with Figure 5.10.

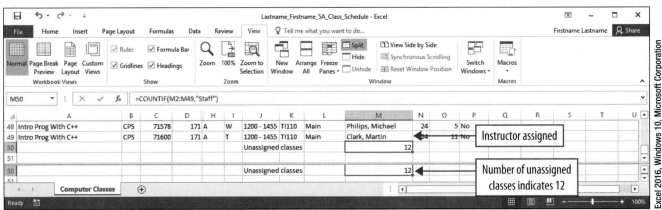

FIGURE 5.10

12 Click anywhere in the **e05A_Teaching_Requests** workbook, and then click **Close** ⊠ to close the workbook. On the title bar of your **Lastname_Firstname_5A_Class_Schedule** workbook, click **Maximize** ▢ to restore the size of the worksheet to its full size.

13 On the **View tab**, in the **Window group**, click **Split** to remove the split.

14 Press ⌃Ctrl + ⌂Home, and then **Save** 🖫 your workbook.

Objective 2 Enhance Worksheets with Themes and Styles

GO! Learn How
Video E5-2

Individuals commonly use worksheets to communicate information both within an organization and to the public. A worksheet might be seen by individuals in an email, in a PowerPoint presentation, or in public blogs and publications. Accordingly, you will want to use some creative elements when preparing your worksheets.

Recall that a theme is a predesigned set of colors, fonts, lines, and fill effects that look good together and that can be applied to your workbook. A theme combines two sets of fonts—one for text and one for headings. In the default Office theme, Calibri Light is the font for headings and Calibri is the font for body text.

Activity 5.05 │ Changing and Customizing a Workbook Theme

1.3.6

In Excel, the applied theme has a set of complementary *cell styles*—a defined set of formatting characteristics, such as fonts, font sizes, font colors, cell borders, and cell shading. The applied theme also has a set of complementary table styles for data that you format as a table.

1 Point to the **row 1 heading** to display the ➡ pointer, right-click, and then click **Insert** to insert a new blank row. In cell **A1**, type **Schedule of Classes with Unassigned Sections** and press ⌂Enter. On the **Home tab**, **Merge & Center** this title across the range **A1:P1**, and then apply the **Title** cell style.

2 On the **Page Layout tab**, in the **Themes group**, click **Themes**. Compare your screen with Figure 5.11.

The gallery of predesigned themes that come with Microsoft Office displays. Office—the default theme—is applied to this workbook.

FIGURE 5.11

> **3** Point to several of the themes and notice how Live Preview displays the colors and fonts associated with each theme. Then, click the **Ion** theme.

> **4** In the **Themes group**, click **Fonts**.

The font associated with the Ion theme for both headings and body text is Century Gothic, but you can customize a theme by mixing the Colors, Fonts, and Effects from any of the supplied themes.

> **5** If necessary, scroll to the top and click the **Office** fonts to change the Theme Fonts for this workbook. **Save** 🖫 your workbook.

Activity 5.06 | Creating and Applying a Custom Table Style

Excel comes with many predefined table styles, but if none of these meets your needs, you can create and apply a custom table style of your own design. Custom table styles that you create are stored only in the current workbook, so they are not available in other workbooks.

> **1** On the **Home tab**, in the **Styles group**, click **Format as Table**. At the bottom, click **New Table Style**.

> **2** In the **New Table Style** dialog box, in the **Name** box, replace the existing text by typing **Class Schedule**

> **3** In the list under **Table Element**, click **First Row Stripe**, and then compare your screen with Figure 5.12.

Here you can select one or more elements of the table, and then customize the format for each element.

FIGURE 5.12

> **4** Below the list of table elements, click **Format**. In the **Format Cells** dialog box, click the **Fill** tab. In the fourth column of colors, click the second color, and notice that the **Sample** area previews the color you selected. Compare your screen with Figure 5.13.

FIGURE 5.13

5 ▶ Click **OK**, notice the **Preview**, and then in the lower left corner of the dialog box, click to select the check box **Set as default table style for this document**. Click **OK**.

> You must select this check box to make your table style available in the gallery of table styles.

6 ▶ Select the range **A2:P50**—do *not* include rows 1 and 51 in your selection. In the **Styles group**, click **Format as Table**. At the top of the gallery, under **Custom**, point to your custom table style to display the ScreenTip *Class Schedule*. Compare your screen with Figure 5.14.

FIGURE 5.14

7 ▶ Click your **Class Schedule** table style, and then in the **Format as Table** dialog box, click **OK**.

8 ▶ Press Ctrl + Home to deselect and move to cell **A1**, and then **Save** 🖫 your workbook.

GO! Learn How
Video E5-3

You can share a worksheet with others by printing and distributing paper copies, sending it electronically as an Excel file or some other file format, or posting it to the web or to a shared workspace. Regardless of how you distribute the information, a large worksheet will be easier for others to view if you insert appropriate page breaks and repeat column or row titles at the top of each page.

You can also add a *hyperlink* to a worksheet, which, when clicked, takes you to another location in the worksheet, to another file, or to a webpage on the Internet or on your organization's intranet.

Activity 5.07 | Previewing and Modifying Page Breaks

1.4.4

Before you print or electronically distribute a large worksheet, preview it to see where the pages will break across the columns and rows. You can move the page breaks to a column or row that groups the data logically, and you can change the orientation between portrait and landscape if you want to display more rows on the page (portrait) or more columns on the page (landscape). You can also apply *scaling* to the data to force the worksheet into a selected number of pages. Scaling adjusts the horizontal and vertical size of the printed data by a percentage or by the number of pages that you specify.

1 ▶ Display the **Print Preview**. Notice that as currently formatted, the worksheet will print on 4 pages.

2 ▶ At the bottom of the **Print Preview**, click **Next Page** ▶ three times to view the four pages required to print this worksheet.

As you view each page, notice that pages 3 and 4 display the Room, Campus, Instructor, Max, Enrolled, and Pre-Req columns that relate to the first two pages of the printout. You can see that the printed worksheet will be easier to read if all the information related to a class is on the same page.

3 ▶ Click **Back** ◀ to return to the worksheet. Click the **View tab**, and then in the **Workbook Views group**, click **Page Break Preview**. Compare your screen with Figure 5.15.

The Page Break Preview window displays blue dashed lines to show where the page breaks are in the current page layout for this worksheet.

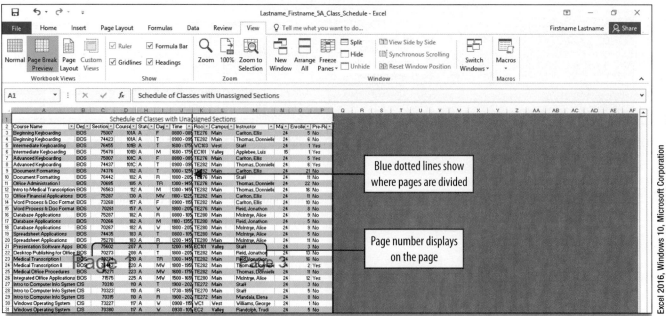

FIGURE 5.15

4 Scroll down to view the other pages and see where the page breaks are indicated. Then, in the **Workbook Views group**, click **Normal** to redisplay the worksheet in Normal view.

Dashed lines display at the page break locations on the worksheet.

5 On the **Page Layout tab**, in the **Page Setup group**, set the **Orientation** to **Landscape**. In the **Scale to Fit group**, click the **Width arrow**, and then click **1 page**.

In the Scale to Fit group, there are two ways to override the default printout size. In the Scale box, you can specify a scaling factor from between 10 and 400 percent. Or, you can use the Width and Height arrows to fit the printout to a specified number of pages. To return to a full-size printout after scaling, in the Scale box, type 100 as the percentage.

6 Display the **Page Setup** dialog box. Click **Header/Footer**, and then click **Custom Footer**. In the **Left section**, insert the **file name**, and then click in the **Right section**. Click **Insert Page Number** 🗐, and then click **OK** two times.

It is good practice to insert any headers or footers *before* making the final page break decisions on your worksheet.

7 Display the **Print Preview**, and at the bottom, notice that the worksheet is now a total of two pages.

By applying the scaling, each complete row of data will fit on one page.

8 Return to the worksheet. On the **View tab**, click **Page Break Preview**. Scroll to view the page break between **Page 1** and **Page 2**.

9 Point to the horizontal page break line between **Page 1** and **Page 2**. When the vertical resize pointer 🔁 displays, drag the line up between **row 26** and **row 27**; this will break the pages between the BOS courses and the CIS courses. Compare your screen with Figure 5.16.

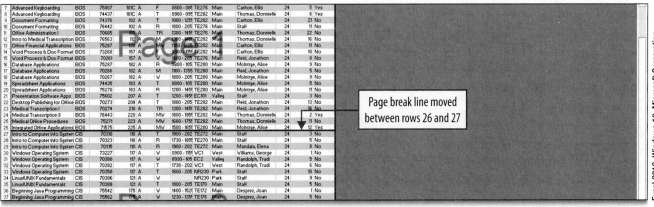

FIGURE 5.16

10 Display the **Print Preview**. At the bottom of the window, click **Next Page** to view **Page 2**.

11 Return to the worksheet. On the list of view buttons on the right side of the **Status bar**, click **Normal** 🞖. Press Ctrl + Home, and then click **Save** 🖫.

Recall that when your worksheet layout spans multiple pages, you will typically want to repeat the column titles on each page. If your worksheet is wider than one page, you will also want to repeat the row titles on each page.

1 Display the **Print Preview**, scroll to **Page 2**, and notice that the column titles display only on the first page. Return to the worksheet.

Repeating the column titles on each page will make it easier to understand and read the information on the pages.

2 On the **Page Layout tab**, in the **Page Setup group**, click **Print Titles** to display the **Sheet tab** of the **Page Setup** dialog box.

Here you can select rows to repeat at the top of each page and columns to repeat at the left of each page.

3 Under **Print titles**, click in the **Rows to repeat at top** box, and then from the **row heading area**, select **row 2**. Compare your screen with Figure 5.17.

A moving border surrounds row 2, and the mouse pointer displays as a black, select-row arrow. The absolute reference $2:$2 displays in the Rows to repeat at top box.

FIGURE 5.17

4 Click **OK**. Display the **Print Preview**, display **Page 2**, and notice that the column titles display at the top of the page. Compare your screen with Figure 5.18. **Save** your workbook.

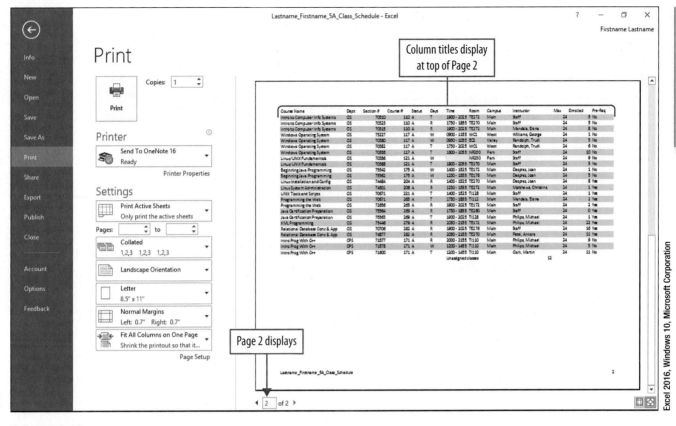

Column titles display at top of Page 2

Page 2 displays

FIGURE 5.18

Activity 5.09 | Inserting a Hyperlink in a Worksheet

1.2.3

Recall that a hyperlink is colored and underlined text that you can click to go to a file, a location in a file, a webpage on the Internet, or a webpage on your organization's intranet. Hyperlinks can be attached to text or to graphics. In this activity, you will add a hyperlink that will open a file containing the contact information for instructors.

1 Click cell **M2**. On the **Insert tab**, in the **Links group**, click **Hyperlink** to display the **Insert Hyperlink** dialog box.

2 Under **Link to**, if necessary, click Existing File or Web Page. Click the **Look in arrow**, navigate to your student files, and then select the file **e05A_Faculty_Contacts**, which contains faculty contact information.

3 In the upper right corner of the **Insert Hyperlink** dialog box, click **ScreenTip**.

4 In the **Set Hyperlink ScreenTip** dialog box, in the **ScreenTip text** box, type **Click here for contact info.** Compare your dialog box with Figure 5.19.

When you point to the hyperlink on the worksheet, this is the text of the ScreenTip that will display.

FIGURE 5.19

5 ▸ In the **Set Hyperlink ScreenTip** dialog box, click **OK** and then in the **Insert Hyperlink** dialog box, click **OK**.

In the Ion theme, the color for a hyperlink is light blue.

6 ▸ Point to the **Instructor hyperlink** and read the ScreenTip that displays. Compare your screen with Figure 5.20.

When you point to the hyperlink, the Link Select pointer 🖑 displays and the ScreenTip text displays.

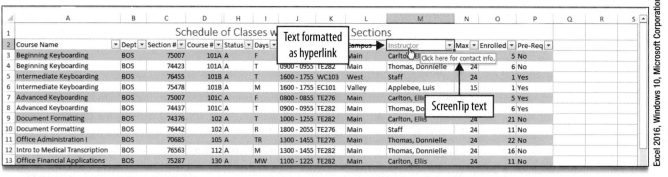

FIGURE 5.20

7 ▸ Click the **Instructor hyperlink**.

The e05A_Faculty_Contacts file opens in a new window and displays the contact information.

8 ▸ **Close** ✕ the **e05A_Faculty_Contacts** file and redisplay your **Lastname_Firstname_5A_Class_Schedule** worksheet.

9 ▸ On the **Page Layout** tab, in the **Themes group**, click the **Colors arrow**. At the bottom of the gallery, click **Customize Colors**. At the bottom of the dialog box, locate the colors for **Hyperlink** and **Followed Hyperlink**. Compare your screen with Figure 5.21.

Each color scheme uses a set of colors for a hyperlink and for a hyperlink that has been clicked (followed) one time. Now that you have followed your inserted hyperlink one time, the text displays in the Followed Hyperlink color. Here you can also change the colors for any of the colors associated with a theme.

FIGURE 5.21

Excel 2016, Windows 10, Microsoft Corporation

10 In the lower right corner of the dialog box, click **Cancel**, and then **Save** 🔲 your workbook.

Activity 5.10 | Modifying a Hyperlink

You can edit a hyperlink after you create it. In this Activity, you will change the name of the file to which you created a hyperlink, and then modify the hyperlink so that when clicked, the correct file displays.

1 In cell **M2**, click the **Instructor hyperlink** to open the **e05A_Faculty_Contacts** workbook.

2 Save this file in your **Excel Chapter 5** folder as **5A_Faculty_Contacts_2015** and then **Close** ☒ the **5A_Faculty_Contacts_2015** file to redisplay your **Lastname_Firstname_5A_Class_Schedule** worksheet.

3 Right-click cell **M2**—the Instructor hyperlink—and then click **Edit Hyperlink**.

4 In the **Edit Hyperlink** dialog box, click the **Look in arrow**, navigate to your **Excel Chapter 5** folder, and then select **5A_Faculty_Contacts_2015**. Compare your screen with Figure 5.22.

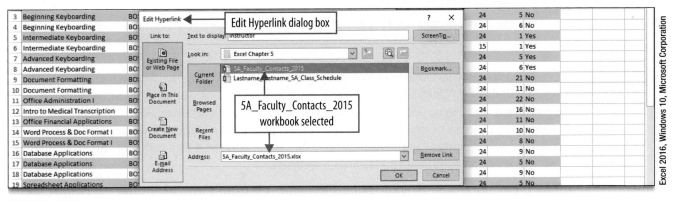

FIGURE 5.22

Excel 2016, Windows 10, Microsoft Corporation

5 Click **OK**. In cell **M2**, click the hyperlinked text—**Instructor**.

6 Click **Close** ☒ to close **5A_Faculty_Contacts_2015**.

7 Click the **File tab** and then click **Show All Properties**. As the **Tags**, type **class schedule** and as the **Subject**, type your course name and section #. Under **Related People**, be sure that your name displays as **Author**. **Save** the workbook.

8 If directed by your instructor to do so, submit your paper printout, your electronic image of your document that looks like a printed document, or your original Excel file. If required by your instructor, print or create an electronic version of your worksheet with formulas displayed. In the upper right corner of the Excel window, click **Close** ☒.

Objective 4   Save Excel Data in Other File Formats

GO! Learn How
Video E5-4

By default, Excel 2016 files are saved in the Excel Workbook file format with the *.xlsx file name extension*, which is a set of characters that helps your Windows operating system understand what kind of information is in a file and what program should open it.

Using the Save As command, you can choose to save an Excel file in another file format from the Save as type list. Some frequently used file formats are: Excel 97-2003 Workbook, Excel Template, Single File Web Page, Web Page, Excel Macro-Enabled Workbook, Text (Tab Delimited), and CSV (Comma Delimited).

For the purpose of posting Excel data to a website or transferring data to other applications, you can save your Excel file in a variety of other file formats. For example, saving an Excel worksheet as a *tab delimited text file* separates the cells of each row with tab characters. Saving an Excel worksheet as a *CSV (comma separated values) file* separates the cells of each row with commas. This type of file is also referred to as a *comma delimited file*. Text formats are commonly used to import data into a database program.

You can also save an Excel file in an electronic format that is easy to read for the viewer of the workbook. Such files are not easily modified and are considered to be an electronic printed version of the worksheet.

Activity 5.11 │ Viewing and Saving a Workbook as a Web Page

MOS
1.5.2

Before you save a worksheet as a webpage, it is a good idea to view it as a webpage to see how it will display. When saving a multiple-page workbook as a webpage, all of the worksheets are available and can be accessed. You can also save a single worksheet as a webpage. Excel changes the contents of the worksheet into *HTML (Hypertext Markup Language)*, which is a language web browsers can interpret, when you save a worksheet as a webpage. In this activity, you will save and publish a worksheet as a webpage.

1 If necessary, open your Lastname_Firstname_5A_Class_Schedule workbook. Display the **Save As** dialog box, and then navigate to your **Excel Chapter 5** folder. In the lower portion of the dialog box, click the **Save as type arrow**, and then click **Web Page**.

Your Excel files no longer display in the dialog box, because only files with the type Web Page are visible. The file type changes to Web Page and additional web-based options display below.

2 In the lower portion of the dialog box, click **Change Title**.

The text that you type here will become the title when the file displays as a webpage.

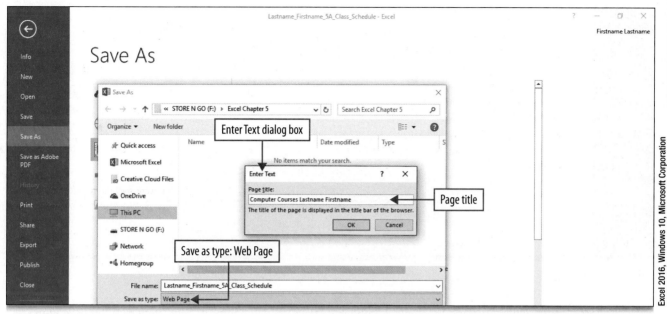

3 In the **Enter Text** dialog box, in the **Page title** box, using your own name, type **Computer Courses Lastname Firstname** and then compare your screen with Figure 5.23.

FIGURE 5.23

4 In the **Enter Text** dialog box, click **OK**, and notice that in the **Page title** box, your typed text displays.

5 In the **Save As** dialog box, click **Publish**.

6 In the **Publish as Web Page** dialog box, click the **Choose arrow**, notice the objects that can be published as a webpage, and then click **Items on Computer Classes** to select the *Computer Classes* sheet. In the lower left corner, make sure that the **Open published web page in browser** check box is selected. Compare your screen with Figure 5.24.

> Under Item to publish, you can choose which elements to include. You can select the entire workbook, a specific worksheet in the workbook, a range of cells, or previously published items that you are modifying. The Open published web page in browser selection ensures that the Internet browser software will automatically start and display the page.

FIGURE 5.24

7 Click **Browse** to display the **Publish As** dialog box.

8 Navigate to your **Excel Chapter 5** folder. In the **File name** box, type **Lastname_Firstname_5A_ Schedule_Webpage** Compare your screen with Figure 5.25.

FIGURE 5.25

9 Click **OK**, and then on the **Publish as Web Page** dialog box, click **Publish**. Compare your screen with Figure 5.26.

The webpage is saved in your selected folder, and the Class Schedule file opens in your default Internet browser. The browser tab displays the text you typed in the Enter Text dialog box.

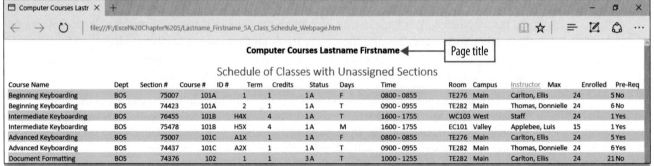

FIGURE 5.26

Excel 2016, Windows 10, Microsoft Corporation

10 If you are instructed to print your webpage on paper, consult the instructions to print from your specific browser software.

Your printed results will vary depending on which browser software you are using. Do not be concerned about the printout; webpages are intended for viewing, not printing.

11 On the browser title bar, click **Close** ⊠, and then redisplay your **Lastname_Firstname_5A_Class_Schedule** Excel workbook.

ALERT! **This Activity is Optional**

This Activity is optional. Check with your instructor to see if you should complete this Activity. This Activity is not included in the MyITLab Grader system for this project, however you may want to practice this on your own.

MOS
1.5.2

You can save an Excel worksheet as a comma separated values (CSV) file, which saves the contents of the cells by placing commas between them and an end-of-paragraph mark at the end of each row.

1 With your **Lastname_Firstname_5A_Class_Schedule** workbook open, display the **Save As** dialog box, click the **Save as type arrow**, and then click **CSV (Comma delimited)**. Be sure you save the file in your **Excel Chapter 5** folder. In the **File name** box, using your own name, type **Lastname_Firstname_5A_Schedule_CSV** and then compare your screen with Figure 5.27.

Your Excel files no longer display, because only CSV files are displayed.

FIGURE 5.27

2 Click **Save**. Compare your screen with Figure 5.28.

A dialog box displays to inform you that some features of the file may not be compatible with the CSV format. Features such as merged cells and formatting are lost. You can save the file and leave out incompatible features by clicking Yes, preserve the file in an Excel format by clicking No, or see what might be lost by clicking Help.

FIGURE 5.28

Excel 2016, Windows 10, Microsoft Corporation

3 Click **Yes** to keep the CSV format.

The file is saved in the new format. The new file name displays in the title bar. If file extensions—the three letters that identify the type of files—are displayed on your computer, you will also see .csv after the file name.

4 ▸ **Close** ⊠ your **Lastname_Firstname_5A_Schedule_CSV** file. Click **Save** to save changes, and then click **Save** again. Click **Yes** two times.

Activity 5.13 | Saving Excel Data as a PDF File

ALERT! | **This Activity is Optional**

This Activity is optional. Check with your instructor to see if you should complete this Activity. This Activity is not included in the MyITLab Grader system for this project, however you may want to practice this on your own.

1.5.2

You can create portable documents to share across applications and platforms with accurate visual representations. To publish a document and ensure that the appearance of the document is the same no matter what computer it is displayed on, save the document in *PDF (Portable Document Format)*. PDF is a widely used format developed by Adobe Systems that lets you create a representation of *electronic paper* that displays your data on the screen as it would look when printed. Use this format if you want someone to be able to view a document but not change it.

1 ▸ **Open** your **Lastname_Firstname_5A_Class_Schedule** workbook, press F12 to display the **Save As** dialog box, and then navigate to your **Excel Chapter 5** folder. Click the **Save as type arrow**, and then click **PDF**.

🔄 **ANOTHER WAY** From Backstage view, click Export, and then click Create PDF/XPS document to open the Publish as PDF or XPS dialog box.

2 ▸ In the lower right section of the dialog box, if necessary, select the Open file after publishing check box. As the file name, type **Lastname_Firstname_5A_Schedule_PDF** and then compare your screen with Figure 5.29.

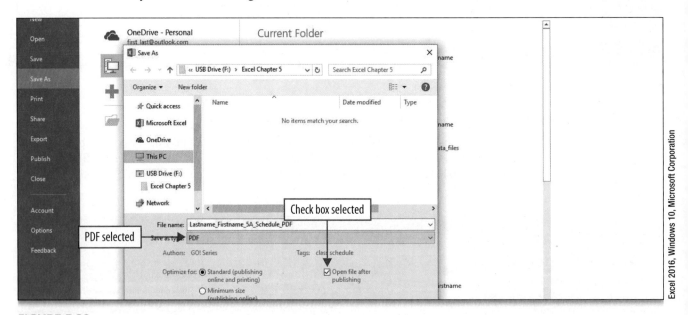

FIGURE 5.29

3 ▸ Click **Save**.

The file is saved in PDF format, and then opens as a PDF document using the default PDF program on your computer.

4 ▶ **Close** ☒ the **Lastname_Firstname_5A_Schedule_PDF** document. **Close** Excel and then submit your files from this project as directed by your instructor.

By choosing Text File as the file type, you can save an Excel worksheet as a text file, which saves the contents of the cells by placing a tab character, rather than commas, between the cells and an end-of-paragraph mark at the end of each row. This type of file can be readily exchanged with various database programs, in which it is referred to as a tab-delimited text file. A text file can be converted from tab-delimited text to a Word table. Word has a *Convert Text to Table* command that can easily convert a tabbed file into a table. A table displays in a row and column format, like an Excel spreadsheet.

End | You have completed Project 5A

PROJECT

5B Sorted, Filtered, and Outlined Database

MyITLab
Project 5B Training
Project 5B Grader

PROJECT ACTIVITIES

In Activities 5.14 to 5.20 you will use advanced table features to provide Dr. Kesia Toomer, the Dean of the Computer and Business Systems Division, information about the Fall course sections and assigned faculty in the Division. Your completed worksheets will look similar to Figure 5.30.

Please always review the downloaded Grader instructions before beginning.

PROJECT FILES

MyITLab
grader

If your instructor wants you to submit Project 5B in the MyITLab grader system, log in to MyITLab, locate Grader Project 5B, and then download the files for this project.

For Project 5B, you will need the following file:
e05B_Fall_Sections

You will save your workbook as:
Lastname_Firstname_5B_Fall_Sections

PROJECT RESULTS

GO! Walk Thru Project 5B

Excel 2016, Windows 10, Microsoft Corporation

FIGURE 5.30 Project 5B Fall Sections

Objective 5 Use Advanced Sort Techniques

GO! Learn How
Video E5-5

Sort means to organize data in a particular order; for example, alphabetizing a list of names. An *ascending* sort refers to text that is sorted alphabetically from A to Z, numbers sorted from lowest to highest, or dates and times sorted from earliest to latest. A *descending* sort refers to text that is sorted alphabetically from Z to A, numbers sorted from highest to lowest, or dates and times sorted from latest to earliest.

Sorting helps you to visualize your data. By sorting in various ways, you can find the data that you want, and then use your data to make good decisions. You can sort data in one column or in multiple columns. Most sort operations are column sorts, but you can also sort by rows.

Activity 5.14 | Sorting on Multiple Columns

> **ALERT!** **To submit as an autograded project, log into MyITLab and download the files for this project, and begin with those files instead of e05B_Fall_Sections.**

3.3.2

To sort data based on several criteria at once, use the *Sort dialog box*, which enables you to sort by more than one column or row. In this activity, you will convert the data into an Excel table, and then use the Sort dialog box to arrange the data.

1 Start Excel. From the student data files that accompany this chapter, open **e05B_Fall_Sections**. **Save** the file in your **Excel Chapter 5** folder as **Lastname_Firstname_5B_Fall_Sections**

2 Be sure that the first worksheet, **Room Conflicts**, is the active sheet. In the **Name Box**, type **a1:m50** and press Enter to select this range. On the **Insert tab**, in the **Tables group**, click **Table**. In the **Create Table** dialog box, be sure that the **My table has headers** check box is selected, and then click **OK**.

> ◆ **ANOTHER WAY** With cell A1 active, on the Insert tab, in the Tables group, click Table, and Excel will select all the contiguous data as the range.

3 On the **Design tab**, in the **Table Styles group**, click **More** ⊡, and then under **Light**, click **Table Style Light 16**. Click any cell to deselect the table, and then compare your screen with Figure 5.31.

A table of data like this one forms a *database*—an organized collection of facts related to a specific topic. In this table, the topic relates to the Fall course sections for this division of the college.

Each table row forms a *record*—all of the categories of data pertaining to one person, place, thing, event, or idea. In this table, each course section is a record. Each table column forms a *field*—a single piece of information that is stored in every record, such as a name or course number.

When information is arranged as records in rows and fields in columns, then you can *query*—ask a question of—the data. A query restricts records through the use of criteria conditions that will display records that will answer a question about the data.

FIGURE 5.31

4 On the **Data tab**, in the **Sort & Filter group**, click **Sort**.

In the Sort dialog box, you can sort up to 64 columns (levels) of data.

NOTE | **Defining data as a table prior to sort operations is optional.**

Defining your range of data as an Excel table is not required to perform sort operations. Doing so, however, is convenient if you plan to perform sorts on all of the data, because any sort commands will be performed on the entire table. Defining the data as a table also freezes the column titles automatically, so they will not move out of view as you scroll down a worksheet that contains many rows. If you want to sort only part of a list of data, do not convert the data to a table. Instead, select the range, and then click the Sort button.

---

5 In the **Sort** dialog box, under **Column**, click the **Sort by arrow**. Notice that the list displays in the order of the field names—the column titles. On the list, click **Dept**.

6 Under **Sort On**, verify that under **Sort On**, *Values* displays and that under **Order**, *A to Z* dislays. Compare your screen with Figure 5.32.

The default Sort On option *Values* indicates that the sort will be based on the values in the cells of the Sort by column—the Dept. column. The default sort Order *A to Z* indicates that the values in the column will be sorted in ascending alphabetic order.

Excel 2016, Windows 10, Microsoft Corporation

FIGURE 5.32

7 In the upper left corner of the **Sort** dialog box, click **Add Level**. In the second level row, click the **Then by arrow**, and then click **Course No**. Be sure that **Sort On** indicates *Values* and **Order** indicates *Smallest to Largest*.

When you initiate the sort operation, these numeric values will be sorted from the smallest number to the largest.

8 Click **Add Level** again. In the new row, under **Column**, click the **Then by arrow**, and then click **Section No.** Sort on the default options **Values**, from **Smallest to Largest**. Compare your screen with Figure 5.33.

FIGURE 5.33

Excel 2016, Windows 10, Microsoft Corporation

9 Click **OK**. Scroll down until **row 25** is at the top of the worksheet, take a moment to examine the arrangement of the data, and then compare your screen with Figure 5.34.

> The first sort level, sometimes referred to as the *major sort*, is by the Dept. field in alphabetic order, so after the BOS department, the CIS department sections are listed, and then the CPS department sections.

> The second sort level is by the Course No. field in ascending order, so within each department, the courses are sorted in ascending order by course number.

> The third sort level is by the Section No. field in ascending order, so within each Course No. the section numbers display in ascending order.

FIGURE 5.34

Excel 2016, Windows 10, Microsoft Corporation

10 Press Ctrl + Home. On the **Page Layout tab**, in the **Page Setup group**, click **Print Titles**. On the **Sheet tab** of the **Page Setup** dialog box, click in the **Rows to repeat at top** box, point to the **row 1** heading to display the pointer, and click to select **row 1** so that the column titles will print on each sheet. In the dialog box, click **OK**.

11 **Save** 🖫 your workbook.

Activity 5.15 | Sorting by Using a Custom List

You can use a ***custom list*** to sort in an order that you define. Excel includes a day-of-the-week and month-of-the-year custom list, so that you can sort chronologically by the days of the week or by the months of the year from January to December.

Optionally, you can create your own custom list by typing the values you want to sort by, in the order you want to sort them, from top to bottom; for example, *High, Medium, Low*. A custom list that you define must be based on a value—text, number, date, or time.

In this activity, you will create a custom list showing all the Fall sections sorted by Delivery, with all online courses listed first.

1 In the **sheet tab area**, click **Online-Campus** to display the second worksheet in the workbook.

2 On the **Data tab**, in the **Sort & Filter group**, click **Sort** to display the **Sort** dialog box. Set the first (major) level to sort by **Delivery** and to sort on **Values**. Then, click the **Order arrow** for this sort level, and click **Custom List** to display the **Custom Lists** dialog box.

3 Under **Custom lists**, be sure **NEW LIST** is selected. Under **List entries**, click in the empty box, type **Online** and then press [Enter]. Type **Classroom** and then compare your screen with Figure 5.35.

FIGURE 5.35

4 In the **Custom Lists** dialog box, click **Add**. On the left, under **Custom lists**, verify **Online, Classroom** is selected, and then click **OK** to redisplay the **Sort** dialog box. Compare your screen with Figure 5.36.

FIGURE 5.36

5 Click **OK** and then click any cell to deselect the table. Scroll down the worksheet, and notice that all of the online courses are listed first, and then scroll down so that **row 82** displays at the top of the worksheet. Notice the **Classroom** sections begin in **row 92**. Compare your screen with Figure 5.37.

A	B	C	D	E	F	G	H	I	J	K	L	M	N	O
82 70445	Linux/UNIX Fundamentals	CIS	121	3	Online	Online	Online	Online	38	17	Online	Instructor		
83 76243	Beginning Keyboarding	BOS	101A	1	Online	Online	Online	Online	38	11	Online	Reid, James		
84 71821	Intro to Software Applications	CIS	100	3	Online	Online	Online	Online	38	13	Online	Instructor		
85 76875	Intro To Visual Basic	CPS	185	4	Online	Online	Online	Online	38	21	Online	Philips, Matt		
86 75457	Intro to Software Applications	CIS	100	3	Online	Online	Online	Online	38	21	Online	Carlton, Elaine		
87 70388	Linux/UNIX Fundamentals	CIS	121	3	Online	Online	Online	Online	38	13	Online	Instructor		
88 75605	Advanced Keyboarding	BOS	101C	1	Online	Online	Online	Online	38	21	Online	Applebee, Linda		
89 75430	Intro to Computer Info Systems	CIS	110	3	Online	Online	Online	Online	38	16	Online	Hernandez, Jose		
90 75271	Medical Transcription II	BOS	220	4	Online	Online	Online	Online				Thomas, Doris		
91 75126	Intro to Software Applications	CIS	100	3	Online	Online	Online	Online				Anderson, Nancy		
92 74423	Beginning Keyboarding	BOS	101A	1	Classroom	T	0900 - 0955	TE282				Thomas, Doris		
93 71818	Intro to Software Applications	CIS	100	3	Classroom	T	0930 - 1055	TE272				Matthews, Chuck		
94 74433	Intermediate Keyboarding	BOS	101B	1	Classroom	F	1200 - 1255	TE276				Carlton, Elaine		
95 75286	Advanced Keyboarding	BOS	101C	1	Classroom	M	1700 - 1755	TE280	38	23	MAIN	McIntrye, Allison		
96 74441	Advanced Keyboarding	BOS	101C	1	Classroom	F	1200 - 1255	TE276	38	24	MAIN	Carlton, Elaine		
97 71834	Intro to Software Applications	CIS	100	3	Classroom	M	1100 - 1225	TE270	38	18	MAIN	Reid, James		

All Online sections display followed by Classroom sections

FIGURE 5.37

Excel 2016, Windows 10, Microsoft Corporation

6 Press Ctrl + Home to move to cell **A1**. On the **Page Layout tab**, in the **Page Setup group**, click **Print Titles**. On the **Sheet tab** of the **Page Setup** dialog box, click in the **Rows to repeat at top** box, point to the **row 1** heading to display the pointer, click to select **row 1**, and then click **OK**. **Save** 🖫 your workbook.

Objective 6   Use Custom and Advanced Filters

GO! Learn How
Video E5-6

Filtering displays only the rows that meet the *criteria*—conditions that you specify to limit which records are included in the results—and hides the rows that do not meet your criteria.

When you format a range of data as a table, or select a range and click the Filter command, Excel displays filter arrows in the column headings, from which you can display the *AutoFilter menu* for a column—a drop-down menu from which you can filter a column by a list of values, by a format, or by criteria.

Use a *custom filter* to apply complex criteria to a single column. Use an *advanced filter* to specify three or more criteria for a particular column, to apply complex criteria to two or more columns, or to specify computed criteria. You can also use an advanced filter for extracting—copying the selected rows to another part of the worksheet, instead of displaying the filtered list.

Activity 5.16 | Filtering by Format and Value Using AutoFilter

3.3.1

There are three types of filters that you can create with AutoFilter. You can filter by one or more values, for example *CIS* for the CIS department. You can filter by a format, such as cell color. Or, you can filter by criteria; for example, course sections that are greater than 2 credits, which would display courses that have 3 or more credits. Each of these filter types is mutually exclusive for the column; that is, you can use only one at a time.

1 Click the **CIS & CPS sheet tab** to display the third worksheet in the workbook.

2 Click the **Data tab**. In the **Sort & Filter group**, notice that **Filter** is active. In **row 1**, notice the **filter arrows** [▾] in each column title.

The data in this worksheet is formatted as an Excel table and filter arrows are automatically added in the header row of the table. A filter arrow, when clicked, displays the AutoFilter menu. On the ribbon, the active Filter button indicates that the data is formatted to use filters.

3 In **column B**, notice that some courses are formatted with a yellow fill color, which indicates courses that have been designated as introductory courses recommended for high school seniors who want to take a college class.

4 In cell **B1**, click the **Course Name filter arrow** ▾. On the **AutoFilter** menu, point to **Filter by Color**, and then compare your screen with Figure 5.38.

Two options display—Filter by Cell Color and Filter by Font Color. Under each option, color blocks display the colors available in the filtered column.

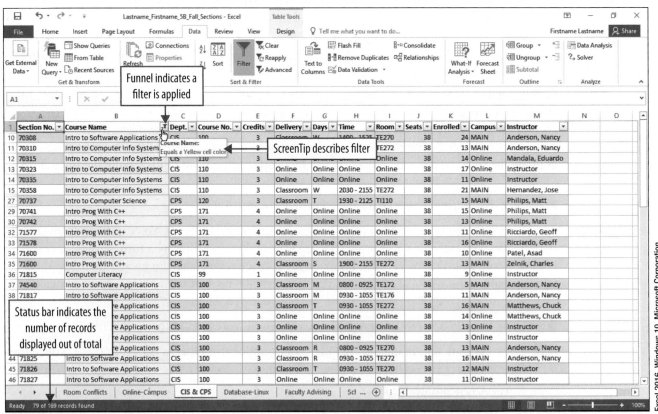

Excel 2016, Windows 10, Microsoft Corporation

FIGURE 5.38

5 Under **Filter by Cell Color**, click the **yellow block**.

Only courses with a yellow fill color in column B display; the status bar indicates that 79 of the 169 records display.

6 Point to the **filter arrow** ▾ in cell **B1**, and notice the ScreenTip *Course Name: Equals a Yellow cell color*. Notice also that a small funnel displays to the right of the arrow. Compare your screen with Figure 5.39.

The funnel indicates that a filter is applied, and the ScreenTip indicates how the records are filtered. The status bar indicates the number of records that display out of the total number of records.

FIGURE 5.39

7 In cell **B1**, click the **Course Name filter arrow** ▼, and then click **Clear Filter From "Course Name"**. Then, in cell **B1**, point to the **Course Name filter arrow**, and notice that *(Showing All)* displays.

> The funnel no longer displays. The status bar no longer indicates that a filter is active. A filter arrow without a funnel means that the filtering feature is enabled but not applied; if you point to the arrow, the ScreenTip will display (Showing All).

8 Click cell **I5**, which contains the value *TE280*. Right-click over the selected cell, point to **Filter**, and then click **Filter by Selected Cell's Value**. Notice that only the courses that meet in Room TE280 display; all the other records are hidden.

> Excel filters the records by the selected value—TE280—and indicates in the status bar that 10 of the 169 records are displayed. This is a quick way to filter a set of records.

9 On the **Data tab**, in the **Sort & Filter group**, click **Clear** to clear all of the filters.

> Use this command to clear all filters from a group of records. This command also clears any sorts that were applied.

10 Save 🖫 your workbook.

Activity 5.17 | Filtering by Custom Criteria Using AutoFilter

By using a custom filter, you can apply complex criteria to a single column. For example, you can use comparison criteria to compare two values by using the ***comparison operators*** such as Equals (=), Greater Than (>), or Less Than (<) singly or in combinations. When you compare two values by using these operators, your result is a logical value that is either true or false.

1 Click the **Database-Linux sheet tab** to display the fourth worksheet in the workbook.

2 In cell **K1**, click the **Enrolled filter arrow** ▼, point to **Number Filters**, and then click **Less Than Or Equal To**. In the **Custom AutoFilter** dialog box, in the first box, be sure that *is less than or equal to* displays. In the second box type **12** and then compare your screen with Figure 5.40.

> In the Custom AutoFilter dialog box, you can create a ***compound filter***—a filter that uses more than one condition—and one that uses comparison operators.

Excel 2016, Windows 10, Microsoft Corporation

FIGURE 5.40

3 Click **OK** to display 49 records.

> This filter answers the question, *Which course sections have 12 or fewer students enrolled?*

4 On the **Data tab**, in the **Sort & Filter group**, click **Clear** to clear all filters.

5 In cell **B1**, click the **Course Name filter arrow** ▼, point to **Text Filters**, and then click **Contains**.

6 In the **Custom AutoFilter** dialog box, under **Course Name**, in the first box, be sure that *contains* displays. In the box to the right, type **database**

7 Between the two rows of boxes, click the **Or** option button. For the second filter, in the first box, click the arrow, scroll down as necessary, and then click **contains**. In the second box, type **linux** and then compare your screen with Figure 5.41.

For the *Or comparison operator*, only one of the two comparison criteria that you specify must be true. By applying this filter, only courses that contain the word *database* or *linux* will display.

For the *And comparison operator*, each and every one of the comparison criteria that you specify must be true.

FIGURE 5.41

8 Click **OK** to display 14 records. Compare your screen with Figure 5.42 and then **Save** 🖫 your workbook.

This filter answers the question, *Which course sections relate to either databases or the Linux operating system?*

FIGURE 5.42

Activity 5.18 | Using the Name Manager and Filtering by Using Advanced Criteria

Expert 3.6.3, 3.6.4

Use an advanced filter when the data you want to filter requires complex criteria; for example, to specify three or more criteria for a particular column, to apply complex criteria to two or more columns, or to specify computed criteria. When you use the Advanced Filter command, the Advanced dialog box displays, rather than the AutoFilter menu, and you type the criteria on the worksheet above the range you want to filter.

In this activity, you will create an advanced filter to determine faculty members whose classification includes Professor and that have an annual salary of $70,000 or more, and who have 8 or more hours of assigned advising hours.

1 ▶ Display the **Faculty Advising** sheet.

2 ▶ Select the range **A7:G7**, right-click, and then click **Copy**. Point to cell **A2**, right-click, under **Paste Options**, click the first button, **Paste (P)**, and then press Esc to cancel the moving border. Compare your screen with Figure 5.43.

The first step in filtering by using advanced criteria is to create a ***criteria range***—an area on your worksheet where you define the criteria for the filter. The criteria range indicates how the displayed records are filtered.

Typically, the criteria range is placed *above* the data. The criteria range includes a row for the column headings that must match the column headings in the data range exactly. The criteria range must also include at least one row for the criteria—you will need additional rows if you have multiple criteria for a column. You can also add a title row. Separate the criteria range from the data by a blank row.

FIGURE 5.43

Excel 2016, Windows 10, Microsoft Corporation

3 ▶ Select the range **A2:G3**—the column names and the blank row below the Criteria column headings. Click in the **Name Box**, type **Criteria** and then press Enter. Compare your screen with Figure 5.44.

By naming the range Criteria, which is a predefined name recognized by Excel, the reference to this range will automatically display as the Criteria range in the Advanced Filter dialog box. This defined criteria range includes the field names and one empty row, where the limiting criteria will be placed. It does not include the title Criteria.

FIGURE 5.44

Excel 2016, Windows 10, Microsoft Corporation

4 ▶ On the **Formulas tab**, in the **Defined Names** group, click **Name Manager**, and then compare your screen with Figure 5.45.

In this workbook, in addition to the Criteria name that you defined, there are several named tables—Excel automatically assigns defined tables with names. Additionally, the Print Titles ranges defined in previous worksheets are listed.

FIGURE 5.45

5 ▶ **Close** the **Name Manager** dialog box.

6 ▶ Click cell **D3**, type **>=70000** and then press Enter.

This action creates a criteria using a comparison operator to look for salary values that are greater than or equal to $70,000. Do not include a comma when you type this value, because the comma is a cell format, not part of the value.

7 ▶ Click cell **A7**. On the **Data tab**, in the **Sort & Filter group**, click **Advanced**.

8 ▶ In the **Advanced Filter** dialog box, in the **List range** box, type **$A$7:$G$34** which is your Excel table. Be sure the **Criteria range** is identified as cells **$A$2:$G$3**. Compare your screen with Figure 5.46.

Both the List and the Criteria ranges use absolute cell references. Under Action, you can choose to display the results in the table—in-place—or copy the results to another location.

FIGURE 5.46

Excel 2016, Windows 10, Microsoft Corporation

9 ▶ Click **OK** to have the filter results display in-place—in the table. Press Ctrl + Home and compare your screen with Figure 5.47.

Only the records for faculty members whose salary is $70,000 or more display. The row numbers for the records that meet the criteria display in blue. The Advanced command disables the AutoFilter command and removes the AutoFilter arrows from the column headings.

Row numbers of included records display in blue

Criteria entered in Criteria range

Faculty whose salary is equal to or greater than $70,000 display

FIGURE 5.47

Excel 2016, Windows 10, Microsoft Corporation

10 Click cell **B3**, type *__Professor__ and then press Enter.

The asterisk (*) is a wildcard. Use a *wildcard* to search a field when you are uncertain of the exact value or you want to widen the search to include more records. The use of a wildcard enables you to include faculty whose classification ends with the word *Professor*. It directs Excel to find Professor and anything before it. The criterion in the Salary field still applies.

The use of two or more criteria on the same row is known as *compound criteria*—all conditions must be met for the records to be included in the results.

11 Click cell **A7**. On the **Data tab**, in the **Sort & Filter group**, click **Advanced**. Verify that the database range is correctly identified in the **List range** box and that the **Criteria range** still indicates *$A$2:$G$3*. Click **OK**. Compare your screen with Figure 5.48.

Only the eight faculty members with a classification containing *Professor* and a salary of $70,000 or more display.

Asterisk wildcard entered in front of *Professor* in Criteria range

Faculty with the classification that ends *Professor* and salary is $70,000 or more display

FIGURE 5.48

Excel 2016, Windows 10, Microsoft Corporation

12 Using the techniques you just practiced, filter the data further by adding an additional criteria—faculty who are assigned 8 hours or more of advising. Compare your result with Figure 5.49.

Five faculty members meet all three of the criteria in the Criteria range.

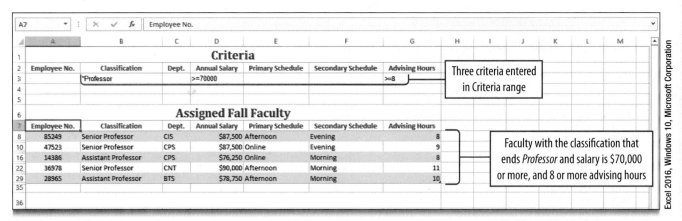

FIGURE 5.49

13 On the **Formulas tab**, in the **Defined Names group**, click **Name Manager**. In the list of names, click **Criteria**, click **Delete**, and then click **OK** to delete the name. Click **Close**, and then **Save** 💾 your workbook.

It is good practice to delete a Criteria name if you plan to filter data in another worksheet within the same workbook. If you do not delete the Criteria name, the Advanced Filter feature will continue to use the named Criteria range in future filters.

More Knowledge | **Using Wildcards**

A wildcard can help you locate information when you are uncertain how the information might be displayed in your records. The placement of the asterisk in relationship to the known value determines the result. If it is placed first, the variable will be in the beginning of the string of characters. For example, in a list of names if you used *son as the criteria, it will look for any name that ends in son. The results might display Peterson, Michelson, and Samuelson. If the asterisk is at the end of the known value in the criteria, then the variable will be at the end. You can also include the asterisk wildcard at the beginning and at the end of a known value. You can also use an asterisk wildcard in the middle, so searching for m*t will result in both mat and moist.

A question mark (?) can also be used as part of your search criteria. Each question mark used in the criteria represents a single position or character that is unknown in a group of specified values. Searching for *m?n* would find, for example, *min*, *men*, and *man*; whereas searching for m??d would find, for example, *mind*, *mend*, *mold*.

Activity 5.19 | Naming Ranges and Extracting Filtered Rows

Expert 3.6.2

You can ***extract***—pull out the results of a filter to another area of your worksheet—instead of displaying a filtered list as you did in the previous activity. The location to which you copy the records is the ***Extract area***, and is commonly placed below the table of data.

In this activity, you will extract data to create a report showing how many faculty have a Morning-Evening schedule.

1 Display the **Schedule Comparison** sheet and notice that a Criteria range has been created at the top of the worksheet.

2 **Copy** the range **A2:G2**, scroll down to view **row 37**, point to cell **A37**, right-click, and then under **Paste Options**, click the first **Paste (P)** button. Compare your screen with Figure 5.50.

FIGURE 5.50

3 With the range **A37:G37** selected, in the **Name Box**, type **Extract** and press Enter.

This action defines the Extract area so that the range will display automatically in the Copy to box of the Advanced Filter dialog box. Excel recognizes *Extract* as the location in which to place the results of an advanced filter.

4 Select the range **A7:G34** and then in the **Name Box**, type **Database** and press Enter.

This action defines the list area. Excel recognizes *Database* as the range to be filtered.

5 At the top of your worksheet, in cell **E3**, type **Morning** and then in cell **F3**, type **Evening**

When applied, the filter will display only those records where the Primary Schedule is Morning and the Secondary Schedule is Evening.

6 On the **Data tab**, in the **Sort & Filter group**, click **Advanced**. Verify that the **List range** is **$A$7:$G$34**.

7 Click in the **Criteria range** box, and then scroll the worksheet to display the criteria range. Select the range **A2:G3**.

8 Under **Action**, click **Copy to another location**. Verify that in the **Copy to** box, the absolute reference to the Extract area—*$A$37:$G$37*—displays. Compare your screen with Figure 5.51.

FIGURE 5.51

Excel 2016, Windows 10, Microsoft Corporation

9 Click **OK**, and then scroll to view the lower portion of your worksheet. Compare your screen with Figure 5.52 and then **Save** 🖫 your workbook.

Two records meet the criteria and are copied to the extract area on your worksheet. When you use an extract area in this manner, instead of reformatting the table to display the qualifying records, Excel places a copy of the qualifying records in the Extract area.

36		**Morning-Evening Schedule**									
37	Employee No.	Classification	Dept.	Annual Salary	Primary Schedule	Secondary Schedule	Advising Hours				
38	47593	Senior Lecturer	CIS	$52,500	Morning	Evening	5		Two records display in the	
39	48752	Senior Lecturer	CPS	$53,125	Morning	Evening	12		Morning-Evening extract area	
40										
41										

FIGURE 5.52

Excel 2016, Windows 10, Microsoft Corporation

Objective 7 Subtotal, Outline, and Group a List of Data

GO! Learn How
Video E5-7

You can group and summarize a *list*—a series of rows that contains related data—by adding subtotals. The first step in adding subtotals is to sort the data by the field for which you want to create a subtotal.

Activity 5.20 │ Subtotaling, Outlining, and Grouping a List of Data

2.3.2, 2.3.3

In this activity, you will use Excel subtotal and outline features to summarize the faculty salaries by department.

1 Display the **Salaries by Department** sheet.

2 Select the range **A2:G29**. On the **Data tab**, in the **Sort & Filter group**, click **Sort**. In the **Sort** dialog box, click the **Sort by arrow**, and then click **Dept**. Click **Add Level**, click the **Then by arrow**, and then click **Annual Salary**. Compare your **Sort** dialog box with Figure 5.53.

FIGURE 5.53

3 Click **OK**. With the range still selected, on the **Data tab**, in the **Outline group**, click **Subtotal**.

The *Subtotal command* totals several rows of related data together by automatically inserting subtotals and totals for the selected cells.

4 In the **Subtotal** dialog box, in the **At each change in** box, click the arrow to display the list, and then click **Dept**. In the **Use function** box, display the list and click **Sum**. In the **Add subtotal to** list, select the **Annual Salary** check box, and then scroll the list and *deselect* any other check boxes that are selected. Compare your screen with Figure 5.54.

These actions direct Excel to create a group for each change in value in the Dept. field. Excel will then use the Sum function to add a subtotal in the Annual Salary field. The check boxes at the bottom of the dialog box indicate how the subtotals will display.

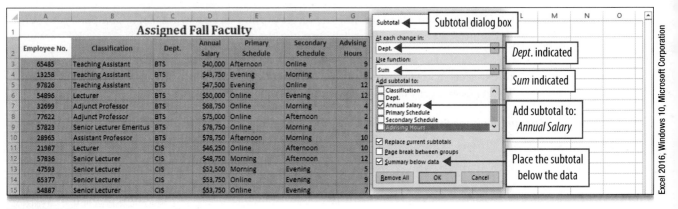

FIGURE 5.54

5 Click **OK**, press Ctrl + Home, **AutoFit column C**, and then compare your screen with Figure 5.55.

The Dept. sort applied earlier in this Activity placed the data for each department together so that at each change in Dept., subtotals for the department salaries display.

FIGURE 5.55

Excel 2016, Windows 10, Microsoft Corporation

6 Along the left edge of your workbook, locate the outline.

When you add subtotals, Excel defines groups based on the rows used to calculate a subtotal. The groupings form an outline of your worksheet based on the criteria you indicated in the Subtotal dialog box, and the outline displays along the left side of your worksheet.

The outline bar along the left side of the worksheet enables you to show and hide levels of detail with a single mouse click. For example, you can show details with the totals, which is the default view. Or, you can show only the summary totals or only the grand total.

There are three types of controls in the outline. Hide Detail (–) collapses a group of cells, Show Detail (+) expands a collapsed group of cells, and the level buttons (1, 2, 3) can hide all levels of detail below the number clicked.

7 To the left of **row 25**, click **Hide Detail** (–) to collapse the detail for the **CNT** department.

Detail data refers to the subtotaled rows that are totaled and summarized. Detail data is typically adjacent to and either above or to the left of the summary data.

8 At the top of the outline area, click the **Level 2** button to hide all Level 3 and 4 details and display only the Level 2 summary information and the Level 1 Grand Total. Press Ctrl + Home and compare your screen with Figure 5.56.

FIGURE 5.56

Excel 2016, Windows 10, Microsoft Corporation

9 Group all the worksheets and change the **Orientation** to **Landscape**. Center the sheets **Horizontally** on the page and insert a footer that includes the file name in the **left section**, and in the **right section**, insert the **Sheet Name** ▦. On the **Page Layout tab**, set the **Width** to **1 page**.

10 **Ungroup** the worksheets, and then display the **Schedule Comparison** sheet. On the **Page Layout tab**, set the **Height** to **1 page**.

11 Click the **File tab** and then click **Show All Properties**. As the **Tags**, type **faculty, schedule, salaries** and as the **Subject**, type your course name and section #. Under **Related People**, be sure that your name displays as **Author**.

12 Group the sheets and display the **Print Preview**. Your workbook should contain 14 pages. View each page and make any necessary corrections or adjustments. **Save** the workbook.

13 If directed by your instructor to do so, submit your paper printout, your electronic image of your document that looks like a printed document, or your original Excel file. If required by your instructor, print or create an electronic version of your worksheet with formulas displayed. In the upper right corner of the Excel window, click **Close** ☒.

More **Knowledge**   **Outlining a Worksheet**

A horizontal outline bar can be created for data that is summarized by row, rather than summarized by column as it was in this activity. In addition, if the data is not organized so that Excel can outline it automatically, you can create an outline manually. To do so, on the Data tab, in the Outline group, click the Group button, and then click Auto Outline.

END | You have completed Project 5B

5

EXCEL

MICROSOFT OFFICE SPECIALIST (MOS) SKILLS IN THIS CHAPTER

PROJECT 5A	PROJECT 5B
1.2.2 Navigate to a named cell, range, or workbook element	**2.3.2** Outline data
1.2.3 Insert and remove hyperlinks	**2.3.3** Insert subtotals
1.3.6 Change workbook themes	**3.3.1** Filter records
1.4.2 Hide or unhide columns and rows	**3.3.2** Sort data by multiple columns
1.4.4 Change workbook views	**Expert 3.6.2** Name data ranges
1.4.5 Change window views	**Expert 3.6.3** Name tables
1.5.2 Save workbooks in alternative file formats	**Expert 3.6.4** Manage named ranges and objects
1.5.5 Display repeating row and column titles on multipage worksheets	
3.2.2 Configure table style options	

BUILD YOUR E-PORTFOLIO

An E-Portfolio is a collection of evidence, stored electronically, that showcases what you have accomplished while completing your education. Collecting and then sharing your work products with potential employers reflects your academic and career goals. Your completed documents from the following projects are good examples to show what you have learned: 5G, 5K, and 5L.

GO! FOR JOB SUCCESS

Organizational decisions like new products or global expansion have historically been made after lengthy analysis of available information and risk. Today, though, organizations of every kind operate in an environment where decisions need to be made quickly, even as the amount of data available on which to base them has reached unprecedented levels. Business people at all levels are being trained to accelerate their decision making. Accelerated decision making requires the ability to quickly understand the situation, identify possible options, evaluate the risk, then take action, without having all the data or time to consider every alternative.

FotolEdhar/Fotolia

What are some situations in your career, in your personal life, or education where you have had to make a decision under these circumstances?

Think about your own decision style? Do you think you would easily adapt to an accelerated decision situation? Why or why not?

Some situations are more suited to an accelerated decision than others. What are some factors that could require a business to make an accelerated decision?

END OF CHAPTER

SUMMARY

You can navigate a large worksheet using the Freeze Panes, Go To, and Find commands. Control the screen display by hiding rows and columns and work with multiple workbooks using the Arrange All command.

A theme is a set of formatting characteristics, such as fonts, number formats, borders, and shading. Insert page breaks, repeat column or row titles, and use Landscape orientation for worksheets with many columns.

By default, Excel files are saved in the Excel Workbook file format with the .xlsx file name extension. Excel data can also be saved in other file formats such as HTML, CSV, and PDF.

Sorting organizes data in a particular order. Filtering displays only the rows that meet specific criteria. Sorting and filtering along with subtotaling, outlining, and grouping are used for data analysis.

GO! LEARN IT ONLINE

Review the concepts, key terms, and MOS skills in this chapter by completing these online challenges, which you can find at **MyITLab**.

Matching and Multiple Choice: Answer matching and multiple choice questions to test what you learned in this chapter.

Lessons on the GO!: Learn how to use all the new apps and features as they are introduced by Microsoft.

MOS Prep Quiz: Answer questions to review the MOS skills that you practiced in this chapter.

PROJECT GUIDE FOR EXCEL CHAPTER 5

Your instructor will assign Projects from this list to ensure your learning and assess your knowledge.

PROJECT GUIDE FOR EXCEL CHAPTER 5

Project	Apply Skills from These Chapter Objectives	Project Type	Project Location
5A MyITLab	Objectives 1-4 from Project 5A	**5A Instructional Project (Grader Project)** Guided instruction to learn the skills in Project 5A.	In MyITLab and in text
5B MyITLab	Objectives 5-7 from Project 5B	**5B Instructional Project (Grader Project)** Guided instruction to learn the skills in Project 5B.	In MyITLab and in text
5C	Objectives 1-4 from Project 5A	**5C Skills Review (Scorecard Grading)** A guided review of the skills from Project 5A.	In text
5D	Objectives 5-7 from Project 5B	**5D Skills Review (Scorecard Grading)** A guided review of the skills from Project 5B.	In text
5E MyITLab	Objectives 1-4 from Project 5A	**5E Mastery (Grader Project)** **Mastery and Transfer of Learning** A demonstration of your mastery of the skills in Project 5A with extensive decision making.	In MyITLab and in text
5F MyITLab	Objectives 5-7 from Project 5B	**5F Mastery (Grader Project)** **Mastery and Transfer of Learning** A demonstration of your mastery of the skills in Project 5B with extensive decision making.	In MyITLab and in text
5G MyITLab	Objectives 1-7 from Projects 5A and 5B	**5G Mastery (Grader Project)** **Mastery and Transfer of Learning** A demonstration of your mastery of the skills in Projects 5A and 5B with extensive decision making.	In MyITLab and in text
5H	Combination of Objectives from Projects 5A and 5B	**5H GO! Fix It (Scorecard Grading)** **Critical Thinking** A demonstration of your mastery of the skills in Projects 5A and 5B by creating a correct result from a document that contains errors you must find.	Instructor Resource Center (IRC) and MyITLab
5I	Combination of Objectives from Projects 5A and 5B	**5I GO! Make It (Scorecard Grading)** **Critical Thinking** A demonstration of your mastery of the skills in Projects 5A and 5B by creating a result from a supplied picture.	IRC and MyITLab
5J	Combination of Objectives from Projects 5A and 5B	**5J GO! Solve It (Rubric Grading)** **Critical Thinking** A demonstration of your mastery of the skills in Projects 5A and 5B, your decision-making skills, and your critical thinking skills. A task-specific rubric helps you self-assess your result.	IRC and MyITLab
5K	Combination of Objectives from Projects 5A and 5B	**5K GO! Solve It (Rubric Grading)** **Critical Thinking** A demonstration of your mastery of the skills in Projects 5A and 5B, your decision-making skills, and your critical thinking skills. A task-specific rubric helps you self-assess your result.	In text
5L	Combination of Objectives from Projects 5A and 5B	**5L GO! Think (Rubric Grading)** **Critical Thinking** A demonstration of your understanding of the chapter concepts applied in a manner that you would outside of college. An analytic rubric helps you and your instructor grade the quality of your work by comparing it to the work an expert in the discipline would create.	In text
5M	Combination of Objectives from Projects 5A and 5B	**5M GO! Think (Rubric Grading)** **Critical Thinking** A demonstration of your understanding of the chapter concepts applied in a manner that you would outside of college. An analytic rubric helps you and your instructor grade the quality of your work by comparing it to the work an expert in the discipline would create.	IRC and MyITLab
5N	Combination of Objectives from Projects 5A and 5B	**5N You and GO! (Rubric Grading)** **Critical Thinking** A demonstration of your understanding of the chapter concepts applied in a manner that you would in a personal situation. An analytic rubric helps you and your instructor grade the quality of your work.	IRC and MyITLab

GLOSSARY

GLOSSARY OF CHAPTER KEY TERMS

Active area The area of the worksheet that contains data or has contained data.

Advanced filter A filter that can specify three or more criteria for a particular column, apply complex criteria to two or more columns, or specify computed criteria.

And comparison operator The comparison operator that requires each and every one of the comparison criteria to be true.

Arrange All The command that tiles all open program windows on the screen.

Ascending The term that refers to the arrangement of text that is sorted alphabetically from A to Z, numbers sorted from lowest to highest, or dates and times sorted from earliest to latest.

AutoFilter menu A drop-down menu from which you can filter a column by a list of values, by a format, or by criteria.

Cell style A defined set of formatting characteristics, such as font, font size, font color, cell borders, and cell shading.

Comma delimited file A file type that saves the contents of the cells by placing commas between them and an end-of-paragraph mark at the end of each row; also referred to as a CSV (comma separated values) file.

Comparison operators Symbols that evaluate each value to determine if it is the same (=), greater than (>), less than (<), or in between a range of values as specified by the criteria.

Compound criteria The use of two or more criteria on the same row— all conditions must be met for the records to be included in the results.

Compound filter A filter that uses more than one condition—and one that uses comparison operators.

Criteria Conditions that you specify in a logical function or filter.

Criteria range An area on your worksheet where you define the criteria for the filter, and that indicates how the displayed records are filtered.

CSV (comma separated values) file A file type in which the cells in each row are separated by commas and an end-of-paragraph mark at the end of each row; also referred to as a comma delimited file.

Custom filter A filter with which you can apply complex criteria to a single column.

Custom list A sort order that you can define.

Database An organized collection of facts related to a specific topic.

Descending The term that refers to the arrangement of text that is sorted alphabetically from Z to A, numbers sorted from highest to lowest, or dates and times sorted from latest to earliest.

Detail data The subtotaled rows that are totaled and summarized; typically adjacent to and either above or to the left of the summary data.

Extract The process of pulling out multiple sets of data for comparison purposes.

Extract area The location to which you copy records when extracting filtered rows.

Field A specific type of data such as name, employee number, or social security number that is stored in columns.

Filtering A process in which only the rows that meet the criteria display; rows that do not meet the criteria are hidden.

Find A command that locates and selects specific text or formatting.

Freeze Panes A command that enables you to select one or more rows or columns and freeze (lock) them into place so that they remain on the screen while you scroll; the locked rows and columns become separate panes.

Go To A command that moves to a specific cell or range of cells that you specify.

Go To Special A command that moves to cells that have special characteristics, for example, to cells that are blank or to cells that contain constants, as opposed to formulas.

HTML (Hypertext Markup Language) A language web browsers can interpret.

Hyperlink Text or graphics that, when clicked, take you to another location in the worksheet, to another file, or to a webpage on the Internet or on your organization's intranet.

List A series of rows that contains related data that you can group by adding subtotals.

Major sort A term sometimes used to refer to the first sort level in the Sort dialog box.

Or comparison operator The comparison operator that requires only one of the two comparison criteria that you specify to be true.

Pane A portion of a worksheet window bounded by and separated from other portions by vertical and horizontal bars.

PDF (Portable Document Format) A file format developed by Adobe Systems that creates a representation of electronic paper that displays your data on the screen as it would look when printed, but that cannot be easily changed.

Query A process of restricting records through the use of criteria conditions that will display records that will answer a question about the data.

Record All the categories of data pertaining to one person, place, thing, event, or idea.

Scaling The group of commands by which you can reduce the horizontal and vertical size of the printed data by a percentage or by the number of pages that you specify.

Sort The process of arranging data in a specific order.

Sort dialog box A dialog box in which you can sort data based on several criteria at once, and that enables a sort by more than one column or row.

Split The command that enables you to view separate parts of the same worksheet on your screen; splits the window into multiple resizable panes to view distant parts of the worksheet at one time.

Subtotal command The command that totals several rows of related data together by automatically inserting subtotals and totals for the selected cells.

Tab delimited text file A file type in which cells are separated by tabs; this type of file can be readily exchanged with various database programs.

Wildcard A character, for example the asterisk or question mark, used to search a field when you are uncertain of the exact value or when you want to widen the search to include more records.

.xlsx file name extension The default file format used by Excel 2016 to save an Excel workbook.

Apply **5A** skills from these Objectives:

1 Navigate and Manage Large Worksheets

2 Enhance Worksheets with Themes and Styles

3 Format a Worksheet to Share with Others

4 Save Excel Data in Other File Formats

Skills Review | Project 5C Science Schedule

In the following Skills Review, you will assist Susanne Black, Program Chair for Science, in formatting and navigating a large worksheet that lists the class schedule for the Science departments at Laurel College. You will also save Excel data in other file formats. Your completed workbooks will look similar to Figure 5.57.

PROJECT FILES

For Project 5C, you will need the following files:

e05C_Science_Faculty

e05C_Science_Requests

e05C_Science_Schedule

You will save your workbooks as:

Lastname_Firstname_5C_Science_CSV (not shown)

Lastname_Firstname_5C_Science_Schedule

PROJECT RESULTS

Excel 2016, Windows 10, Microsoft Corporation

FIGURE 5.57

(Project 5C Science Schedule continues on the next page)

1 Start Excel. From your student files, open the file **e05C_Science_Schedule**. Display the Save As dialog box, navigate to your **Excel Chapter 5** folder, and then **Save** the workbook as **Lastname_Firstname_5C_Science_Schedule**

a. On the **Home tab**, in the **Editing group**, click **Find & Select**, and then click **Go To Special**. In the first column, click **Blanks**, and then click **OK** to select all blank cells in the worksheet's active area. Point to the selected cell **K31** and right-click. On the mini toolbar, click the **Fill Color button arrow**, and then under **Standard Colors**, click the fourth color—**Yellow**—to fill all the selected blank cells. These cells still require Room assignments.

b. Press (Ctrl) + (Home). From the column heading area, select **columns E:H**. Right-click over the selected area, and then click **Hide**.

c. On the **Home tab**, in the **Editing group**, click **Find & Select**, and then click **Go To**. In the **Go To** dialog box, in the **Reference** box, type **m172** and then click **OK**. With cell **M172** active, on the **Formulas tab**, in the **Function Library** group, click **More Functions**, point to **Statistical**, and then click **COUNTIF**. As the **Range**, type **m2:m170** and as the **Criteria**, type **Staff** Click **OK**. Your result is *27*, indicating that 27 courses still indicate *Staff* and need an instructor assigned. In cell **I172**, type **Still need instructor assigned** and press (Enter). Press (Ctrl) + (Home) and click **Save**.

2 From your student files, open **e05C_Science_Requests**. On the **View tab**, in the **Window group**, click **Switch Windows**, and then at the bottom of the list, click your **Lastname_Firstname_5C_Science_Schedule** file to make it the active worksheet. On the **View tab**, in the **Window group**, click **Arrange All**. Click **Horizontal**, and then click **OK**. If necessary, click the title bar of your Lastname_Firstname_5C_Science_Schedule worksheet to make it the active worksheet. Press (Ctrl) + (End) to move to cell **P172**.

a. Click cell **A172**. In the **Window group**, click **Split**. Above the split bar, click any cell in **column C**. Press (Ctrl) + (F) to display the **Find and Replace** dialog box. Locate the first request in the **e05C_Science_Requests** worksheet, which is from *Eric Marshall* to teach *Survey of Astronomy Section # 76822*. In the

Find what box, type **76822** so that you can locate the course in the worksheet.

b. Click **Find Next**. Drag the title bar of the dialog box into the upper right area of your screen so that you can see the **Name Box**, which indicates *C38*. In your **Lastname_Firstname_5C_Science_Schedule** worksheet, click in cell **M38**, type **Marshall, Eric** to delete *Staff* and assign the class to Mr. Marshall. Press (Enter).

c. **Close** the **Find and Replace** dialog box. In cell **M172**, notice that *26* classes remain unassigned.

d. Click any cell in the **e05C_Science_Requests** worksheet, and then on this worksheet's title bar, click **Close**. On the title bar of your **Lastname_Firstname_5C_Science_Schedule** worksheet, click **Maximize** to restore the size of the worksheet to its full size. On the **View tab**, in the **Window group**, click **Split** to remove the split.

e. Press (Ctrl) + (Home), and then **Save** your workbook.

3 Point to the **row 1 heading**, right-click, and then click **Insert**. In cell **A1**, type **Schedule of Classes with Unassigned Sections Merge & Center** this title across the range **A1:P1**, and then apply the **Title** cell style.

a. On the **Page Layout tab**, in the **Themes group**, click **Themes**, and then, click the **Slice** theme. In the **Themes group**, click **Fonts**. Scroll to the top and then click the **Office** fonts.

b. On the **Home tab**, in the **Styles group**, click **Format as Table**. At the bottom, click **New Table Style**. In the **New Table Style** dialog box, in the **Name** box, replace the existing text by typing **Science Schedule** In the list under **Table Element**, click **First Row Stripe**, and then click **Format**. In the **Format Cells** dialog box, click the **Fill tab**. In the fifth column of colors, click the second color, and then click **OK**.

c. In the lower left corner of the dialog box, click to select the check box **Set as default table style for this document**, and then click **OK**.

d. Select the range **A2:P171**, and then in the **Styles group**, click **Format as Table**. At the top of the gallery, under **Custom**, locate and then click your custom **Science Schedule** table style. In the **Format As Table** dialog box, click **OK**. Press (Ctrl) + (Home) to deselect and move to cell **A1**. Click **Save**.

(Project 5C Science Schedule continues on the next page)

4 On the **Page Layout tab**, in the **Page Setup group**, set the **Orientation** to **Landscape**. Then, in the **Scale to Fit group**, click the **Width arrow**, and then click **1 page.**

a. Insert a footer that includes the file name in the **left section**.

b. On the **View tab**, in the **Workbook Views group**, click **Page Break Preview**. Scroll down to view pages 4 and 5, and then position the break between **Page 4** and **Page 5** between **row 152** and **row 153**.

c. On the **View tab**, in the **Workbook Views group**, click **Normal**, and then press Ctrl + Home.

d. Click the **Page Layout tab**, in the **Page Setup group**, click **Print Titles** to display the **Sheet tab** of the **Page Setup** dialog box.

e. Under **Print titles**, click in the **Rows to repeat at top** box, and then in the worksheet, select **row 2**. Click **OK**.

5 Click cell **M2**. On the **Insert tab**, in the **Links group**, click **Hyperlink**. Under **Link to**, click **Existing File or Web Page**. Click the **Look in arrow**, navigate to your student data files, and then select the **e05C_Science_Faculty** workbook. Click **OK**.

a. Point to cell **M2** to display the 🖑 pointer, and then click to confirm that the link opens the workbook containing the contact information. **Close** the workbook with the faculty contacts.

b. Point to cell **M2**, right-click, and then click **Edit Hyperlink**. In the upper right corner of the **Edit Hyperlink** dialog box, click **ScreenTip**. In the **ScreenTip text** box, type **Click here for contact information** and then click **OK** two times. Point to cell **M2** and confirm that your **ScreenTip** displays.

c. Click the **File tab** and then click **Show All Properties**. As the **Tags**, type **science schedule** and as the **Subject**, type your course name and section number. Under **Related People**, be sure that your name displays as **Author**. **Save** the workbook and keep the workbook open.

6 Display the **Save As** dialog box, be sure you are saving in your **Excel Chapter 5** folder, set the **Save as type** to **CSV (Comma delimited)**, and as the **File name**, type **Lastname_Firstname_5C_Science_CSV** Click **Save**, and then click **Yes**.

a. **Close** the **Lastname_Firstname_5C_Science_CSV** file, click **Save** two times and then click **Yes** two times.

b. If directed by your instructor to do so, submit your paper printout, your electronic image of your document that looks like a printed document, or your original Excel file. If required by your instructor, print or create an electronic version of your worksheet with formulas displayed.

> **End | You have completed Project 5C**

Apply **5B skills from these Objectives:**

5 Use Advanced Sort Techniques

6 Use Custom and Advanced Filters

7 Subtotal, Outline, and Group a List of Data

Skills Review | Project 5D Spring Sections

In the following Skills Review, you will use advanced table features to provide Dr. Marshall Eaton, the Dean of the Arts Division, information about the Spring course sections and assigned faculty in the Division. Your completed worksheets will look similar to Figure 5.58.

For Project 5D, you will need the following file:

e05D_Spring_Sections

You will save your workbook as:

Lastname_Firstname_5D_Spring_Sections

PROJECT RESULTS

FIGURE 5.58

(Project 5D Spring Sections continues on the next page)

1 Start Excel. From your student files, open the file **e05D_Spring_Sections**, and then **Save** the file in your **Excel Chapter 5** folder as **Lastname_Firstname_5D_Spring_Sections**

a. Make sure the **Online-Campus-Studio** worksheet displays. On the **Data tab**, in the **Sort & Filter group**, click **Sort**. In the **Sort** dialog box, under **Column**, click the **Sort by arrow**, and then click **Delivery**. Under **Sort On**, click the **arrow**, and then click **Values**. Under **Order**, click the **Order arrow** for this sort level, and then click **Custom List**. In the dialog box, under **Custom lists**, be sure **NEW LIST** is selected. Then, under **List entries**, click in the empty box and type **Studio** Press [Enter], type **Classroom** Press [Enter], and then type **Online**

b. In the **Custom Lists** dialog box, click **Add**, and then click **OK**. Click **Add Level**, and then as the second level sort, click **Dept**. Click **Add Level** again, and as the third level sort, click **Course Name**. Click **OK**.

2 Click the **Music & Dance sheet tab** to display the second worksheet. In cell **C1**, click the **Dept. filter arrow**. Click the **(Select All)** check box to clear all the check boxes, and then select the **Drama** and the **Music** check boxes. Click **OK**.

a. In cell **E1**, click the **Credits filter arrow**, and then filter the list further by selecting **3**. In cell **F1**, click the **Delivery filter arrow**, and filter the list further by selecting **Online**. The status bar information reveals that *4* of the *39* course sections meet the filter criteria.

b. On the **Data tab**, in the **Sort & Filter group**, **Clear** all filters. In cell **K1**, click the **Enrolled filter arrow**, point to **Number Filters**, and then click **Less Than Or Equal To**. In the first box, be sure that *is less than or equal to* displays, and then in the second box type **15** Click **OK** to display *16* records. **Save** the workbook.

3 Display the **Schedule Comparison** worksheet. **Copy** the range **A6:G7**, **Paste** it in cell **A1**, and then change the title in cell **A1** to **Criteria**

a. Select the range **A2:G3**, and then in the **Name Box**, name this range **Criteria**

b. **Copy** the range **A1:G2**, scroll down to view **row 34**, point to cell **A34**, right-click, and then click **Paste**. Click cell **A34**, and then change the title to **Morning-Evening Schedule** and then press [Enter]. Select the range **A35:G35** and then in the **Name Box**, name this range **Extract**

c. Select the range **A7:G32** and then in the **Name Box**, name this range **Database**

d. At the top of your worksheet, in cell **E3**, type **Morning** and in cell **F3**, type **Evening**

e. On the **Data tab**, in the **Sort & Filter group**, click **Advanced**. Under **Action**, click **Copy to another location**. Verify that in the **Copy to** box— *$A$35:$G$35*—displays. Click **OK**, and then scroll to view the lower portion of your worksheet. Two records meet the criteria. **Save** the workbook.

4 Display the **Salaries by Department** worksheet. Select the range **A2:G30**. On the **Data tab**, in the **Sort & Filter group**, click **Sort**. In the **Sort** dialog box, sort by the **Dept.** column, and then by the **Annual Salary** column. Click **OK**.

a. With the range still selected, on the **Data tab**, in the **Outline group**, click **Subtotal**. In the **Subtotal** dialog box, in the **At each change in** box, display the list, and then click **Dept**. In the **Use function** box, display the list and click **Sum**. In the **Add subtotal to** list, select the **Annual Salary** check box, and then deselect any other check boxes. Click **OK**.

b. At the top of the outline area, click the **Level 2** button to hide all Level 3 details and display only the Level 2 summary information, and the Level 1 Grand Total.

c. Group the four worksheets. Insert a footer in the **left section** that includes the file name, and in the **right section**, insert the **Sheet Name**. On the **Page Layout tab**, set the **Width** to **1 page** and set the **Height** to **1 page**—this will scale each worksheet to fit on a single page. **Ungroup** the worksheets.

d. Click the **Online-Campus-Studio** sheet, hold down [Shift], and then click the **Music & Dance** sheet to select both sheets. Change the **Orientation** to **Landscape**, and then **Ungroup** the sheets.

(Project 5D Spring Sections continues on the next page)

Skills Review **Project 5D Spring Sections** (continued)

e. Click the **File tab** and then click **Show All Properties**. As the **Tags**, type **sections, schedule, salaries** and as the Subject, type your course name and section number. Under Related People, be sure that your name displays as Author. **Save** the workbook.

f. If directed by your instructor to do so, submit your paper printout, your electronic image of your document that looks like a printed document, or your original Excel file. If required by your instructor, print or create an electronic version of your worksheet with formulas displayed. In the upper right corner of the Excel window, click **Close**.

END | You have completed Project 5D

Mastering Excel   Project 5E Sports Schedule

Apply 5A skills from these Objectives:

1 Navigate and Manage Large Worksheets

2 Enhance Worksheets with Themes and Styles

3 Format a Worksheet to Share with Others

4 Save Excel Data in Other File Formats

In the following Mastering Excel project, you will assist Damian Howard, Athletic Director at Laurel College, in formatting and navigating a large worksheet that lists the sports events schedule for spring sports. Your completed worksheets will look similar to Figure 5.59.

PROJECT FILES

For Project 5E, you will need the following files:

e05E_Sports_Coaches
e05E_Referee_Requests
e05E_Sports_Schedule

You will save your workbook as:

Lastname_Firstname_5E_Sports_Schedule

PROJECT RESULTS

FIGURE 5.59

Excel 2016, Windows 10, Microsoft Corporation

(Project 5E Sports Schedule continues on the next page)

Mastering Excel | Project 5E Sports Schedule (continued)

1 Start Excel. Open the file **e05E_Sports_Schedule** and **Save** it in your **Excel Chapter 5** folder as **Lastname_Firstname_5E_Sports_Schedule**

2 **Go To** cell **M82**, and then insert a **COUNTIF** function to count the number of Staff referees. In cell **K82**, type **Events with Unassigned Referees**

3 Move to cell **A1**, and then from your student data files, **Open** the file **e05E_Referee_Requests**. Switch windows, and then make your **Lastname_Firstname_5E_Sports_Schedule** the active window. Arrange the two files horizontally.

4 In your **Lastname_Firstname_5E_Sports_Schedule** workbook, go to cell **A82**, **Split** the window horizontally, and then click in any cell above the split in **column C**. Use **Find** to locate the first **Event #** request from the **e05E_Referee_Requests** worksheet, and then type **Danny Litowitz** in the appropriate cell in your **Lastname_Firstname_5E_Sports_Schedule** workbook to assign him as the *Referee*.

5 Use the **Find** command to locate the remaining three **Event #s** listed in the **e05E_Referee_Requests** worksheet, and then enter the appropriate referee for each sports event in **column M** of your **Lastname_Firstname_5E_Sports_Schedule** worksheet. **Close** the **Find and Replace** dialog box, and then **Close** the **e05E_Referee_Requests** workbook. **Maximize** your **Lastname_Firstname_5E_Sports_Schedule** worksheet, and then remove the **Split**.

6 Insert a new blank **row 1**. In cell **A1**, type **Schedule of Sports Events with Unassigned Referees** and then **Merge & Center** the title across the range **A1:M1**. Apply the **Title** cell style.

7 Create a **New Table Style** named **Sports Schedule** and format the **First Row Stripe** with a **Fill**—in the fifth column, the third color. For the **Header Row**, in the first column of colors click the second color. Set the style you created as the default table style for this workbook.

8 Select the range **A2:M81** and apply the **Custom** table style—**Sports Schedule**.

9 **AutoFit** columns **A:M**. Set the **Orientation** to **Landscape**, set the **Width** to **1 page**, and center the worksheet **Horizontally**. Insert a footer in the **left section** that includes the file name, and in the **right section**, insert a page number.

10 In **Page Break Preview**, break **Page 1** after **row 49** to end Page 1 with *TENNIS* and begin **Page 2** with *TRACK*. Return to **Normal** view. Set **Print Titles** to repeat **row 2** at the top of each page.

11 In cell **J2**, **Insert** a **Hyperlink** to your student data file **e05E_Sports_Coaches**. Create the **ScreenTip Click here for contact information** and then test your hyperlink. **Close** the **e05E_Sports_Coaches** file.

12 Show all the properties, and then as the **Tags**, type **sports schedule** As the **Subject**, type your course name and section number. Be sure your name displays as the **Author**.

13 **Save** your workbook. If directed by your instructor to do so, submit your paper printout, your electronic image of your document that looks like a printed document, or your original Excel file. If required by your instructor, print or create an electronic version of your worksheet with formulas displayed. In the upper right corner of the Excel window, click **Close**.

END | You have completed Project 5E

MyITLab
grader

Mastering Excel | **Project 5F Career Programs**

In the following Mastering Excel project, you will edit a worksheet for Michael Schaeffler, Vice President of Instruction, with data that has been sorted, filtered, and grouped that analyzes Career Tech programs at Laurel College. The worksheets of your workbook will look similar to Figure 5.60.

Apply 5B skills from these Objectives:

5 Use Advanced Sort Techniques

6 Use Custom and Advanced Filters

7 Subtotal, Outline, and Group a List of Data

PROJECT FILES

For Project 5F, you will need the following file:

e05F_Career_Programs

You will save your workbook as:

Lastname_Firstname_5F_Career_Programs

PROJECT RESULTS

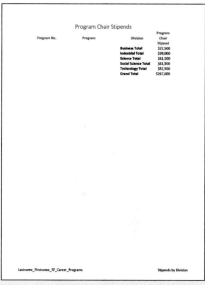

FIGURE 5.60

Excel 2016, Windows 10, Microsoft Corporation

(Project 5F Career Programs continues on the next page)

Mastering Excel | Project 5F Career Programs (continued)

1 Start Excel. **Open** the file **e05F_Career_Programs**. **Save** the file in your **Excel Chapter 5** folder as **Lastname_Firstname_5F_Career_Programs**

2 On the **Main-East-West** worksheet, insert a table using the range **A1:J40**. Apply **Table Style Light 21**.

3 **Sort** the values in the **Campus** column using a **Custom List** in the following order: **MAIN**, **EAST**, and then **WEST**. Add a second level sort by **Division** and a third level sort by **Program Name** both in ascending order.

4 Display the second worksheet, **Delivery Mode Comparison**. **Copy** the range **A6:G7**, and then **Paste** the range to cell **A1**. Change the title in cell **A1** to **Criteria** and then name the range **A2:G3 Criteria**

5 **Copy** the range **A1:G2**, and **Paste** it into cell **A36**. Change the title in cell **A36** to **Online-Hybrid Delivery Mode** and then name the range **A37:G37 Extract** Select the range **A7:G34**, and then name this range **Database**

6 Create an advanced filter that will place in the extract area the records from the Database range in which **Online** is the primary delivery mode and **Hybrid** is the secondary delivery mode.

7 Display the **Stipends by Division** worksheet. Sort the data in ascending order first by **Division** and then by **Program Chair Stipend**.

8 Apply subtotals to the **Program Chair Stipend** column at each change in **Division**. **AutoFit columns C:D** and then collapse the outline so that the **Level 2** summary information is displayed.

9 Group all three worksheets. Insert a footer in the **left section** that includes the file name, and in the **right section**, insert the **Sheet Name**. Center the worksheets **Horizontally**, and then set the **Width** and **Height** to **1 page**.

10 Show all the properties, and then as the **Tags**, type **career programs** As the **Subject**, type your course name and section number. Be sure your name displays as the **Author**.

11 **Save** your workbook. If directed by your instructor to do so, submit your paper printout, your electronic image of your document that looks like a printed document, or your original Excel file. If required by your instructor, print or create an electronic version of your worksheet with formulas displayed. In the upper right corner of the Excel window, click **Close**.

END | You have completed Project 5F

MyITLab
grader

Mastering Excel | Project 5G Sports Programs

Apply **5A** and **5B** skills from these Objectives:

1 Navigate and Manage Large Worksheets

2 Enhance Worksheets with Themes and Styles

3 Format a Worksheet to Share with Others

4 Save Excel Data in Other File Formats

5 Use Advanced Sort Techniques

6 Use Custom and Advanced Filters

7 Subtotal, Outline, and Group a List of Data

In the following Mastering Excel project, you will create a worksheet for Sandy Chase, Assistant Director of Athletics, with data that has been sorted, filtered, and grouped and that analyzes sports programs at Laurel College. The worksheets of your workbook will look similar to Figure 5.61.

PROJECT FILES

For Project 5G, you will need the following files:

e05G_Coach_Information
e05G_Sports_Programs

You will save your workbook as:

Lastname_Firstname_5G_Sports_Programs

PROJECT RESULTS

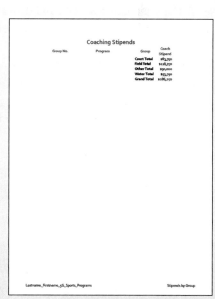

FIGURE 5.61

Excel 2016, Windows 10, Microsoft Corporation

(Project 5G Sports Programs continues on the next page)

1 Start Excel. From your student files, locate and open **e05G_Sports_Programs**. **Save** the file in your **Excel Chapter 5** folder as **Lastname_Firstname_5G_Sports_Programs**

2 Display the **Valley-Park-West** worksheet. Select the range **A1:J40**, insert a table, and then apply **Table Style Light 17**.

3 **Sort** the table on the **Campus** column using a **Custom List** in the following order: **Valley**, **Park**, and then **West**. Add a second level sort by **Sport Group** and a third level sort by **Program Name** both in ascending order.

4 Display the **Sports Season Comparison** worksheet. **Copy** the range **A6:G7**, **Paste** it in cell **A1**, and then change the title in cell **A1** to **Criteria** Select the range **A2:G3**, and then name this range **Criteria**

5 **Copy** the range **A1:G2**, and then **Paste** the copied range in cell **A36**. Change the title in cell **A36** to **Fall-Summer Sports Season** Name the range **A37:G37 Extract** and then name the range **A7:G34 Database**

6 Create an advanced filter that will place in the extract area the records from the Database range in which **Fall** is the primary season and **Summer** is the secondary season.

7 Display the **Stipends by Group** worksheet. **Sort** the data in ascending order by **Group**, then by the **Coach Stipend**.

8 Apply subtotals to the **Coach Stipend** column at each change in **Group**. **AutoFit columns C:D** and then collapse the outline so that the Level 2 summary information is displayed.

9 On the **Valley-Park-West** worksheet, in cell **J1**, insert a **Hyperlink** to your student data file **e05G_Coach_Information**. Display the **ScreenTip Click here for contact information** and then test your hyperlink. **Close** the **e05G_Coach_Information** file.

10 Select all three worksheets. Insert a footer in the **left section** that includes the file name, and in the **right section**, insert the **Sheet Name**. Set the **Width** and **Height** to **1 page**, and **Center** the worksheets horizontally. Change the **Theme** to **Slice**, and then change the **Fonts** theme to **Corbel**.

11 Show all the properties, and then as the **Tags**, type **sports programs** As the **Subject**, type your course name and section number. Be sure your name displays as the **Author**. **Save** your workbook. If directed by your instructor to do so, submit your paper printout, your electronic image of your document that looks like a printed document, or your original Excel file. If required by your instructor, print or create an electronic version of your worksheet with formulas displayed. In the upper right corner of the Excel window, click **Close**.

END | You have completed Project 5G

5

Apply a combination of the 5A and 5B skills.	GO! Fix It	Project 5H Programs	MyITLab
	GO! Make It	Project 5I Arts Faculty	MyITLab
	GO! Solve It	Project 5J Organizations	MyITLab
	GO! Solve It	Project 5K Dept Tutors	

PROJECT FILES

For Project 5K, you will need the following file:

e05K_Dept_Tutors

You will save your workbook as:

Lastname_Firstname_5K_Dept_Tutors

Open the file e05K_Dept_Tutors and save it in your chapter folder as
Lastname_Firstname_5K_Dept_Tutors

The Director of the Tutoring Center wants to know which tutors are available to tutor online from the CPS department. Create and name Criteria, Extract, and Database ranges and then use the Advanced filtering feature to copy the requested information to the extract range. Include the file name in the footer, add appropriate properties, and then save your workbook. Submit as directed.

Performance Level

Performance Criteria		Exemplary: You consistently applied the relevant skills	Proficient: You sometimes, but not always, applied the relevant skills	Developing: You rarely or never applied the relevant skills
	Range names created	All range names are created.	Some, but not all range names are created.	Range names are not created.
	Data filtered correctly	Data is filtered according to both criteria and copied to extract range.	Not all criteria is applied or the data is filtered in place and is not copied to the extract range.	The data is not filtered.

END | You have completed Project 5K

OUTCOMES-BASED ASSESSMENTS

RUBRIC

The following outcomes-based assessments are *open-ended assessments*. That is, there is no specific correct result; your result will depend on your approach to the information provided. Make *Professional Quality* your goal. Use the following scoring rubric to guide you in *how* to approach the problem and then to evaluate *how well* your approach solves the problem.

The *criteria*—Software Mastery, Content, Format and Layout, and Process—represent the knowledge and skills you have gained that you can apply to solving the problem. The *levels of performance*—Professional Quality, Approaching Professional Quality, or Needs Quality Improvements—help you and your instructor evaluate your result.

	Your completed project is of Professional Quality if you:	Your completed project is Approaching Professional Quality if you:	Your completed project Needs Quality Improvements if you:
1-Software Mastery	Choose and apply the most appropriate skills, tools, and features and identify efficient methods to solve the problem.	Choose and apply some appropriate skills, tools, and features, but not in the most efficient manner.	Choose inappropriate skills, tools, or features, or are inefficient in solving the problem.
2-Content	Construct a solution that is clear and well organized, contains content that is accurate, appropriate to the audience and purpose, and is complete. Provide a solution that contains no errors of spelling, grammar, or style.	Construct a solution in which some components are unclear, poorly organized, inconsistent, or incomplete. Misjudge the needs of the audience. Have some errors in spelling, grammar, or style, but the errors do not detract from comprehension.	Construct a solution that is unclear, incomplete, or poorly organized, contains some inaccurate or inappropriate content, and contains many errors of spelling, grammar, or style. Do not solve the problem.
3-Format and Layout	Format and arrange all elements to communicate information and ideas, clarify function, illustrate relationships, and indicate relative importance.	Apply appropriate format and layout features to some elements, but not others. Overuse features, causing minor distraction.	Apply format and layout that does not communicate information or ideas clearly. Do not use format and layout features to clarify function, illustrate relationships, or indicate relative importance. Use available features excessively, causing distraction.
4-Process	Use an organized approach that integrates planning, development, self-assessment, revision, and reflection.	Demonstrate an organized approach in some areas, but not others; or, use an insufficient process of organization throughout.	Do not use an organized approach to solve the problem.

GO! Think Project 5L Summer Sections

PROJECT FILES

For Project 5L, you will need the following file:

e05L_Summer_Sections

You will save your workbook as:

Lastname_Firstname_5L_Summer_Sections

From your student files, open the file e05L_Summer_Sections, and then save it in your Chapter 5 folder as **Lastname_Firstname_5L_Summer_Sections** Create a custom table style, name it **Summer Sections** and then create a table using the Summer Sections style. Sort the table on the Campus field using the following order: Online, Valley, Park, West. Add a second sort level by Dept. and a third sort level by Course Name. Include the file name in the footer, set orientation to landscape and width to 1 page, and repeat rows as necessary at the top of each page. Add appropriate properties with the tags **summer sections** and then submit as directed.

> **END | You have completed Project 5L**

GO! Think   Project 5M Social Science   MyITLab

You and GO! Project 5N Personal Expenses   MyITLab

Creating Charts, Diagrams, and Templates

EXCEL 2016

6

Syda Productions/Shutterstock

In This Chapter 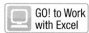 GO! to Work with Excel

In this chapter, you will create charts and diagrams to communicate data visually. Charts make a set of numbers easier to understand by displaying data in a graphical format. Excel's SmartArt illustrations make diagrams, like an organizational chart or process cycle, easy to comprehend.

In this chapter, you will also work with templates. Templates have built-in formulas for performing calculations and are used for standardization and protection of data. You will create a template for an order form.

The Dallas – Ft. Worth Job Fair is a nonprofit organization that brings together employers and job seekers in the Dallas – Ft. Worth metropolitan area. Each year the organization holds a number of targeted job fairs and the annual Dallas – Ft. Worth fair draws over 900 employers in more than 75 industries and registers more than 30,000 candidates. Candidate registration is free; employers pay a nominal fee to display and present at the fairs. Candidate resumes and employer postings are managed by a state-of-the-art database system, allowing participants quick and accurate access to job data and candidate qualifications.

Attendance Charts and Diagrams

PROJECT ACTIVITIES

In Activities 6.01 through 6.17, you will create and format column and line charts for the Dallas – Ft. Worth Job Fair that display attendance patterns at the fairs over a five-year period. You will also create a process diagram and an organization chart. Your completed worksheets will look similar to Figure 6.1.

PROJECT FILES

MyITLab grader

If your instructor wants you to submit Project 6A in the MyITLab Grader system, log into MyITLab, locate Grader Project 6A, and then download the files for this project.

Please always review the downloaded Grader instructions before beginning.

For Project 6A, you will need the following file:

e06A_Attendance

You will save your workbook as:

Lastname_Firstname_6A_Attendance

PROJECT RESULTS

GO!
Walk Thru
Project 6A

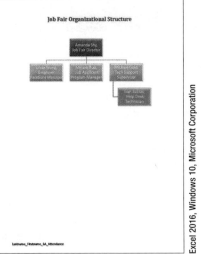

Excel 2016, Windows 10, Microsoft Corporation

FIGURE 6.1 Project 6A Attendance Charts and Diagrams

Objective 1 — Create and Format Sparklines and a Column Chart

GO! Learn How
Video E6-1

Recall that *sparklines* are tiny charts that fit within a cell and give a visual trend summary alongside your data. Also recall that a *column chart*, which presents data graphically in vertical columns, is useful to make comparisons among related data.

Activity 6.01 | Creating and Formatting Sparklines

MOS
2.3.1, 5.1.4

To create sparklines, first select the data you want to plot—represent graphically—and then select the range of cells alongside each row of data where you want to display the sparklines.

1 Start Excel. From the student data files that accompany this chapter, open the file **e06A_Attendance**. Display the **Save As** dialog box, navigate to the location where you will store your workbooks for this chapter, and then create a new folder named **Excel Chapter 6** Open your folder, and then **Save** the workbook as **Lastname_Firstname_6A_Attendance**

This data shows the number of applicants who have attended job fairs held over a five-year period at various locations in the greater Dallas-Ft. Worth area.

2 Select the range **B4:F10**. In the lower right corner of the selected range, click **Quick Analysis**, and then click **Sparklines**. Compare your screen with Figure 6.2.

ANOTHER WAY On the Insert tab, in the Sparklines group, click Line.

FIGURE 6.2

3 With **Sparklines** selected in the Quick Analysis tool, click **Line**. Compare your screen with Figure 6.3.

Sparklines display alongside each row of data and provide a quick visual trend summary for each city's job fair attendance. The sparklines provide a quick indication that for most locations, attendance has had an overall upward trend over the five-year period.

FIGURE 6.3

> **4** On the **Design tab**, in the **Show group**, select the **High Point** check box and the **Last Point** check box.
>
> By showing the High Point and the Last Point, you further emphasize the visual story that sparklines depict.
>
> **5** On the **Design tab**, in the **Style group**, click **More** ⊟ , and then in the third row, click the first style—**Sparkline Style Accent 1, (no dark or light)**.
>
> **6** In cell **G3**, type **Trend** and press Enter . Press Ctrl + Home , **Save** 🖫 your workbook, and then compare your screen with Figure 6.4.
>
> Use styles in this manner to further enhance your sparklines.

FIGURE 6.4

Activity 6.02 | Creating a Column Chart

5.1.1, 5.2.4

A chart is a graphic representation of data. When you create a chart, first decide whether you are going to plot the values representing totals or the values representing details—you cannot plot both in the same chart. Excel's **Recommended Charts** feature can help you make this decision by previewing suggested charts based upon patterns in your data. In this Activity, you will select the details—the number of attendees at each location each year. To help the reader understand the chart, you will also select the *labels* for the data—the column and row headings that describe the values. Here, the labels are the location names and the years.

1 Take a moment to study the data elements shown in Figure 6.5.

FIGURE 6.5

Excel 2016, Windows 10, Microsoft Corporation.

2 Select the range **A3:F10**. On the **Insert tab**, in the **Charts group**, click **Recommended Charts**. Compare your screen with Figure 6.6.

Excel recommends several charts based on the data you selected. The Clustered Column chart displays in the preview window.

FIGURE 6.6

Excel 2016, Windows 10, Microsoft Corporation.

ANOTHER WAY Click Quick Analysis 📊, click Charts, and then click More Charts to open the Insert Chart dialog box.

3 In the **Insert Chart** dialog box, with the **Clustered Column** chart selected, click **OK**.

4 On the **Design tab**, in the **Location group**, click **Move Chart**.

The Move Chart dialog box displays. You can accept the default to display the chart as an object within the worksheet, which is an *embedded chart*. Or, you can place the chart on a separate sheet, referred to as a *chart sheet*, in which the chart fills the entire page. A chart sheet is useful when you want to view a chart separately from the worksheet data.

5 In the **Move Chart** dialog box, click **New sheet**. In the **New sheet** box, type **Attendance Chart** and then click **OK**.

6 On the **Design tab**, in the **Type group**, click **Change Chart Type**. In the **Change Chart Type** dialog box, on the **All Charts tab**, if necessary, on the left click **Column**, and then on the right, at the top of the dialog box, click the fourth chart icon—**3-D Clustered Column**. Click **OK**.

You can use this technique to change the chart type.

7 In the upper right corner of the chart, click **Chart Styles** ✎. In the displayed list of Styles, click **Style 3**. Compare your screen with Figure 6.7.

🔄 **ANOTHER WAY** On the Design tab, in the Chart Styles group, click More ▾, and then click Style 3.

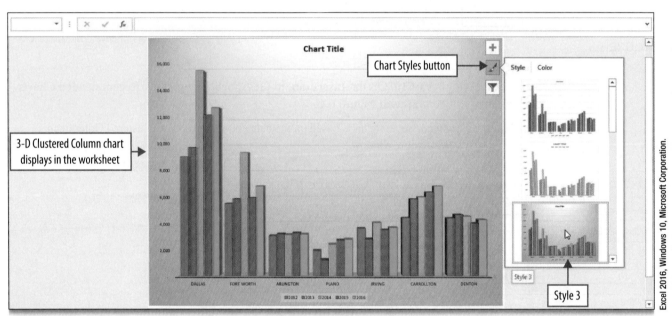

Chart Styles button

3-D Clustered Column chart displays in the worksheet

Style 3

Excel 2016, Windows 10, Microsoft Corporation.

FIGURE 6.7

8 Click **Chart Styles** ✎ to close the **Chart Styles** gallery. In the **Chart Layouts group**, click **Add Chart Element** to display the **Chart Elements** list. Compare your screen with Figure 6.8, and then take a moment to study the table in Figure 6.9, which lists the elements that are typically found in a chart.

The Chart Elements list displays. ***Chart elements*** are the objects that make up a chart. From the Chart Elements list, you can select a chart element to format it.

FIGURE 6.8

MICROSOFT EXCEL CHART ELEMENTS

OBJECT	DESCRIPTION
Axis	A line that serves as a frame of reference for measurement and that borders the chart plot area.
Category labels	The labels that display along the bottom of the chart to identify the category of data.
Chart Area	The entire chart and all its elements.
Data labels	Labels that display the value, percentage, and/or category of each particular data point and can contain one or more of the choices listed—Series name, Category name, Value, or Percentage.
Data marker	A column, bar, area, dot, pie slice, or other symbol in a chart that represents a single data point.
Data points	The numeric values of the selected worksheet.
Data series	A group of related data points that are plotted in a chart.
Gridlines	Lines in the plot area that aid the eye in determining the plotted values.
Horizontal Category axis (x-axis)	The axis that displays along the bottom of the chart to identify the category of data. Excel uses the row titles as the category names.
Legend	A key that identifies patterns or colors that are assigned to the categories in the chart.
Major unit value	The value that determines the spacing between tick marks and between the gridlines in the plot area.
Plot area	The area bounded by the axes, including all the data series.
Tick mark labels	Identifying information for a tick mark generated from the cells on the worksheet used to create the chart.
Tick marks	The short lines that display on an axis at regular intervals.
Vertical Value axis (y-axis)	The axis that displays along the left side of the chart to identify the numerical scale on which the charted data is based.
Walls and floor	The areas surrounding a 3-D chart that give dimension and boundaries to the chart. Two walls and one floor display within the plot area.

FIGURE 6.9

9 ▸ Click in a blank area of the screen to close the **Chart Elements** list.

10 ▸ In the **Chart Area**, click the text *Chart Title* to select it. Watch the **Formula Bar** as you type **Attendance** as the chart title—your typing displays in the **Formula Bar** and not on the chart—and then press Enter to display the text in the chart.

11 ▸ Click the tallest column displayed, which is in the Dallas category. Compare your screen with Figure 6.10.

All the green columns representing the Series *2014* are selected—selection handles display at the corners of each column in the series—and a ScreenTip displays the value for the column you are pointing to. Recall that a data series is a group of related data—in this instance, the attendees to all the job fairs that were held in 2014. Also notice that the Formula Bar displays the address for the selected data series.

FIGURE 6.10

12 ▸ Locate the **Plano** category, and then click the shortest column in that group.

The selected series changes to those columns that represent the attendees at the job fairs in 2013. The Formula Bar changes to indicate the selected series and a new ScreenTip displays when you point to the column.

13 ▸ Click outside the chart area to deselect the series.

More Knowledge **Sizing Handles and Selection Handles**

Sizing handles and selection handles look the same, and the terms are often used interchangeably. If a two-headed resize arrow—⬍, ⬌, ⬈, ⬋—displays when you point to boxes surrounding an object, it is a sizing handle; otherwise, it is a selection handle. Some objects in a chart cannot be resized, such as the category axis or the value axis, but they can be selected and then reformatted.

Activity 6.03 │ Changing the Display of Chart Data

As you create a chart, you make choices about what data to include, the chart type, chart titles, and location. You can change the chart type, change the way the data displays, add or change titles, select different colors, and modify the background, scale, and chart location.

In the column chart you created, the attendance numbers are displayed along the value axis—the vertical axis—and the locations for each job fair are displayed along the category axis—the horizontal axis. The cells you select for a chart include the row and column labels from your worksheet. In a column or line chart, Excel selects whichever has more items—either the rows or the columns—and uses those labels to plot the data series, in this instance, the locations.

After plotting the data series, Excel uses the remaining labels—in this example, the years identified in the row headings—to create the data series labels on the legend. The legend is the key that defines the colors used in the chart; here it identifies the data series for the years. A different color is used for each year in the data series. The chart, as currently displayed, compares the change in attendance year to year grouped by location category. You can change the chart to display the years on the category axis and the locations as the data series identified in the legend.

1 In the **Dallas** category, click the fourth column.

All columns with the same color are selected. The ScreenTip displays *Series "2015" Point "Dallas" Value: 12,245.*

2 Point to each of the other purple columns that are selected and notice that the ScreenTip that displays identifies each purple column as being in the *Series "2015."*

3 On the **Chart Tools Design tab**, in the **Data group**, click **Switch Row/Column**. Compare your screen with Figure 6.11.

The chart changes to display the locations as the data series. The locations are the row headings in the worksheet and are now identified in the legend. The years display as the category labels on the horizontal axis.

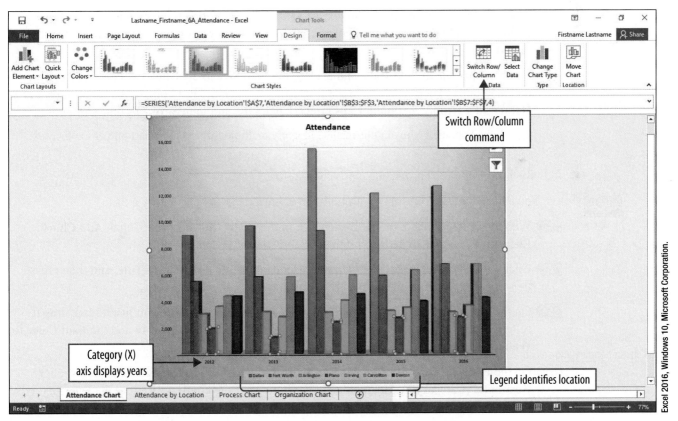

FIGURE 6.11

4 Click one of the purple columns. Point to each purple column and read the ScreenTip.

The ScreenTips for the purple columns now identify this as the *Plano* series.

5 On the **Design tab**, in the **Data group**, click **Switch Row/Column** again, and then **Save** 🖫 your workbook.

The chart changes back to the more useful arrangement with the years identified in the legend and the locations displayed as the category labels.

> **More Knowledge** | **Changing the Range of Data in a Chart**
>
> After you have created a chart, you can adjust the range of data that displays in the chart. To do so, on the Design tab, in the Data group, click Select Data. Edit the source address displayed in the Chart data range box, or drag the data in the worksheet to adjust the range as needed.

Activity 6.04 | Editing and Formatting the Chart Title

The data displayed in the chart focuses on the attendance by location. It is good practice to create a chart title to reflect your charted data.

1 Click the text of the **Chart Title**—*Attendance*—to select it, and then click to position the mouse pointer to the right of *Attendance*.

To edit a title, click once to select the chart object, and then click a second time to position the insertion point in the title and change to editing mode.

2 Press Spacebar one time, and then type **by Location**

3 Click the border surrounding the text *Attendance by Location* to change it to a solid line, point to the title text and right-click, and then on the shortcut menu, click **Font** to display the **Font** dialog box.

4 Set the **Font style** to **Bold Italic** and change the **Font Size** to **20**. Click the **Font color arrow**, and then under **Theme Colors**, in the first column, click the last color—**White, Background 1, Darker 50%**. Apply the **Small Caps** effect. Click **OK**, and then **Save** 🖫 your workbook.

Use the Font dialog box in this manner to apply multiple formats to a chart title or to other text.

Activity 6.05 | Adding, Formatting, and Aligning Axis Titles

MOS
5.2.2

You can add a title to display with both the value axis and the category axis.

1 With the chart selected, on the **Design tab**, in the **Chart Layouts group**, click **Add Chart Element**. Point to **Axis Titles**, and then click **Primary Vertical**.

2 Click in the **Formula Bar**, type **Number Attending** as the **Vertical Axis Title**, and then press Enter to display the axis title text in the chart.

3 On the left side of the chart, point to the **Vertical (Value) Axis Title** you just added, drag to select the text, and then on the mini toolbar, change the **Font Size** to **14** and the **Font Color** to **White, Background 1, Darker 50%**—in the first column, the last color.

4 On the **Format tab**, in the **Current Selection group**, click the **Chart Elements arrow**, click **Horizontal (Category) Axis**, and then at the bottom of the chart, notice that the **Category axis** is selected.

5 Point to the border of the selected axis to display the ⌖ pointer, right-click, and then on the shortcut menu, click **Font**. In the **Font dialog box**, click the **Font style arrow**, click **Bold**, and then change the **Font Color** to **White, Background 1, Darker 50%**. Click **OK**.

6 On the left side of the chart, point to any value in the **Vertical (Value) Axis**, and then click one time to select the axis. Click the **Home tab**, and then in the **Font group**, change the **Font Size** to **12**.

You can use multiple techniques to change font characteristics.

7 Save 🖫 your workbook, and then compare your screen with Figure 6.12.

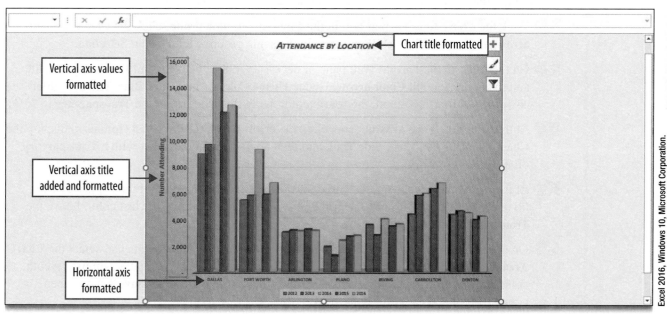

Vertical axis values formatted

Vertical axis title added and formatted

Chart title formatted

Horizontal axis formatted

FIGURE 6.12

Activity 6.06 | Editing Source Data

One of the characteristics of an Excel chart is that it reflects changes made to the underlying data.

1 In the **Fort Worth** column cluster, point to the last column—**2016**. Notice that the *Value* for this column is *6,827*.

2 Display the **Attendance by Location** worksheet, and then in cell **F5**, type **7261** and press Enter.

3 Redisplay the **Attendance Chart** worksheet, **Save** 🖫 your workbook, and then point to the **Fort Worth** column for 2016. Compare your screen with Figure 6.13.

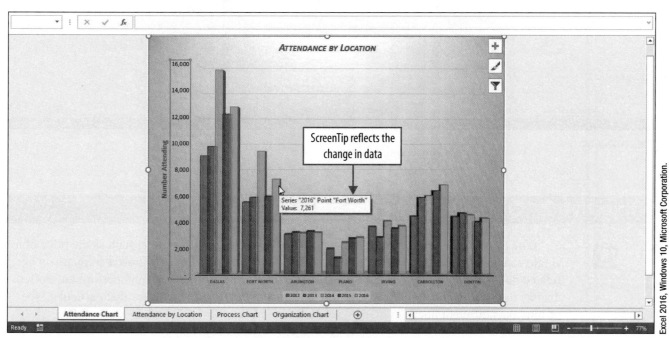

ScreenTip reflects the change in data

Series "2016" Point "Fort Worth"
Value: 7,261

FIGURE 6.13

5.2.2

If your chart style includes shaded walls and a floor, you can format these elements.

1 Click the **Chart Tools Format tab**, in the **Current Selection group**, click the **Chart Elements arrow**, and then click **Back Wall**. Then in the same group, click **Format Selection**.

2 On the right, in the **Format Wall** pane, if necessary, click ▷ to expand **Fill**, click **Solid fill**, and then click the **Fill Color arrow**. Under **Theme Colors**, click **Dark Blue, Text 2, Lighter 40%**—in the fourth column, the fourth color. Drag the slider to set the **Transparency** to **75%**.

3 At the top of the **Format Wall** pane, click the arrow to the right of **Wall Options** to display the **Chart Elements** list. Click **Side Wall**, and then apply the same fill, but with a **Transparency** of **60%**.

4 At the top of the pane, from the **Chart Elements** list, select **Floor**, and then apply a **Solid fill** using **White, Background 1, Darker 50%**—in the first column, the last color. Leave the **Transparency** set to **0%**.

5 On the ribbon, in the **Current Selection group**, from the **Chart Elements** list, select the **Chart Area**, and then apply a **Solid fill** using **Olive Green, Accent 3, Lighter 60%**—in the seventh column, the third color. **Close** ☒ the **Format Chart Area** pane, click **Save** 🖫, and then compare your screen with Figure 6.14.

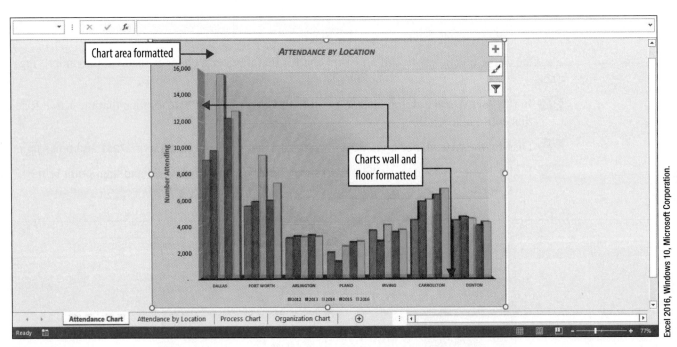

FIGURE 6.14

Objective 2 | Create and Format a Line Chart

GO! Learn How
Video E6-2

Line charts show trends over time. A line chart can consist of one line, such as the price of a single company's stock over time, or it can display more than one line to show a comparison of related numbers over time. For example, charts tracking stock or mutual fund performance often display the price of the mutual fund on one line and an industry standard for that particular type of fund on a different line.

In this Activity, you will create a line chart showing the change in attendance at the Dallas Job Fair over a five-year period.

1 Display the **Attendance by Location** worksheet.

2 Select the range **A3:F4**, and then, on the **Insert tab**, in the **Charts group**, click **Insert Line or Area Chart** 📊▾. In the first row, click the fourth chart type—**Line with Markers**. Compare your screen with Figure 6.15.

> Cell A3 must be included in the selection, despite being empty, because the same number of cells must be in each selected row. Excel identifies the first row as a category because of the empty first cell.

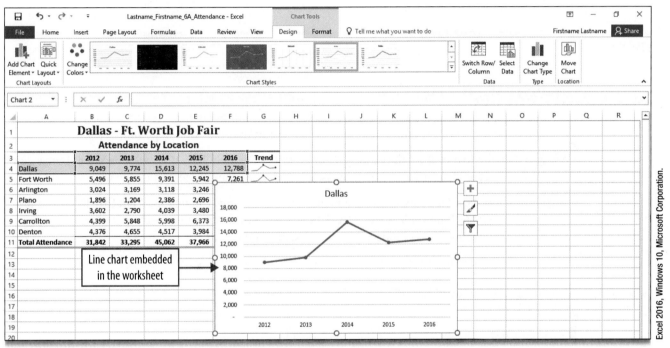

FIGURE 6.15

3 Point to the upper left chart border to display the 📍 pointer, and then drag the upper left corner of the chart slightly inside the upper left corner of cell **A13**.

4 Scroll down as necessary to view **row 30**. Point to the lower right corner of the chart to display the 📍 pointer, and then drag the lower right corner of the chart inside the lower right corner of cell **G29**. Click anywhere outside the chart to deselect. **Save** 💾 your workbook. Compare your screen with Figure 6.16.

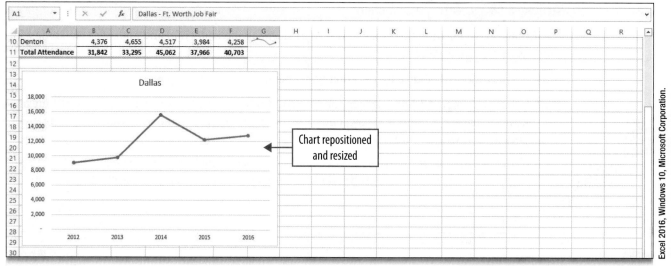

FIGURE 6.16

Activity 6.09 | Changing a Chart Title

When you select the chart type, the resulting chart might contain elements that you want to delete or change. For example, you might want to edit the chart title to be more specific.

1 Click the text of the **Chart Title**—*Dallas*. In the **Formula Bar**, type **Attendance at Dallas Job Fairs** as the chart title, and then press Enter to display the title text in the chart.

2 Point to the **Chart Title**, right-click, and then click **Font**. Change the **Font Size** to **16** and the **Font Style** to **Bold Italic**. Click **OK**. Click outside of the chart to deselect it, **Save** 🖫 your workbook, and then compare your chart with Figure 6.17.

The size of the title increases, and the plot area decreases slightly.

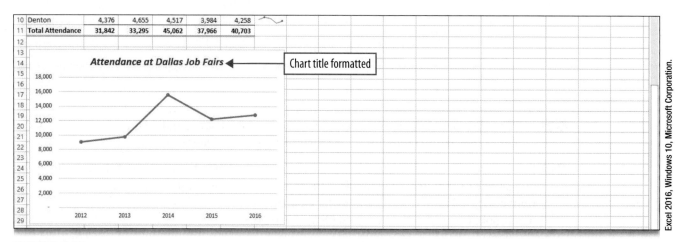

FIGURE 6.17

Activity 6.10 | Changing the Values on the Value Axis

5.2.2

You can change the values on the value axis to increase or decrease the variation among the numbers displayed. The *scale* is the range of numbers in the data series; the scale controls the minimum, maximum, and incremental values on the value axis. In the line chart, the attendance figures for Dallas are all higher than 8,000, but the scale begins at zero, so the line occupies only the upper area of the chart. Adjust the scale as necessary to make your charts meaningful to the reader.

1 On the left side of the line chart, point to any number. When the ScreenTip displays *Vertical (Value) Axis*, right-click, and then click **Format Axis**.

2 On the right, in the **Format Axis** pane, if necessary, click ▷ to expand **Axis Options**. Under **Bounds**, in the **Minimum** box, replace any existing text with **5000** Under **Units**, change the **Major unit** to **1000** and then press Enter. Compare your screen with Figure 6.18.

Here you can change the beginning and ending numbers displayed on the chart and also change the unit by which the major gridlines display.

FIGURE 6.18

3 In the upper right corner of the **Format Axis** pane, click **Close** ✕. Click **Save** 🖫, and then compare your screen with Figure 6.19.

The Value Axis begins at 5,000 with major gridlines at intervals of 1,000. This will emphasize the change in attendance over the five years by starting the chart at a higher number and decreasing the interval for gridlines.

FIGURE 6.19

5.2.2

1. Right-click anywhere *within*, but not directly *on* a line, the lined **Plot Area**, and then click **Format Plot Area**.

   The Format Plot Area pane displays. Here you can change the border of the plot area or the background color.

2. In the **Format Plot Area** pane, if necessary, click ▷ to expand **Fill**. Click **Solid fill**. Click the **Fill Color arrow**, and then under **Theme Colors**, in the first column, click the fourth color—**White, Background 1, Darker 25%**.

3. Point to the blue chart line, right-click, and then click **Format Data Series**.

   In the Format Data Series pane, you can change the data markers—the indicators for a data point value, which on the line chart is represented by a circle shape. You can also change the line connecting the data markers.

4. In the **Format Data Series** pane, click **Fill & Line** 🖌. Under **Line**, click **Solid line**. Use the spin box arrows to set the **Width** to **4 pt**.

5. Under the **Fill & Line** icon, click **Marker**. Click ▷ to expand **Marker Options**. Click **Built-in**, click the **Type arrow**, and then click the **triangle**—the third symbol in the list. Set the **Size** of the **Marker Type** to **12**

6. Under **Fill**, click **Solid fill**, and then click the **Fill Color arrow**. Under **Theme Colors**, in the first column, click the last color—**White, Background 1, Darker 50%**.

7. Under **Border**, click **No line**, and then **Close** ✕ the **Format Data Series** pane.

8. Click the **Chart Tools Format tab**, in the **Current Selection group**, click the **Chart Elements arrow**, and then click **Chart Area**. In the same group, click **Format Selection** to display the **Format Chart Area** pane, and then under **Border**, apply a **Solid line** using **White, Background 1, Darker 15%**—in the first column, the third color. **Close** ✕ the **Format Chart Area** pane.

9. Click in any cell outside of the chart, **Save** 💾 your workbook, and then compare your screen with Figure 6.20.

FIGURE 6.20

MOS
4.1.1 Expert

A *trendline* is a graphic representation of trends in a data series, such as a line sloping upward to represent increased sales over a period of months. A trendline is always associated with a data series, but it does not represent the data of that data series. Rather, a trendline depicts trends in the existing data.

1 ▸ Click in the white area slightly inside the chart border to select the entire chart. Next to the chart, click **Chart Elements** ⊞, click **Trendline**, click the arrow, and then click **Linear**. **Save** 🖫 your workbook, and then compare your screen with Figure 6.21.

A linear trendline displays in the chart. The chart shows a significant increase in attendance for 2014 and a drop in attendance in 2015, but the trendline indicates an overall increasing trend in attendance over the past five years.

FIGURE 6.21

Objective 3 Create and Modify a SmartArt Graphic

GO! Learn How
Video E6-3

A *SmartArt graphic* is a visual representation of your information and ideas. You can create SmartArt graphics by choosing from among many different layouts to communicate complex messages and relationships easily and effectively.

Unlike charts, a SmartArt graphic does not depend on any underlying data in a worksheet; rather, it is a graphical tool that depicts ideas or associations. In the following activities, you will create a process diagram to illustrate how an employer can register to have a booth at the job fair.

Activity 6.13 | Creating a Process SmartArt Graphic

In this Activity, you will use a Process SmartArt graphic, which shows steps in a process or timeline.

1 ▸ Display the **Process Chart** worksheet.

2 ▸ On the **Insert tab**, in the **Illustrations group**, click **SmartArt** 🖬.

3 On the left, notice the types of SmartArt graphics that are available, and then take a moment to examine the table in Figure 6.22.

SMART ART	
USE THIS SMARTART TYPE:	**TO DO THIS:**
List	Show nonsequential information
Process	Show steps in a process or timeline
Cycle	Show a continual process
Hierarchy	Create an organization chart or show a decision tree
Relationship	Illustrate connections
Matrix	Show how parts relate to a whole
Pyramid	Use a series of pictures to show relationships
Picture	Use to display pictures in a diagram

FIGURE 6.22

4 On the left, click *Process*, and then in the first row, click the third option—**Step Down Process**. Click **OK**.

5 If necessary, on the **Design tab**, in the **Create Graphic group**, click **Text Pane** to display the Text Pane on the left side of the graphic. Then, with your insertion point blinking in the first bullet of the **Text Pane**, type **Apply**

The text *Apply* displays in the Text Pane and in the first box in the diagram. Use the **Text Pane**, which displays to the left of the graphic, to input and organize the text in your graphic. The Text Pane is populated with placeholder text that you replace with your information. If you prefer, close the Text Pane and type directly into the graphic.

6 In the **Text Pane**, click the next bullet, which is indented, and then type **Register for Booth** Compare your screen with Figure 6.23.

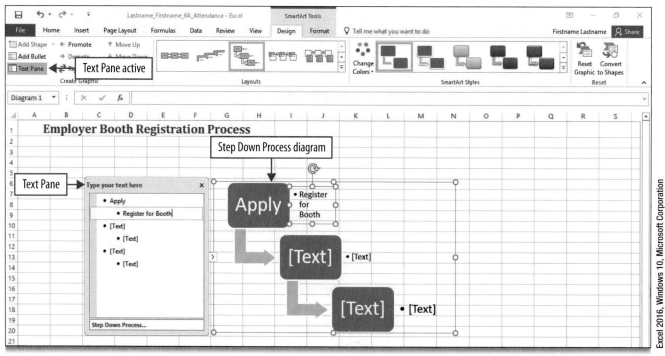

FIGURE 6.23

7 ▸ In the **Text Pane**, click the next bullet, and then type **Prepare** Under *Prepare* click the indented bullet and type **Booth Number Assigned**

8 ▸ Click the next bullet and type **Attend** Click the next bullet, and then type **Set Up Job Fair Booth** Compare your diagram with Figure 6.24.

The Text Pane entries display on the left in the Text Pane, and the process diagram with entries displays on the right in the process diagram.

FIGURE 6.24

9 ▸ **Close** ☒ the **Text Pane**, and then **Save** 🖫 your workbook.

Activity 6.14 | Modifying the Diagram Style

Excel offers preformatted SmartArt styles that you can apply to a diagram.

1 ▸ With the SmartArt still selected, on the **Design tab**, in the **SmartArt Styles group**, click **More** ⊽. Under **3-D**, click the first style—**Polished**.

2 ▸ In the **SmartArt Styles group**, click **Change Colors**, and then under **Colorful**, click the third option—**Colorful Range – Accent Colors 3 to 4**.

3 ▸ By using the ⬚ pointer, drag the upper left corner of the graphic border inside the upper left corner of cell **A4**. Point to the lower right corner of the graphic's border to display the ⬚ pointer, and then drag to resize the graphic and position the lower right corner inside the lower right corner of cell **H22**. **Save** 🖫 your workbook, and then compare your screen with Figure 6.25.

FIGURE 6.25

Objective 4 | Create and Modify an Organization Chart

GO! Learn How
Video E6-4

An ***organization chart*** depicts reporting relationships within an organization.

Activity 6.15 | Creating and Modifying a SmartArt Organization Chart

In this Activity, you will create an organizational chart that shows the reporting relationship among the Job Fair Director, Employer Relations Manager, Job Applicant Program Manager, Tech Support Supervisor, and Help Desk Technician.

1 Display the **Organization Chart** worksheet.

2 On the **Insert tab**, in the **Illustrations group**, click **SmartArt** . On the left, click **Hierarchy**, and then in the first row, click the first graphic—**Organization Chart**. Click **OK**. If the Text Pane displays, close it.

> **NOTE** Displaying the Text Pane
>
> Typing in the Text Pane is optional. If you have closed the Text Pane and want to reopen it, select the graphic, click the Design tab, and then in the Create Graphic group, click Text Pane. Alternatively, click the arrow on the left border of the SmartArt graphic to display the Text Pane.

3 In the graphic, with the first [**Text**] box selected, type **Amanda Shy, Job Fair Director**

4 In the box below the *Job Fair Director*, click on the *edge* of the box to display a solid line border—if a dashed border displays, click the edge of the box again. With the box bordered with a solid line, press ⌈Delete⌋. Compare your screen with Figure 6.26.

Three shapes comprise the second level of the organization chart.

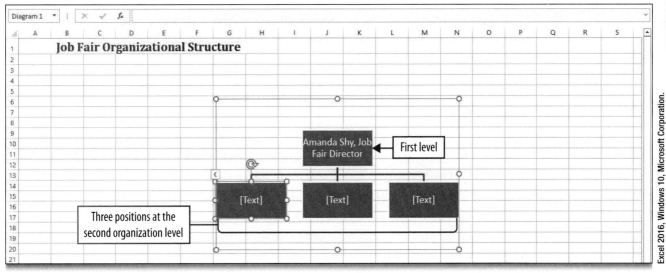

FIGURE 6.26

5 In the leftmost shape on the second level of the organization chart, type **Linda Wong, Employer Relations Manager**

6 Click in the middle shape, and type **Miriam Ruiz, Job Applicant Program Manager** In the rightmost shape, type **Michael Gold, Tech Support Supervisor**

7 With the *Michael Gold* shape selected, on the **Design tab**, in the **Create Graphic group**, click the **Add Shape arrow**, and then click **Add Shape Below**.

A new shape displays below the Tech Support Supervisor shape.

🔄 **ANOTHER WAY**   Right-click the shape, click Add Shape, and then click Add Shape Below.

8 Type **Ivan Soklov, Help Desk Technician**

9 In the **SmartArt Styles group**, click **More** ⌈▾⌋, and then under **3-D**, click the first style— **Polished**. Click **Change Colors**, and then under **Colorful**, click the fifth color arrangement— **Colorful Range – Accent Colors 5 to 6**. Click **Save** ⌈🖫⌋ and then compare your screen with Figure 6.27.

FIGURE 6.27

In this Activity, you will change the formatting and layout of the graphic.

1 With the *Ivan Soklov* shape selected, on the **Format tab**, in the **Shape Styles group**, click the **Shape Fill arrow**, and then under **Theme Colors**, in the seventh column, click the fifth color—**Olive Green, Accent 3, Darker 25%**.

2 Click the edge of the *Ivan Soklov* shape so that it is surrounded by a solid line and sizing handles and the polished shape displays. Hold down [Ctrl], and click each of the other shapes until all five are selected.

3 With all five shapes selected, on the **Format tab** in the **Shape Styles group**, click **Shape Effects**, point to **Bevel**, and then under **Bevel**, in the third row, click the second bevel shape—**Riblet**.

4 By using the [cursor] pointer, drag the upper left corner of the graphic inside the upper left corner of cell **A4**. By using the [cursor] pointer, drag the lower right corner of the chart inside the lower right corner of cell **H20**.

5 In the shape for *Amanda Shy*, click to position the insertion point after the comma, hold down [Shift], and then press [Enter] to insert a line break. Press [Delete] to delete the extra space. Use the same technique in any remaining shapes as necessary to move the job title to the second line.

6 Click cell **A1**, and then **Save** [icon] your workbook. Compare your screen with Figure 6.28.

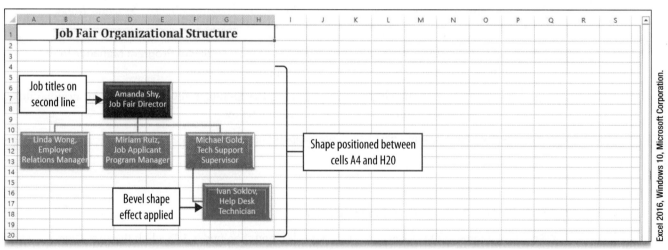

FIGURE 6.28

Excel 2016, Windows 10, Microsoft Corporation.

1 Display the **Attendance Chart** worksheet, and if necessary, click in a white area to deselect the chart. On the ribbon, click the **Page Layout tab**, and then in the **Page Setup group**, click the **Dialog Box Launcher** [icon].

2 In the **Page Setup** dialog box, click the **Header/Footer tab**, and then click **Custom Footer**. With the insertion point in the **Left section**, in the small toolbar in the center of the dialog box, click **Insert File Name** [icon], and then click **OK** two times.

3 Click the **Attendance by Location sheet tab**, hold down [Ctrl], and then click the **Process Chart sheet tab** and the **Organization Chart sheet tab** to select the remaining three worksheets and group them.

4 On the **Page Layout tab**, in the **Page Setup group**, click the **Margins arrow**, and then at the bottom click **Custom Margins**.

5 On the **Margins tab**, below **Center on page**, select the **Horizontally** check box.

6 In the dialog box, click the **Header/Footer tab**, click **Custom Footer**, and then in the **Left section**, click **Insert File Name** 🗎. Click **OK** two times.

7 Click the **File tab** to display **Backstage** view. On the right, at the bottom of the **Properties** list, click **Show All Properties**. On the list of **Properties**, in the **Tags** box, type **attendance statistics, organization charts** In the **Subject** box, type your course name and section #. Under **Related People**, be sure that your name displays as the author. If necessary, right-click the author name, click **Edit Property**, type your name, click outside of the **Edit person** dialog box, and then click **OK**.

8 On the left, click **Print**. Under **Settings**, click the **Print Active Sheets arrow**, and then click **Print Entire Workbook**. At the bottom of the window, click **Next Page** ▶ to scroll through the worksheets.

9 On the left, click **Save** to save your workbook and redisplay the workbook window. Click the **Attendance Chart sheet tab** to ungroup the sheets.

10 If directed by your instructor to do so, submit a paper printout of each of the four worksheets, an electronic image of each of your four worksheets that looks like a printed document, or your original Excel file. If required by your instructor, print or create an electronic version of your worksheets with formulas displayed. In the upper right corner of the Excel window, click **Close** ☒.

> **END | You have completed Project 6A**

PROJECT ACTIVITIES

In Activities 6.18 through 6.25, you will create, format, and edit a booth registration order form template for use by Job Fair staff to ensure that totals for items ordered are calculated accurately. You will also protect the template. Your completed worksheet will look similar to Figure 6.29.

Please always review the downloaded Grader instructions before beginning.

PROJECT FILES

MyITLab
grader

If your instructor wants you to submit Project 6B in the MyITLab grader system, log into MyITLab, locate Grader Project 6B, and then download the files for this project.

For Project 6B, you will need the following files:

e06B_Logo
e06B_Booth_Order

You will save your workbooks as:

Lastname_Firstname_6B_Topaz_Order

Lastname_Firstname_6B_Booth_Order
(will not submit for grading)
Lastname_Firstname_6B_Order_Template
(will not submit for grading)

PROJECT RESULTS

GO!
Walk Thru
Project 6B

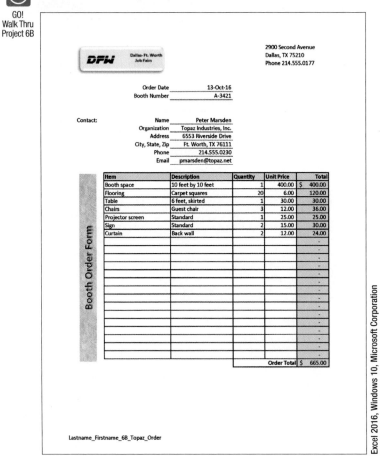

Objective 5   Create an Excel Template

GO! Learn How
Video E6-5

A *template* is a workbook that you create and use as the basis for other similar workbooks. Excel also has predesigned templates that include, among others, financial forms to record expenses, time worked, balance sheet items, and other common financial reports.

Standardization and *protection* are the two main reasons for creating templates for commonly used forms in an organization. Standardization means that all forms created within the organization will have a uniform appearance; the data will always be organized in the same manner. Protection means that individuals entering data cannot change areas of the worksheet that are protected, and therefore cannot alter important formulas and formats built in to the template.

Activity 6.18 | Entering Template Text

To create a template, you can start with a blank worksheet; enter the text, formatting, and formulas needed for the specific worksheet purpose, and then save the file as a template. Saving a workbook as a template adds the extension *.xltx* to the file name. In this Activity, you will start a workbook for the purpose of creating a purchase order template.

> **ALERT!** To submit as an autograded project, log into MyITLab, download the files for this project, and begin with those files instead of e06B_Booth_Order.

1 Start Excel. On Excel's opening screen, scroll through the various templates and compare your screen with Figure 6.30.

From the *Search for online templates* box, you can find and download many different predesigned templates from Microsoft's site. Microsoft updates this list frequently.

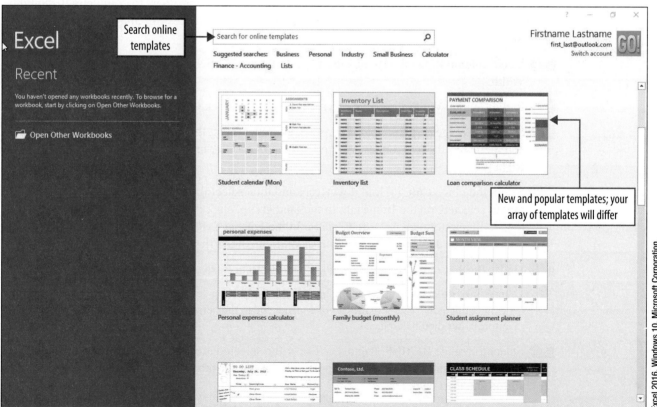

FIGURE 6.30

2 On the left, click **Open Other Workbooks**. Click **Browse**, in the **Open** dialog box, navigate to the student data files that accompany this chapter, and then open **e06B_Booth_Order**. In cell **A1**, type **Dallas - Ft. Worth Job Fair** and press Enter.

3 Using your own name, save the file in your **Excel Chapter 6** folder as **Lastname_Firstname_6B_Booth_Order**

4 Compare your screen with Figure 6.31.

Some formatting is already applied. Until the format and design of the order form is complete, you will save your work as a normal workbook—not as a template.

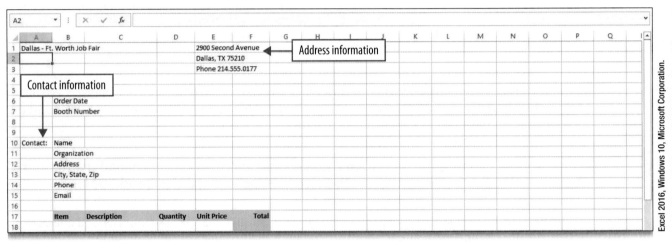

FIGURE 6.31

Activity 6.19 | Formatting a Template

One of the goals in designing a template is to make it easy for others to complete. It should be obvious to the person completing the form what information is necessary and where to place the information.

1 Select **column B**. On the **Home tab**, in the **Cells group**, click **Format**, and then click **Column Width**.

2 In the **Column Width** dialog box, type **21.5** and then click **OK**.

3 Select the range **B6:B15**, hold down Ctrl, and then select the range **C10:C15**. Release Ctrl, and then with the two ranges selected, on the **Home tab**, in the **Alignment group**, click **Align Right** ☰.

4 Select the range **C6:C7**. Hold down Ctrl, and then select the range **C10:C15**. With the two ranges selected, on the **Home tab**, in the **Font group**, click the **Borders button arrow** ⊞ ▾, and then at the bottom, click **More Borders**. In the **Format Cells** dialog box, on the **Border tab**, under **Line**, in the **Style** list, click the second line in the first column—**the dotted line**.

5 Under **Border**, click **Middle Border** ⊟, and **Bottom Border** ⊞ ▾. Click **OK**.

Inserting borders on cells in a template creates lines as a place to record information when the form is filled out. This provides a good visual cue to the person filling out the form as to where information should be placed.

6 Select the range **B17:F40**. Right-click over the selected area and click **Format Cells**. In the **Format Cells** dialog box, if necessary, click the **Border tab**. Under **Presets**, click **Outline** and **Inside** and then click **OK**.

This action applies a visible grid of columns and rows, which is helpful to those individuals completing the form.

7 Press `Ctrl` + `Home` to deselect and make cell **A1** the active cell. Click the **File tab**, and then on the left, click **Print** to view the Print Preview. Compare your screen with Figure 6.32.

FIGURE 6.32

8 On the left, click **Save** to save and return to your workbook.

A vertical dotted line on the worksheet indicates where the first page would end if the worksheet were printed as it is currently set up. As you develop your template, use the Print Preview to check your progress.

Activity 6.20 | Entering Template Formulas

After the text is entered and formatted in your template, add formulas to the cells where you want the result of the calculations to display. In this Activity, you will create a formula in the Total column to determine the dollar value for the quantity of each item ordered, and then create another formula to sum the Total column.

1 In cell **F18**, type **=d18*e18** and then on the **Formula Bar**, click **Enter** ✓.

No value displays in cell F18. However, when the person entering information into the worksheet types the Quantity in cell D18 and the Unit Price in cell E18, the formula will multiply the two values to calculate a total for the item.

2 Use the fill handle to copy the formula in cell **F18** down through cell **F39**. Select the range **F19:F39**, and then on the **Home tab**, in the **Number group**, click **Comma Style** 🔘.

When copying a formula, the format of the copied cell carries into the cells. This action changes the Number format of the cells in the range F19:F39 to the Comma Style.

3 Click cell **F40**. On the **Home tab**, in the **Editing group**, click **AutoSum** Σ AutoSum ▾. In the **Formula Bar**, be sure the range displays as *F18:F39*, and then press `Enter`.

4 Select the range **D40:E40**. In the **Alignment group**, click **Merge & Center**. Type **Order Total** and then on the **Formula Bar**, click **Enter** ✓. In the **Alignment group**, click **Align Right** ☰. In the **Font** group, click **Bold** **B**.

A label is added and formatted to identify the total for the entire order.

5 Select the range **B40:C40**, right-click, and then click **Format Cells**. In the **Format Cells** dialog box, if necessary, click the **Border tab**, and then in the **Border preview** area, click **Left Border** ▣, **Middle Vertical Border** ▦, and **Bottom Border** ▦ to *remove* these borders from the preview—be sure the right and top lines remain in the preview area. Compare your dialog box with Figure 6.33.

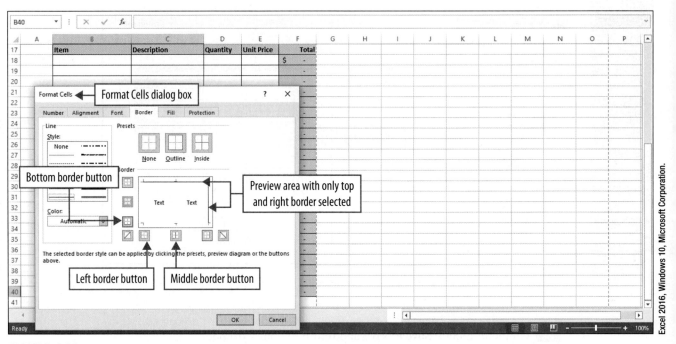

FIGURE 6.33

6 Click **OK**. Click the **File tab**, and then click **Print** to view the Print Preview. Compare your screen with Figure 6.34.

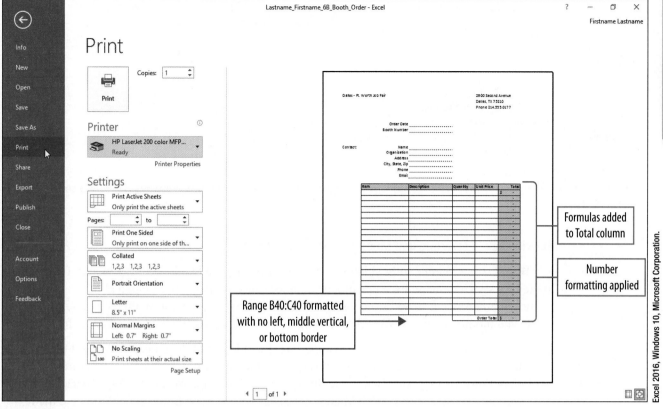

Excel 2016, Windows 10, Microsoft Corporation.

FIGURE 6.34

> 7 In **Backstage** view, on the left, click **Save** to save and return to your workbook.

Activity 6.21 | Inserting and Modifying an Image

MOS

5.3.2

In the following Activity, you will add a logo image to the form.

> 1 Click cell **A1** and press Delete to remove the job fair name. On the **Insert tab**, in the **Illustrations group**, click **Pictures**.

> 2 In the **Insert Picture** dialog box, navigate to the student data files that accompany this chapter, and then insert the file **e06B_Logo**.

   The logo displays in the upper left corner of the worksheet. The Picture Tools contextual tab displays when the object is selected.

> 3 With the image selected, on the **Format tab**, in the **Picture Styles group**, click **More**, and then, in the third row, click the last style—**Bevel Rectangle**. Point to the image to display the pointer, and then drag the image down and to the right slightly, as shown in Figure 6.35. **Save** your workbook.

FIGURE 6.35

Activity 6.22 | Inserting and Modifying a WordArt Image

WordArt is a feature with which you can insert decorative text in your document, for example to create a stylized image for a heading or logo. Because WordArt is a graphical object, it can be moved and resized. In addition, you can change its shape and color. In this Activity, you will create and modify a vertical WordArt heading and place it at the left side of the order form grid.

1 Scroll so that **row 16** is at the top of the Excel window, and then, click cell **A17**. On the **Insert tab**, in the **Text group**, if necessary click the Text arrow to display Text commands, click **WordArt** 4 , and then in the third row, click the first WordArt—**Fill – Black, Text 1, Outline – Background 1, Hard Shadow – Background 1**. Type **Booth Order Form** and then compare your screen with Figure 6.36.

FIGURE 6.36

2 Select the text you just typed, and then from the mini toolbar, change the **Font Size** to **20**.

The WordArt image floats on your screen. Sizing handles display around the outside of the WordArt, and a *rotation handle* displays on the top side of the image. Use the rotation handle to rotate an image to any angle.

3 Point to the **rotation handle** until the ⟳ pointer displays, hold down the Shift key, drag to the left until the WordArt is vertical, as shown in Figure 6.37, and then release the mouse button.

You can use the rotation handle to revolve the image 360 degrees. Holding down the SHIFT key while dragging helps to snap the image vertically.

FIGURE 6.37

4 ▶ Point to the edge of the **WordArt** image to display the [cursor] pointer. Drag the WordArt image to **column A** and align the top of the image with the top of cell **A17**—centered in the column.

5 ▶ At the lower edge of the WordArt image, point to the center resize handle and drag down so the end of the image aligns at the lower edge of cell **A39**.

6 ▶ With the WordArt image still selected, on the **Format tab**, in the **Shape Styles group**, click the **Shape Fill arrow**, point to **Texture**, and then in the fourth row, click the last texture—**Stationery**. Compare your screen with Figure 6.38.

The WordArt text box fills with Stationery texture and color.

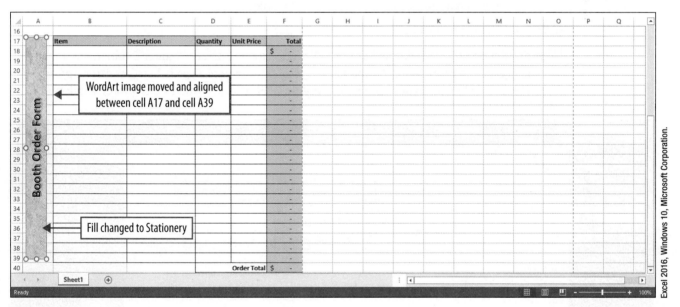

FIGURE 6.38

7 ▶ Click any cell to deselect the WordArt. On the **Page Layout tab**, in the **Page Setup group**, click the **Dialog Box Launcher** [icon] to display the **Page Setup** dialog box. On the **Margins tab**, center the page horizontally. On the **Header/Footer tab**, create a **Custom Footer**, and then in the **Left section**, click **Insert File Name** [icon]. Click **OK** two times.

8 ▶ Press Ctrl + Home to move to the top of the worksheet. **Save** [icon] your workbook, and leave it open for the next Activity. You will not submit this workbook; rather, you will use it to create your template.

Activity 6.23 | Saving a File as a Template

MOS
1.1.1 Expert

After you complete the formatting and design of a worksheet that you would like to use over and over again, save it as a template file. When saved as a template file, the *.xltx* file extension is added to the file name instead of *.xlsx*.

If a template is saved in the Custom Office Templates folder on the hard drive of your computer, or the network location where the Excel software resides, the template will be available to other people who have access to the same system from the New tab in Backstage view.

Regardless of where the template file is saved, when the template is opened, a new *copy* of the workbook opens, preserving the original template for future use.

Instead of the Custom Office Templates folder, which might be restricted in a college lab, you will save the template in your chapter folder.

1 Click the **File tab**, and then on the left, click **Save As**. Click **Browse** to display the **Save As** dialog box.

2 Click the **Save as type arrow**, and then on the list, click **Excel Template**. At the top of the **Save As** dialog box, notice that the path changes to the **Custom Office Templates** folder in the **Documents** folder of your hard drive.

3 Navigate to your **Excel Chapter 6** folder so that it displays in the **Address bar** at the top of the dialog box. In the **File name** box, change the **File name** to **Lastname_Firstname_6B_Order_Template** and then click **Save**.

A copy of the template is saved with your other files.

4 **Close** the file and **Close** Excel.

5 From the taskbar, click **File Explorer**. Navigate to your **Excel Chapter 6** folder, and then notice that the *Lastname_Firstname_6B_Order_Template* **Type** is listed as *Microsoft Excel Template*. Compare your screen with Figure 6.39. **Close** ☒ the File Explorer window.

FIGURE 6.39

GO! Learn How
Video E6-6

When the template design is complete, you can enable the protection of the worksheet. Protection prevents anyone from changing the worksheet—they cannot insert, modify, delete, or format data in a locked cell.

For purposes of creating a form that you want someone to complete, you can protect the worksheet, and then unlock specific areas where you *do* want the person completing the form to enter data.

By default, all cells in Excel are *locked*—data cannot be typed into them. However, the locked feature is disabled until you protect the worksheet. After protection is enabled, the locked cells cannot be changed. Of course, you will want to designate some cells to be *unlocked*, so that individuals completing your form can type their data into those cells.

The basic process is to determine the cells that you will allow people to change or unlock, and then protect the entire worksheet. Then, only the cells that you designated as unlocked will be available to any person using the worksheet. You may add an optional *password* to prevent someone from disabling the worksheet protection. The password can be any combination of numbers, letters, or symbols up to 15 characters long. The password should be shared only with people who have permission to change the template.

Activity 6.24 | Protecting a Worksheet

MOS

1.2.1 Expert
1.2.2 Expert
1.2.4 Expert
1.2.6 Expert

1 Start Excel, and then on the left, click **Open Other Workbooks**. Click **Browse**, navigate to your **Excel Chapter 6** folder, click one time to select your **Lastname_Firstname_6B_Order_Template** file, and then click **Open**.

2 Select the range **C6:C7**, hold down Ctrl, select the nonadjacent ranges **C10:C15** and **B18:E39**.

The selected cells are the ones that you want individuals placing booth orders to be able to fill in— they should *not* be locked when protection is applied.

3 With the three ranges selected, on the **Home tab**, in the **Cells group**, click **Format**, and then click **Format Cells**. In the **Format Cells** dialog box, click the **Protection tab**.

4 Click to *clear* the check mark from the **Locked** check box, and then compare your screen with Figure 6.40.

Recall that all cells are locked by default, but the locking feature is enabled only when protection is applied. Therefore, you must *unlock* the cells you want to have available for use in this manner *before* you protect the worksheet.

FIGURE 6.40

5 Click **OK** to close the **Format Cells** dialog box.

6 In the **Cells group**, click **Format**, and then under **Protection**, click **Protect Sheet**.

The Protect Sheet dialog box displays. Under *Allow all users of this worksheet to*, the *Select locked cells* and *Select unlocked cells* check boxes are selected by default. The *Select locked cells* option allows the user to click the locked cells and *view* the formulas, but because the cells are locked, they cannot *change* the content or format of the locked cells. If you deselect this option, the user cannot view or even click in a locked cell.

For the remaining check boxes, you can see that, because they are not selected, users are restricted from performing all other actions on the worksheet.

7 Leave the first two check boxes selected. At the top of the dialog box, be sure the **Protect worksheet and contents of locked cells** check box is selected. In the **Password to unprotect sheet** box, type **goseries** Compare your screen with Figure 6.41.

The password does not display—rather bullets display as placeholders for each letter or character that is typed. Passwords are case sensitive; therefore, *GOSeries* is different from *goseries*.

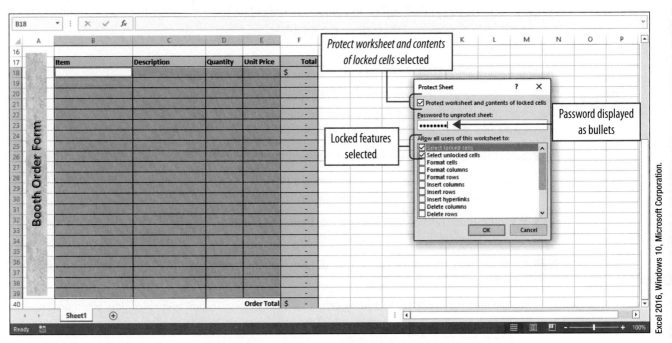

FIGURE 6.41

8 Click **OK**. In the **Confirm Password** dialog box, type **goseries** to confirm the password, and then click **OK** to close both dialog boxes.

9 Click in any cell in the **Total** column, type **123** and observe what happens.

The number is not entered; instead a message informs you that the cell you are trying to change is protected and, therefore, read-only.

10 Click **OK** to acknowledge the message. Click cell **D18**, type **2** and press (Tab), type **150** and press (Enter).

The numbers are entered and the formulas in cells F18 and F40 calculate and display the results—$300.00

11 On the **Quick Access Toolbar**, click **Undo** 🔄 two times to remove the two numbers that you typed, and then click **Save** 🖫.

You have tested your template, and it is protected and saved.

12 Display the **document properties** and under **Related People**, be sure that your name displays as the author. If necessary, right-click the author name, click **Edit Property**, and then type your name. In the **Subject** box, type your course name and section #, and in the **Tags** box, type **booth order form, template**

13 Display the **Print Preview**, and then on the left click **Save** to save and redisplay the workbook.

14 You do not need to submit this workbook—you will use it to create a worksheet based on your template in the next Activity. Click the **File tab**. On the left click **Close** to close the workbook but leave Excel open.

Objective 7   Create a Worksheet Based on a Template

GO! Learn How
Video E6-7

After the template is protected, it is ready for use. If the template is stored in the Custom Office Templates folder, anyone using the system or network on which it is stored can open it from the New tab in Backstage view. When opened from this location, Excel opens a new copy of the template as a workbook. Then you can enter information in the unlocked cells and save it as a new file. Templates can be provided to coworkers by storing them on a company intranet, or they can be made available to customers through a website.

Activity 6.25 │ Creating a Worksheet Based on a Template

1 Click the **File tab**, on the left click **Open**, click **Browse**, navigate to your **Excel Chapter 6** folder, and then click one time to select your **Lastname_Firstname_6B_Order_Template** file. Click **Open**.

2 Click the **File tab**, on the left click **Save As**, and then click **Browse** to display the **Save As** dialog box. Navigate to your **Excel Chapter 6** folder, and then set the **Save as type box** to **Excel Workbook**—the first choice at the top of the list. In the **File name** box, using your own name, type **Lastname_Firstname_6B_Topaz_Order** Compare your screen with Figure 6.42.

FIGURE 6.42

3 Click **Save**. Click cell **C6**, type **October 13, 2016** press ⏎, and notice that Excel applies the default date format. As the booth number, type **A-3421** and then press ⇥ to move to cell **C10**.

4 Starting in cell **C10**, enter the company information as follows:

Name	**Peter Marsden**
Organization	**Topaz Industries, Inc.**
Address	**6553 Riverside Drive**
City, State, Zip	**Ft. Worth, TX 76111**
Phone	**214.555.0230**
Email	**pmarsden@topaz.net**

5 In cell **B18**, type **Booth space** and press ⇥, type **10 feet by 10 feet** and press ⇥, type **1** and press ⇥, type **400** and then press ⇥.

6 Beginning in cell **B19**, complete the order by entering the following items, pressing ⇥ to move from cell to cell. When you are finished, scroll to display **row 16** at the top of your screen, and then compare your screen with Figure 6.43.

ITEM	DESCRIPTION	QUANTITY	UNIT PRICE
Booth space	10 feet by 10 feet	1	400
Flooring	**Carpet squares**	**20**	**6**
Table	**6 feet, skirted**	**1**	**30**
Chairs	**Guest chair**	**3**	**12**
Projector screen	**Standard**	**1**	**25**
Sign	**Standard**	**2**	**15**
Curtain	**Back wall**	**2**	**12**

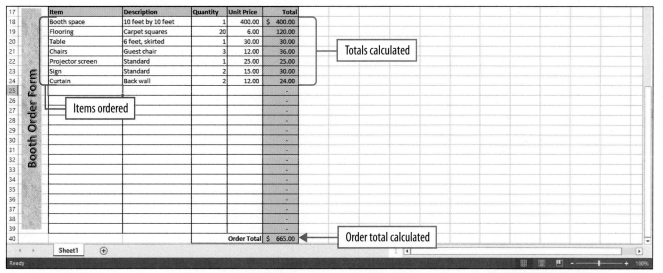

	Item	Description	Quantity	Unit Price	Total
18	Booth space	10 feet by 10 feet	1	400.00	$ 400.00
19	Flooring	Carpet squares	20	6.00	120.00
20	Table	6 feet, skirted	1	30.00	30.00
21	Chairs	Guest chair	3	12.00	36.00
22	Projector screen	Standard	1	25.00	25.00
23	Sign	Standard	2	15.00	30.00
24	Curtain	Back wall	2	12.00	24.00

Totals calculated

Items ordered

Order Total $ 665.00

Order total calculated

FIGURE 6.43

Excel 2016, Windows 10, Microsoft Corporation.

7 Display the **document properties**. Be sure your name displays as the **Author** and your course name and section # displays in the **Subject** box. Change the **Tags** box to **Topaz booth order**

8 Display the **Print Preview**, and be sure the file name displays in the left section of the footer. On the left, click **Save** to save your workbook and redisplay the Excel window.

9 If directed by your instructor to do so, submit a paper printout of your worksheet, an electronic image of your worksheets that looks like a printed document, or your original Excel file. If required by your instructor, print or create an electronic version of your worksheet with formulas displayed. In the upper right corner of the Excel window, click **Close** ⊠.

END | You have completed Project 6B

MICROSOFT OFFICE SPECIALIST (MOS) SKILLS IN THIS CHAPTER	
PROJECT 6A	**PROJECT 6B**
2.3.1 Insert sparklines	6.2.1 Insert images
4.1.1 Expert	1.1.1 Expert: Save a workbook as a template
5.1.1 Create a new chart	1.2.1 Expert: Restrict editing
5.1.3 Switch between rows and columns in source data	1.2.2 Expert: Protect a worksheet
5.1.4 Analyze data by using Quick Analysis	1.2.4 Expert: Protect workbook structure
5.2.2 Add and modify chart elements	1.2.6 Expert: Encrypt a workbook with a password
5.2.4 Move charts to a chart sheet	5.3.2 Insert images
4.1.1 Expert: Add trendlines to charts	

BUILD YOUR E-PORTFOLIO

An E-Portfolio is a collection of evidence, stored electronically, that showcases what you have accomplished while completing your education. Collecting and then sharing your work products with potential employers reflects your academic and career goals. Your completed documents from the following projects are good examples to show what you have learned: 6G, 6K, and 6L.

GO! FOR JOB SUCCESS

Your instructor may assign this discussion to your class and then ask you to think about, or discuss with your classmates, these questions.

Mobile devices, unlimited data plans, public Wi-Fi networks, streaming video and music services, and social media provide many more ways for companies to reach their customers than in the past. Years ago, companies focused on only a few advertising outlets—radio, tv, newspapers, and magazines—to reach consumers. Now companies use multi-channel marketing to reach current and potential customers. In addition to traditional commercials on television or radio, products must be advertised on websites, in YouTube videos, on social media sites, by direct mail and email, in retail stores, and through catalogs.

Multi-channel marketing enables customers to do more than just passively view ads. Multi-channel marketing encourages consumers to become part of the marketing experience. For example, a television show can display a Twitter hashtag so that viewers can simultaneously discuss the show on social media.

FotolEdhar / Fotolia

What are some other multi-channel marketing tools you have seen companies use to generate interest in their products or services?

Some studies show that consumers who are exposed to multiple marketing channels spend up to four times more on a company's products than those who see only traditional advertising. Are there products you have become interested in or purchased because you saw their social media accounts or videos?

Multi-channel marketing is not always useful for all products or services. What products or services might reach more customers through traditional marketing channels or direct sales instead of multi-channel marketing?

END OF CHAPTER

SUMMARY

Excel's Recommended Charts feature displays suggested charts based on your data and helps you to decide the best chart type to use. You can easily modify, create, and format various chart elements.

Excel includes many different chart types, including column and line charts. A column chart shows a comparison among related numbers and a line chart displays a trend over time.

A SmartArt graphic is a visual representation of your information and ideas. SmartArt diagrams are not linked to the underlying worksheet data but float on top of the worksheet like other images.

Templates have built-in formulas and are used for standardization and protection of data. You created a template using text, formatting, formulas, locked and unlocked cells, and password protection.

GO! LEARN IT ONLINE

Review the concepts, key terms, and MOS skills in this chapter by completing these online challenges, which you can find at **MyITLab**.

Matching and Multiple Choice: Answer matching and multiple choice questions to test what you learned in this chapter.

Lessons on the GO!: Learn how to use all the new apps and features as they are introduced by Microsoft.

MOS Prep Quiz: Answer questions to review the MOS skills that you practiced in this chapter.

PROJECT GUIDE FOR EXCEL CHAPTER 6

Your instructor will assign Projects from this list to ensure your learning and assess your knowledge.

		PROJECT GUIDE FOR EXCEL CHAPTER 6	
Project	Apply Skills from These Chapter Objectives	Project Type	Project Location
6A MyITLab	Objectives 1-4 from Project 6A	**6A Instructional Project (Grader Project)** Guided instruction to learn the skills in Project 6A.	In MyITLab and in text
6B MyITLab	Objectives 5-7 from Project 6B	**6B Instructional Project (Grader Project)** Guided instruction to learn the skills in Project 6B.	In MyITLab and in text
6C	Objectives 1-4 from Project 6A	**6C Skills Review (Scorecard Grading)** A guided review of the skills from Project 6A.	In text
6D	Objectives 5-7 from Project 6B	**6D Skills Review (Scorecard Grading)** A guided review of the skills from Project 6B.	In text
6E MyITLab	Objectives 1-4 from Project 6A	**6E Mastery (Grader Project)** **Mastery and Transfer of Learning** A demonstration of your mastery of the skills in Project 6A with extensive decision-making.	In MyITLab and in text
6F MyITLab	Objectives 5-7 from Project 6B	**6F Mastery (Grader Project)** **Mastery and Transfer of Learning** A demonstration of your mastery of the skills in Project 6B with extensive decision-making.	In MyITLab and in text
6G MyITLab	Combination of Objectives from Projects 6A and 6B	**6G Mastery (Grader Project)** **Mastery and Transfer of Learning** A demonstration of your mastery of the skills in Projects 6A and 6B with extensive decision-making.	In MyITLab and in text
6H	Combination of Objectives from Projects 6A and 6B	**6H GO! Fix It (Scorecard Grading)** **Critical Thinking** A demonstration of your mastery of the skills in Projects 6A and 6B by creating a correct result from a document that contains errors you must find.	Instructor Resource Center (IRC) and MyITLab
6I	Combination of Objectives from Projects 6A and 6B	**6I GO! Make It (Scorecard Grading)** **Critical Thinking** A demonstration of your mastery of the skills in Projects 6A and 6B by creating a result from a supplied picture.	IRC and MyITLab
6J	Combination of Objectives from Projects 6A and 6B	**6J GO! Solve It (Rubric Grading)** **Critical Thinking** A demonstration of your mastery of the skills in Projects 6A and 6B, your decision-making skills, and your critical thinking skills. A task-specific rubric helps you self-assess your result.	IRC and MyITLab
6K	Combination of Objectives from Projects 6A and 6B	**6K GO! Solve It (Rubric Grading)** **Critical Thinking** A demonstration of your mastery of the skills in Projects 6A and 6B, your decision-making skills, and your critical thinking skills. A task-specific rubric helps you self-assess your result.	In text
6L	Combination of Objectives from Projects 6A and 6B	**6L GO! Think (Rubric Grading)** **Critical Thinking** A demonstration of your understanding of the Chapter concepts applied in a manner that you would outside of college. An analytic rubric helps you and your instructor grade the quality of your work by comparing it to the work an expert in the discipline would create.	In text
6M	Combination of Objectives from Projects 6A and 6B	**6M GO! Think (Rubric Grading)** **Critical Thinking** A demonstration of your understanding of the Chapter concepts applied in a manner that you would outside of college. An analytic rubric helps you and your instructor grade the quality of your work by comparing it to the work an expert in the discipline would create.	IRC and MyITLab
6N	Combination of Objectives from Projects 6A and 6B	**6N You and GO! (Rubric Grading)** **Critical Thinking** A demonstration of your understanding of the Chapter concepts applied in a manner that you would in a personal situation. An analytic rubric helps you and your instructor grade the quality of your work.	IRC and MyITLab
Capstone Project for Excel Chapters 4-6	Combination of Objectives from Projects 4A, 4B, 5A, 5B, 6A, 6B	**Capstone (Grader Project)** A demonstration of your mastery of the skills in Chapters 4-6 with extensive decision making.	IRC and MyITLab

GLOSSARY

GLOSSARY OF CHAPTER KEY TERMS

Axis A line that serves as a frame of reference for measurement and that borders the chart plot area.

Category labels The labels that display along the bottom of a chart to identify the categories of data.

Chart area The entire chart and all of its elements.

Chart elements Objects that make up a chart.

Chart sheet A workbook sheet that contains only a chart.

Column chart A chart in which the data is arranged in columns and that is useful for showing data changes over a period of time or for illustrating comparisons among items.

Cycle A category of SmartArt graphics that illustrates a continual process.

Data labels Labels that display the value, percentage, and/or category of each particular data point and can contain one or more of the choices listed— Series name, Category name, Value, or Percentage.

Data marker A column, bar, area, dot, pie slice, or other symbol in a chart that represents a single data point; related data points form a data series.

Data point A value that originates in a worksheet cell and that is represented in a chart by a data marker.

Data series Related data points represented by data markers; each data series has a unique color or pattern represented in the chart legend.

Embedded chart A chart that is inserted into the same worksheet that contains the data used to create the chart.

Gridlines Lines in the plot area that aid the eye in determining the plotted values.

Hierarchy A category of SmartArt graphics used to create an organization chart or show a decision tree.

Horizontal Category axis (x-axis) The area along the bottom of a chart that identifies the categories of data; also referred to as the x-axis.

Labels Column and row headings that describe the values and help the reader understand the chart.

Legend A chart element that identifies the patterns or colors that are assigned to the categories in the chart.

Line chart A chart type that is useful to display trends over time; time displays along the bottom axis and the data point values are connected with a line.

List A category of SmartArt graphics used to show nonsequential information.

Locked [cells] In a protected worksheet, data cannot be inserted, modified, deleted, or formatted in these cells.

Major unit value A number that determines the spacing between tick marks and between the gridlines in the plot area.

Matrix A category of SmartArt graphics used to show how parts relate to a whole.

Organization chart A type of graphic that is useful to depict reporting relationships within an organization.

Password An optional element of a template added to prevent someone from disabling a worksheet's protection.

Picture A category of SmartArt graphics that is used to display pictures in a diagram.

Plot area The area bounded by the axes of a chart, including all the data series.

Process A category of SmartArt graphics that is used to show steps in a process or timeline.

Protection A feature that prevents anyone from altering the formulas or changing other template components.

Pyramid A category of SmartArt graphics that uses a series of pictures to show relationships.

Recommended Charts An Excel feature that helps you choose a chart type by previewing suggested charts based on patterns in your data.

Relationship A category of SmartArt graphics that is used to illustrate connections.

Rotation handle A circle that displays on the top side of a selected object used to rotate the object up to 360 degrees.

Scale The range of numbers in the data series that controls the minimum, maximum, and incremental values on the value axis.

SmartArt graphic A visual representation of information and ideas.

Sparklines Tiny charts that fit within a cell and give a visual trend summary alongside data.

Standardization All forms created within the organization will have a uniform appearance; the data will always be organized in the same manner.

Template A special workbook that may include formatting, formulas, and other elements and is used as a pattern for creating other workbooks.

Text Pane A window that displays to the left of the SmartArt graphic, to input and organize the text in the graphic.

Tick mark labels Identifying information for a tick mark generated from the cells on the worksheet used to create the chart.

Tick marks The short lines that display on an axis at regular intervals.

Trendline A graphic representation of trends in a data series, such as a line sloping upward to represent increased sales over a period of months.

Unlocked [cells] Cells in a protected worksheet that may be filled in.

Vertical Value axis (y-axis) A numerical scale on the left side of a chart that shows the range of numbers for the data points; also referred to as the y-axis.

Walls and floor The areas surrounding a 3-D chart that give dimension and boundaries to the chart.

WordArt A feature with which you can insert decorative text in your document.

Project 6C Employer Attendance

Apply 6A skills from these Objectives:

1 Create and Format Sparklines and a Column Chart

2 Create and Format a Line Chart

3 Create and Modify a SmartArt Graphic

4 Create and Modify an Organization Chart

In the following Skills Review, you will assist Linda Wong, Employer Relations Manager, in displaying the employer participation for the Dallas – Ft. Worth Job Fair in charts and diagrams. Your completed workbook will look similar to Figure 6.44.

PROJECT FILES

For Project 6C, you will need the following file:

e06C_Employer_Participation

You will save your workbook as:

Lastname_Firstname_6C_Employer_Participation

PROJECT RESULTS

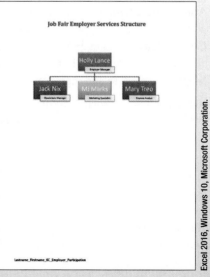

FIGURE 6.44

(Project 6C Employer Attendance continues on the next page)

1 Start Excel. From the student data files that accompany this chapter, open **e06C_Employer_Participation**. Save the file in your **Excel Chapter 6** folder as **Lastname_Firstname_6C_Employer_Participation**

a. Select the range **B4:F10**. Click **Quick Analysis**, click **Sparklines**, and then click **Line**. On the **Design tab**, in the **Show group**, select the **High Point** check box and the **Last Point** check box. On the **Design tab**, in the **Style group**, click **More**, and then in the third row, click the first style—**Sparkline Style Accent 1, (no dark or light)**. In cell **G3**, type **Trend**

b. Select the range **A3:F10**. On the **Insert tab**, in the **Charts group**, click **Recommended Charts**. With the **Clustered Column** chart selected, click **OK**. On the **Design tab**, in the **Location group**, click **Move Chart**. Click **New sheet**, name the new sheet **Participation Chart** and then click **OK**.

c. On the **Design tab**, in the **Type group**, click **Change Chart Type**. In the **Change Chart Type** dialog box, click the **All Charts** tab. On the left, click **Column**, and then on the right, at the top of the dialog box, click the fourth chart type—**3-D Clustered Column**. Click **OK**.

d. In the upper right corner of the chart, click **Chart Styles** ✎. Scroll down if necessary, and then click **Style 3**. Close the gallery of charts. On the **Design tab**, in the **Chart Layouts group**, click **Add Chart Element**. In the **Chart Elements** list, point to **Legend**, and then click **Right**. Click **Add Chart Element** again, point to **Axis Titles**, and then click **Primary Vertical**. In the **Formula Bar**, type **Number Attending** and then press Enter.

e. In the chart, click the text *Chart Title*. In the **Formula Bar**, type **Employer Participation** as the chart title, and then press Enter. **Save** your workbook.

f. In the **Fort Worth** column cluster, point to the last column—**2016**. Notice that the Value for this column is 306. Display the **Participation by Location** worksheet, and then in cell **F5**, type **270** and press Enter. Display the **Participation Chart** worksheet and verify the value for the column has changed.

g. On the **Format tab**, in the **Current Selection group**, click the **Chart Elements arrow**, and then click **Back Wall**. Then in the same group, click **Format Selection**. In the **Format Wall** pane on the right, click **Fill**, click **Solid fill**, and then click the **Fill Color arrow**. Under **Theme Colors**, in the fourth column, click the fourth color—**Dark Blue, Text 2, Lighter 40%**—and then set the **Transparency** to **75%**.

h. In the **Format Wall** pane, click the arrow to the right of **Wall Options** to display the **Chart Elements** list. Click **Side Wall**, and then apply the same fill, but with a **Transparency** of **60%**. To the **Floor**, apply a **Solid fill** using the last color in the first column—**White, Background 1, Darker 50%** with **0% Transparency**. To the **Chart Area**, apply a **Solid fill** using **Tan, Background 2, Darker 10%**—in the third column, the second color. **Close** the **Format Chart Area** pane.

2 Display the **Participation by Location** worksheet. Select the range **A3:F4**, and then on the **Insert tab**, in the **Charts group**, click **Insert Line or Area Chart**. In the first row, click the fourth chart type—**Line with Markers**. Drag the upper left corner of the chart inside the upper left corner of cell **A13**. Drag the lower right corner of the chart inside the lower right corner of cell **G29**.

a. In the embedded chart, click the **Chart Title** text *Dallas*, in the **Formula Bar** type **Employer Participation at Dallas Job Fairs** and press Enter. Point to the **Chart Title** that you just typed, right-click, click **Font**, and then change the font size to **16**. Press Enter.

b. On the left side of the line chart, point to the **Vertical (Value) axis**, right-click, and then click **Format Axis**. If necessary, expand **Axis Options**. Under **Bounds**, in the **Minimum** box, type **500** Under **Units**, change the **Major unit** to **25** and press Enter. **Close** the **Format Axis** pane.

c. Right-click anywhere within the **Plot Area**, click **Format Plot Area**, and if necessary, expand **Fill**. Under **Fill**, click **Solid fill**, click the **Fill Color arrow**, and then under **Theme Colors**, in the first column, click the fourth color—**White, Background 1, Darker 25%**.

(Project 6C Employer Attendance continues on the next page)

d. Point to the chart line, right-click, and then click **Format Data Series**. Under **Series Options**, click **Fill & Line** ⬧. Under **Line**, click **Solid line**. Use the spin box arrows to set the **Width** to **4 pt**. Under the **Fill & Line** icon, click **Marker**. Expand **Marker Options**. Click **Built-in**, click the **Type arrow**, and then click the **triangle**—the third symbol in the list. Set the **Size** of the **Marker Type** to **14**

e. Under **Fill**, click **Solid fill**, and then click the **Fill Color arrow**. Under **Theme Colors**, in the first column, click the last color—**White, Background 1, Darker 50%**.

f. Under **Border**, click **No line**. Click in the white area just inside the chart border to open the **Format Chart Area** pane. Apply a **Solid fill** using **White, Background 1, Darker 15%**—in the first column, the third color. **Close** the **Format Chart Area** pane. Click in any cell outside of the chart.

g. Click slightly inside the chart border to select the entire chart. On the **Design tab**, in the **Charts Layouts group**, click **Add Chart Element**, point to **Trendline**, and then click **Linear**. **Save** your workbook.

3 ▶ Display the **Process Chart** worksheet. On the **Insert tab**, in the **Illustrations group**, click **SmartArt**. On the left, click **Cycle**, and then in the first row, click the third option—**Block Cycle**. Click **OK**.

a. On the **Design tab**, in the **Create Graphic group**, if necessary, click **Text Pane**. In the **Text Pane**, as the first bullet, type **Increase Number of People Hired** Click the next bullet, and then type **Attract More Attendees** As the third bullet, type **Attract More Employers** As the fourth bullet, type **Reduce Costs** As the last bullet, type **Increase Profits** **Close** the **Text Pane**.

b. If necessary, click the edge of the SmartArt graphic to select it. On the **Design tab**, in the **SmartArt Styles group**, click **More** ⬇. Under **3-D**, click the first style—**Polished**. Click **Change Colors**, and then under **Colorful**, click the first option—**Colorful – Accent Colors**. Drag the upper left corner of the graphic into the left corner of cell **A3**. Drag the lower right corner inside the lower right corner of cell **H20**. Click cell **A1**, and then click **Save**.

4 ▶ Display the **Organization Chart** worksheet. On the **Insert tab**, in the **Illustrations group**, click **SmartArt**. On the left, click **Hierarchy**, and then in the first row, click the third graphic—**Name and Title Organization Chart**. Click **OK**.

a. If the Text Pane displays, close it. In the SmartArt, click in the first [**Text**] box, and then type **Holly Lance** Click the edge of the small white box below *Holly Lance* to select it and type **Employer Manager** In the [**Text**] box below *Employer Manager*, click on the edge of the box to display a solid line border—if a dashed border displays, click the edge of the box again. With the box bordered with a solid line, press Delete.

b. On the second level, click in the leftmost shape, and then using the technique you just practiced, type **Jack Nix** and **Operations Manager** In the next shape, type **MJ Marks** and **Marketing Specialist** In the rightmost shape, type **Mary Treo** and **Finance Analyst** Hold down Ctrl, and then click the edge of each of the smaller title boxes to select all four. Then, on the **Home tab**, in the **Font group**, change the font size to **8**, and click **Center**.

c. Drag the upper left corner of the graphic into cell **A3** and the lower right corner into cell **H20**. On the **Design tab**, in the **SmartArt Styles group**, apply the **Intense Effect style**—under **Best Match for Document**, the fifth style. Change the colors to **Colorful – Accent Colors**.

d. Display the **Participation Chart** sheet. If necessary, click outside of the chart. On the **Page Layout tab**, in the **Page Setup group**, click the **Dialog Box Launcher** ⬚.

e. In the **Page Setup** dialog box, click the **Header/Footer tab**, and then click **Custom Footer**. With the insertion point in the **Left section**, in the small toolbar in the center of the dialog box, click **Insert File Name** ⬚, and then click **OK** two times.

f. Click the **Participation by Location sheet tab**, hold down Ctrl, and then click the **Process Chart sheet tab** and the **Organization Chart sheet tab** to select the remaining three worksheets and group them. On the **Page Layout tab**, in the **Page Setup group**, click the **Margins arrow**, and then at the bottom click **Custom Margins**. On the **Margins tab**, below

(Project 6C Employer Attendance continues on the next page)

Center on page, click the **Horizontally** check box. Click the **Header/Footer tab**, click **Custom Footer**, and then in the **Left section**, click **Insert File Name**. click **OK** two times.

g. Click the **File tab** to display **Backstage** view. On the right, at the bottom of the **Properties** list, click **Show All Properties**. On the list of **Properties**, in the **Tags** box, type **participation statistics, organization charts** In the **Subject** box, type your course name and section #. Under **Related People**, be sure that your name displays as the author. If necessary, right-click the author name, click **Edit Property**, type your name, click outside of the **Edit person** dialog box, and then click **OK**.

h. On the left, click **Print**. Under **Settings**, click the **Print Active Sheets arrow**, and then click **Print Entire Workbook**. At the bottom of the window, click **Next Page** ▶ to scroll through the worksheets. On the left, click **Save**. Click any sheet tab to ungroup the sheets.

i. If directed by your instructor to do so, submit a paper printout of each of the four worksheets, an electronic image of each of your four worksheets that looks like a printed document, or your original Excel file. If required by your instructor, print or create an electronic version of your worksheet with formulas displayed. In the upper right corner of the Excel window, click **Close**.

END | You have completed Project 6C

In the following Skills Review, you will assist Job Fair Director, Amanda Shy, in creating a template for a Purchase Order, and then a Purchase Order for items with a logo and name imprint of the Dallas – Ft. Worth Job Fair. Your completed worksheets will look similar to Figure 6.45.

PROJECT FILES

Build from Scratch

For Project 6D, you will need the following files:

New blank Excel workbook
e06D_Logo

You will save your workbooks as:

Lastname_Firstname_6D_Hancock_PO
Lastname_Firstname_6D_Purchase_Order_Template
(will not be submitted for grading)

PROJECT RESULTS

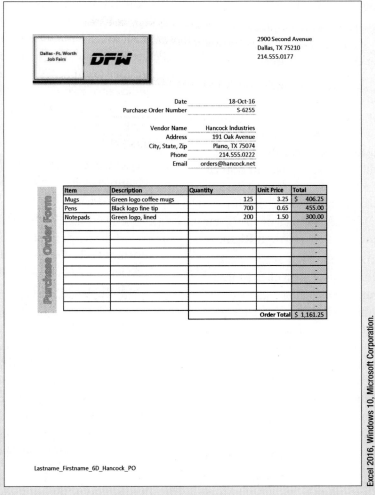

FIGURE 6.45

(Project 6D Purchase Order continues on the next page)

1 Start Excel and display a new blank workbook. Click the **File tab**, on the left click **Save As**, and then click **Browse**. In the lower portion of the **Save As** dialog box, click the **Save as type arrow**, and then click **Excel Template**. Navigate to your **Excel Chapter 6** folder. As the file name, using your own name, type **Lastname_Firstname_6D_Purchase_Order_Template** and then click **Save**.

a. Beginning in cell **E1**, type **2900 Second Avenue** and press Enter. In cell **E2**, type **Dallas, TX 75210** and in cell **E3**, type **214.555.0177** and press Enter.

b. Click cell **C8**, type **Date** and press Enter. In cell **C9**, type **Purchase Order Number** Click cell **C11**. Type **Vendor Name** and press Enter. In cell **C12**, type **Address** In cell **C13**, type **City, State, Zip** In cell **C14**, type **Phone** In cell **C15**, type **Email**

c. Click cell **B18**. Type **Item** and press Tab to move to cell **C18**. Continuing across **row 18**, in cell **C18**, type **Description** and press Tab, in cell **D18**, type **Quantity** and press Tab, in cell **E18**, type **Unit Price** and press Tab, and in cell **F18**, type **Total** and press Enter. Select the range **B18:F18** and apply **Bold**.

d. Select **column B**. On the **Home tab**, in the **Cells group**, click **Format**, and then by using the **Column Width** command, set the width of **column B** to **13.5** Use this same method to change the width of **column C** to **22.8** and the width of **column D** to **20** Select **columns E:F** and set the width to **10** Select the range **C8:C9**, hold down Ctrl and select the nonadjacent range **C11:C15**, and then on the **Home tab**, in the **Alignment group**, click **Align Right**.

e. Select the range **D8:D9**. In the **Font group**, click the **Borders button arrow**, and then click **More Borders**. In the **Format Cells** dialog box, on the **Border tab**, under **Line**, in the **Style** list, click the second line in the first column—a dotted line. Click the **Color arrow**, and then under **Theme Colors**, in the sixth column, click the sixth color—**Orange, Accent 2, Darker 50%**. Under **Border**, click **Middle Border** and **Bottom Border**. Click **OK**.

f. With the range **D8:D9** still selected, in the **Alignment group**, click **Align Right**. Right-click over the selected range, on the mini toolbar, click the **Format Painter**, and then select the range **D11:D15** to copy the format.

g. Select the range **B18:F32**. Right-click over the selected range and click **Format Cells**. In the **Format Cells** dialog box, click the **Border tab**. Under **Presets**, click **Outline** and **Inside**, and then click **OK**. Select the range **B18:F18**, hold down Ctrl and select the range **F19:F32**. In the **Font group**, click the **Fill Color arrow**, and then under **Theme Colors**, in the sixth column, click the third color— **Orange, Accent 2, Lighter 60%**.

h. Press Ctrl + Home. Click the **File tab**, on the left click **Print** to view the Print Preview. On the left, click **Save** to save and return to your workbook.

2 To construct a formula to multiply the Quantity times the Unit Price, in cell **F19**, type **=d19*e19** and then on the **Formula Bar**, click **Enter**. Use the fill handle to copy the formula in cell **F19** down through cell **F31**. Click cell **F32**. On the **Home tab**, in the **Editing group**, click **AutoSum**. In the **Formula Bar**, be sure the range displays as **F19:F31**, and then press Enter. Select the range **E19:E31**. In the **Number group**, click **Comma Style**. Click cell **F19**, hold down Ctrl, and then click cell **F32**. In the **Number group**, click **Accounting Number Format**. Select the range **F20:F31**, and then click **Comma Style**. Select the range **D19:D31**, and then in the **Styles group**, click **Cell Styles**, and then under **Number Format**, click **Comma [0]**.

a. Select the range **D32:E32**. In the **Alignment group**, click **Merge & Center**. Type **Order Total** and press Enter. Click cell **D32** again, and then in the **Alignment group**, click **Align Right**. Apply **Bold**.

b. Select the range **B32:C32**, right-click, and then click **Format Cells**. On the **Border tab**, in the **Border** preview area, click **Left Border**, **Middle Border**, and **Bottom Border** to remove these borders from the preview—be sure the right and top border lines remain in the preview area. Click **OK**.

c. Press Ctrl + Home to make cell **A1** the active cell. On the **Insert tab**, in the **Illustrations group**, click **Pictures**. In the **Insert Picture** dialog box, navigate to your student data files, and then insert the file **e06D_Logo**. With the image selected, click the **Picture Tools Format tab**, in the **Picture Styles group**, click **More**, and then locate and click the **Simple Frame, Black**. **Save** your workbook.

(Project 6D Purchase Order continues on the next page)

d. Scroll so that **row 16** is at the top of the Excel window. Then, click cell **A18**. On the **Insert tab**, in the **Text group**, click **WordArt**, and then in the first row, click the third WordArt—**Fill – Orange, Accent 2, Outline – Accent 2**. Type **Purchase Order Form** Select the text you just typed, right-click, and then from the mini toolbar, set the **Font Size** to **20**. Drag the rotation handle to the left until the WordArt is vertical. Then, drag the WordArt image to **column A** and align the top of the image with the top of cell **A18**—centered in the column. At the lower edge of the WordArt image, point to the center resize handle and drag down so the end of the image aligns at the lower edge of cell **A32**.

e. With the WordArt still selected, on the **Format tab**, in the **Shape Styles group**, click the **Shape Fill arrow**, click **Texture**, and then in the fourth row, click the second texture—**Recycled paper**. Click any cell to deselect the WordArt, and then press Ctrl + Home.

3 Select the range **D8:D9**, hold down Ctrl, select the range **D11:D15** and the range **B19:E31**. With the three ranges selected, on the **Home tab**, in the **Cells group**, click **Format**, and then click **Format Cells**. In the **Format Cells** dialog box, click the **Protection tab**. Click to clear the check mark from the **Locked** check box. Click **OK**.

a. In the **Cells group**, click **Format**, and then under **Protection**, click **Protect Sheet**. Under **Allow all users of this worksheet to:** leave the first two check boxes selected. At the top of the dialog box, be sure the **Protect worksheet and contents of locked cells** check box is selected. In the **Password to unprotect sheet** box, type **goseries** Click **OK**. In the displayed **Confirm Password** dialog box, type **goseries** to confirm the password, and then click **OK** to close both dialog boxes. Press Ctrl + Home and then click Save.

b. From the Page Layout tab, display the Page Setup dialog box. Center the worksheet horizontally and add a custom footer with the file name in the Left section.

c. Display the **document properties**. As the **Tags**, type **purchase order form, template**

d. On the left click **Print** to view the Print Preview, and then on the left, click **Save** to save your template and return to the worksheet window.

4 To create a purchase order from your template, display the **Save As** dialog box, and then set the **Save as type** box to **Excel Workbook**—the first choice at the top of the list. Navigate to your **Excel Chapter 6** folder, and then in the **File name** box, type **Lastname_Firstname_6D_Hancock_PO** Click **Save**.

a. Click cell **D8**, type **October 18, 2016** and press Enter—Excel applies the default date format. As the Purchase Order Number, type **S-6255** and then press Enter two times to move to cell **D11**. Beginning in cell **D11**, enter the vendor information as follows:

Vendor Name	**Hancock Industries**
Address	**191 Oak Avenue**
City, State, ZIP	**Plano, TX 75074**
Phone	**214.555.0222**
Email	**orders@hancock.net**

b. Click cell **B19**, and then complete the order by entering the following items as shown in the following table, pressing Tab to move from cell to cell.

ITEM	DESCRIPTION	QUANTITY	UNIT PRICE
Mugs	**Green logo coffee mugs**	125	3.25
Pens	**Black logo fine tip**	700	0.65
Notepads	**Green logo, lined**	200	1.50

c. From the Page Layout tab, display the Page Setup dialog box. Center the worksheet horizontally and add a custom footer with the file name in the Left section.

d. Display the **document properties**. Be sure your name displays in the **Author** box. As the Subject,

(Project 6D Purchase Order continues on the next page)

type your course name and section #. Change the **Tags** to **Hancock, promotional items**

e. On the left, click Save. If directed by your instructor to do so, submit a paper printout of your worksheet (you do **not** need to submit your template file), an electronic image of your worksheet that looks like a printed document, or your original Excel file. If required by your instructor, print or create an electronic version of your worksheet with formulas displayed. In the upper right corner of the Excel window, click **Close**.

END | You have completed Project 6D

Mastering Excel Project 6E Hires

In the following Project, you will assist Linda Wong, Employer Relations Manager, in tracking the number of people who get hired by an employer at each fair. You will create and modify a chart to display the number of people hired at the fairs over a five-year period, create a diagram of the communities served, and create an organizational chart for staff at the Job Fair. Your completed worksheets will look similar to Figure 6.46.

Apply 6A skills from these Objectives:

1. Create and Format Sparklines and a Column Chart
2. Create and Format a Line Chart
3. Create and Modify a SmartArt Graphic
4. Create and Modify an Organization Chart

PROJECT FILES

For Project 6E, you will need the following file:

e06E_Hires

You will save your workbook as:

Lastname_Firstname_6E_Hires

PROJECT RESULTS

FIGURE 6.46

Excel 2016, Windows 10, Microsoft Corporation.

(Project 6E Hires continues on the next page)

1 Start Excel. From the student files that accompany this chapter, open **e06E_Hires**. Using your own name, save the file in your **Excel Chapter 6** folder as **Lastname_Firstname_6E_Hires**

2 Using the data in the range **B4:F10**, insert **Sparklines** using the **Line** format. Place the sparklines in the range adjacent to the **2016** column, show the **High Point** and **Last Point**, and then apply **Sparkline Style Accent 4, Darker 25%**.

3 Type **Trend** in the cell above the sparklines.

4 Using the data for the years and for each location (not the totals) and the **Recommended Charts** command, create a **Clustered Column** chart on a separate chart sheet named **Hires by Location Chart**

5 Display the **Change Chart Type** dialog box. On the **All Charts tab**, if necessary, on the left click **Column**, and then on the right, at the top of the dialog box, click the fourth chart icon—**3-D Clustered Column**. Click **OK**.

6 Apply **Chart Style 5** to the chart, and add a chart title above the chart with the text **Job Hires by Location** Set the title's font size to **28**.

7 Format the **Chart Area** with a solid fill using **Olive Green, Accent 3, Lighter 80%**. Format the **Plot Area** with a solid fill two shades darker—**Olive Green, Accent 3, Lighter 40%**.

8 Format the floor and the side wall with a solid color using **Aqua, Accent 5, Darker 50%** and **60%** transparency. Add the chart element Axis Title to the vertical axis with the text **Number of Attendees Hired** and change the font size to **16**.

9 On the **Job Hires by Location** worksheet, using the data for **Dallas** *including the years* insert a **Line with Markers** line chart. Resize the chart to position the upper left corner within cell **A13** and the lower right corner within cell **G26**.

10 Change the chart title to **Successful Job Hires in Dallas** and set the title's font size to **16**. Format the **Vertical (Value) Axis** so that the **Minimum** value is **400** and the **Major unit** is **25**

11 Add a **Linear Trendline**. Format the **Line Color** of the trendline with **Orange, Accent 6** and set **Width** of the line to **2 pt**.

12 Insert a new sheet and name it **List Chart** In cell **A1**, type **Three Largest Communities We Serve** Merge and center this title across the range **A1:G1** and apply the **Title** cell style.

13 Insert a **SmartArt** graphic using the **Vertical Box List**. In the three boxes type, in order, **Dallas** and **Fort Worth** and **Carrollton**

14 Resize the graphic to position the upper left corner in cell **A3** and the lower right corner in cell **G16**. Apply the **Inset** style and change the colors to **Colorful Range – Accent Colors 4 to 5**. Click cell **A1** to deselect the graphic.

15 Insert a new sheet and name it **Organization Chart** In cell **A1**, type **Job Fair Booth Installation Services Structure** Merge and center this title across the range **A1:H1** and apply the **Title** cell style.

16 Insert a **SmartArt** graphic using **Horizontal Multi-Level Hierarchy**. In the vertical box, type **Booth Manager** and in the three remaining boxes, type **Safety Inspectors** and **Electricians** and **Carpenters** Resize the graphic to position the upper left corner within cell **A4** and the lower right corner within cell **H16**.

17 Apply the **Subtle Effect** style and change the colors to **Colorful Range – Accent Colors 4 to 5**. Click cell **A1**.

18 Display the **Hires by Location chart sheet**. From the **Page Layout tab**, use the Dialog Box Launcher to display the **Page Setup** dialog box. Insert a **Custom Footer** with the **File Name** in the **Left section**.

19 Display the **Job Hires by Location** sheet. Hold down Ctrl and select the remaining two worksheets to group the three sheets. Insert a **Custom Footer** with the **File Name** in the **Left section**, and then center the sheets horizontally.

20 Click the **File tab** to display **Backstage** view. On the right, at the bottom of the **Properties** list, click **Show All Properties**. On the list of **Properties**, in the **Tags** box, type **attendance statistics, organization charts** In the **Subject** box, type your course name and section #. Under **Related People**, be sure that your name displays as the author. If necessary, right-click the author name, click **Edit Property**, type your name, click outside of the **Edit person** dialog box, and then click **OK**.

(Project 6E Hires continues on the next page)

21 On the left, click **Print**. Under **Settings**, click the **Print Active Sheets arrow**, and then click **Print Entire Workbook**. At the bottom of the window, click **Next Page** 🖫 to scroll through the worksheets. Save your workbook. If directed by your instructor to do so, submit a paper printout of each of the four worksheets, an electronic image of each of your four worksheets that looks like a printed document, or your original Excel file. If required by your instructor, print or create an electronic version of your worksheet with formulas displayed. In the upper right corner of the Excel window, click **Close**.

END | You have completed Project 6E

Mastering Excel Project 6F Event Budget

Apply 6B skills from these Objectives:

5 Create an Excel Template

6 Protect a Worksheet

7 Create a Worksheet Based on a Template

In the following Mastering Excel project, you will create a budget template for the Dallas location of the Dallas-Ft. Worth Job Fair. You will also create a worksheet based on the budget template for review by Milton Hyken, Dallas Job Fair Director. Your completed worksheets will look similar to Figure 6.47.

PROJECT FILES

For Project 6F, you will need the following files:

e06F_Dallas_Budget
e06F_Logo

You will save your workbooks as:

Lastname_Firstname_6F_Dallas_Budget
Lastname_Firstname_6F_Dallas_Budget_Template
(will not be submitted for grading)

PROJECT RESULTS

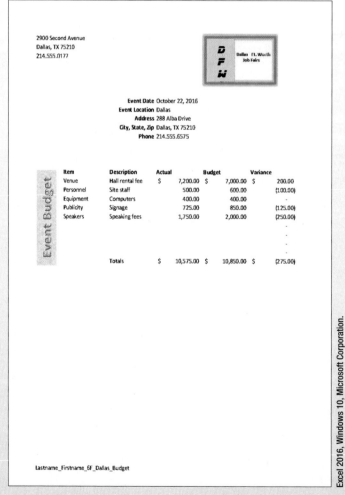

FIGURE 6.47

(Project 6F Event Budget continues on the next page)

Mastering Excel Project 6F Event Budget (continued)

1 Start Excel, and then from the student data files that accompany this chapter, open **e06F_Dallas_Budget**.

2 In cell **B16**, type **Item** and press Tab. In cell **C16**, type **Description** In cell **D16**, type **Actual** In cell **E16**, type **Budget** In cell **F16**, type **Variance** Click cell **C26** and type **Totals**

3 To the ranges **C8:C12** and **B16:F16**, apply **Bold**. To the range **C8:C12**, apply **Align Right**. To the range **D8:D12**, apply **Align Left**. Widen columns **B:F** to **15 (110 pixels)**.

4 To construct a formula to compute the Variance (Variance = Actual − Budget) for each budget item, in cell **F17**, type **=d17-e17** and copy the formula through cell **F25**.

5 In the range **D26:F26**, insert appropriate formulas to sum these columns. To the range **D18:F25**, apply **Comma Style**. To the ranges **D17:F17** and **D26:F26**, apply **Accounting Number Format**. (Remember that you are creating a template—so there is no data entered yet.)

6 In cell **E1**, insert the picture **e06F_Logo**. Click cell **A16**, insert a **WordArt** using **Fill – Blue, Accent 5, Outline – Background 1, Hard Shadow – Accent 5**—in the third row, the third WordArt. As the text, type **Event Budget** and set the **Font Size** to **24**.

7 Rotate the WordArt 90 degrees to the left, and resize it to fill the range **A16:A26**. In the **Shape Styles group**, click **Shape Fill**, click **Texture**, and then click **Blue tissue paper**.

8 Select the ranges **D8:D12** and **B17:E25**. Remove the **Locked** formatting from the selected cells, and then protect the worksheet. Be sure the check box at the top and the first two check boxes in the list are selected, and as the password type **goseries**

9 Insert a footer in the **left section** with the file name. Add your name, course information, and the tags **budget template** to the **document properties**, and then check the **Print Preview**. On the left click **Save As**, and then using your own name, save your workbook as an **Excel Template** in your **Excel Chapter 6** folder as **Lastname_Firstname_6F_Dallas_Budget_Template**

10 To create a new budget report using the template as your model, display the **Save As** dialog box again, and then **Save** the template as an **Excel Workbook** in your chapter folder as **Lastname_Firstname_6F_Dallas_Budget** Enter the following data:

Event Date	October 22, 2016
Event Location	Dallas
Address	288 Alba Drive
City, State, ZIP	Dallas, TX 75210
Phone	214.555.6575

11 Beginning in cell **B17**, complete the order by entering the following items as shown in Table 1.

ITEM	DESCRIPTION	ACTUAL	BUDGET
Venue	Hall rental fee	7200	7000
Personnel	Site staff	500	600
Equipment	Computers	400	400
Publicity	Signage	725	850
Speakers	Speaking fees	1750	2000

12 Display the document properties. Be sure your name displays in the Author box. As the **Subject**, type your course name and section #. Change the **Tags** to **Dallas, event budget** Check the Print Preview to be sure the file name updated and displays in the left section of the footer. On the left, click Save.

13 If directed by your instructor to do so, submit a paper printout of your Lastname_Firstname_6F_Dallas_Budget worksheet (you do not need to submit your Lastname_Firstname_ 6F_Dallas_Budget_Template file), an electronic image of your worksheet that looks like a printed document, or your original Excel file. If required by your instructor, print or create an electronic version of your worksheet with formulas displayed. In the upper right corner of the Excel window, click Close.

END | You have completed Project 6F

Mastering Excel Project 6G Internships and Travel Template

Apply 6A and 6B skills from these Objectives:

1 Create and Format Sparklines and a Column Chart

2 Create and Format a Line Chart

3 Create and Modify a SmartArt Graphic

4 Create and Modify an Organization Chart

5 Create an Excel Template

6 Protect a Worksheet

7 Create a Worksheet Based on a Template

In the following project, you will assist Ann Takei, Internship Coordinator, in tracking the number of internships by industry at each job fair and in creating a template to use for travel expenses. Your completed worksheets will look similar to Figure 6.48.

PROJECT FILES

For Project 6G, you will need the following file:

e06G_Internships_Travel

You will save your workbooks as:

Lastname_Firstname_6G_Travel_Report
Lastname_Firstname_6G_Travel_Template (will not be submitted for grading)

PROJECT RESULTS

FIGURE 6.48

(Project 6G Internships and Travel Template continues on the next page)

Mastering Excel | Project 6G Internships and Travel Template (continued)

1 Start Excel. From the student data files that accompany this chapter, locate and open **e06G_Internships_Travel**.

2 On the **Internships by Industry** worksheet, in the range **G4:G10**, insert line **Sparklines** using the values in the range **B4:F10**.

3 Format the Sparklines to show the high point and the last point. Apply the **Sparkline Style Accent 4, (no dark or light)**.

4 Create a **Line with Markers** chart style using the ranges **A3:F3** and **A7:F7**. Position the chart so that the upper left corner of the chart aligns with the upper left corner of cell **A13**.

5 Change the chart title to **Internships Available in Technology**

6 Edit the **Vertical (Value) Axis** to set the **Minimum** to **35** and the **Major unit** to **5**

7 Format the **Plot Area** with a **Green, Accent 6, Lighter 80%** solid fill. Format the **Chart Area** with **Green, Accent 6, Lighter 40%** solid fill.

8 Insert a **Linear Trendline** and change the width of the line to **2.5 pt**.

9 On the **List Chart** worksheet, insert a SmartArt graphic using the **Pyramid List** style. Position the SmartArt so that the upper left corner of the graphic aligns with the upper left corner of cell **A3**.

10 In the SmartArt, type **Paid** in the top text box. Type **Work-Study** in the second text box, and **Unpaid** in the last text box.

11 Apply the **Inset 3-D** SmartArt style to the graphic. Change the colors to **Colored Fill – Accent 1**. Click cell **A1**.

12 On the **Organization Chart** worksheet, insert a SmartArt graphic using the **Hierarchy List** style. Position the SmartArt so that the upper left corner of the graphic aligns with the upper left corner of cell **A3**.

13 In the SmartArt, on the left, type **Ann Takei, Internship Coordinator** in the top box and **Dennis Jones, Specialist** in the second box and **Corey Finn, Specialist** in the third box. On the right, type **Shani Kuhlman,**

Work-Study Coordinator in the first box and **Anand Singh, Specialist** in the second box and **Viv Lopez, Specialist** in the third box. Click cell **A1**.

14 Display the **Save As** dialog box. In the **Save as type** box, click the arrow, and then change the file type to **Excel Template**. From the **navigation pane**, navigate to your **Excel Chapter 6** folder, and then using your own name, as the **File name** type **Lastname_Firstname_6G_Travel_Template** and click **Save**. On the **Travel Expenses** worksheet, in cell **H22** enter a formula that will add the contents of the range **H15:H21**. Apply the **Total** cell style to cell **H22**.

15 Remove the Locked formatting from the ranges **D8:D10** and **A15:G21**. Protect the worksheet using the default selections and the password **goseries**. **Save** your workbook.

16 Display the **Save As** dialog box, navigate to your chapter folder, change the file type to **Excel Workbook**, and then using your own name, as the **File name** type **Lastname_Firstname_6G_Travel_Report**

17 Select all of the sheets, display the **Page Setup** dialog box, and then insert a **Custom Footer** with the file name in the left section. Ungroup the sheets, and then check that the first three worksheets display in **Portrait orientation** and the last worksheet displays in **Landscape orientation**. Check the document properties; as the **Tags** type **travel template** and as the **Subject**, type your course name and section number. Be sure your name displays as the author.

18 Display the print preview, examine your worksheets for any errors or changes. On the left, click **Save** to save your workbook and redisplay the Excel window.

19 If directed by your instructor to do so, submit a paper printout of your Lastname_Firstname_6G_Travel_Report workbook (you do not need to submit your template file), an electronic image of your worksheet that looks like a printed document, or your original Excel file. If required by your instructor, print or create an electronic version of your worksheet with formulas displayed. In the upper right corner of the Excel window, click Close.

END | You have completed Project 6G

CONTENT-BASED ASSESSMENTS (CRITICAL THINKING)

GO! Fix It	Project 6H Operations Chart	MyITLab
GO! Make It	Project 6I Advertisers	MyITLab
GO! Solve It	Project 6J Sponsors	MyITLab
GO! Solve It	Project 6K Time Card	

PROJECT FILES

For Project 6K, you will need the following file:

e06K_Time_Card

You will save your workbook as:

Lastname_Firstname_6K_Time_Template

Open the file e06K_Time_Card and save it as a template in your chapter folder with the name **Lastname_Firstname_6K_Time_Template** Insert a formula to calculate daily pay (Regular Hours x Rate Per Hour using an absolute cell reference), a formula to total the hours for the week, and a formula to calculate the total pay. Apply appropriate number and financial formatting. Reposition the WordArt above the Time Card chart. Unlock the cells in which an individual would enter variable data, and then protect the sheet with the password **goseries** Insert the file name in the footer, add appropriate information to the document properties including the tags **timecard, payroll** and submit as directed by your instructor.

Performance Level

	Exemplary: You consistently applied the relevant skills	Proficient: You sometimes, but not always, applied the relevant skills	Developing: You rarely or never applied the relevant skills
Place WordArt Object and Apply Financial Formatting	Appropriate formulas, cell formatting, and WordArt placement are applied.	Appropriate formulas, cell formatting, and WordArt placement are partially applied.	Appropriate formulas, cell formatting, and WordArt placement are not applied.
Lock Formulas	Formula cells are locked and variable data cells are unlocked.	Only one of the formula cells or variable data cells has the locked or unlocked feature applied appropriately.	Formula cells are unlocked and variable data cells are locked.
Protect Worksheet	The worksheet is protected with the password goseries.	The worksheet is protected but not with the password goseries.	The worksheet is not protected with a password.

Performance Criteria

END | You have completed Project 6K

OUTCOME-BASED ASSESSMENTS (CRITICAL THINKING)

RUBRIC

The following outcomes-based assessments are open-ended assessments. That is, there is no specific correct result; your result will depend on your approach to the information provided. Make Professional Quality your goal. Use the following scoring rubric to guide you in how to approach the problem and then to evaluate how well your approach solves the problem.

The *criteria*—Software Mastery, Content, Format and Layout, and Process—represent the knowledge and skills you have gained that you can apply to solving the problem. The *levels of performance*—Professional Quality, Approaching Professional Quality, or Needs Quality Improvements—help you and your instructor evaluate your result.

	Your completed project is of Professional Quality if you:	Your completed project is Approaching Professional Quality if you:	Your completed project Needs Quality Improvements if you:
1-Software Mastery	Choose and apply the most appropriate skills, tools, and features and identify efficient methods to solve the problem.	Choose and apply some appropriate skills, tools, and features, but not in the most efficient manner.	Choose inappropriate skills, tools, or features, or are inefficient in solving the problem.
2-Content	Construct a solution that is clear and well organized, contains content that is accurate, appropriate to the audience and purpose, and is complete. Provide a solution that contains no errors of spelling, grammar, or style.	Construct a solution in which some components are unclear, poorly organized, inconsistent, or incomplete. Misjudge the needs of the audience. Have some errors in spelling, grammar, or style, but the errors do not detract from comprehension.	Construct a solution that is unclear, incomplete, or poorly organized, contains some inaccurate or inappropriate content, and contains many errors of spelling, grammar, or style. Do not solve the problem.
3-Format and Layout	Format and arrange all elements to communicate information and ideas, clarify function, illustrate relationships, and indicate relative importance.	Apply appropriate format and layout features to some elements, but not others. Overuse features, causing minor distraction.	Apply format and layout that does not communicate information or ideas clearly. Do not use format and layout features to clarify function, illustrate relationships, or indicate relative importance. Use available features excessively, causing distraction.
4-Process	Use an organized approach that integrates planning, development, self-assessment, revision, and reflection.	Demonstrate an organized approach in some areas, but not others; or, use an insufficient process of organization throughout.	Do not use an organized approach to solve the problem.

GO! Think   Project 6L Tech Industry

PROJECT FILES

For Project 6L, you will need the following file:

e06L_Tech_Industry

You will save your workbook as:

Lastname_Firstname_6L_Tech_Industry

From your student files, open the file e06L_Tech_Industry, and then save it in your chapter folder as **Lastname_Firstname_6L_Tech_Industry** Format the data attractively, add appropriate formulas, add sparklines, and insert a line chart in the sheet that tracks the data for the Irving location. Create a 3-D chart on a separate page based on the data in the worksheet, and format it attractively. Change the Fort Worth 2016 data point from 84 to 96. Insert the file name in the footer on each page, format each sheet for printing, add appropriate information to the document properties including the tags **technology employers** and submit as directed by your instructor.

END | You have completed Project 6L

GO! Think   Project 6M Location List   MyITLab

Build from
Scratch

You and GO!   Project 6N Job Finding   MyITLab

Creating PivotTables and PivotCharts

PROJECT 7A

OUTCOMES
Query large amounts of data, subtotal and aggregate numeric data, and filter and group data to analyze for relationships and trends.

OBJECTIVES

1. Create a PivotTable Report
2. Use Slicers and Search Filters
3. Modify a PivotTable
4. Create a PivotChart

PROJECT 7B

OUTCOMES
Use a Data Model to analyze data from multiple sources.

OBJECTIVES

5. Create a PivotTable from a Data Model
6. Create and Format a 3-D Pie PivotChart

Zhu difeng/Fotolia

In This Chapter

In this chapter, you will create PivotTables and PivotChart reports. Organizations gather large amounts of data, but the data is not useful until it is organized in a manner that reveals patterns or trends. You will use Excel to subtotal, aggregate, and summarize data, and you will extract information from data by organizing the data into groups from which trends, comparisons, patterns, and relationships can be determined. You will also create different views of the data so that more than one pattern or trend can be observed.

The projects in this chapter relate to **Golden Grove**, a growing city located between Los Angeles and San Diego.

Just 10 years ago the population was under 100,000; today it has grown to almost 300,000. Community leaders have always focused on quality and economic development in decisions on housing, open space, education, and infrastructure, and encourage best environmental practices, making the city a model for other communities its size around the United States. The city provides many recreational and cultural opportunities with a large park system, thriving arts, and a friendly business atmosphere.

PivotTable and PivotChart

PROJECT ACTIVITIES

In Activities 7.01 through 7.13, you will create a PivotTable and a PivotChart that summarize calls handled at fire department stations and police department precincts during the first quarter of the year for the City of Golden Grove. Your completed worksheets will look similar to Figure 7.1.

 PROJECT FILES If your instructor wants you to submit Project 7A in the MyITLab Grader system, log into MyITLab, locate Grader Project 7A, and then download the files for the project.

Please always review the downloaded Grader instructions before beginning.

For Project 7A, you will need the following file:
e07A_Fire_Police

You will save your workbook as:
Lastname_Firstname_7A_Fire_Police

PROJECT RESULTS

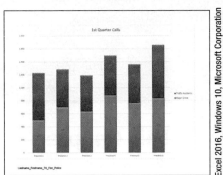

FIGURE 7.1 Project 7A PivotTable and PivotChart

NOTE	If You Are Using a Touchscreen
	Tap an item to click it.
	Press and hold for a few seconds to right-click; release when the information or commands display.
	Touch the screen with two or more fingers and then pinch together to zoom out or stretch your fingers apart to zoom in.
	Slide your finger on the screen to scroll—slide left to scroll right and slide right to scroll left.
	Slide to rearrange—similar to dragging with a mouse.
	Swipe to select—slide an item a short distance with a quick movement—to select an item and bring up commands, if any.

Objective 1 Create a PivotTable Report

GO! Learn How
Video E7-1

A ***list*** is a series of rows that contains related data with column titles in the first row. A long list of numerical data is not useful until it is organized in a way that is meaningful to the reader. To combine and compare large amounts of data, use Excel's PivotTable report—also called simply a ***PivotTable***—which is an interactive Excel report that summarizes and helps you to analyze large amounts of data.

Using a PivotTable, you can show the same data in a table in more than one arrangement. For example, you can manipulate the rows and columns of the table to view or summarize the data from different perspectives. In this manner, you pivot—turn—the information around to get varying views of the data. A PivotTable is especially useful when you want to analyze related totals, such as when you have a long list of numbers to sum and you want to compare several facts about each total. The ***source data*** for a PivotTable must be formatted in columns and rows, and can be located in an Excel worksheet or an external source.

Activity 7.01 | Creating a PivotTable Report

MOS
4.2.1

The data you use to create your PivotTable should be in the format of a list. Subsequent rows should contain data appropriate to its column title, and there should be no blank rows. Excel will use your column titles as the ***field names***—the categories of data. The data in each column should be of the same type. In this Activity, you will use a PivotTable to analyze quarterly fire and police department call and response data.

ALERT! **To submit as an autograded project, log into MyITLab and download the files for this Project, and begin with those files instead of e07A_Fire_Police.**

1 ▶ Start Excel. From your student files, open the file **e07A_Fire_Police**, and then display the **Save As** dialog box. Navigate to the location where you are storing your files for this chapter, create a new folder named **Excel Chapter 7** and then **Save** the workbook in the **Excel Chapter 7** folder as **Lastname_Firstname_7A_Fire_Police**

This worksheet displays three months of calls that must be summarized in a PivotTable. There are two classifications for fire department calls and three classifications for police department calls.

2 Click cell **A2**. On the **Insert tab**, in the **Tables group**, click **Recommended PivotTables**. Compare your screen with Figure 7.2.

The Recommended PivotTables dialog box displays and a moving border surrounds the range of data—this is referred to as the source data. A cell in your data must be active before you create a PivotTable so that you can identify the source of your data.

FIGURE 7.2

3 In the **Recommended PivotTables** dialog box, scroll down, point to each preview to display a ScreenTip, and then click the fifth PivotTable—**Sum of Number by Location (+)**. Compare your screen with Figure 7.3.

Excel suggests PivotTables based on the organization of your data. If the Recommended PivotTables do not provide an appropriate layout for your data, you can create a custom PivotTable by clicking Blank PivotTable. In this case, the Sum of Number by Location (+) layout is a good starting point for your PivotTable.

🔄 **BY TOUCH**   Select the range A2:E80 and tap Quick Analysis. Tap the Tables tab and point to each PivotTable example to view a preview of the selection, then tap the table you wish to create.

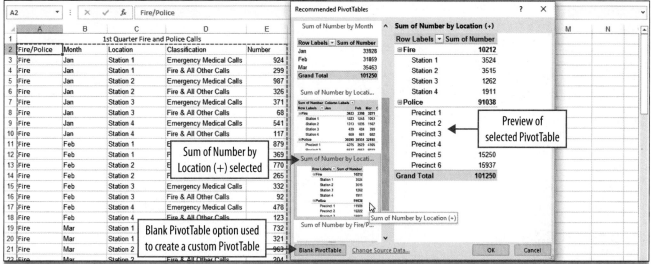

FIGURE 7.3

Excel 2016, Windows 10, Microsoft Corporation

4 Click **OK**.

Excel adds a new sheet—Sheet1—to the workbook. On the left side of the new worksheet, Excel generates a PivotTable report.

On the right side of the window, Excel displays the ***PivotTable Fields pane***—a window in which you can arrange the fields in the PivotTable. The upper portion, referred to as the ***field section***, lists the field names—the column titles from your source data. Use the field section to add fields to and remove fields from the PivotTable. The lower portion, referred to as the ***layout section***, displays four areas where you can build the PivotTable by rearranging and repositioning fields. On the ribbon, the PivotTable Tools include two contextual tabs—Analyze and Design.

More **Knowledge**	If your source data is already formatted as an Excel table, you can create a PivotTable easily by selecting a single cell within the source data, and then on the Design tab, in the Tools group, click Summarize with PivotTable.

5 **Save** 🖫 your workbook, and then take a moment to study Figure 7.4 and the table in Figure 7.5.

FIGURE 7.4

ALERT!	**If the PivotTable Fields Pane Does Not Display**

If the PivotTable Fields pane is not visible, click any cell in the PivotTable report to display it. If you accidently click Close at the upper right corner of the PivotTable Fields pane, you can redisplay it by clicking any cell in the PivotTable report to display the PivotTable Tools Contextual tabs on the ribbon. On the Analyze tab, in the Show group, click Field List.

PIVOTTABLE SCREEN ELEMENTS	
SCREEN ELEMENT	**DESCRIPTION**
PivotTable Fields pane	A window that lists at the top, all of the fields—column titles—from the source data for use in the PivotTable and at the bottom, an area in which you can arrange the fields in the PivotTable.
FILTERS area	An area to position fields by which you want to filter the PivotTable, enabling you to display a subset of data in the PivotTable report.
COLUMNS area	An area to position fields that you want to display as columns in the PivotTable. Field names placed here become column titles, and the data is grouped in columns by these titles.
ROWS area	An area to position fields that you want to display as rows in the PivotTable report. Field names placed here become row titles, and the data is grouped by these row titles.
VALUES area	An area to position fields that contain data that is summarized in a PivotTable or PivotChart. The data placed here is usually numeric or financial in nature and the data is summarized—summed. You can also perform other basic calculations such as finding the average, the minimum, or the maximum.
Layout section	The lower portion of the PivotTable Fields pane containing the four areas for layout; use this area to rearrange and reposition fields in the PivotTable.
Field section	The upper portion of the PivotTable Fields pane containing the fields—column titles—from your source data; use this area to add fields to and remove fields from the PivotTable.

FIGURE 7.5

4.2.2

A PivotTable can combine and compare large amounts of data for the purpose of analyzing related totals. By viewing the combined information in different ways, you can answer questions.

There are two ways to place the data from your list into the PivotTable report. From the PivotTable Fields pane, you can drag field names from the field section at the top and then drop them into one of the four areas in the layout section at the bottom. Or, you can select a field name in the field section at the top, and Excel will place the field in a default location based on the field's data type. If you want an arrangement other than the one you get by default, you can move fields from one location to another by dragging them between the various areas in the layout section.

1 To the right of the worksheet, in the **PivotTable Fields pane**, in the **field section**, notice that the **Fire/Police** check box is selected, and Excel placed the field in the **ROWS area** of the **layout section**. In the **layout section**, in the **ROWS area**, point to **Fire/Police**, hold down the left mouse button, and then drag the field name upward into the **FILTERS area** above.

> By default, non-numeric fields are added to the ROWS area and numeric fields are added to the VALUES area, but you can move fields as desired. For example, you can use a PivotTable to analyze the fire and police calls separately.
>
> You can *filter* the report based on the *Fire/Police* field by moving this field to the FILTERS area. When you filter a report, you limit the display of data to only specific information. As you drag, a small blue icon attaches to the mouse pointer to indicate you are moving a field. *Fire/Police* displays in the FILTERS area. On the left, the Fire/Police field is added at the top of the PivotTable report.

⟳ ANOTHER WAY   In the ROWS area, click the Fire/Police arrow, and then click Move to Report Filter.

2 In the **PivotTable Fields pane**, in the **field section**, verify that the **Location** field check box is selected.

> In the layout section, the non-numeric Location field displays in the ROWS area. The Location names—Precincts and Stations—display as rows in the PivotTable report. There are six police department precincts and four fire department stations.

3 In the **PivotTable Fields pane**, in the **field section**, select the **Classification** field check box. In the PivotTable, right-click any one of the *Precinct* or *Station* names, point to **Expand/Collapse**, and then click **Expand Entire Field**. Compare your screen with Figure 7.6.

> In the layout section, the Classification field displays as the second field in the ROWS area. In the PivotTable, the Classification names are added as indented row headings under each police precinct location and under each fire station location. A row that is lower in position in the ROWS area is nested within the row immediately above it. Notice that, under each precinct location, only the call classifications related to the police department display. Likewise, as you scroll down, under station locations, only the call classifications related to the fire department display.

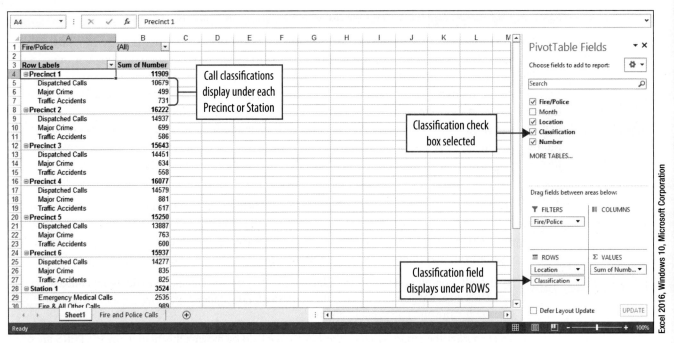

FIGURE 7.6

4 ▶ In the **PivotTable Fields pane**, from the **field section**, drag the **Month** field down to the **COLUMNS area**. Verify that **Sum of Number** displays in the **VALUES area**. Compare your screen with Figure 7.7.

The PivotTable report is complete; the result is a group of related totals. The arrangement of fields in the layout section reflects the arrangement of the data in the PivotTable report. The long list of figures from the Fire and Police Calls worksheet is summarized, and you can make comparisons among the data. *Sum of Number* displays in cell A3, which refers to the field name *Number*—the number of calls for each call classification has been summed.

FIGURE 7.7

5 On the **Design tab**, in the **PivotTable Styles group**, click **More** ⊡, and then under **Medium**, in the second row, click the fourth style—**Pivot Style Medium 11**. Compare your screen with Figure 7.8.

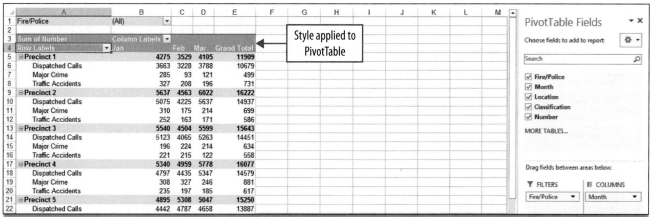

FIGURE 7.8

Excel 2016, Windows 10, Microsoft Corporation

6 Click cell **B5**, point to the selected cell, and then notice the ScreenTip that displays.

Now that the data is organized and the number of calls calculated, you can view and compare various facts about the data. For example, you can see that in January, in Precinct 1, there were a total of 4275 calls, compared with 3529 calls in February. This summary information was not available in the original worksheet. By summarizing and pivoting (turning) data in various ways, you can see different information. Additionally, ScreenTips describe the cell contents.

7 **Close** ⊠ the **PivotTable Fields pane**, and then **Save** 🖫 your workbook.

Objective 2   Use Slicers and Search Filters

GO! Learn How
Video E7-2

You can filter a PivotTable by using a search filter or by using slicers. **Slicers** are filtering controls with buttons that enable you to drill down through large amounts of data. Slicers display as movable objects on your worksheet in the same manner as charts and shapes and make it easy to see what filters are currently applied.

Activity 7.03 │ Using a Slicer to Filter a PivotTable

4.2.3

Limiting the data displayed enables you to focus on parts of the data without the distraction of data you do not need to see. In this Activity, you will limit the data to only the fire department information and then determine which fire department station had the lowest number of emergency medical calls.

1 On the **Analyze tab**, in the **Filter group**, click **Insert Slicer**. Compare your screen with Figure 7.9.

The Insert Slicers dialog box displays all the field names from your PivotTable report.

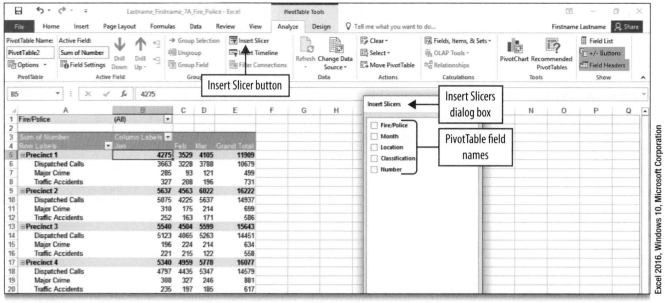

FIGURE 7.9

2 ▶ Select the **Fire/Police** check box, and then click **OK**. Compare your screen with Figure 7.10.

The Fire/Police slicer displays.

FIGURE 7.10

3 ▶ Point to the upper border of the **Fire/Police** slicer to display the 🔧 pointer, and then drag the slicer up to align with the top of the PivotTable and to the right so that it is not blocking your view of the PivotTable. Compare your screen with Figure 7.11.

A slicer includes a *slicer header* that indicates the category of the slicer items, *filtering buttons* to select the item by which to filter, a Multi-Select button, and a Clear Filter button. When a filtering button is selected, the item is included in the filter. The Multi-Select button enables multiple selection of filtering buttons. *Clear Filter* removes a filter.

FIGURE 7.11

4 On the **Options tab**, in the **Slicer Styles group**, click **More**, and then under **Dark**, click the second slicer style—**Slicer Style Dark 2**. Compare your screen with Figure 7.12.

You can apply various styles to slicers to make them easier to differentiate or to match the PivotTable report.

FIGURE 7.12

5 In the PivotTable report, notice that the police department precincts display first. On the **Fire/Police slicer**, click the **Fire** filtering button, move your pointer out of the slicer, and then compare your screen with Figure 7.13.

With the data filtered, the records for the police precincts are hidden and only the fire station items display. A filtering button that is not selected indicates that the item is *not* included in the filtered list. By looking at this slicer, you can see that only Fire items are included. Because slicers indicate the current filtering state, it is easy to see exactly what is shown in the PivotTable report—and also to see what is *not* shown.

FIGURE 7.13

6 Click any cell in the PivotTable. On the **Analyze tab**, in the **Filter group**, click **Insert Slicer**. In the **Insert Slicers** dialog box, select the **Classification** check box, and then click **OK**.

7 Drag the **Classification** slicer to the right of the Fire/Police slicer. Notice that call classifications associated with the police department—Dispatched Calls, Major Crime, and Traffic Accidents—are dimmed. Compare your screen with Figure 7.14.

Because the PivotTable is currently filtered by Fire, no filters related to Police are available.

FIGURE 7.14

Excel 2016, Windows 10, Microsoft Corporation

8 ▶ On the **Classification slicer**, click the **Emergency Medical Calls** filtering button, and then compare your screen with Figure 7.15.

Only fire department station items with *Emergency Medical Calls* as the call classification display in the PivotTable report and you can determine which fire department station had the lowest number of emergency medical calls.

FIGURE 7.15

Excel 2016, Windows 10, Microsoft Corporation

9 ▶ Point to the **Sheet1** sheet tab, right-click, and then on the shortcut menu, click **Move or Copy**. In the **Move or Copy** dialog box, at the lower left, select the **Create a copy** check box. Compare your screen with Figure 7.16.

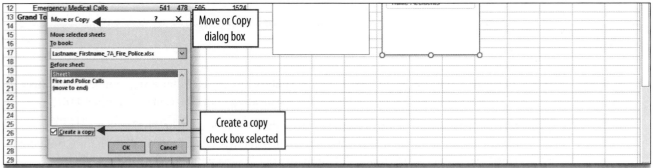

FIGURE 7.16

Excel 2016, Windows 10, Microsoft Corporation

10 ▶ Click **OK**. Right-click the **Sheet1 (2)** sheet tab, and then click **Rename**. Type **Slicers** and then press Enter.

The sheet is copied and renamed.

11 ▶ **Save** 🖫 your workbook.

Using the Search Filter is another way to filter data in a PivotTable report and find relevant information easily.

1 Display **Sheet1**. In the **Classification slicer**, click the **Fire & All Other Calls** filtering button, and then compare your screen with Figure 7.17.

Clicking a filtering button cancels the selection of another filtering button, unless you hold down the Ctrl key to include multiple filters.

FIGURE 7.17

2 In the **Classification slicer**, click **Clear Filter** 🏋. In the **Fire/Police** slicer, click **Clear Filter** 🏋.

No filters are applied and data from both the police department and the fire department displays.

3 Point to the **Fire/Police slicer header** and right-click. On the shortcut menu, click **Remove "Fire/Police"**. By using the same technique, remove the **Classification slicer**.

4 Click cell **A1** to select the PivotTable, and then on the **Analyze tab**, in the **Show group**, click **Field List** to display the PivotTable Fields pane. In the **field section**, point to **Location**, and then on the right, click the **Location arrow**. On the displayed menu, click in the **Search** box, type **Station 3** and then compare your screen with Figure 7.18.

FIGURE 7.18

5 Click **OK**. The filter is applied and only Station 3 data displays.

6 With cell **A1** still active, on the **Analyze tab**, in the **Actions group**, click **Clear**, and then click **Clear Filters**.

You can also clear filters by using this command.

7 Save your workbook.

Objective 3 | Modify a PivotTable

GO! Learn How
Video E7-3

You have seen how, after adding fields to the PivotTable, you can pivot (turn) the information in various ways; for example, by removing or rearranging the fields. With different views of your data, you can answer different questions. You can display a field as a column rather than a row. You can display parts of the data on separate pages; for example, by creating separate pages for the fire department calls and police department calls. After data is displayed in a useful way, you can format it using any methods you have practiced.

Activity 7.05 | Rearranging a PivotTable Report

MOS
4.2.4

In the Fire/Police PivotTable report, a large amount of detail information displays. Although totals display for both the rows and the columns for each location and for each classification, it is still difficult for a reader to make comparisons across precincts and stations. In this Activity, you will remove and rearrange fields to answer questions regarding the average number of service calls by department, by classification, and by precinct or station.

1 In the **layout section** of the **PivotTable Fields pane**, from the **COLUMNS area**, drag the **Month** field name upward into the white **field section**—a black X attaches to the pointer as you drag—and then release the mouse button. Compare your screen with Figure 7.19.

The X indicates that the field is being removed from the PivotTable report. When you release the mouse button, the details for each month no longer display in the PivotTable report; only the quarterly totals for the various call classifications at each location display. In the PivotTable Fields pane, *Month* is no longer selected or bold.

ANOTHER WAY In the Layout section, click the Month arrow, and then click Remove Field.

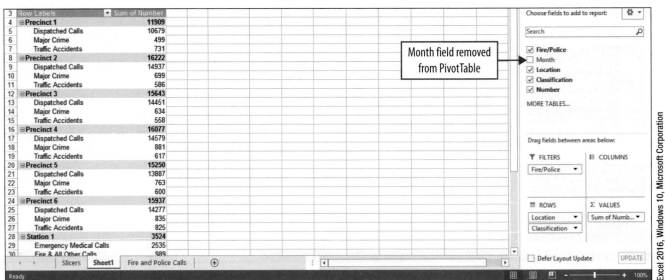

FIGURE 7.19

2 In the **layout section** of the **PivotTable Fields pane**, from the **ROWS area**, drag the **Classification** field into the **COLUMNS area**. Compare your screen with Figure 7.20.

By moving *Classification* from the ROWS area to the COLUMNS area, the various classifications become column titles instead of row titles. The classifications are arranged alphabetically across columns B:F. Now the police-related calls—Dispatched Calls, Major Crime, and Traffic Accidents—display as separate classifications.

FIGURE 7.20

3 **Close** ☒ the **PivotTable Fields pane**. Click cell **B4**—the column title *Dispatched Calls*. Right-click to display a shortcut menu, point to **Move**, and then click **Move "Dispatched Calls" Down**.

The Dispatched Calls column moves one column to the right.

4 Click cell **C4**—the column title *Dispatched Calls*—display the shortcut menu, point to **Move**, and then click **Move "Dispatched Calls" Down** again so that it moves one more column to the right.

The three police-related call classifications are adjacent to one another and you have a clearer view of the activity by location.

5 **Save** 🖫 your workbook, and then compare your screen with Figure 7.21.

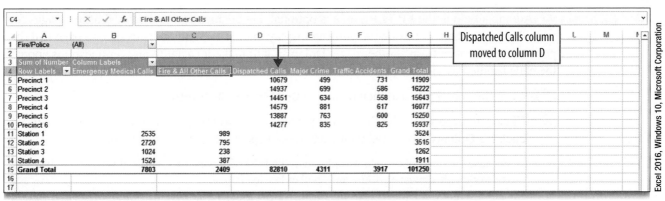

FIGURE 7.21

From the PivotTable report, you can display details for a particular category of information in a separate worksheet. In this Activity, you will create a separate report showing major crimes reported each month by precinct.

1 Click cell **E15**—the total for the *Major Crime* classification—and then point to the selected cell to view the ScreenTip.

To display the Major Crime field as a separate report, first select the total.

2 Right-click cell **E15**, and then click **Show Details**.

A new sheet—*Sheet3*—is added to your workbook, and the records for the Major Crime calls display in a table, along with the other fields from the Excel source data. Notice that the *Month* field is included, even though that field is not used in the PivotTable report.

ANOTHER WAY Double-click a total to display the data on a new worksheet.

3 On **Sheet3**, with the table selected, in the lower right corner, click **Quick Analysis**, and then click **Data Bars**. Click cell **A1**, and then compare your screen with Figure 7.22.

Conditional formatting is applied to the data in column E.

FIGURE 7.22

4 Rename the **Sheet3** tab **Major Crimes** and then **Save** your workbook.

Adding a field to the FILTERS area is optional, but enables you to display multiple pages for your PivotTable data. For example, you can display the fire department calls on one page and the police department calls on another page. Doing so will make it easier to answer questions about the calls handled by each Department.

1 Click the **Sheet1 tab**, and then rename it **Combined Calls PivotTable**

2 Click cell **A1** to select the PivotTable report. On the **Analyze tab**, in the **PivotTable group**, click the **Options arrow**, and then click **Show Report Filter Pages**. Click **OK**.

Because the Fire/Police field was placed in the FILTERS area, this action adds two new sheets to the workbook, one labeled *Fire* and another labeled *Police*.

3 Click the **Police sheet tab**.

The data for the police department calls displays on a separate sheet. The data remains in the form of a PivotTable—you can move fields from a row position to a column position and vice versa.

4 Click the **Fire sheet tab**. **Save** 🖫 your workbook, and then compare your screen with Figure 7.23.

The data for the Fire calls displays on a separate sheet.

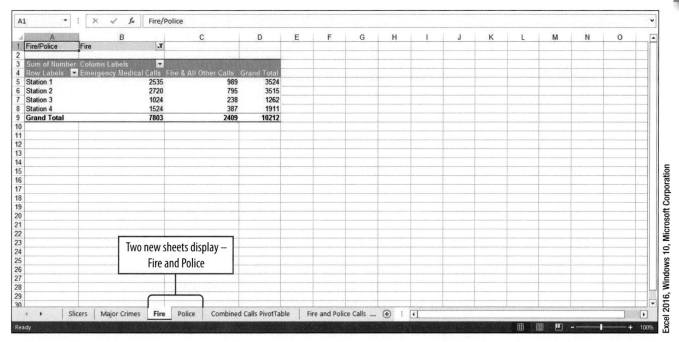

Two new sheets display – Fire and Police

FIGURE 7.23

Activity 7.08 | Changing Calculations in a PivotTable Report

MOS
4.2.5

A PivotTable report combines and compares large amounts of data so that you can analyze related totals. The default calculation in a PivotTable report is to *sum* the numeric data. You can modify the calculation to display an average, minimum, maximum, or some other calculation.

1 Display the **Combined Calls PivotTable** worksheet. Point to any cell containing numerical data, right-click, and then click **Value Field Settings**.

The Value Field Settings dialog box displays. In the Custom Name box, *Sum of Number* displays; in the Summarize value field by list, *Sum* is selected.

🔄 **ANOTHER WAY**   On the Analyze tab, in the Active Field group, click Field Settings.

---

2 Under **Summarize value field by**, click **Average**. Compare your screen with Figure 7.24.

The Custom Name box displays *Average of Number*.

FIGURE 7.24

3 ▸ Click **OK**.

An average for the three months is calculated and displays with up to six decimal places in the data cells. Cell A3 indicates *Average of Number*.

4 ▸ Right-click any numeric value, and then on the shortcut menu, click **Value Field Settings**. In the lower left corner of the dialog box, click **Number Format**.

The Format Cells dialog box displays, with only the Number tab included.

5 ▸ Under **Category**, click **Number**. Change the **Decimal places** box to **0**. Select the **Use 1000 Separator (,)** check box. Click **OK** two times to close both dialog boxes. Click cell **A1**, and then compare your screen with Figure 7.25.

The average figures display as whole numbers with the 1000 separator comma appropriately applied.

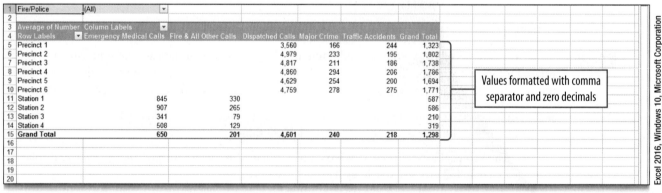

FIGURE 7.25

6 ▸ Save 🖫 your workbook.

Activity 7.09 | Formatting a PivotTable Report

4.2.6, 4.2.7

You can apply a PivotTable Style to the entire PivotTable report and change field names to make them easier to understand. For example, the field name *Average of Number* would be easier to understand as *Average Number of Calls*.

1 ▸ In cell **A1**, type **1st Quarter Fire & Police Calls** and then press Enter.

2 ▸ Click cell **A3**, type **Average Number of Calls** and then press Enter. **AutoFit column A**.

3 Display the **Police** worksheet. On the **Design tab**, in the **PivotTable Styles group**, display the **PivotTable Styles** gallery, and then under **Medium**, in the first row apply the second style—**Pivot Style Medium 2**.

4 Point to any numerical value, right-click, and then click **Number Format**. Under **Category**, click **Number**. Change the **Decimal places** to **0**, and then select the **Use 1000 Separator (,)** check box. Click **OK**. Click cell **A1**, and then compare your screen with Figure 7.26.

	A	B	C	D	E	F
1	Fire/Police	Police				
2						
3	Sum of Number	Column Labels				
4	Row Labels	Dispatched Calls	Major Crime	Traffic Accidents	Grand Total	
5	Precinct 1	10,679	499	731	11,909	
6	Precinct 2	14,937	699	586	16,222	
7	Precinct 3	14,451	634	558	15,643	
8	Precinct 4	14,579	881	617	16,077	
9	Precinct 5	13,887	763	600	15,250	
10	Precinct 6	14,277	835	825	15,937	
11	Grand Total	82,810	4,311	3,917	91,038	

FIGURE 7.26

Excel 2016, Windows 10, Microsoft Corporation

5 Display the **Fire** worksheet. Using the techniques you just practiced, apply the **Pivot Style Medium 3** style to this PivotTable and format the numbers to display using the 1000 comma separator with no decimal places.

6 Save your workbook.

Activity 7.10 | Updating PivotTable Report Data

In this Activity, you will update some of the data. If you change the underlying data on which the PivotTable report is based, you must also *refresh*—update—the PivotTable to reflect the new data.

1 On the **Fire** worksheet, in cell **B5**, notice that the total **Emergency Medical Calls** for **Station 1** is *2,535*.

2 Display the **Combined Calls PivotTable** worksheet, and then click cell **B11**. Notice that the *average* number of **Emergency Medical Calls** for **Station 1** is *845*.

3 Display the **Fire and Police Calls** worksheet—your original source data. Click cell **E3** and change the number from *924* to **824** and then press Enter. In cell **E11**, change the number from *879* to **778** and then press Enter.

The calls for January and February were both mistakenly overstated by 100 calls and are reduced from 924 and 879 to 824 and 778, respectively.

4 Display the **Combined Calls PivotTable** worksheet. Although you adjusted the underlying data, notice that in cell **B11**, the average number of Emergency Medical Calls for Station 1 has not changed—it still indicates *845*.

5 On the **Analyze tab**, in the **Data group**, click the **Refresh arrow**, and then click **Refresh**. Compare your screen with Figure 7.27.

The average number of Emergency Medical Calls for Station 1 updates to *778*, and the average for this type of call from all stations changes to *634*.

FIGURE 7.27

6 > Display the **Fire** worksheet, and then click cell **B5**. Notice that the total number of Emergency Medical Calls for Station 1 has been updated to *2,335*. **Save** 🔲 your workbook.

Objective 4 | Create a PivotChart

GO! Learn How
Video E7-4

A **PivotChart** is a graphical representation of the data in a PivotTable—referred to as the **associated PivotTable report**. A PivotChart usually has an associated PivotTable and the two are interactive; that is, if you change the field layout or data in the associated PivotTable, the changes are immediately reflected in the PivotChart. A PivotChart and its associated PivotTable must be in the same workbook.

Most of the formatting that you have practiced in standard charts work the same way in a PivotChart. A PivotChart displays data series, categories, data markers, and axes in the same manner as a standard chart. There are some differences. For example, whereas standard charts are linked directly to a range of worksheet cells, PivotCharts are based on the data source of the associated PivotTable.

Activity 7.11 | Creating a PivotChart Report from a PivotTable Report

4.3.1

In this Activity, you will create a PivotChart to analyze the police Major Crime and Traffic Accident calls.

1 > Display the **Combined Calls PivotTable** worksheet, and then press Ctrl + Home to make cell **A1** the active cell and to select the PivotTable.

2 > On the **Analyze tab**, in the **Tools group**, click **PivotChart**. In the **Insert Chart** dialog box, on the left side, if necessary, click **Column**, and then click **OK** to accept the default chart— **Clustered Column**. Compare your screen with Figure 7.28.

> The PivotChart displays **field buttons**. You can click on any button with an arrow to choose a filter and change the data that is displayed in the chart. Filters you apply will be reflected in the PivotTable and vice versa. After your chart is complete, you can hide the field buttons from view. Here, the Classification field items form the legend, and the Location field items form the category axis.

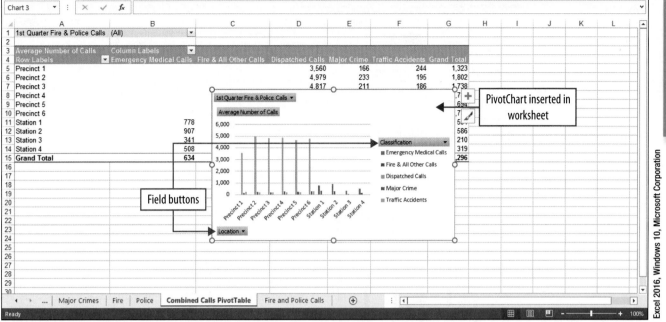

FIGURE 7.28

3 On the **Design tab**, in the **Location group**, click **Move Chart**. In the **Move Chart** dialog box, click the **New sheet** option, replace the highlighted text *Chart1* by typing **1st Quarter Chart** and then click **OK**.

4 In the **1st Quarter Chart** sheet, on the **Design tab**, in the **Chart Layouts group**, click **Quick Layout**, and then click the first chart layout—**Layout 1**. In the **Chart Styles group**, click **More** ⊡, and then apply **Style 14**.

5 Click the **Chart Title** and watch the **Formula Bar** as you type **1st Quarter Calls** and press ⏎ to display the title text in the chart. Compare your screen with Figure 7.29.

FIGURE 7.29

6 ▶ Insert a **Custom Footer** with the file name on the left, and then **Save** 🖫 your workbook.

Activity 7.12 │ Modifying a PivotChart Report

4.3.2 and 4.3.4

You can filter and change the values of the data in the PivotChart report by using the gray field buttons that display on the chart. For example, most of the calls number in the hundreds, but the Dispatched Calls number in the thousands, resulting in a larger vertical scale. To make the data easier to analyze, you will filter the data to show only Police calls in the Major Crime and Traffic Accidents classifications. You will also change the summary data back to total number of calls rather than the average.

1 ▶ In the upper left corner of the chart, click the **Report Filter** field button, which indicates *1st Quarter Fire & Police Calls*. In the lower left corner of the list, select (place a check mark in) the **Select Multiple Items** check box. Click to clear the (**All**) check box, and select the **Police** check box. Click **OK**, and then compare your screen with Figure 7.30.

Only the Police precinct calls display.

FIGURE 7.30

> **2** To the right of the PivotChart, click the *Classification* button above the chart legend. Click to *clear* the check box for **Dispatched Calls**, and then click **OK**.

This action removes the Dispatched Calls classification; only the two remaining call classifications for Police precincts display. The Legend field button displays a funnel icon to indicate that a filter is applied. Because the number of dispatched calls is in the thousands, compared to hundreds for the other call types, removing this classification allows for a clearer comparison of the other call classifications.

> **3** On the **Design tab**, in the **Type group**, click **Change Chart Type**. In the **Change Chart Type** dialog box, with **Column** selected, click the second chart type—**Stacked Column**—and then click **OK**. Compare your screen with Figure 7.31.

Stacked columns display the two call classifications by location. Within each location, the stacked column shows the amount of activity as part of a whole.

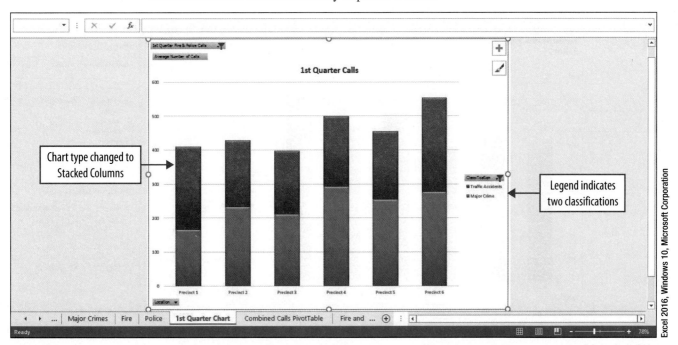

FIGURE 7.31

4 Display the **Combined Calls PivotTable** worksheet, and then compare your screen with Figure 7.32.

The data is rearranged and only the precinct calls display. Each time you change the PivotChart, the underlying PivotTable changes to reflect the new display of the data.

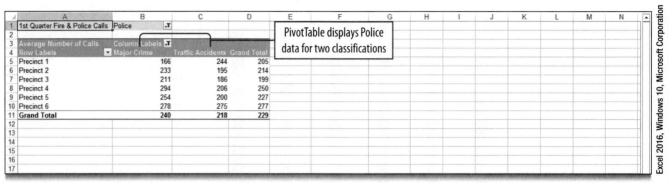

FIGURE 7.32

5 Click the **1st Quarter Chart sheet tab**, and then click in the chart title to make the chart active. On the **Design tab**, in the **Chart Layouts group**, click **Add Chart Element**, point to **Data Labels**, and then click **Center**.

Labels display on each segment of the columns showing the value for that portion of the column. For the call classification at a particular station, the number represents the *average* number of calls per month in the three months that comprise the first quarter.

6 On the **Analyze tab**, in the **Show/Hide group**, if necessary, click Field List to display the PivotChart Fields pane.

The PivotChart Fields pane displays. Here you can change the way the data is summarized.

7 In the **PivotChart Fields pane**, in the **VALUES area**, click **Average Number of Calls**, and then click **Value Field Settings**. In the dialog box, click **Sum**, and then click **OK**. Compare your screen with Figure 7.33.

The chart changes to display the total number of calls rather than the average number of calls.

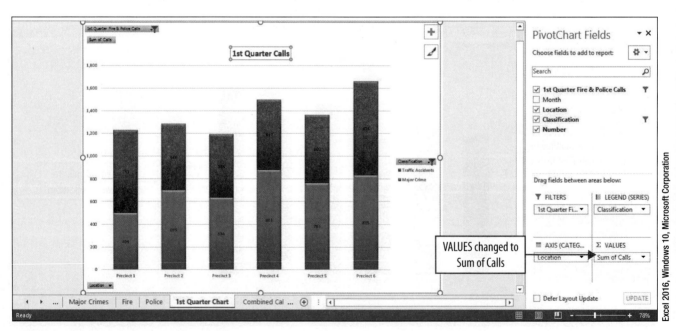

FIGURE 7.33

8 ▸ On the **Analyze tab**, in the **Show/Hide group**, click the **Field Buttons arrow**, and then click **Hide All** so that the field buttons do not display in the chart.

9 ▸ **Close** ⓧ the **PivotChart Fields** pane, and then **Save** 🖫 your workbook.

Activity 7.13 | Arranging and Hiding Worksheets in a Multi-sheet Workbook

1 ▸ At the bottom of the Excel window, to the left of the sheet tabs, click the **left arrow** as necessary so that the **Slicers** worksheet displays, and then click the **Slicers** sheet tab to make it the active sheet.

2 ▸ To the right of the sheet tabs, locate the horizontal scroll bar. At the left end of the scroll bar, point to the three vertical dots to display the ⬌ pointer, and then drag to the right to decrease the width of the scroll bar to display all seven worksheets in this workbook. Compare your screen with Figure 7.34.

FIGURE 7.34

Excel 2016, Windows 10, Microsoft Corporation

3 ▸ Drag the **Combined Calls PivotTable sheet tab** to the left until it is the first worksheet.

4 ▸ Right-click the **Fire and Police Calls sheet tab** and then click **Hide**.

In this manner, you can hide a worksheet to prevent a user from altering the data.

5 ▸ Point to the **Combined Calls PivotTable sheet tab**, right-click, and then click **Select All Sheets**. Insert a footer in the **left section** that includes the **file name**. Center the worksheets **Horizontally** on the page, change the orientation to **Landscape**, and then in the **Scale to Fit group**, set the **Width** to **1 page**. Press Ctrl + Home to move to the top of the worksheet.

6 ▸ Click the **File tab** and then click **Show All Properties**. As the **Tags**, type **fire, police call activity** and as the **Subject**, type your course name and section number. Under **Related People**, be sure that your name displays as **Author**.

7 ▸ With the sheets still grouped, display the **Print Preview**, and then examine the six visible pages of your workbook. Return to the worksheet and make any necessary corrections or adjustments. **Ungroup** the worksheets. **Save** 🖫 your workbook.

8 ▸ If directed by your instructor to do so, submit your paper printout, your electronic image of your document that looks like a printed document, or your original Excel file. If required by your instructor, print or create an electronic version of your worksheet with formulas displayed. In the upper right corner of the Excel window, click **Close** ⓧ.

END | You have completed Project 7A

Supply Expenditure Analysis

PROJECT ACTIVITIES

In Activities 7.14 through 7.17, you will create a PivotTable and PivotChart using two related lists of data from Microsoft Access. Your completed worksheets will look similar to Figure 7.35.

PROJECT FILES

 If your instructor wants you to submit Project 7B in the MyITLab Grader system, log into MyITLab, locate Grader Project 7B, and then download the files for the project.

For Project 7B, you will need the following files:
New blank Excel workbook
e07B_Medical_Supplies

You will save your workbook as:
Lastname_Firstname_7B_First_Aid

Please always review the downloaded Grader instructions before beginning.

PROJECT RESULTS

Build from Scratch

GO!
Walk Thru
Project 7B

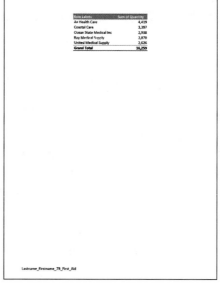

Excel 2016, Windows 10, Microsoft Corporation

FIGURE 7.35 Project 7B Supply Expenditure Analysis

GO! Learn How
Video E7-5

Objective 5 Create a PivotTable from a Data Model

A **Data Model** is a method of incorporating data from multiple, related tables into an Excel worksheet. The data can be in an Excel workbook, imported from an Access database, or imported from an external source such as a corporate database, a public data feed, or an analysis service.

A Microsoft Access table stores data in rows and columns. Each row is a **record**—all of the categories of data pertaining to one person, place, event, thing, or idea. Each column is a **field**—a single piece of information for every record. An Access database can contain multiple, related tables, and you can use these related tables to create PivotTables and Pivot Charts.

Activity 7.14 | Creating a Data Model by Getting External Data from Microsoft Access

MOS
Expert 3.4.1

When you import Access tables into an Excel data model, you can establish a **relationship**—an association between the tables of data that share a common field. When the connection is established, you can use fields from each of the imported tables to create a PivotTable. In this Activity, you will get external data from two Microsoft Access tables so that you can analyze the purchase of first aid supplies.

> **ALERT!** To submit as an autograded project, log into MyITLab and download the files for this Project, and begin with those files instead of a new blank workbook.

1 Take a moment to view Figures 7.36 and 7.37, which display the data in the two Access tables that you will be working with in your PivotTable. By importing the data from the two tables into one PivotTable, you can use Excel's PivotTable tools to conduct your analysis.

In Figure 7.36, the Suppliers table contains the contact information for each supplier, and each supplier is assigned a unique Supplier ID. In Microsoft Access, the field used to uniquely identify a record is the **primary key**.

In Figure 7.37, the Supply Order Summary table includes the first aid supply purchases made by the Golden Grove fire department from each supplier for a three-year period. The supplier name and contact information is not part of the table. Instead, the Supplier ID field identifies the supplier and is the common field that connects the two databases.

FIGURE 7.36

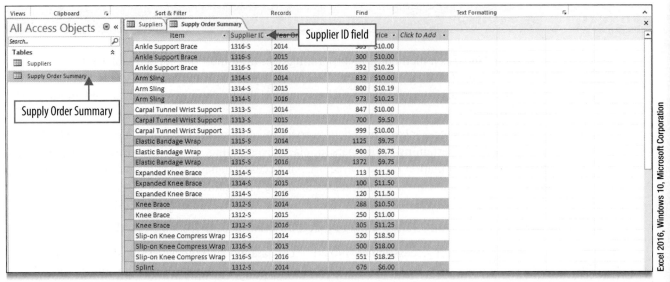

FIGURE 7.37

> **2** Start Excel and open a new blank workbook. **Save** the workbook in your **Excel Chapter 7** folder as **Lastname_Firstname_7B_First_Aid**

> **3** Click the **Data tab**, and then at the left end of the ribbon, click **Get External Data**. On the displayed list of possible sources, click **From Access**. Navigate to your student data files, click **e07B_Medical_Supplies**, and then click **Open**. Compare your screen with Figure 7.38.

>> This database contains the two tables shown in Figures 7.36 and 7.37—Suppliers and Supply Order Summary.

FIGURE 7.38

> **4** In the **Select Table** dialog box, select the **Enable selection of multiple tables** check box, and then select the **Name** check box so that both tables are selected. Compare your screen with Figure 7.39.

>> You can click the Name check box to select all of the tables in the database, or you can select individual tables to be included in your data model.

FIGURE 7.39

5 Click **OK**. In the **Import Data** dialog box, under **Select how you want to view this data in your workbook**, click **PivotTable Report**. Under **Where do you want to put the data**, be sure that **Existing worksheet** is selected and that *=$A$1* displays. In the worksheet, verify that cell **A1** is selected. Compare your screen with Figure 7.40.

> The two tables will not be added to the Excel workbook. Instead, a connection is created between the Excel PivotTable and the two Access tables. Both tables will be added to the Data Model.

FIGURE 7.40

6 Click **OK**, and then compare your screen with Figure 7.41.

> A PivotTable placeholder displays on the left side of the worksheet and the PivotTable Fields pane displays on the right. The two tables that you added to the Data Model display in the PivotTable Fields pane. You may need to scroll the fields section to view both tables in the PivotTable Fields pane.

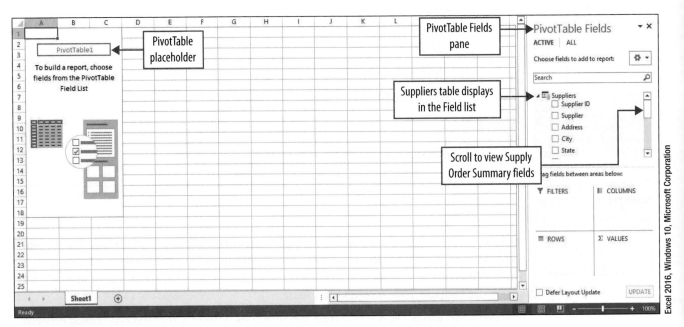

FIGURE 7.41

7 Save 🖫 your workbook.

Activity 7.15 | Creating a PivotTable Using Multiple Tables

Expert 3.4.2,
4.2.1

The Data Model enables you to create PivotTables by using the data from multiple, related tables. The Suppliers table contains the contact information for each supplier, and each supplier is assigned a unique Supplier ID. Recall that in Microsoft Access, the field that uniquely identifies a record is the primary key.

The Supply Order Summary table includes the purchases made by the fire department from each supplier. The supplier name and contact information is not part of the table. Instead, the Supplier ID field identifies the supplier and is the common field that connects the two tables.

In this Activity, you will generate a PivotTable report using fields from both tables to analyze the number of first aid supply purchases from each vendor.

1 Double-click the **Sheet1** sheet tab, and then rename the sheet **Supply PivotTable**

2 In the worksheet, if necessary, click the PivotTable placeholder to activate it and display the PivotTable Fields pane. In the **PivotTable Fields pane**, if necessary click the Suppliers table to expand it. Drag the **Supplier** field to the **COLUMNS area**.

3 In the **PivotTable Fields pane**, in the field list section, drag the scroll bar down, and if necessary, expand the Supply Order Summary table. Drag the **Item** field to the **ROWS area**, and then drag the **Year Ordered** field to the **ROWS area**. Drag the **Quantity** field to the **VALUES area**. Compare your screen with Figure 7.42.

You have created a PivotTable using data from two related tables. Although the common field—*Supplier ID*—is not used in the PivotTable, the relationship between the two tables that was created in the Access database enables Excel to use the common field to locate the data necessary from each table.

FIGURE 7.42

4 Point to cell **F3** and right-click. On the shortcut menu, click **Number Format**. Under **Category**, click **Number**, change the **Decimal places** to **0**, and then select the **Use 1000 Separator (,)** check box. Click **OK** to apply the format to all of the values in the PivotTable.

5 On the **Design tab**, in the **PivotTables Styles group**, click **More** ▾, and then under **Medium**, in the second row, click the sixth style—**Pivot Style Medium 13**.

6 **Close** ☒ the **PivotTable Fields** pane and **Save** 🖫 your workbook.

Objective 6 │ Create and Format a 3-D Pie PivotChart

GO! Learn How
Video E7-6

Recall that a pie chart is used to illustrate the relationship of each part to a whole. You can create a PivotChart from the data in a data model, and then filter the PivotChart to best represent your data.

Activity 7.16 │ Creating a 3-D Pie PivotChart

4.3.1, 4.3.4

In this Activity, you will create a 3-D pie chart that identifies which vendors supply the fire department with the most first aid supplies.

1 If necessary, click anywhere in the PivotTable so that the PivotTable Tools are active. On the **Analyze tab**, in the **Tools group**, click **PivotChart**. Click **Pie**, and then click **3-D Pie**. Click **OK**, and then compare your screen with Figure 7.43.

A 3-D pie chart based on the PivotTable displays. The field buttons correspond to the fields used in the PivotTable.

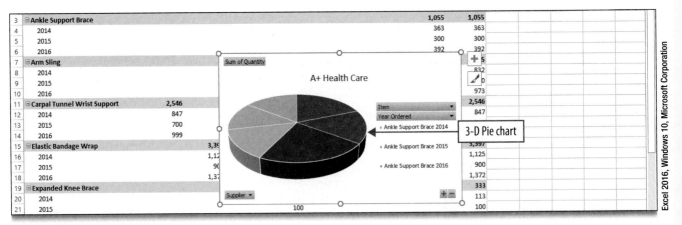

				1,055	1,055
3	⊟Ankle Support Brace				
4	2014			363	363
5	2015			300	300
6	2016			392	392
7	⊟Arm Sling				
8	2014				832
9	2015				0
10	2016				973
11	⊟Carpal Tunnel Wrist Support	2,546			2,546
12	2014	847			847
13	2015	700			
14	2016	999			
15	⊟Elastic Bandage Wrap	3,39			3,397
16	2014	1,12			1,125
17	2015	90			900
18	2016	1,37			1,372
19	⊟Expanded Knee Brace				333
20	2014				113
21	2015				100

FIGURE 7.43

2 On the **Design tab**, in the **Location group**, click **Move Chart**. Click **New sheet**, and then in the **New sheet** box, if necessary, select the existing text. Type **Suppliers Chart** and then click **OK** to move the chart to a chart sheet.

3 On the **Analyze tab**, in the **Show/Hide group**, click **Field List** to display the PivotChart Fields pane.

> You can modify the data that displays in the PivotChart by dragging the fields between areas in the PivotChart Fields list.

4 In the **AXIS (CATEGORY) area**, click **Item** and then click **Remove Field**. Use the same technique to remove the **Year Ordered** field.

5 In the **LEGEND (SERIES)** area, point to **Supplier**, and then drag the Supplier field to the **AXIS (CATEGORY)** area. Compare your screen with Figure 7.44.

> The AXIS (CATEGORY) area corresponds to the legend in a pie chart.

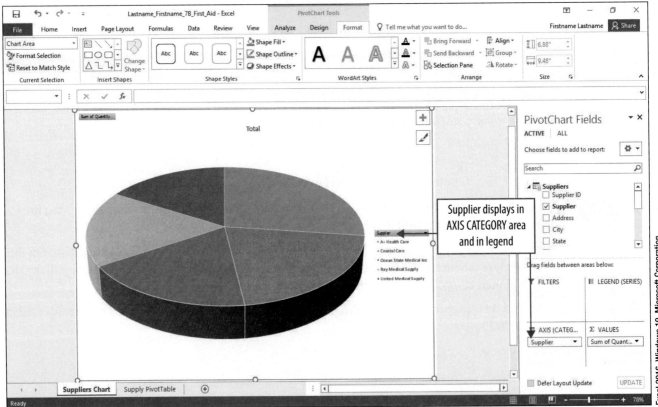

FIGURE 7.44

6 Close ☒ the **PivotChart Fields** pane, and then **Save** ☐ your workbook.

Activity 7.17 | Formatting a 3-D Pie PivotChart

4.3.3

You can format a PivotChart using the same techniques that you use to format a chart.

1 On the **Design tab**, in the **Chart Styles group**, click **Style 3**.

2 In the upper right corner of the Chart Area, click **Chart Elements** ⊞, and then clear the **Legend** check box.

3 With the **CHART ELEMENTS** list displayed, point to **Data Labels**, click the **arrow**, and then click **More Options**. In the **Format Data Labels** pane, select and clear check boxes as necessary so that only the **Category Name** and **Percentage** check boxes are selected. **Close** ☒ the **Format Data Labels** pane.

4 With all of the data labels selected, right-click one of the selected data labels, and then click **Font**. In the **Font** dialog box, select the value in the **Size box**, type **11** and then click **OK**.

5 Click the chart title—*Total*. Type **Three-Year Total First Aid Supply Purchases** and then press Enter to insert the chart title.

6 In the upper left corner of the chart area, right-click the **Sum of Quantity** button, and then click **Hide Value Field Buttons on Chart**. Compare your screen with Figure 7.45.

FIGURE 7.45

7 Display the **Page Setup** dialog box, and then click the **Header/Footer tab**. Click **Custom Footer**, and then in the **Left section**, insert the file name. Click **OK** two times.

8 Display the **Supply PivotTable** sheet and notice that the PivotTable is arranged to match the data in the pie chart. Insert a footer in the **left section** that includes the **file name**, and then center the worksheet **Horizontally** on the page.

9 Click the **File tab** and then click **Show All Properties**. As the **Tags**, type **first aid supplies** and as the **Subject**, type your course name and section number. Under **Related People**, be sure that your name displays as **Author**. **Save** your workbook.

10 If directed by your instructor to do so, submit your paper printout, your electronic image of your document that looks like a printed document, or your original Excel file. If required by your instructor, print or create an electronic version of your worksheet with formulas displayed. In the upper right corner of the Excel window, click **Close** ☒.

END | You have completed Project 7B

GO! To Work

MICROSOFT OFFICE SPECIALIST (MOS) SKILLS IN THIS CHAPTER

PROJECT 7A	PROJECT 7B
4.2.1 Creating a new PivotTable	3.4.1 Expert Import, transform, combine, display, and connect to data
4.2.2 Modifying field selections and options	3.4.2 Expert Consolidate data
4.2.3 Creating a slicer	4.2.1 Creating a new PivotTable
4.2.4 Grouping PivotTable data	4.3.1 Creating PivotCharts
4.2.5 Utilizing calculated fields	4.3.3 Applying styles to PivotCharts
4.2.6 Formatting data	4.3.4 Drill down into PivotChart details
4.2.7 Format data	
4.3.1 Creating PivotCharts	
4.3.2 Manipulating options in existing PivotCharts	
4.3.4 Drilling down into PivotChart details	

BUILD YOUR E-PORTFOLIO

An E-Portfolio is a collection of evidence, stored electronically, that showcases what you have accomplished while completing your education. Collecting and then sharing your work products with potential employers reflects your academic and career goals. Your completed documents from the following projects are good examples to show what you have learned: 7G, 7K, and 7L.

GO! FOR JOB SUCCESS

Discussion: Agile Business Culture

Your instructor may assign these questions to your class, and then ask you to think about them or discuss them with your classmates:

Markets and technologies move fast in today's high-tech environment. Companies that need to adapt to changes quickly are adopting an agile business culture. Evolved from a software development technique, agile businesses put their focus on customer needs and welcome the changes to products or services that customers request. Constant innovation toward more effective strategies is seen as the norm.

What are some businesses that you interact with, either at a physical location or online, that might benefit from the quicker innovation and response to customer input provided by an agile culture?

Do you see areas at your college that you think would benefit from a more agile culture?

Are there areas of your personal or professional life where an agile approach to change and innovation might be beneficial?

END OF CHAPTER

SUMMARY

PivotTables and PivotCharts are used to organize and display data. PivotTables are useful for summarizing and analyzing large amounts of data. PivotCharts graphically represent the data in PivotTables.

By manipulating data in PivotTables and PivotCharts, you can present and organize information into groups from which trends, comparisons, patterns, and relationships can be determined.

Excel uses the Data Model to incorporate data from multiple sources into related tables in Excel. The data can come from an Excel worksheet or an external source such as databases and data feeds.

A PivotChart can be formatted in much the same way as any other chart in Excel. You can apply chart styles and layouts, and add, remove, and format chart elements. When you rearrange the fields in a PivotChart, the associated PivotTable is rearranged to reflect the same data.

GO! LEARN IT ONLINE

Review the concepts, key terms, and MOS skills in this chapter by completing these online challenges, which you can find at **MyITLab**.

Matching and Multiple Choice: Answer matching and multiple choice questions to test what you learned in this chapter.

Lessons on the GO!: Learn how to use all the new apps and features as they are introduced by Microsoft.

MOS Prep Quiz: Answer questions to review the MOS skills that you practiced in this chapter.

PROJECT GUIDE FOR EXCEL CHAPTER 7

Your instructor will assign Projects from this list to ensure your learning and assess your knowledge.

	PROJECT GUIDE FOR EXCEL CHAPTER 7		
Project	**Apply Skills from These Chapter Objectives**	**Project Type**	**Project Location**
7A MyITLab	Objectives 1-4 from Project 7A	**7A Instructional Project (Grader Project)** Guided instruction to learn the skills in Project 7A.	In MyITLab and in text
7B	Objectives 5-6 from Project 7B	**7B Instructional Project (Grader Project)** Guided instruction to learn the skills in Project 7B.	In MyITLab and in text
7C	Objectives 1-4 from Project 7A	**7C Skills Review (Scorecard Grading)** A guided review of the skills from Project 7A.	In text
7D MyITLab	Objectives 5-6 from Project 7B	**7D Skills Review (Scorecard Grading)** A guided review of the skills from Project 7B.	In text
7E MyITLab	Objectives 1-4 from Project 7A	**7E Mastery (Grader Project)** **Mastery and Transfer of Learning** A demonstration of your mastery of the skills in Project 7A with extensive decision making.	In MyITLab and in text
7F MyITLab	Objectives 5-6 from Project 7B	**7F Mastery (Grader Project)** **Mastery and Transfer of Learning** A demonstration of your mastery of the skills in Project 7B with extensive decision making.	In MyITLab and in text
7G MyITLab	Objectives 1-6 from Project 7A and 7B	**7G Mastery (Grader Project)** **Mastery and Transfer of Learning** A demonstration of your mastery of the skills in Projects 7A and 7B with extensive decision making.	In MyITLab and in text
7H	Combination of Objectives from Projects 7A and 7B	**7H GO! Fix It (Scorecard Grading)** **Critical Thinking** A demonstration of your mastery of the skills in Projects 7A and 7B by creating a correct result from a document that contains errors you must find.	Instructor Resource Center (IRC) and MyITLab
7I	Combination of Objectives from Projects 7A and 7B	**7I GO! Make It (Scorecard Grading)** **Critical Thinking** A demonstration of your mastery of the skills in Projects 7A and 7B by creating a result from a supplied picture.	IRC and MyITLab
7J	Combination of Objectives from Projects 7A and 7B	**7J GO! Solve It (Rubric Grading)** **Critical Thinking** A demonstration of your mastery of the skills in Projects 7A and 7B, your decision-making skills, and your critical thinking skills. A task-specific rubric helps you self-assess your result.	IRC and MyITLab
7K	Combination of Objectives from Projects 7A and 7B	**7K GO! Solve It (Rubric Grading)** **Critical Thinking** A demonstration of your mastery of the skills in Projects 7A and 7B, your decision-making skills, and your critical thinking skills. A task-specific rubric helps you self-assess your result.	In text
7L	Combination of Objectives from Projects 7A and 7B	**7L GO! Think (Rubric Grading)** **Critical Thinking** A demonstration of your understanding of the chapter concepts applied in a manner that you would outside of college. An analytic rubric helps you and your instructor grade the quality of your work by comparing it to the work an expert in the discipline would create.	In text
7M	Combination of Objectives from Projects 7A and 7B	**7M GO! Think (Rubric Grading)** **Critical Thinking** A demonstration of your understanding of the chapter concepts applied in a manner that you would outside of college. An analytic rubric helps you and your instructor grade the quality of your work by comparing it to the work an expert in the discipline would create.	IRC and MyITLab
7N	Combination of Objectives from Projects 7A and 7B	**7N You and GO! (Rubric Grading)** **Critical Thinking** A demonstration of your understanding of the chapter concepts applied in a manner that you would in a personal situation. An analytic rubric helps you and your instructor grade the quality of your work.	IRC and MyITLab

GLOSSARY

GLOSSARY OF CHAPTER KEY TERMS

Associated PivotTable report The PivotTable in a workbook that is graphically represented in a PivotChart.

Clear Filter A button that removes a filter.

COLUMNS area An area to position fields that you want to display as columns in the PivotTable. Field names placed here become column titles, and the data is grouped in columns by these titles.

Data Model A method of incorporating data from multiple, related tables into an Excel worksheet.

Field A single piece of information for every record.

Field button A button on a PivotChart with an arrow to choose a filter, and thus change the data that is displayed in the chart.

Field names The column titles from source data that form the categories of data for a PivotTable.

Field section The upper portion of the PivotTable Fields pane containing the fields—column titles—from your source data; use this area to add fields to and remove fields from the PivotTable.

Filter To limit the display of data to only specific information.

FILTERS area An area in the lower portion of the PivotTable Fields pane to position fields by which you want to filter the PivotTable, enabling you to display a subset of data in the PivotTable report.

Filtering button A button on a slicer used to select the item by which to filter.

Layout section The lower portion of the PivotTable Fields pane containing the four areas for layout; use this area to rearrange and reposition fields in the PivotTable.

List A series of rows that contains related data with column titles in the first row.

PivotChart A graphical representation of the data in a PivotTable.

PivotTable An interactive Excel report that summarizes and analyzes large amounts of data.

PivotTable Fields pane A window that lists at the top, all of the fields—column titles—from the source data for use in the PivotTable and at the bottom, an area in which you can arrange the fields in the PivotTable.

Primary key The field used to uniquely identify a record in an Access table.

Record All of the categories of data pertaining to one person, place, event, thing, or idea.

Refresh The command to update a worksheet to reflect the new data.

Relationship An association between tables of data that share a common field.

ROWS area An area to position fields that you want to display as rows in the PivotTable. Field names placed here become row titles, and the data is grouped by these row titles.

Slicer Easy-to-use filtering control with buttons that enable you to drill down through large amounts of data.

Slicer header The top of a slicer that indicates the category of the slicer items.

Source data The data for a PivotTable, formatted in columns and rows, that can be located in an Excel worksheet or an external source.

VALUES area An area to position fields that contain data that is summarized in a PivotTable or PivotChart. The data placed here is usually numeric or financial in nature and the data is summarized—summed. You can also perform other basic calculations such as finding the average, the minimum, or the maximum.

Apply 7A skills from these Objectives:

1 Create a PivotTable Report

2 Use Slicers and Search Filters

3 Modify a PivotTable

4 Create a PivotChart

Skills Review   Project 7C Parks and Pools Calls

In the following Skills Review, you will assist Lindsay Johnson, Director of Parks and Recreation, in preparing a comparative report for phone calls received by the various park and pool facilities in the city. You will create and modify a PivotTable and PivotChart. The first six worksheets in your workbook will look similar to Figure 7.46.

PROJECT FILES

For Project 7C, you will need the following file:

e07C_Parks_Pools

You will save your workbook as:

Lastname_Firstname_7C_Parks_Pools

PROJECT RESULTS

Excel 2016, Windows 10, Microsoft Corporation

FIGURE 7.46

(Project 7C Parks and Pools Calls continues on the next page)

1 Start Excel. From your student files, open **e07C_Parks_Pools**. **Save** the file in your **Excel Chapter 7** folder as **Lastname_Firstname_7C_Parks_Pools**

a. Click cell **A2**. On the **Insert tab**, in the **Tables group**, click **Recommended PivotTables**, and then, in the **Recommended PivotTables** dialog box, click **Sum of Number by Location (+)**. Click **OK**.

b. In the **PivotTable Fields pane**, in the **layout section**, verify that **Parks/Pools** and **Location** are listed in the **ROWS area**, and **Sum of Number** is listed in the **VALUES area**.

c. Drag the **Parks/Pools field** from the **ROWS area** up to the **FILTERS area**.

d. In the field section, select the **Classification** field check box. Right-click **A4**, point to **Expand/ Collapse**, and then click **Expand Entire Field**.

e. In the **PivotTable Fields pane**, from the **field section**, drag the **Month** field down to the **COLUMNS area**.

f. On the **Design tab**, in the **PivotTable Styles group**, click **More**, and then under **Light**, click **Pivot Style Light 8**.

2 On the **Analyze tab**, in the **Filter group**, click **Insert Slicer**. Select the **Parks/Pools** check box, and then click **OK**. Drag the **Parks/Pools** slicer to the right of the PivotTable.

a. On the **Options tab**, in the **Slicer Styles group**, click **More**, and then under **Dark**, click **Slicer Style Dark 6**. Click cell **A1**. On the **Parks/Pools slicer**, click the **Parks** filtering button. Point to the **Sheet1** sheet tab, right-click, and then click **Move or Copy**. In the **Move or Copy** dialog box, select the **Create a copy** check box. Click **OK**. Right-click the **Sheet1 (2)** sheet tab, click **Rename**, and then type **Filtered by Parks**

b. Display the **Sheet1** worksheet. In the **Parks/Pools slicer**, click **Clear Filter**. Point to the **Parks/Pools slicer header**, right-click, and then click **Remove "Parks/Pools"**.

3 In the **layout section** of the **PivotTable Fields pane**, from the **COLUMNS area**, drag the **Month** field name upward into the white **field section** and then release the mouse button. In the **layout section**, from the **ROWS area**, drag the **Classification** field into the **COLUMNS area**. **Close** the **PivotTable Fields pane**.

a. Click cell **B4**. Right-click, point to **Move**, and then click **Move "Maintenance & All Other Calls" Down**. Point to cell **E19**, right-click, and then click **Show Details** to create a worksheet with the details of cell E19—the swim lesson calls.

b. In the lower right corner, click **Quick Analysis**, and then click **Data Bars**. **AutoFit** columns C and D and then click cell **A1**. Rename the **Sheet3** tab **Swim Lesson Calls**

c. Click the **Sheet1 tab**. Rename the sheet **Combined Calls PivotTable** and then click cell **A1**. On the **Analyze tab**, in the **PivotTable group**, click the **Options arrow**, and then click **Show Report Filter Pages**. In the dialog box, click **OK** to create worksheets for Parks and for Pools.

d. Display the **Combined Calls PivotTable** worksheet. Point to any cell with numerical data, right-click, and then click **Value Field Settings**. Click **Number Format**, click **Number**, and then set the **Decimal places** to **0** and select the **Use 1000 Separator** check box. Click **OK** two times.

e. Click cell **A1**. Type **3rd Quarter Parks & Pools** and then press Enter. **AutoFit column A**.

f. Display the **Parks and Pools Calls** worksheet, which is your source data. Change the value in cell **E3** from *95* to **85** and then press Enter. Display the **Combined Calls PivotTable** worksheet. Click cell **A1**. On the **Analyze tab**, in the **Data group**, click the **Refresh arrow**, and then click **Refresh**.

4 With the **Combined Calls PivotTable** sheet displayed, on the **Analyze tab**, in the **Tools group**, click **PivotChart**. On the **Insert Chart** dialog box, on the left verify that **Column** is selected, on the right, verify the first chart—**Clustered Column** is selected, and then click **OK**. On the **Design tab**, in the **Location group**, click **Move Chart**. In the **Move Chart** dialog box, click the **New sheet** option, replace the highlighted text *Chart1* by typing **3rd Quarter Chart** and then click **OK**. In the new chart sheet, on the **Design tab**, in the **Chart Layouts group**, click **Quick Layout**, and then click **Layout 3**. In the **Chart Styles group**, click **More**, and then apply **Style 13**.

a. Click the **Chart Title** and watch the **Formula Bar** as you type **3rd Quarter Calls** and press Enter. Insert a **Custom Footer** with the file name in the **left section**.

(Project 7C Parks and Pools Calls continues on the next page)

b. In the upper left corner of the chart, click **Report Filter**, which indicates *3rd Quarter Parks & Pools*. In the lower left corner of the list, select the **Select Multiple Items** check box. Click to clear the (**All**) check box, select the **Pools** check box, and then click **OK**. At the bottom of the PivotChart, click the **Classification** filter arrow, and then *clear* the check box for **Pool Party Calls**. Click **OK**.

c. On the **Design tab**, in the **Type group**, click **Change Chart Type**. In the **Change Chart Type** dialog box, click **Stacked Column,** and then click **OK**. On the **Design tab**, in the **Chart Layouts group**, click **Add Chart Element**, point to **Data Labels**, and then click **Center**.

d. On the **Analyze tab**, in the **Show/Hide group**, click the **Field Buttons arrow**, and then click **Hide All**.

e. Drag the **Combined Calls PivotTable sheet tab** to the left until it is the first worksheet. Right-click the **Parks and Pools Calls** sheet and then click **Hide** to hide the source data.

f. Point to the **Combined Calls PivotTable sheet tab**, right-click, and then click **Select All Sheets**. Insert a footer in the **left section** that includes the **file name**. Center the worksheets **Horizontally** on the page, change the orientation to **Landscape**, and then in the **Scale to Fit group**, set the **Width** to **1 page**.

g. Click the **File tab** and then click **Show All Properties**. As the **Tags**, type **parks, pools** and as the **Subject**, type your course name and section #. Under **Related People**, be sure that your name displays as Author. **Save** your workbook.

h. If directed by your instructor to do so, submit your paper printout, your electronic image of your document that looks like a printed document, or your original Excel file. If required by your instructor, print or create an electronic version of your worksheet with formulas displayed. In the upper right corner of the Excel window, click **Close**.

END | You have completed Project 7C

Skills Review | Project 7D Office Supplies

In the following Skills Review, you will assist City Council Office Manager Jake Curley in creating a Data Model, PivotTable, and 3-D Pie PivotChart. Your results will look similar to those in Figure 7.47.

PROJECT FILES

For Project 7D, you will need the following files:

New blank workbook
e07D_Office_Supplies

You will save your workbook as:

Lastname_Firstname_7D_Office_Supplies

PROJECT RESULTS

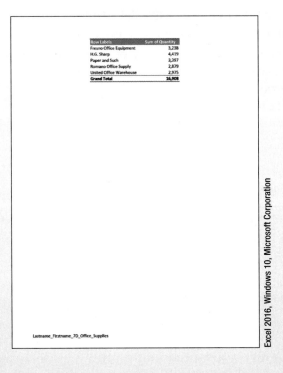

Excel 2016, Windows 10, Microsoft Corporation

FIGURE 7.47

(Project 7D Office Supplies continues on the next page)

1 Start Excel and open a new blank workbook. **Save** the workbook in your **Excel Chapter 7** folder as **Lastname_Firstname_7D_Office_Supplies**

a. Click the **Data tab**, and then at the left end of the ribbon, click **Get External Data**. On the displayed list of possible sources, click **From Access**. Navigate to your student data files, click **e07D_Office_Supplies** and then click **Open**.

b. In the **Select Table** dialog box, select the **Enable selection of multiple tables** check box, and then select the **Name** check box so that both tables are selected. Click **OK**.

c. In the **Import Data** dialog box, under **Select how you want to view this data in your workbook**, click **PivotTable Report**. Under **Where do you want to put the data**, be sure that **Existing worksheet** is selected and that *=$A$1* displays. In the worksheet, verify that cell **A1** is selected. Click **OK**.

d. **Rename** the **Sheet1** sheet tab to **Office PivotTable**

2 Click the **PivotTable placeholder** to activate it and display the **PivotTable Fields** pane. In the **PivotTable Fields** pane, if necessary click the Suppliers table to expand it.

a. Drag the **Supplier** field to the **COLUMNS area**.

b. In the PivotTable Fields pane, drag the vertical scroll bar down to display the **Supply Order Summary** table and if necessary, expand the table. Drag the **Item** field to the **ROWS area**, and then drag the **Year Ordered** field to the **ROWS area**. Drag the **Quantity** field to the **VALUES area**.

c. Point to any of the values in the PivotTable, right-click, and then click **Number Format**. Under **Category**, click **Number**, change the **Decimal places** to **0**, and then select the **Use 1000 Separator (,)** check box. Click **OK** to apply the format to all of the values in the PivotTable.

d. On the **Design tab**, in the **PivotTables Styles group**, click **More**, and then under **Medium**, in the second row, click the sixth style—**Pivot Style Medium 13**. **Close** the PivotTable Fields pane.

3 If necessary, click anywhere in the PivotTable so that the PivotTable Tools are active. On the **Analyze tab**, in the **Tools group**, click **PivotChart**. Click **Pie**, and then click **3-D Pie**. Click **OK**.

a. On the **Design tab**, in the **Location group**, click **Move Chart**. Click **New sheet**, and then in the New sheet box, select the existing text. Type **Suppliers Chart** and then click **OK** to move the chart to a chart sheet.

b. On the **Analyze tab**, in the **Show/Hide group**, click **Field List** to display the PivotChart Fields pane. In the **AXIS (CATEGORY)** area, click **Item** and then click **Remove Field**. Use the same technique to remove the **Year Ordered** field.

c. In the **LEGEND (SERIES)** area, point to **Supplier**, and then drag the Supplier field to the **AXIS (CATEGORY)** area. **Close** the PivotChart Fields pane.

d. On the **Design tab**, in the **Chart Styles group**, click **Style 3**.

e. In the upper right corner of the Chart Area, click **Chart Elements**, and then *clear* the **Legend** check box to remove the legend from the chart.

f. With the **CHART ELEMENTS** list displayed, point to **Data Labels**, click the arrow, and then click **More Options**. In the **Format Data Labels** pane, select and clear check boxes as necessary so that only the **Category Name** and **Percentage** check boxes are selected. **Close** the Format Data Labels pane.

g. With all of the data labels selected, right-click one of the selected data labels, and then click **Font**. In the **Font dialog box**, select the value in the **Size** box, type **11** and then click **OK**.

4 Click the chart title—**Total**. Type **Office Supply Purchases** and then press Enter to insert the chart title.

a. Display the **Page Setup** dialog box, and then click the **Header/Footer tab**. Click **Custom Footer**, and then in the **Left section**, insert the file name. Click **OK** two times.

b. Display the **Office PivotTable** sheet and notice that the PivotTable is arranged to match the data in the pie chart. Insert a footer in the left section that includes the file name, and then center the worksheet **Horizontally** on the page.

c. Click the **File tab** and then click **Show All Properties**. As the **Tags**, type **office supplies** and as the **Subject**, type your course name and section

(Project 7D Office Supplies continues on the next page)

Skills Review **Project 7D Office Supplies** (continued)

number. Under **Related People**, be sure that your name displays as Author. **Save** your workbook.

d. If directed by your instructor to do so, submit your paper printout, your electronic image of your document that looks like a printed document, or your original Excel file. If required by your instructor, print or create an electronic version of your worksheet with formulas displayed. In the upper right corner of the Excel window, click **Close**.

END | You have completed Project 7D

Mastering Excel Project 7E Concessions Revenue

In the following Mastering Excel project, you will help Lindsay Johnson, the Director of Parks and Recreation, create and modify a PivotTable and PivotChart to analyze revenue from park concessions such as food, boat rentals, and golf fees. Your completed workbook will look similar to Figure 7.48.

Apply 7A skills from these Objectives:

1 Create a PivotTable Report

2 Use Slicers and Search Filters

3 Modify a PivotTable

4 Create a PivotChart

PROJECT FILES

For Project 7E, you will need the following file:

e07E_Concessions

You will save your workbook as:

Lastname_Firstname_7E_Concessions

PROJECT RESULTS

Excel 2016, Windows 10, Microsoft Corporation

FIGURE 7.48

(Project 7E Concessions Revenue continues on the next page)

Mastering Excel | Project 7E Concessions Revenue (continued)

1 Start Excel. From your student files, open **e07E_Concessions** and **Save** the file in your **Excel Chapter 7** folder as **Lastname_Firstname_7E_Concessions**

2 Click cell **A2**. Insert the last **Recommend PivotTable—Sum of Amount byPark**. Add the **Month** field to the **ROWS area**, and the **Item** field to the **COLUMNS area**, and then **Close** the **PivotTable Fields pane**.

3 Insert two slicers, one for the **Park** field and one for the **Item** field. Move the slicers so that they are to the right of the PivotTable. Apply **Slicer Style Light 4** to the **Park** slicer and **Slicer Style Light 6** to the **Item** slicer.

4 Use the slicers to filter the PivotTable by **Memorial Park**, and then by **Golf Fees**. Change the **Number Format** to the **Number** category and display zero decimal places and the 1000 Separator. Move the **Park** slicer so that its upper left corner aligns with the upper left corner of cell **E3**. Move the **Item** slicer so that its upper left corner aligns with the upper left corner of cell **H3**.

5 Make a copy of this worksheet and **Rename** the copied worksheet **Memorial Golf Fees**

6 Rename **Sheet1** as **Concessions Revenue** and then clear the filters and remove the slicers. In cell **A1**, type **Third Quarter Park Concession Revenue** and apply the **Title** cell style.

7 Display the **Field List**, and then *remove* the **Month** field from the **ROWS area** to display the Grand totals for each park and for each item. **Close** the **PivotTable Fields pane**.

8 Insert a **PivotChart** using the **Stacked Column** chart type. Move the chart to a new worksheet named **Concessions Chart**

9 Apply the **Layout 3** chart layout and **Chart Style 5**. As the **Chart Title**, type **3rd Quarter Concession Revenue** and then insert a custom footer with the file name in the left section. Hide all of the field buttons on the chart.

10 Hide the **Park Concessions** worksheet. Select all worksheets, and then insert a footer with the file name in the **left section**. Change the **Orientation** to **Landscape**, set the **Width** to **1 page**, and center the sheets **Horizontally**.

11 Display the properties. As the **Tags**, type **concession revenue** and as the **Subject**, type your course name and section number. Under **Related People**, be sure that your name displays as **Author**. **Save** your workbook.

12 If directed by your instructor to do so, submit your paper printout, your electronic image of your document that looks like a printed document, or your original Excel file. If required by your instructor, print or create an electronic version of your worksheet with formulas displayed. In the upper right corner of the Excel window, click **Close**.

END | You have completed Project 7E

Mastering Excel Project 7F Vehicles

Apply 7B skills from these Objectives:

5 Create a PivotTable from a Data Model

6 Create and Format a 3-D Pie PivotChart

In the following Mastering Excel project, you will assist Caryn Black, the Vehicle Fleet Manager, to create a Data Model, PivotTable, and PivotChart. Your results will look similar to those in Figure 7.49.

PROJECT FILES

For Project 7F, you will need the following files:

New blank workbook
e07F_Vehicle_Parts

You will save your workbook as:

Lastname_Firstname_7F_Vehicles

PROJECT RESULTS

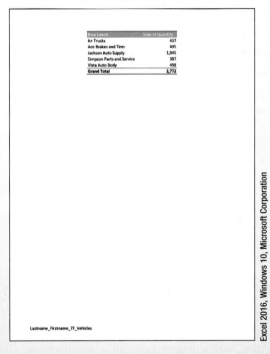

FIGURE 7.49

(Project 7F Vehicles continues on the next page)

Mastering Excel   Project 7F Vehicles (continued)

1 Start Excel and display a new blank workbook. **Save** the workbook in your **Excel Chapter 7** folder as **Lastname_Firstname_7F_Vehicles**

2 Use the **Get External Data** command to import from your student data files the Access database **e07F_Vehicle_Parts**. Select both tables in the database and view the data as a **PivotTable Report**. Put the data in the **Existing worksheet** in cell **A1**. Rename the sheet **Vehicle Supplies**

3 Create a PivotTable to sum the **Quantity** field. Display the **Supplier** as the column titles, and the **Item** and **Year Ordered** as the rows.

4 Format the numbers in the PivotTable using the **Number** category. Change the **Decimal places** to **0** and apply the **1000 Separator (,)**. Apply **Pivot Style Medium 14**.

5 Insert a **3-D Pie PivotChart** and move the chart to a new sheet with the name **Vehicle Supplies Chart**

6 Modify the chart so that only the **Supplier** field displays in the **AXIS (CATEGORY) area**. Remove any fields that display in the **LEGEND (SERIES) area**.

7 Apply **Style 4**, remove the legend from the chart, and display only the **Category Name** and **Percentage** data labels with the **Label Position** set to **Center**. Format the data labels by changing the font size to **13** with **Bold** applied.

8 Change the chart title to **Vehicle Supply Purchases** and then change the title font size to **22**. Insert a footer with the file name.

9 Display the **Vehicle Supplies** sheet and insert a footer in the left section that includes the file name, and then center the worksheet **Horizontally** on the page.

10 Display the file properties. As the **Tags**, type **vehicle supplies** and as the **Subject**, type your course name and section #. Under **Related People**, be sure that your name displays as Author. **Save** your workbook.

11 If directed by your instructor to do so, submit your paper printout, your electronic image of your document that looks like a printed document, or your original Excel file. If required by your instructor, print or create an electronic version of your worksheet with formulas displayed. In the upper right corner of the Excel window, click **Close**.

END | You have completed Project 7F

Mastering Excel | Project 7G Aquatics

In the following Mastering Excel project, you will assist Lindsay Johnson, the Director of Pools and Recreation, in creating and modifying a PivotTable report and a PivotChart report to analyze revenue and expenses from the Aquatics Program. Your completed workbook will look similar to Figure 7.50.

Apply 7A and 7B skills from these Objectives:

1 Create a PivotTable Report
2 Use Slicers and Search Filters
3 Modify a PivotTable
4 Create a PivotChart
5 Create a PivotTable from a Data Model
6 Create and Format a 3-D Pie PivotChart

PROJECT FILES

For Project 7G, you will need the following files:

e07G_Aquatics
e07G_Pool_Supplies

You will save your workbook as:

Lastname_Firstname_7G_Aquatics

PROJECT RESULTS

FIGURE 7.50

(Project 7G Aquatics continues on the next page)

Mastering Excel | Project 7G Aquatics (continued)

1 From your student files, open the file **e07G_Aquatics**. Save the file as **Lastname_Firstname_7G_Aquatics** in your **Excel Chapter 7** folder.

2 Click cell **A2**, and then insert a **Recommended PivotTable** by choosing the **Blank PivotTable** option in the lower left corner of the dialog box. **FILTER** by the **Month** field. Use the **Pool** field as the row labels and the **Item** field as the column labels. Place the **Amount** field in the **VALUES area**. **Close** the **PivotTable Fields list**.

3 Format the values in the PivotTable using the **Number** category to display zero decimal places and the **1000 Separator**.

4 Insert a slicer for the **Pool** field and for the **Item** field. Apply **Slicer Style Light 4** and **Slicer Style Light 6** to the slicers, respectively.

5 By using the two slicers, filter the data to show, for the **Tropics Pool**, the total revenue for **Spa Fees** and **Swim Lessons**. Recall that you can use Ctrl to select multiple filters in a slicer. Move the two slicers to the right of the filtered PivotTable, and then make a copy of this worksheet. Name the copied worksheet **Tropics Pool**

6 Display **Sheet1** and clear the filters from the slicers and remove the slicers from the worksheet. Rename the sheet **2Q Revenue**

7 Insert a **PivotChart** using the **Stacked Column** chart type. Move the chart to a new worksheet named **2Q Revenue Chart**

8 Apply the **Layout 3** chart layout and **Chart Style 9**. Add centered data labels, and then hide all of the field buttons on the chart. As the **Chart Title**, type **2nd Quarter Aquatics Program Revenue** and then insert a custom footer with the file name in the **left section**.

9 Add a new worksheet to the workbook, and then import the Access database **e07G_Pool_Supplies** into the Data Model as a **PivotTable Report** using both tables in the database. Rename the sheet **Supplies PivotTable**

10 To create the PivotTable, place the **Supplier** field from the **Suppliers** table in the **COLUMNS area**. From the **Supply Order Summary table**, place the **Item** field in the **ROWS area**, and the **Quantity** field in the **VALUES area**. Apply the **Number** format to the values in the PivotTable with zero decimals and the **1000 separator**.

11 **Insert** a row above the PivotTable, and in cell **A1**, type **Aquatics Program Purchases** and then apply the **Title** cell style.

12 Click in the PivotTable, and then insert a **3-D Pie PivotChart**. Move the chart to a new sheet with the name **Aquatic Supplies Chart**

13 Modify the chart so that only the **Supplier** field displays in the **AXIS (CATEGORY) area**. Remove any fields that display in the **LEGEND (SERIES) area**.

14 Apply **Style 7**, remove the legend from the chart, and display only the **Category Name** and **Percentage** data labels positioned in the **Center**. Format the data labels by changing the font size to **12**, the **Font color** to **Black, Text 1**, and then apply **Bold**.

15 Change the chart title to **Aquatic Supply Purchases** and then change the font size to **24**. Hide all of the field buttons on the chart, and then insert a footer with the file name.

16 **Hide** the **Aquatics Revenue** sheet. Select all the sheets and insert a footer in the left section that includes the file name, and then center the worksheet **Horizontally** on the page. Change the **Orientation** to **Landscape** and scale the **Width** to fit to **1 page**.

17 Display the properties. As the **Tags**, type **aquatic revenue, supplies** and as the **Subject**, type your course name and section #. Under **Related People**, be sure that your name displays as Author. **Save** your workbook.

18 If directed by your instructor to do so, submit your paper printout, your electronic image of your document that looks like a printed document, or your original Excel file. If required by your instructor, print or create an electronic version of your worksheet with formulas displayed. In the upper right corner of the Excel window, click **Close**.

END | You have completed Project 7G

Apply a combination of the **7A** and **7B** skills.	**GO! Fix It**	**Project 7H Park Revenue**	**MyITLab**
	GO! Make It	**Project 7I City Services Revenue**	**MyITLab**
	GO! Solve It	**Project 7J Inventory**	**MyITLab**
	GO! Solve It	**Project 7K Park Expenses**	

PROJECT FILES

For Project 7K, you will need the following file:

e07K_Park_Expenses

You will save your workbook as:

Lastname_Firstname_7K_Park_Expenses

Open the file **e07K_Park_Expenses** and save it as **Lastname_Firstname_7K_Park_Expenses** From the source data, create a PivotTable. Use the Month and Park fields as row labels. Use the Expense Item field as column labels. Place the Amount field in the VALUES area. Format the numbers to display zero decimal places and the 1000 separator. Format the PivotTable with an attractive style. Create a PivotChart on a separate sheet using the column chart style, and then use the report filters on the chart to show only the June data for Knight's Bridge, Five Points, and Sunset Parks, and only the expenses for Equipment, Grounds & Maintenance, and Utilities. Format the chart attractively. Hide the Park Expenses worksheet. On all sheets, insert the file name in the footer in the left section. Set the orientation to landscape and center horizontally. Add appropriate information to the document properties including the tag **park grounds** and submit as directed by your instructor.

Performance Level

Performance Criteria		Exemplary: You consistently applied the relevant skills	Proficient: You sometimes, but not always, applied the relevant skills	Developing: You rarely or never applied the relevant skills
	Create a PivotTable Report	The PivotTable Report displays Month and Park row labels, Expense Item in COLUMNS area, and Amount field in the VALUES area.	The PivotTable Report displays some of the items from the field list, but not all according to the directions.	The PivotTable was not created.
	Format a PivotTable Report	The PivotTable is formatted with the numbers displaying zero decimal places, the 1000 separator, and an attractive style.	The PivotTable is formatted with some but not all of the formatting, numbers displaying zero decimal places, the 1000 separator, and some attractive formatting.	The PivotTable was not formatted.
	Create and Format a PivotChart	A PivotChart displays on a separate sheet using the column chart style. The chart is filtered showing the data for June, only for Knight's Bridge, Five Points, and Sunset Parks, and only the expenses for Equipment, Grounds & Maintenance, and Utilities. The chart is formatted attractively.	A PivotChart displays on a separate sheet using the column chart style. The chart is filtered showing some but not all of the data for June, only for Knight's Bridge, Five Points, and Sunset Parks, and only the expenses for Equipment, Grounds & Maintenance, and Utilities. Some of the chart is formatted attractively.	The PivotChart was not created.

END | You have completed Project 7K

OUTCOME-BASED ASSESSMENTS (CRITICAL THINKING)

RUBRIC

The following outcomes-based assessments are open-ended assessments. That is, there is no specific correct result; your result will depend on your approach to the information provided. Make Professional Quality your goal. Use the following scoring rubric to guide you in how to approach the problem and then to evaluate how well your approach solves the problem.

The *criteria*—Software Mastery, Content, Format and Layout, and Process—represent the knowledge and skills you have gained that you can apply to solving the problem. The *levels of performance*—Professional Quality, Approaching Professional Quality, or Needs Quality Improvements—help you and your instructor evaluate your result.

	Your completed project is of Professional Quality if you:	Your completed project is Approaching Professional Quality if you:	Your completed project Needs Quality Improvements if you:
1-Software Mastery	Choose and apply the most appropriate skills, tools, and features and identify efficient methods to solve the problem.	Choose and apply some appropriate skills, tools, and features, but not in the most efficient manner.	Choose inappropriate skills, tools, or features, or are inefficient in solving the problem.
2-Content	Construct a solution that is clear and well organized, contains content that is accurate, appropriate to the audience and purpose, and is complete. Provide a solution that contains no errors of spelling, grammar, or style.	Construct a solution in which some components are unclear, poorly organized, inconsistent, or incomplete. Misjudge the needs of the audience. Have some errors in spelling, grammar, or style, but the errors do not detract from comprehension.	Construct a solution that is unclear, incomplete, or poorly organized, contains some inaccurate or inappropriate content, and contains many errors of spelling, grammar, or style. Do not solve the problem.
3-Format and Layout	Format and arrange all elements to communicate information and ideas, clarify function, illustrate relationships, and indicate relative importance.	Apply appropriate format and layout features to some elements, but not others. Overuse features, causing minor distraction.	Apply format and layout that does not communicate information or ideas clearly. Do not use format and layout features to clarify function, illustrate relationships, or indicate relative importance. Use available features excessively, causing distraction.
4-Process	Use an organized approach that integrates planning, development, self-assessment, revision, and reflection.	Demonstrate an organized approach in some areas, but not others; or, use an insufficient process of organization throughout.	Do not use an organized approach to solve the problem.

OUTCOMES-BASED ASSESSMENTS (CRITICAL THINKING)

GO! Think   Project 7L Golf Courses

PROJECT FILES

For Project 7L, you will need the following file:

e07L_Golf_Courses

You will save your workbook as:

Lastname_Firstname_7L_Golf_Courses

Open the file **e07L_Golf_Courses**, and then save it in your chapter folder as **Lastname_Firstname_7L_Golf_Courses** From the source data, create a PivotTable and filter the report on Month. Use Course as the row labels and Item as the column labels. Sum the amounts. Create a PivotChart report on a separate sheet for the 3rd Quarter Revenue. Exclude Logo Shirts and Golf Balls from the PivotChart. Hide the source data worksheet. Insert the file name in the left section of the footer on each page, center horizontally, set the orientation to landscape, add appropriate information to the document properties, including the tags **golf course revenue** and submit as directed by your instructor.

> **END | You have completed Project 7L**

GO! Think   Project 7M Pool Expenses   MyITLab

Build from
Scratch

You and GO!   Project 7N Inventory   MyITLab

Using the Data Analysis, Solver, and Scenario Features, and Building Complex Formulas

8

PROJECT 8A	**OUTCOMES** Analyze sales data to evaluate business solutions and compare data with a line chart.

OBJECTIVES

1. Calculate a Moving Average
2. Project Income and Expenses
3. Determine a Break-Even Point

PROJECT 8B	**OUTCOMES** Use Solver and Scenario Tools, and create complex formulas.

OBJECTIVES

4. Use Solver
5. Create Scenarios
6. Use Logical Functions
7. Create Complex Formulas

Tetra Images/Shutterstock

In This Chapter

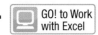 GO! to Work with Excel

Organizations forecast future results based on current trends. In this chapter, you will use Excel tools to analyze data, project values, determine the moving average of sales, project sales based on an expected growth rate, and determine a break-even point.

You will use the Solver and Scenario tools to search for solutions to problems. Solver can analyze financial planning problems that involve a quantity that changes over time. By using a scenario, you can look at a set of values and project forward to focus on possible results. Finally, you will create complex formulas to determine which employees meet specific performance criteria.

The projects in this chapter relate to **Brina's Bistro**, which is a chain of 25 casual, full-service restaurants based in Ft. Lauderdale, Florida. The Brina's Bistro owners plan an aggressive expansion program. To expand by 15 additional restaurants in Tennessee, Florida, Georgia, North Carolina, and South Carolina by 2021, the company must attract new investors, develop new menus, and recruit new employees, all while adhering to the company's quality guidelines and maintaining its reputation for excellent service. To succeed, the company plans to build on its past success and maintain its quality elements.

Sales Analysis

PROJECT ACTIVITIES

In Activities 8.01 through 8.06, you will use Excel's data analysis tools to determine the moving average of sales for the first six weeks at the new Brina's Bistro restaurant in Charlotte, North Carolina. Then you will project sales based on an expected growth rate and determine the break-even point for the restaurant. Your completed worksheets will look similar to Figure 8.1.

Please always review the downloaded Grader instructions before beginning.

PROJECT FILES

MyITLab grader — If your instructor wants you to submit Project 8A in the MyITLab Grader system, log into MyITLab, locate Grader Project 8A, and then download the files for this project.

For Project 8A, you will need the following file:

e08A_Charlotte_Sales

You will save your workbook as:

Lastname_Firstname_8A_Charlotte_Sales

PROJECT RESULTS

GO!
Walk Thru
Project 8A

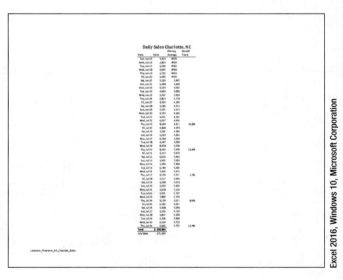

Excel 2016, Windows 10, Microsoft Corporation

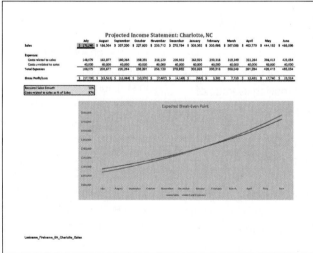

FIGURE 8.1 Project 8A Sales Analysis

Objective 1 Calculate a Moving Average

GO! Learn How
Video E8-1

Start-up businesses usually operate at a loss while the business grows with an expectation that at some future point the business will become profitable. Owners and investors want to know if the business is on track to become profitable and when the point of profitability is likely to occur.

Excel offers Data Analysis tools, which range from basic to very sophisticated, to help you project future results based on past performance. One of the basic tools is a *moving average*. A moving average is a sequence of averages computed from parts of a data series. In a chart, a moving average evens out the fluctuations in data, showing a pattern or trend more clearly. When you use a moving average, you choose how many preceding intervals to include in the average. A series of averages is calculated by moving—or changing—the range of cells used to calculate each average.

Activity 8.01 | Creating a Custom Number Format

2.1.1 Expert

Kelsey Tanner, the Chief Financial Officer for the Brina's Bistro restaurant chain, wants to see how sales have grown in the first six weeks at the new restaurant in Charlotte, North Carolina. Because there is a wide variation in sales at restaurants between weekday and weekend sales, Ms. Tanner first needs to add the day of the week to the Charlotte sales report. To accomplish this, you will customize the format applied to the date. You can customize numbers or dates when the available options do not match your needs.

> **ALERT!** **To submit as an autograded project, log into MyITLab, download the files for this project, and begin with those files instead of e08A_Charlotte_Sales.**

1 ▶ Start Excel. On the left, click **Open Other Workbooks**, click **Browse**, and then in the **Open** dialog box, navigate to the student data files that accompany this chapter. Open the file **e08A_Charlotte_Sales**. Click the **File tab**, click **Save As**, click **Browse**, navigate to the location where you will store your workbooks for this chapter, and then create a new folder named **Excel Chapter 8** In your new folder, **Save** the workbook as **Lastname_Firstname_8A_Charlotte_Sales**

2 ▶ Select the range **A3:AV4**. Right-click anywhere over the selection and click **Copy**. Click cell **A5**. Right-click and under **Paste Options**, click **Transpose (T)** 📋. Compare your screen with Figure 8.2.

If the data in a worksheet is arranged in rows but you want to work with columns instead, you can use this method to *transpose*, or switch, the rows and columns.

FIGURE 8.2

The TRANSPOSE Function

You can use the TRANSPOSE function to swap rows and columns. TRANSPOSE is an array function. The advantage to using the TRANSPOSE function is that a link is maintained between the original and transposed data.

3 ▶ Delete **rows 2:4**. In cell **C2**, type **Moving Average** In cell **D2**, type **Growth Trend** Select the range **A2:D2**, apply the **Heading 3** cell style, and then in the **Alignment group**, click **Wrap Text**.

4 ▶ Click cell **A3**. On the **Home tab**, in the **Number group**, click the **Dialog Box Launcher** ⬜. In the **Format Cells** dialog box, be sure the **Number tab** is selected. Under **Category**, click **Custom**. Examine the table in Figure 8.3 to familiarize yourself with the codes you can use to create a custom date format.

In the displayed Format Cells dialog box, custom codes display under Type, and the code for the selected date in cell A3 displays in the Type box. You can use this format as a starting point and then modify it, or you can type a new code in the Type box.

DATE CODES	
TO DISPLAY	**USE THIS CODE**
Months as 1–12	m
Months as 01–12	mm
Months as Jan–Dec	mmm
Months as January–December	mmmm
Months as the first letter of the month	mmmmm
Days as 1–31	d
Days as 01–31	dd
Days as Sun–Sat	ddd
Days as Sunday–Saturday	dddd
Years as 00–99	yy
Years as 1900–9999	yyyy

FIGURE 8.3

5 ▶ In the **Type** box, select the existing text and replace it by typing **ddd, mmm dd** Compare your screen with Figure 8.4.

As you type, you can see the date displayed in the new format in the Sample box. This code creates a date that displays as *Sun, Jun 15*. The comma displays as a comma.

FIGURE 8.4

Excel 2016, Windows 10, Microsoft Corporation.

6 ▸ Click **OK**, and notice the new date format in cell **A3**. Drag the fill handle to copy the new format down through cell **A49**. Apply AutoFit to **column A**.

7 ▸ Click cell **A50** and type **Total** Click cell **B50**, and then in the **Editing group**, click **AutoSum**. Verify the range to be summed is **B3:B49** and then press Enter. From the **Cell Styles** gallery, apply the **Currency [0]** cell style to cell **B50**. Your total equals *$232,844*. Apply the **Total** cell style to the range **A50:B50**. Press Ctrl + Home, click **Save** 🖫, and then compare your screen with Figure 8.5.

FIGURE 8.5

Excel 2016, Windows 10, Microsoft Corporation.

Activity 8.02 │ Calculating a Moving Average

Recall that a moving average calculates an average for a group of numbers over a specified interval. The number range that is averaged is constantly changing, dropping off the first number in the range and adding on the most recent number. In this manner, you can see a trend for widely fluctuating numbers. The sales activity for the new Charlotte restaurant has been strong on the weekends and slower during the week. You need to determine if, overall, the sales activity is trending upward or downward. The moving average tool is one of several Data Analysis tools.

1 ▸ Click the **File tab**. In **Backstage** view, click **Options**. In the **Excel Options** dialog box, on the left, click **Add-ins**. At the bottom of the dialog box, verify that the **Manage** box displays *Excel Add-ins*, and then click **Go**. In the **Add-ins** dialog box, if necessary, select the **Analysis ToolPak** check box. Compare your screen with Figure 8.6.

Recall that *Add-ins* are optional commands and features that are not immediately available; you must first install and/or activate an add-in to use it.

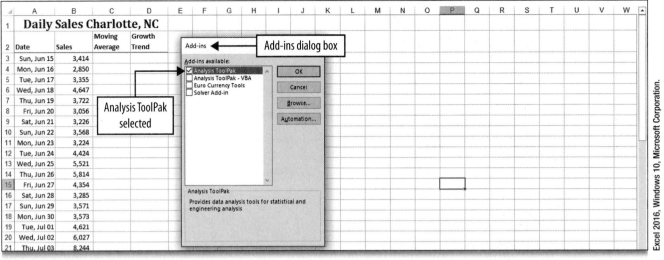

FIGURE 8.6

> 2 ▸ Click **OK**, and then click cell **A2** to make it the active cell. On the **Data tab**, in the **Analysis group**, click **Data Analysis**. Scroll the list as necessary, and then click **Moving Average**. Click **OK**.

The Moving Average dialog box displays. Here you define the input range, the *interval*—the number of cells to include in the average—and the output range.

> 3 ▸ With the insertion point blinking in the **Input Range** box, type **b2:b49** and then select the **Labels in First Row** check box.

The input range consists of the sales figures for the first six weeks, from Jun 15 through Jul 31. The first cell in the range, B2, contains the label *Sales*.

> 4 ▸ Click in the **Interval** box, and then type **7**

The moving average will be a weekly (7-day) average of sales. The first average will be from Sun, Jun 15 through Sat, Jun 21. The next average will be from Mon, Jun 16 through Sun, Jun 22. This pattern—dropping the oldest date and adding in the next date—will continue for the entire range.

> 5 ▸ Click in the **Output Range** box, type **c3** and then select the **Chart Output** check box. Compare your **Moving Average** dialog box with Figure 8.7.

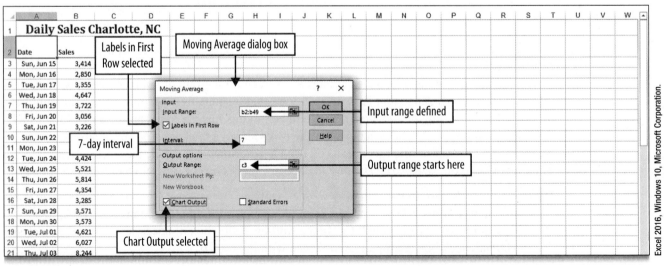

FIGURE 8.7

6 ▸ Click **OK. Save** 🖫 your workbook, and then compare your screen with Figure 8.8.

The moving averages display in column C and a chart is added to the worksheet. The first six cells in column C display the error code *#N/A* because there were not seven numbers available to use in the average. Green triangles display because the formulas in these cells refer to a range that has additional numbers adjacent. The first average—for Sun, Jun 15 through Sat, Jun 21—is *3,467*.

FIGURE 8.8

Activity 8.03 │ Modifying the Moving Average Chart and Creating a Dual-Axis Chart

5.2.2
4.1.2 Expert

To gain a clearer image of a trend, you can modify the moving average chart. In the moving average chart, the moving average is labeled Forecast. A *forecast* is a prediction of the future, often based on past performances.

1 ▸ Click the outer edge of the chart to select it, and then on the **Design tab**, in the **Location group**, click **Move Chart**.

2 ▸ Click **New sheet**, type **Sales Trend Chart** and then click **OK**.

By displaying this chart on a separate chart sheet, you can more easily see the actual data points—in dark blue—versus the moving average—in red—which is labeled *Forecast*. The horizontal category axis—the X-axis—is titled *Data Point*. This represents the dates for each sales figure. You can see by the red line that, overall, the sales activity for the first six weeks is trending slightly upward.

3 ▸ At the bottom of the chart, point to any of the data points to display the ScreenTip *Horizontal (Category) Axis*, and then click to select the axis. On the **Design tab**, in the **Data group**, click **Select Data**.

In the Select Data Source dialog box, you can change the category axis labels to display the range of dates that correspond to the sales figures. You can also use this method to add or edit the data series used in a chart.

 ANOTHER WAY   Right-click the axis, and then click Select Data.

4 In the **Select Data Source** dialog box, under **Horizontal (Category) Axis Labels**, click **Edit**. Click the **Sales sheet tab** to display the *Sales* worksheet, and then select the range **A9:A49**. Compare your screen with Figure 8.9.

> The selected range displays in the dialog box. You can select the range of cells to use as labels for the category axis. Start with cell A9 because that is the first row for which there is a moving average calculation.

FIGURE 8.9

5 In the **Axis Labels** dialog box, click **OK**. In the **Select Data Source** dialog box, click **OK**.

> Dates display along the category axis at the bottom of the chart.

6 Right-click the **Horizontal (Category) Axis**, and then click **Format Axis**. In the **Format Axis** pane, with **Axis Options** active, scroll down in the pane and click **Number**. Scroll down and click the **Category arrow**, and then click **Date**. Click the **Type** arrow, click the **3/14** format, and then **Close** ⊠ the **Format Axis pane**.

> This action shortens the date format displayed on the axis.

7 Click the **Horizontal (Category) Axis Title**—*Data Point*—to select it. On the **Formula Bar**, type **June 15th through July 31st** and then press ⏎. Click the **Horizontal Axis Title**, triple-click to select the text, and then on the mini toolbar, change the font size to **12**. Click the **Vertical (Value) Axis Title**—*Value*—to select it. On the **Formula Bar** type **Sales** and then press ⏎. Point to the **Vertical Axis Title**, double-click, and then on the mini toolbar, change the font size to **12**.

> The Horizontal Axis and Vertical Axis titles are changed and formatted.

8 Right-click any value on the **Vertical (Value) Axis**, and then click **Format Axis**. In the **Format Axis** pane, scroll to the bottom and click **Number**. Scroll down and click the **Category arrow**, and then click **Currency**. If necessary, set **Decimal places** to **0**, and then **Close** ⊠ the **Format Axis** pane.

> This action changes the values to Currency with 0 decimal places.

9 On the **Format tab**, in the **Current Selection group**, click the **Chart Elements arrow**, and then click **Series "Forecast"**. In the same group, click **Format Selection**. In the **Format Data Series** pane, if necessary, click the **Series Options** icon 📊. Under **Plot Series On**, click **Secondary Axis**. **Close** ⊠ the **Format Data Series** pane. **Save** your workbook, and then compare your chart with Figure 8.10.

> Plotting the Forecast series on the secondary axis makes the trend easier to visualize because the scale is adjusted to reflect the smaller differences in the Forecast series values. A ***dual-axis chart*** is useful when comparing data series that use different scales or different types of measurements.

=SERIES("Forecast",Sales!$A$9:$A$49,Sales!$C$3:$C$49,2)

Moving Average

Axis titles changed and formatted

Forecast series plotted on secondary axis

Shortened dates display on category axis

June 15th through July 31st

Sales Trend Chart   Sales   Projected Income

Excel 2016, Windows 10, Microsoft Corporation.

FIGURE 8.10

More Knowledge   **Using a Moving Average to Forecast Trends**

It is common to see moving averages used to calculate stock or mutual fund performance, where fluctuations in value may be frequent, but the overall trend is what is important. Moving averages can also be used as a tool to help predict how much inventory will be needed to meet demand. Although this is a forecasting tool, it is important to recognize its limitations. A moving average is based on historical data, and it is not necessarily a good prediction of what will occur in the future. Changes in the economy, competition, or other factors can affect sales dramatically, causing the moving average trend to change.

Activity 8.04 │ Calculating Growth Based on a Moving Average

You can also use a moving average to calculate the growth rate at different intervals.

1 Display the **Sales** worksheet. Scroll to position **row 21** near the top of your screen. Click cell **D21**, type **=(c21-c14)/c14** and then on the **Formula Bar**, click **Enter** ✓.

This formula calculates a weekly sales growth percentage from one Thursday to the next, based on the moving average.

2 Point to cell **D21**, right-click, and then on the mini toolbar, click **Percent Style** %. Click **Increase Decimal** .00 one time to display one decimal place—your result is *16.8%*.

3 With cell **D21** still selected, point to the cell and right-click, and then click **Copy**. Point to cell **D28**, right-click, and then under **Paste Options**, click **Paste (P)** .

The formula is copied to the next date that is a Thursday.

4 Point to cell **D35**—a Thursday—right-click, and then click **Paste (P)** . Continue in the same manner to paste the formula in cells **D42** and **D49** for the next two Thursday dates. Click **Save** 🖫, and then compare your screen with Figure 8.11.

The formula results show that the trend has moved up and down over five weeks of business.

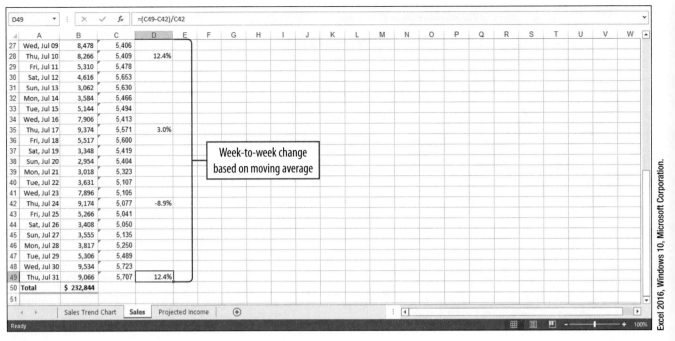

FIGURE 8.11

Objective 2 | **Project Income and Expenses**

GO! Learn How
Video E8-2

Income generally consists of sales for products and services. In a restaurant, this includes the sale of food and beverages. Expenses can be classified according to two broad categories: fixed expenses and variable expenses. *Fixed expenses* remain the same each month regardless of the amount of activity. They include items such as rent, utilities, insurance, and general overhead. *Variable expenses* change depending on the amount of sales. In a restaurant, the cost of the food—otherwise known as cost of goods sold—and wages are the two most common variable expenses. In this Activity, you will work with a worksheet that uses these two broad categories of expenses.

Activity 8.05 | Projecting Income and Expenses

1 ▶ Click cell **A51**, type **July Sales** Press Tab, and then in cell **B51**, type **=SUM(b19:b49)** and then press Enter. Display the **Projected Income** worksheet. Click cell **B3**. Type **=** Click the **Sales sheet tab**, click cell **B51**, which represents the July sales total, on the **Formula Bar** click **Enter** ✓, and then compare your screen with Figure 8.12.

This sheet contains the first portion of an income statement for the Charlotte restaurant. Now that you have referenced the July total from the Sales worksheet, you will use that value to project sales and expenses through June of next year.

FIGURE 8.12

Excel 2016, Windows 10, Microsoft Corporation.

2 ▶ Click cell **B2**, and then use the fill handle to fill the months for a year—from July to June—across to **column M**. With the range **B2:M2** selected, apply **Center** ▤.

3 ▶ Click cell **C3**, type **=b3*(1+$b12)** and then on the **Formula Bar** click **Enter** ✓. From the **Cell Styles** gallery, apply the **Currency [0]** cell style.

This formula takes the previous month's sales in cell B3 and multiplies it by 110% to determine a growth rate of 10 percent over the previous month—*$188,364*. Cell B12 indicates the Required Sales Growth rate of 10%, and the absolute cell reference is used so this formula can be copied across the row.

4 ▶ With cell **C3** as the active cell, use the fill handle to copy the formula and the formatting across to **column M**. Compare your screen with Figure 8.13.

Based on this projection, by June of next year, the Charlotte restaurant should have *$488,568* in monthly sales.

FIGURE 8.13

Excel 2016, Windows 10, Microsoft Corporation.

5 ▶ Click cell **B6** and examine the formula.

This formula multiplies the sales for July by the value in cell B13—*87%*. It is estimated that variable expenses for the first year will be 87 percent of sales. An absolute reference is used so this formula can be copied across the worksheet.

6 ▶ Use the fill handle to copy the formula from cell **B6** across the row to **column M**.

The variable expenses, which are based on sales, are projected for the next year. Variable expenses for June are calculated to be *425,054*.

> **7** Click cell **B7**. Use the fill handle to copy the value from cell **B7** across the row to **column M**.
>
> These are fixed costs—costs such as rent and insurance that are not directly tied to sales—which total 40,000.
>
> **8** Select the range **C8:M8**, and then on the **Home tab**, in the **Editing group**, click **AutoSum** Σ AutoSum ▾.
>
> This action calculates the total expenses for each month.
>
> **9** Click cell **B10**.
>
> This formula calculates the gross profit or loss for a month—sales minus expenses.
>
> **10** Use the fill handle to copy the formula from cell **B10** across to **column M**. **Save** 💾 your workbook, and then compare your screen with Figure 8.14.

	B10		fx	=B3-B8									

	A	B	C	D	E	F	G	H	I	J	K	L	M
1				Projected Income Statement: Charlotte, NC									
2		July	August	September	October	November	December	January	February	March	April	May	June
3	Sales	$ 171,240	$ 188,364	$ 207,200	$ 227,920	$ 250,712	$ 275,784	$ 303,362	$ 333,698	$ 367,068	$ 403,775	$ 444,152	$ 488,568
4													
5	Expenses:												
6	Costs related to sales	148,979	163,877	180,264	198,291	218,120	239,932	263,925	290,318	319,349	351,284	386,413	425,054
7	Costs unrelated to sales	40,000	40,000	40,000	40,000	40,000	40,000	40,000	40,000	40,000	40,000	40,000	40,000
8	Total Expenses	188,979	203,877	220,264	238,291	258,120	279,932	303,925	330,318	359,349	391,284	426,413	465,054
9													
10	Gross Profit/Loss	$ (17,739)	$ (15,513)	$ (13,064)	$ (10,370)	$ (7,407)	$ (4,148)	$ (563)	$ 3,381	$ 7,719	$ 12,491	$ 17,740	$ 23,514
11													
12	Required Sales Growth	10%											
13	Costs related to sales as % of Sales	87%											
14													

Total expenses

Profit or loss

Break-even point

FIGURE 8.14

Objective 3 Determine a Break-Even Point

GO! Learn How
Video E8-3

The goal of a business is to make a profit. However, a new business often operates at a loss for a period of time before becoming profitable. The point at which a company starts to make a profit is known as the ***break-even point***. A break-even point can be calculated for a product, a branch office, a division, or an entire company. The Brina's Bistro restaurants use a model for new restaurants that projects 10 percent growth, month-to-month, in the first year, with the expectation that sometime during the first year the restaurant will start to make a profit. Ms. Tanner wants to estimate when the new Charlotte restaurant will become profitable, based on sales for its first full month of business.

Activity 8.06 | Charting the Break-Even Point with a Line Chart

5.1.1, 5.2.1, 5.2.2

You can chart the results of the estimated income statement to create a visual image of the income and expenses and the projected break-even point.

Recall that a line chart displays trends over time. Time is displayed along the bottom axis and the data point values are connected with a line. If you want to compare more than one set of values, each group is connected by a different line. The curves and directions of the lines make trends noticeable to the reader.

1 Be sure that **columns A:M** display on your screen—if necessary, in the lower right corner of your screen, set the Zoom to 80% so that you can see the entire range. Select the range **A2:M3**.

By including the months in row 2 and the label in column A in the selection, the chart will be properly labeled.

2 On the **Insert tab**, in the **Charts group**, click **Recommended Charts**. In the **Insert Chart** dialog box, with the **Line chart** selected, click **OK**.

3 On the **Design tab**, in the **Data group**, click **Select Data**. In the **Select Data Source** dialog box, under **Legend Entries (Series)**, click **Add**. With the Insertion point in the **Series name** box, click cell **A8**. Press Tab, select the range **B8:M8** and then click **OK**. Verify that the **Chart data range** is *$A2:$M3* and *$A8:$M8*. Compare your screen with Figure 8.15.

By selecting the income totals and the expense totals, you will be able to see where they cross each other on a graph when you chart the break-even point. The Chart data range box displays the selected range—including the sheet name—using absolute references.

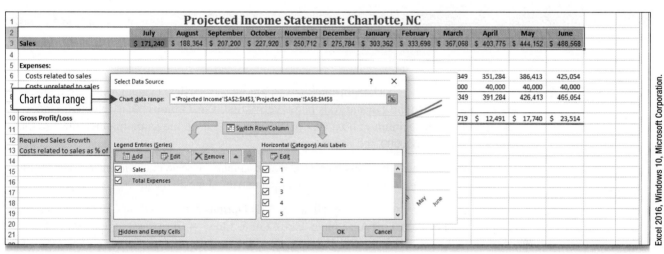

FIGURE 8.15

4 Click **OK**. On the **Design tab**, in the **Chart Layouts group**, click **Quick Layout**, and then click **Layout 3**. In the chart, click the text *Chart Title*, and then watch the **Formula Bar** as you type **Expected Break-Even Point** Press Enter.

5 By using the pointer, drag to position the upper left corner of the chart inside the upper left corner of cell **B15**.

6 Scroll to position **row 14** at the top of your screen. Drag the lower right sizing handle of the chart inside the lower right corner of cell **M36**. Compare your chart with the one shown in Figure 8.16.

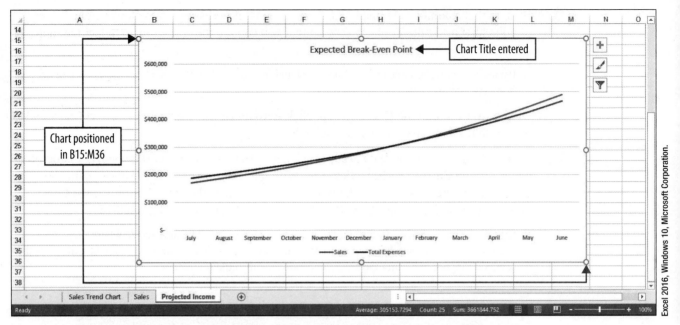

FIGURE 8.16

7 On the left side of the chart, right-click anywhere on the **Vertical (Value) Axis**, and then click **Format Axis**. In the **Format Axis** pane, verify that **Axis Options** ▮ is selected. Under **Axis Options**, in the **Minimum** box, type **100000** Press Enter. In the same manner, change the **Maximum** value to **500000** and press Enter.

Because there are no figures less than $100,000, changing the scale in this manner provides more vertical space on the chart and results in a more dramatic slope on the line.

8 At the top of the **Format Axis** pane, click the **Axis Options arrow**, and then click **Chart Area** to display the **Format Chart Area** pane. Click **Fill & Line** ◇. If necessary, expand **Fill**, and then click **Solid Fill**. Click the **Fill Color arrow** ◇ ▾, and then under **Theme Colors**, click **Tan, Background 2, Darker 10%**—in the third column, the second color.

9 At the top of the **Format Chart Area** pane, click the **Chart Options arrow**, and then click **Plot Area**. Format the **Plot Area** with the same fill. **Close** ✕ the **Format Plot Area** pane. Compare your screen with Figure 8.17.

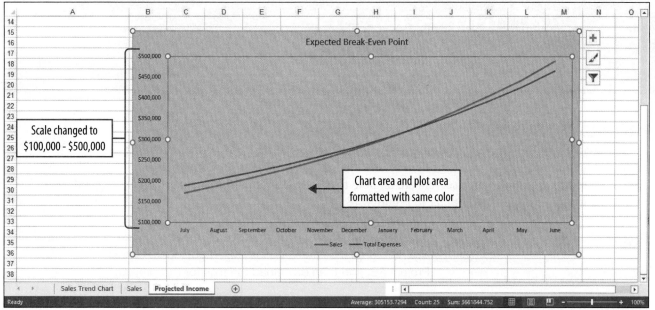

Scale changed to
$100,000 - $500,000

Chart area and plot area
formatted with same color

FIGURE 8.17

Excel 2016, Windows 10, Microsoft Corporation.

10 Display the **Sales Trend Chart** worksheet. On the **Page Layout tab**, in the **Page Setup group**, click the **Dialog Box Launcher** button ⌐ to display the **Page Setup** dialog box. Insert a custom footer with the file name in the **left section**. Display the **Projected Income** worksheet, click anywhere outside the chart, and then, if necessary, set the **Zoom** ⊟────╪────⊞ back to **100%**. Right-click the **sheet tab**, and then click **Select All Sheets** so that *[Group]* displays in the title bar. Display the **Page Setup** dialog box again, and then insert a footer in the **left section** that includes the file name.

11 On the **Page Layout tab**, set the **Orientation** to **Landscape**, and then in the **Scale to Fit** group, set the **Width** to **1 page** and the **Height** to **1 page**. Display the Page Setup dialog box again, and center the worksheets horizontally on the page. Press [Ctrl] + [Home] to move to the top of the worksheet.

12 Display the **document properties** and under **Related People**, be sure that your name displays as the author. If necessary, right-click the author name, click **Edit Property**, and then type your name. In the **Subject** box, type your course name and section #, and in the **Tags** box, type **moving average, break-even point** Display the grouped worksheets in **Print Preview**.

13 Under **Settings**, click the **Print Active Sheets arrow**, and then click **Print Entire Workbook**. At the bottom of the window, click **Next Page** here, ▶ to scroll through the worksheets.

14 On the left, click **Save**. Click the **Sales Trend Chart** sheet tab to ungroup the sheets.

15 If directed by your instructor to do so, submit a paper printout of each of the three worksheets, an electronic image of each of your three worksheets that looks like a printed document, or your original Excel file. If required by your instructor, print or create an electronic version of your worksheet with formulas displayed. In the upper right corner of the Excel window, click **Close** ☒.

END | You have completed Project 8A

Staffing Analysis

PROJECT ACTIVITIES

In Activities 8.07 through 8.18, you will assist Jillian Zachary, manager of the Ft. Lauderdale restaurant, in determining the most efficient work schedule for the server staff. You will also evaluate sales to determine which servers are eligible for Employee of the Week status. Your completed worksheets will look similar to Figure 8.18.

Please always review the downloaded Grader instructions before beginning.

 ## PROJECT FILES

MyITLab
grader

If your instructor wants you to submit Project 8B in the MyITLab grader system, log into MyITLab, locate Grader Project 8B, and then download the files for this project.

For Project 8B, you will need the following file:
e08B_Staffing_Analysis

You will save your workbook as:
Lastname_Firstname_8B_Staffing_Analysis

 ## PROJECT RESULTS

GO!
Walk Thru
Project 8B

FIGURE 8.18 Project 8B

Solver is an Excel what-if analysis tool with which you can find an optimal (maximum or minimum) value for a formula in one cell subject to constraints, or limits, on the values of other formula cells on a worksheet.

Use Solver when you need to make a decision that involves more than one variable. For example, the manager of the Ft. Lauderdale restaurant needs to determine the number of servers to assign to each evening shift so there are enough servers to handle customer demand, but not too many servers for the work required. Additionally, the schedule must allow each server to have two or more consecutive days off each week. Solver can help determine values like these—values that result in minimums, maximums, or specific results.

When you use Solver, the focus is on the **objective cell**—the cell that contains a formula for the results you are trying to determine, such as minimum weekly payroll expense. Your worksheet will have **decision variables**—also referred to as **variable cells**—that are cells in which the values will change to achieve the desired results. Your worksheet will also have **constraint cells**—cells that contain values that limit or restrict the outcome. As an example of a constraint, in determining a work schedule, you cannot schedule more than the total number of employees on the payroll.

Activity 8.07 | Installing Solver

Recall that add-ins are optional commands and features that are not immediately available; you must first install and/or activate an add-in to use it. Solver is an add-in.

1 Start Excel and display a new blank workbook. Click the **Data tab**, and then at the right end of the **Data tab**, in the **Analyze group**, check to see if **Solver** displays. Compare your screen with Figure 8.19.

FIGURE 8.19

Excel 2016, Windows 10, Microsoft Corporation.

2 If **Solver** displays, Solver has been installed on your computer and you can move to Activity 8.08. If Solver does *not* display, complete the remaining steps in this Activity to install it.

3 From **Backstage** view, display **Options**. On the left, click **Add-ins**, and then at the bottom of the screen, in the **Manage** box, if necessary, select **Excel Add-ins**. Compare your screen with Figure 8.20.

FIGURE 8.20

4 Click **Go**.

The Add-ins dialog box displays.

5 In the **Add-ins** dialog box, select the **Solver Add-in** check box, and then click **OK**.

The Solver Add-in is installed. On the Data tab, in the Analysis group, Solver displays.

Activity 8.08 | Understanding a Solver Worksheet

The manager of the Ft. Lauderdale restaurant wants to minimize the weekly payroll expense by scheduling only enough servers to handle established customer activity. She has reviewed customer activity for the past three months and determined how many servers are needed for the evening schedule on each day of the week. For example, more servers are needed on Friday and Saturday evenings than on Tuesday and Wednesday evenings. You will use Solver to determine the number of servers to schedule for each evening shift to meet the demand while minimizing the payroll expense. Before you can solve the problem of minimizing payroll expenses, familiarize yourself with the components of the worksheet.

> **ALERT!**   **To submit as an autograded project, log into MyITLab, download the files for this project, and begin with those files instead of e08B_Staffing_Analysis.**

1 Click **File tab**, on the left click **Close** to close the blank workbook. Click the **File tab** again, on the left click **Open**, and then click **Browse**. From the student data files that accompany this chapter, open the file **e08B_Staffing_Analysis**. Display the **Save As** dialog box, navigate to your **Excel Chapter 8** folder, and then using your own name, **Save** the workbook as **Lastname_Firstname_8B_Staffing_Analysis**

2 On the **Evening Shift** worksheet, click in cell **E4**, type **1** and press Enter to complete the information for **Schedule B**. Examine the range **A2:K8**, and then compare your screen with Figure 8.21.

Six possible schedules are labeled—A through F. Column B lists the consecutive days off for each schedule. For example, servers who work Schedule C have Tuesday and Wednesday as their days off. Servers who work Schedule D have Wednesday and Thursday off.

For each schedule, the cells in columns E through K indicate a 0 for days off and a 1 for days worked. For example, Schedule C indicates 0 under Tue and Wed—the days off—and 1 under Sun, Mon, Thu, Fri, and Sat—the days worked.

	A	B		F	G	H	I	J	K			
1			Days off for each schedule	er Staff Schedule								
2	Schedule	Days off	Employees	Sun	Mon	Tue	Wed	Thu	Fri	Sat		
3	A	Sun, Mon		0	0	1	1	1	1	1		
4	B	Mon, Tue		1	0	0	1	1	1	1		Days off indicated by 0;
5	C	Tue, Wed		1	1	0	0	1	1	1		Days worked indicated by 1
6	D	Wed, Thu		1	1	1	0	0	1	1		
7	E	Thu, Fri		1	1	1	1	0	0	1		
8	F	Sat, Sun		0	1	1	1	1	1	0		
9												
10		Schedule Totals:	0	0	0	0	0	0	0	0		
11												
12		Total Demand:		22	17	14	15	20	24	24		
13												
14		Weekly Wage Per Server:	$ 297.50									
15		Weekly Payroll Expense:	$0.00									
16												

FIGURE 8.21

Excel 2016, Windows 10, Microsoft Corporation.

3 Click cell **C10**, and then look at the **Formula Bar**.

Cell C10 sums the range C3:C8. It represents the number of servers who are assigned to each schedule. It is currently zero because no servers have been assigned to a schedule. The range C3:C8 is shaded in orange. These are the decision variables—the values that will change to achieve the desired results. Here, the desired result is to have only enough staff assigned to meet customer demand and hence minimize payroll expense.

4 Click cell **C14** and examine the formula.

This formula calculates the weekly wage, based on $8.50 per hour, multiplied by seven hours worked each day, multiplied by five days worked per week. The proposed schedule shows all servers working five days each week.

5 Click cell **C15**, which is formatted using the Calculation cell style, and examine the formula.

This cell calculates the total weekly payroll expense by multiplying the number of servers scheduled to work—cell C10—by the Weekly Wage Per Server—cell C14. Cell C15 is the objective cell. Recall that the objective cell contains the result that you are trying to achieve. In this instance, you are trying to achieve the minimum payroll expense that must be paid while maintaining enough servers on duty to meet established customer demand.

6 Select the range **E12:K12**.

These cells represent the minimum number of servers required to serve the number of customers expected each day of the week. The cells in this row will be one of the constraints used to determine the minimum weekly payroll expense. Recall that *constraints* are conditions or restrictions that must be met. In this case, the number of servers scheduled must be equal to or greater than the number required for each day.

7 Click cell **E10**.

The formulas in this row multiply the number of people assigned to work each schedule, arriving at a total number available each day of the week.

8 Click cell **C3**, and then click the **Name Box arrow**. Notice that cell **C3** has been named *Sun_Mon*. Compare your screen with Figure 8.22 and take a moment to review each of the cells you will work with in this Project.

The cells in the range C3:C8, the decision variables, have been named with their corresponding days off.

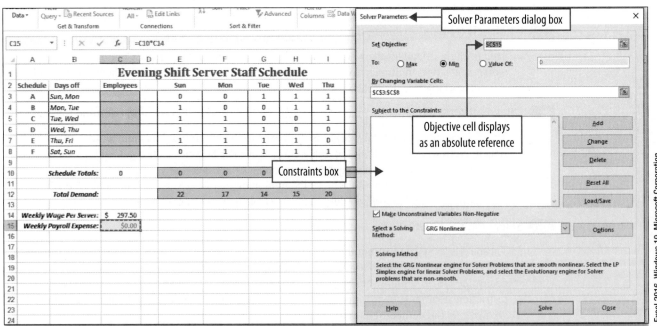

FIGURE 8.22

Activity 8.09 | Using Solver

In this Activity, you will use Solver to determine the minimum payroll expense; that is, the minimum number of servers who can be on duty and still meet expected customer demand. This process involves identifying the objective cell, the decision variable cells, and the constraint cells.

1 Click cell **C15**—the objective cell. On the **Data tab**, in the **Analyze group**, click **Solver**. If necessary, drag the **Solver Parameters** dialog box to the right side of your worksheet. In the **Set Objective** box, be sure that *$C$15* displays. Compare your screen with Figure 8.23.

The Solver Parameters dialog box displays and cell C15 displays as an absolute reference in the Set Objective box.

FIGURE 8.23

2 In the **Solve Parameters** dialog box, under **Set Objective**, click the **Min** option button.

The three option buttons here enable you to use the Solver tool to maximize, minimize, or solve for a specific value.

3 Click in the **By Changing Variable Cells** box, and then if necessary select the range **C3:C8**.

The range displays as an absolute reference. In this cell range, Solver will place the optimum number of servers who must be assigned to each schedule to minimize payroll and meet the constraints that are set.

4 Click in the **Subject to the Constraints** box, and then on the right, click **Add**.

The Add Constraint dialog box displays; here you enter constraints—limitations caused by various circumstances.

5 With the insertion point blinking in the **Cell Reference** box, select the range **C3:C8**.

6 In the middle box, click the **arrow**, and then click **int**. Compare your screen with Figure 8.24.

This constraint requires that only an *integer*—a whole number—can be used, because you cannot assign part of a person as a server. In the Add Constraint dialog box, in the Constraint box, *integer* displays.

FIGURE 8.24

Excel 2016, Windows 10, Microsoft Corporation.

7 Click **OK**. If necessary, on the taskbar, click the blinking Excel icon to redisplay the Solver Parameters dialog box.

The Add Constraint dialog box closes and the first constraint is added to the Solver Parameters dialog box.

8 Click **Add** again. With the insertion point in the **Cell Reference** box, select the range **C3:C8**. In the middle box, click the **arrow**, and then click **>=**. In the **Constraint** box, type **0** (zero, not the letter O) and then compare your dialog box with Figure 8.25.

This constraint (limitation) requires that the number of servers assigned to each schedule be a positive number—a negative number of servers cannot be assigned. The number must be equal to or greater than zero.

FIGURE 8.25

Excel 2016, Windows 10, Microsoft Corporation.

9 Click **OK**. If necessary, on the taskbar, click the blinking Excel icon to redisplay the Solver Parameters dialog box.

The second constraint is added to the Solver Parameters dialog box.

10 Click **Add**. With the insertion point blinking in the **Cell Reference** box, select the range **E10:K10**. In the middle box, click the **arrow**, and then click **>=**. With the insertion point blinking in the **Constraint** box, select the range **E12:K12**.

This constraint requires that the number of servers assigned to each shift be greater than or equal to the number of servers required each day to meet the projected demand. For example, on Saturday, the number of servers assigned must be at least 24.

11 Click **OK**. Compare your **Solver Parameters** dialog box with Figure 8.26.

Three constraints display in the Solver Parameters dialog box. First, the number of servers assigned to any given Schedule—C3:C8—must be a whole number. Second, the number of servers—C3:C8—assigned to any given Schedule must be a positive number equal to or greater than zero. Third, the number of servers—E10:K10—assigned to each day's shift must be equal to or greater than the number of servers needed to meet the established demand in cells E12:K12. With the constraints established, you can solve for—calculate—the minimum payroll expense.

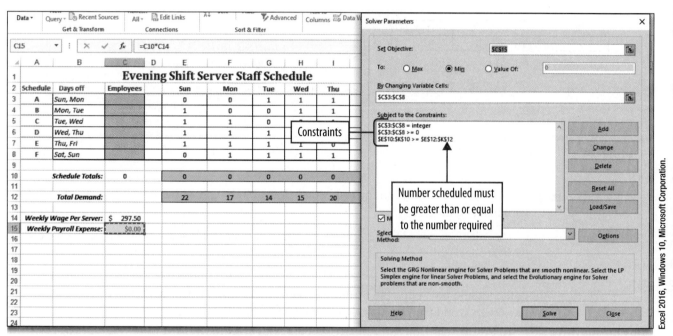

FIGURE 8.26

Excel 2016, Windows 10, Microsoft Corporation.

12 At the bottom of the **Solver Parameters** dialog box, click **Solve**. If necessary, on the taskbar, click the blinking Excel icon to display the Solver Results dialog box. In the **Solver Results** dialog box, with **Keep Solver Solution** selected, click **OK**. **Save** your workbook, and then compare your screen with Figure 8.27.

The decision variables—the cell range C3:C8—displays the number of servers that should be assigned to each Schedule to meet the demand while minimizing payroll. Cell C15—the objective cell—shows the Weekly Payroll Expense as *$8,330.00*, and the number of servers who will work each schedule displays in cells E10:K10. Thus, to adequately staff the evening shifts and to give servers two consecutive days off requires a total of 28 servers each working 5 days a week and 7 hours each day—cell C10. The minimum weekly payroll expense for 28 servers is $8,330.00—28 servers times $297.50.

Evening Shift Server Staff Schedule

Schedule	Days off	Employees	Sun	Mon	Tue	Wed	Thu	Fri	Sat
A	Sun, Mon	2	0	0	1	1	1	1	1
B	Mon, Tue	9			1	1	1	1	
C	Tue, Wed	5			0	1	1	1	
D	Wed, Thu	4			0	0	1	1	
E	Thu, Fri	4			1	0	0	1	
F	Sat, Sun	4	0	1	1	1	1	1	0
		28	22	17	14	19	20	24	24
			22	17	14	15	20	24	24
Weekly Wage Per Server:		$ 297.50							
Weekly Payroll Expense:		$8,330.00							

Callouts in figure: *Number of employees assigned to each schedule* · *Number of employees who will work each day* · *Total number of employees needed* · *Payroll expense minimized*

FIGURE 8.27

Excel 2016, Windows 10, Microsoft Corporation.

13 This is one possible solution. Later, you will consider alternatives with a different distribution of staff over the week.

More Knowledge   Solver Reports

The Solver Results dialog box offers three reports—Answer, Sensitivity, and Limits—that can be created to help you understand the results. The Answer Report displays the original and final values for the objective cell and the decision variables. It also shows the impact of the constraints on determining values for the decision variables and whether the result for each cell is binding or nonbinding. It helps you understand where there may be some flexibility in the results if you want to do further analysis or consider other alternatives. The Sensitivity and Limits reports are not meaningful in the current example because of the integer constraints that have been applied.

Objective 5   Create Scenarios

GO! Learn How
Video E8-5

The current solution indicates nine servers assigned to *Schedule B, Mon and Tue off*, and only two servers assigned to *Schedule A, Sun and Mon off*. Ms. Zachary wants to see what would happen if she assigned more servers to Schedule A. You can create several possible solutions to a problem and then use Excel's *Scenario Manager* what-if analysis tool to compare the alternatives. A *scenario* is a set of values that Excel saves and can substitute automatically in your worksheet.

Activity 8.10   Creating a Scenario Using the Scenario Manager

3.4.3

You can create a scenario from the Solver dialog box, or you can open the Scenario Manager dialog box and create a scenario. Here, you will use the Scenario Manager dialog box to save the existing solution for minimizing the weekly server staff payroll.

1 Select the range **C3:C8**.

These are the decision variable cells defined in Solver that are used to calculate the minimum payroll expense while matching the staffing requirements that are shown in row 12.

2 On the **Data tab**, in the **Forecast group**, click **What-If Analysis**, and then click **Scenario Manager**. Compare your screen with Figure 8.28.

The Scenario Manager dialog box displays. It shows that no scenarios have been defined.

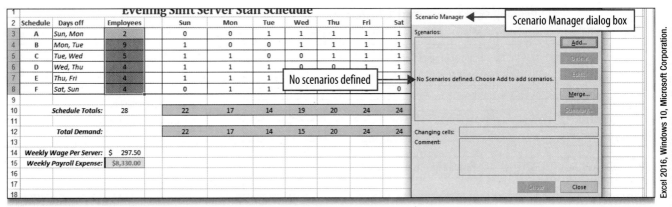

FIGURE 8.28

3 In the **Scenario Manager** dialog box, click **Add**.

The Add Scenario dialog box displays. Here you name the scenario and identify the decision variable cells.

4 In the **Scenario name** box, type **Option 1** Verify that the **Changing cells** box displays *C3:C8*.

You will save the existing solution as your first scenario.

5 Click **OK**. Compare your screen with Figure 8.29.

The Scenario Values dialog box displays and the current value in each of the decision variable cells is listed. You will accept the values that are displayed.

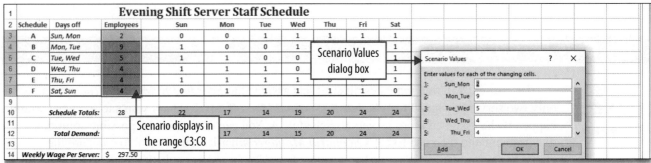

FIGURE 8.29

6 In the **Scenario Values** dialog box, click **OK**.

The Scenario Manager dialog box redisplays, and the first scenario is listed in the Scenarios box as *Option 1*.

7 In the **Scenario Manager** dialog box, click **Close**. Save 💾 your workbook.

Activity 8.11 | Creating a Scenario Using Solver

You can also create a scenario using the Solver Parameters dialog box. Ms. Zachary wants to add another schedule option that would assign more servers to Schedule A so more people could be off on Sunday, a more traditional day off, and to help balance the numbers of shifts among employees.

1 Click cell **C15**—the objective cell. On the **Data tab**, in the **Analyze group**, click **Solver**. In the **Solver Parameters** dialog box, verify that the **Set Objective** box displays *$C$15* and the **By Changing Variable Cells** box displays *$C$3:$C$8*.

The values from the first solution display in the Solver Parameters dialog box.

2 To the right of **Subject to the Constraints** box, click **Add**.

3 In the **Add Constraint** dialog box, click the **Cell Reference** box, and then click cell **C3**. In the middle box, click the **arrow**, and then click **=**. In the **Constraint** box, type **4**

This constraint will assign four servers to *Schedule A—Sun and Mon off*.

4 Click **OK**.

A fourth constraint is added to the Solver Parameters dialog box. Recall that because each of the cells in the range C3:C8 were named, the constraint displays as Sun_Mon =4. The range name displays when you summarize the alternatives you are creating.

5 In the lower right corner of the dialog box, click **Solve**. Drag the **Solver Results** dialog box to the right side of the screen and compare your screen with Figure 8.30.

A new solution is found and the Solver Results dialog box displays. The Weekly Payroll Expense remains at $8,330.00, but the servers are more evenly distributed across the schedules, with more servers scheduled on Friday and Saturday when the restaurant is the busiest. This provides a better distribution of staff on the busiest weekend days, while giving more people Sunday off. This shows that there may be more than one acceptable solution to the problem of minimizing the payroll.

FIGURE 8.30

6 Click **Save Scenario** to display the **Save Scenario** dialog box.

7 In the **Scenario Name** box, type **Option 2** and then click **OK**.

A second scenario is saved and the Solver Results dialog box displays.

8 In the **Solver Results** dialog box, click **Restore Original Values**, and then click **OK**. Save 🖫 your workbook.

The dialog box closes and the previous solution is redisplayed on the worksheet.

Activity 8.12 | Creating a Scenario Summary

Ms. Zachary wants to see what would happen if she schedules six servers to have Saturday off. Schedule F includes both Saturday and Sunday off, which would give more employees a traditional weekend off. After the third scenario is created, you will view a summary of the results of all three alternatives.

1 Verify that cell **C15** is still the active cell. On the **Data tab**, in the **Analyze group**, click **Solver**.

In the Solver Parameters dialog box, all four constraints (from Option 2) display, even though the currently displayed solution—Option 1—does not use the constraint that requires four servers be assigned to schedule A—*Sun_Mon = 4*.

2 In the **Subject to the Constraints** box, select the fourth constraint—**Sun_Mon = 4**—and then on the right side of the dialog box, click **Delete**.

3 Click **Add**.

4 In the **Add Constraint** dialog box, click in the **Cell Reference** box, and then click cell **C8**. Change the middle box to **=**. In the **Constraint** box, type **6** and then click **OK**. Compare your screen with Figure 8.31.

Four constraints are listed in the Solver Parameters dialog box.

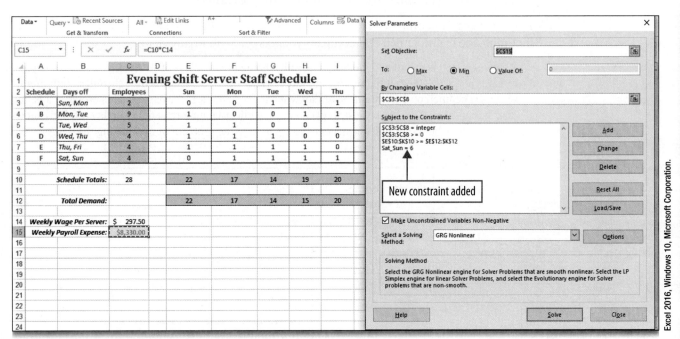

FIGURE 8.31

5 Click **Solve**.

A new solution is found; however, the Weekly Payroll Expense in cell C15 increases to *$8,925.00*, and the number of servers required to meet this scenario in cell C10 increases to 30.

6 If necessary, on the taskbar, click the blinking Excel icon to redisplay the Solver Results dialog box. Click **Save Scenario**. In the **Save Scenario** dialog box, type **Option 3** and then click **OK**.

The third scenario is saved and the Solver Results dialog box displays.

7 Click **Restore Original Values**, and then click **OK**.

The previous solution is restored to the worksheet.

8 On the **Data tab**, in the **Forecast group**, click **What-If Analysis**, and then click **Scenario Manager**. Compare your screen with Figure 8.32.

The Scenario Manager dialog box displays the three scenario names that you have created.

Evening Shift Server Staff Schedule

Schedule	Days off	Employees	Sun	Mon	Tue	Wed	Thu	Fri	Sat
A	Sun, Mon	2	0	0	1	1	1	1	1
B	Mon, Tue	9	1	0	0	1	1	1	1
C	Tue, Wed	5	1	1	0	0	1	1	1
D	Wed, Thu	4	1	1	1	0	0	1	1
E	Thu, Fri	4	1	1	1	1	0	0	1
F	Sat, Sun	4	0	1	1	1	1	1	0
	Schedule Totals:	28	22	17	14	19	20	24	24
	Total Demand:		22	17	14	15	20	24	24
Weekly Wage Per Server:		$ 297.50							
Weekly Payroll Expense:		$8,330.00							

Scenario Manager — ? X

Scenarios:
Option 1
Option 2
Option 3

Three scenarios listed

Add...
Delete
Edit...
Merge...
Summary...

Changing cells: $C$3:$C$8
Comment: Created by Firstname Lastname on 11/29/2015

Show   Close

FIGURE 8.32

9 In the **Scenario Manager** dialog box, click **Summary**.

The Scenario Summary dialog box displays. Here you can choose between a Scenario summary, which displays the data in a table, or a Scenario PivotTable report.

10 Be sure **Scenario summary** is selected, and then click **OK**. Compare your screen with Figure 8.33.

Excel inserts a new worksheet in your workbook—the *Scenario Summary* sheet, which compares the three options side by side. The results for Option 1 and Option 2 indicate the same amount in the results cell—$8,330.00—and Option 3 indicates $8,925.00 in payroll expenses. The outline pane displays along the top and left side of the worksheet.

A1

Scenario Summary

	Current Values:	Option 1	Option 2	Option 3
Changing Cells:				
Sun_Mon	2	2	4	2
Mon_Tue	9	9	7	9
Tue_Wed	5	5	7	5
Wed_Thu	4	4	4	4
Thu_Fri	4	4	4	4
Sat_Sun	4	4	2	6
Result Cells:				
$C$15	$8,330.00	$8,330.00	$8,330.00	$8,925.00

Scenarios listed side by side

Notes: Current Values column represents values of changing cells at time Scenario Summary Report was created. Changing cells for each scenario are highlighted in gray.

FIGURE 8.33

11 Select the range **D12:G12** and then on the **Home tab**, in the **Editing group**, click **AutoSum** ∑ AutoSum ▾. **Save** 🖫 your workbook.

The total number of servers required for each scenario is added to the Scenario Summary sheet. Options 1 and 2 require 28 servers to fill the schedule and Option 3 requires 30 servers.

GO! Learn How
Video E8-6

There are a number of *logical functions* you can use to test for specific conditions. The results of a logical test are either TRUE or FALSE. Recall the SUM function adds values in a specified range of cells. The *SUMIF function* contains a logic test—it will add values in a specified range that meet a certain condition or criteria. The *SUMIFS function* is similar to the SUMIF function, but allows you to specify multiple ranges and multiple criteria to test. The *COUNTIF function* and *COUNTIFS function* work in the same way, counting cells that meet specific criteria in specified ranges. The *syntax*, or arrangement of the arguments in a function, displays in a ScreenTip as you begin to build the function.

Activity 8.13 | Using the SUMIF Function

4.2.2

Ms. Zachary wants to see the total each server has sold over the past week. SUMIF can be used to add values in a range that meet a specific condition or criteria. In this Activity, you will use SUMIF to calculate the total weekly sales for each server.

1 Display the **Weekly Sales** worksheet.

> This worksheet lists the sales for each server that has worked the day or evening shift the week of January 1-8.

2 Click cell **G3**, and then type **=sumif(** and then compare your screen with Figure 8.34.

> The syntax displays for the SUMIF function. It has two required arguments: *range* and *criteria*, and one optional argument: *sum_range*.

	A	B	C	D	E	F	G	H	I	J	K	L
1	Sales by Server - Week of Jan 1-8					Total Sales Per Server			Server Sales - Evening Shift			
2	Day	Shift	Server	Nightly Sales		Server	Weekly Sales		Server	Shift	Total	Number of Shifts
3	Sun	Evening	Alishia	2,600.71		Alishia	=sumif(					
4	Sun	Day	Alishia	2,682.33		Arty						
5	Sun	Evening	Carol	2,578.45		Bryan						
6	Sun	Evening	Hugo	2,608.13		Carol						
7	Sun	Evening	Meredith	1,938.03		Hugo						
8	Sun	Day	Bryan	1,678.69								
9	Sun	Evening	Bryan	2,796.24								
10	Sun	Evening	Todd	2,404.86		Jerri						

SUMIF(range, criteria, [sum_range])

Optional argument displays in brackets

SUMIF syntax in ScreenTip

FIGURE 8.34

Excel 2016, Windows 10, Microsoft Corporation.

3 Notice *range* is bold in the ScreenTip that displays. Select the range **C3:C102** and press F4 to make the value absolute. Type **,** (a comma) and notice *criteria* is now bold in the ScreenTip.

4 Click cell **F3**, and then type **,** (a comma).

5 Notice *[sum_range]* is now bold. Select the range **D3:D102** and press F4. Type **)** and then, on the **Formula Bar**, click **Enter** ✓.

> The brackets around *sum_range* indicate it is an optional argument. If you do not include it, Excel will attempt to determine what range to use for the calculation.

6 Drag the fill handle to copy the formula down through cell **G19**. Format the range **G3:G19** using cell style **Currency [0]**. **Save** 🖫 your workbook and compare your screen with Figure 8.35.

FIGURE 8.35

Excel 2016, Windows 10, Microsoft Corporation.

Activity 8.14 | Using the SUMIFS Function

3.1.3 Expert

Because each server may work multiple shifts, you can use the SUMIFS function to include a second criteria—Shift—to SUM. In this Activity, you will use SUMIFS to calculate sales for each server for the evening shift.

1 Select the range **F3:F19**, which contains the server names. Right-click over the selection and click **Copy**. Right-click cell **I3** and click **Paste (P)** 📋. Click cell **J3**, type **Evening** and then copy the cell down through **J19**.

2 Click cell **K3** and type **=sumifs(** Compare your screen with Figure 8.36.

In the SUMIFS function, the *sum_range* argument is specified first, followed by the first *criteria_range1* and *criteria1*. Additional *criteria_range* and *criteria* arguments can follow, up to a maximum of 127.

FIGURE 8.36

Excel 2016, Windows 10, Microsoft Corporation.

3 Select the range **D3:D102** and press F4 to make the value absolute. Type **,** (a comma), select the range **C3:C102,** and press F4. Type **,** (a comma). Click cell **I3**, and then type **,** (a comma).

The optional arguments [criteria_range2, criteria2] display in brackets in the ScreenTip.

4 Select the range **B3:B102** and then press F4. Type **,** and then click cell **J3**. Type **)** and then on the **Formula Bar** click **Enter** ✓.

5 Drag the fill handle to copy the formula down through cell **K19**. Format the range **K3:K19** using cell style **Currency [0]**. **Save** 💾 your workbook and compare your screen with Figure 8.37.

In this SUMIFS function, you used the Nightly Sales as the sum_range, the Server as the first criteria, and the Shift as the second criteria.

FIGURE 8.37

Activity 8.15 | Using the COUNTIFS Function

MOS

3.1.3 Expert

Ms. Zachary wants to see the number of evening shifts each server has worked over the past week. The COUNTIFS function can be used to count items that meet multiple conditions—in this case, the server and the shift worked.

1 Click cell **L3** and type **=countifs(** and then compare your screen with Figure 8.38.

The COUNTIFS function has two required arguments: *criteria_range1* and *criteral*. Additional *criteria_range* and *criteria* arguments can follow.

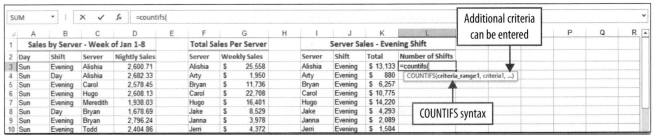

FIGURE 8.38

Excel 2016, Windows 10, Microsoft Corporation.

2 Select the range **C3:C102** and press F4 to make the value absolute. Type **,** (a comma), click cell **I3**, and then type **,** (a comma).

The optional arguments [criteria_range2, criteria2] display in brackets in the ScreenTip.

3 Select the range **B3:B102** and then press F4. Type **,** and then click cell **J3**. Type **)** and then on the **Formula Bar** click **Enter** ✓.

4 Drag the fill handle to copy the formula down through cell **L19**. **Save** 🖫 your workbook and compare your screen with Figure 8.39.

Using the COUNTIFS function, Ms. Zachary is able to see how many evening shifts each server worked this week.

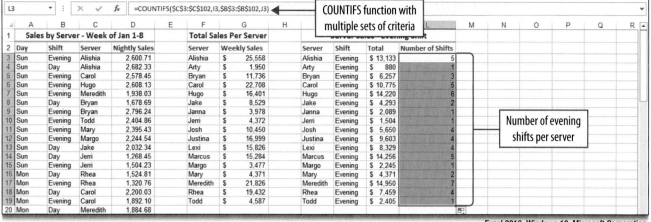

FIGURE 8.39

Formula bar: L3 =COUNTIFS($C$3:$C$102,I3,$B$3:$B$102,J3) — **COUNTIFS function with multiple sets of criteria**

Day	Shift	Server	Nightly Sales		Server	Weekly Sales		Server	Shift	Total	Number of Shifts
Sales by Server - Week of Jan 1-8					Total Sales Per Server						
Sun	Evening	Alishia	2,600.71		Alishia	$ 25,558		Alishia	Evening	$ 13,133	5
Sun	Day	Alishia	2,682.33		Arty	$ 1,950		Arty	Evening	$ 880	1
Sun	Evening	Carol	2,578.45		Bryan	$ 11,736		Bryan	Evening	$ 6,257	3
Sun	Evening	Hugo	2,608.13		Carol	$ 22,708		Carol	Evening	$ 10,775	5
Sun	Evening	Meredith	1,938.03		Hugo	$ 16,401		Hugo	Evening	$ 14,220	6
Sun	Day	Bryan	1,678.69		Jake	$ 8,529		Jake	Evening	$ 4,293	2
Sun	Evening	Bryan	2,796.24		Janna	$ 3,978		Janna	Evening	$ 2,089	1
Sun	Evening	Todd	2,404.86		Jerri	$ 4,372		Jerri	Evening	$ 1,504	1
Sun	Evening	Mary	2,395.43		Josh	$ 10,450		Josh	Evening	$ 5,650	4
Sun	Evening	Margo	2,244.54		Justina	$ 16,999		Justina	Evening	$ 9,603	4
Sun	Day	Jake	2,032.34		Lexi	$ 15,826		Lexi	Evening	$ 8,329	4
Sun	Day	Jerri	1,268.45		Marcus	$ 15,284		Marcus	Evening	$ 14,256	5
Sun	Evening	Jerri	1,504.23		Margo	$ 3,477		Margo	Evening	$ 2,245	1
Mon	Day	Rhea	1,524.81		Mary	$ 4,371		Mary	Evening	$ 4,371	2
Mon	Evening	Rhea	1,320.76		Meredith	$ 21,826		Meredith	Evening	$ 14,950	7
Mon	Day	Carol	2,200.03		Rhea	$ 19,432		Rhea	Evening	$ 7,459	4
Mon	Evening	Carol	1,892.10		Todd	$ 4,587		Todd	Evening	$ 2,405	1
Mon	Day	Meredith	1,884.68								

Number of evening shifts per server

Excel 2016, Windows 10, Microsoft Corporation.

Objective 7 Create Complex Formulas

GO! Learn How
Video E8-7

Use the logical functions AND and OR to develop compound logical tests using up to 255 arguments. The **AND function** returns a result of TRUE if *ALL* of the conditions are met. The **OR function** returns a value of TRUE if *ANY* of the conditions are met. The similar **NOT function** takes only one argument and tests one condition. If the condition is true, NOT returns the logical opposite false. If the condition is false, then true is returned.

Activity 8.16 | Building Compound Conditional Tests Using AND

MOS
3.1.1 Expert

To determine the Employee of the Week, Ms. Zachary needs to determine the server with the best sales that worked at least three shifts but no more than five evening shifts during the week, and worked at least one shift during the slower days Monday and Tuesday. To do this, she needs to use a compound conditional test.

1 ▶ Click cell **N1** and type **Employee of the Week** and press Enter. **Merge & Center** the text over the range **N1:Q1** and apply the **Heading 2** cell style. In cell **N2**, type **Server** and press Tab. In cell **O2**, type **3-5 Shifts** and press Tab. In cell **P2**, type **M or T** and press Enter. Copy the server names from the range **I3:I19** and then paste them into the range **N3:N19**.

2 ▶ Select the range **A3:A102**. Click in the **Name Box** to select the existing text *A3*, type **DAY** and then press Enter. Select the range **B3:B102**, in the **Name Box**, type **SHIFT** and then press Enter. Select the range **C3:C102**, in the **Name Box**, type **SERVER** and then press Enter.

By naming the ranges, you have made it easier to construct and understand complex formulas.

3 ▶ In cell **O3**, type **=and(** and compare your screen with Figure 8.40.

The AND function takes the argument *logical1*, followed by optional additional logical tests.

Formula bar: SUM =and(

Day	Shift	Server	Nightly Sales		Server	Weekly Sales		Server	Shift	Total	Number of Shifts		Server	3-5 Shifts	M or T
Sales by Server - Week of Jan 1-8					Total Sales Per Server			Server Sales - Evening Shift					Employee of the Week		
Sun	Evening	Alishia	2,600.71		Alishia	$ 25,558		Alishia	Evening	$ 13,133	5		Alishia	=and(	
Sun	Day	Alishia	2,682.33		Arty	$ 1,950		Arty	Evening	$ 880	1		Arty	AND(logical1, [logical2], ...)	
Sun	Evening	Carol	2,578.45		Bryan	$ 11,736		Bryan	Evening	$ 6,257	3		Bryan		
Sun	Evening	Hugo	2,608.13		Carol	$ 22,708		Carol	Evening	$ 10,775	5		Carol		
Sun	Evening	Meredith	1,938.03		Hugo	$ 16,401		Hugo	Evening	$ 14,220	6		Hugo		
Sun	Day	Bryan	1,678.69		Jake	$ 8,529		Jake	Evening	$ 4,293	2		Jake	AND syntax	
Sun	Evening	Bryan	2,796.24		Janna	$ 3,978		Janna	Evening	$ 2,089	1		Janna		

FIGURE 8.40

Excel 2016, Windows 10, Microsoft Corporation.

4 Click cell **L3**, type **>=3,** (include the comma) Click cell **L3**, and type **<=5)** on the **Formula Bar**, click **Enter** ☑ and copy the formula down through cell **O19**. Compare your screen with Figure 8.41.

The AND function performs two logical tests *L3>=3* and *L3<=5*. Both of the tests must be true for the function to return TRUE. If either or both tests fail, the function returns the result FALSE.

FIGURE 8.41

5 Click cell **P3**, and then type the formula **=countifs(server,n3,day,"Mon")** On the **Formula Bar**, click **Enter** ☑ and copy the formula down through cell **P19**. Compare your screen with Figure 8.42.

This formula uses the named ranges SERVER and DAY as the criteria ranges to determine the number of Monday shifts each server has worked.

FIGURE 8.42

6 Click cell **P3** and in the **Formula Bar**, click to position the insertion point at the end of the formula. Type **+countifs(server,n3,day,"Tue")** Click **Enter** ☑ and copy the formula down through cell **P19**. **Save** 🖫 your workbook and compare your screen with Figure 8.43.

The mathematical operators plus sign (+), minus sign (−), division sign (/), and multiplication sign (*), can be used to build complex formulas; in this instance, by adding the results of two functions.

Formula bar (Figure 8.43): **P3** =COUNTIFS(SERVER,N3,DAY,"Mon")+COUNTIFS(SERVER,N3,DAY,"Tue")

Callout: Number of Monday + Tuesday shifts worked by each server

Callout: Mathematical operator + used to add another COUNTIFS function

Day	Shift	Server	Nightly Sales	Server	Weekly Sales	Server	Shift	Total	Number of Shifts	Server	3-5 Shifts	M or T
	Sales by Server - Week of Jan 1-8			Total Sales Per Server		Server Sales - Evening Shift						
Sun	Evening	Alishia	2,600.71				Evening	$ 13,133	5	Alishia	TRUE	1
Sun	Day	Alishia	2,682.33				Evening	$ 880	1	Arty	FALSE	0
Sun	Evening	Carol	2,578.45				Evening	$ 6,257	3	Bryan	TRUE	4
Sun	Evening	Hugo	2,608.13				Evening	$ 10,775	5	Carol	TRUE	5
Sun	Evening	Meredith	1,938.03				Evening	$ 14,220	6	Hugo	FALSE	3
Sun	Day	Bryan	1,678.69	Hugo	$ 16,401	Hugo	Evening	$ 4,293	2	Jake	FALSE	1
Sun	Evening	Bryan	2,796.24	Jake	$ 8,529	Jake	Evening	$ 2,089	1	Janna	FALSE	0
Sun	Evening	Todd	2,404.86	Janna	$ 3,978	Janna	Evening	$ 1,504	1	Jerri	FALSE	1
Sun	Evening	Mary	2,395.43	Jerri	$ 4,372	Jerri	Evening	$ 5,650	4	Josh	TRUE	1
Sun	Evening	Margo	2,244.54	Josh	$ 10,450	Josh	Evening	$ 9,603	4	Justina	TRUE	0
Sun	Day	Jake	2,032.34	Justina	$ 16,999	Justina	Evening	$ 8,329	4	Lexi	TRUE	0
Sun	Day	Jerri	1,268.45	Lexi	$ 15,826	Lexi	Evening	$ 14,256	5	Marcus	TRUE	1
Sun	Evening	Jerri	1,504.23	Marcus	$ 15,284	Marcus	Evening	$ 2,245	1	Margo	FALSE	1
Mon	Day	Rhea	1,524.81	Margo	$ 3,477	Margo	Evening	$ 4,371	2	Mary	FALSE	1
Mon	Evening	Rhea	1,320.76	Mary	$ 4,371	Mary	Evening	$ 14,950	7	Meredith	FALSE	4
Mon	Day	Carol	2,200.03	Meredith	$ 21,826	Meredith	Evening	$ 7,459	4	Rhea	TRUE	2
Mon	Evening	Carol	1,892.10	Rhea	$ 19,432	Rhea	Evening	$ 2,405	1	Todd	FALSE	1
Mon	Day	Meredith	1,884.68	Todd	$ 4,587	Todd						

FIGURE 8.43

Excel 2016, Windows 10, Microsoft Corporation.

Activity 8.17 | Using Nested Functions

3.1.1 Expert
3.1.2 Expert

You can build complex formulas by using a **nested function**, which is a function contained inside another function. The inner, nested function is evaluated first and the result becomes the argument for the outer function. Recall that the IF function uses a single logic test and returns one value if true and another value if false. In this Activity, you will use an IF function with a nested AND function to determine which servers are eligible for Employee of the Week status.

1 Click cell **Q2**, type **Eligible** and then press Enter.

2 In cell **Q3**, type the following formula and be sure you use the letter o and not the number 0: **=if(and(o3,p3>=1),"Eligible","")** Click **Enter** ✓ and copy the formula down through cell **Q19**. Save 🖫 your workbook and compare your screen with Figure 8.44.

There are six servers that meet both criteria—O3 is true and P3 is greater than or equal to 1—and are listed as *Eligible*. The double quotes make the cell blank rather than displaying the word FALSE if the result is false.

Formula bar (Figure 8.44): **Q3** =IF(AND(O3,P3>=1),"Eligible","")

Callout: Employees that meet both criteria are labeled *Eligible*

**Callout:** AND function nested within IF function

Callout: Double quotes "" result in empty cells rather than displaying FALSE

Day	Shift	Server	Nightly Sales	Server	Weekly Sales	Server	Shift	Total	Number of Shifts	Server	3-5 Shifts	M or T	Eligible
	Sales by Server - Week of Jan 1-8			Total Sales Per Server		Server Sales - Evening Shift				Employee of the Week			
Sun	Evening			Alishia	$ 25,558	Alishia	Evening	$ 13,133	5	Alishia	TRUE	1	Eligible
Sun	Day			Arty	$ 1,950	Arty	Evening	$ 880	1	Arty	FALSE	0	
Sun	Evening			Bryan	$ 11,736	Bryan	Evening	$ 6,257	3	Bryan	TRUE	4	Eligible
Sun	Evening			Carol	$ 22,708	Carol	Evening	$ 10,775	5	Carol	TRUE	5	Eligible
Sun	Evening	Meredith	1,938.03	Hugo	$ 16,401	Hugo	Evening	$ 14,220	6	Hugo	FALSE	3	
Sun	Day	Bryan	1,678.69			Jake	Evening	$ 4,293	2	Jake	FALSE	1	
Sun	Evening	Bryan	2,796.24			Janna	Evening	$ 2,089	1	Janna	FALSE	0	
Sun	Evening	Todd	2,404.86			Jerri	Evening	$ 1,504	1	Jerri	FALSE	1	
Sun	Evening	Mary	2,395.43			Josh	Evening	$ 5,650	4	Josh	TRUE	1	Eligible
Sun	Evening	Margo	2,244.54			Justina	Evening	$ 9,603	4	Justina	TRUE	0	
Sun	Day	Jake	2,032.34			Lexi	Evening	$ 8,329	4	Lexi	TRUE	0	
Sun	Day	Jerri	1,268.45	Marcus	$ 15,284	Marcus	Evening	$ 14,256	5	Marcus	TRUE	1	Eligible
Sun	Evening	Jerri	1,504.23	Margo	$ 3,477	Margo	Evening	$ 2,245	1	Margo	FALSE	1	
Mon	Day	Rhea	1,524.81	Mary	$ 4,371	Mary	Evening	$ 4,371	2	Mary	FALSE	1	
Mon	Evening	Rhea	1,320.76	Meredith	$ 21,826	Meredith	Evening	$ 14,950	7	Meredith	FALSE	4	
Mon	Day	Carol	2,200.03	Rhea	$ 19,432	Rhea	Evening	$ 7,459	4	Rhea	TRUE	2	Eligible
Mon	Evening	Carol	1,892.10	Todd	$ 4,587	Todd	Evening	$ 2,405	1	Todd	FALSE	1	
Mon	Day	Meredith	1,884.68										

FIGURE 8.44

Excel 2016, Windows 10, Microsoft Corporation.

3 With the range Q3:Q19 still selected, press Ctrl + Q to open **Quick Analysis** at the bottom of the selection, and then click the first option—**Text Contains**. In the **Text That Contains** dialog box, verify **Format cells that contain the text** displays *Eligible*. Click the **with arrow**, and then click **Green Fill with Dark Green Text**. Compare your screen with Figure 8.45.

This action applies conditional formatting to the cells in the selected range that contain text, which makes it easy for Ms. Zachary to see which employees are eligible.

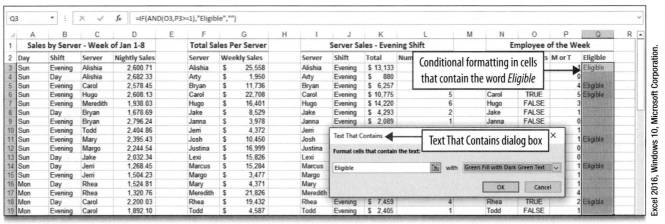

FIGURE 8.45

4 Click **OK**.

5.3.1,
3.1.3 Expert

Activity 8.18 | Using the AVERAGEIFS Function and Inserting a Shape Containing Text

Ms. Zachary is interested to know what is the average nightly sales for servers working the evening shift who have sales over $2,000. To compute this, she can use Excel's **AVERAGEIFS** function, which enables you to specify multiple criteria when computing an average.

1 Click cell **A105** and type **Average if Shift = Evening and Nightly Sales > $2,000** and press Enter.

2 Click cell **F105**. On the **Formulas tab**, in the **Function Library group**, click **More Functions**, point to **Statistical**, and then click **AVERAGEIFS**.

3 In the **Function Arguments** dialog box, in the **Average_range** box, type **d3:d102** to define the range to be averaged—the Nightly Sales for the week of Jan 1-8.

4 In the **Criteria_range1** box type **b3:b102** and then in the **Criteria1** box type **=Evening** to set the first criteria—only Evening shifts.

5 In the **Criteria_range2** box type **d3:d102** and then in the **Criteria2** box type **>2000** to narrow the amounts to be averaged to only sales greater than $2,000. Compare your screen with Figure 8.46.

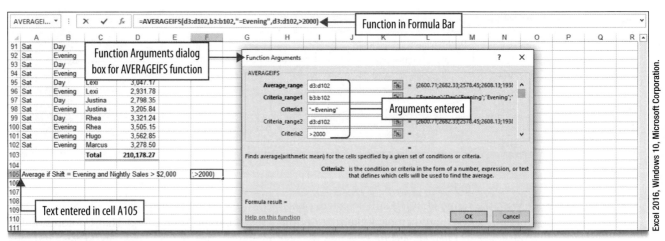

FIGURE 8.46

6 ▶ Click **OK**, click cell **F105** to select it, and then on the **Home tab**, in the **Number group**, click **Accounting Number Format** $ ▾ .

The average nightly sales for servers on the Evening shift who have sales over $2,000 is $2,652.78.

7 ▶ Press Ctrl + Home. On the **Insert tab**, in the **Illustrations group**, click **Shapes** ⬛, and then under **Block Arrows**, click the second shape—**Left Arrow**.

8 ▶ Position the ⊞ pointer in the upper left corner of cell **E21**, hold down the left mouse button, and then drag down and to the right until the ⊞ pointer is approximately in the lower right corner of cell **I26**, and then release the mouse button.

9 ▶ Click any cell to deselect the shape, and then click the shape again to select it. Right-click over the shape, and then on the shortcut menu, click **Edit Text**. Type **Average nightly sales for servers on the Evening shift who have sales over $2,000 is $2,652.78** Compare your screen with Figure 8.47.

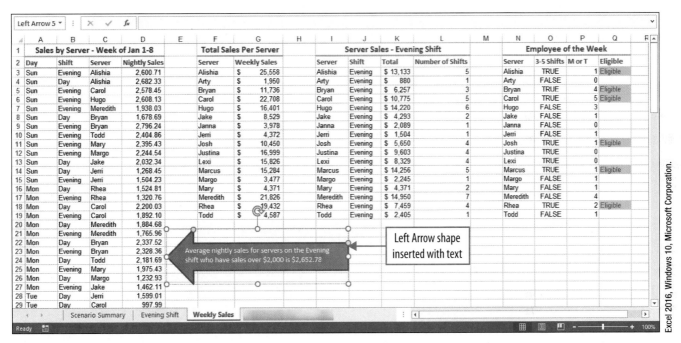

FIGURE 8.47

Excel 2016, Windows 10, Microsoft Corporation.

10 ▶ Click any cell to deselect the shape, and then press Ctrl + Home to make cell **A1** active.

11 ▶ On the **Page Layout tab**, click **Print Titles**. Under **Print titles**, click in the **Rows to repeat at top** box, and then from the **row heading area**, select **rows 1:2**. Click **OK**.

This worksheet will print on two pages so adding column titles will make it easier to understand the information on the second page.

12 ▶ Right-click the sheet tab and then click **Select All Sheets** so that *[Group]* displays in the title bar. With the worksheets grouped, set the **Orientation** to **Landscape** and set the **Width** to **1 page**. In the **Page Setup group**, click the **Dialog Box Launcher** button ⬛ to display the **Page Setup** dialog box. On the **Margins tab**, center the worksheets horizontally on the page. On the **Header/Footer tab**, insert a **Custom Footer** in the **left section** that includes the file name.

13 ▶ Display the **document properties** and if necessary, right-click the author name, click Edit Property, and then type your name. In the **Subject** box, type your course name and section #, and in the **Tags** box, type **staff schedule** Display the grouped worksheets in **Print Preview**— you will have four total pages.

14 On the left, click **Save**. Point to any sheet tab, right-click, and then click Ungroup Sheets.

15 If directed by your instructor to do so, submit a paper printout of each of the three worksheets, an electronic image of each of your three worksheets that looks like a printed document, or your original Excel file. If required by your instructor, print or create an electronic version of your worksheets with formulas displayed. In the upper right corner of the Excel window, click **Close** ⊠.

END | You have completed Project 8B

GO! To Work

Andrew Rodriguez / Fotolia; FotolEdhar / Fotolia; apops / Fotolia; Yuri Arcurs / Fotolia

MICROSOFT OFFICE SPECIALIST (MOS) SKILLS IN THIS CHAPTER

PROJECT 8A	PROJECT 8B
5.1.1 Create a new chart **5.2.1** Resize charts **5.2.2** Add and modify chart elements **2.1.1** Expert: Create custom number formats **4.1.2** Expert: Create dual-axis charts	**4.2.2** Perform logical operations by using the SUMIF function **5.3.1** Insert text boxes and shapes **3.1.1** Expert: Perform logical operations by using AND, OR, and NOT functions **3.1.2** Expert: Perform logical operations by using nested functions **3.1.3** Expert: Perform statistical operations by using SUMIFS, AVERAGEIFS, and COUNTIFS functions **3.4.3** Expert: Perform what-if analysis by using Goal Seek and Scenario Manager

BUILD YOUR E-PORTFOLIO

An E-Portfolio is a collection of evidence, stored electronically, that showcases what you have accomplished while completing your education. Collecting and then sharing your work products with potential employers reflects your academic and career goals. Your completed documents from the following projects are good examples to show what you have learned: 8G, 8K, and 8L.

GO! FOR JOB SUCCESS

Project Management

Your instructor may assign this topic to your class, and then ask you to think about, or discuss with your classmates, these questions:

Project management is a discipline that identifies and plans for the resources required to complete a defined set of tasks to achieve a stated goal. Project managers develop timelines, coordinate resources, organize and motivate cross-functional groups working on the project, and forecast and monitor costs. Size and complexity of projects vary: Construction and architecture projects might entail building a new highway or skyscraper; software projects develop new software products or upgrades of existing products. Administrative projects might include meeting and event planning. To assure that the corporate strategy translates into projects actually being implemented, many organizations have implemented a Project Management Office, which assures alignment between strategy and projects so that the right projects move forward at the right time and right budget.

FotolEdhar / Fotolia

Project managers must have skills in a variety of areas including accounting, management, forecasting, and writing. What are some other skills that would be valuable in project management?

What "soft" skills do you think are required to be a successful project manager?

What do you think are some other benefits to both executives and project managers of using a Project Management Office?

END OF CHAPTER

SUMMARY

A moving average is a sequence of averages computed from parts of a data series. It evens out the data to show a pattern or trend. The break-even point is the point at which a company starts to make a profit.

Solver is a what-if analysis tool used to find an optimal value for a formula in one cell—referred to as the objective cell—subject to constraints, on the values of other formula cells in a worksheet.

You can create several possible solutions to a problem and use Scenario Manager to compare the alternatives. A scenario is a set of values that Excel saves and that you can substitute automatically in your worksheet.

Complex formulas can be built by nesting functions. A nested function is contained inside another function. The inner function is evaluated first and the result becomes the argument for the outer function.

GO! LEARN IT ONLINE

Review the concepts, key terms, and MOS skills in this chapter by completing these online challenges, which you can find in **MyITLab**.

Matching and Multiple Choice: Answer matching and multiple choice questions to test what you learned in this chapter.

Lessons on the GO!: Learn how to use all the new apps and features as they are introduced by Microsoft.

MOS Prep Quiz: Answer questions to review the MOS skills you practiced in this chapter.

PROJECT GUIDE FOR EXCEL CHAPTER 8

Your instructor will assign Projects from this list to ensure your learning and assess your knowledge.

PROJECT GUIDE FOR EXCEL CHAPTER 8			
Project	**Apply Skills from These Chapter Objectives**	**Project Type**	**Project Location**
8A MyITLab	Objectives 1-3 from Project 8A	**8A Instructional Project (Grader Project)** Guided instruction to learn the skills in Project 8A.	In MyITLab and in text
8B MyITLab	Objectives 4-7 from Project 8B	**8B Instructional Project (Grader Project)** Guided instruction to learn the skills in Project 8B.	In MyITLab and in text
8C	Objectives 1-3 from Project 8A	**8C Skills Review (Scorecard Grading)** A guided review of the skills from Project 8A.	In text
8D	Objectives 4-7 from Project 8B	**8D Skills Review (Scorecard Grading)** A guided review of the skills from Project 8B.	In text
8E MyITLab	Objectives 1-3 from Project 8A	**8E Mastery (Grader Project)** **Mastery and Transfer of Learning** A demonstration of your mastery of the skills in Project 8A with extensive decision-making.	In MyITLab and in text
8F MyITLab	Objectives 4-7 from Project 8B	**8F Mastery (Grader Project)** **Mastery and Transfer of Learning** A demonstration of your mastery of the skills in Project 8B with extensive decision-making.	In MyITLab and in text
8G MyITLab	Objectives 1-7 from Projects 8A and 8B	**8G Mastery (Grader Project)** **Mastery and Transfer of Learning** A demonstration of your mastery of the skills in Projects 8A and 8B with extensive decision-making.	In MyITLab and in text
8H	Combination of Objectives from Projects 8A and 8B	**8H GO! Fix It (Scorecard Grading)** **Critical Thinking** A demonstration of your mastery of the skills in Projects 8A and 8B by creating a correct result from a document that contains errors you must find.	Instructor Resource Center (IRC) and MyITLab
8I	Combination of Objectives from Projects 8A and 8B	**8I GO! Make It (Scorecard Grading)** **Critical Thinking** A demonstration of your mastery of the skills in Projects 8A and 8B by creating a result from a supplied picture.	IRC and MyITLab
8J	Combination of Objectives from Projects 8A and 8B	**8J GO! Solve It (Rubric Grading)** **Critical Thinking** A demonstration of your mastery of the skills in Projects 8A and 8B, your decision-making skills, and your critical thinking skills. A task-specific rubric helps you self-assess your result.	IRC and MyITLab
8K	Combination of Objectives from Projects 8A and 8B	**8K GO! Solve It (Rubric Grading)** **Critical Thinking** A demonstration of your mastery of the skills in Projects 8A and 8B, your decision-making skills, and your critical thinking skills. A task-specific rubric helps you self-assess your result.	In text
8L	Combination of Objectives from Projects 8A and 8B	**8L GO! Think (Rubric Grading)** **Critical Thinking** A demonstration of your understanding of the Chapter concepts applied in a manner that you would outside of college. An analytic rubric helps you and your instructor grade the quality of your work by comparing it to the work an expert in the discipline would create.	In text
8M	Combination of Objectives from Projects 8A and 8B	**8M GO! Think (Rubric Grading)** **Critical Thinking** A demonstration of your understanding of the Chapter concepts applied in a manner that you would outside of college. An analytic rubric helps you and your instructor grade the quality of your work by comparing it to the work an expert in the discipline would create.	IRC and MyITLab
8N	Combination of Objectives from Projects 8A and 8B	**8N You and GO! (Rubric Grading)** **Critical Thinking** A demonstration of your understanding of the Chapter concepts applied in a manner that you would in a personal situation. An analytic rubric helps you and your instructor grade the quality of your work.	IRC and MyITLab

GLOSSARY

GLOSSARY OF CHAPTER KEY TERMS

Add-in Optional command or feature that is not immediately available; you must first install and/or activate it to use it.

AND function A logical function that can be used to develop compound logical tests using up to 255 arguments. The function returns a result of TRUE if ALL of the conditions are met.

AVERAGEIFS function A statistical function that enables you to specify multiple criteria when computing an average.

Break-even point The point at which a company starts to make a profit.

Constraint In Solver, a condition or restriction that must be met.

Constraint cell In Solver, a cell that contains a value that limits or restricts the outcome.

COUNTIF function A logical function that counts the cells that meet specific criteria in a specified range.

COUNTIFS function A logical function that counts the cells that meet specific criteria in multiple ranges.

Decision variable In Solver, cell in which the value will change to achieve the desired results.

Dual-axis chart A chart that has one series plotted on a secondary axis.

Useful when comparing data series that use different scales or different types of measurements.

Fixed expense Expense that remains the same each month regardless of the amount of activity.

Forecast A prediction of the future, often based on past performances.

Integer A whole number.

Interval The number of cells to include in the average.

Logical function A function that tests for specific conditions.

Moving average A sequence of averages computed from parts of a data series.

Nested function A function that is contained inside another function. The inner function is evaluated first and the result becomes the argument for the outer function.

NOT function A logical function that takes only one argument and is used to test one condition. If the condition is true, the function returns the logical opposite false. If the condition is false, true is returned.

Objective cell In Solver, a cell that contains a formula for the results you are trying to determine.

OR function A logical function that can be used to develop compound logical

tests using up to 255 arguments. The function returns a value of TRUE if ANY of the conditions are met.

Scenario A set of values that Excel saves and can substitute automatically in your worksheet.

Scenario Manager A what-if analysis tool that compares alternatives.

Solver A what-if analysis tool with which you can find an optimal (maximum or minimum) value for a formula in one cell—referred to as the objective cell—subject to constraints, or limits, on the values of other formula cells on a worksheet.

SUMIF function A logical function that contains one logic test—it will add values in a specified range that meet a certain condition or criteria.

SUMIFS function A logical function that will add values in multiple ranges that meet multiple criteria.

Syntax The arrangement of the arguments in a function.

Transpose To switch the data in rows and columns.

Variable cell In Solver, cell in which the value will change to achieve the desired result.

Variable expense Expense that varies depending on the amount of sales.

Apply 8A skills from these Objectives:

1 Calculate a Moving Average

2 Project Income and Expenses

3 Determine a Break-Even Point

Skills Review Project 8C Orlando Sales

In the following Skills Review, you will create a worksheet for Kelsey Tanner, the Chief Financial Officer of Brina's Bistro, who wants to see how sales have grown in the first six weeks at the new restaurant in Orlando, Florida. Your completed worksheets will look similar to Figure 8.48.

PROJECT FILES

For Project 8C, you will need the following file:

e08C_Orlando_Sales

You will save your workbook as:

Lastname_Firstname_8C_Orlando_Sales

PROJECT RESULTS

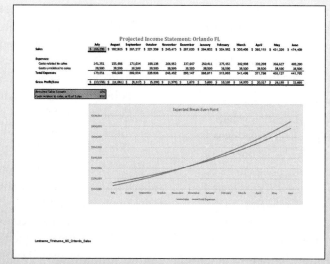

FIGURE 8.48

(Project 8C Orlando Sales continues on the next page)

1 Start Excel. From the student data files that accompany this chapter, open the file **e08C_Orlando_Sales**, and then in your **Exce Chapter 8** folder, **Save** the file as **Lastname_Firstname_8C_Orlando_Sales**

a. Select the range **A3:AV4**. Right-click anywhere over the selection and click **Copy**. Click cell **A5**. Right-click and under **Paste Options**, click **Transpose (T)**. Delete **rows 2:4**. In cell **C2** type **Moving Average** In cell **D2** type **Growth Trend** Select the range **A2:D2** and apply the **Heading 3** cell style, and then in the **Alignment group**, click **Wrap Text**. Click cell **A3**. On the **Home tab**, in the **Number group**, click the **Dialog Box Launcher**. In the **Format Cells** dialog box, be sure the **Number tab** is selected. Under **Category**, click **Custom**. In the **Type** box, select the existing text, and then type **ddd, mmm dd** to replace it. Click **OK**, and then drag the fill handle to copy the new format down through cell **A49**. Press Ctrl + Home.

b. Click the **File tab**. From **Backstage** view, click **Options**. In the **Excel Options** dialog box, on the left, click **Add-ins**. At the bottom of the dialog box, verify that the **Manage** box displays *Excel Add-ins*, and then click **Go**. In the **Add-ins** dialog box, if necessary, select the **Analysis ToolPak** check box. Click **OK**.

c. Click cell **A2**. On the **Data tab**, in the **Analyze group**, click **Data Analysis**. Scroll the list as necessary, and then click **Moving Average**. Click **OK**. Click in the **Input Range** box, type **b2:b49** and then select the **Labels in First Row** check box. Click in the **Interval** box, and then type **7** Click in the **Output Range** box, type **c3** and then select the **Chart Output** check box. Click **OK**.

d. Click the outer edge of the chart to select it and then, on the **Design tab**, in the **Location group**, click **Move Chart**. Click **New sheet**, type **Sales Trend Chart** and then click **OK**. At the bottom of the chart, point to any of the data points to display the ScreenTip *Horizontal (Category) Axis*, and then click to select the axis. On the **Design tab**, in the **Data group**, click **Select Data**. In the **Select Data Source** dialog box, under **Horizontal (Category) Axis Labels**, click **Edit**. Display the **Sales** worksheet, and then select the range **A9:A49**. In the **Axis Labels**

dialog box, click **OK**. In the **Select Data Source** dialog box, click **OK**.

e. Right-click the **Horizontal (Category)Axis**, and then click **Format Axis**. In the **Format Axis** pane, with **Axis Options** selected, scroll down and click to expand **Number**. Scroll down as necessary, click the **Category arrow**, and then click **Date**. Click the **Type** arrow, click the **3/14** format, and then **Close** the **Format Axis** pane. Click the **Horizontal (Category) Axis Title** to select it. On the **Formula Bar** type **June 15th through July 31st** and then press Enter. Point to the **Horizontal (Category)Axis Title**, triple-click, and then on the mini toolbar, change the font size to **12**. Click the **Vertical (Value) Axis Title** to select it. On the **Formula Bar** type **Sales** and then press Enter. Point to the **Vertical (Value) Axis Title**, double-click, and then on the mini toolbar, change the font size to **12**. Right-click the **Vertical (Value) Axis**, and then click **Format Axis**. In the **Format Axis** pane, scroll down to **Number**, click the **Category arrow**, and then click **Currency**. If necessary, set **Decimal places** to **0**, and then **Close** the **Format Axis** pane.

f. On the **Format tab**, in the **Current Selection group**, click the **Chart Elements arrow**, and then click **Series "Forecast"**. In the same group click **Format Selection**. In the **Format Data Series** pane, if necessary, click the **Series Options** icon. Under **Plot Series on**, click **Secondary Axis**. **Close** the **Format Data Series** pane.

g. Display the **Sales** worksheet. Click cell **D21**, and then type **=(c21-c14)/c14** Press Enter. Scroll to position **row 21** near the top of your screen. Point to cell **D21**, right-click, and then on the mini toolbar, click **Percent Style**. Click **Increase Decimal** one time to display one decimal. With cell **D21** still selected, point to the cell and right-click, and then click **Copy**. Point to cell **D28**, right-click, and then click the first **Paste** button. In the same manner, paste it in cells **D35, D42,** and **D49**. AutoFit **column D**.

2 Click cell **A51**, type **July Sales** press Tab, and then in cell **B51**, type **=sum(b19:b49)** and then press Enter. Display the **Projected Income** worksheet. Click cell **B3**. Type **=** click the **Sales sheet tab**, click cell **B51**—the July sales total—and then to the left of the Formula Bar, click **Enter**. On the **Projected Income** worksheet, click cell **B2**, and then use the fill handle to fill the months for a

(Project 8C Orlando Sales continues on the next page)

year—from July to June—across to **column M**. With the range **B2:M2** selected, apply **Center**.

a. Click cell **B3**; in the **Formula Bar**, notice the cell reference. Click cell **C3**, type **=b3*(1+b12)** and then click **Enter**. From the Cell Styles gallery, apply the **Currency [0]** cell style. Use the fill handle to copy the formula in cell **C3** across the row to cell **M3**.

b. Click cell **B6** and examine the formula. Use the fill handle to copy the formula from cell **B6** across the row to cell **M6**. Drag the fill handle to **Copy** the value in cell **B7** across the row to cell **M7**. Select the range **C8:M8**, and then on the **Home tab**, in the **Editing group**, click **AutoSum**. Drag the fill handle to **Copy** the formula in cell **B10** across the row to cell **M10**.

3 In the lower right corner of your screen, if necessary, set the Zoom to **80%** so that **columns A:M** display on your screen. Select the range **A2:M3**. On the **Insert tab**, in the **Charts group**, click **Recommended Charts**. In the **Insert Chart** dialog box, with the **Line** chart selected, click **OK**.

a. On the **Design tab**, in the **Data group**, click **Select Data**. In the **Select Data Source** dialog box, under **Legend Entries (Series)**, click **Add**. With the insertion point in the **Series name** box, click cell **A8**. Press ⎇Tab, select the range **B8:M8**, and then click **OK**. Verify that the **Chart data range** is *$A$2:$M$3* and *$A$8:$M$8* and click **OK**. On the **Design tab**, in the **Chart Layouts group**, click **Quick Layout**, and then click **Layout 3**. In the chart, click the text *Chart Title*, and then watch the **Formula Bar** as you type **Expected Break-Even Point** Press ⎇Enter.

b. Drag to position the upper left corner of the chart inside the upper left corner of cell **B15**. Scroll to position **row 13** near the top of your screen. Drag the lower right corner of the chart inside the lower right corner of cell **M36**.

c. On the left side of the chart, right-click the **Vertical (Value) Axis**, and then click **Format Axis**. In the

Format Axis pane, verify that **Axis Options** is selected. Under **Axis Options**, in the **Minimum** box, type **150000** Press ⎇Enter. In the same manner, change the **Maximum** value to **500000** if necessary.

d. Format both the **Plot Area** and the **Chart Area** with a **Solid fill** using the color **Light Yellow, Background 2**—in the third column, the first color.

e. Display the **Sales Trend Chart** worksheet. On this chart sheet, from the **Page Layout tab**, display the **Page Setup** dialog box, and then insert a custom footer with the file name in the **left section**.

4 Display the **Projected Income** worksheet, click anywhere outside the chart, and then, if necessary, set the **Zoom** back to **100%**. Right-click the sheet tab, and then click **Select All Sheets** so that *[Group]* displays in the title bar. With the worksheets grouped, insert a custom footer in the **left section** that includes the file name.

a. On the **Page Layout tab**, set the **Orientation** to **Landscape**, and then, set the **Width** to **1 page**, and the **height** to **1 page**. Center the worksheets horizontally on the page. Press ⎇Ctrl + ⎇Home to move to the top of the worksheet.

b. Display the **document properties**, and under **Related People**, be sure that your name displays as the author. If necessary, right-click the author name, click **Edit Property**, and then type your name. In the **Subject** box, type your course name and section #, and in the **Tags** box, type **Orlando, break-even** On the left, click **Print** to display the grouped worksheets in **Print Preview**.

c. On the left, click **Save**. Right-click any sheet tab, and then click **Ungroup Sheets**. If directed by your instructor to do so, submit a paper printout of each of the three worksheets, an electronic image of each of your three worksheets that looks like a printed document, or your original Excel file. If required by your instructor, print or create an electronic version of your worksheet with formulas displayed. In the upper right corner of the Excel window, click **Close**.

END | You have completed Project 8C

Skills Review Project 8D Charlotte Staffing

In the following Skills Review, you will assist Stephanie Wheaton, manager of the Charlotte restaurant, in determining the most efficient work schedule for the evening server staff. Your completed worksheets will look similar to Figure 8.49.

PROJECT FILES

For Project 8D, you will need the following file:

e08D_Charlotte_Staffing

You will save your workbook as:

Lastname_Firstname_8D_Charlotte_Staffing

PROJECT RESULTS

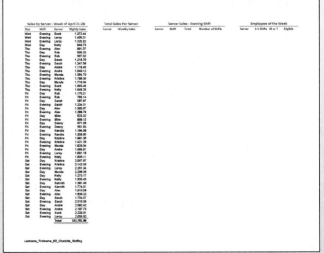

FIGURE 8.49

(Project 8D Charlotte Staffing continues on the next page)

1 Start Excel and display a blank workbook. Click the **Data tab**, and then at the right end of the **Data tab**, check to see if the **Analyze group** and **Solver** display. If Solver displays, Solver is installed. On the **File tab**, click **Close** and move to step a. If Solver does *not* display, from **Backstage** view, click **Options**. On the left, click **Add-ins**, and then at the bottom of the screen, in the **Manage** box, if necessary, select **Excel Add-ins**. Click **Go**. Select the **Solver Add-in** check box, and then click **OK**. On the File tab, click Close and move to step a.

a. From the student data files that accompany this chapter, open the file **e08D_Charlotte_Staffing**. Display the **Save As** dialog box, navigate to your **Excel Chapter 8** folder, and then using your own name, **Save** the workbook as **Lastname_Firstname_8D_Charlotte_Staffing**

b. Examine the formulas in cells **C10**, **C14**, and **C15**. Click cell **C3**, and then click the **Name Box arrow**; notice that cell **C3** is named *Sun_Mon* and the other schedules also have been named.

c. Click cell **C15**—the objective cell. On the **Data tab**, in the **Analyze group**, click **Solver**.

d. To the right of **To**, click **Min**. Click in the **By Changing Variable Cells** box, and then select the range **C3:C8**. Click in the **Subject to the Constraints** area, and then on the right click **Add** to add the first constraint. If necessary, click the blinking Excel icon on your taskbar to display the Add Constraint dialog box. With the insertion point blinking in the **Cell Reference** box, select the range **C3:C8**. In the middle box, click the arrow, and then click **int**. Click **OK**—the result must be a whole number.

e. Click **Add** to add the second constraint. With the insertion point in the **Cell Reference** box, select the range **C3:C8**. In the middle box, click the arrow, and then click **>=**. In the **Constraint** box, type **0** Click **OK**.

f. Click **Add** to add the third constraint. In the **Cell Reference** box, select the range **E10:K10**. In the middle box, click the arrow, and then click **>=**. In the **Constraint** box, select the range **E12:K12**. Click **OK**; the result must be equal to or greater than the demand for each day. At the bottom of the **Solver Parameters** dialog box, click **Solve**. With **Keep Solver Solution** selected, click **OK**. Cell **C15** indicates *$8,170.75*.

2 Select the range **C3:C8**. On the **Data tab**, in the **Forecast group**, click **What-If Analysis**, and then click **Scenario Manager**. In the **Scenario Manager** dialog box, click **Add**. In the **Scenario name** box, type **Option 1** Verify that the **Changing cells** box displays *C3:C8*. Click **OK**. In the **Scenario Values** dialog box, click **OK**. In the **Scenario Manager** dialog box, click **Close**.

a. Click cell **C15**—the objective cell. On the **Data tab**, in the **Analyze group**, click **Solver**. In the **Solver Parameters** dialog box, verify that the **Set Objective** box displays *$C$15* and the **By Changing Variable Cells** box displays *$C$3:$C$8*.

b. To the right of **Subject to the Constraints** box, click **Add** to add an additional constraint. In the **Add Constraint** dialog box, click the **Cell Reference** box, and then click cell **C3**. In the middle box, click the arrow, and then click **=**. In the **Constraint** box, type **4** Click **OK**; this constraint will raise the number of employees who have Sunday and Monday off to 4.

c. In the lower right corner of the dialog box, click **Solve**. Click **Save Scenario** to display the **Save Scenario** dialog box. In the **Scenario Name** box, type **Option 2** and then click **OK**. In the **Solver Results** dialog box, click **Restore Original Values**, and then click **OK**.

d. Verify that cell **C15** is still the active cell. On the **Data tab**, in the **Analyze group**, click **Solver**. In the **Subject to the Constraints** box, select the fourth constraint—*Sun_Mon = 4*—and then on the right click **Delete** to delete this constraint.

e. Click **Add**. In the **Add Constraint** dialog box, click in the **Cell Reference** box, and then select cell **C8**. Change the middle box to **=**. In the **Constraint** box, type **6** and then click **OK**; this constraint will raise the number of employees who have Saturday and Sunday off to 6.

f. Click **Solve**. Click **Save Scenario**. In the **Save Scenario** dialog box, type **Option 3** and then click **OK**. Click **Restore Original Values**, and then click **OK**.

g. On the **Data tab**, in the **Forecast group**, click **What-If Analysis**, and then click **Scenario Manager**. In the **Scenario Manager** dialog box, click **Summary**. Be sure **Scenario summary** is selected, and then click **OK** to summarize the three Options

(Project 8D Charlotte Staffing continues on the next page)

on a new worksheet. Select the range **D12:G12** and then on the **Home tab**, in the **Editing group**, click **AutoSum**. **Save** your workbook.

3 Display the **Weekly Sales** worksheet. Click cell **G3**, and then type **=sumif(** Select the range **C3:C102** and press `F4` to make the value absolute. Type **,** (a comma). Click cell **F3**, and then type **,** (a comma). Select the range **D3:D102** and press `F4`. Type **)** and then on the **Formula Bar**, click **Enter**.

a. Drag the fill handle to copy the formula down through cell **G19**. Format the range **G3:G19** using cell style **Currency [0]**.

b. Select the range **F3:F19**. Right-click over the selection and click **Copy**. Right-click cell **I3** and click **Paste (P)**. Click cell **J3**, and then type **Evening** and then copy the cell down through **J19**.

c. Click cell **K3** and type **=sumifs(** Select the range **D3:D102** and press `F4` to make the value absolute. Type **,** (a comma), select the range **C3:C102**, and press `F4`. Type **,** (a comma). Click cell **I3**, and then type **,** (a comma). Select the range **B3:B102** and then press `F4`. Type **,** (a comma) and then click cell **J3**. Type **)** and then click **Enter**. Drag the fill-handle to copy the formula down through cell **K19**. Format the range **K3:K19** using cell style **Currency [0]**.

d. Click cell **L3** and type **=countifs(** Select the range **C3:C102** and press `F4` to make the value absolute. Type **,** (a comma), click cell **I3**, and then type **,** (a comma). Select the range **B3:B102**, and then press `F4`. Type **,** (a comma) and then click cell **J3**. Type **)** and then click **Enter**. Drag the fill handle to copy the formula down through cell **L19**.

4 Click cell **N1** and type **Employees of the Week** and press `Enter`. **Merge & Center** the text over the range **N1:Q1** and apply the **Heading 2** cell style. In cell **N2** type **Server** and press `Tab`. In cell **O2** type **3-5 Shifts** and press `Tab`. In cell **P3** type **M or T** and press `Enter`. Copy the server names from the range **I3:I19** to the range **N3:N19**.

a. Select the range **A3:A102**, in the **Name Box** type **DAY** and then press `Enter`. Select the range **B3:B102**, in the **Name Box** type **SHIFT** and then press `Enter`. Select the range **C3:C102**, in the **Name Box** type **SERVER** and then press `Enter`.

b. In cell **O3**, type **=and(** Click cell **L3**, type **>=3,** (include the comma). Click cell **L3** and type **<=5)** Click **Enter** and copy the formula down through cell **O19**.

c. Click cell **P3**, and then type the formula **=countifs(server,n3,day,"Mon")** Click **Enter** and copy the formula down through cell **P19**. Click cell **P3** and in the **Formula Bar**, position the insertion point at the end of the formula. Type **+countifs(server,n3,day,"Tue")** Click **Enter** and copy the formula down through cell **P19**.

d. Click cell **Q2**, type **Eligible** and then press `Enter`. In cell **Q3**, type **=if(and(o3,p3>=1),"Eligible","")** Click **Enter** and copy the formula down through cell **Q19**. Note: cell Q3 results in an empty cell, but the formula still exists to copy.

e. With the range still selected, press `Ctrl` + `Q` to open **Quick Analysis** at the bottom of the selection, and then click the first option—**Text Contains**. In the **Text That Contains** dialog box, in the **Format cells that contain the text** box type **Eligible** Click the **with arrow**, and then click **Green Fill with Dark Green Text**. Click **OK**. Press `Ctrl` + `Home` to make cell **A1** the active cell. On the **Page Layout tab**, click **Print Titles**. Under **Print titles**, click in the **Rows to repeat at top** box, and then from the **row heading area**, select **rows 1:2**. Click **OK**.

5 Right-click the sheet tab and then click **Select All Sheets** so that *[Group]* displays in the title bar. With the worksheets grouped, set the **Orientation** to **Landscape** and set the **Width** to **1 page**. In the **Page Setup group**, click the **Dialog Box Launcher** button to display the **Page Setup** dialog box. On the **Margins tab**, center the worksheets horizontally on the page. On the **Header/Footer tab**, insert a **Custom Footer** in the **left section** that includes the file name.

a. Display the document properties and if necessary, right-click the author name, click Edit Property, and then type your name. In the **Subject** box, type your course name and section #, and in the **Tags** box, type **Charlotte, server schedule** Display and then review the grouped worksheets in Print Preview—you will have four total pages.

(Project 8D Charlotte Staffing continues on the next page)

b. On the left, click **Save**. Right-click any sheet tab, and then click **Ungroup Sheets**.

c. If directed by your instructor to do so, submit a paper printout of each of the three worksheets, an electronic image of each of your three worksheets that looks like a printed document, or your original Excel file. If required by your instructor, print or create an electronic version of your worksheets with formulas displayed. In the upper right corner of the Excel window, click Close.

END | You have completed Project 8D

MyITLab
grader

Mastering Excel **Project 8E Seafood Inventory**

Apply 8A skills from these Objectives:

1 Calculate a Moving Average

2 Project Income and Expenses

3 Determine a Break-Even Point

In this Project, you will create a worksheet for Joe Flores, manager of the Dallas region, who wants to analyze the fluctuation in the quantity of shrimp that is used at the four Dallas restaurants. You will use the moving average tool to help identify the variation in shrimp usage in recipes over a four-week period. Your completed worksheets will look similar to Figure 8.50.

PROJECT FILES

For Project 8E, you will need the following file:

e08E_Seafood_Inventory

You will save your workbook as:

Lastname_Firstname_8E_Seafood_Inventory

PROJECT RESULTS

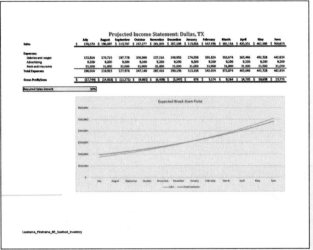

FIGURE 8.50

Excel 2016, Windows 10, Microsoft Corporation.

(Project 8E Seafood Inventory continues on the next page)

1 Start Excel. From the student data files that accompany this chapter, open the file **e08E_Seafood Inventory**. Using your own name, save the file in your **Excel Chapter 8** folder as **Lastname_Firstname_8E_Seafood_Inventory**

2 Ensure that the **Analysis ToolPak** is enabled. On the **Moving Average** worksheet, insert a **Moving Average** using the range **A5:AB5** as the **Input Range**, **4** as the **Interval**, and cell **A6** as the **Output Range**. Select only the **Chart Output** check box; do NOT select the Labels in First Row check box.

3 Position the chart between cells **C8** and **Z29**, keeping the chart slightly inside the cell borders.

4 Edit the **Vertical (Value) Axis Title** to **Bags of Shrimp Used** Edit the **Horizontal (Category) Axis Title** to **Four-Week Period**

5 To display the days of the week as the Horizontal (Category) Axis Labels, at the bottom of the chart, point to any of the data points, right-click, display the **Select Data Source** dialog box, and then edit the **Horizontal (Category) Axis Labels** by selecting the range **A4:AB4**; click **OK** two times.

6 To plot the Forecast series on a secondary axis, on the **Format tab**, in the **Current Selection group**, click the **Chart Elements arrow**, and then click **Series "Forecast"**. In the same group, click **Format Selection**. In the **Format Data Series** pane, display **Series Options**, and then plot the series on **Secondary Axis**.

7 Format both the **Chart Area** and the **Plot Area** with a **Solid fill** using the color **Green, Accent 4, Lighter 80%**—in the eighth column, the second color. Format the range **D6:AB6** with the **Comma [0]** cell style.

8 Display the **Projected Income** worksheet. Click cell **C3**, type **=b3*(1+b13)** and **Copy** the formula across to cell **M3**. **Copy** the formula in cell **B9** across to cell **M9**.

9 To create a line chart with a second series, select the nonadjacent ranges **A2:M3** and **A9:M9**, and then insert the first Line chart style.

10 Change the **Chart Title** to **Expected Break-Even Point**

11 Position the chart between cells **B15** and **M36**, keeping the chart slightly inside the cell borders.

12 Format both the **Plot Area** and the **Chart Area** with a **Solid fill** using the color **Gold, Accent 1, Lighter 80%**—in the fifth column, the second color.

13 Deselect the chart. Select all the sheets, and then display the **Page Setup** dialog box. Insert a **custom footer** in the **left section** that includes the file name, and then center the worksheets horizontally. On the ribbon, set the **Orientation** to **Landscape**, and set the **Width** to **1 page**.

14 Display the **document properties** and, if necessary, edit the **Author** box, to display your name. In the **Subject** box, type your course name and section #, and in the **Tags** box, type **Dallas, seafood inventory** On the left, click **Save**. Right-click any sheet tab, and then click **Ungroup Sheets**. If directed by your instructor to do so, submit a paper printout of each of the two worksheets, an electronic image of each of your two worksheets that looks like a printed document, or your original Excel file. If required by your instructor, print or create an electronic version of your worksheets with formulas displayed. In the upper right corner of the Excel window, click **Close**.

END | You have completed Project 8E

Mastering Excel Project 8F Seafood Chowder

Apply **8B** skills from these Objectives:

4 Use Solver

5 Create Scenarios

6 Use Logical Functions

7 Create Complex Formulas

In this Mastering Excel project, you will assist Jillian Zachary, manager of the Ft. Lauderdale restaurant, by using Solver to create several scenarios for how much of each of the three seafood ingredients—scallops, shrimp, and fish—to include in the chowder at the new seasonal prices to maintain a profit margin of 35 percent on a serving of chowder at the current wholesale seafood costs. Your completed worksheets will look similar to Figure 8.51.

PROJECT FILES

For Project 8F, you will need the following file:

e08F_Seafood_Chowder

You will save your workbook as:

Lastname_Firstname_8F_Seafood_Chowder

PROJECT RESULTS

FIGURE 8.51

(Project 8F Seafood Chowder continues on the next page)

1 Start Excel. From your student files, open the file **e08F_Seafood_Chowder**, and then using your own name, **Save** the file in your **Excel Chapter 8** folder as **Lastname_Firstname_8F_Seafood_Chowder**

2 Ensure that **Solver** is installed. Open **Solver**. Set the objective cell as **J5** to the **Value Of 35%** and then set variable cells to the range **C4:C6** and click **Solve**.

3 Save the scenario as **No minimum weight** and then restore the original values.

4 Open **Solver**. Add a constraint where cell **C7 >=7.5** Click **Solve**.

5 **Save** the scenario as **Minimum 7.5 pounds** and restore the original values.

6 Add a constraint where cell **C6 =c5*2** and then click **Solve**.

7 **Save** the scenario as **Twice as much fish as shrimp** and restore the original values.

8 Open the **Scenario Manager** and create a scenario summary. As the **Results cells** type **=j5,c7** to summarize results from cells J5 and C7.

9 Click the **Weekly Sales** worksheet. In cell **I2**, enter a **SUMIF** function that uses named ranges, **MENU** and **CUPS** to count the number of cups of soup sold for each menu in column H and then copy the formula down through cell **I4**.

10 In cell **J2** enter the **SUMIF** function that uses the named ranges **MENU** and **BOWLS** to count the number of

bowls of soup sold for each menu in column H. Copy the formula down through cell **J4**.

11 In cell **F2**, enter an **IF** function with a nested **AND** function to test for lunch sales of more than $100 and that returns the word **BEST** when both conditions are met and leave the cells blank for days that do not. Copy the formula down through cell **F15**. Use conditional formatting to format the cells with a red border for those days that meet both conditions.

12 Select All Sheets, click the **Page Layout tab**, set the **Orientation** to **Landscape** and set the **Width** to **1 page**. Display the **Page Setup** dialog box, center the worksheets horizontally, and insert a **Custom Footer** with the file name in the **left section**. Make cell **A1** active. Display the **document properties**, if necessary add your name as the author, type your course name and section # in the **Subject** box, and as the **Tags**, type **seafood chowder, recipe costs** On the left, click **Print**, and then examine the Print preview. On the left, click **Save**. Right-click any sheet tab and click **Ungroup Sheets**. If directed by your instructor to do so, submit a paper printout of each of the two worksheets, an electronic image of each of your two worksheets that looks like a printed document, or your original Excel file. If required by your instructor, print or create an electronic version of your worksheets with formulas displayed. In the upper right corner of the Excel window, click **Close**.

END | You have completed Project 8F

Mastering Excel Project 8G Income Model

Apply 8A and 8B skills from these Objectives:

1 Calculate a Moving Average
2 Project Income and Expenses
3 Determine a Break-Even Point
4 Use Solver
5 Create Scenarios
6 Use Logical Functions
7 Create Complex Formulas

In this Mastering Excel project, you will assist Kelsey Tanner, CFO of Brina's Bistro, to use a worksheet model and Solver to create several scenarios that would result in breaking even six months after opening. In this model for projecting the income, a new restaurant is expected to break even eight months after opening. Management wants to examine the assumptions and see what changes are needed to shorten the time it takes to break even. Month 0 is the first month of operation and it assumes that a new restaurant will gross $156,250 in sales in the opening month. The costs related to sales are assumed to be 87%; fixed costs are $40,000; and the anticipated growth rate in the first year, month-to-month, is 10%. The worksheet extends these assumptions out to month 11, which is the end of the first year of operation. Your completed worksheets will look similar to Figure 8.52.

PROJECT FILES

For Project 8G, you will need the following file:

e08G_Income_Model

You will save your workbook as:

Lastname_Firstname_8G_Income_Model

PROJECT RESULTS

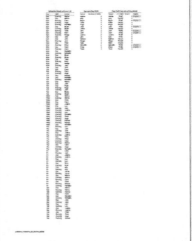

FIGURE 8.52

(Project 8G Income Model continues on the next page)

Mastering Excel   Project 8G Income Model (continued)

1 From the student data files that accompany this chapter, open **e08G_Income_Model**. Using your own name, save the file as **Lastname_Firstname_8G_Income_Model** in your **Excel Chapter 8** folder. Take a moment to examine the **Projected Income** worksheet.

2 On the **Projected Income** worksheet, change the value in cell **B15** to **6** and press Enter. In the green shaded area, notice that *Sales* changes to *$276,806* and the *Gross Profit/Loss* changes to *($4,015)*. Note that these match the figures under Month 6 in cells **H3** and **H10** respectively. Management wants to create several scenarios that would result in breaking even six months after opening.

3 Change the value in cell B16 to **11%** and press Enter. Ensure that the Solver add-in is installed. Open **Solver. Set** the **objective cell** as **b20** to a **Value Of 0** and set the **Variable Cells** to **b16,b18** (be sure to type the comma between the two cell references) to change both the growth rate in cell B16 and the costs related to sales % in cell B18. **Solve**, if necessary click the blinking Excel icon on the taskbar to display the Solver Results. Save this scenario as **11% Growth** and then restore the original values.

4 Display the **Solver Parameters** dialog box again. Add a constraint that requires **Percent growth** in cell **B16** to be less than or equal to **10% Solve**, and then save this scenario as **10% Growth** Restore the original values.

5 Display the **Solver Parameters** dialog box again. **Delete** the existing constraint, and add a constraint for the **Costs related to sales** in cell B18 to be equal to **85% Solve**, save the scenario as **85% Costs** and then restore the original values.

6 With the **Projected Income** worksheet displayed, create a scenario summary worksheet using **Gross profit or loss** in cell **B20** as the result cell. Change the value in cell **B15** back to 1 and change the value in cell **B16** back to **10%**.

7 On the **Projected Income** worksheet, create a **Line** chart using the noncontiguous ranges **A2:M3** and **A8:M8**.

8 Change the **Chart Title** to **Expected Break-Even Point** Position the chart so that the upper left corner of the chart aligns with the upper left corner of cell **B22**.

9 Ensure that the Analysis ToolPak add-in is installed. On the **Sales** worksheet, create a **Moving Average** using the sales **B2:B49** as the input range, **7** as the **Interval**, C3 as the **Output Range**, and selecting the **Labels in First Row** and **Chart Output** check boxes.

10 Move the chart to a new sheet named **Sales Trend Chart**

11 On the **Sales Trend Chart** worksheet, edit the **Horizontal (Category) Axis Labels** to display the range **A9:A49** from the Sales worksheet.

12 On the **Sales Trend Chart** worksheet, change the date format used for the **Horizontal (Category) Axis** labels to the **3/14 Date** format.

13 On the **Sales Trend Chart** worksheet, change the **Horizontal (Category) Axis** title to **Date** On the Vertical (Value) Axis, set the *Minimum* to **3500** On this chart sheet, insert a custom footer with the file name in the **left section.**

14 On the **Schedules** worksheet, in the range **F3:F19**, enter a **COUNTIFS** function to count the number of day shifts each server is scheduled to work.

15 In the range **I3:I19**, enter an **AND** function to determine which servers are scheduled for 2-5 day shifts.

16 In cell **J3**, enter a **COUNTIFS** function to calculate the number of Monday shifts each server is scheduled to work. Edit the formula in cell **J3** by adding a second **COUNTIFS** function to calculate the number of Tuesday shifts each server is scheduled to work. Copy the formula down through cell **J19**.

17 In the range **K3:K19**, enter an **IF** function with a nested **AND** function to determine which employees are scheduled for 2-5 shifts, including a Monday or Tuesday. The function should return the world **Eligible** if true, and leave the cell blank if false.

18 Select the first three worksheets to group them— **Scenario Summary, Projected Income**, and **Sales Trend Chart**. Click the **Page Layout tab**, set the **Orientation** to **Landscape** and set the **Width** to **1 page**. Display the **Page Setup** dialog box, center the worksheets horizontally, and insert a **Custom Footer** with the file name in the **left section**. Make cell **A1** active.

19 Select the last two worksheets to group them— **Sales** and **Schedules**. Click the **Page Layout tab**, set the

(Project 8G Income Model continues on the next page)

Orientation to **Portrait**, set the **Width** to **1 page** and set the **Height** to **1 page**. Display the **Page Setup** dialog box, center the worksheets horizontally, and insert a **Custom Footer** with the file name in the **left section**. Make cell **A1** active.

20 ▶ Right-click any sheet tab and click **Select All Sheets**. Display the **document properties**, if necessary add your name as the author, type your course name and section # in the **Subject** box, and as the **Tags**, type **income, sales model** On the left, click **Print**, and then

examine the Print preview. On the left, click **Save**. Right-click any sheet tab, and then click **Ungroup Sheets**. If directed by your instructor to do so, submit a paper printout of each of the five worksheets, an electronic image of each of your five worksheets that looks like a printed document, or your original Excel file. If required by your instructor, print or create an electronic version of your worksheets with formulas displayed. In the upper right corner of the Excel window, click **Close**.

END | You have completed Project 8G

8

EXCEL

GO! Fix It	Project 8H Maintenance Expenses	**MyITLab**
GO! Make It	Project 8I Oyster Usage	**MyITLab**
GO! Solve It	Project 8J Tampa Income	**MyITLab**
GO! Solve It	Project 8K Ahi Salad	

PROJECT FILES

For Project 8K, you will need the following file:

e08K_Ahi_Salad

You will save your workbook as:

Lastname_Firstname_8K_Ahi_Salad

Open the file e08K_Ahi_Salad and using your own name, save it as **Lastname_Firstname_8K_Ahi_Salad** Be sure that Solver is installed. Create three scenarios and a summary. Set the objective cell to J5, value of 60%. Solve for **No minimum weight of vegetables** by changing variable cells to the range C4:C6. Solve for **Minimum 5 pounds of vegetables** by using the constraint C5>=5. Solve for **Twice as many vegetables as greens** by using the constraint C5=C6*2. Create a Scenario Summary. On all sheets, insert the file name in the footer in the left section. Set the orientation to Landscape, width to 1 page, and center horizontally. Add appropriate information to the document properties including the tag **Ahi salad** and submit as directed by your instructor.

Performance Level

Performance Criteria	Exemplary: You consistently applied the relevant skills	Proficient: You sometimes, but not always, applied the relevant skills	Developing: You rarely or never applied the relevant skills
Use Solver to Create Scenarios	Three scenarios were created using Solver based on the instructions.	Two scenarios were created using Solver based on the instructions.	None or one scenario was created using Solver based on the instructions.
Create a Scenario Summary	A Scenario Summary listing three scenarios was created.	A Scenario Summary listing two scenarios was created.	A Scenario Summary was not created.

END | You have completed Project 8K

OUTCOME-BASED ASSESSMENTS (CRITICAL THINKING)

RUBRIC

The following outcomes-based assessments are open-ended assessments. That is, there is no specific correct result; your result will depend on your approach to the information provided. Make Professional Quality your goal. Use the following scoring rubric to guide you in how to approach the problem and then to evaluate how well your approach solves the problem.

The *criteria*—Software Mastery, Content, Format and Layout, and Process—represent the knowledge and skills you have gained that you can apply to solving the problem. The *levels of performance*—Professional Quality, Approaching Professional Quality, or Needs Quality Improvements—help you and your instructor evaluate your result.

	Your completed project is of Professional Quality if you:	Your completed project is Approaching Professional Quality if you:	Your completed project Needs Quality Improvements if you:
1-Software Mastery	Choose and apply the most appropriate skills, tools, and features and identify efficient methods to solve the problem.	Choose and apply some appropriate skills, tools, and features, but not in the most efficient manner.	Choose inappropriate skills, tools, or features, or are inefficient in solving the problem.
2-Content	Construct a solution that is clear and well organized, contains content that is accurate, appropriate to the audience and purpose, and is complete. Provide a solution that contains no errors of spelling, grammar, or style.	Construct a solution in which some components are unclear, poorly organized, inconsistent, or incomplete. Misjudge the needs of the audience. Have some errors in spelling, grammar, or style, but the errors do not detract from comprehension.	Construct a solution that is unclear, incomplete, or poorly organized, contains some inaccurate or inappropriate content, and contains many errors of spelling, grammar, or style. Do not solve the problem.
3-Format and Layout	Format and arrange all elements to communicate information and ideas, clarify function, illustrate relationships, and indicate relative importance.	Apply appropriate format and layout features to some elements, but not others. Overuse features, causing minor distraction.	Apply format and layout that does not communicate information or ideas clearly. Do not use format and layout features to clarify function, illustrate relationships, or indicate relative importance. Use available features excessively, causing distraction.
4-Process	Use an organized approach that integrates planning, development, self-assessment, revision, and reflection.	Demonstrate an organized approach in some areas, but not others; or, use an insufficient process of organization throughout.	Do not use an organized approach to solve the problem.

OUTCOMES-BASED ASSESSMENTS (CRITICAL THINKING)

GO! Think   Project 8L Seasonings Inventory

PROJECT FILES

For Project 8L, you will need the following file:

e08L_Seasonings_Inventory

You will save your workbook as:

Lastname_Firstname_8L_Seasonings_Inventory

Open the file e08L_Seasonings_Inventory, and then using your own name save it in your chapter folder as **Lastname_Firstname_8L_Seasonings_Inventory** From the source data, create a Moving Average chart to help identify the variation in seafood seasoning used over a four-week period using a 7 day interval. Begin the output range in cell A6. Move the chart to a new sheet. Format the chart attractively. Insert the file name in the left section of the footer on each page, center horizontally, set the orientation to Landscape, add appropriate information to the document properties, including the tag **seasonings inventory** and submit as directed by your instructor.

> END | You have completed Project 8L

GO! Think   Project 8M PT Staff   MyITLab

Build from
Scratch

You and GO!   Project 8N Entertainment   MyITLab

Using Macros and Visual Basic for Applications

PROJECT 9A
OUTCOMES
Record a macro to automate complex and repetitive tasks.

OBJECTIVES
1. Record a Macro
2. Assign a Macro to a Button on the Quick Access Toolbar
3. Modify a Macro

PROJECT 9B
OUTCOMES
Ensure accuracy and automate instructions using VBA commands and ActiveX Controls.

OBJECTIVES
4. Write a VBA Procedure to Use an ActiveX Control
5. Restore Initial Settings

Rob/Fotolia

In This Chapter

GO! to Work with Excel

In this chapter, you will automate Excel worksheets to make it easier and faster to perform complex or repetitive tasks. Because individuals who do the same type of work each day may use a specific sequence of Excel commands repeatedly, Excel enables you to record a sequence of commands in a macro and then activate the sequence with a single button or keystroke. A button can be attached to the macro and placed on the worksheet or ribbon. You can also program Excel to perform tasks that are not represented by existing commands or to validate data against complex criteria that requires more than a simple comparison.

Westland Plains Human Resources Consulting provides its customers with services such as Employee Benefits Administration, Recruitment Services, Payroll Processing, Computer Technology Training, Employee Assistance Programs, and Corporate Health and Wellness Programs. Customers are typically small and mid-size companies who, for cost savings and efficiency, use an outside source for such services. Westland has a staff of 35 full-time employees in five regional offices throughout the metropolitan area. Westland's knowledgeable consultants help companies remain compliant with federal and state laws and regulations.

PROJECT 9A

Travel Expenses

MyITLab
Project 9A Training
Project 9A Grader

PROJECT ACTIVITIES

In Activities 9.01 through 9.07, you will set a macro security level, remove file protection, record a macro, and assign a macro to the Quick Access Toolbar. You will test and modify a macro to fill in employee information for a Travel Expense Report, and protect the worksheet. Your completed project will look similar to Figure 9.1.

Please always review the downloaded Grader instructions before beginning.

PROJECT FILES

MyITLab
grader

If your instructor wants you to submit Project 9A in the MyITLab Grader system, log in to MyITLab, locate Grader Project 9A, and then download the files for this project.

For Project 9A, you will need the following file:
e09A_Travel_Macro

You will save your workbook as:
Lastname_Firstname_9A_Travel_Macro

PROJECT RESULTS

GO!
Walk Thru
Project 9A

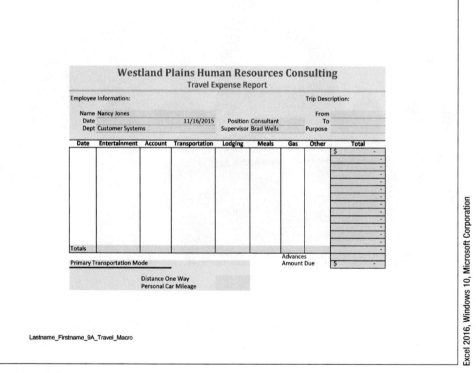

FIGURE 9.1 Project 9A Travel Expenses

Excel 2016, Windows 10, Microsoft Corporation

GO! Learn How
Video E9-1

A **macro** is an action or a set of actions with which you can automate tasks by grouping a series of commands into a single command. You can perform the command with a single mouse click, a keyboard shortcut, or when a workbook opens.

For example, you could record a macro that automatically enters employee names in the first column, alphabetizes the names, and then applies a fill color to the cells containing the names. When you have a sequence of actions that you perform frequently, record the actions as a macro to automate the task.

Macros are recorded in the **Visual Basic for Applications** programming language—also referred to as **VBA**—which is the language used to write computer programs within the Microsoft Windows environment.

To work with macros, you must:

- Add the Developer tab to the ribbon, which displays the commands you will need to work with macros.

- Select a macro security setting to enable macros when using Excel.

- Save the workbook that includes macros as an Excel Macro-Enabled Workbook file type.

Activity 9.01 | Adding the Developer Tab to the Ribbon

> **ALERT!** To submit as an autograded project, log into MyITLab and download the files for this project, and begin with those files instead of a new blank document and e09A_Travel_Macro.

MOS

1.1.6 Expert

The macro commands are located on the Developer tab, which, by default, does not display in Excel. You must enable the Developer tab from the Excel Options dialog box. In this Activity, you will add the Developer tab to the ribbon.

1 Start Excel and open a new blank workbook. Click the **File** tab to display **Backstage** view, and then click **Options**.

2 In the **Excel Options** dialog box, on the left, click **Customize Ribbon**. On the right, under **Customize the Ribbon**, verify that **Main Tabs** is selected, select the **Developer** check box, and then compare your screen with Figure 9.2.

FIGURE 9.2

Excel 2016, Windows 10, Microsoft Corporation

3 In the lower right corner, click **OK**. On the ribbon, click the **Developer tab**, and then compare your screen with Figure 9.3.

The *Developer tab* displays on the ribbon. The *Code group* contains the commands you will need to work with macros.

FIGURE 9.3

Activity 9.02 | Changing the Macro Security Settings in Excel

1.1.5 Expert

Opening an Excel workbook that has a macro attached to it might cause a message to display, indicating that macros are disabled. This is a precautionary measure because macros may contain viruses. Because a macro is a computer program, programming code that erases or damages files can be inserted by the person creating the macro. This unauthorized code is called a *macro virus*. In this Activity, you will change the security setting so that you can choose to enable macros when you open a workbook that contains a macro.

1 On the **Developer tab**, in the **Code group**, click **Macro Security**. Compare your screen with Figure 9.4, and then take a moment to study the table in Figure 9.5.

The Trust Center dialog box displays. On the left, Macro Settings is selected. The Macro Settings enable you to decide, each time you open a workbook, how or whether to run the macros that are contained in the workbook. The table in Figure 9.5 summarizes how macro virus protection works under each setting. Regardless of which option you choose, any installed antivirus software that works with your Microsoft Office software will scan the workbook for known viruses before it is opened. In an organization, you may not be permitted to change these settings without permission from your System Administrator. Any macro setting changes that you make in Excel in the Macro Settings category apply only to Excel and do not affect any other Office program.

FIGURE 9.4

MACRO SETTINGS AND THEIR EFFECTS	
MACRO SETTING	**DESCRIPTION**
Disable all macros without notification	This setting disables all macros and security alerts unless the Excel document is in a trusted location.
Disable all macros with notification	This setting is enabled by default. You are alerted if macros are present in the workbook. This setting enables you to choose each time you open a workbook whether or not to run the macros that are contained in the workbook.
Disable all macros except digitally signed macros	This setting enables macros from trusted publishers to run; otherwise, this setting is the same as the Disable all macros with notification setting.
Enable all macros (not recommended; potentially dangerous code can run)	Use this setting when you want to enable all macros to run on a temporary basis. It is not recommended as a permanent setting because it makes your computer vulnerable to potential malicious code.

FIGURE 9.5

2 Under **Macro Settings**, verify that the default option—**Disable all macros with notification**—is selected, and then click **OK**.

By selecting the security level *Disable all macros with notification*, you have the option of enabling macros on a file-by-file basis. This security level causes a Security Warning to display, indicating that macros have been disabled, and gives you the option to enable or disable macros.

Excel provides safeguards that help protect against viruses that can be transmitted by macros. If you share macros with others, you can certify that the macro is from a trustworthy source by using a ***digital signature***—an electronic, encryption-based, secure stamp of authentication on a macro or document. The digital signature confirms that the macro or document originated from the signer and has not been altered. If a file has been digitally signed, a certificate that identifies the source displays; then you can decide whether this is a trusted source before you activate the macros.

NOTE   Message Bar Security Warnings

When you open a macro-enabled workbook, on the Message Bar, a Security Warning may display advising you that macros in the file have been disabled. If you get an information message that indicates you cannot open the workbook, you will want to confirm that your computer will display the Message Bar. To set the Message Bar to display, do the following: On the left side of the Excel Options dialog box, click Trust Center. Under Microsoft Excel Trust Center, at the right, click Trust Center Settings. On the left side of the Trust Center dialog box, click Message Bar and at the right, confirm that Show the Message Bar in all applications when active content, such as ActiveX controls and macros, has been blocked is selected. Click OK two times to close both dialog boxes.

3 From your student files, open the file **e09A_Travel_Macro**. Display the **Save As** dialog box, navigate to the location where you will save your projects for this chapter, and then create a new folder for **Excel Chapter 9**

4 Click the **Save as type arrow**, and then click **Excel Macro-Enabled Workbook**. In the **File name** box, type **Lastname_Firstname_9A_Travel_Macro** and then compare your screen with Figure 9.6.

Selecting *Excel Macro-Enabled Workbook* saves the Excel file in the XML-based format, allowing macros to be saved to the workbook.

FIGURE 9.6

5 ▶ Click **Save**. Insert a footer in the **left section** that includes the file name. Return to **Normal** view and scroll to view the top of the worksheet.

6 ▶ **Save** 🖫 your workbook.

Activity 9.03 | Unprotecting a Workbook

This workbook is a form that employees of Westland Plains Human Resources Consulting use to report travel expenses. A *form* is a worksheet or Excel object that contains fields and controls that enable a user to easily enter or edit data. The worksheet is protected so that employees can fill in their travel expense information only in the unlocked cells. A worksheet must be *unprotected* to record a macro.

1 ▶ On the **Review tab**, in the **Changes group**, click **Protect Workbook**.

2 ▶ In the **Unprotect Workbook** dialog box, type **travel** which is the password applied to this form, and then click **OK**.

Activity 9.04 | Recording a Macro

2.3.4 Expert

The macro recorder records all the steps (keystrokes and mouse clicks) that you require to complete the actions you want your macro to perform—*except* for navigation on the ribbon, which is not included in the recorded steps. When you record a macro, assign it a name so that you can refer to the macro name later. In this Activity, you will record a macro that will fill in employee information for a specific employee on a Travel Expense form.

1 ▶ With cell **B6** active, click the **Developer tab**, and then, in the **Code group**, click **Record Macro**.

In the Record Macro dialog box, you can name the macro, assign a shortcut key, and start the recording. The *Record Macro* command records your actions in Visual Basic for Applications (VBA).

🔄 **ANOTHER WAY**   On the View tab, in the Macros group, click the Macros button arrow, and then click Record Macro.

2 ▶ In the **Macro name** box, delete the existing text, and then type **Employee_Info**

The first character of the macro name must be a letter. Following characters can be letters, numbers, or underscore characters. Spaces are not permitted in a macro name; an underscore character works well as a word separator. Do not use a macro name that could be a cell reference—you will get an error message that the macro name is not valid.

In the **Shortcut key** box, type **r**

You can create a shortcut key to execute the macro, in this instance Ctrl + R. If you do not specify a shortcut key at the time you create the macro, you can add it later. Shortcut keys are case sensitive.

NOTE   Assigning Shortcut Keys to a Macro

The Excel program uses shortcut keys for common commands, such as Ctrl + S for saving a file or Ctrl + P for printing a file. When you assign a shortcut key to a macro, it takes precedence over the shortcut keys that are built into Excel. For this reason, use caution when you assign a shortcut key so that you do not override an existing shortcut. To see a list of Excel shortcut keys, in the Excel Help files, in the Search window box, type *keyboard shortcuts*, and then examine the topic *Keyboard shortcuts in Excel 2016 for Windows*.

---

4 Click the **Store macro in arrow** to see the available options.

You can store a macro in *This Workbook*—the default setting—in *New Workbook*, or in a *Personal Macro Workbook*. The *New Workbook* option opens a new workbook and adds the macro to that workbook. The *Personal Macro Workbook* is a workbook where you can store macros that you want to be able to use in other workbooks.

5 Be sure **This Workbook** is selected, and then click the **Store macro in arrow** to close the list. Click in the **Description** box. Type **Fills in the Employee Information** and then compare your screen with Figure 9.7.

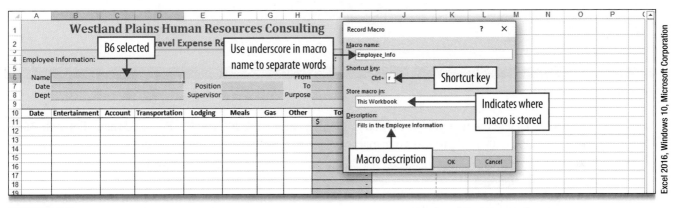

FIGURE 9.7

6 Click **OK**, and in the Status bar in the lower left corner of your screen, notice the square button indicating that a macro is recording.

The macro recorder is turned on. From this point forward, every action you take will be recorded as part of the macro. Be assured that the amount of time you take between actions is not being recorded, so there is no need to rush. If you make an error, take the appropriate steps to correct it; the corrective steps will simply become part of the macro, and you can edit the mistakes out of the macro later.

7 In cell **B6**, type **Nancy Jones** and then press Enter. With cell **B7** active, hold down Ctrl and press ; (semicolon), which will insert the current date. Press Enter.

8 With cell **B8** active, type **Customer Systems** and then press Enter. Click cell **F7**, type **Consultant** and then press Enter. In cell **F8**, type **Brad Wells** and then click cell **A11**, so that when the macro completes, the first cell in the data area is active to begin filling in the travel information.

9 On the **Developer tab**, in the **Code group**, click **Stop Recording**. Compare your screen with Figure 9.8.

The macro stops recording and cell A11 is selected. The Stop Recording button returns to a Record Macro button on the ribbon. In the status bar, if you point to the button to the right of *Ready*, the ScreenTip indicates *No macros are currently recording. Click to begin recording a new macro.*

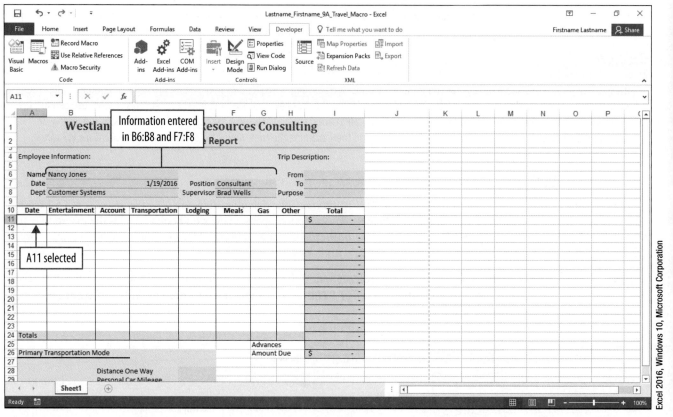

FIGURE 9.8

10 Delete the text you just typed in the five cells—**B6**, **B7**, **B8**, **F7**, **F8**—and then click cell **B6**. Press Ctrl + R to test your macro.

The shortcut key activates the macro, the employee information is filled in, and cell A11 is selected.

11 **Save** 🔲 your workbook.

Objective 2 | Assign a Macro to a Button on the Quick Access Toolbar

GO! Learn How
Video E9-2

You have practiced activating a macro with a keyboard shortcut, but another option is to activate a macro by clicking a button on the Quick Access Toolbar. To do so, you must create a new toolbar button.

Activity 9.05 | Adding a Button to the Quick Access Toolbar

In the following Activity, you will add a button to the Quick Access Toolbar. Buttons that you add to the Quick Access Toolbar become a permanent part of the toolbar to which it was added unless you specifically remove it or reset the Quick Access Toolbar.

1 On the **Quick Access Toolbar**, click **Customize Quick Access Toolbar** ⏷, and then click **More Commands**.

🔄 **ANOTHER WAY**   Click the File tab, click Options to display the Excel Options dialog box, and then on the left, click Quick Access Toolbar.

2 Click the **Choose commands from arrow**, and then click **Macros**. Compare your screen with Figure 9.9.

Under <Separator>, your Employee_Info macro and a default icon display.

FIGURE 9.9

3 Click your **Employee_Info** macro, and then in the center of the dialog box click **Add**. Compare your screen with Figure 9.10.

The Employee_Info macro displays on the right in the panel that contains buttons that currently display on the Quick Access Toolbar.

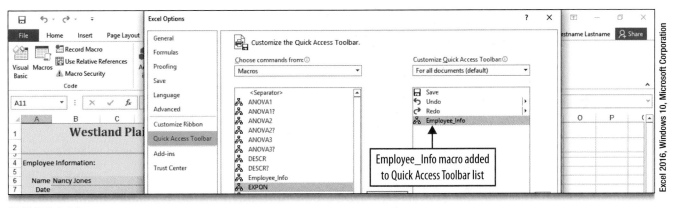

FIGURE 9.10

4 With your **Employee_Info** command selected on the right, click **Modify**. Compare your screen with Figure 9.11.

The Modify Button dialog box displays. The first symbol is selected and at the bottom of the dialog box, Display name indicates *Employee_Info*.

FIGURE 9.11

> **5** Under **Symbol**, in the fourth row, click the last icon—the **Smiley Face**—and then click **OK** two times. **Save** 🖫 your workbook, and then compare your screen with Figure 9.12.
>
> The Smiley Face icon displays on the Quick Access Toolbar.

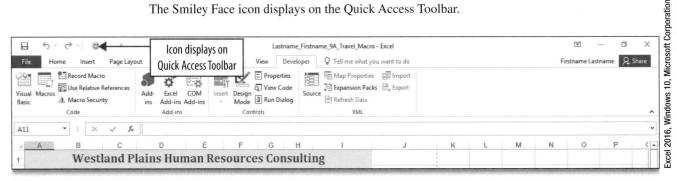

FIGURE 9.12

Activity 9.06 | Testing the Macro Button

After you add the button, test it to verify that the button performs as you intended. When you point to the button, the ScreenTip describes the name of the button. The action that causes your macro to run is called an **event** and might be a combination of keystrokes or the click of a button on the Quick Access Toolbar.

> **1** Select the nonadjacent ranges **B6:B8** and **F7:F8** and press Del so that these cells are empty again.

> **2** Click cell **B6**, and then on the **Quick Access Toolbar**, click your new **Employee_Info** button—the Smiley Face.
>
> The employee information is filled in, and cell A11 is selected.

Objective 3 Modify a Macro

GO! Learn How
Video E9-3

When you record a macro, a **module** is the place where the Visual Basic for Applications (VBA) programming code is stored. A module consists of one or more **procedures**—a unit of computer code that performs an action. Procedures are commonly referred to as **sub procedures**, or simply **subs**. If you want to modify the way your macro performs, you can modify the actual code that was created by the macro.

Activity 9.07 | Changing the Visual Basic Code

You can view and edit the module containing the Visual Basic code in the **Visual Basic Editor** window. In this Activity, you will open the module that was created for the *Employee_Info* macro, examine the VBA code, and then modify the code to add the action of centering the worksheet both horizontally and vertically.

1 On the **Developer tab,** in the **Code group**, click **Macros**.

The Macro dialog box displays and the *Employee_Info* macro is listed. From this dialog box, you can also run the macro.

2 In the **Macro** dialog box, with the **Employee_Info** macro selected, click **Edit**. If necessary, maximize the Microsoft Visual Basic Editor window and the Code window.

The Microsoft Visual Basic Editor window displays. This window has several panes that can be displayed, and some of the available panes may be opened or closed.

3 In the **Code window** on the right, locate the green and black lines of text that comprise the comments and code for the Employee_Info macro. Compare your screen with Figure 9.13.

Your window may be configured differently than the one shown in Figure 9.13. The first section, displayed in green and in lines preceded by an apostrophe ('), consists of comments that describe the macro. These comments are not part of the macro procedure. In this module, the comments include the data you entered when you created the macro—the macro name and description and the shortcut key that was assigned.

The VBA code that follows, in black type, includes the instructions to select the cell ranges and enter data. *Sub* indicates the beginning of the sub procedure. *End Sub* indicates the end of the sub procedure.

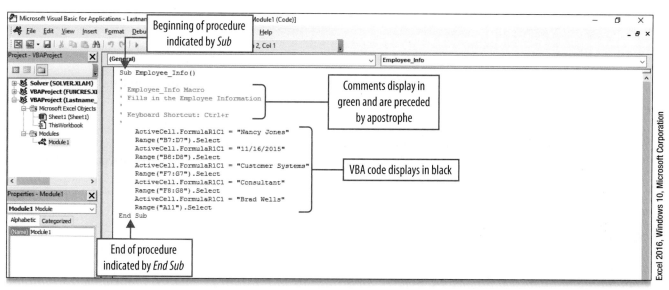

FIGURE 9.13

4 At the end of the *last* line of code—*Range("A11").Select*—click to place the insertion point after *Select*, and then press Enter.

In this manner, you can insert a blank line to type new code.

5 On the new, empty line type **With ActiveSheet.PageSetup** and then press Enter.

The word *With* notes the beginning of a **VBA construct**—an instruction that enables the macro to perform multiple operations on a single object. The remainder of the code—*ActiveSheet. PageSetup*—is the equivalent of displaying the Page Setup dialog box.

6 Press Tab to indent and type **.CenterHorizontally = True** Press Enter and type **.CenterVertically = True** and then press Enter. Verify that you typed the period preceding each line of code.

The period identifies the command that follows. In this case, the two commands that you typed following each period instruct Excel to center the worksheet horizontally and vertically on the page. The commands are indented using Tab to make it easier to read the code. When you press Enter, the text will continue to wrap to that same level of indentation.

7 Press Shift + Tab. Type **End With** and then compare your screen with Figure 9.14.

Instructions that have a beginning and ending statement, such as *With* and *End With*, should be indented at the same level. To decrease the level of indentation, press Shift + Tab, which will move the indentation toward the left margin.

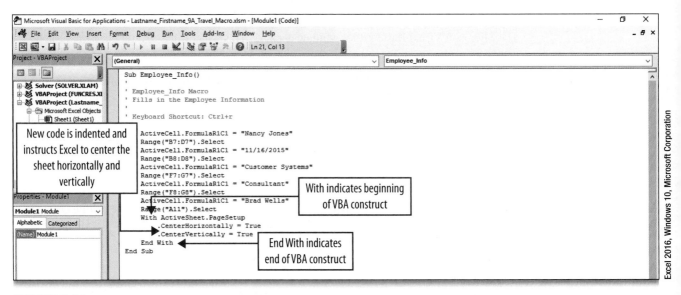

FIGURE 9.14

8 On the menu bar, click **File**, and then click **Close and Return to Microsoft Excel**. Click **File**, and then click **Print**. Notice that the worksheet is not centered on the page. Return ⊖ to the worksheet.

9 Select the nonadjacent ranges **B6:B8** and **F7:F8** and press Del so that these cells are empty again. Select cell **B6**. On the **Quick Access Toolbar**, click the **Employee_Info** button that you created, and then display the **Print Preview**. Compare your screen with Figure 9.15.

The worksheet is centered horizontally and vertically on the page.

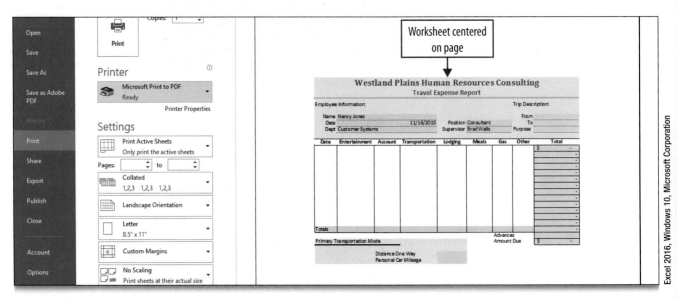

FIGURE 9.15

10 ▸ Click **Info**, and then click **Show All Properties**. In the **Tags** box, type **travel expense form** and in the **Subject** box, type your course name and section number. Under **Related People**, be sure that your name displays as **Author**.

11 ▸ **Save** 🖫 your workbook. If directed by your instructor to do so, submit your paper printout, your electronic image of your document that looks like a printed document, or your original Excel file. If required by your instructor, print or create an electronic version of your worksheet with formulas displayed. In the upper right corner of the Excel window, click **Close** ✕.

ALERT!   **If you are submitting your file for grading in MyITLab, complete steps 12 through 17.**

12 ▸ To submit your file in MyITLab, you will copy the VBA code to a new worksheet so that it can be verified. **Open** your **Lastname_Firstname_9A_Travel_Macro** file. If necessary, click Enable Content. On the **Developer tab**, in the **Code group**, click **Macros**. In the **Macro** dialog box, with the **Employee_Info** macro selected, click **Edit** to display the Microsoft Visual Basic Editor window.

13 ▸ In the Microsoft Visual Basic Editor window, press Ctrl + A to select all of the code. Press Ctrl + C to copy the code to the clipboard. On the menu bar, click **File**, and then click **Close and Return to Microsoft Excel**.

14 ▸ In the sheet tab area, click **New sheet** ⊕ to insert a new worksheet. **Rename** the inserted sheet **VBA Code**

15 ▸ In the **VBA Code** sheet, with cell **A1** active, on the **Home tab**, in the **Clipboard group**, click **Paste** to paste the VBA code to the new worksheet.

16 ▸ Click the **File tab**, and then click **Save As**. Navigate to your **Excel Chapter 9 folder**, and then click the **Save as type arrow**. Click **Excel workbook**. In the **File name** box, type **Lastname_Firstname_9A_Travel_Macro_MyITLab** and then click **Save**. In the displayed message box, click **Yes**.

17 ▸ **Close** ✕ your file. Submit your **Lastname_Firstname_9A_Travel_Macro_MyITLab** file in MyITLab.

More Knowledge

You can copy a macro to another workbook using the VBA Editor. Be sure that both Excel files are open, and then open the VBA Editor for the macro that you wish to copy. On the left, in the Project Explorer pane of the editor, both worksheets will be listed. Drag the selected module to the destination worksheet.

END | You have completed Project 9A

PROJECT ACTIVITIES

In Activities 9.08 through 9.13, you will assist Edward Salisbury, Controller at Westland Plains Human Resources Consulting, by writing a set of commands in the VBA programming language using ActiveX Control buttons to automate the travel policy guidelines for expense reports. Your completed workbook will look similar to Figure 9.16.

Please always review the downloaded Grader instructions before beginning.

PROJECT FILES

 If your instructor wants you to submit Project 9B in the MyITLab grader system, log in to MyITLab, locate Grader Project 9B, and then download the files for this project.

For Project 9B, you will need the following file:
e09B_Travel_VBA

You will save your workbook as:
Lastname_Firstname_9B_Travel_VBA

PROJECT RESULTS

GO!
Walk Thru
Project 9B

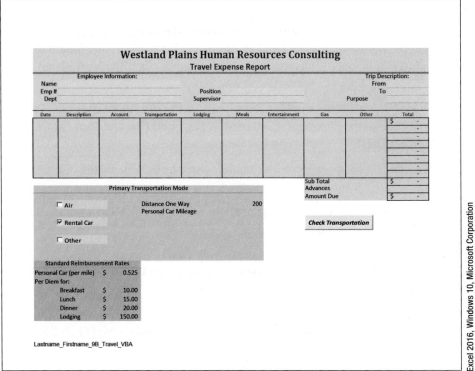

FIGURE 9.16 Project 9B VBA Procedure

Go Learn How
Video E9-4

Recall that within VBA, you can write a procedure—a named sequence of statements in a computer program that performs an action or task. A procedure can include an **ActiveX control**—a graphic object such as a check box or a button that can be placed on a worksheet or form to display or enter data, to perform an action, or to make the form easier to read. When the person filling in the form clicks the ActiveX control, VBA code runs that automates a task or offers options.

A **Form control** is a simpler object that does not require VBA code (therefore it works on other versions of Excel that do not support ActiveX). You can assign a macro directly to a Form control without using the VBA Editor. Unlike ActiveX controls, you can put a Form control on a chart sheet. A Form control is formatted by right-clicking to open a Format dialog box. ActiveX controls are more flexible and customizable than Form controls.

Activity 9.08 | Inserting ActiveX Controls

ALERT! **To submit as an autograded project, log into MyITLab and download the files for this project, and begin with those files instead of e09B_Travel_VBA.**

MOS
2.3.5 Expert

ActiveX controls are especially useful for forms that individuals complete online, because you can control different events that occur when the control is used. In the following Activity, you will insert check boxes. A **check box** is a type of ActiveX control that the person filling in the form can select to indicate a choice.

Westland Plains Human Resources Consulting has a policy that requires employees to use ground transportation—company car, company van, rental car, or personal car—for trips under 200 miles. In this project, you will design a travel expense form that will verify that when an employee submits an expense report that lists air as the mode of travel, that the one-way distance is over 200 miles, and if it is not, a message will display indicating that a supervisor signature is required.

1 Start Excel. From your student files, locate and open the file **e09B_Travel_VBA**. If necessary, on the Security Warning bar, Enable Editing and/or Enable Content. **Save** the file in your **Excel Chapter 9** folder as an **Excel Macro-Enabled Workbook** with the file name **Lastname_Firstname_9B_Travel_VBA**

2 On the **Developer tab**, in the **Controls group**, click **Insert**.

A gallery of Form Controls and ActiveX Controls displays.

3 Under **ActiveX Controls**, point to each button to display the ScreenTip. Take a moment to study the description of the ActiveX controls in the table in Figure 9.17.

ACTIVEX CONTROLS		
BUTTON	**SCREENTIP**	**DESCRIPTION**
	Command Button	Inserts a Command Button control to which code can be attached, initiating an action when clicked.
	Combo Box	Inserts a combo box control, which displays a list of choices from another source; the user can either select a choice from the list or type his or her own entry in the box.
	Check Box	Inserts a check box control that can be turned on (selected) or turned off (cleared).
	Image	Inserts an image control to embed a picture.
	Label	Inserts a text label to provide information about a control.
	List Box	Inserts a list box control, which displays a list of choices.
	More Controls	Displays a list of additional controls.
	Option Button	Inserts an option button control to indicate an on/off choice.
	Scroll Bar	Inserts a scroll bar control, which scrolls through a range of values.
	Spin Button	Inserts a spin button control, which displays a range of numbers from which the user can increase or decrease a value.
	Text Box	Inserts a text box control in which the user can type text.
	Toggle Button	Inserts a toggle button control, which remains pressed in when clicked, and then releases when clicked again.

FIGURE 9.17

4 Under **ActiveX Controls**, click **Check Box** ☑ and notice that the mouse pointer changes to the ⊞ shape.

5 Point to the upper left corner of cell **B20** and drag to insert a check box object that is approximately the height of the cell and the width of columns **B:C.** Compare your screen with Figure 9.18. The size and placement need not be exact—you will adjust the size and placement later. If you are not satisfied with your result, click **Undo** and begin again, or use the sizing handles to adjust the size.

The object name—*CheckBox1*—displays in the check box and also displays in the Name Box. An EMBED formula displays on the Formula Bar.

The formula defines the object as an embedded object and includes the name of the object source. Recall that to *embed* means to insert something created in one program into another program. ActiveX controls are not part of Excel but may be added to it. This provides other software vendors and individuals the opportunity to write ActiveX controls to handle a wide variety of desired actions. The More Controls button at the end of the ActiveX Controls gallery lists many additional ActiveX controls, and there are more available for download from the Internet.

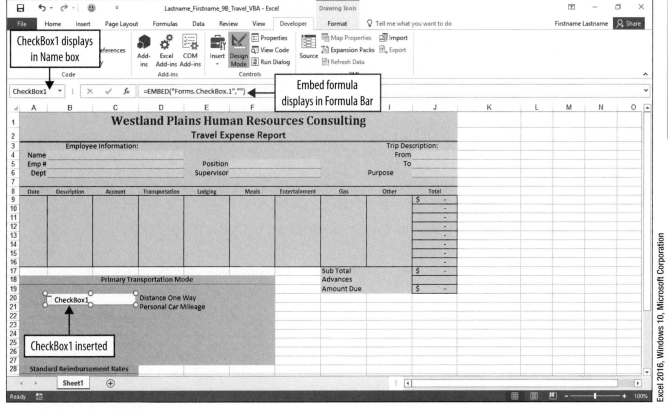

FIGURE 9.18

6 Repeat this process to add two more check boxes of the same approximate size under **CheckBox1**. Verify that the boxes do not overlap—leave a slight space between each box. Use any technique for moving and sizing objects that you have practiced, and then compare your screen with Figure 9.19.

> ActiveX controls are not attached to cells—rather, they float on the worksheet like inserted Shapes or SmartArt.

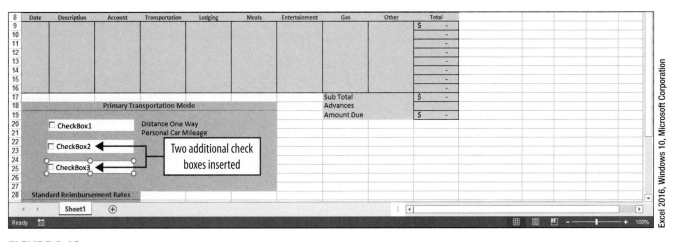

FIGURE 9.19

7 Click **CheckBox1**, and then on the **Developer tab**, in the **Controls group**, notice that *Design Mode*—a feature in which you can add and modify ActiveX controls—is active.

> When you are finished creating and editing the ActiveX controls in your worksheet, you can click Design Mode to toggle it off. When you add controls, Design Mode is activated. Use the Design Mode button to move in and out of Design Mode.

8 With **CheckBox1** selected, hold down Ctrl, and click each of the remaining check boxes so that all three check boxes are selected.

9 On the **Page Layout tab**, in the **Arrange group**, click **Align**, and then click **Align Left** to align the check boxes on the left. **Save** 🖫 your workbook.

Activity 9.09 | Changing the Properties of an ActiveX Control

Each ActiveX control has a set of ***properties***—characteristics—that you can change. This is similar to formatting a shape by changing its color, font, or some other property. There are many properties associated with ActiveX controls, and the properties vary depending on the type of control. In this Activity, you will change the name of each of the check boxes, change the caption that displays in each check box, and change the height and width of each check box.

1 Click the **Developer tab**. In the **Controls group**, verify that **Design Mode** is active.

2 Click another area of the worksheet to deselect the group of check boxes, and then click **CheckBox1** to select the check box. In the **Controls group**, click **Properties** to display the Properties pane.

3 Drag the **Properties** pane near the upper right of your screen. Point to the lower left sizing handle to display the 🖾 pointer and then drag down and to the left as necessary so that you can see the entire list of properties, as shown in Figure 9.20.

> The properties are organized in alphabetical order on the *Alphabetic* tab. On the *Categorized* tab, the same properties are listed, but they are organized by logical groups. You can click the arrow at the top of the Properties pane to display a list from which you can select the object whose properties you want to modify.

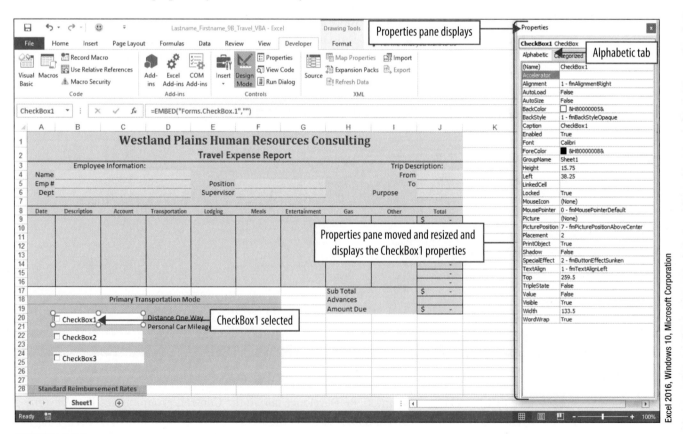

FIGURE 9.20

4 At the top of the **Alphabetic** list, in the first column, click **(Name)**, and then type **Air** Notice that your typing displays in the column to the right. Press [Enter], and notice that *Air* displays in the **Name Box**.

Use the (Name) field when you need to refer to an object in a program. The naming convention is the same for naming cells in Excel; that is, the name cannot include spaces or punctuation marks.

5 In the first column, click the **Caption** property, type **Air** and then press [Enter].

The text in the check box changes to *Air*.

6 Under **Alphabetic**, click **Height**. Type **15.75** and then click **Width**. Type **84.75** and then press [Enter]. Compare your screen with Figure 9.21.

The check box resizes to a height of 15.75 pixels and a width of 84.75 pixels.

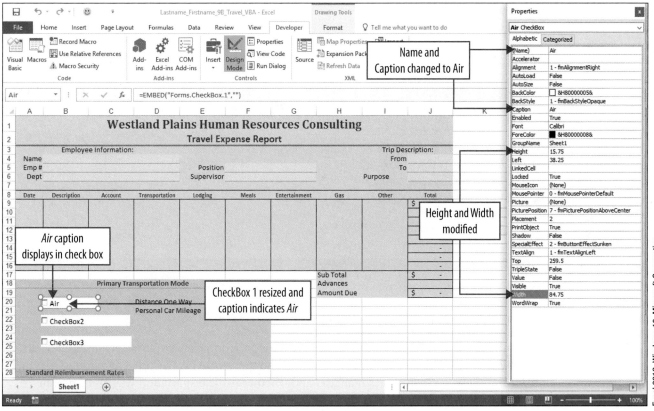

FIGURE 9.21

7 Click **CheckBox2** to select the check box, and notice that the **Properties** pane displays the properties for *CheckBox2*. In the **Properties** pane, click **(Name)**, type without any spaces **RentalCar** and then press [Enter]. Click the **Caption** property. Including the space, type **Rental Car** and then press [Enter].

8 Using the technique you just practiced, change the **(Name)** and **Caption** for the remaining check box to **Other**

9 Select the **Rental Car** check box, hold down Ctrl, and then select the **Other** check box so that both check boxes are selected.

If you want to change the same property for a group of objects, you can press Ctrl to select multiple objects and then change the property. You must change the Name and Caption of each check box individually.

10 With both check boxes selected, in the **Properties** pane, change the **Height** to **15.75** and the **Width** to **84.75**

The Rental Car and Other check boxes are resized and are the same height and width as the Air check box.

11 With both check boxes selected, hold down Ctrl, and then click the **Air** check box so that all three check boxes are selected. In the **Properties** pane, click **BackColor**, and notice that an arrow displays at the right edge of the BackColor box. Click the **BackColor arrow**, click the **System tab**, scroll down, and then click **Button Light Shadow**.

12 Close [x] the **Properties** pane. With the three check boxes selected, on the **Page Layout tab**, in the **Arrange group**, click **Align**, and then click **Distribute Vertically**. Click cell **A1** to deselect the group of check boxes. **Save** [💾] your workbook, and then compare your screen with Figure 9.22.

The space between each of the check boxes is equal.

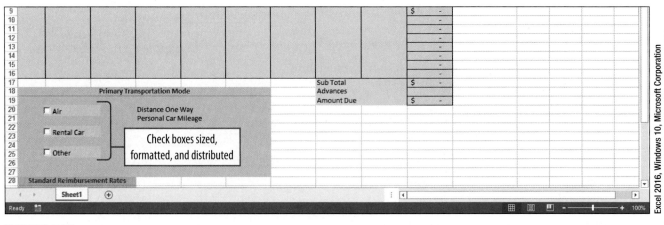

FIGURE 9.22

Excel 2016, Windows 10, Microsoft Corporation

Activity 9.10 │ Writing a VBA Procedure for a Command Button

Recall that a Command Button runs a macro that performs an action when a user clicks it. In this Activity, you will insert a Command Button and then write a VBA procedure to test whether the *Distance One Way* cell is less than 200 and whether *Air* transportation was used. If both conditions are true, a warning message will display indicating that a supervisor's signature is required in the Supervisor box.

1 Click cell **H22** to identify the location where you will place the Command Button. On the **Developer tab**, in the **Controls group**, click **Insert**, and then under **ActiveX Controls**, click **Command Button** [□]. Point to the upper left corner of cell **H22**, and then click one time to insert a Command Button. Compare your screen with Figure 9.23.

The Command Button is added and a portion of the text *CommandButton1* displays as the caption on the button. By selecting cell H22, you have a visual cue as to where to place the Command Button. Recall, however, that ActiveX objects are not actually attached to a cell—the cell address is only a guide to direct you to the location where the control will be placed.

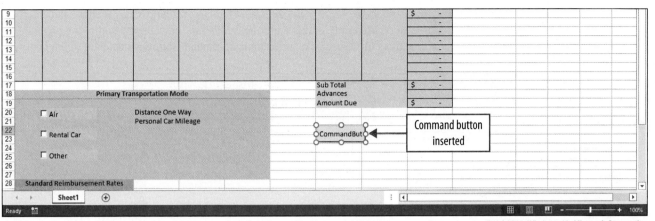

FIGURE 9.23

2 In the **Controls group**, click **Properties**. In the **Properties** pane, click **(Name)**. As one word, type **CheckTransportation** and then press Enter. Click the **Caption** property. Type **Check Transportation** and then press Enter. Click **AutoSize**, click the **AutoSize arrow**, and then click **True**.

When AutoSize is set to True, the button resizes to accommodate the new caption.

3 In the **Properties** pane, click **Font**, and then at the right of the second column click **Font build** ... to display the **Font** dialog box. Under **Font style**, click **Bold Italic**, and then click **OK**. Compare your screen with Figure 9.24.

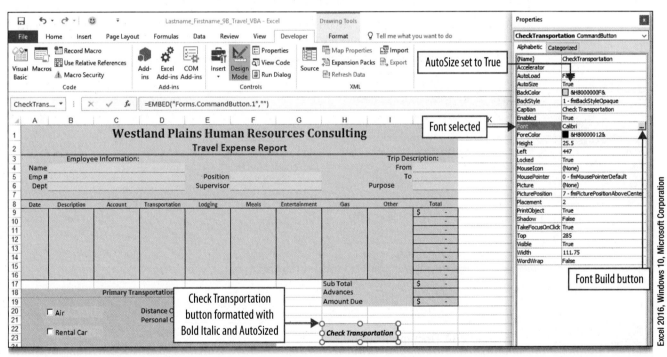

FIGURE 9.24

4 Close ☒ the **Properties** pane. Be sure that the **Check Transportation** control is selected. On the **Developer tab**, in the **Controls group**, click **View Code**. At the top of the **Code window**, click the **Object arrow**, and then on the list, click **CheckTransportation**. Compare your screen with Figure 9.25.

The Microsoft Visual Basic Code window displays and *CheckTransportation* displays in the Object box at the top of the window. This is the name of the selected ActiveX control. The beginning of this VBA procedure is indicated by *Private Sub CheckTransportation_Click( )*. *Private* indicates that this procedure can be used only in this workbook. *End Sub* indicates the end of the procedure. The event that will activate the Check Transportation Command Button is one click of the button.

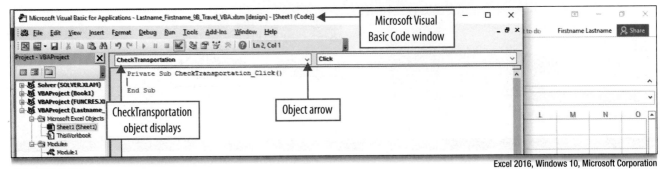

FIGURE 9.25

🔁 **ANOTHER WAY**   In Design Mode, right-click the command button, and then click View Code, or in Design Mode, double-click the command button. You can also open the VBA Editor by pressing [Alt] + [F11].

---

5 Click to the left of *Private Sub CheckTransportation_Click( )* to place the insertion point there, and then press [Enter] to insert a blank line. Press [↑] to move to the blank line. Including the apostrophe, type **'Check Transportation Button Procedure** and then press [Enter]. Be sure that you included the apostrophe at the beginning of the line. Type **'Determines if a supervisor signature is necessary** and then press [Enter]. Compare your screen with Figure 9.26.

Comments display in green and are preceded by an apostrophe ('). A line separates the comments from the VBA code. When writing a VBA procedure, it is recommended that you document the procedure with comments. Comments do not affect the running of the procedure.

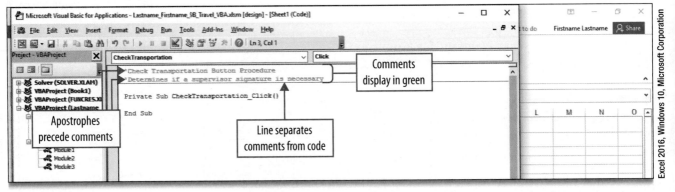

FIGURE 9.26

NOTE   Writing VBA Documentation

For purposes of this instruction, the documentation you entered is brief. When you create documentation in your own worksheets, you may want to include additional information about your VBA procedures.

---

6 Click to position the insertion point on the blank line under *Private Sub CheckTransportation_Click( )*. Press [Enter], and then press [Tab]. Type the lines of VBA code spaced as shown below. Use the [Tab] key to indent the middle three lines and [Shift] + [Tab] to reduce the indent by one tab for the last line. As you type, a prompt box may display to assist you with the VBA syntax. Ignore the prompts and type the code as shown. When you are finished, compare your screen with Figure 9.27.

If Air = True Then

    TitleBarText = "Air"

    MessageText = "To use air transportation, miles one way should equal 200 or more."

    MsgBox MessageText, , TitleBarText

End If

The VBA code tests to see if the Air check box is selected, indicating that it is true. If the check box is selected, a message box will display the Message Text.

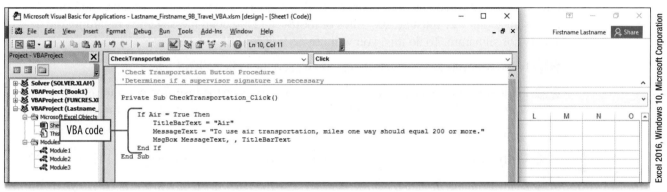

FIGURE 9.27

7 ▶ On the menu bar, click **File**, and then click **Close and Return to Microsoft Excel**.

8 ▶ In the **Controls group**, click **Design Mode** to exit Design Mode.

9 ▶ In the tan shaded section, select the **Air** check box, and then click the **Check Transportation** Command Button. If an error message displays, see the Alert box that follows for instructions on how to resolve the error. Compare your screen with Figure 9.28.

A check mark displays in the Air check box, and the Air message box displays.

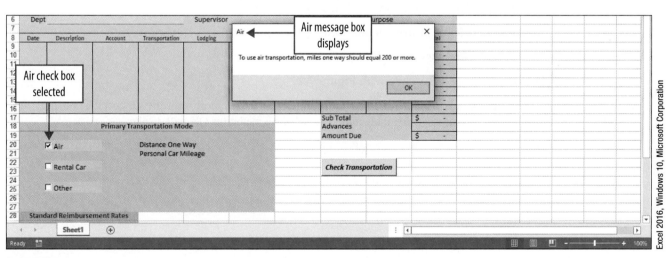

FIGURE 9.28

10 ▶ In the **Air** message box, click **OK**. Save 🖫 your workbook.

Activity 9.11 | Modifying a VBA Procedure

You can modify a VBA procedure in the same manner that you modified the VBA code that was created when you used a macro. In this Activity, you will add a second condition—the distance one way must be 200 miles or more—and a second message box regarding the supervisor signature. To do this, you will use an If, Then, Else statement.

1 In the **Controls group**, click **Design Mode**, and then click **View Code**.

2 In the line of code beginning with *If Air*, click to place the insertion point to the *left* of the word *Then*. Type the following line of code, pressing Spacebar one time at the end:

And Range("F20").Value < 200

3 Verify that the first line of code now reads: *If Air = True And Range("F20").Value < 200 Then*

4 In the *MessageText* line, click to the left of the closing quotation mark, press Spacebar, and then type a second sentence as follows: **Supervisor must sign submitted Expense Form.**

If the travel method is Air and the mileage is less than 200, the following message displays: *"To use air transportation, miles one way should equal 200 or more. Supervisor must sign submitted Expense Form."* The line of text extends across the Visual Basic Editor window, and the screen scrolls to the right.

5 Scroll to the left. At the end of the *MsgBox* line, place the insertion point after *TitleBarText*. Press Enter, and then press Shift + Tab. Type the following code spaced as shown below:

Else

    TitleBarText = "Travel Method Checked"

    MessageText = "Travel method OK."

    MsgBox MessageText, , TitleBarText

6 Compare your VBA code with Figure 9.29.

If the Air check box is selected and the mileage is 200 or more, or if the Air check box is not selected, a message box indicating that the travel method is OK will display.

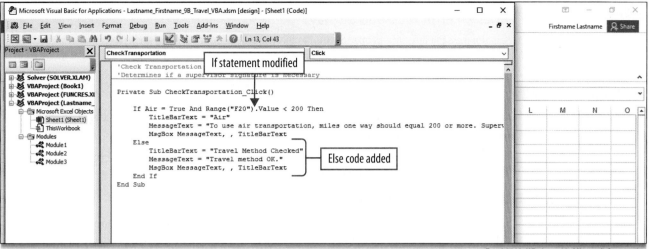

FIGURE 9.29

Excel 2016, Windows 10, Microsoft Corporation

7 Click **File**, and then click **Close and Return to Microsoft Excel**. On the **Developer tab**, in the **Controls group**, click **Design Mode** to exit Design Mode. **Save** 🖫 your workbook.

Activity 9.12 | Testing the VBA Procedure and the ActiveX Control

After you create a VBA procedure, you should test it to verify that it works as you intended.

1 Be sure the **Air** check box is still selected—it displays a check mark. Be sure **Design Mode** is not selected. In cell **F20**, type **150** and then press Enter. Click the **Check Transportation** button. Compare your screen with Figure 9.30.

The first message box displays and informs you that a supervisor's signature is required.

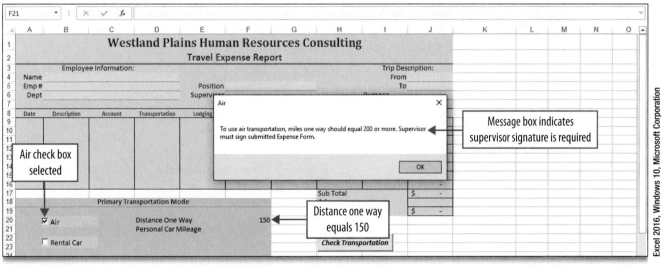

FIGURE 9.30

Excel 2016, Windows 10, Microsoft Corporation

2 In the **Air** message box, click **OK**. Click cell **F20**, type **200** and then press Enter. Click the **Check Transportation** button.

> The second message box displays indicating *Travel method OK*. If you get the first message box, return to the code and correct the cell reference to F20.

3 In the **Travel Method Checked** message box, click **OK**.

> You have tested both conditions for using air transportation—when the miles are 200 or more, and when the miles are less than 200. You also need to test the Command Button when other modes of transportation are used.

4 Clear the check mark from the **Air** check box. Select the **Rental Car** check box, and then click the **Check Transportation** button.

> The second message box displays indicating *Travel method OK*.

5 Click **OK** to acknowledge the message, and then press Ctrl + Home to move to cell A1. On the **Page Layout tab**, in the **Scale to Fit group**, change the **Width** to 1 **page**.

6 Insert a footer in the **left section** that includes the file name. Return to **Normal** view, and then press Ctrl + Home to move to the top of the worksheet. Click the **File tab**, and then in the lower right portion of the screen, click **Show all properties**. In the **Tags** box, type **expense report** and in the **Subject** box type your course name and section number. In the **Author** box, replace the existing text with your first and last name. Display the worksheet in **Print Preview**, return to the workbook and make any necessary corrections or adjustments.

7 Click the **Review tab**. In the **Changes group**, click **Protect Workbook**. In the **Protect Structure and Windows** dialog box, verify that **Structure** is selected and then type **goseries** in the **Password** box. Compare your screen with Figure 9.31.

> It is good practice to protect a workbook that contains a form so that users do not modify the ActiveX controls.

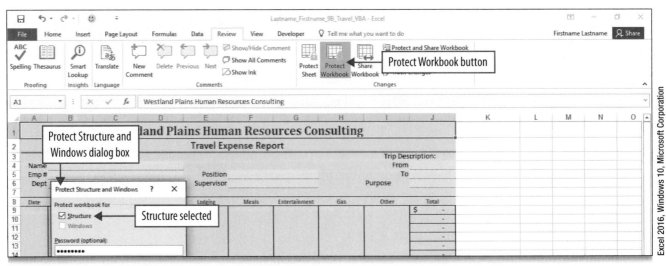

FIGURE 9.31

8 Click **OK**. In the Confirm Password dialog box, type **goseries** and click **OK**.

9 Save your workbook. If directed by your instructor to do so, submit your paper printout, your electronic image of your document that looks like a printed document, or your original Excel file. If required by your instructor, print or create an electronic version of your worksheet with formulas displayed. In the upper right corner of the Excel window, click **Close** ☒.

ALERT! **If you are submitting your file for grading in MyITLab, complete steps 10 through 15.**

---

10 To submit your file in MyITLab, you will copy the VBA code to a new worksheet so that it can be verified. **Open** your **Lastname_Firstname_9B_Travel_VBA** file. If necessary, Enable Content. On the **Review tab**, in the **Changes group**, click **Protect Workbook**. In the **Password** box, type **goseries** and then click **OK**.

11 On the **Developer tab**, in the **Controls group**, click **View Code**. In the Microsoft Visual Basic Editor window, press Ctrl + A to select all of the code. Press Ctrl + C to copy the code to the clipboard. On the menu bar, click **File**, and then click **Close and Return to Microsoft Excel**.

12 In the sheet tab area, click **New sheet** ⊕ to insert a new worksheet. **Rename** the inserted sheet **VBA Code**

13 In the **VBA Code** sheet, with cell **A1** active, on the **Home tab**, in the **Clipboard group**, click **Paste** to paste the VBA code to the new worksheet. On the **Review tab**, in the **Changes group**, click **Protect Workbook**. In the **Password** box, type **goseries** and then click **OK**. In the **Confirm Password** dialog box, type **goseries** and then click **OK**.

14 Click the **File tab**, and then click **Save As**. Navigate to your **Excel Chapter 9 folder**, and then click the **Save as type arrow**. Click **Excel workbook**. In the **File name** box, type **Lastname_Firstname_9B_Travel_VBA_MyITLab** and then click **Save**. If a message box displays, click Yes.

15 **Close** ☒ your file but leave Excel open. Submit your **Lastname_Firstname_9B_Travel_VBA_MyITLab** file in MyITLab.

Objective 5 | Restore Initial Settings

GO! Learn How
Video E9-5

When you use a computer in a public location such as a college computer lab, or when you use someone else's computer, it is proper computer etiquette to return it to the condition in which you found it. In this chapter, you created a macro and then placed a button on the Quick Access Toolbar.

Activity 9.13 | Removing the Quick Access Toolbar Button, Macro, and the Developer Tab

1 If necessary, start Excel. Right-click the **Smiley Face** icon on the **Quick Access Toolbar**, and then click **Remove from Quick Access Toolbar**.

The Employee_Info button is removed from the Quick Access Toolbar.

2 On the **Developer tab**, in the **Code group**, click **Macros**.

3 Verify that the Macro dialog box is empty. If the Employee_Info macro you created is displayed, select the macro name, and then click **Delete**.

The Employee_Info macro is part of the workbooks Lastname_Firstname_9A_Travel_Macro and Lastname_Firstname_9B_Travel_VBA and will not be deleted from those files. Because the workbooks are closed, the macro name should not display in this list of macros. If you accidentally saved the macro in another place and it displays in this list, it should now be deleted.

4 Click **Cancel**.

5 Right-click the **Developer tab**, and then click **Customize the Ribbon**. In the right pane, click **Developer** to deselect it, and then click **OK** to remove the **Developer tab**. **Close** Excel.

> **END | You have completed Project 9B**

GO! To Work

Andres Rodriguez/Fotolia; FotolEdhar/Fotolia; Andrey Popov/Fotolia; Shutterstock

MICROSOFT OFFICE SPECIALIST (MOS) SKILLS IN THIS CHAPTER

PROJECT 9A	PROJECT 9B
1.4.3 Customize the Quick Access toolbar **Expert 1.1.5** Enable macros in a workbook **Expert 1.1.6** Display hidden ribbon tabs **Expert 2.3.4** Create and modify simple macros	**Expert 1.2.2** Protect a worksheet **Expert 1.2.6** Encrypt a workbook with a password **Expert 2.3.5** Insert and configure form controls

BUILD YOUR E-PORTFOLIO

An E-Portfolio is a collection of evidence, stored electronically, that showcases what you have accomplished while completing your education. Collecting and then sharing your work products with potential employers reflects your academic and career goals. Your completed documents from the following projects are good examples to show what you have learned: 9G, 9K, and 9L.

GO! FOR JOB SUCCESS

Discussion: Cyber Security

Your instructor may assign these questions to your class, and then ask you to think about them or discuss them with your classmates:

The U.S. Homeland Security Department describes cyber incidents (hacking) as actions where there is an attempt to gain unauthorized access to a system or its data, unwanted disruption to service, unauthorized use of a system, or change to a system without the owner's permission. As companies store and process more and more data at centralized, offsite "cloud" data centers, the opportunities for criminals to hack data are growing. Cyber security is an important part of every organization's information systems protocols, and many companies now employ a senior executive with the title Chief Information Security Officer.

FotolEdhar/Fotolia

What cyber incidents have you heard of in the news over the last year?

What precautions have you taken with your personal data to prevent a hack?

What would you do if you learned that a company you do business with, such as your bank or college, had been the subject of a cyber incident?

END OF CHAPTER

SUMMARY

You can automate an Excel worksheet to perform complex tasks faster and to perform repetitive actions using macros and the programming language called Visual Basic for Applications (VBA).

In the Visual Basic Editor window, comments that describe the macro are displayed in green and in lines preceded by an apostrophe ('). The VBA code that follows displays in black type.

A set of instructions that accomplishes a specific task is called a sub procedure, or simply sub. In the VBA code, Sub indicates the beginning of the sub procedure and End Sub indicates the end.

An ActiveX control is a graphic object, such as a check box or button, that can be placed on a worksheet or form. When the ActiveX control is clicked, a macro or code runs that automates a task or offers options.

GO! LEARN IT ONLINE

Review the concepts, key terms, and MOS skills in this chapter by completing these online challenges, which you can find at **MyITLab**.

Matching and Multiple Choice: Answer matching and multiple-choice questions to test what you learned in this chapter.

Lessons on the GO!: Learn how to use all the new apps and features as they are introduced by Microsoft.

MOS Prep Quiz: Answer questions to review the MOS skills that you practiced in this chapter.

Your instructor will assign Projects from this list to ensure your learning and assess your knowledge.

Project Guide for EXCEL Chapter 9

Project	Apply Skills from These Chapter Objectives	Project Type	Project Location
9A MyITLab	Objectives 1–3 from Project 9A	**9A Instructional Project (Grader Project)** Guided instruction to learn the skills in Project 9A.	In MyITLab and in text
9B MyITLab	Objectives 4–5 from Project 9B	**9B Instructional Project (Grader Project)** Guided instruction to learn the skills in Project 9B.	In MyITLab and in text
9C	Objectives 1–3 from Project 9A	**9C Skills Review (Scorecard Grading)** A guided review of the skills from Project 9A.	In text
9D	Objectives 4–5 from Project 9B	**9D Skills Review (Scorecard Grading)** A guided review of the skills from Project 9B.	In text
9E MyITLab	Objectives 1–3 from Project 9A	**9E Mastery (Grader Project)** **Mastery and Transfer of Learning** A demonstration of your mastery of the skills in Project 9A with extensive decision making.	In MyITLab and in text
9F MyITLab	Objectives 4–5 from Project 9B	**9F Mastery (Grader Project)** **Mastery and Transfer of Learning** A demonstration of your mastery of the skills in Project 9B with extensive decision making.	In MyITLab and in text
9G MyITLab	Objectives 1–5 from Project 9A and 9B	**9G Mastery (Grader Project)** **Mastery and Transfer of Learning** A demonstration of your mastery of the skills in Projects 9A and 9B with extensive decision making.	In MyITLab and in text
9H	Combination of Objectives from Projects 9A and 9B	**9H GO! Fix It (Scorecard Grading)** **Critical Thinking** A demonstration of your mastery of the skills in Projects 9A and 9B by creating a correct result from a document that contains errors you must find.	Instructor Resource Center (IRC) and MyITLab
9I	Combination of Objectives from Projects 9A and 9B	**9I GO! Make It (Scorecard Grading)** **Critical Thinking** A demonstration of your mastery of the skills in Projects 9A and 9B by creating a result from a supplied picture.	IRC and MyITLab
9J	Combination of Objectives from Projects 9A and 9B	**9J GO! Solve It (Rubric Grading)** **Critical Thinking** A demonstration of your mastery of the skills in Projects 9A and 9B, your decision-making skills, and your critical thinking skills. A task-specific rubric helps you self-assess your result.	IRC and MyITLab
9K	Combination of Objectives from Projects 9A and 9B	**9K GO! Solve It (Rubric Grading)** **Critical Thinking** A demonstration of your mastery of the skills in Projects 9A and 9B, your decision-making skills, and your critical thinking skills. A task-specific rubric helps you self-assess your result.	In text
9L	Combination of Objectives from Projects 9A and 9B	**9L GO! Think (Rubric Grading)** **Critical Thinking** A demonstration of your understanding of the chapter concepts applied in a manner that you would outside of college. An analytic rubric helps you and your instructor grade the quality of your work by comparing it to the work an expert in the discipline would create.	In text
9M	Combination of Objectives from Projects 9A and 9B	**9M GO! Think (Rubric Grading)** **Critical Thinking** A demonstration of your understanding of the chapter concepts applied in a manner that you would outside of college. An analytic rubric helps you and your instructor grade the quality of your work by comparing it to the work an expert in the discipline would create.	IRC and MyITLab
9N	Combination of Objectives from Projects 9A and 9B	**9N You and GO! (Rubric Grading)** **Critical Thinking** A demonstration of your understanding of the chapter concepts applied in a manner that you would in a personal situation. An analytic rubric helps you and your instructor grade the quality of your work.	IRC and MyITLab

GLOSSARY

GLOSSARY OF CHAPTER KEY TERMS

ActiveX control A graphic object, such as a check box or button that you place on a form to display or enter data, perform an action, or make the form easier to read. When the person filling in the form clicks the ActiveX control, VBA code runs that automates a task or offers options.

Check box A type of ActiveX control that the person filling in the form can select to indicate a choice.

Design Mode An Excel feature in which you can add and modify ActiveX controls.

Digital signature An electronic, encryption-based, secure stamp of authentication on a macro or document.

Embed The action of inserting something created in one program into another program.

Event The action that causes a program or macro to run, such as clicking a button or a command or pressing a combination of keys.

Form An Excel worksheet or object containing fields and controls that enable a user to easily enter or edit data.

Form control A graphic object that does not require VBA code. A Form control is compatible with versions of Excel that do not support ActiveX.

Macro An action or a set of actions with which you can automate tasks by grouping a series of commands into a single command.

Macro virus Unauthorized programming code in a macro that erases or damages files.

Module The place where the Visual Basic for Applications (VBA) programming code is stored.

Procedure A unit of computer code that performs an action.

Property A characteristic of an object that can be changed.

Record Macro A command that records your actions in Visual Basic for Applications (VBA).

Sub Short for a sub procedure.

Sub procedure A unit of computer code that performs an action.

VBA The abbreviation for the Visual Basic for Applications programming language.

VBA construct An instruction that enables a macro to perform multiple operations on a single object.

Visual Basic Editor The window in which you can view and edit Visual Basic code.

Visual Basic for Applications The programming language used to write computer programs in the Microsoft Windows environment.

Apply **9A** skills from these Objectives:

1 Record a Macro
2 Assign a Macro to a Button on the Quick Access Toolbar
3 Modify a Macro

Skills Review Project 9C Training

In the following Skills Review, you will assist Matt Gallagher, Training Director, in creating a macro that will make it easier for staff members to include the required information in their training department expense reports. You will assign the macro to a button on the Quick Access Toolbar, and then modify the macro by changing the Visual Basic Code. Your completed worksheet will look similar to Figure 9.32.

PROJECT FILES

For Project 9C, you will need the following file:

e09C_Training

You will save your workbook as:

Lastname_Firstname_9C_Training

PROJECT RESULTS

Excel 2016, Windows 10, Microsoft Corporation

FIGURE 9.32

(Project 9C Training continues on the next page)

1 Start Excel. From your student files, open the file **e09C_Training**. Display the **Save As** dialog box, navigate to your **Excel Chapter 9** folder, click the **Save as type arrow**, and then click **Excel Macro-Enabled Workbook**. In the **File name** box, type **Lastname_Firstname_9C_Training** and then click **Save**.

a. If the Developer tab is not visible, click File to display Backstage view. Click Options. In the Excel Options dialog box, on the left, click Customize Ribbon. Under Customize the Ribbon, verify that Main Tabs is selected, select the Developer check box, and then click OK.

b. On the **Developer tab**, in the **Code group**, click **Macro Security**. Under **Macro Settings**, verify that **Disable all macros with notification** is selected, and then click **OK**.

c. On the **Review tab**, in the **Changes group**, click **Protect Workbook**. In the **Unprotect Workbook** dialog box, type **goseries** which is the password applied to this form, and then click **OK**.

d. Be sure cell **B6** is the active cell. On the **Developer tab**, in the **Code group**, click **Record Macro**. In the **Macro name** box, delete the existing text, and then type **Employee_Section** In the **Shortcut key** box, type **t** Click the **Store macro in arrow**, then click **This Workbook**. Click in the **Description** box. Type **Fills in the Employee Section** Click **OK**.

e. In cell **B6**, type **Elaine Richards** and then press Enter. With cell **B7** active, hold down Ctrl and press ; (semicolon), which will insert the current date. Press Enter. With cell **B8** active, type **Training** Click in cell **F7** and type **Training Specialist** and then press Enter. In cell **F8**, type **Westland Drugs** and then click cell **A11**, so that when the macro completes, the first cell in the data area is active to begin filling in the travel information. On the **Developer tab**, in the **Code group**, click **Stop Recording**.

f. Delete the text you just typed in the five cells—**B6**, **B7**, **B8**, **F7**, **F8**—and then click cell **B6**. Then, to test that your macro will fill in the employee information and the date, run the macro by pressing the shortcut key Ctrl + T. **Save** your workbook.

2 From **Backstage** view, click **Options** to display the **Excel Options** dialog box, and then on the left, click **Quick Access Toolbar**.

a. Click the **Choose commands from arrow**, and then click **Macros**. Click your **Employee_Section** macro, and then, in the center of the dialog box, click **Add**.

b. With your **Employee_Section** command selected on the right, click **Modify**. Under **Symbol**, in the seventh row, click the seventh icon—**Checkered Square**—and then click **OK** two times. **Save** your workbook.

c. Select the nonadjacent ranges **B6:B8** and **F7:F8** and press Del so that these cells are empty again. Click cell **B6**, and then on the **Quick Access Toolbar**, click your new **Employee_Section** button—the Checkered Square.

3 On the **Developer tab,** in the **Code group**, click **Macros**. Be sure the **Employee_Section** macro is selected, and then click **Edit**. In the **Code window**, at the end of the last line of code—*Range("A11") .Select*—click to place the insertion point after *Select*, and then press Enter.

a. On the new, empty line, type the following code to center the worksheet horizontally and vertically on the page: **With ActiveSheet.PageSetup** and then press Enter. Press Tab to indent and type **.CenterHorizontally = True** Press Enter and type **.CenterVertically = True** and then press Enter. Press Shift + Tab, and then type **End With**

b. On the **menu bar**, click **File**, and then click **Close and Return to Microsoft Excel**. Delete the text in **B6:B8, F7:F8**, click cell **B6**, and then on the **Quick Access Toolbar**, click the **Employee_Section** button that you created, so that the macro runs and includes the centering you added to the macro. Display the **Print Preview** to verify that the worksheet is centered. Return to the worksheet.

c. Right-click the **Checkered Square** icon on the **Quick Access Toolbar,** and then click **Remove from Quick Access Toolbar**. If you are directed to remove the Developer tab, follow the directions in Activity 9.13.

(Project 9C Training continues on the next page)

d. Insert a footer in the **left section** that includes the file name. Display the file properties. As the **Tags**, type **training expense** and as the **Subject**, type your course name and section number. Under **Related People**, be sure that your name displays as **Author**. **Save** your workbook.

e. If directed by your instructor to do so, submit your paper printout, your electronic image of your document that looks like a printed document, or your original Excel file. If required by your instructor, print or create an electronic version of your worksheet with formulas displayed. In the upper right corner of the Excel window, click **Close**.

> END | You have completed Project 9C

Apply 9B skills from these Objectives:

4 Write a VBA Procedure to Use an ActiveX Control

5 Restore Initial Settings

Skills Review Project 9D Recruitment

In the following Skills Review, you will assist Matt Gallagher, Training Director at Westland Plains Human Resources Consulting, by writing a set of commands in the VBA programming language, using ActiveX Control buttons to automate the Recruitment Department policy guidelines for expense reports. Your completed workbook will look similar to Figure 9.33.

PROJECT FILES

For Project 9D, you will need the following file:

e09D_Recruitment

You will save your workbook as:

Lastname_Firstname_9D_Recruitment

PROJECT RESULTS

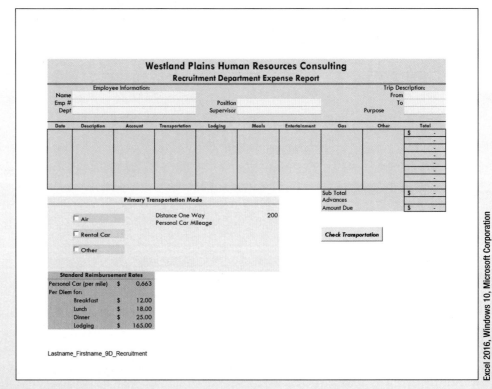

FIGURE 9.33

(Project 9D Recruitment continues on the next page)

1 Start Excel. From your student files, locate and open the file **e09D_Recruitment**. If necessary, on the Security Warning bar, click Enable Content. **Save** the file in your **Excel Chapter 9** folder as an **Excel Macro-Enabled Workbook** with the file name Lastname_Firstname_9D_Recruitment

a. On the **Developer tab**, in the **Controls group**, click **Insert**. Under **ActiveX Controls**, click **Check Box**. Point to the upper left corner of cell **B20** and drag to insert a check box object that is approximately the height of the cell and the width of columns **B:C**. Repeat this process to add two more check boxes of the same approximate size under **CheckBox1**.

b. Click **CheckBox1**, hold down Ctrl and then click each of the remaining check boxes so that all three check boxes are selected. On the **Page Layout tab**, in the **Arrange group**, click **Align**, and then click **Align Left** to align the check boxes on the left.

2 Click the **Developer tab**. In the **Controls group**, verify that **Design Mode** is active. Click another area of the worksheet to deselect the group of check boxes, and then click **CheckBox1** to select the check box. In the **Controls group**, click **Properties**. Drag the **Properties** pane near the upper right of your screen, and then expand its lower edge so that you can see the entire list of properties.

a. At the top of the **Alphabetic** list, in the first column, click **(Name)**. Type **Air** and then press Enter to display *Air* in the **Name Box**. In the first column, click the **Caption** property, type **Air** and then press Enter. Click **Height**. Type **15.75** and then click **Width**. Type **84.75** and then press Enter.

b. Using the technique you just practiced, change the properties for the remaining two check boxes as shown in the table at the bottom of the page.

c. In the yellow shaded area of the worksheet, select the **Air** check box control, hold down Ctrl, and then

click each of the other check boxes to select all three check box controls. In the **Properties** pane, click **BackColor**, click the **BackColor arrow**, click the **System tab**, scroll down and click **Button Light Shadow**. **Close** the **Properties** pane.

d. On the **Page Layout tab**, in the **Arrange group**, click **Align**, and then click **Distribute Vertically**. Click cell **A1** to deselect the group of check boxes, and then click **Save**.

3 Click cell **H22** to identify the location where you will place a Command Button. On the **Developer tab**, in the **Controls group**, click **Insert**, and then under **ActiveX Controls**, click **Command Button**. Point to the upper left corner of cell **H22**, and then click one time to insert the button.

a. In the **Controls group**, click **Properties**, and then in the **Properties** pane, click **(Name)**. Type **CheckTransportation** and then click the **Caption** property. Type **Check Transportation** and then click **AutoSize**. Click the **AutoSize arrow**, and then click **True**. In the **Properties** pane, click **Font**, and then click **Font build** to display the **Font** dialog box. Under **Font style**, click **Bold Italic**, and then click **OK**. **Close** the **Properties** pane.

b. Be sure the **Check Transportation** command button is selected. On the **Developer tab**, in the **Controls group**, click **View Code**. Click the **Object arrow**, and then on the list, click **CheckTransportation**.

c. Click to the left of *Private Sub* to place the insertion point there, and then press Enter to insert a blank line. Press ↑ to move to the blank line, and then type the following comments. Be sure to type the apostrophe at the beginning of each line, and at the end of both lines, press Enter.

'Check Transportation Button Procedure
'Function: Validates transportation mode.

	NAME	CAPTION	HEIGHT	WIDTH
CheckBox2	**RentalCar**	**Rental Car**	**15.75**	**84.75**
CheckBox3	**Other**	**Other**	**15.75**	**84.75**

(Return to Step 2C)

(Project 9D Recruitment continues on the next page)

d. Click to position the insertion point on the blank line under *Private Sub*. Press [Enter], and then press [Tab]. Type the following lines of VBA code, spaced as shown, to test the mileage. Use the [Tab] key to indent the middle lines and [Shift] + [Tab] to reduce the indent by one tab for the last line. As you type, a prompt box may display to assist you with the VBA syntax. Ignore the prompts and type the code as shown:

```
If Air = True Then
    TitleBarText = "Air"
    MessageText = "To use air transportation, miles
    one way should equal 200 or more."
        MsgBox MessageText, , TitleBarText
End If
```

e. On the menu bar, click **File**, and then click **Close and Return to Microsoft Excel**. In the **Controls group**, click **Design Mode** to exit Design Mode. In the yellow shaded section, select the **Air** check box, and then click the **Check Transportation** button. Click **OK** to acknowledge the message.

4 In the **Controls group**, click **Design Mode**, and then click **View Code**. At the end of the first line of the If statement, click to place the insertion point to the left of the word *Then*. Type the following line of code, pressing [Spacebar] at the end:

```
And Range("F20").Value < 200
```

a. Verify that the first line of code now reads: *If Air = True And Range("F20").Value < 200 Then* In the *MessageText* line, click to the left of the closing quotation mark and after the period. Press [Spacebar], and then type **Supervisor must sign this expense form.**

b. Scroll to the left. At the end of the *MsgBox* line of code, click after **TitleBarText** and press [Enter]. Then press [Shift] + [Tab]. Type the following code spaced as shown:

```
Else
    TitleBarText = "Travel Method Checked"
    MessageText = "Travel method OK."
    MsgBox MessageText, , TitleBarText
```

c. On the menu bar, click **File**, and then click **Close and Return to Microsoft Excel**. In the **Controls group**, click **Design Mode** to exit Design mode.

d. Be sure the **Air** check box is still selected—it displays a check mark. In cell **F20**, type **150** and then press [Enter]. Click the **Check Transportation** button. In the **Air** message box, click **OK**. Click cell **F20**, type **200** and then press [Enter]. Click the **Check Transportation** button.

e. In the **Travel Method Checked** message box, click **OK**. Clear the check mark from the **Air** check box. Select the **Rental Car** check box, and then click the **Check Transportation** button. Click **OK** to acknowledge the message. Click the **Rental Car** check box again to clear the check box so that none of the check boxes are selected.

5 Insert the file name in the left section of the footer and then display the file properties. As the **Tags**, type **recruitment department expense report** and as the **Subject**, type your course name and section number. Under **Related People**, be sure that your name displays as **Author**. **Save** your workbook.

a. Click the **Review tab**. In the **Changes group**, click **Protect Workbook**. In the **Protect Structure and Windows** dialog box, verify **Structure** is selected and then type **goseries** in the **Password** box. Confirm the password, and then **Save** your workbook. If you are directed to remove the **Developer tab**, follow the directions in Activity 9.13.

b. If directed by your instructor to do so, submit your paper printout, your electronic image of your document that looks like a printed document, or your original Excel file. If required by your instructor, print or create an electronic version of your worksheet with formulas displayed. In the upper right corner of the Excel window, click **Close**.

END | You have completed Project 9D

Mastering Excel | Project 9E Operations

In the following Mastering Excel project, you will assist Bill Roman, Project Director, in creating a macro that will assign an operations department heading required on all reports. You will modify the macro by changing the Visual Basic Code. Your completed worksheet will look similar to Figure 9.34.

Apply 9A skills from these Objectives:

1 Record a Macro

2 Assign a Macro to a Button on the Quick Access Toolbar

3 Modify a Macro

PROJECT FILES

For Project 9E, you will need the following file:

e09E_Operations

You will save your workbook as:

Lastname_Firstname_9E_Operations

PROJECT RESULTS

WPHRC Operations Department
Quarterly Operations Report

	January	February	March	Totals
Supplies	$ 3,210	$ 2,056	$ 3,773	$ 9,039
Salaries	15,823	14,335	16,300	46,458
Overhead	6,250	6,250	6,250	18,750
Equipment	-	-	1,875	1,875
Meals	331	230	200	761
Other	335	630	275	1,240
Totals	$ 25,949	$ 23,501	$ 28,673	$ 78,123

Lastname_Firstname_9E_Operations

Excel 2016, Windows 10, Microsoft Corporation

FIGURE 9.34

(Project 9E Operations continues on the next page)

Mastering Excel | **Project 9E Operations** (continued)

1 Start Excel. Verify that the **Developer tab** is enabled and the **Macro Settings** are set to **Disable all macros with notification**. From your student files, open the file **e09E_Operations**. Display the **Save As** dialog box, navigate to your **Excel Chapter 9** folder, set the **Save as type** to **Excel Macro-Enabled Workbook**, and as the file name, type **Lastname_Firstname_9E_Operations**

2 With cell **A1** active, record a macro with the name **Operations_Header** and the shortcut key [Ctrl] + [O]. Store the macro in this workbook. As the description, type **Fills in Operations report heading** and then click **OK** to begin recording the macro.

3 **Insert** two blank rows at the top of the worksheet, and then click cell **A1**. Type **WPHRC Operations Department** and then **Merge & Center** the text you typed across the range **A1:E1**. Apply the **Title** cell style. In cell **A2**, type **Quarterly Report** and then **Merge & Center** the text you typed across the range **A2:E2**. Apply the **Heading 1** cell style. Center the worksheet **Horizontally**, click cell **A1**, and then stop recording the macro.

4 Delete **rows 1:2**, click cell **A1**, and then test the macro.

5 On the **Developer tab,** in the **Code group**, click **Macros**. Verify that the **Operations_Header** macro is selected, and then click **Edit**. Scroll down and locate the first instance of *End With*, and then in the fourth line following End With, edit *"Quarterly Report"* to indicate **"Quarterly Operations Report"**

6 Click **File**, and then click **Close and Return to Microsoft Excel**. Delete **rows 1:2**, click cell **A1**, and then use the keyboard shortcut to run the macro to test that *Quarterly Operations Report* displays as the subtitle of the report.

7 Insert the file name in the left section of the footer. Display the worksheet in **Print Preview** and verify that

the worksheet is centered horizontally. Display the file properties. As the **Tags**, type **operations department report** and as the **Subject**, type your course name and section number. Under **Related People**, be sure that your name displays as **Author**.

8 **Save** your workbook. If directed by your instructor to do so, submit your paper printout, your electronic image of your document that looks like a printed document, or your original Excel file. If required by your instructor, print or create an electronic version of your worksheet with formulas displayed. Close **Excel**.

9 **If you are submitting this project in the MyITLab grader system, complete the following steps so that your VBA code can be verified.**

- **Open** your **Lastname_Firstname_9E_Operations** file. If necessary, Enable Content.

- On the **Developer tab**, in the **Code group**, click **Macros**. Select your **Operations_Header** macro, and then click **Edit**. Press [Ctrl] + [A] to select all of the code. Press [Ctrl] + [C] to copy the code to the clipboard. **Close and Return to Microsoft Excel**.

- In the sheet tab area, click **New sheet** to insert a new worksheet. Rename the inserted sheet **Macro Code**

- In the **Macro Code sheet**, with cell **A1** active, on the **Home tab**, in the **Clipboard group**, click **Paste** to paste the code to the new worksheet.

- Click the **File tab**, and then click **Save As**. Navigate to your **Excel Chapter 9 folder**, and then click the **Save as type arrow**. Click **Excel workbook**. In the **File name** box, type **Lastname_Firstname_9E_Operations_MyITLab** and then click **Save**. In the displayed message box, click **Yes**.

- **Close** your file and in MyITLab, submit your **Lastname_Firstname_9E_Operations_MyITLab** file.

END | You have completed Project 9E

MyITLab
grader

Mastering Excel | Project 9F Evaluation

Apply 9B skills from these Objectives:

4 Write a VBA Procedure to Use an ActiveX Control

5 Restore Initial Settings

In the following Mastering Excel project, you will assist Matt Gallagher, Training Director, by adding ActiveX controls to an evaluation form to gather feedback about training seminars. You will write VBA code to create input boxes that the respondent will use to enter information about the seminar. Your completed worksheet will look similar to Figure 9.35.

PROJECT FILES

For Project 9F, you will need the following file:

e09F_Evaluation

You will save your workbook as:

Lastname_Firstname_9F_Evaluation

PROJECT RESULTS

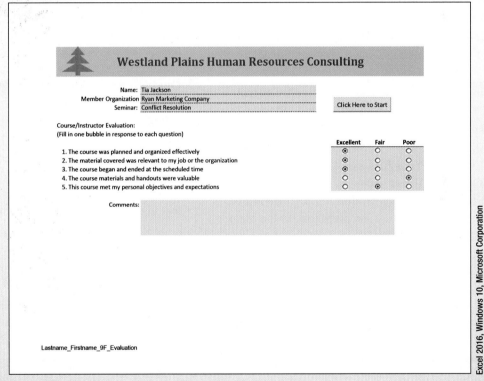

FIGURE 9.35

(Project 9F Evaluation continues on the next page)

Mastering Excel **Project 9F Evaluation** (continued)

1 Start Excel. From your student files, locate the file **e09F_Evaluation**. If necessary, on the Security Warning bar, click Enable Content. **Save** the file in your **Excel Chapter 9** folder as an **Excel Macro-Enabled Workbook** with the file name **Lastname_Firstname_9F_Evaluation**

2 Click cell **G17** and insert an **ActiveX Controls Option Button** in this location, and then display the **Properties** pane. Click (**Name**), type **Q5E** and then select the **Caption** property text—*OptionButton1*. Delete the caption text. Click **GroupName**, and then type **Question5**

3 Change the **Height** property to **9.75** Change the **Left** property to **465** Change **Top** to **234.75** and **Width** to **9.75** Change the SpecialEffect to the first effect **0 – fmButtonEffectFlat**.

4 Using the same technique, add two more option buttons in **row 17** and set the properties shown in the table at the bottom of this page, being sure to delete the **Caption** text.

5 Insert a **Command Button ActiveX Control** at cell **G7**. Change the property **Name** to **Start** and the **Caption** to **Click Here to Start** Set the **AutoSize** property to *True*.

6 **Close** the **Properties** pane, and then view the code. Click the **Object arrow**, scroll down, and then click **Start**. In the **Code window**, click to the left of *Private Sub Start_Click()* and press Enter. In the blank line that you inserted, type the following comments, pressing Enter after each line.

> ' Start Button Procedure
> ' Function: Complete seminar information

7 Click in the empty line following *Private Sub Start_Click()*, press Tab, and then type the following VBA code

to create a procedure instructing seminar attendees to fill in the requested information.

> Range("B6").Value = InputBox("Enter your name", "Name")
> Range("B7").Value = InputBox("Enter the name of your organization", "Organization")
> Range("B8").Value = InputBox("Enter the seminar title", "Seminar")

8 Return to Microsoft Excel, and then exit Design Mode.

9 Test your Command Button and type the following in each of the input boxes that display; click **OK** to close each box:

> Name: **Tia Jackson**
> Organization: **Ryan Marketing Company**
> Seminar: **Conflict Resolution**

10 Click the **Excellent** option button for each of the five questions. Now, test to see what happens when you change your mind. For **Question 4**, click **Poor** and for **Question 5** click **Fair**. The original option buttons are cleared for both questions, and only the new option buttons are selected.

11 Insert a footer in the **left section** that includes the file name. Display the file properties. As the **Tags**, type **evaluation report** and as the **Subject**, type your course name and section number. Under **Related People**, be sure that your name displays as **Author**.

12 **Save** your workbook. If directed by your instructor to do so, submit your paper printout, your electronic image of your document that looks like a printed document, or your original Excel file. If required by your instructor, print or create an electronic version of your worksheet with formulas displayed. Close **Excel**.

LOCATION/ PROPERTY	NAME	CAPTION	GROUP NAME	HEIGHT	LEFT	TOP	WIDTH	SPECIALEFFECT
Cell H17	Q5F	Delete	Question5	9.75	519	234.75	9.75	0 fmButtonEffectFlat
Cell I17	Q5P	Delete	Question5	9.75	570	234.75	9.75	0 fmButtonEffectFlat

(Return to Step 5)

(Project 9F Evaluation continues on the next page)

13 **If you are submitting this project in the MyITLab grader system, complete the following steps so that your VBA code can be verified.**

- **Open** your **Lastname_Firstname_9F_Evaluation** file. If necessary, Enable Content.

- On the **Developer tab**, in the **Controls group**, click **View Code**. In the Microsoft Visual Basic Editor window, press Ctrl + A to select all of the code. Press Ctrl + C to copy the code to the clipboard. **Close and Return to Microsoft Excel**.

- In the sheet tab area, click **New sheet** to insert a new worksheet. Rename the inserted sheet **Evaluation Code**

- In the **Evaluation Code sheet**, with cell **A1** active, on the **Home tab**, in the **Clipboard group**, click **Paste** to paste the code to the new worksheet.

- Click the **File tab**, and then click **Save As**. Navigate to your **Excel Chapter 9 folder**, and then click the **Save as type arrow**. Click **Excel workbook**. In the **File name** box, type **Lastname_Firstname_9F_Evaluation_MyITLab** and then click **Save**. In the displayed message box, click **Yes**.

- **Close** your file and in MyITLab, submit your **Lastname_Firstname_9F_Evaluation_MyITLab** file.

> **END | You have completed Project 9F**

Mastering Excel Project 9G Billing

Apply 9A and 9B skills from these Objectives:

1 Record a Macro

2 Assign a Macro to a Button on the Quick Access Toolbar

3 Modify a Macro

4 Write a VBA Procedure to Use an ActiveX Control

5 Restore Initial Settings

In this project you will assist Erica Ramirez, Sales Manager, to create a macro that enters footer information on chart sheets. You will also create several check boxes to indicate manager approval on sales bonuses. Your completed worksheets will look similar to Figure 9.36.

PROJECT FILES

For Project 9G, you will need the following file:

e09G_Billing

You will save your workbook as:

Lastname_Firstname_9G_Billing

PROJECT RESULTS

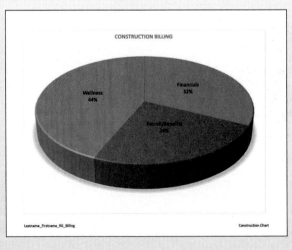

Excel 2016, Windows 10, Microsoft Corporation

FIGURE 9.36

(Project 9G Billing continues on the next page)

Mastering Excel Project 9G Billing (continued)

1 Start Excel. From your student files, open the file **e09G_Billing**. If necessary, enable the content, display the Developer tab, and set the Macro Settings to Disable all macros with notification. **Save** the file in your **Excel Chapter 9** folder as an **Excel Macro-Enabled Workbook** with the name **Lastname_Firstname_9G_Billing**

2 Display the **Mortgage Chart** sheet. Record a macro named **Chart_Setup** and assign the letter **o** as the **Shortcut key**. Store the macro in this workbook. As the description, type **Create footers in chart sheets** and then click **OK** to begin recording the macro.

3 Insert a **Custom Footer** on the **Mortgage Chart** sheet that includes the **File name** in the left section and the **Sheet name** in the right section, and then **Stop Recording** the macro.

4 Display the macro code. Click in the line below the second comment—*Create footers in chart sheets*—press Spacebar, and then type **Inserts file name and sheet name**

5 **Close and Return to Microsoft Excel.** Add the **Chart_Setup** macro to the **Quick Access Toolbar**. **Modify** the button by changing it to the **pie chart**—in the second row, the ninth button. If the pie chart button is not available, choose another button.

6 Display the **Construction Chart** sheet, and then use the button you assigned to the Quick Access Toolbar to insert the footer. View the **Print Preview** to verify that the footer was inserted.

7 Display the **Summary** sheet. Insert three **ActiveX Check Box** controls positioned at cell **B10**, **B12**, and **B14** and assign the following properties:

PROPERTY	NAME	CAPTION
CheckBox1	Billing	Billing Verified
CheckBox2	Contact	Contacts Verified
CheckBox3	Manager	Manager Assigned

8 Select all three check box controls so that you can modify the following properties at the same time.

Change the **Height** to **18** and the **Width** to **105** and then change the **Font** to **Bold Italic**. With all three check boxes still selected, **Distribute Vertically** and then **Align Left**. Turn off **Design Mode** and then select each check box.

9 Display the file properties. As the **Tags**, type **billing summary** and as the **Subject**, type your course name and section number. Under **Related People**, be sure that your name displays as **Author**. Remove the pie chart icon from the **Quick Access Toolbar**.

10 **Save** your workbook. If directed by your instructor to do so, submit your paper printout, your electronic image of your document that looks like a printed document, or your original Excel file. If required by your instructor, print or create an electronic version of your worksheet with formulas displayed. Close **Excel**.

11 **If you are submitting this project in the MyITLab grader system, complete the following steps so that your VBA code can be verified.**

- **Open** your **Lastname_Firstname_9G_Billing** file. If necessary, Enable Content. Save the file as an **Excel Workbook** with the File name **Lastname_Firstname_9G_Billing_MyITLab** and in the message box that displays, click **Yes**.

- On the **Developer tab**, in the **Code group**, click **Macros**, and then with the **Chart_Setup** macro selected, click **Edit**. Select and **Copy** the four green comment lines beginning with the *Chart_Setup Macro* line and ending with the *Keyboard Shortcut* line. Be sure to include the apostrophe at the beginning of the first selected line. **Close and Return to Microsoft Excel**.

- Insert a new worksheet. **Rename** the sheet **Macro Code** and then **Paste** the comment code to cell **A1**. Move the **Macro Code** sheet to the end of the workbook after the **Construction Chart** sheet. Make the Summary sheet the active sheet.

- **Save** and **Close** your file and in MyITLab, submit your **Lastname_Firstname_9G_Billing_MyITLab** file.

> **END | You have completed Project 9G**

Apply a combination of the **9A** and **9B** skills.

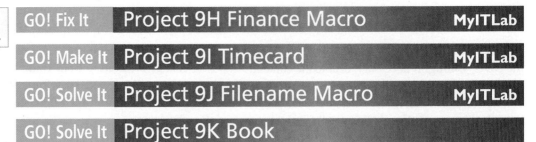

GO! Fix It	Project 9H Finance Macro	MyITLab
GO! Make It	Project 9I Timecard	MyITLab
GO! Solve It	Project 9J Filename Macro	MyITLab
GO! Solve It	Project 9K Book	

From Scratch icon

PROJECT FILES

For Project 9K, you will need the following file:

e09K_Book

You will save your workbook as:

Lastname_Firstname_9K_Book

Open the file e09K_Book and save it as an Excel Macro-Enabled Workbook **Lastname_Firstname_9K_Book** In the following Mastering Excel project, you will assist Matt Gallagher, Training Director, by adding an ActiveX Control Command Button to an evaluation form to gather feedback from the consultants about a new book that will be used at customer seminars. In cell H7, add an ActiveX Control Command Button to the worksheet. In the properties, change the name to **Start** and the caption to **Click Here to Start** and AutoSize to *True*. Add the following comments to the VBA code:

   ' Start Button Procedure
   ' Function: When clicked, the Start button will display four input boxes
Add the following VBA code:
   Range("B6").Value = InputBox("Enter your name", "Name")
   Range("B7").Value = InputBox("Enter the name of your position", "Position")
   Range("B8").Value = InputBox("Enter the name of your department", "Department")
   Range("B9").Value = InputBox("Enter your email", "Email")
Add appropriate name and course information to the document properties including the tags **book evaluation, VBA** and then submit as directed by your instructor.

Performance Level

Performance Criteria		Exemplary: You consistently applied the relevant skills	Proficient: You sometimes, but not always, applied the relevant skills	Developing: You rarely or never applied the relevant skills
	Insert an ActiveX Control Command Button and Change Properties	An ActiveX Control Command Button was inserted and name, caption, and AutoSize properties were assigned.	An ActiveX Control Command Button was inserted but one or more of the properties were missing.	An ActiveX Control Command Button was not inserted.
	Write a VBA Procedure for a Command Button	The VBA Procedure for a Start Command Button was correctly written.	The VBA Procedure for a Start Command Button was only partially written.	The VBA Procedure for a Start Command Button was not written.

END | You have completed Project 9K

OUTCOME-BASED ASSESSMENTS (CRITICAL THINKING)

RUBRIC

The following outcomes-based assessments are open-ended assessments. That is, there is no specific correct result; your result will depend on your approach to the information provided. Make Professional Quality your goal. Use the following scoring rubric to guide you in how to approach the problem and then to evaluate how well your approach solves the problem.

The *criteria*—Software Mastery, Content, Format and Layout, and Process—represent the knowledge and skills you have gained that you can apply to solving the problem. The *levels of performance*—Professional Quality, Approaching Professional Quality, or Needs Quality Improvements—help you and your instructor evaluate your result.

	Your completed project is of Professional Quality if you:	Your completed project is Approaching Professional Quality if you:	Your completed project Needs Quality Improvements if you:
1-Software Mastery	Choose and apply the most appropriate skills, tools, and features and identify efficient methods to solve the problem.	Choose and apply some appropriate skills, tools, and features, but not in the most efficient manner.	Choose inappropriate skills, tools, or features, or are inefficient in solving the problem.
2-Content	Construct a solution that is clear and well organized, contains content that is accurate, appropriate to the audience and purpose, and is complete. Provide a solution that contains no errors of spelling, grammar, or style.	Construct a solution in which some components are unclear, poorly organized, inconsistent, or incomplete. Misjudge the needs of the audience. Have some errors in spelling, grammar, or style, but the errors do not detract from comprehension.	Construct a solution that is unclear, incomplete, or poorly organized, contains some inaccurate or inappropriate content, and contains many errors of spelling, grammar, or style. Do not solve the problem.
3-Format and Layout	Format and arrange all elements to communicate information and ideas, clarify function, illustrate relationships, and indicate relative importance.	Apply appropriate format and layout features to some elements, but not others. Overuse features, causing minor distraction.	Apply format and layout that does not communicate information or ideas clearly. Do not use format and layout features to clarify function, illustrate relationships, or indicate relative importance. Use available features excessively, causing distraction.
4-Process	Use an organized approach that integrates planning, development, self-assessment, revision, and reflection.	Demonstrate an organized approach in some areas, but not others; or, use an insufficient process of organization throughout.	Do not use an organized approach to solve the problem.

GO! Think   Project 9L Accounting Department

PROJECT FILES

For Project 9L, you will need the following file:

e09L_Accounting_Macro

You will save your workbook as:

Lastname_Firstname_9L_Accounting_Macro

Open the file e09L_Accounting_Macro, and then save it in your chapter folder as **Lastname_Firstname_9L_Accounting_Macro**

Record a macro with the shortcut key Ctrl + R, that will insert a header that is required on all reports—Westland Plains Human Resources Consulting in the left section and Accounting Department in the right section. Edit the macro to change the left header to WPHR Consulting. Insert a new worksheet, type a title in cell A1, and test your macro.

Insert the file name in the left section of the footer, add appropriate information to the document properties including the tags **accounting, macro** and submit as directed by your instructor.

END | You have completed Project 9L

GO! Think   Project 9M Sign In   MyITLab

Build from Scratch

You and GO!   Project 9N Personal Footer   MyITLab

External Data, Database Functions, and Side-by-Side Tables

PROJECT 10A	OUTCOMES Import and manage external data and use database functions in Excel.

PROJECT 10B	OUTCOMES Create a side-by-side table with conditional formatting and customize headers and footers.

OBJECTIVES

1. Get External Data into Excel
2. Clean Up and Manage Imported Data
3. Use Database Functions

OBJECTIVES

4. Insert a Second Table into a Worksheet
5. Manage and Use Formulas in Conditional Formatting Rules
6. Create Custom Headers and Footers

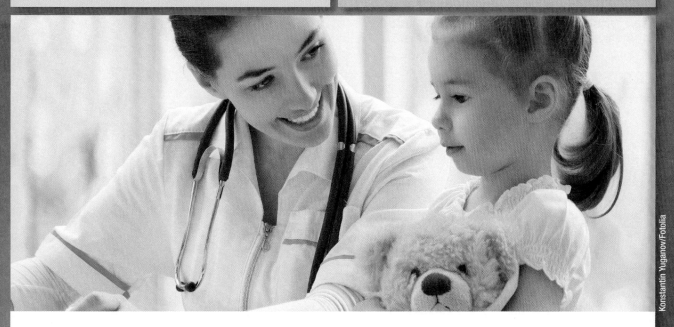

Konstantin Yuganov/Fotolia

In This Chapter

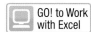

GO! to Work with Excel

In this chapter, you will use Excel's database capabilities to organize data. You will import and manage data from other sources, including from an Access database and a text file. You will use database functions to summarize information and analyze data. You will insert a second table in a worksheet and sort data in side-by-side tables. You will also apply conditional formatting to data using icon sets, by creating a conditional formatting rule by using a formula, and by managing the conditional formatting rules. Finally, you will create custom headers and footers.

The projects in this chapter relate to **Sunshine Health System**, which is the premier patient care and research institution serving the metropolitan area of Miami, Florida. Because of its outstanding reputation in the medical community and around the world, Sunshine Health System is able to attract top physicians, scientists, and researchers in all fields of medicine and achieve a level of funding that allows it to build and operate state-of-the-art facilities and provide the newest, innovative treatment options. Individuals throughout the area travel to Sunshine Health System for world-class diagnosis and care.

PROJECT

10A

Medical Center Information

MyITLab
Project 10A Training
Project 10A Grader

PROJECT ACTIVITIES

In Activities 10.01 through 10.10, you will import data about medical center nurses, doctors, patients, and supplies into Excel, and use database functions. Your completed worksheet will look similar to Figure 10.1.

Please always review the downloaded Grader instructions before beginning.

PROJECT FILES

MyITLab
grader

If your instructor wants you to submit Project 10A in the MyITLab Grader system, log into MyITLab, locate Grader Project 10A, and then download the files for this project.

For Project 10A, you will need the following files:

e10A_Medical_Center (Excel Workbook)
e10A_Nurse_Information (Access Database)
e10A_Orthopedic_Supplies (XML Document)
e10A_Physician_Information (Text Document)

GO!
Walk Thru
Project10A

You will save your workbook as:

Lastname_Firstname_10A_Medical_Center

PROJECT RESULTS

Excel 2016, Windows 10, Microsoft Corporation

FIGURE 10.1 Project 10A Medical Center Information

NOTE	If You Are Using a Touchscreen
👆	Tap an item to click it.
👆	Press and hold for a few seconds to right-click; release when the information or commands display.
👆	Touch the screen with two or more fingers and then pinch together to zoom out or stretch your fingers apart to zoom in.
👆	Slide your finger on the screen to scroll—slide left to scroll right and slide right to scroll left.
👆	Slide to rearrange—similar to dragging with a mouse.
👆	Swipe to select—slide an item a short distance with a quick movement—to select an item and bring up commands, if any.

Objective 1 Get External Data into Excel

GO! Learn How
Video E10-1

You have used many of Excel's powerful tools for analyzing data, but what if the data you want to analyze is not in Excel? You can get data that resides outside of Excel into Excel by using the **Get External Data** command located on the Data tab. This group of commands enables you to bring data from an Access database, from the Web, from a text file, from an XML file, and from other sources such as a database on a SharePoint or SQL server, or an external data feed, into Excel without repeatedly copying the data. Then you can apply Excel's data analysis tools to the data. You can also establish links, or **data connections**, to the external data so that you can automatically update your Excel workbook from the original data whenever the original data source gets new information.

NOTE	To Maintain Connections to External Data
To connect to external data when you open a workbook, you must enable data connections by using the Trust Center bar or by putting the workbook in a trusted location.	

Activity 10.01 │ Importing Data into Excel from an Access Database

Data in an Access database is organized in a format of horizontal rows and vertical columns—just like an Excel worksheet. Each horizontal row stores all of the data about one database item and is referred to as a **record**. Each vertical column stores information that describes the record and is referred to as a **field**. Data stored in a format of rows and columns is referred to as a **table**. In this Activity, you will import data into Excel from an Access database.

ALERT!	To submit as an autograded project, log into MyITLab, download the files for this project, and begin with those files instead of e10A_Medical_Center.

1 ▶ Start Excel. On the left, click **Open Other Workbooks**, click **Browse**, and then in the **Open** dialog box, navigate to the student data files that accompany this chapter. Open the file **e10A_Medical_Center**. Navigate to the location where you are storing your files for this chapter, create a new folder named **Excel Chapter 10**, and then using your own name, **Save** the file as **Lastname_Firstname_10A_Medical_Center** If necessary, enable the content of the workbook.

2 ▶ Click the **File tab**, on the left, click **Options**, and then in the **Excel Options** dialog box, on the left, click **Trust Center**. Under **Microsoft Excel Trust Center**, click **Trust Center Settings**. In the **Trust Center** dialog box, on the left, click **External Content**. Verify that the default selections *Prompt user about Data Connections* and *Prompt user on automatic update for Workbook links* are selected, and then click **OK**. In the **Excel Options** dialog box, click **OK**.

> Here you can make decisions about enabling connections. By default, both settings are set to *Prompt user*, and it is recommended that you maintain these default settings. This instruction assumes the default settings.

3 ▶ At the bottom of the Excel window, in the row of sheet tabs, locate the horizontal scroll bar. At the left end of the scroll bar, point to the three vertical dots to display the ⟨⊹⟩ pointer, and then drag to the right to decrease the width of the scroll bar to display all five worksheets in this workbook as shown in Figure 10.2.

Excel 2016, Windows 10, Microsoft Corporation

FIGURE 10.2

4 ▶ On the **Nurse Information** worksheet, click cell **A2**. On the **Data tab**, at the left end of the ribbon, in the **Get External Data Group**, click **From Access**.

5 ▶ In the **Select Data Source** dialog box, navigate to the student data files that accompany this textbook, click the Access file **e10A_Nurse_Information**, and then in the lower right corner of the dialog box, click **Open**.

> The Import Data dialog box displays. The selected option buttons indicate that the information will be imported as a table into the existing worksheet in cell A2—the active cell.

> *Microsoft Access* is a database program that manages database files. Use this technique to import data from Access or from other database programs.

6 ▶ In the **Import Data** dialog box, be sure that **Table** is selected, and then click **OK**. Compare your screen with Figure 10.3.

> Excel imports the table of nurse information. Beside each column title, an arrow displays for easy sorting and filtering. The field names display in row 2 and the records display in rows 3 to 22.

> On the Table Tools Design tab, the External Table Data group includes commands to *Unlink* and *Refresh* the data from the external table. If you unlink the table, then your Excel data will not be updated when the external data is changed.

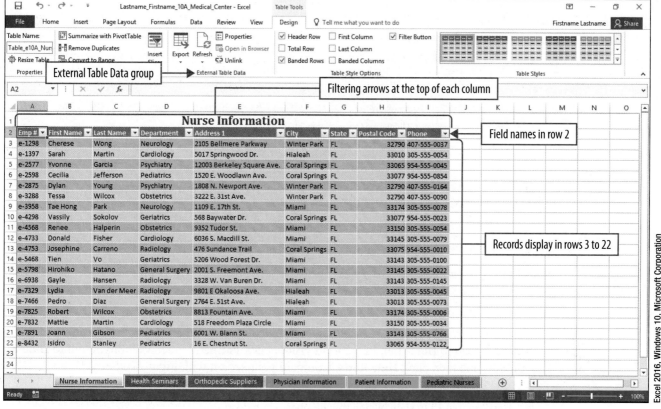

FIGURE 10.3

7 Save 🖫 your workbook.

Activity 10.02 | Hiding Worksheets, Hiding Rows and Columns, and Modifying Cell Alignment and Indentation

MOS
1.4.1
1.4.2
2.2.2

To indent data in a cell, use the Increase Indent command. To remove an indent, use the Decrease Indent command. Use caution not to type spaces to achieve an indent—doing so can affect sorting and searching.

When you have many worksheets in a workbook, you may want to hide some from view so you have fewer worksheet tabs to manage. If necessary, you can continue to reference the data in a hidden worksheet.

1 Make the next worksheet—**Health Seminars**—the active sheet.

2 Select the range **A2:B2**. On the **Home tab**, in the **Alignment group**, click **Center** ≡ and then click **Middle Align** ≡ so that the text is centered both horizontally and vertically in the cell.

🔄 **ANOTHER WAY** Right-click over the selection, click Format Cells, click the Alignment tab, and then under Text alignment, set Horizontal to Center and set Vertical to Center.

3 Select the range **A4:A5**. On the **Home tab**, in the **Alignment group**, click **Increase Indent** 🔳 one time. Click cell **A7**, hold down [Ctrl], and then click cell **A10**. Click **Increase Indent** 🔳 one time.

4 Select the range **A8:A9**, hold down [Ctrl], select the range **A11:A12**, and then press **Increase Indent** 🔳 two times.

5 Press [Ctrl] + [Home] to make cell **A1** the active cell, and then compare your screen with Figure 10.4.

FIGURE 10.4

> **6** Because the *Staying Safe at Home* training meetings are still tentative, select **rows 10:12**, and then on the **Home tab**, in the **Cells group**, click **Format**. Under **Visibility**, point to **Hide & Unhide**, and then click **Hide Rows**. Compare your screen with Figure 10.5.
>
> A green line indicates that some rows are hidden from view, and the row numbers jump from row 9 to row 13 to show which row numbers are hidden.

ANOTHER WAY   Select the rows, right-click over the selection, and then on the shortcut menu, click Hide.

FIGURE 10.5

> **7** To hide the entire worksheet, on the **Home tab**, in the **Cells group**, click **Format**. Under **Visibility**, point to **Hide & Unhide**, and then click **Hide Sheet**.

ANOTHER WAY   Right-click the sheet tab, and then on the shortcut menu, click Hide.

8 To unhide the worksheet, on the **Home tab**, in the **Cells group**, click **Format**. Under **Visibility**, point to **Hide & Unhide**, click **Unhide Sheet**, and then compare your screen with Figure 10.6.

> You can select multiple worksheets and then hide them as a group; however, you can unhide only one worksheet at a time.

ANOTHER WAY   Right-click any sheet tab, and then on the shortcut menu, click Unhide.

FIGURE 10.6

9 Click **OK** to redisplay the worksheet, **Save** 🖫 your workbook, and then compare your screen with Figure 10.7.

FIGURE 10.7

Activity 10.03 | Importing Data into Excel from an XML File, Adding and Removing Table Rows and Columns, and Converting a Table to a Cell Range

3.1.2
3.1.3

In this Activity, you will import data into Excel from an XML file. *Extensible Markup Language (XML)* is a language that structures data in text files so that it can be read by other systems, regardless of the hardware platform or operating system. Such portability is why XML has become a popular technology for exchanging data.

1 Display the next worksheet—**Orthopedic Suppliers**.

2 Click cell **A2**. On the **Data tab**, at the left end of the ribbon, if necessay display the **Get External Data** commands, and then click **From Other Sources**. On the displayed list, click **From XML Data Import**.

3 In the **Select Data Source** dialog box, navigate to your student data files, and then click the XML file **e10A_Orthopedic_Supplies**. At the bottom of the dialog box, notice that the file type is *XML Files*.

The Orthopedic Supplies file contains supplier information for orthopedic supplies at the Medical Center. In this manner, you can import data from an XML file.

4 With the **e10A_Orthopedic_Supplies** file selected, click **Open**.

A Microsoft Excel information message displays. The specified XML source does not refer to a schema. A *schema* is an XML file that contains the rules for what can and cannot reside in an XML data file. Schemas are not required in XML, but they can be useful in ensuring that any data inserted into an XML document follows predefined rules for both content and structure.

5 Click **OK** to display the **Import Data** dialog box. Notice that the data will be imported as an XML table into the existing worksheet in cell **$A$2**—the active cell.

6 Click **OK**, and then compare your screen with Figure 10.8.

The table of orthopedic suppliers is imported as an Excel table with filter arrows in the column titles. The field names display in row 2 and the records display in rows 3 to 10.

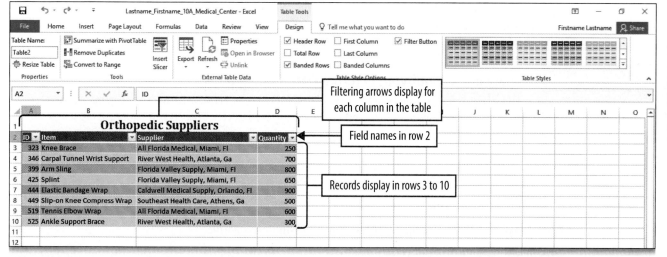

FIGURE 10.8

Excel 2016, Windows 10, Microsoft Corporation

7 Click cell **B8**. On the **Home tab**, in the **Cells group**, click the **Delete button arrow**, and then click **Delete Table Rows**.

To delete a table row or column, you need only click in a cell, and then use the appropriate command. Similarly, you can insert a table row or column by clicking the Insert button arrow in the Cells group.

Click in the cell, right-click to display a shortcut menu, point to Delete (or Insert), and then click Table Rows or Table Columns—depending on what you want to delete or insert.

8 To convert the table back to a normal range, click in any cell, right-click, point to **Table**, and then compare your screen with Figure 10.9.

When you convert your table back to a range of normal cells, all the functionality of the table, such as filters, are removed, but the style, like colors and bold, will remain.

FIGURE 10.9

Excel 2016, Windows 10, Microsoft Corporation

> **9** Click **Convert to Range**, and then click **Yes**. Notice that the range of cells retains the colors and formatting of the table, but the filtering arrows no longer display. **Save** 🖫 your workbook.

More Knowledge   **Viewing or Modifying External Data Connections**

To view or modify external data connections, on the Data tab, in the Connections group, click Connections to open the Workbook Connections dialog box. Select the name of the worksheet, and then in the lower pane, click *Click here* to see where the selected connections are used.

Activity 10.04 | Importing Data into Excel from a Delimited Text File

In this Activity, you will import information into Excel from a delimited text file.

> **1** Make the next worksheet—**Physician Information**—active.

> **2** Click cell **A8**. On the **Data tab**, at the left end of the ribbon, if necessary display the **Get External Data** commands, and then click **From Text**.

The Import Text File dialog box displays.

> **3** In the **Import Text File** dialog box, navigate to your student data files, select the Text file **e10A_Physician_Information**, and then at the bottom of the dialog box, notice that *Text Files* displays as the file type.

The Physician Information file contains contact information for doctors at the Medical Center. Use this technique to import data from a text file.

> **4** With the **e10A_Physician_Information** file selected, click **Import**. Compare your screen with Figure 10.10.

The Text Import Wizard – Step 1 of 3 dialog box displays. The Text Import Wizard determines that the Physician Information file is *delimited*—separated by commas or tabs—and selects Delimited. At the bottom of the dialog box, a preview of the data displays.

FIGURE 10.10

> **5** Click **Next**, and then compare your screen with Figure 10.11.

The Text Import Wizard – Step 2 of 3 dialog box displays. Here you can set the delimiters your data contains. Under Delimiters, the Tab check box is selected. At the bottom of the dialog box, the Data preview displays.

FIGURE 10.11

Excel 2016, Windows 10, Microsoft Corporation

6 ▸ Click **Next**, and then compare your screen with Figure 10.12.

> The Text Import Wizard – Step 3 of 3 dialog box displays. Here you can select each column and see the data format. Under Column data format, General is selected. At the bottom of the dialog box, the Data preview displays.

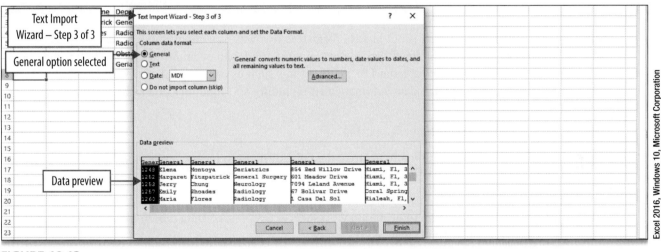

FIGURE 10.12

Excel 2016, Windows 10, Microsoft Corporation

7 ▸ Click **Finish**.

> The Import Data dialog box displays, indicating that the table will be imported into the existing worksheet in cell $A$8—the active cell. This will append the data to the existing data in rows 1:7.

8 ▸ Click **OK**, and then compare your screen with Figure 10.13. Notice there are several duplicate records in this data. **Save** 🖫 your workbook.

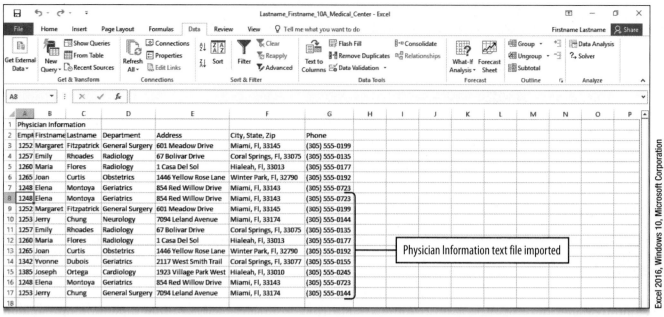

FIGURE 10.13

Excel 2016, Windows 10, Microsoft Corporation

Clean Up and Manage Imported Data

GO! Learn How
Video E10-2

Data in a worksheet is not always formatted in a way you can use it. The data may be in the wrong columns, duplicate records may be imported, and even the case of the letters may be incorrect. In addition to standard formatting tools such as cell styles, Excel includes several tools to help you clean up the data automatically, including text functions and ribbon commands.

Activity 10.05 | Removing Duplicates

MOS

3.3.4

In a worksheet with many records, it can be difficult to locate duplicate records by eye. In this Activity, you will remove duplicate records from the Physician Information worksheet automatically.

1 With the **Physician Information** worksheet active, on the **Data tab**, in the **Data Tools group**, click **Remove Duplicates**.

The Remove Duplicates dialog box includes a list of the columns available in the data.

2 Click **Unselect All**, verify that the *My data has headers* check box is selected, select the *Emp#* and *Department* check boxes, and then click **OK**. Compare your screen with Figure 10.14.

By removing duplicate records, you assure that an employee will only appear one time for each department. Six duplicate records were found and deleted. In this manner you can clean up duplicate data automatically.

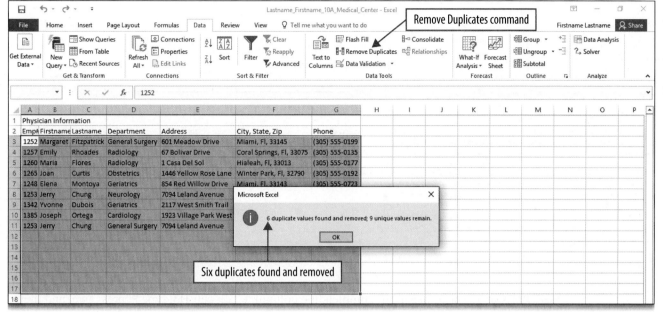

FIGURE 10.14

3 Click **OK**, and then **Save** 🖫 your workbook.

Activity 10.06 | Using Flash Fill to Expand Data

Excel can format text data. For example, to make sorting and filtering easier, you can separate data into separate fields using **Flash Fill**—an Excel feature that predicts how to alter data based on the pattern you enter into the cell at the beginning of the column. To use Flash Fill, the data must be in the adjacent column. In this Activity, you will use Flash Fill to clean up imported data.

1 On the **Physician Information** worksheet, notice the city, state, and zip are all in the same field in **column F**.

2 Click the **column G** header to select the column, right-click, and then click **Insert** to insert a new column. Use the same method to insert two additional columns.

Three new columns are added between the *City, State, Zip* and *Phone* fields.

3 Click cell **G2**, type **City** and then press ⎵Tab⎵. In cell **H2** type **State** press ⎵Tab⎵, in cell **I2** type **Zip** and then press ⎵Enter⎵.

4 In cell **G3**, type **Miami** and press ⎵Enter⎵. In cells **G4** type **Co** and compare your screen with Figure 10.15.

Based on your entries in cells G3 and G4, Flash Fill suggests entries for the remaining cells in the column.

FIGURE 10.15

5 Press [Enter] to have Flash Fill complete the column. Click cell **H3**, type **Fl** press [Enter], and then use the **fill handle** to copy the text down through **H11**. **Save** 🖫 your workbook.

> Excel's Flash Fill feature automatically completes column G using the pattern. Because all employees live in Florida, you can simply drag to fill column H.

Activity 10.07 | Using Text Functions

4.3.1
4.3.2
4.3.3

Among Excel's **Text functions**, which are functions that assist in formatting text, you will find functions to combine or separate data, change case, and apply formatting to a string of characters. The text function **RIGHT** will return the specified number of characters from the end (right) of a string of characters. The similar **LEFT** function returns the specified number of characters from the beginning (left) of a string, and the **MID** function extracts a series of characters from a text string given the location of the beginning character.

The **CONCATENATE** text function can join up to 255 strings of characters. The **TRIM** function can remove extra blank spaces from a string. This is especially useful for removing leading blank spaces, which are difficult to see by eye, but can cause problems with sorting and filtering. The **UPPER** and **LOWER** functions will change the case of the characters in a string, making all characters uppercase or lowercase, and the **PROPER** function will capitalize the first letter of each word; for example, all proper nouns such as the names of cities. In this Activity, you will use text functions to clean up imported data.

1 Click cell **I3**. On the **Formulas tab**, in the **Function Library group**, click **Text**, and then click **RIGHT**.

2 If necessary, drag the **Function Arguments** dialog box down so **row 3** is visible. With the insertion point in the **Text** box, click cell **F3**. Press [Tab], and then, in the **Num_chars** box, type **5** Compare your dialog box with Figure 10.16.

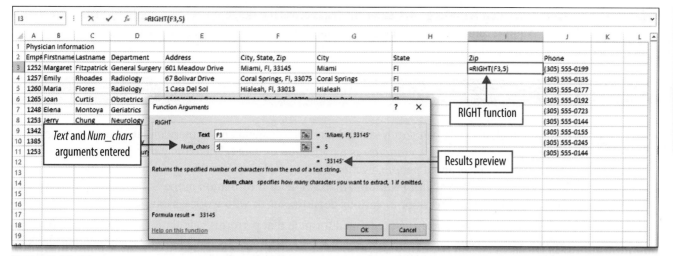

FIGURE 10.16

Excel 2016, Windows 10, Microsoft Corporation

3 Click **OK**. Drag the **fill handle** to copy the function down through cell **I11**.

The text function RIGHT displays the last 5 characters of the text in column F.

4 Click cell **H3**. In the **Function Library group**, click **Text**, scroll down as necessary, and then click **UPPER**. In the **Function Arguments** dialog box, in the **Text** box, type **Fl** and then click OK.

5 Drag the **fill handle** to copy the function down through cell **H11**. **Save** 🔲 your workbook.

6 Click cell **K2** and type **Full Name** Click cell **K3**, on the **Formulas tab**, in the **Function Library group**, click **Text**, and then click **CONCATENATE**.

7 If necessary, drag the **Function Arguments** dialog box so **columns B:C** are visible. With the insertion point in the **Text1** box, click cell **B3**. Press Tab. In the **Text2** box type " and then press Spacebar and then type " Press Tab and in the **Text3** box, click **C3**. Compare your dialog box with Figure 10.17.

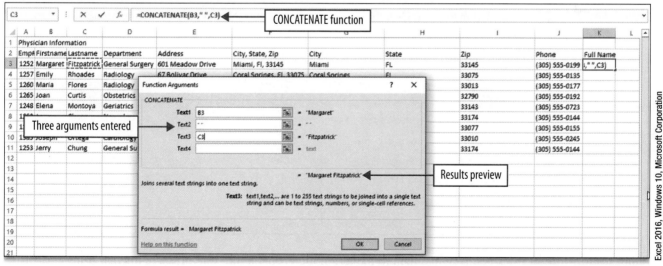

FIGURE 10.17

Excel 2016, Windows 10, Microsoft Corporation

8 Click **OK**. Use the **fill handle** to copy the function down through cell **K11**.

The CONCATENATE function combined the text entered in the function argument boxes into a single cell.

9 Click cell **A1**. **Merge & Center** the text across the range **A1:K1** and apply the **Title** cell style. **AutoFit columns A:K**. Click the **column F** heading, right-click, click **Hide**, and then **Save** 🖫 your workbook.

Objective 3 Use Database Functions

GO! Learn How
Video E10-3

In Excel, not only can you track and manage financial and numerical data, but you can also create simple databases. A *database* is a collection of data related to a particular topic or purpose. *Data* refers to facts about people, events, things, or ideas. Data that is organized in a useful manner is referred to as *information*. An example of information at the Sunshine Health System is the list of nurses who work in various departments or who work various shifts.

Recall that a *function* is a predefined formula that performs calculations by using specific values, called *arguments*. Database functions are identified by the letter *D*—each function starts with a D, for example, DSUM, DAVERAGE, and DCOUNT. The initial letter *D* identifies to Excel that a database range will be used in the formula, rather than a single column or row of numbers.

Activity 10.08 │ Using the DAVERAGE Database Function

The *syntax*—arrangement of arguments in a function—for the majority of database functions is: DFunction Name(database, field, criteria), where *database* identifies the range of cells where the data is displayed, *field* is the field name to be considered, and *criteria* is the range of cells where the search criteria has been defined.

The criteria is defined in a separate area on the worksheet. In this Activity, you will use the DAVERAGE function to determine the average hourly wage for LPNs (Licensed Practical Nurses) in the pediatric wing of the hospital. The *DAVERAGE function* determines an average in a database that is limited by criteria set for one or more cells.

1 In your workbook, display the next worksheet—**Pediatric Nurses**.

This worksheet lists the Employee Number, Shift Code, Status, Hours per Shift, Hourly Wage, and Wage per Shift for pediatric nurses who work on Mondays. The Wage per Shift field contains a formula that multiplies the Hours per Shift in column D times the Hourly Wage in column E. The number in the Shift Code field is a code for the shift. Not all nurses work on Mondays; so, some rows indicate 0 hours per shift.

The Shift Codes represent the following hours:

SHIFT	CODE
Day (6a–2p)	1
Evening (7p–3a)	2
Afternoon (12p–8p)	3
Night (10p–6a)	4
Day 12-hr (6a–6p)	5
Night 12-hr (6p–6a)	6

2 Click cell **B28**, and then to the left of the **Formula Bar**, click **Insert Function** 𝑓ₓ.

You can use the Insert Function dialog box to locate any function in Excel. Cell C28 will form the first cell in the criteria range for the DAVERAGE function, which must consist of at least two vertical cells. The top cell is the field name that is to be searched, and the cell immediately below it is the criteria used in the function search. The value—LPN—is the search criteria.

🔁 ANOTHER WAY   On the Formulas tab, in the Function Library group, click Insert Function.

3 ▸ In the **Insert Function** dialog box, click the **Or select a category arrow**, and then click **Database**. In the **Select a function** box, click **DAVERAGE**, and then click **OK**. Compare your screen with Figure 10.18.

The Function Arguments dialog box for DAVERAGE displays. Recall that **arguments** are the values that an Excel function uses to perform calculations or operations.

FIGURE 10.18

Excel 2016, Windows 10, Microsoft Corporation

4 ▸ In the **Database** box, click **Collapse Dialog Box** 🔳, and then select the range **A3:F26**. Then, in the collapsed dialog box, click **Expand Dialog Box** 🔲.

This action defines the database range in the first argument box.

5 ▸ In the **Field** box, type **Hourly Wage** and press ⌨Tab.

This action identifies the field or column in the database that you want to average; the insertion point moves to the Criteria box. Excel adds quotation marks around the Field name, which identifies it as a string of characters to use in the search.

6 ▸ With the insertion point in the **Criteria** box, select the vertical range **C28:C29**—the criteria range that was previously defined. Compare your screen with Figure 10.19.

The two cells in the criteria range will limit the DAVERAGE calculation to only those records where *Status* is equal to *LPN*—RNs and Nurse Supervisors will not be included.

FIGURE 10.19

Excel 2016, Windows 10, Microsoft Corporation

7 ▸ Click **OK**.

The result, *$20.17*, displays in cell B28. This is the average hourly wage for LPNs who work in the pediatric wing of the hospital on Mondays.

8 ▸ **Save** 💾 your workbook.

The **DSUM function** will sum a column of values in a database that is limited by criteria set for one or more cells. In this Activity, you will sum the *Wage per Shift* for RNs who work in the Pediatric wing on Mondays.

1 Click cell **B31**, and then type **=dsum(** to begin the formula for the DSUM function. Compare your screen with Figure 10.20.

The *Status* will be limited to RN, and the *Hours Worked* will be limited to those RNs who worked a number of hours greater than zero. This is a **compound criteria**—use of two or more criteria on the same row—all conditions must be met for the records to be included in the results.

Recall that you can type the function arguments directly into the cell instead of using the *Function Argument* dialog box. A ScreenTip displays the parts of the argument that must be included, which guides you through the process of entering all of the arguments necessary for this function.

FIGURE 10.20

2 Notice that in the function ScreenTip, *database* displays in bold, indicating that you must select a range that is the database. Select the range **A3:F26**, and then type **,** (a comma). You can look at the **Formula Bar** to see your typing and correct as necessary. Compare your screen with Figure 10.21.

The database range is defined, and the *field* argument displays in bold.

FIGURE 10.21

3 Notice that in the function ScreenTip, *field* displays in bold, indicating that you must type the name of the field. Being sure to include the comma, type **"Wage per Shift",** to enter the second part of the argument; you can look at the **Formula Bar** to see your typing and correct as necessary.

The field that you want to sum is the *Wage per Shift* field, so the field name is entered as the second argument. The quotation marks define this as a string of characters; it must match the field name exactly. The comma separates this argument from the next argument.

4 As indicated by *criteria* in the ScreenTip, type the criteria as **c31:d32** and then press Enter.

After you type the criteria range, Excel automatically adds a closing parenthesis. The final result of the formula—$1,455.72—displays in cell B31. The total cost to pay all the RNs who work in the Pediatric wing on Mondays is $1,455.72.

5 With cell **B31** active, click in the **Formula Bar** and examine the parts of the DSUM function. Compare your screen with Figure 10.22.

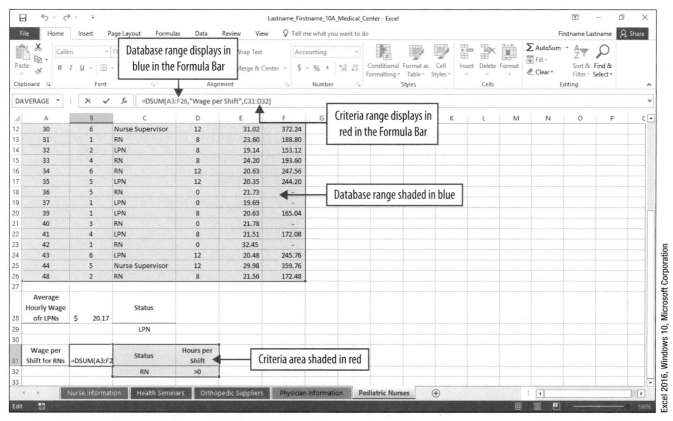

FIGURE 10.22

6 Save 💾 your workbook.

Activity 10.10 | Using DCOUNT

DCOUNT counts the cells containing numbers in the column of records that match the conditions you specify. In this Activity, you will count the number of nurses who work the day shift.

1 Scroll down as necessary to view rows 34:37, and then compare your screen with Figure 10.23.

Cell A34 forms the label for the function. Three shifts include daytime hours—Shift Codes 1, 3, and 5—so include all three in the criteria range. In the range C35:D35, the Shift Code value for the first daytime shift, which is *1*, is entered. To meet the conditions of this compound criteria, a nurse must be assigned to Shift 1 and work greater than zero hours.

In the range C36:D36 the code for the second daytime shift is entered and functions as an *OR* criteria. Excel evaluates the criteria in row 35 and then will consider the criteria in row 36. If a record meets either condition, it will be included in the calculation.

The code for the third daytime shift—*5*—also functions as an *OR* criteria. Consequently, the calculation will count the number of nurses who worked more than zero hours in one of the three day shifts, whether it is Shift Code 1, 3, or 5.

FIGURE 10.23

> **2** Click cell **B34**. To the left of the **Formula Bar**, click **Insert Function** ☒.

> **3** If necessary, click the **Or select a category arrow**, and then click **Database**. In the **Select a function** box, click **DCOUNT**, and then click **OK**.
>
> The Function Arguments dialog box for DCOUNT displays.

> **4** In the **Database** box, click **Collapse Dialog Box** ☒. Move the collapsed box to the upper right corner of your screen. Scroll as necessary, and then select the range **A3:F26**.

> **5** In the collapsed dialog box, click **Expand Dialog Box** ☒.
>
> The database range is defined and displays in the first argument box.

> **6** In the **Field** box, type **Employee Number** and then press ⎵Tab.
>
> The *Employee Number* field will be counted.

> **7** With the insertion point in the **Criteria** box, click **Collapse Dialog Box** ☒, scroll as necessary, and then select the range **C34:D37**—the criteria area that was previously defined. In the collapsed dialog box, click **Expand Dialog Box** ☒. Compare your **Function Arguments** dialog box with Figure 10.24.

FIGURE 10.24

> **8** Click **OK**. Save ☐ your workbook.
>
> The result, *10*, displays in cell B34. This is the total number of nurses assigned to work the day shift in the pediatric wing of the hospital on Mondays.

9 ▶ Group the worksheets. On the **Page Layout tab**, in the **Page Setup group**, cilck **Orientation**, and then click **Portrait**. On the **Page Layout tab**, click **Margins**, click **Custom Margins**, and then under **Center on page**, be sure the **Horizontally** check box is selected. Click the **Header/Footer tab**, click **Custom Footer**, and then in the **left section**, insert the **File Name**. Click **OK** two times.

10 ▶ With all the sheets still grouped, press ⌃Ctrl + Home to make cell **A1** the active cell. In the **Scale to Fit group**, set the **Width** to **1 page** and the **Height** to **1 page**. Display the **document properties**. As the **Tags**, type **medical center information** In the **Subject** box, type your course name and section number. Be sure your name displays as the author.

11 ▶ On the left, click **Print** to display the **Print Preview**. Scroll through the five worksheets. On the left, click **Save** to save your workbook and return to the workbook window.

12 ▶ Ungroup the worksheets. If directed by your instructor to do so, submit a paper printout of each of the five worksheets, an electronic image of each of your five worksheets that looks like a printed document, or your original Excel file. If required by your instructor, print or create an electronic version of your worksheets with formulas displayed. In the upper right corner of the Excel window, click **Close** ☒.

◀ END | You have completed Project 10A

PROJECT
10B

Office Equipment Inventory

MyITLab
Project 10B Training
Project 10B Grader

PROJECT ACTIVITIES

In Activities 10.11 through 10.14, you will edit a worksheet for Pat Shepard, Vice President of Operations, detailing the current inventory of two office equipment types—Office Equipment Nursing Station and Office Equipment Administrative. Your completed worksheet will look similar to Figure 10.25.

Please always review the downloaded Grader instructions before beginning.

PROJECT FILES

MyITLab
grader

If your instructor wants you to submit Project 10B in the MyITLab grader system, log into MyITLab, locate Grader Project 10B, and then download the files for this project.

For Project 10B, you will need the following files:

e10B_Equipment_Inventory
e10B_Logo

You will save your workbook as:

Lastname_Firstname_10B_Equipment_Inventory

PROJECT RESULTS

GO!
Walk Thru
Project10B

Excel 2016, Windows 10, Microsoft Corporation

FIGURE 10.25 Project 10B Office Equipment Inventory

GO! Learn How
Video E10-4

In Excel, you can insert a table beside another table in the *same* worksheet, and then work with the data in each table separately. This enables you to view and compare similar sets of data.

Activity 10.11 | Inserting a Second Table into a Worksheet

ALERT! To submit as an autograded project, log into MyITLab, download the files for this project, and begin with those files instead of e10B_Equipment_Inventory.

1 Start Excel. On the left, click **Open Other Workbooks**, click **Browse**, and then in the **Open** dialog box, navigate to the student data files that accompany this chapter. Open the file **e10B_Equipment_Inventory**. Click the **File tab**, on the left click **Save As**, click **Browse**, in the **Save As** dialog box, navigate to your **Excel Chapter 10 folder**, and then using your own name, save the file as **Lastname_Firstname_10B_Equipment_Inventory**

2 On the **Equipment Inventory** worksheet, select the range **A7:E62**, and then on the **Insert tab**, in the **Tables group**, click **Table**. In the **Create Table** dialog box, verify that =$A$7:$E$62 displays as the data range and that the **My table has headers** check box is selected. Click **OK**.

The Office Equipment Nursing Station data converts to a table, a table style is applied, and the headings display filter arrows.

3 Click the **Administrative** sheet tab, select the range **A1:E52**, right-click over the selection, and then, click **Copy**.

BY TOUCH Press and hold to display the right-click menu.

4 Display the **Equipment Inventory** worksheet, scroll up as necessary, point to cell **F6** and right-click, and then, under **Paste Options**, click **Paste (P)**. Click any cell to deselect. Compare your screen with Figure 10.26.

The data regarding Office Equipment Administrative is added to the right of the Office Equipment Nursing Station table.

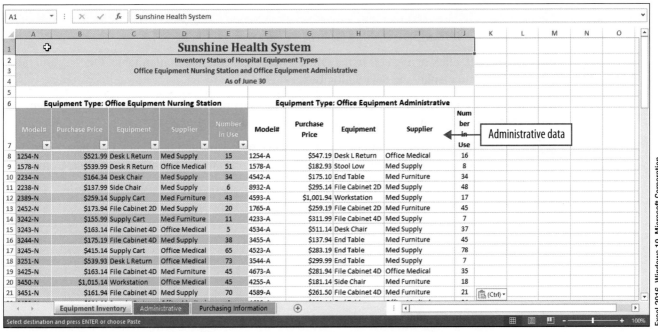

FIGURE 10.26

5 Select the range **F7:J57**. In the lower right corner of the selection click **Quick Analysis** 📊, click **Tables**, and then click **Table**.

This is another method to convert data to a table in Excel. Here you see that side-by-side tables do *not* have to contain the same number of rows or columns.

6 On the **Design tab**, in the **Table Styles group**, click **More** ▾, and then in the gallery, under **Medium**, click the gold colored **Table Style Medium 13**—you can use the ScreenTips to view the table names.

7 Press Ctrl + Home to move to cell **A1** and deselect the table. **Save** 💾 your workbook, and then compare your screen with Figure 10.27.

The data for Office Equipment Administrative is converted to a table, a style is applied, and the headings display filtering arrows—also referred to as *filtering controls*.

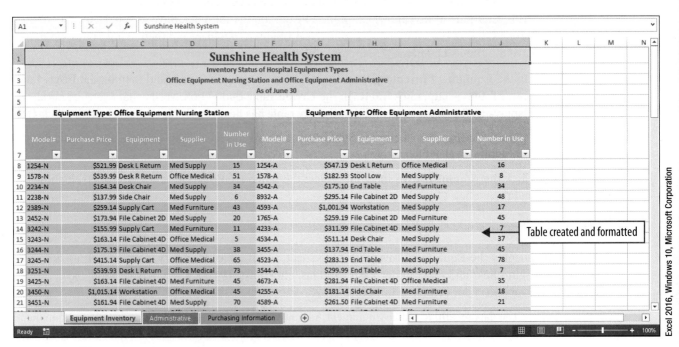

FIGURE 10.27

Activity 10.12 | Sorting Side-by-Side Tables

1 On the left, click in any cell in the **Office Equipment Nursing Station** table. On the **Data tab**, click **Sort** to display the **Sort** dialog box.

2 In the **Sort** dialog box, under **Column**, click the **Sort by arrow**, and then click **Equipment**. Verify that **Sort On** indicates *Values* and **Order** indicates *A to Z*.

3 Click **Add Level**. Under **Column**, click the **Then by arrow**, and then click **Purchase Price**. In the same row, click the **Order arrow**, and set the sort order to **Largest to Smallest**. Compare your screen with Figure 10.28.

FIGURE 10.28

Excel 2016, Windows 10, Microsoft Corporation

4 Click **OK**, and then compare your screen with Figure 10.29.

> The Equipment column is sorted alphabetically, and within each equipment type, the items are sorted by Purchase Price from the highest to lowest.

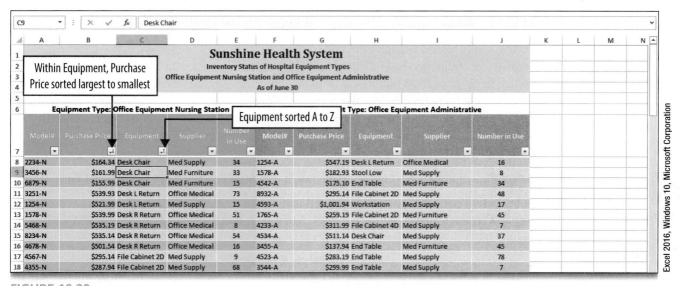

FIGURE 10.29

5 Using the same technique and the same sort orders, sort the **Office Equipment Administrative** table. **Save** 🖫 your workbook, and then compare your screen with Figure 10.30.

> By having the two tables side-by-side in the same worksheet, you can sort similar sets of data to make comparisons. For example, you can see that the Administrative desk chairs are more expensive than the Nursing Station desk chairs.

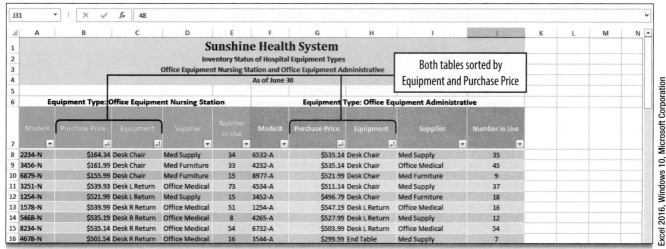

FIGURE 10.30

Objective 5 Manage and Use Formulas in Conditional Formatting Rules

GO! Learn How
Video E10-5

Recall that *conditional formatting* makes your data easier to interpret by changing the appearance of your data based on a condition; if the condition is true, the cell is formatted based on that condition, and if the condition is false, the cell is not formatted.

Excel provides built-in conditional formatting rules, but sometimes you will need to create your own rules by using a formula. You can also manage—change—either built-in rules or rules that you have created.

Icon sets are sets of three, four, or five small graphic images that make your data visually easier to interpret. The icons are placed inside the cells. Their shape or color indicates the values in the cells relative to all other adjacent cells formatted using the same condition.

Activity 10.13 Managing and Using Formulas in Conditional Formatting Rules

2.2.2 Expert
2.2.3 Expert

Mr. Shepard is planning a remodel and needs an inventory of nursing station equipment. Additionally, the company *Med Furniture* is going out of business, and Mr. Shepard needs to know which items have been purchased from this company so that he can check on any warranties or parts that might be needed before the company closes.

In this Activity, you will use icon sets as the conditional formatting to distinguish visually the Number in Use of equipment items. You will also create a conditional formatting rule using a formula and change—manage—a rule.

1 Select the range **E8:E62**. On the **Home tab**, in the **Styles group**, click **Conditional Formatting**.

2 Point to **Icon Sets**, and then under **Directional**, in the first row, click the first icon set—**3 Arrows (Colored)**. Click cell **E63** to deselect, and then compare your screen with Figure 10.31.

In this icon set, a colored arrow provides the visual cue about the value of a cell relative to other cells. A green upward pointing arrow represents a higher value, a yellow sideways pointing arrow represents a mid-level value, and a red downward pointing arrow represents a lower value. Icon sets are useful to quickly identify higher and lower numbers within a large group of data, such as very high or very low levels of inventory.

	A	B	C	D	E	F	G	H	I	J	K	L	M	N
40	3458-N	$161.94	Stool High	Med Supply	48	4255-A			urniture	18				
41	7865-N	$141.59	Stool High	Med Furniture	12	3562-A	$179.94	Side Chair	Med Supply	7				
42	3566-N	$161.99	Stool Low	Med Furniture	11	5478-A	$167.99	Side Chair	Office Medical	21				
43	3245-N	$415.14	Supply Cart	Office Medical	65	5678-A	$161.94	Side Chair	Office Medical	37				
44	4233-N	$381.59	Supply Cart	Med Furniture	10	4573-A	$172.26	Sofa Table	Office Medical	46				
45	6234-N	$319.14	Supply Cart	Med Supply	54	4590-A	$167.99	Sofa Table	Med Furniture	55				
46	6121-N	$311.99	Supply Cart	Med Supply	85	5489-A	$161.94	Sofa Table	Office Medical	34				
47	5677-N	$295.14	Supply Cart	Med Furniture	27	6121-A	$141.54	Sofa Table	Office Medical	48				
48	3452-N	$281.99	Supply Cart	Office Medical	6	8755-A	$497.94	Stool Low	Med Furniture	8				
49	7988-N	$281.94	Supply Cart	Med Supply	8	1578-A	$182.93	Stool Low	Med Supply	8				
50	5378-N	$271.14	Supply Cart	Med Supply	16	6845-A	$173.99	Stool Low	Office Medical	55				
51	4235-N	$261.59	Supply Cart	Med Furniture	73	7654-A	$1,015.19	Workstation	Med Supply	35				
52	3578-N	$261.55	Supply Cart	Office Medical	53	4258-A	$1,013.99	Workstation	Office Medical	48				
53	2389-N	$259.14	Supply Cart	Med Furniture	43	4593-A	$1,001.94	Workstation	Med Supply	17				
54	3242-N	$155.99	Supply Cart	Med Furniture	11	6455-A	$979.19	Workstation	Med Supply	7				
55	4532-N	$141.54	Supply Cart	Office Medical	45	6734-A	$979.14	Workstation	Med Supply	20				
56	3450-N	$1,015.14	Workstation	Office Medical	45	7865-A	$977.99	Workstation	Med Furniture	55				
57	4562-N	$1,013.99	Workstation	Office Medical	10	4522-A	$976.79	Workstation	Med Furniture	48				
58	4255-N	$1,007.99	Workstation	Med Furniture	10									
59	6789-N	$1,007.99	Workstation	Med Supply	17									
60	4578-N	$1,004.34	Workstation	Office Medical	54									
61	7859-N	$1,001.99	Workstation	Office Medical	7									
62	7892-N	$995.99	Workstation	Med Supply	11									
63														
64														

Conditional formatting indicates inventory level

Excel 2016, Windows 10, Microsoft Corporation

FIGURE 10.31

3 Select the range **E8:E62** again. On the **Home tab**, in the **Styles group**, click **Conditional Formatting**, and then at the bottom, click **Manage Rules**. Compare your screen with Figure 10.32.

> Here you can edit or delete the conditional formatting rule applied to the selected cells.

FIGURE 10.32

Excel 2016, Windows 10, Microsoft Corporation

4 In the **Conditional Formatting Rules Manager** dialog box, click **Edit Rule**, and then in the **Edit Formatting Rule** dialog box, in the lower portion of the dialog box, click the **Icon Style arrow**, scroll down about half way, and then point to the three circles with the symbols X, !, and ✓, as shown in Figure 10.33.

5 Click the **3 Symbols (Circled)** icon style, and then click **OK** two times to change the icon style.

> Mr. Shepard thinks these symbols are more descriptive of the information he wants to see at a glance regarding the number of equipment types in use.

FIGURE 10.33

6 In the second table, select the range **J8:J57**. On the **Home tab**, in the **Styles group**, click **Conditional Formatting**, point to **Icon Sets**, and then under **Indicators**, click **3 Symbols (Circled)** to apply the same icon set to the second table.

7 In the first table, select the range **D8:D62**. On the **Home tab**, in the **Styles group**, click **Conditional Formatting**, and then at the bottom click **New Rule**. In the **New Formatting Rule** dialog box, under **Select a Rule Type**, click the last rule type—**Use a formula to determine which cells to format**.

8 In the lower portion of the dialog box, in the **Format values where this formula is true** box, type **=d8="Med Furniture"** and then compare your screen with Figure 10.34.

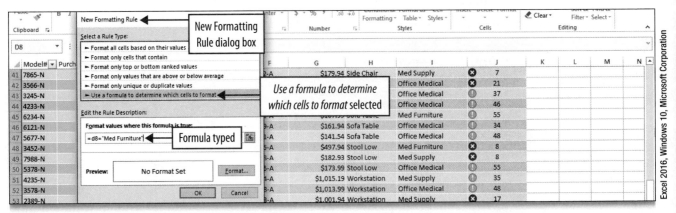

FIGURE 10.34

9 In the lower right corner of the dialog box, click **Format**. In the **Format Cells** dialog box, under **Font style**, click **Bold Italic**. Click the **Color arrow**, and then under **Standard Colors**, click the second color—**Red**. Compare your screen with Figure 10.35.

When the conditional formatting is applied, the text will be formatted in red bold italic.

FIGURE 10.35

10 Click **OK** two times. In the second table, select the range **I8:I57**, and then create the same conditional formatting rule using the formula **=i8="Med Furniture"** and apply it to the selection. Press Ctrl + Home, and then compare your screen with Figure 10.36.

11 **Save** 💾 your workbook.

	A	B	C	D	E	F	G	H	I	J	K	L	M	N
1				Sunshine Health System										
2				Inventory Status of Hospital Equipment Types										
3				Office Equipment Nursing Station and Office Equipment Administrative										
4				As of June 30										
5														
6		Equipment Type: Office Equipment Nursing Station					Equipment Type: Office Equipment Administrative							
7	Model#	Purchase Price	Equipment	Supplier	Number in Use	Model#	Purchase Price	Equipment	Supplier	Number in Use				
8	2234-N	$164.34	Desk Chair	Med Supply	34	6532-A	$535.14	Desk Chair	Med Supply	35				
9	3456-N	$161.99	Desk Chair	Med Furniture	23	4232-A	$535.14	Desk Chair	Office Medical	45				
10	6879-N	$155.99	Desk Chair	Med Furniture	15	8977-A	$521.99	Desk Chair	Med Furniture	9				
11	3251-N	$539.93	Desk L Return	Office Medical	73	4534-A	$511.14	Desk Chair	Med Supply	37				
12	1254-N	$521.99	Desk L Return	Med Supply	15	3452-A	$496.79	Desk Chair	Med Furniture	18				
13	1578-N	$539.99	Desk R Return	Office Medical	51	1254-A	$547.19	Desk L Return	Office Medical	16				
14	5468-N	$535.19	Desk R Return	Office Medical	8	4265-A	$527.99	Desk L Return	Med Supply	12				
15	8234-N	$535.14	Desk R Return	Office Medical	54	6732-A	$503.99	Desk L Return	Office Medical	54				
16	4678-N	$501.54	Desk R Return	Office Medical	16	3544-A	$299.99	End Table	Med Supply	7				
17	4567-N	$295.14	File Cabinet 2D	Med Supply	9	4523-A	$283.19	End Table	Med Supply	78				
18	4355-N	$287.94	File Cabinet 2D	Med Supply	68	4632-A	$283.14	End Table	Office Medical	34				
19	3478-N	$281.99	File Cabinet 2D	Med Supply	27	8976-A	$281.94	End Table	Med Furniture	35				
20	3567-N	$281.99	File Cabinet 2D	Office Medical	35	1732-A	$281.94	End Table	Med Supply	37				
21	3455-N	$257.99	File Cabinet 2D	Office Medical	9	5677-A	$256.79	End Table	Med Furniture	7				

Supplier *Med Furniture* formatted in red and bold italic

Equipment Inventory   Administrative   Purchasing Information

Ready

FIGURE 10.36

Objective 6   Create Custom Headers and Footers

GO! Learn How
Video E10-6

You can create custom headers and footers to provide useful information about your worksheet. You can type your own text or insert header and footer elements such as pictures, page numbers, and the date and time.

Activity 10.14 | Creating Custom Headers and Footers

In this Activity, you will create a custom header by inserting a logo, text, and the date and time. You will create a custom footer by inserting Header & Footer Elements.

1 From the row heading area, click the **row 7** heading to select the row. On the **Home tab**, in the **Cells group**, click **Format**, under **Cell Size** click **Row Height**, and then in the **Row Height** box, replace the existing text with **30** and click **OK**.

2 Point to the **Administrative** sheet tab, right-click, and then click **Delete**. In the warning box, click **Delete**.

3 Click the **Equipment Inventory** sheet tab to display the worksheet, and then right-click the **Equipment Inventory** sheet tab. On the shortcut menu, click **Select All Sheets**.

4 With the worksheets grouped, on the **View tab**, in the **Workbook Views group**, click **Page Layout**, and then compare your screen with Figure 10.37.

Use Page Layout view to fine-tune your pages before printing. As in Normal view, you can change the layout and format of your data, but here you can also use the rulers to measure and get a better visual view of your headers and footers.

 ANOTHER WAY   On the status bar, on the right, click the Page Layout button .

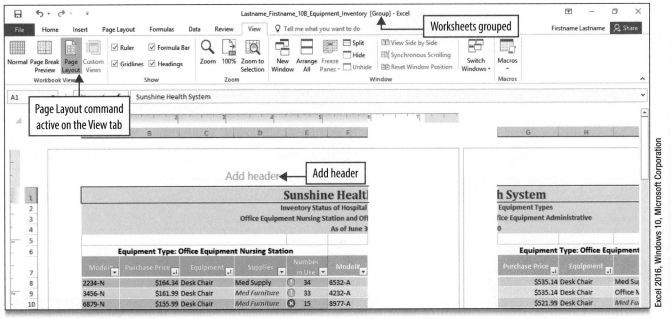

FIGURE 10.37

5 Click the text *Add header*. On the **Header & Footer Tools Design tab**, in the **Header & Footer Elements group**, click **Picture** 📷.

6 In the **Insert Pictures** dialog box, click **From a file**. In the **Insert Picture** dialog box, navigate to your student data files, click the file **e10B_Logo**, and then click **Insert**.

7 Click above *&[Picture]* outside of the box, and then compare your screen with Figure 10.38.

FIGURE 10.38

8 Click the logo, and then click in the left section under *Header*. Type **Created by Pat Shepard**

9 Press Tab two times to move to the right section. On the **Header & Footer Tools Design tab**, in the **Header & Footer Elements group**, click **Sheet Name**. Click above the header, and then compare your screen with Figure 10.39.

In the header, the logo displays in the center section, text displays in the left section, and the sheet name displays in the right section.

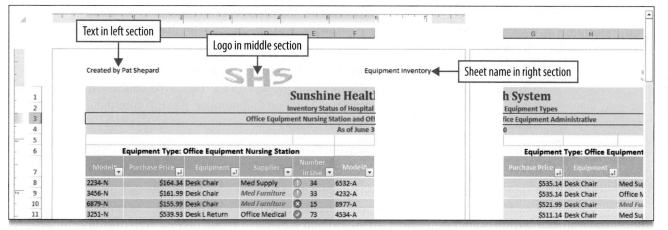

FIGURE 10.39   Excel 2016, Windows 10, Microsoft Corporation

10 Click anywhere in the header, click the **Header & Footer Design tab**, and then in the **Navigation group**, click **Go to Footer**.

11 Click in the left section, in the **Header & Footer Elements group**, click **File Name**. Click a cell just above the footer area to deselect, and then compare your screen with Figure 10.40.

In the footer, the file name displays in the left section.

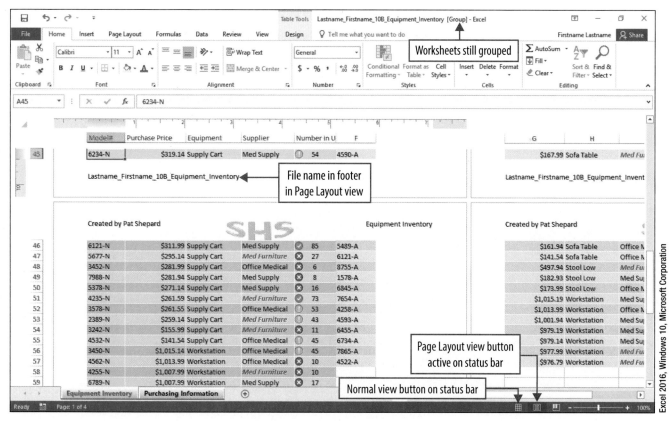

FIGURE 10.40

12 In the lower right corner of your screen, in the status bar, click **Normal** ⊞ to return to **Normal** view, and then press Ctrl + Home to display the top of your worksheet.

13 With the worksheets still grouped, on the **Page Layout tab**, click **Margins**, click **Custom Margins**, and then under **Center on page**, if necessary, click the **Horizontally** check box. Click **OK**.

14 Set the **Orientation** to **Landscape**. In the **Scale to Fit group**, set the **Width** to **1 page** and the **Height** to **1 page**. Display the **document properties**. As the **Tags**, type **equipment inventory** In the **Subject** box, type your course name and section number. Be sure your name displays as the author.

15 On the left, click **Print** to display the **Print Preview**. Scroll through the two worksheets. On the left, click **Save** to save your workbook and return to the workbook window.

16 Ungroup the worksheets. If directed by your instructor to do so, submit a paper printout of each of the two worksheets, an electronic image of each of your two worksheets that looks like a printed document, or your original Excel file. If required by your instructor, print or create an electronic version of your worksheets with formulas displayed. In the upper right corner of the Excel window, click **Close** ☒.

END | You have completed Project 10B

Andres Rodriguez/Fotolia; FotolEdhar/Fotolia; Andrey Popov/Fotolia; Shutterstock

MICROSOFT OFFICE SPECIALIST (MOS) SKILLS IN THIS CHAPTER

PROJECT 10A	PROJECT 10B
1.1.2 Import data from a delimited text file **1.4.1** Hide or unhide worksheets **1.4.2** Hide or unhide columns and rows **2.2.2** Modify cell alignment and indentation **3.1.2** Convert a table to a cell range **3.1.3** Add or remove table rows and columns **3.3.4** Remove duplicate records **4.3.1** Format text by using RIGHT, LEFT, and MID functions **4.3.2** Format text by using UPPER, LOWER, and PROPER functions **4.3.3** Format text by using the CONCATENATE function	**2.2.2** Expert: Create conditional formatting rules that use formulas **2.2.3** Expert: Manage conditional formatting rules

BUILD YOUR E-PORTFOLIO

An E-Portfolio is a collection of evidence, stored electronically, that showcases what you have accomplished while completing your education. Collecting and then sharing your work products with potential employers reflects your academic and career goals. Your completed documents from the following projects are good examples to show what you have learned: 10G, 10K, and 10L.

GO! FOR JOB SUCCESS

Career Passion

Your instructor may assign this topic to your class, and then ask you to think about, or discuss with your classmates, these questions:

When students talk about career plans, they inevitably hear advice like, "Follow your passion!" or "Do what you love and you'll be successful." But is that really true? Should everyone expect that following their dreams will lead to a successful career? Are you a failure if you don't follow your passion?

With millions of people unemployed but millions of jobs going unfilled, many career experts believe a new way of thinking about "passion" is needed. More realistic advice might be to find a passion for the job you have rather than struggling to find a job that fits your passion. A particular skill or area of knowledge will result in a successful career only if there is a need for it in the market—employers and customers must be willing to pay you to do it.

FotolEdhar/Fotolia

Do you think it's possible to be happy in a job or career that you are not passionate about, but that you like or are good at?

Do you think doing what you love is a requirement for a rewarding and successful career?

If you have a passion for an activity or cause, do you think it's realistic that you could make a living devoted to it, and do you think you would continue to be passionate about it if you had to do it for a living every day?

END OF CHAPTER

SUMMARY

Data can be imported into Excel from external sources such as webpages, databases, or text files. Cleaning up data includes removing duplicates, fixing spacing and case, and separating or merging fields.

A database is an organized collection of facts related to a specific topic or purpose. Excel's database functions such as DSUM, DAVERAGE, and DCOUNT can be used to perform calculations on the database.

You can insert a second table in a worksheet and sort data in side-by-side tables to compare data. Apply conditional formatting using icon sets to add visual emphasis to the conditional format of a list.

You can create custom headers and footers that include pictures; for example, a logo or a product picture. You can also insert elements such as the sheet name, the date, and text that you type.

GO! LEARN IT ONLINE

Review the concepts, key terms, and MOS skills in this chapter by completing these online challenges, which you can find in **MyITLab**.

Matching and Multiple Choice: Answer matching and multiple choice questions to test what you learned in this chapter.

Lessons on the GO!: Learn how to use all the new apps and features as they are introduced by Microsoft.

MOS Prep Quiz: Answer questions to review the MOS skills you practiced in this chapter.

PROJECT GUIDE FOR EXCEL CHAPTER 10

Your instructor will assign Projects from this list to ensure your learning and assess your knowledge.

	PROJECT GUIDE FOR EXCEL CHAPTER 10		
Project	**Apply Skills from These Chapter Objectives**	**Project Type**	**Project Location**
10A **MyITLab**	Objectives 1-3 from Project 10A	**10A Instructional Project (Grader Project)** Guided instruction to learn the skills in Project 10A.	In MyITLab and in text
10B **MyITLab**	Objectives 4-6 from Project 10B	**10B Instructional Project (Grader Project)** Guided instruction to learn the skills in Project 10B.	In MyITLab and in text
10C	Objectives 1-3 from Project 10A	**10C Skills Review (Scorecard Grading)** A guided review of the skills from Project 10A.	In text
10D	Objectives 4-6 from Project 10B	**10D Skills Review (Scorecard Grading)** A guided review of the skills from Project 10B.	In text
10E **MyITLab**	Objectives 1-3 from Project 10A	**10E Mastery (Grader Project)** **Mastery and Transfer of Learning** A demonstration of your mastery of the skills in Project 10A with extensive decision making.	In MyITLab in text
10F **MyITLab**	Objectives 4-6 from Project 10B	**10F Mastery (Grader Project)** **Mastery and Transfer of Learning** A demonstration of your mastery of the skills in Project 10B with extensive decision making.	In MyITLab and in text
10G **MyITLab**	Objectives 1-6 from Projects 10A and 10B	**10G Mastery (Grader Project)** **Mastery and Transfer of Learning** A demonstration of your mastery of the skills in Projects 10A and 10B with extensive decision making.	In MyITLab and in text
10H	Combination of Objectives from Projects 10A and 10B	**10H GO! Fix It (Scorecard Grading)** **Critical Thinking** A demonstration of your mastery of the skills in Projects 10A and 10B by creating a correct result from a document that contains errors you must find.	Instructor Resource Center (IRC) and MyITLab
10I	Combination of Objectives from Projects 10A and 10B	**10I GO! Make It (Scorecard Grading)** **Critical Thinking** A demonstration of your mastery of the skills in Projects 10A and 10B by creating a result from a supplied picture.	IRC and MyITLab
10J	Combination of Objectives from Projects 10A and 10B	**10J GO! Solve It (Rubric Grading)** **Critical Thinking** A demonstration of your mastery of the skills in Projects 10A and 10B, your decision-making skills, and your critical thinking skills. A task-specific rubric helps you self-assess your result.	IRC and MyITLab
10K	Combination of Objectives from Projects 10A and 10B	**10K GO! Solve It (Rubric Grading)** **Critical Thinking** A demonstration of your mastery of the skills in Projects 10A and 10B, your decision-making skills, and your critical thinking skills. A task-specific rubric helps you self-assess your result.	In text
10L	Combination of Objectives from Projects 10A and 10B	**10L GO! Think (Rubric Grading)** **Critical Thinking** A demonstration of your understanding of the Chapter concepts applied in a manner that you would outside of college. An analytic rubric helps you and your instructor grade the quality of your work by comparing it to the work an expert in the discipline would create.	In text
10M	Combination of Objectives from Projects 10A and 10B	**10M GO! Think (Rubric Grading)** **Critical Thinking** A demonstration of your understanding of the Chapter concepts applied in a manner that you would outside of college. An analytic rubric helps you and your instructor grade the quality of your work by comparing it to the work an expert in the discipline would create.	IRC and MyITLab
10N	Combination of Objectives from Projects 10A and 10B	**10N You and GO! (Rubric Grading)** **Critical Thinking** A demonstration of your understanding of the Chapter concepts applied in a manner that you would in a personal situation. An analytic rubric helps you and your instructor grade the quality of your work.	IRC and MyITLab

GLOSSARY

GLOSSARY OF CHAPTER KEY TERMS

Arguments The values that an Excel function uses to perform calculations or operations.

Compound criteria The use of two or more criteria on the same row—all conditions must be met for the records to be included in the results.

CONCATENATE A text function used to join up to 255 strings of characters.

Conditional formatting A format that changes the appearance of a cell—for example, by adding cell shading or font color—based on a condition; if the condition is true, the cell is formatted based on that condition, and if the condition is false, the cell is not formatted.

Data Facts about people, events, things, or ideas.

Data connection A link to external data that automatically updates an Excel workbook from the original data whenever the original data source gets new information.

Database An organized collection of facts related to a specific topic or purpose.

DAVERAGE function A function that determines an average in a database that is limited by criteria set for one or more cells.

DCOUNT function A function that counts the number of occurrences of a specified condition in a database.

Delimited A text file in which the text is separated by commas or tabs.

DSUM function A function that sums a column of values in a database that is limited by criteria set for one or more cells.

Extensible Markup Language (XML) A language that structures data in text files so that it can be read by other systems, regardless of the hardware platform or operating system.

Field A specific type of data such as name, employee number, or social security number that is stored in columns.

Filtering controls The arrows that display in the column titles of Excel data when the data is converted to a table and that enable you to sort and filter the data.

Flash Fill An Excel feature that predicts how to alter data based upon the pattern you enter into the cell at the beginning of the column. The data must be in the adjacent column to use Flash Fill.

Function A predefined formula that performs calculations by using specific values, called arguments, in a particular order or structure.

Get External Data A group of commands that enables you to bring data from an Access database, from the Web, from a text file, or from an XML file into Excel without repeatedly copying the data.

Icon set A set of three, four, or five small graphic images that make your data visually easier to interpret.

Information Data that has been organized in a useful manner.

LEFT A text function that returns the specified number of characters from the beginning (left) of a string of characters.

LOWER A text function that changes the case of the characters in a string, making all characters lowercase.

Microsoft Access A database program used to manage database files.

MID A text function that extracts a series of characters from a text string given the location of the beginning character.

PROPER A text function that capitalizes the first letter of each word.

Record A horizontal row in a database table that stores all of the data about one database item.

RIGHT A text function that returns the specified number of characters from the end (right) of a string of characters.

Schema An XML file that contains the rules for what can and cannot reside in an XML data file.

Syntax The arrangement of the arguments in a function.

Table Data stored in a format of rows and columns.

Text function A function that can be used to combine or separate data, change case, and apply formatting to a string of characters.

TRIM A text function that removes extra blank spaces from a string of characters.

UPPER A text function that changes the case of the characters in a string, making all characters uppercase.

Apply 10A skills from these Objectives:

1 Get External Data into Excel

2 Clean Up and Manage Imported Data

3 Use Database Functions

Skills Review | Project 10C Lab Information

In the following Skills Review, you will import data about lab department technicians, hematologists, blood bank services, and lab suppliers into Excel, and query the database to locate information. Your completed worksheets will look similar to Figure 10.41.

PROJECT FILES

For Project 10C, you will need the following files:

e10C_Hematologist_Information (Text Document)

e10C_Lab_Dept (Excel Workbook)

e10C_Lab_Supplies (XML Document)

e10C_Technician_Information (Access Database)

You will save your workbook as:

Lastname_Firstname_10C_Lab_Dept

PROJECT RESULTS

FIGURE 10.41

(Project 10C Lab Information continues on the next page)

1 Start Excel. On the left, click **Open Other Workbooks**. Click **Browse**, and then in the **Open** dialog box, navigate to the student data files that accompany this chapter. Open the Excel file **e10C_Lab_Dept**. Click the **File tab**, on the left, click **Save As**, click **Browse**, and then in the **Save As** dialog box, navigate to your **Excel Chapter 10** folder. Using your own name, save the file as **Lastname_Firstname_10C_Lab_Dept**

a. On the **Lab Tech Information** worksheet, click cell **A2**. On the **Data tab**, at the left end of the ribbon, click **Get External Data**, and then click **From Access**. In the **Select Data Source** dialog box, navigate to your student data files, click the Access file **e10C_Technician_Information**, and then click **Open**.

b. In the **Import Data** dialog box, be sure that **Table** is selected, and then click **OK**. **Merge & Center** the text in cell **A1** across the range **A1:I1**, and then apply the **Title** cell style. **Save** your workbook.

2 Display the **Lab Seminars** worksheet. Select the range **A2:B2**. On the **Home tab**, in the **Alignment group**, click **Center**, and then click **Middle Align**.

a. Select the range **A4:A7**, On the **Home tab**, in the **Alignment group**, click **Increase Indent** one time. Select the range **A8:A10**, and then click **Increase Indent** two times.

b. Select the range **A12:A13** and click **Increase Indent** one time. **Save** your workbook.

3 Display the **Hematologist Information** worksheet. Click in cell **A9**. On the **Data tab**, at the left end of the ribbon, click **Get External Data**, and then click **From Text**. In the **Import Text File** dialog box, navigate to your student data files, select the Text file **e10C_Hematologist_Information**, and then click **Import**. Click **Next**, click **Next** again, click **Finish**, and then click **OK**.

a. On the **Data tab**, in the **Connections group**, click **Connections** to open the **Workbook Connections** dialog box. Verify that two connections exist in the workbook, and then close the **Workbook Connections** dialog box.

4 With the **Hematologist Information** worksheet active, on the **Data tab**, in the **Data Tools group**, click **Remove Duplicates**.

a. In the **Remove Duplicates** dialog box, click **Unselect All**, verify that the *My data has headers* check box is selected, and then select the **Doctor ID** and **Department** check boxes. Click **OK**, and then click **OK** again.

5 Notice the City, State, and Zip are all in the same field in **column F**. Click the **column G** header, right-click, and then click **Insert** to insert a new column. Use the same method to insert two additional columns.

a. Click cell **G2**, type **City** and then press Tab. In cell **H2** type **State** press Tab, in cell **I2** type **Zip** and then press Enter.

b. In cell **G3**, type **Miami** and press Enter. In cell **G4** type **W** and then press Enter to have Flash Fill complete the column.

c. Click cell **H3** and type **FI** Use the fill handle to copy the text down through **H11**.

6 Click cell **I3**. On the **Formulas tab**, in the **Function Library group**, click **Text**, and then click **RIGHT**.

a. With the insertion point in the **Text** box, click cell **F3**. Press Tab, and then, in the **Num_chars** box, type **5** Click **OK**. Drag the **fill handle** to copy the function down through cell **I11**.

b. Click cell **H3**, in the **Function Library**, click **Text**, scroll down as necessary and then click **UPPER**. With the insertion point in the **Text** box, type **FL** and then click **OK**. Drag the fill handle to copy the function down through cell **H11**.

c. Click cell **K2** and type **Full Name** and then click cell **K3**. On the **Formulas tab**, in the **Function Library group**, click **Text**, and then click **CONCATENATE**. With the insertion point in the **Text1** box, click cell **B3**. Press Tab, in the **Text2** box type " and then press Spacebar. Type " and then press Tab. In the **Text3** box, click **C3**. Click **OK**. Use the **fill handle** to copy the function down through cell **K11**.

d. Click cell **A1**. **Merge & Center** the text across the range **A1:K1** and apply the **Title** cell style. **AutoFit columns A:K**. Click the **column F** heading, right-click, and then click **Hide**. **Save** your workbook.

(Project 10C Lab Information continues on the next page)

7 Display the **Lab Suppliers** worksheet. Click in cell **A2**. On the **Data tab**, at the left end of the ribbon, click **Get External Data**, click **From Other Sources**, and then click **From XML Data Import**.

a. In the **Select Data Source** dialog box, navigate to your student data files, click to select the XML file **e10C_Lab_Supplies**, and then click **Open**. Click **OK** to display the **Import Data** dialog box, and then click **OK**. **Merge & Center** the title in cell **A1** across the range **A1:D1**, and then apply the **Title** cell style. **Save** your workbook.

8 Display the **Lab Technicians** worksheet. In cell **A22**, type **Average Hourly Wage for Phlebotomists** and press Tab. **AutoFit column A**. Point to cell **C3**, right-click, and then click **Copy**. Scroll down, point to cell **C22**, right-click, and then click **Paste (P)**.

a. In cell **C23**, type **Phlebotomist** and press Tab. Click cell **B22**, and then to the left of the **Formula Bar**, click **Insert Function**. In the **Insert Function** dialog box, click the **Or select a category arrow**, and then on the list, click **Database**. In the **Select a function** box, click **DAVERAGE**, and then click **OK**.

b. In the **Function Arguments** dialog box, in the **Database** box, click **Collapse Dialog Box**, and then select the range **A3:F20**. Then, in the collapsed dialog box, click **Expand Dialog Box**. In the **Field** box, type **Hourly Wage** and press Tab. With the insertion point in the **Criteria** box, select the vertical range **C22:C23**. Click **OK**. Right-click cell **B22**, and then from the mini toolbar, apply **Accounting Number Format**.

9 In cell **A25**, type **Wage per Shift for Lab Technicians** and press Tab. Select and then copy the range **C3:D3**. Point to cell **C25** and right-click, and then click **Paste (P)**. In cell **C26**, type **Lab Technician** and press Tab. In cell **D26**, type **>0** and then press Enter.

a. Click cell **B25**, and then type **=dsum(** to begin the formula for the DSUM function. Select the range **A3:F20**, and then type **,** (a comma). Being sure to include the comma, type **"Wage per Shift",** to enter the second part of the argument. As indicated by *criteria* in the ScreenTip, type the criteria as **c25:d26**

and then press Enter. Right-click cell **B25** and apply **Accounting Number Format**.

10 In cell **A28**, type **Count Day Shift (Code 1, 3, 5)** and press Tab. Click cell **B3**, hold down Ctrl and click cell **D3**. Right-click either of the selected cells, and then click **Copy**. Scroll down, point to cell **C28**, right-click, and then click **Paste (P)**.

a. In cell **C29**, type **1** and press Tab. In cell **D29**, type **>0** and press Enter. In cell **C30**, type **3** and press Tab. In cell **D30**, type **>0** and press Enter. In cell **C31**, type **5** and press Tab. In cell **D31**, type **>0** and press Enter.

b. Click cell **B28**. To the left of the **Formula Bar**, click **Insert Function**. Click the **Or select a category arrow**, and then click **Database**. In the **Select a function** box, click **DCOUNT**, and then click **OK**.

c. In the **Function Arguments** dialog box, in the **Database** box, click **Collapse Dialog Box**. Move the collapsed box to the upper right corner of your screen. Scroll as necessary, and then select the range **A3:F20**. In the collapsed dialog box, click **Expand Dialog Box**.

d. In the **Field** box, type **Employee Number** and then press Tab. With the insertion point in the **Criteria** box, click **Collapse Dialog Box**, scroll as necessary, and then select the range **C28:D31**. In the collapsed dialog box, click **Expand Dialog**. Click **OK**.

11 Display the first worksheet—**Lab Tech Information**. In the sheet tab area, point to any sheet tab, right-click, and then click **Select All Sheets** to group the worksheets. On the **Page Layout tab**, click **Margins**, click **Custom Margins**, and then in the **Page Setup** dialog box, under **Center on page**, be sure the **Horizontally** check box is selected. Click the **Header/Footer tab**, click **Custom Footer**, and then in the **left section**, insert the **File Name**. Click **OK** two times.

a. With all the sheets still grouped, press Ctrl + Home to make cell **A1** the active cell. In the **Scale to Fit group**, set the **Width** to **1 page** and the **Height** to **1 page**. Display the **document properties**. As the **Tags**, type **lab department information** In the **Subject** box, type your course name and section number. Be sure your name displays as the author.

(Project 10C Lab Information continues on the next page)

b. On the left, click **Print** to display the **Print Preview**. Scroll through the five worksheets. On the left, click **Save** to save your workbook and return to the workbook window.

c. Ungroup the worksheets. If directed by your instructor to do so, submit a paper printout of each of the five worksheets, an electronic image of each of your five worksheets that looks like a printed document, or your original Excel file. If required by your instructor, print or create an electronic version of your worksheets with formulas displayed. In the upper right corner of the Excel window, click **Close**.

END | You have completed Project 10C

Apply 10B skills from these Objectives:

4 Insert a Second Table into a Worksheet

5 Apply Conditional Formatting to Side-by-Side Tables

6 Create Custom Headers and Footers

In the following Skills Review, you will edit a worksheet for Pat Shepard, Vice President of Operations, detailing the current inventory of two medical supply types. Your completed worksheets will look similar to Figure 10.42.

PROJECT FILES

For Project 10D, you will need the following files:

e10D_Logo

e10D_Medical_Supplies

You will save your workbook as:

Lastname_Firstname_10D_Medical_Supplies

PROJECT RESULTS

FIGURE 10.42

Excel 2016, Windows 10, Microsoft Corporation

(Project 10D Medical Supplies continues on the next page)

1 Start Excel. On the left, click **Open Other Workbooks**. Click **Browse**, and then in the **Open** dialog box, navigate to the student data files that accompany this chapter. Open the Excel file **e10D_Medical_Supplies**. Click the **File tab**, on the left, click **Save As**, click **Browse**, and then in the **Save As** dialog box, navigate to your **Excel Chapter 10** folder. Using your own name, save the file as **Lastname_Firstname_10D_Medical_Supplies**

a. On the **Medical Supplies Inventory** worksheet, select the range **A7:E62**, and then on the **Insert tab**, in the **Tables group**, click **Table**. In the **Create Table** dialog box, verify that *=$A$7:$E$62* displays as the data range and that the **My table has headers** check box is selected. Click **OK**.

b. Display the **Physician's Clinic** worksheet, select the range **A1:E52**, right-click over the selection, and then, click **Copy**. Display the **Medical Supplies Inventory** worksheet, scroll up as necessary, point to cell **F6** and right-click, and then, under **Paste Options**, click **Paste (P)**. Click any cell to deselect.

c. Select the range **F7:J57**. In the lower right corner of the selection, click **Quick Analysis**, click **Tables**, and then click **Table**. On the **Design tab**, in the **Table Styles group**, click **More** and then under **Medium**, click **Table Style Medium 13**.

2 Click any cell in the **Medical Supplies Hospital** table on the left. On the **Data tab**, click **Sort** to display the **Sort** dialog box.

a. In the **Sort** dialog box, under **Column**, click the **Sort by arrow**, and then click **Item**. Be sure **Sort On** indicates *Values* and **Order** indicates *A to Z*. In the upper left corner, click **Add Level**. Under **Column**, click the **Then by arrow**, and then click **Purchase Price**. On the same row, click the **Order arrow**, and then set the sort order to **Largest to Smallest**. Click **OK**.

b. Using the same technique and sort orders, sort the **Medical Supplies Physician's Clinic** table. AutoFit columns **A:J**.

3 Select the range **E8:E62**. On the **Home tab**, in the **Styles group**, click **Conditional Formatting**. Point to **Icon Sets**, and then under **Directional**, in the first row, click the first icon set—**3 Arrows (Colored)**. Click any cell to deselect.

a. Select the range **J8:J57** and then in the lower right corner of the selection click **Quick Analysis**. Click **Icon Set**.

b. Select the range **C8:C62**. On the **Home tab**, in the **Styles group**, click **Conditional Formatting**, and then at the bottom click **New Rule**. Under **Select a Rule Type**, click **Use a formula to determine which cells to format**.

c. In the **Format values where this formula is true** box type **=c8="Latex tubing"** and then in the lower right, click **Format**. Under **Font style** click **Bold italic**. Click the **color arrow**, and at the bottom under **Standard Colors**, click **Red**. Click **OK** two times.

4 From the row heading area, select **row 7**. On the **Home tab**, in the **Cells group**, click **Format**, click **Row Height**, and then set the **Row height** to **15** Click **OK**. Point to the **Physician's Clinic** sheet tab, right-click, and then click **Delete**. Click **Delete** a second time to confirm the deletion. Right-click the **Medical Supplies Inventory** sheet tab, and then click **Select All Sheets**. Click the **View tab**, and then in the **Workbook Views group**, click **Page Layout**. Scroll up if necessary, click the text *Add header*. On the **Header & Footer Tools Design tab**, in the **Header & Footer Elements group**, click **Picture**.

a. In the **Insert Pictures** dialog box, click **From a file**. In the **Insert Picture** dialog box, navigate to your student data files, click the file **e10D_Logo**, and then click **Insert**.

b. On the **Design tab**, in the **Navigation group**, click **Go to Footer**. Click in the **left section**, and then in the **Header & Footer Elements group**, click **File Name**. Click in any worksheet cell to deselect the footer. In the lower right corner of your screen, in the status bar, click **Normal** to return to **Normal** view, and then press Ctrl + Home to display the top of your worksheet.

5 With the worksheets still grouped, on the **Page Layout tab**, click **Margins**, click **Custom Margins**, and then under **Center on page**, if necessary, click the **Horizontally** check box. Click **OK**.

a. Set the **Orientation** to **Landscape**. In the **Scale to Fit group**, set the **Width** to **1 page** and the **Height** to **1 page**. Display the document properties. As the Tags, type **medical supplies inventory** In the

(Project 10D Medical Supplies continues on the next page)

Subject box, type your course name and section number. Be sure your name displays as the author.

b. On the left, click **Print** to display the **Print Preview**. Scroll through the two worksheets. On the left, click **Save** to save your workbook and return to the workbook window.

c. Ungroup the worksheets. If directed by your instructor to do so, submit a paper printout of each

of the two worksheets, an electronic image of each of your two worksheets that looks like a printed document, or your original Excel file. If required by your instructor, print or create an electronic version of your worksheets with formulas displayed. In the upper right corner of the Excel window, click **Close**.

END | You have completed Project 10D

<table>
<tr><td>

Apply 10A skills from these Objectives:

1 Get External Data into Excel

2 Clean Up and Manage Imported Data

3 Use Database Functions

</td></tr>
</table>

Mastering Excel | Project 10E ER Department

In the following Mastering Excel project, you will import data about Emergency department technicians, ER doctors, paramedic services, and emergency suppliers into Excel, and query the database to locate information. Your completed worksheets will look similar to Figure 10.43.

PROJECT FILES

For Project 10E, you will need the following files:

e10E_ER_Dept (Excel workbook)

e10E_ER_Doctors (Text Document)

e10E_ER_Staff (Access database)

You will save your workbook as:

Lastname_Firstname_10E_ER_Dept

PROJECT RESULTS

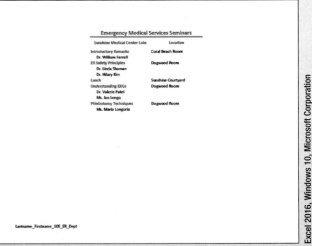

FIGURE 10.43

(Project 10E ER Department continues on the next page)

1 Start Excel. On the left, click **Open Other Workbooks**. Click **Browse**, and then in the **Open** dialog box, navigate to the student data files that accompany this chapter. Open the Excel file **e10E_ER_Dept**. Click the **File tab**, on the left, click **Save As**, click **Browse**, and then in the **Save As** dialog box, navigate to your **Excel Chapter 10** folder. Using your own name, save the file as **Lastname_Firstname_10E_ER_Dept**

2 On the **Emergency Staff** worksheet, insert a **DAVERAGE** function in cell **B22**. As the **Database**, use the range **a3:f20** As the **Field**, type **Hourly Wage** and as the **Criteria**, use the range **c22:c23**

3 In cell **B25**, enter a DSUM function using the database range **A3:F20**, type **Wage per Shift** as the field, and **c25:d26** as the criteria.

4 Apply **Accounting Number Format** to the results in cells **B22** and **B25**.

5 Display the **ER Staff Information** worksheet, and then click cell **A2**. From your student data files, import the data from the Access file **e10E_ER_Staff** as a table in the existing worksheet.

6 Display the **ER Doctors** worksheet; and then click cell **A6**. From your student data files import the text file **e10E_ER_Doctors** accepting all defaults in the Text Import Wizard.

7 Remove duplicate doctors (ER Doctor ID) from each unit (ER Unit).

8 Insert three new columns between **columns F:G**. In cell **G2**, type **City** and separate the City field using Flash Fill in **column G**. In cell **H2**, type **State** In cell **H3**, type **FL** and fill down. In cell **I2** type **Zip** Extract the Zip field from **column F** by using the **RIGHT** function in **column I**. **AutoFit** columns **A:J**. Hide **column F**.

9 In cell **K2** type **Full Name** and then in cell **K3** insert the **CONCATENATE** function to combine the text in

cell **B3** and **C3**. Be sure to construct the formula so that there is a space between the first and last names. Copy the formula down. **AutoFit column K**.

10 Display the **ER Seminars** worksheet. Center the titles in cells **A2** and **B2** vertically and horizontally. Indent the name of each presenter two times.

11 Display the first worksheet—**Emergency Staff**. In the sheet tab area, point to any sheet tab, right-click, and then click **Select All Sheets** to group the worksheets. On the **Page Layout tab**, click **Margins**, click **Custom Margins**, and then in the **Page Setup** dialog box, under **Center on page**, be sure the **Horizontally** check box is selected. Click the **Header/Footer tab**, click **Custom Footer**, and then in the **left section**, insert the **File Name**. Click **OK** two times.

12 With all the sheets still grouped, press Ctrl + Home to make cell **A1** the active cell. Set the **Orientation** to **Landscape**. In the **Scale to Fit group**, set the **Width** to **1 page** and the **Height** to **1 page**. Display the **document properties**. As the **Tags**, type **ER information** In the **Subject** box, type your course name and section number. Be sure your name displays as the author.

13 On the left, click **Print** to display the **Print Preview**. Scroll through the four worksheets. On the left, click **Save** to save your workbook and return to the workbook window. Ungroup the worksheets. If directed by your instructor to do so, submit a paper printout of each of the four worksheets, an electronic image of each of your four worksheets that looks like a printed document, or your original Excel file. If required by your instructor, print or create an electronic version of your worksheets with formulas displayed. In the upper right corner of the Excel window, click **Close**.

END | You have completed Project 10E

Mastering Excel Project 10F Beverage Supplies

In the following Mastering Excel project, you will edit a worksheet for Pat Shepard, Vice President of Operations, detailing the current inventory of two beverage supply types—Beverage Supplies Staff and Beverage Supplies Guests. Your completed worksheet will look similar to Figure 10.44.

PROJECT FILES

For Project 10F, you will need the following files:

e10F_Beverage_Supplies

e10F_Logo

You will save your workbook as:

Lastname_Firstname_10F_Beverage_Supplies

PROJECT RESULTS

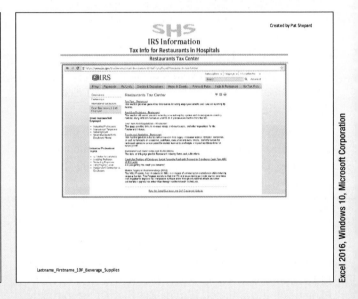

Excel 2016, Windows 10, Microsoft Corporation

FIGURE 10.44

(Project 10F Beverage Supplies continues on the next page)

1 Start Excel. On the left, click **Open Other Workbooks**. Click **Browse**, and then in the **Open** dialog box, navigate to the student data files that accompany this chapter. Open the Excel file **e10F_Beverage_Supplies**. Click the **File tab**, on the left, click **Save As**, click **Browse**, and then in the **Save As** dialog box, navigate to your **Excel Chapter 10** folder. Using your own name, save the file as **Lastname_Firstname_10F_Beverage_Supplies**

2 On the **Beverage Supplies Inventory** worksheet, insert a table using the range **A7:E30**.

3 Click the **Guests** sheet tab. Copy the range **A1:E20**, and then paste it into cell **F6** of the **Beverage Supplies Inventory** worksheet.

4 On the **Beverage Supplies Inventory** worksheet, format the data as a table using the range **F7:J25**; apply the **Medium 12** table style. Apply **AutoFit** to **columns H:I**.

5 Sort the **Beverage Supplies Type: Staff** table by **Item #, A to Z**. Add a second level sort by **Purchase Price, Largest to Smallest**.

6 Using the same sort orders, sort the **Beverage Supplies Type: Guests** table.

7 Select the range **E8:E30**. Apply conditional formatting to the range using the **3 Arrows (Colored)** directional icon set.

8 Use **Quick Analysis** to apply the default conditional formatting icon set to the range **J8:J25**.

9 In the range **C8:C30** create a new conditional formatting rule using the formula **=c8="Juice"** and setting the format to **Bold italic** with the **Red** font color.

10 Delete the **Guests** worksheet.

11 Group both worksheets, and then display the workbook in **Page Layout** view. In the middle section of the header, insert the picture **e10F_Logo**. In the right header section, type **Created by Pat Shepard** Move to the footer area and insert the **File Name** in the left section. Click any cell to close the Footer area, and then return to **Normal** view.

12 Press Ctrl + Home. With your two worksheets still grouped, set the **Orientation** to **Landscape**, set the **Width** to **1 page**, the **Height** to **1 page**, and center horizontally on the page.

13 Display the **document properties**. As the **Tags**, type **beverage supplies** In the **Subject** box, type your course name and section number. Be sure your name displays as the author.

14 On the left, click **Print** to display the **Print Preview**. Scroll through the two worksheets. On the left, click **Save** to save your workbook and return to the workbook window. Ungroup the worksheets. If directed by your instructor to do so, submit a paper printout of each of the two worksheets, an electronic image of each of your two worksheets that looks like a printed document, or your original Excel file. If required by your instructor, print or create an electronic version of your worksheets with formulas displayed. In the upper right corner of the Excel window, click **Close**.

END | You have completed Project 10F

Apply 10A and 10B skills from these Objectives:

1 Get External Data into Excel

2 Clean Up and Manage Imported Data

3 Use Database Functions

4 Insert a Second Table into a Worksheet

5 Apply Conditional Formatting to Side-by-Side Tables

6 Create Custom Headers and Footers

Mastering Excel Project 10G Pharmacy Department

In the following Mastering Excel project, you will import data about Pharmacy suppliers. You will edit a worksheet for Pat Shepard, Vice President of Operations, detailing the current inventory of two pharmacy supply types—Hospital and Physician's Clinic. Your completed worksheets will look similar to Figure 10.45.

PROJECT FILES

For Project 10G, you will need the following files:

e10G_Pharmacy_Suppliers (Access database)
e10G_Pharmacy_Supplies (Excel Workbook)

You will save your workbook as:

Lastname_Firstname_10G_Pharmacy_Supplies

PROJECT RESULTS

FIGURE 10.45

Excel 2016, Windows 10, Microsoft Corporation

(Project 10G Pharmacy Department continues on the next page)

Mastering Excel   Project 10G Pharmacy Department (continued)

1 Start Excel. On the left, click **Open Other Workbooks**. Click **Browse**, and then in the **Open** dialog box, navigate to the student data files that accompany this chapter. Open the Excel file **e10G_Pharmacy_Supplies**. Click the **File tab**, on the left, click **Save As**, click **Browse**, and then in the **Save As** dialog box, navigate to your **Excel Chapter 10** folder. Using your own name, save the file as **Lastname_Firstname_10G_Pharmacy_Supplies**

2 Ensure that the **Pharmacy Suppliers Info** worksheet is active. Select cell **A2** and import the data from the downloaded Access database named **e10G_Pharmacy_Suppliers**. Use the default options when importing the data.

3 Display the **Pharmacy Staff** worksheet. Insert a **DAVERAGE** function in cell **B18** that calculates the average **Hourly Wage** for pharmacists using the criteria in the range **C18:C19**. Apply **Accounting Number Format** to cell **B18**.

4 Insert a **DSUM** function in cell **B21** that calculates the **Wage per Shift** for pharmacy technicians using the criteria in cells **C21:D22**. Apply **Accounting Number Format** to cell **B21**.

5 Display the **Pharmacy Supplies Inventory** worksheet. Insert a table in the range **A7:E42**.

6 Display the **Physician's Clinic** worksheet and copy the range **A1:E32**. Display the **Pharmacy Supplies Inventory** worksheet, and paste the data into cell **F6**.

7 Insert a table in the range **F7:J37** and apply **Table Style Medium 7**. Apply AutoFit to **columns H:I**.

8 Sort both tables by **Model# A to Z** and then by **Purchase Price Largest to Smallest**.

9 Apply conditional formatting to the range **E8:E42** using the **3 Traffic Lights (Rimmed)** icon set.

10 Apply the same conditional formatting to the range **J8:J37**.

11 In the range **C8:C42** create a new conditional formatting rule using the formula **=c8="Pharmacy spill kit"** and setting the format to **Bold italic** with the **Red** font color.

12 Delete the **Physician's Clinic** worksheet. Group the remaining three worksheets.

13 Insert a header in the right section that displays the **Sheet Name**. Insert the **File Name** element in the left section of the footer. If necessary return to **Normal** view, and then press Ctrl + Home to make cell **A1** the active cell.

14 Center all three sheets horizontally on the page, and set the scaling of all sheets to 1 page wide by 1 page high. Set the **Orientation** to **Landscape**.

15 Display the **document properties**. As the **Tags**, type **pharmacy supplies** In the **Subject** box, type your course name and section number. Be sure your name displays as the author.

16 On the left, click **Print** to display the **Print Preview**. Scroll through the three worksheets. On the left, click **Save** to save your workbook and return to the workbook window. Ungroup the worksheets. If directed by your instructor to do so, submit a paper printout of each of the three worksheets, an electronic image of each of your three worksheets that looks like a printed document, or your original Excel file. If required by your instructor, print or create an electronic version of your worksheets with formulas displayed. In the upper right corner of the Excel window, click **Close**.

> **END | You have completed Project 10G**

CONTENT-BASED ASSESSMENTS (CRITICAL THINKING)

GO! Fix It	Project 10H Imaging Technicians	MyITLab

GO! Make It	Project 10I Snack Supplies	MyITLab

GO! Solve It	Project 10J Medical Imaging Suppliers	MyITLab

GO! Solve It	Project 10K Gift Shop Supplies

PROJECT FILES

For Project 10K, you will need the following file:

e10K_Gift_Shop

You will save your workbook as:

Lastname_Firstname_10K_Gift_Shop

Open the file **e10K_Gift_Shop** and save it as **Lastname_Firstname_10K_Gift_Shop** Insert a table in the Gift Shop Inventory worksheet for the range A7:E40. On the Clinic worksheet, remove duplicates, select and copy the remaining data, and then on the Gift Shop Inventory worksheet, paste it in the range beginning in cell F6. Insert a Table, and then apply Table Style Medium 13. AutoFit columns as necessary. Delete the Clinic worksheet. In each table's Quantity in Stock column, apply different conditional formatting icon sets. Convert each table to a Range. Insert the file name in the footer in the left section and the current date in the header right section. Set the orientation to landscape and center horizontally. Add appropriate information to the document properties including the tags **gift shop supplies, inventory** and submit as directed by your instructor.

Performance Level

Performance Criteria	Exemplary: You consistently applied the relevant skills	Proficient: You sometimes, but not always, applied the relevant skills	Developing: You rarely or never applied the relevant skills
Remove duplicate data	All duplicate data was removed.	Some duplicate data was removed.	Duplicate data was not removed.
Insert a Second Table in a Worksheet	A second table is inserted in a worksheet, and tables display side-by-side.	A second table is inserted in a worksheet, but tables do not display side-by-side.	A second table was not inserted in a worksheet.
Delete the Clinic worksheet	Clinic worksheet deleted.	N/A	Clinic worksheet was not deleted.
Apply Conditional Formatting to Side-by-Side Tables	Conditional Formatting Icon Sets, applied to the Quantity in Stock columns.	Conditional Formatting Icon Sets, applied to one but not the other Quantity in Stock column.	Conditional Formatting was not applied to the Quantity in Stock columns.
Convert a Table to a Range	The tables are converted to a range.	One, but not the other table, is converted to a range.	The tables are not converted to a range.
Header and footer information inserted	Header and footer correctly inserted.	Header and footer inserted but missing some information.	Header and footer not inserted.

End | You have completed Project 10K

OUTCOME-BASED ASSESSMENTS (CRITICAL THINKING)

RUBRIC

The following outcomes-based assessments are open-ended assessments. That is, there is no specific correct result; your result will depend on your approach to the information provided. Make Professional Quality your goal. Use the following scoring rubric to guide you in how to approach the problem and then to evaluate how well your approach solves the problem.

The *criteria*—Software Mastery, Content, Format and Layout, and Process—represent the knowledge and skills you have gained that you can apply to solving the problem. The *levels of performance*—Professional Quality, Approaching Professional Quality, or Needs Quality Improvements—help you and your instructor evaluate your result.

	Your completed project is of Professional Quality if you:	Your completed project is Approaching Professional Quality if you:	Your completed project Needs Quality Improvements if you:
1-Software Mastery	Choose and apply the most appropriate skills, tools, and features and identify efficient methods to solve the problem.	Choose and apply some appropriate skills, tools, and features, but not in the most efficient manner.	Choose inappropriate skills, tools, or features, or are inefficient in solving the problem.
2-Content	Construct a solution that is clear and well organized, contains content that is accurate, appropriate to the audience and purpose, and is complete. Provide a solution that contains no errors of spelling, grammar, or style.	Construct a solution in which some components are unclear, poorly organized, inconsistent, or incomplete. Misjudge the needs of the audience. Have some errors in spelling, grammar, or style, but the errors do not detract from comprehension.	Construct a solution that is unclear, incomplete, or poorly organized, contains some inaccurate or inappropriate content, and contains many errors of spelling, grammar, or style. Do not solve the problem.
3-Format and Layout	Format and arrange all elements to communicate information and ideas, clarify function, illustrate relationships, and indicate relative importance.	Apply appropriate format and layout features to some elements, but not others. Overuse features, causing minor distraction.	Apply format and layout that does not communicate information or ideas clearly. Do not use format and layout features to clarify function, illustrate relationships, or indicate relative importance. Use available features excessively, causing distraction.
4-Process	Use an organized approach that integrates planning, development, self-assessment, revision, and reflection.	Demonstrate an organized approach in some areas, but not others; or, use an insufficient process of organization throughout.	Do not use an organized approach to solve the problem.

OUTCOMES-BASED ASSESSMENTS (CRITICAL THINKING)

GO! Think   Project 10L Facilities Pay

PROJECT FILES

For Project 10L, you will need the following file:

e10L_Facilities_Pay

You will save your workbook as:

Lastname_Firstname_10L_Facilities_Pay

Open the file **e10L_Facilities_Pay**, and then save it in your chapter folder as **Lastname_Firstname_10L_Facilities_Pay** In this project, you will use a worksheet that contains payroll information for the facilities staff. You will calculate the average pay and count how many employees have worked for the hospital for over five years.

In rows 26-27, enter the criteria and a DAVERAGE function to determine the average wage for housekeeping. Apply Currency Style to the result. In rows 29-30, enter the criteria and a DCOUNT function to count the number of employees hired prior to 1/1/2010.

Insert the file name in the left section of the footer and the current date in the right section of the header. Set orientation to landscape and center horizontally. Set width and height to 1 page. Add appropriate information to the document properties, including the tags **facilities pay** and submit as directed by your instructor.

END | You have completed Project 10L

GO! Think   Project 10M Institutes of Health   MyITLab

You and GO!   Project 10N Budget   MyITLab

Build from
Scratch

Collaborating with Others and Preparing a Workbook for Distribution

| PROJECT 11A | OUTCOMES Assemble changes from multiple sources to collaborate with others. | PROJECT 11B | OUTCOMES Inspect a workbook, prepare a workbook for distribution, and store a workbook in the Cloud. |

OBJECTIVES

1. Create a Shared Workbook
2. Track Changes Made to a Workbook
3. Merge Workbooks and Accept Changes

OBJECTIVES

4. Inspect a Workbook
5. Prepare a Final Workbook for Distribution

Antonioguillem/Fotolia

In This Chapter

GO! to Work with Excel

In this chapter, you will assemble changes from multiple sources to collaborate with others. The process of collaborating typically involves sending a worksheet to others and asking each person to review the worksheet and make changes or add comments. Changes can be tracked and then accepted or rejected. Additionally, you will compare two different versions of a workbook and merge them together.

You will also prepare a final workbook for distribution, inspect the workbook for hidden information, add security by encrypting the workbook with a password, and digitally sign the workbook.

The projects in this chapter relate to **Capital Cities Community College**, which provides high quality education and professional training to residents in the cities surrounding the nation's capital. Its five campuses serve over 50,000 students and offer more than 140 programs, including associate degrees, certifications, and continuing education courses. Over 1,700 faculty and staff make student success a top priority. Capital Cities Community College makes positive contributions to the community through cultural and athletic programs, health care, economic development activities, and partnerships with businesses and non-profit organizations.

PROJECT
11A

Summer Schedule

MyITLab
Project 11A Training
Project 11A Grader

PROJECT ACTIVITIES

In Activities 11.01 through 11.10, you will create a shared workbook so that it can be reviewed by the different department chairpersons in the college's Business Division. Various individuals in the Business Division will be able to edit and comment on the information in the workbook. Your completed workbook will look similar to Figure 11.1.

Please always review the downloaded Grader instructions before beginning.

PROJECT FILES

MyITLab
grader

If your instructor wants you to submit Project 11A in the MyITLab Grader system, log in to MyITLab, locate Grader Project 11A, and then download the files for this project.

For Project 11A, you will need the following files:

e11A_Draft
e11A_Summer_Schedule

You will save your documents as:

Lastname_Firstname_11A_Summer_Schedule
Lastname_Firstname_11A_Summer_Schedule - Copy

PROJECT RESULTS

GO!
Walk Thru
Project 11A

FIGURE 11.1 Project 11A Summer Schedule

	NOTE	If You Are Using a Touchscreen
	Tap an item to click it.	
	Press and hold for a few seconds to right-click; release when the information or commands displays.	
	Touch the screen with two or more fingers and then pinch together to zoom out or stretch your fingers apart to zoom in.	
	Slide your finger on the screen to scroll—slide left to scroll right and slide right to scroll left.	
	Slide to rearrange—similar to dragging with a mouse.	
	Swipe to select—slide an item a short distance with a quick movement—to select an item and bring up commands, if any.	

Objective 1 Create a Shared Workbook

GO! Learn How
Video E11-1

In Excel, ***collaboration*** refers to the process of working jointly with others to review, comment on, and make necessary changes to a shared workbook. A ***shared workbook*** is a workbook set up to allow multiple users on a network to view and make changes to the workbook at the same time. Typically the users are on an ***intranet***, which is a network within an organization and that uses Internet technologies. When the collaboration process is complete, as the owner of the shared workbook, you can accept or reject the input suggested by others.

Activity 11.01 │ Locating and Modifying Workbook Properties

Recall that every Excel workbook file has ***properties***, which are details about a file that describe or identify the file, including the title, author name, subject, and tags that identify the file's topic or contents—also known as ***metadata***. Properties also include the size and location of the file. You can change file properties before the file is distributed so that the recipients will know who distributed the file. Some property information displays when you point to a file in a list of files, such as in File Explorer or in the Open dialog box.

> **ALERT!** To submit as an autograded project, log into MyITLab and download the files for this Project, and begin with those files instead of e11A_Summer_Schedule.

1 Start Excel. From your student files, open the file **e11A_Summer_Schedule**. Display the **Save As** dialog box, navigate to the location where you are storing your files for this chapter, and then create a new folder named **Excel Chapter 11 Save** the file in your **Excel Chapter 11** folder as **Lastname_Firstname_11A_Summer_Schedule**

This workbook contains three worksheets listing the proposed summer classes for three departments in the Liberal Arts Division.

2 Group the worksheets, and then insert a footer with the file name in the **left section** and the sheet name in the **right section**, and if necessary, return to **Normal** view and press Ctrl + Home to move to the top of the sheet. Set the **Orientation** to **Landscape**.

3 Click the **File tab** to display **Backstage** view. On the **Info tab**, at the top of the screen, notice that the location of this file on your computer displays under the file name. On the right, notice that some of the more common properties for this file display, for example, the file *Size* and *Author*.

4 Under **Properties**, point to the text *Add a title*, and then click one time. Type **Proposed Summer Schedule** and then compare your screen with Figure 11.2.

Recall some of the properties displayed on the Info tab can be changed. For example, you can add a *Title*, add *Tags*, and add *Categories*.

FIGURE 11.2

5 Under **Related People**, point to the text *Jason Klein*, who is the author, to display the **Contact Card**, and then compare your screen with Figure 11.3.

In a networked environment, from this Contact Card you could send an e-mail to this individual, initiate an IM (Instant Messaging) session, schedule a meeting in Outlook, or look up contact information such as a phone number.

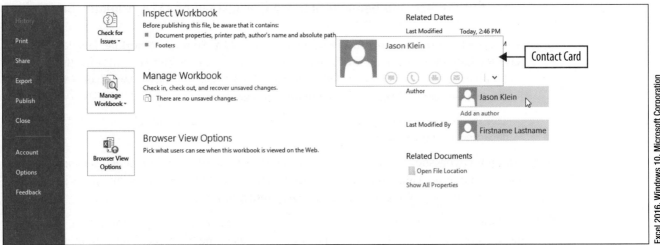

FIGURE 11.3

6 ▸ Move the mouse pointer away from the **Contact Card**, near the top right of the Info pane click the **Properties arrow**, click **Advanced Properties**, and then in the dialog box, if necessary click the **General tab**.

In the Properties dialog box for a file, there are additional properties that you can view and change. Here, on the General tab, you can see the date the file was last accessed. The Attributes area is dimmed because these properties cannot be changed while the file is open.

7 ▸ Click the **Summary tab**.

The Author name *Jason Klein* was generated from the computer on which the file was originally created. If you receive a file from someone else, which you then modify and use, the original author's name remains with the file, even when you save the file with a new name. If you want your name, division, or company to be associated with the file, change the information located here. Information entered here can also be used by search engines to help locate files.

8 ▸ In the **Author** box, delete *Jason Klein,* type **Fred Nicholas** and then press ⌨Tab. In the **Manager** box, type **Dean Massaro, Liberal Arts Division** Compare your screen with Figure 11.4.

FIGURE 11.4

9 ▸ Click **OK**. Click **Save** to save your workbook and return to the worksheet.

More **Knowledge**   **Read-only Property**

One of the attributes that displays in the Properties dialog box is the Read-only property. Recall that when this property is selected, the file can be read or copied, but it cannot be changed or saved. This property cannot be set while the file is open. To change a file to Read-only, display the file list in File Explorer, right-click the file name, and then click Properties. In the Properties dialog box, select the Read-only attribute, and then click OK. When the file is opened, [Read-only] will display in the title bar, which indicates that the file cannot be changed or saved. If you need to use a Read-only file, you must save it with a new file name, which preserves the original file.

Activity 11.02 | Making Edits in a Foreign Language and Inserting a Watermark Image

When you share a workbook with others, it is helpful to include a watermark that indicates the document is a draft. A ***watermark*** is a faded image or text used as a background of a document. Excel does not include a feature to add an automatic watermark, but you can create one by using an image as the worksheet background. Many of the instructors in the Foreign Language department have names that use foreign characters. In the following Activity, you will insert a background image in the workbook and use the Symbol dialog box to insert foreign characters into a cell.

Both of these tasks must be done before you share the file, as inserting symbols and other objects is disabled in a shared file.

1 Point to the **Foreign Language sheet tab**, right-click, and then click **Ungroup Sheets**. With the **Foreign Language** worksheet active, on the **Page Layout tab**, in the **Page Setup group**, click **Background**. In the **Insert Pictures** dialog box, click **From a file**.

2 In the **Sheet Background** dialog box, navigate to your student data files, click the file **e11A_Draft** and then click **Insert**. **Save** 💾 your workbook and compare your screen with Figure 11.5.

When you share a workbook with others, it is helpful to include a watermark that indicates the document is a draft. The ***background image*** is behind, not in, the worksheet cells.

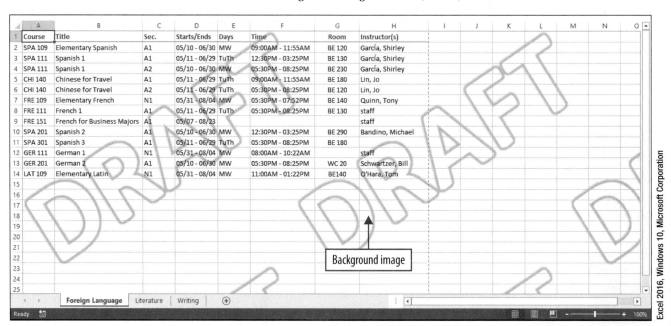

FIGURE 11.5

3 On the **Foreign Language** worksheet, click cell **H11**, type **Pe** and then on the **Insert tab**, in the **Symbols group**, click **Symbol**. If necessary, drag the Symbol dialog box up so that cell H11 is visible. In the **Symbol** dialog box, click the **Font arrow**, and then drag the scroll box to the top. Click **(normal text)**. Click the **Subset arrow**, and then click **Latin-1 Supplement**. Click the **scrollbar arrows** as necessary to locate the symbol **ñ—Latin Small Letter N With Tilde**. Click **ñ** and compare your screen with Figure 11.6.

FIGURE 11.6

> **4** Click **Insert**, and then click **Close**. Type **a, Dar** and then display the **Symbol** dialog box. Verify that the Latin-1 Supplement subset is selected, scroll up one row, and insert the symbol **ì—Latin Small Letter I With Grave. Close** the **Symbol** dialog box, type **o** and then press (Enter).

> **5** **Save** your workbook and then compare your screen with Figure 11.7.

> The Symbol dialog box is used to insert symbols such as foreign language letters, currency symbols, and other special characters.

9	FRE 151	French for Business Majors	A1	05/07 - 08/23				staff	
---	---------	----------------------------	-----	---------------	---------------------	------	--------	----------------	
10	SPA 201	Spanish 2	A1	05/10 - 06/30	MW	12:30PM - 03:25PM	BE 290	Bandino, Michael	Peña, Darìo entered in cell H11
11	SPA 301	Spanish 3	A1	05/11 - 06/29	TuTh	05:30PM - 08:25PM	BE 180	Peña, Darìo	
12	GER 111	German 1	N1	05/31 - 08/04	MW	08:00AM - 10:22AM		staff	
13	GER 201	German 2	A1	05/10 - 06/30	MW	05:30PM - 08:25PM	WC 20	Schwartzer, Bill	
14	LAT 109	Elementary Latin	N1	05/31 - 08/04	MW	11:00AM - 01:22PM	BE140	O'Hara, Tom	

FIGURE 11.7

Excel 2016, Windows 10, Microsoft Corporation

More Knowledge

If you regularly need to work in a foreign language in Excel, you can set the Office Language Preferences from the Excel Options dialog box Language tab. This sets the editing preferences for all of the installed Microsoft Office applications.

Activity 11.03 | Activating Track Changes to Create a Shared Workbook

When you share a workbook with others, you control the collaboration process by using Excel's **Track Changes** feature, which logs details about workbook changes including insertions and deletions. When you activate the Track Changes feature, the workbook automatically becomes a shared workbook.

> **1** On the **Review tab**, in the **Changes group**, click **Track Changes**, and then click **Highlight Changes**.

> **2** In the **Highlight Changes** dialog box, click to select the **Track Changes while editing** check box, which activates the Track Changes feature and saves the file as a shared workbook.

> **3** Verify that the **When** check box is selected and indicates *All*. Select the **Who** check box and be sure *Everyone* is indicated. Verify that the **Highlight changes on screen** check box is selected, and then compare your screen with Figure 11.8.

> Use onscreen highlighting when there are minimal changes in the workbook or when you want to see, at a glance, what has changed.

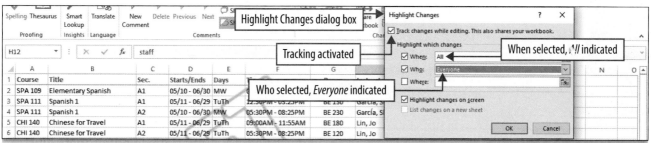

FIGURE 11.8

Excel 2016, Windows 10, Microsoft Corporation

> **4** Click **OK**.

> A message box displays, informing you that this action will save the workbook.

> **5** Click **OK** to continue.

> The workbook is saved, and *[Shared]* displays on the title bar. The file is ready to be shared with others who will make changes to the proposed summer schedule.

> **6** On the **File tab**, click **Close** to close the file and leave Excel open.

GO! Learn How
Video E11-2

As others make changes to a shared workbook, you can view and track the changes they make by viewing the details in the **change history**—information that is maintained about changes made in past editing sessions. The information includes the name of the person who made each change, when the change was made, and what data was changed. After the changes are recorded, you can review the shared file and accept or reject the changes.

Activity 11.04 | Making a Copy of a Shared Workbook

For individuals who do not have access to the network, make a copy of the shared workbook and send it to them by email. After changes are made to this copy of the shared workbook, it can be returned and merged with the original shared workbook. In this manner, you can view all the changes made by reviewers—even from reviewers who did not have access to the shared workbook. In the following Activity, you will make a copy of the shared workbook for Kyle Messina, Chair of the Writing Department, because he will not have access to the college's network during the review period.

1 Display the **Open** dialog box. Navigate to your **Excel Chapter 11** folder, point to your **Lastname_Firstname_11A_Summer_Schedule** file, right-click, and then, click **Copy**.

2 Right-click in an empty space below or to the right of the file list, and then click **Paste**. If necessary, point to the border between the Name and Date modified columns to display the ⊞ pointer, and then, drag the border to the right to display the complete file names. Compare your screen with Figure 11.9.

A copy of the shared file is created and is named *Lastname_Firstname_11A_Summer_Schedule - Copy*.

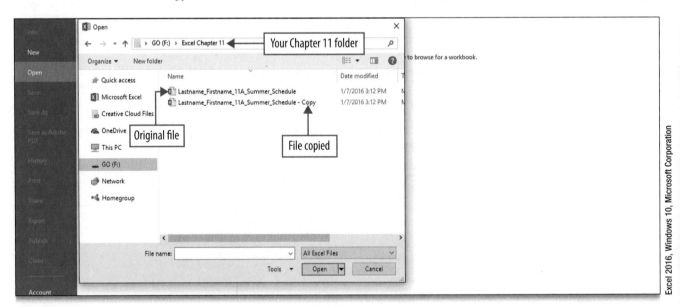

FIGURE 11.9

3 In the **Open** dialog box, click **Cancel**.

Activity 11.05 | Making Changes to a Shared Workbook

Each department's chairperson needs to review the summer schedule and make any necessary changes. In the following Activity, you will open the file and make the changes for Ryan Woodward, Chair of the Literature Department and Claudette Fischer, Chair of the Language Department.

1 Open your **Lastname_Firstname_11A_Summer_Schedule** file—open the original, *not* the copy that you made.

Notice that the title bar displays *[Shared]* at the end of the file name.

2 On the **File tab**, click **Options**. In the **Excel Options** dialog box, on the left, verify **General** is selected.

The Excel Options dialog box displays, and under Personalize your copy of Microsoft Office, the *User name* assigned to your computer displays.

3 Under **Personalize your copy of Microsoft Office**, click in the **User name** box.

Notice the name that displays as you may need to reset the User name upon completion of this project.

4 Select the User name text, type **Ryan Woodward, Literature** to replace the selected User name text. Compare your screen with Figure 11.10.

From this point forward, any changes made to the file will display this user name until you change the User name again.

NOTE	Changing the User Name

Under normal circumstances, you would not change the user name. The person making changes would be using his or her own computer, which would already display their name in the User name box. In this Project, you are changing the user name for instructional purposes.

FIGURE 11.10

5 Click **OK** to close the **Excel Options** dialog box.

6 Display the **Literature** worksheet. Click cell **H10**, begin to type **Sanchez, Christina** and press [Enter] to accept the AutoComplete suggestion to change the name. In cell **H11**, change the name to **Patel, Ash** Press [Ctrl] + [Home] to move to cell **A1**, and then compare your screen with Figure 11.11. The instructor for two literature courses is changed.

FIGURE 11.11

7 ▶ On the **Review tab**, in the **Changes group**, click **Track Changes**, and then click **Highlight Changes**. In the **Highlight Changes** dialog box, click the **When arrow**, and then click **All**. Select the **Who** check box, and be sure that it indicates *Everyone*. Click **OK**.

> By activating Highlight Changes, the two cells changed by Ryan Woodward are outlined in blue with a Track Changes indicator shown in the upper left corner of each cell.

8 ▶ Point to cell **H11** to view the ScreenTip, which indicates the change that was made and the date and time the change was made. Compare your screen with Figure 11.12.

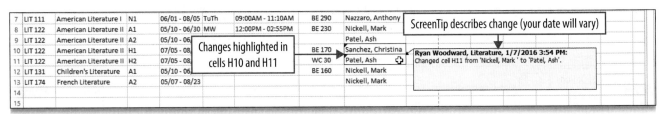

FIGURE 11.12

9 ▶ Save 🖫 your workbook. On the **File tab** click **Close** to close the file and leave Excel open.

> To change the user name for the next set of changes, you must close and then reopen the file.

Activity 11.06 | **Making Changes to a Copy of the Shared Workbook**

Recall that a copy of the shared workbook was prepared for Kyle Messina, Chair of the Writing Department. In this Activity, you will make Mr. Messina's changes on his copy of the shared workbook.

1 ▶ Open the **Lastname_Firstname_11A_Summer_Schedule - Copy** file that you created earlier.

> Notice that the title bar displays *Copy [Shared]* at the end of the file name.

2 ▶ On the **File tab**, click **Options** to display the **Excel Options** dialog box, and then using the technique you practiced, change the **User name** to **Kyle Messina, Writing** and then click **OK**.

3 ▶ Display the **Writing** worksheet. Click cell **F3** and type **Online** Click cell **F5**, type **Online** and then press Enter. Press Ctrl + Home.

> This completes the changes made by Mr. Messina.

4 ▶ Save 🖫 your workbook. On the **File tab**, click **Close** to close the file and leave Excel open.

GO! Learn How
Video E11-3

After others make changes to the shared workbook, you can view and then accept or reject their changes. When more than one copy of the shared workbook contains marked changes, first merge the workbooks so that you can view everyone's changes in a single workbook.

Activity 11.07 | Merging Revisions

Recall that because he was not connected to the network, the Chair of the Writing Department made his changes on a separate copy of the shared workbook. In this Activity, you will merge the two workbooks so that you can view everyone's changes in a single workbook.

1 On the **File tab**, click **Options** to display the **Excel Options** dialog box, and then change the **User name** to **Dean Massaro** Click **OK** to close the dialog box, and then open your **Lastname_Firstname_11A_Summer_Schedule** file.

The Dean of the Liberal Arts Division must review the changes before the file is submitted to the Vice President for final schedule preparation.

2 Display the **Foreign Language** worksheet, on the **Review tab**, in the **Changes group**, click **Track Changes**, and then click **Highlight Changes**.

3 In the **Highlight Changes** dialog box, click the **When arrow**, and then click **All**. Click the **Who arrow**, and then click **Everyone but Me**. Compare your screen with Figure 11.13.

By selecting *Everyone but Me*, you can accept or reject changes without your own actions being recorded as a change. A Track Changes indicator displays in the upper left corner of the cells that were changed on this worksheet, and the cells display a colored border.

FIGURE 11.13

4 Click **OK**. Display the **Literature** worksheet and notice the borders around cells **H10** and **H11** indicating that changes have been made.

5 Display the **Writing** worksheet, and notice that no changes are indicated because changes for this department were made on another copy of the shared workbook.

6 On the **File tab**, click **Options** to display the **Excel Options** dialog box, and then on the left, click **Quick Access Toolbar**.

7 At the top of the dialog box, under **Customize the Quick Access Toolbar**, click the **Choose commands from arrow**, and then click **Commands Not in the Ribbon**. In the list below, scroll as necessary, click **Compare and Merge Workbooks**, in the center click **Add**, and then compare your screen with Figure 11.14.

ANOTHER WAY   To the right of the Quick Access Toolbar, click More ▾, under Customize Quick Access Toolbar, click More commands to open the Excel Options dialog box.

FIGURE 11.14

8 Click **OK**. On the **Quick Access Toolbar**, click **Compare and Merge Workbooks** ◉. In the **Select Files to Merge Into Current Workbook** dialog box, if necessary, navigate to your **Excel Chapter 11** folder. Compare your screen with Figure 11.15.

Here you select the workbook to be merged into the open workbook.

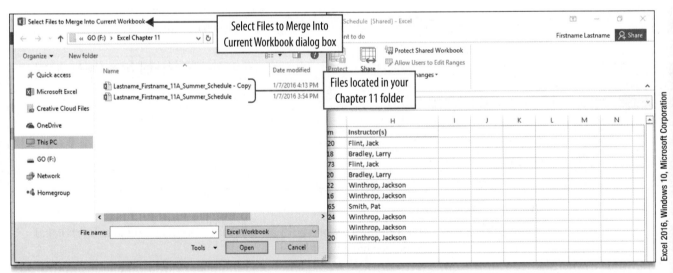

FIGURE 11.15

9 Click your **Lastname_Firstname_11A_Summer_Schedule - Copy** file—if necessary, adjust the Name column to display the complete file name. Click **OK**, and then compare your screen with Figure 11.16.

After a moment, a border displays around cells F3 and F5 on the Writing sheet, and the changes from the file Lastname_Firstname_11A_Summer_Schedule - Copy are merged into the original file.

FIGURE 11.16

Excel 2016, Windows 10, Microsoft Corporation

Activity 11.08 | Accepting or Rejecting Tracked Changes

Now that each person's changes have been incorporated into one copy of the workbook, you can review each change and decide whether to accept the change and keep the new value or to reject the change and keep the cell's original value. After a proposed change is accepted or rejected, the tracking notation is removed from the cell.

1 Display the **Foreign Language** worksheet. On the **Review tab**, in the **Changes group**, click **Track Changes**, and then click **Accept/Reject Changes**.

The Select Changes to Accept or Reject dialog box displays. Here you set the parameters for reviewing changes.

2 Verify that the **When** box indicates *Not yet reviewed*. Change the **Who** box to indicate **Everyone**, and then click **OK**. Compare your screen with Figure 11.17.

The Accept or Reject Changes dialog box displays, and the first changed cell is surrounded by a moving border. If necessary, drag the dialog box so you can view the changed cell.

FIGURE 11.17

Excel 2016, Windows 10, Microsoft Corporation

3 Click **Accept** to accept the change of instructor in cell H10 to *Sanchez, Christina*.

The change is accepted and the next changed cell displays a moving border. The Accept or Reject Changes dialog box displays the information for the change in cell H11—from *Nickell, Mark* to *Patel, Ash*.

4 Click **Accept**. Compare your screen with Figure 11.18.

The change is accepted and the next change on the Writing sheet is selected.

FIGURE 11.18

> 5 ▶ Click **Reject**, and then **Reject** the last change—a change in cell F5 to *Online*. Compare your screen with Figure 11.19.
>
> All the changes have been reviewed, and the Accept or Reject Changes dialog box closes.

FIGURE 11.19

> 6 ▶ **Save** 🖫 your workbook.

Activity 11.09 | Removing the Shared Designation, Resetting the User Name, and Removing a Command from the Quick Access Toolbar

After the changes have been reviewed and before the workbook is published, the Shared designation must be removed from the workbook. Removing the Shared designation will also turn off the Track Changes feature and remove the tracking indicators. Because you changed the User name for this project, you will also restore your computer's original User name.

> 1 ▶ On the **Review tab**, in the **Changes group**, click **Share Workbook**. Compare your screen with Figure 11.20.
>
> The Share Workbook dialog box displays and indicates the name of the person who is currently using the file—*Dean Massaro*.

FIGURE 11.20

2 Clear the **Allow changes by more than one user at the same time** check box, and then click **OK**. In the **Microsoft Excel** information box, click **Yes**.

> The dialog box closes, *[Shared]* no longer displays on the title bar, and the tracking indicators are removed from the changed cells.

3 On the **File tab**, click **Options** to display the **Excel Options** dialog box, click in the **User name** box. Select the text *Dean Massaro*, and then type the original user name for your system. Click **OK** to restore the original User name.

4 On the **Quick Access Toolbar**, right-click **Compare and Merge Workbooks** ◉, and then click **Remove from Quick Access Toolbar**.

Activity 11.10 │ Adding a Signature Line

A *digital signature* is an electronic, encrypted, stamp of authentication. A digital signature is a means of proving identity and authenticity that ensures that a file originated from the signer and has not been changed.

You must have a current *digital certificate*, which proves identity, to digitally sign an Office document. You can obtain a digital certificate from a *certificate authority*, which is a commercial organization that issues digital certificates, keeps track of who is assigned to a certificate, signs certificates to verify their validity, and tracks which certificates are revoked or expired. Institutions, governments, and corporations can also issue their own digital certificates. A digital certificate works by providing a cryptographic key pair that is associated with a digital signature.

A digital certificate authenticates—verifies that people and products are who and what they claim to be—the digital signature. A digital signature helps to assure that the signer is who they claim to be, helps to assure that the document content has not been changed or tampered with since it was digitally signed, and helps to prove to all parties the origin of the signed content. It cannot be repudiated—the signer cannot deny association with the signed content.

A digital signature may be visible or invisible. In either case, the digital signature references a digital certificate, which authenticates the source of the signature. When you create your own certificate, it is referred to as a *self-signed* project. Certificates you create yourself are considered unauthenticated; however, self-signed projects are considered safer to open than those with no certificates at all. In this Activity, you will create a digital signature line for the Summer Schedule workbook.

1 If necessary, display the Foreign Language worksheet, and then click cell **A16**. On the **Insert tab**, in the **Text group**, click the **Signature Line arrow** ⬛▾, and then click **Microsoft Office Signature Line**. Compare your screen with Figure 11.21.

> The Signature Setup dialog box displays. A *signature line* specifies the individual who must sign the document. Inserting an actual digital signature requires that you obtain a digital ID.

FIGURE 11.21

Excel 2016, Windows 10, Microsoft Corporation

> **2** In the **Signature Setup** dialog box, with the insertion point blinking in the **Suggested signer** box and *using your own name*, type **Firstname Lastname** and then click **OK**. Compare your screen with Figure 11.22.
>
> > The signature line with a large X displays on the worksheet. *Firstname Lastname* displays below the signature line.

FIGURE 11.22

Excel 2016, Windows 10, Microsoft Corporation

> **3** Right-click the **Foreign Language sheet tab**, and then click **Select All Sheets**. On the **Page Layout tab**, set the **Width** to **1 page**. Center the worksheets horizontally on the page. Display the **document properties** and under **Related People**, right-click the author name, click **Edit Property**, and then type your name. In the **Subject** box, type your course name and section number, and in the **Tags** box, type **summer courses**
>
> **4** **Save** your workbook. If directed by your instructor to do so, submit your paper printout, your electronic image of your document that looks like a printed document, or your original Excel file. In the upper right corner of the Excel window, click **Close** ☒.

ALERT! If you are submitting your project in the MyITLab grader system, submit your Lastname_Firstname_11A_Summer_Schedule file. Do not submit the copy.

> END | You have completed Project 11A

PROJECT
11B

Distributed Workbook

MyITLab
Project 11B Training
Project 11B Grader

11

EXCEL

PROJECT ACTIVITIES

In Activities 11.11 through 11.15, you will assist Justin Mitrani, Vice President of Academic Affairs, in distributing a workbook to the instructional deans at the college. Your completed workbook will look similar to Figure 11.23.

PROJECT FILES

MyITLab
grader

If your instructor wants you to submit Project 11B in the MyITLab grader system, log in to MyITLab, locate Grader Project 11B, and then download the files for this project.

Please always review the downloaded Grader instructions before beginning.

For Project 11B, you will need the following file:
e11B_Courses

You will save your workbooks as:
Lastname_Firstname_11B_Courses
Lastname_Firstname_11B_Courses_Compatibility
Lastname_Firstname_11B_Courses_Encrypted

PROJECT RESULTS

Thru
11B

Courses 2014-15 Academic Year

Section Number	Dept Name	Course Number	Course Name	Instructor ID	Semester	Room#	Delivery Mode
3550	Accounting	101	Beginning Acctg Principles	INST-1122	Fall	C210	Classroom
3551	Accounting	101	Beginning Acctg Principles	INST-1122	Spring	Online	Online
3552	Accounting	102	Intermediate Acctg Principles	INST-1123	Fall	Online	Classroom
3553	Accounting	101	Beginning Acctg Principles	INST-1122	Spring	B234	Classroom
3554	Accounting	102	Intermediate Acctg Principles	INST-1123	Fall		Online
3555	Accounting	102	Intermediate Acctg Principles	INST-1123	Spring	Online	Online
3556	Accounting	103	Advanced Acctg Principles	INST-1124	Fall	Online	Online
3557	Accounting	102	Intermediate Acctg Principles	INST-1123	Spring	C210	Classroom
3558	Accounting	103	Advanced Acctg Principles	INST-1125	Fall	C210	Classroom
3559	Accounting	103	Advanced Acctg Principles	INST-1124	Spring	Online	Online
3560	Business	101	Intro to Business	INST-1117	Fall	Online	Online
3561	Business	103	Advanced Acctg Principles	INST-1125	Spring	Online	Online
3562	Business	101	Intro to Business	INST-1117	Fall	C210	Classroom
3563	Business	101	Intro to Business	INST-1117	Spring	C212	Classroom
3564	Business	101	Intro to Business	INST-1118	Fall	C213	Classroom
3565	Business	101	Intro to Business	INST-1117	Spring	C213	Classroom
3566	Business	210	Organizational Behavior	INST-1119	Fall	Online	Online
3567	Business	101	Intro to Business	INST-1118	Spring	C213	Classroom
3568	Business	220	Business Law	INST-1120	Fall		Classroom
3569	Business	210	Organizational Behavior	INST-1119	Spring	C212	Classroom
3570	Business	230	Business Statistics	INST-1120	Spring	C212	Classroom
3571	Business	220	Business Law	INST-1120	Spring	C213	Classroom
3572	CIS	101	MS Office Overview	INST-1111	Fall	A133	Classroom
3573	Business	230	Business Statistics	INST-1120	Spring	C212	Classroom
3574	Accounting	101	Beginning Acctg Principles	INST-1122	Fall		Classroom
3575	CIS	101	MS Office Overview	INST-1111	Spring	Online	Online
3576	CIS	101	MS Office Overview	INST-1111	Fall	Online	Online
3577	CIS	101	MS Office Overview	INST-1111	Spring	A133	Classroom

Lastname_Firstname_11B_Courses_Encrypted

Section Number	Dept Name	Course Number	Course Name	Instructor ID	Semester	Room#	Delivery Mode
3578	CIS	101	MS Office Overview	INST-1112	Fall	A133	Classroom
3579	CIS	101	MS Office Overview	INST-1112	Spring	A133	Classroom
3580	CIS	102	MS Word	INST-1112	Fall	Online	Online
3581	CIS	102	MS Word	INST-1112	Spring	A133	Classroom
3582	CIS	103	MS Excel	INST-1122	Fall	A133	Classroom
3583	CIS	103	MS Excel	INST-1122	Spring	A133	Classroom
3584	CIS	104	MS PowerPoint	INST-1111	Fall	Online	Online
3585	CIS	104	MS PowerPoint	INST-1111	Spring	A133	Classroom
3586	CIS	105	MS Access	INST-1113	Fall	A133	Classroom
3587	CIS	105	MS Access	INST-1113	Spring	Online	Online
3588	Marketing	115	Principles of Marketing	INST-1121	Fall		Classroom
3589	Marketing	115	Principles of Marketing	INST-1121	Spring		Classroom
3590	Programming	115	Introduction to Programming	INST-1113	Fall	Online	Online
3591	Programming	115	Introduction to Programming	INST-1113	Spring	A132	Classroom
3592	Programming	120	Database Systems Design	INST-1114	Fall	A132	Classroom
3593	Programming	120	Database Systems Design	INST-1114	Spring	Online	Online
3594	Programming	121	Enterprise Software Development	INST-1115	Fall	A132	Classroom
3595	Programming	121	Enterprise Software Development	INST-1115	Spring	A132	Classroom
3596	Programming	122	Object Oriented Programming Concepts	INST-1116	Fall	A132	Classroom
3597	Programming	122	Object Oriented Programming Concepts	INST-1116	Spring	A132	Classroom

Lastname_Firstname_11B_Courses_Encrypted

Excel 2016, Windows 10, Microsoft Corporation

FIGURE 11.23 Project 11B Distributed Workbook

GO! Learn How
Video E11-4

When you finish editing a workbook, you may want to review its contents to ensure that it does not contain sensitive or personal information that you do not want to share with other people, that it is accessible to individuals with disabilities, and that it is compatible with earlier versions of Excel.

Activity 11.11 | Ensuring Accessibility in a Workbook

MOS
1.5.7, 5.3.4

To ensure that an Excel 2016 workbook is accessible and can be read by individuals with disabilities, you can run the Accessibility Checker. The **Accessibility Checker** finds any potential accessibility issues and creates a report so that you can resolve the issues to make your file easier for those with disabilities to use. In this Activity, you will run the Accessibility Checker and correct three problems.

ALERT! **To submit as an autograded project, log into MyITLab and download the files for this Project, and begin with those files instead of e11B_Courses.**

---

1 Start Excel. From your student files, open the file **e11B_Courses**. **Save** the file in your **Excel Chapter 11** folder as **Lastname_Firstname_11B_Courses**

2 On the **File tab** click **Check for Issues**, and then click **Check Accessibility**. Compare your screen with Figure 11.24.

The Accessibility Checker pane displays and the Inspection Results display one error and two warnings that you should address. Errors are more severe than warnings.

FIGURE 11.24

3 In the **Accessibility Checker** pane, under **Errors** click **Picture 1 (Sheet1)**. Under **Additional Information**, read the information under **Why Fix**. Scroll down and read **How To Fix**.

Alt text is used in documents and webpages to provide a text description of an image.

4 Right-click the selected image in cells **F1:H1**, and then click **Format Picture**. In the **Format Picture** pane, click **Size & Properties** 🔳, and then, click to expand **Alt Text**. In the **Title** box, type **DRAFT** and then notice that the error no longer displays in the Accessibility Checker pane.

5 Close ⊠ the **Format Picture** pane. In the **Accessibility Checker** pane, under **Warnings**, under **Merged Cells**, click **A1:E1 (Sheet1)**. Read the *Why Fix* and *How To Fix* sections. On the **Home tab**, in the **Alignment group**, click **Merge & Center** to split the merged cells.

> Merged cells can make a spreadsheet structure difficult to understand and navigate.

6 In the **Accessibility Checker** pane, under **Warnings**, under **Default Sheet Names**, click **Sheet1**. Read the *Why Fix* and *How To Fix* sections. Right-click the **Sheet1 sheet tab**, click **Rename**, type **Courses** and then press Enter.

> Sheet names make it easier to understand and navigate a workbook.

7 Notice the **Accessibility Checker** indicates there are no accessibility issues found. **Close** ⊠ the **Accessibility Checker** pane.

8 Display the **document properties** and under Related People, be sure that your name displays as the author. If necessary, right-click the author name, click Edit Property, and then type your name. In the **Subject** box, type your course name and section number, in the **Tags** box, type **accessibility** and then **Save** your workbook.

Activity 11.12 | Ensuring Backward-Compatibility in a Workbook

1.5.8

To ensure that an Excel 2016 workbook does not have compatibility issues that cause a significant loss of functionality or a minor loss of fidelity in an earlier version of Excel, you can run the Compatibility Checker. The *Compatibility Checker* finds any potential compatibility issues and creates a report so that you can resolve the issues. When you work on a workbook in *Compatibility Mode*, where the workbook is in Excel 97-2003 file format (.xls) instead of the newer XML-based file format (.xlsx), the Compatibility Checker runs automatically when you save a workbook. In this Activity, you will run the Compatibility Checker to identify features in the workbook that cannot be transferred to earlier versions of Excel.

1 On the **File tab** click **Check for Issues**, and then click **Check Compatibility**. Compare your screen with Figure 11.25.

> The Microsoft Excel - Compatibility Checker dialog box displays. The Compatibility Checker displays one minor loss of fidelity issue with formatting styles. The formats—cell title fill and font Theme Colors—will be converted to the closest format available when the worksheet is saved in an earlier version of Excel.

FIGURE 11.25

2 Click **OK**.

3 Display the **document properties**. In the **Tags** box, delete *accessibility* and type **compatibility**

4 Click **Save As** and then click **Browse** to display the **Save As** dialog box. At the bottom of the dialog box, click the **Save as type arrow**, and then near the top of the list, click **Excel 97-2003 Workbook**. **Save** the file in your **Excel Chapter 11** folder as **Lastname_Firstname_11B_Courses_Compatibility**

The Microsoft Excel - Compatibility Checker dialog box displays.

5 In the **Microsoft Excel - Compatibility Checker** dialog box, click **Continue**.

The file is saved in an earlier version of Excel—Excel 97-2003.

6 On the **File tab** click **Close** to close the workbook. Leave Excel open for the next Activity.

Activity 11.13 | Inspecting a Document

1.5.6

In this Activity, you will use the ***Document Inspector***, which is an Excel feature that can find and remove hidden properties and personal information in a workbook. You will inspect the workbook and review the results that the Document Inspector finds to determine what information, if any, should be removed. Because some information is not needed by the distribution recipients of the Courses document, Justin Mitrani, Vice President of Academic Affairs, has asked you to remove some information.

1 Open your **Lastname_Firstname_11B_Courses** workbook.

2 On the **File tab**, click **Check for Issues**, and then, click **Inspect Document**. Compare your screen with Figure 11.26.

The Document Inspector dialog box displays and lists the various types of content that will be checked. By default, all the check boxes are selected.

FIGURE 11.26

3 In the lower right corner of the dialog box, click **Inspect**. Compare your screen with Figure 11.27.

The Document Inspector indicates four categories that contain sensitive or personal information. A red exclamation point and a Remove All button display in the inspection results for these four categories. In this workbook, the Document Inspector found comments, document properties, footer, and a hidden worksheet.

FIGURE 11.27

4 **Close** the **Document Inspector** dialog box, and then click ⬅ to return to the worksheet.

5 Click cell **G6**, and notice the comment that displays.

6 On the **File tab**, click **Show All Properties**. Notice that in the **Status** box, *DRAFT* displays.

7 Click ⬅ to return to the worksheet. Right-click the **Courses sheet tab**, and then click **Unhide**. In the **Unhide** dialog box, with *Instructors* selected, click **OK**.

The Instructors worksheet, which was hidden, displays.

8 Right-click the **Instructors sheet tab**, and then click **Hide**.

The Instructors worksheet is once again hidden.

9 **Save** 🖫 your workbook. On the **File tab**, click **Check for Issues**, and then click **Inspect Document**.

10 In the **Document Inspector** dialog box, click **Inspect**.

You have now examined the items flagged by the Document Inspector—the comment regarding the new podium, the subject DRAFT in the document properties, and the hidden worksheet with instructor names and e-mail addresses.

11 To the right of **Comments and Annotations**, click **Remove All**. Scroll the dialog box, and then to the right of **Headers and Footers**, click **Remove All**. To the right of **Hidden Worksheets**, click **Remove All**. Do not remove the Document Properties and Personal Information. Scroll to the top of the list and compare your screen with Figure 11.28.

The comments, footer, and hidden worksheet are removed from the file. This information is not needed by the distribution recipients of the Courses document. If you remove the hidden worksheet, you are losing this data, so if you want to keep it, make a copy elsewhere.

NOTE | Removing Document Properties and Personal Information

When you remove document properties and personal information using the Document Inspector, it applies a setting that automatically removes properties and personal information whenever you save the document. To add properties such as author or tags to such a file, on the File tab, enter the properties and then, under Inspect Workbook, click Allow this information to be saved in your file.

FIGURE 11.28

12 In the lower right corner of the **Document Inspector** dialog box, click **Close**.

13 Return to the worksheet. Set the **orientation** to **Landscape**, the **Width** to **1 page**, and center the worksheet horizontally. Insert a footer in the **left section** that includes the file name. In **Normal** view, make cell **A1** the active cell, and then, click **Save** 🗄.

Objective 5 | Prepare a Final Workbook for Distribution

GO! Learn How
Video E11-5

Before distributing Excel workbooks to others, you may need to protect it with a password and mark it as final so that others do not change it.

Activity 11.14 | Encrypting a Workbook and Protecting Workbook Structure

MOS
1.2.1 Expert
1.2.4 Expert

You can provide another level of security for your workbook by adding encryption. *Encryption* is the process by which a file is encoded so that it cannot be *opened* without the proper password. Encryption is more than simple password protection—the process digitally obscures information to make it unreadable without a proper key to decode it. Passwords prevent users from *editing* a worksheet or the entire workbook. Encryption is different—it prevents users from *opening* the file. In this Activity, you will protect the workbook structure and apply encryption to your Courses workbook.

1 With your **Lastname_Firstname_11B_Courses** workbook open, display the **Save As** dialog box. **Save** the file in your **Excel Chapter 11** folder as **Lastname_Firstname_11B_Courses_Encrypted** and then display the **document properties**. In the **Tags** box, delete *accessibility,* and then, type **encrypted**

2 In **Backstage view**, with the **Info tab** displayed, click **Protect Workbook**, and then click **Protect Workbook Structure**. Click **OK**.

Protecting the workbook structure prevents changes at the workbook level such as the addition of new worksheets.

3 Click the **File tab**, and then click **Protect Workbook**. Click **Encrypt with Password**. Compare your screen with Figure 11.29.

The Encrypt Document dialog box displays. A box in which to type the password and a note of caution about entering passwords displays.

FIGURE 11.29

4 In the **Encrypt Document** dialog box, with the insertion point blinking in the **Password** box, type **goseries** and then click **OK**. In the **Reenter password** box, type **goseries** and then click **OK**.

More Knowledge **Making Passwords More Secure**

The Windows Help system has the following suggestions for secure passwords: "A more secure or strong password is one that's difficult for others to determine by guessing or by using automated programs. Strong passwords contain 7-16 characters, do not include common words or names, and combine uppercase letters, lowercase letters, numbers, and symbols."

---

5 **Save** your workbook. **Close** the workbook and leave Excel open.

6 Display the **Open** dialog box. Navigate to your **Excel Chapter 11** folder, and then open your **Lastname_Firstname_11B_Courses_Encrypted** file.

The Password dialog box displays. The workbook cannot be opened without the password.

ANOTHER WAY   Click Open and then click the Lastname_Firstname_11B_Courses_Encrypted file in the Recent Workbooks list.

---

7 Type **goseries** and then click **OK**.

Your Lastname_Firstname_11B_Courses_Encrypted workbook opens.

ALERT! **Does the Workbook Not Open?**

If the workbook does not open, you may have mistyped the password; try typing the password again. If the workbook still does not open, you may have mistyped the password and the reentered password when you encrypted the workbook. There is no simple way to recover a mistyped password from an encrypted document. Open the Lastname_Firstname_11B_Courses file, and repeat Steps 1 through 7.

Activity 11.15 | **Marking a Workbook as Final**

Before you share a workbook, you can apply the Mark as Final command, which makes the document read-only. The ***Mark as Final command*** prevents additional changes to the document and disables typing, editing comments, and proofing marks. When the document is opened by others, the user will be notified by Microsoft Excel that the document has been *Marked as Final*. In this Activity, you will mark the workbook as final.

1 With your **Lastname_Firstname_11B_Courses_Encrypted** workbook open, on the **File tab**, click **Protect Workbook**, and then click **Mark as Final**.

The Microsoft Excel dialog box displays and indicates that the workbook will be marked as final and then saved.

2 Click **OK**. Read the message box, and then click **OK**. Compare your screen with Figure 11.30.

The workbook is marked as final. The title bar displays *[Read-Only]* to indicate the file can be read but not edited. A yellow bar displays below the ribbon tabs, indicating that *An author has marked this workbook as final to discourage editing*. If someone opening the file clicks Edit Anyway, the workbook will no longer be *Marked as Final* and will not be a Read-Only file.

FIGURE 11.30

3 Click any cell and type a number or text to confirm the workbook cannot be edited.

The Mark as Final command is not a security feature. Anyone can edit a document that has been marked as final by removing the Mark as Final status from the document, editing the file, and then reapplying the Mark as Final status. To ensure that a workbook cannot be edited, you must password protect the workbook. Mark as Final signifies the intent of the author that the document is final in content.

4 If directed by your instructor to do so, submit your paper printout, your electronic image of your document that looks like a printed document, or your original Excel file. In the upper right corner of the Excel window, click **Close** ⊠.

END | You have completed Project 11B

GO! To Work

Andres Rodriguez/Fotolia; FotolEdhar/Fotolia; Andrey Popov/Fotolia; Shutterstock

MICROSOFT OFFICE SPECIALIST (MOS) SKILLS IN THIS CHAPTER
PROJECT 11B
1.5.6 Inspect a workbook for hidden properties or personal information
1.5.7 Inspect a workbook for accessibility issues
1.5.8 Inspect a workbook for compatibility issues
5.3.4 Add alternative text to objects for accessibility
1.2.1 Expert Restrict editing
1.2.4 Expert Protect workbook structure

BUILD YOUR E-PORTFOLIO

An E-Portfolio is a collection of evidence, stored electronically, that showcases what you have accomplished while completing your education. Collecting and then sharing your work products with potential employers reflects your academic and career goals. Your completed documents from the following projects are good examples to show what you have learned: 11G, 11K, and 11L.

GO! FOR JOB SUCCESS

Discussion: Big Data

Your instructor may assign these questions to your class, and then ask you to think about them or discuss them with your classmates:

"Big data" describes information that a company has that is so massive in the number of records that it is difficult to analyze using standard database techniques. It often refers to information that a company collects in the course of doing business that is not usually used for any other purpose than to process transactions. An example is airline ticket sales: The information airlines collect in a ticket sale includes names, addresses, travel preferences, destinations, credit cards, seating preferences, etc. Analyzing this information could result in information that would be useful in updating flight schedules, changing seat layouts, and marketing plans.

FotolEdhar/Fotolia

> **What are some other industries that collect large amounts of data about customers during the course of a normal transaction?**

> **What other industries would benefit from data such as that collected during an airline ticket sale?**

> **Do you think it is ethical for businesses to sell the information they collect to other businesses?**

END OF CHAPTER

SUMMARY

Collaboration is the process of working jointly with others to review, comment on, and make changes to a shared workbook. This includes comparing different versions of a workbook and merging them together.

Changes to documents by different individuals can be tracked and then accepted or rejected. The change history is information that is maintained about changes made in past editing sessions.

A digital signature is an electronic, encrypted, stamp of authentication. You can add a digital signature to an Excel workbook to ensure that a file originated from the signer and has not been changed.

Preparing a final workbook for distribution includes inspecting the workbook for hidden information, encrypting a workbook with a password, and checking for compatibility and accessibility issues.

GO! LEARN IT ONLINE

Review the concepts and key terms in this chapter by completing these online challenges, which you can find at MyITLab.

Matching and Multiple Choice: Answer matching and multiple choice questions to test what you learned in this chapter.

Lessons on the GO!: Learn how to use all the new apps and features as they are introduced by Microsoft.

MOS Prep Quiz: Answer questions to review the MOS skills that you practiced in this chapter.

PROJECT GUIDE FOR EXCEL CHAPTER 11

Your instructor may assign one or more of these projects to help you review the chapter and assess your mastery and understanding of the chapter.

Project	Apply Skills from These Chapter Objectives	Project Type	Project Location
Project Guide for EXCEL Chapter 11			
11A MyITLab	Objectives 1–3 from Project 11A	**11A Instructional Project (Grader Project)** Guided instruction to learn the skills in Project 11A.	In MyITLab and in text
11B MyITLab	Objectives 4–5 from Project 11B	**11B Instructional Project (Grader Project)** Guided instruction to learn the skills in Project 11B.	In MyITLab and in text
11C	Objectives 1–3 from Project 11A	**11C Skills Review (Scorecard Grading)** A guided review of the skills from Project 11A.	In text
11D	Objectives 4–5 from Project 11B	**11D Skills Review (Scorecard Grading)** A guided review of the skills from Project 11B.	In text
11E MyITLab	Objectives 1–3 from Project 11A	**11E Mastery (Grader Project)** **Mastery and Transfer of Learning** A demonstration of your mastery of the skills in Project 11A with extensive decision making.	In MyITLab and in text
11F MyITLab	Objectives 4–5 from Project 11B	**11F Mastery (Grader Project)** **Mastery and Transfer of Learning** A demonstration of your mastery of the skills in Project 11B with extensive decision making.	In MyITLab and in text
11G MyITLab	Objectives 1–5 from Project 11A and 11B	**11G Mastery (Grader Project)** **Mastery and Transfer of Learning** A demonstration of your mastery of the skills in Projects 11A and 11B with extensive decision making.	In MyITLab and in text
11H	Combination of Objectives from Projects 11A and 11B	**11H GO! Fix It (Scorecard Grading)** **Critical Thinking** A demonstration of your mastery of the skills in Projects 11A and 11B by creating a correct result from a document that contains errors you must find.	Instructor Resource Center (IRC) and MyITLab
11I	Combination of Objectives from Projects 11A and 11B	**11I GO! Make It (Scorecard Grading)** **Critical Thinking** A demonstration of your mastery of the skills in Projects 11A and 11B by creating a result from a supplied picture.	IRC and MyITLab
11J	Combination of Objectives from Projects 11A and 11B	**11J GO! Solve It (Rubric Grading)** **Critical Thinking** A demonstration of your mastery of the skills in Projects 11A and 11B, your decision-making skills, and your critical thinking skills. A task-specific rubric helps you self-assess your result.	IRC and MyITLab
11K	Combination of Objectives from Projects 11A and 11B	**11K GO! Solve It (Rubric Grading)** **Critical Thinking** A demonstration of your mastery of the skills in Projects 11A and 11B, your decision-making skills, and your critical thinking skills. A task-specific rubric helps you self-assess your result.	In text
11L	Combination of Objectives from Projects 11A and 11B	**11L GO! Think (Rubric Grading)** **Critical Thinking** A demonstration of your understanding of the chapter concepts applied in a manner that you would outside of college. An analytic rubric helps you and your instructor grade the quality of your work by comparing it to the work an expert in the discipline would create.	In text
11M	Combination of Objectives from Projects 11A and 11B	**11M GO! Think (Rubric Grading)** **Critical Thinking** A demonstration of your understanding of the chapter concepts applied in a manner that you would outside of college. An analytic rubric helps you and your instructor grade the quality of your work by comparing it to the work an expert in the discipline would create.	IRC and MyITLab
11N	Combination of Objectives from Projects 11A and 11B	**11N You and GO! (Rubric Grading)** **Critical Thinking** A demonstration of your understanding of the chapter concepts applied in a manner that you would in a personal situation. An analytic rubric helps you and your instructor grade the quality of your work.	IRC and MyITLab

GLOSSARY

Apply 11A skills from these Objectives:

1 Create a Shared Workbook

2 Track Changes Made to a Workbook

3 Merge Workbooks and Accept Changes

Skills Review Project 11C Fall Schedule

In the following Skills Review, you will create a shared workbook so that it can be reviewed by the different department chairpersons in the college's Liberal Arts Division. Various individuals in the Liberal Arts Division will be able to edit and comment on the information in the workbook. Your completed worksheets will look similar to Figure 11.31.

PROJECT FILES

For Project 11C, you will need the following files:

e11C_Draft

e11C_Fall_Schedule

You will save your workbook as:

Lastname_Firstname_11C_Fall_Schedule

Lastname_Firstname_11C_Fall_Schedule - Copy

PROJECT RESULTS

FIGURE 11.31

(Project 11C Fall Schedule continues on the next page)

1 Start Excel. From your student files, open the file **e11C_Fall_Schedule**. Display the **Save As** dialog box, navigate to the location where you are storing your files for this chapter, and then **Save** the file in your **Excel Chapter 11** folder as **Lastname_Firstname_11C_Fall_Schedule**

a. Group the worksheets. Insert a footer with the file name in the **left section** and the sheet name in the **right section**, click above the footer area to deselect, and then return to **Normal** view. Set the orientation to landscape. Press Ctrl + Home to move to the top of the sheet.

b. Click the **File tab** to display **Backstage** view. On the **Info tab**, at the top of the screen, notice that the location of this file on your computer displays under the file name. On the right, notice that some of the more common properties for this file display, for example, the file *Size* and *Author*.

c. Under **Properties**, point to the text *Add a title*, and then click one time. Type **Proposed Fall Schedule** Under **Related People**, point to the text *Molly Morton*, who is the author to view the **Contact Card**.

d. Move the mouse pointer away from the **Contact Card**, near the top right of the Info pane click the **Properties arrow**, and then click **Advanced Properties**. Click the **Summary tab**. In the **Author** box, delete *Molly Morton*, type **Kelly Clinton** and then press Tab. In the **Manager** box, type **Dean Massaro, Liberal Arts Division**

e. Click **OK**. Click **Save** to save your workbook and return to the worksheet.

2 Point to the **Drama sheet tab**, right-click, and then click **Ungroup Sheets** With the **Drama** worksheet active, on the **Page Layout tab** in the **Page Setup group**, click **Background**. In the **Insert Pictures** dialog box, click **From a File**.

a. In the **Sheet Background** dialog box, navigate to your student data files, click the file **e11C_Draft** and then click **Insert**. **Save** your workbook.

b. On the **Music** worksheet, click cell **H11**, type **Nu** On the **Insert tab**, in the **Symbols group**, click **Symbol**. If necessary, drag the Symbol dialog box up so that cell **H11** is visible. In the **Symbol** dialog box, click the **Subset arrow**, and then click

Latin-1 Supplement. Click the **scrollbar arrows** as necessary to locate the symbol **ñ—Latin Small Letter N With Tilde**. Click **Insert**, click **Close**, and then type **ez, Mar** Display the **Symbol** dialog box, verify the **Latin-1 Supplement** subset is selected, scroll up one row, and then insert the symbol **í—Latin Small Letter I With Acute**. **Close** the **Symbol** dialog box, type **a** and then press Enter. **Save** your workbook.

3 On the **Review tab**, in the **Changes group**, click **Track Changes**, and then click **Highlight Changes**. In the **Highlight Changes** dialog box, click to select the **Track Changes while editing** check box. Verify that the **When** check box is selected and indicates *All*. Select the **Who** check box and be sure *Everyone* is indicated. Verify that the **Highlight changes on screen** check box is selected, and then click **OK.**

a. Click **OK**. On the **File tab**, click **Close** to close the file and leave Excel open.

4 Display the **Open** dialog box. Navigate to your **Excel Chapter 11** folder, point to your **Lastname_Firstname_11C_Fall_Schedule** file, right-click, and then, click **Copy**.

a. Right-click in an empty space below or to the right of the file list, and then click **Paste**. In the **Open** dialog box, click **Cancel**.

5 Display the **Open** dialog box, navigate to your chapter folder, and then open your **Lastname_Firstname_11C_Fall_Schedule** file—open the original, *not* the copy that you made.

a. On the **File tab**, click **Options**. In the **Excel Options** dialog box, on the left, verify **General** is selected.

b. Under **Personalize your copy of Microsoft Office**, click in the **User name** box. On a piece of paper, write down the User name that displays so that you can restore it later. Select the User name text, type **Andy Koch, Humanities** to replace the selected User name text. Click **OK.**

c. Display the **Humanities** worksheet. Click cell **H10**, begin to type **Lee, Elaine** and press Enter to accept the AutoComplete suggestion to change the name. In cell **H12**, change the name to **Woods, Sam** Press Ctrl + Home to move to cell **A1**.

(Project 11C Fall Schedule continues on the next page)

d. On the **Review tab**, in the **Changes group**, click **Track Changes**, and then click **Highlight Changes**. In the **Highlight Changes** dialog box, click the **When arrow**, and then click **All**. Click the **Who** check box, and be sure that it indicates *Everyone*. Click **OK**. Point to each of the changed cells to view the ScreenTip, which indicates the change that was made and the date and time the change was made. **Save** your workbook, and then on the **File tab**, click **Close** to close the file and leave Excel open.

e. Display the Open dialog box. Navigate to and then reopen your **Lastname_Firstname_11C_Fall_Schedule** file—not the copy. On the **File tab**, click **Options** to display the **Excel Options** dialog box change the **User name** to **Jan Clarke, Music** and then click **OK**.

f. Display the **Music** worksheet. Click cell **G9** and type **Permission** Click cell **H12** and type **Jones, Pat** then press Enter. Press Ctrl + Home to make cell **A1** the active cell. **Save** your workbook, and then on the **File tab** click **Close** to close the file and leave Excel open.

6 Open the **Lastname_Firstname_11C_Fall_Schedule - Copy** file that you created earlier.

a. On the **File tab**, click **Options** to display the **Excel Options** dialog box, change the User name to **Kate Sparks, Drama** and then click **OK**.

b. Display the **Drama** worksheet. Click cell **F4** and type **Online** Click cell **F5**, type **Online** and then press Enter. Press Ctrl + Home. **Save** your workbook, and then on the **File tab,** click **Close** to close the file and leave Excel open.

7 On the **File tab**, click **Options** to display the **Excel Options** dialog box, and then change the **User name** to **Dean Massaro** Click **OK** to close the dialog box, and then open your **Lastname_Firstname_11C_Fall_Schedule** file.

a. With the **Music** worksheet active, on the **Review tab**, in the **Changes group**, click **Track Changes**, and then click **Highlight Changes**. In the **Highlight Changes** dialog box, click the **When arrow**, and then click **All**. Click the **Who arrow**, and then click **Everyone but Me**. Click **OK**.

b. Display the **Humanities** worksheet and notice the borders around cells **H10** and **H12** indicating

that changes have been made. Display the **Drama** worksheet, and notice that no changes are indicated because changes for this department were made on another copy of the shared workbook.

c. On the **File tab**, click **Options** to display the **Excel Options** dialog box, and then on the left, click **Quick Access Toolbar**. At the top of the dialog box, under **Customize the Quick Access Toolbar**, click the **Choose commands from arrow**, and then click **Commands Not in the Ribbon**. In the list below, scroll as necessary, click **Compare and Merge Workbooks**, in the center click **Add**. Click **OK**.

d. On the **Quick Access Toolbar**, click **Compare and Merge Workbooks**. In the **Select Files to Merge Into Current Workbook** dialog box, if necessary, navigate to your **Excel Chapter 11** folder. Locate your **Lastname_Firstname_11C_Fall_Schedule - Copy** file—if necessary, widen the Name column to display the complete file name—and then click to select it. Click **OK**.

8 Display the **Humanities** worksheet. On the **Review tab**, in the **Changes group**, click **Track Changes**, and then click **Accept/Reject Changes**.

a. Verify that the **When** box indicates *Not yet reviewed*. Change the **Who** box to indicate *Everyone*, and then click **OK**.

b. Click **Accept** to accept the change of instructor in cell **H10** to *Lee, Elaine*. Click **Accept**. Click **Reject** to reject the change in cell **G9**. **Accept** the next change—change 4 of 6—a change in instructor to *Jones, Pat*.

c. Click **Accept**, and then **Accept** the last change—a change in cell **F5** to *Online*.

d. Display the **Drama** worksheet, click cell **F4**, and then press Delete. Press Tab and in cell **G4**, type **Online** Click cell **F5** and press Delete. Press Tab and in cell **G5**, type **Online** and press Enter. **Save** your workbook.

9 On the **Review tab**, in the **Changes group**, click **Share Workbook**. Clear the *Allow changes by more than one user at the same time* check box, and then click **OK**. On the **Microsoft Excel** information box, click **Yes**.

a. On the **File tab**, click **Options** to display the **Excel Options** dialog box, and then click in the **User**

(Project 11C Fall Schedule continues on the next page)

name box. Select the text *Dean Massaro*, type the name that you wrote down previously to replace the selected **User name** text, and then click **OK**.

b. On the **Quick Access Toolbar**, right-click **Compare and Merge Workbooks**, and then click **Remove from Quick Access Toolbar**.

10 Display the **Drama** worksheet, and then click cell **A15**. On the **Insert tab**, in the **Text group**, click the **Add Signature Line arrow**, and then click **Microsoft Office Signature Line**.

a. In the **Signature Setup** dialog box, with the insertion point blinking in the **Suggested signer** box and using your own name, type **Firstname Lastname** and then click **OK**.

b. Right-click the **Drama sheet tab**, and then click **Select All Sheets**. On the **Page Layout tab**, set the **Width** to **1 page**. Center the worksheets horizontally on the page. Display the **document properties** and under **Related People**, right-click the author name, click **Edit Property**, type your name and then press Enter. In the **Subject** box, type your course name and section number, and in the **Tags** box, type **fall classes**

c. Display and check the Print Preview, make any necessary corrections, and then ungroup the worksheets. **Save** your workbook. If directed by your instructor to do so, submit your paper printout, your electronic image of your document that looks like a printed document, or your original Excel file. **Close** Excel.

END | You have completed Project 11C

Apply 11B skills from these Objectives:

4 Inspect a Workbook

5 Prepare a Final Workbook for Distribution

Skills Review   Project 11D Distributed Class Workbook

In the following Skills Review, you will assist Justin Mitrani, Vice President of Academic Affairs, in distributing a workbook for social science classes to the instructional deans at the college. Your completed worksheets will look similar to Figure 11.32.

PROJECT FILES

For Project 11D, you will need the following file:

e11D_Classes

You will save your workbooks as:

Lastname_Firstname_11D_Classes

Lastname_Firstname_11D_Classes_Compatibility

Lastname_Firstname_11D_Classes_Encrypted

PROJECT RESULTS

FIGURE 11.32

Excel 2016, Windows 10, Microsoft Corporation

(Project 11D Distributed Class Workbook continues on the next page)

1 Start Excel. From your student files, open the file **e11D_Classes** and then **Save** the file in your **Excel Chapter 11** folder as **Lastname_Firstname_11D_Classes**

a. On the **File tab**, click **Check for Issues**, and then click **Check Accessibility**.

b. In the **Accessibility Checker** pane, under **Errors** click **Picture 1 (Sheet1)**. Under **Additional Information**, read the information under **Why Fix**. Scroll down and read **How To Fix**. Right-click the selected image in cells **E1:H1**. Click **Format Picture**, on the **Format Picture** pane, click **Size & Properties**, and then, if necessary, click to expand **Alt Text**. In the **Title** box, type **DRAFT** Notice the error no longer displays in the **Accessibility Checker** pane. **Close** the **Format Picture** pane.

c. In the **Accessibility Checker** pane, under **Warnings**, under **Merged Cells**, click **A1:G1 (Sheet1)**. Read the *Why Fix* and *How To Fix* sections. On the **Home tab**, in the **Alignment group**, click **Merge & Center** to split the merged cells.

d. In the **Accessibility Checker** pane, under **Warnings**, under **Default Sheet Names**, click **Sheet1**. Read the *Why Fix* and *How To Fix* sections. Right-click the **Sheet1 sheet tab**, click **Rename**, type **Courses** and then press Enter. Notice the **Accessibility Checker** indicates there are no accessibility issues found. **Close** the **Accessibility Checker** pane.

e. Display the **document properties** and under Related People, be sure that your name displays as the author. If necessary, right-click the author name, click Edit Property, and then type your name. In the **Subject** box, type your course name and section number, in the **Tags** box, type **accessibility** and then **Save** your workbook.

2 On the **File tab,** click **Check for Issues**, and then click **Check Compatibility**. Click **OK**.

a. Display the **document properties**. In the **Tags** box, delete *accessibility* and type **compatibility**

b. Click **Save As** and then click **Browse** to display the **Save As** dialog box. At the bottom of the dialog box, click the **Save as type arrow**, click **Excel 97-2003 Workbook**. Save the file in your **Excel Chapter 11** folder as

Lastname_Firstname_11D_Classes_Compatibility and then in the **Microsoft Excel - Compatibility Checker** dialog box, click **Continue**. On the **File tab**, click **Close** to close the workbook. Leave Excel open for the next step.

3 Display the **Open** dialog box. Navigate to your **Excel Chapter 11** folder and open your **Lastname_Firstname_11D_Classes** workbook.

a. On the **File tab**, click **Check for Issues,** and then, click **Inspect Document**. In the lower right corner of the dialog box, click **Inspect**. Close the **Document Inspector** dialog box, and then return to the worksheet.

b. Click cell **G6**, and notice the comment that displays. On the **File tab**, click **Show All Properties**. Notice that in the Status box, *DRAFT* displays. Return to the worksheet. Right-click the **Courses sheet tab**, and then click **Unhide**. In the **Unhide** dialog box, with *Instructors* selected, click **OK**. Right-click the **Instructors sheet tab**, and then click **Hide**.

c. **Save** your workbook. On the **File tab**, click **Check for Issues**, and then click **Inspect Document**. In the **Document Inspector** dialog box, click **Inspect**. To the right of **Comments and Annotations**, click **Remove All**. To the right of **Headers and Footers**, click **Remove All**. To the right of **Hidden Worksheets**, click **Remove All**.

d. In the lower right corner of the **Document Inspector** dialog box, click **Close**. Return to the worksheet. Set the **orientation** to **Landscape**, the **Width** to **1 page**, and center the worksheet horizontally. Insert a footer in the **left section** that includes the file name, return to **Normal** view, make cell A1 the active cell, and then, click **Save**.

4 With your **Lastname_Firstname_11D_Classes** file open, display the **Save As** dialog box, and then **Save** the file in your **Excel Chapter 11** folder as **Lastname_Firstname_11D_Classes_Encrypted** Display the **document properties**, in the **Tags** box, delete *accessibility,* and then, type **encrypted**

a. Click **Protect Workbook**, and then, click **Encrypt with Password**. In the **Encrypt Document** dialog box, with the insertion point blinking in the **Password** box, type **goseries** and then click **OK**. In the **Reenter password** box, type **goseries** and then click **OK**.

(Project 11D Distributed Class Workbook continues on the next page)

b. **Save** and **Close** the workbook. Leave Excel open. On the **File tab**, click **Open**, and then click **Browse** to display the **Open** dialog box. Navigate to your **Excel Chapter 11** folder, and then open your **Lastname_Firstname_11D_Classes_Encrypted** file. Type **goseries** and then click **OK**.

5 With the **Lastname_Firstname_11D_Classes_Encrypted** file open, on the **File tab**, click **Protect Workbook**, and then click **Mark as Final**. Click **OK**. Read the message box, and then click **OK**. Click any cell in the worksheet and type a number or text to confirm that you cannot edit the workbook. If directed by your instructor to do so, submit your paper printout, your electronic image of your document that looks like a printed document, or your original Excel file. **Close** Excel.

> END | You have completed Project 11D

Apply **11A** skills from these Objectives:

1 Create a Shared Workbook

2 Track Changes Made to a Workbook

3 Merge Workbooks and Accept Changes

Mastering Excel   Project 11E Scholarship Classes

In the following Mastering Excel project, you will create a shared workbook, change the user name, and then make changes to the workbook for the Continuing Education Division of Capital Cities Community College. Capital Cities Community College offers a selection of free (scholarship) classes to nonprofit agencies. The class list from the previous semester must be updated for the upcoming semester. Then you will review the changes that were made and accept or reject the changes. Your completed worksheet will look similar to Figure 11.33.

PROJECT FILES

For Project 11E, you will need the following file:

e11E_Scholarship_Classes

You will save your workbook as:

Lastname_Firstname_11E_Scholarship_Classes

PROJECT RESULTS

Scholarship Classes for Nonprofit Agencies

Fall

Title	Dates	Time	Class Number
Introduction to Access	Sept 17 & 24	8 AM-12 PM	OS 325
Intermediate Access	Oct 1 & 8	8 AM-12 PM	OS 326
Introduction to Excel	Oct 15 & 22	1-5 PM	OS 322
Intermediate Excel	Oct 29 & Nov 5	8 AM-12 PM	OS 310
Introduction to PowerPoint	Oct 15 & 22	8 AM-12 PM	OS 328
Introduction to Word	Nov 12 & 19	1-5 PM	OS 319
Intermediate Word	Dec 3 & 10	1-5 PM	OS 320
MS Publisher	Nov 12 & 19	8 AM-12 PM	OS 345

Lastname_Firstname_11E_Scholarship_Classes.xlsx

Excel 2016, Windows 10, Microsoft Corporation

FIGURE 11.33

(Project 11E Scholarship Classes continues on the next page)

1 Start Excel. From your student files, open the Excel workbook **e11E_Scholarship_Classes**. **Save** the file in your **Excel Chapter 11** folder as **Lastname_Firstname_11E_Scholarship_Classes** Insert a footer in the **left section** with the **File Name**. Display the **document properties**. In the **Subject** box, type your course name and section #, type **scholarship classes** as the tags and **Fall Nonprofit Classes** as the title.

2 On the **NonProfits** worksheet, in cell **A3**, type **Fall** On the **Review tab**, in the **Changes group**, click the **Track Changes arrow**, and then click **Highlight Changes**. In the **Highlight Changes** dialog box, select the **Track changes while editing** check box. Be sure the **When** check box is selected and indicates *All* and that the **Who** check box is selected and indicates *Everyone*.

3 **Close** the file and then reopen it. Display the **Excel Options** dialog box, verify **General** is selected. Under **Personalize your copy of Microsoft Office**, write down the name that displays in the **User name** box so that you can restore it later, and then change the name to **Kimberly Phillips**

4 Delete the text in the range **B6:B13**. In **column B**, starting in cell **B6** enter the following dates:

Sept 17 & 24
Oct 1 & 8
Oct 15 & 22
Oct 29 & Nov 5
Oct 15 & 22
Nov 12 & 19
Dec 3 & 10
Nov 12 & 19

5 Return to cell **A1**. **Save** the file, and then **Close** it. Open your **Lastname_Firstname_11E_Scholarship_Classes** file again, display the **Excel Options** dialog box, and change the **User name** to **Jo Marzetti**

6 On the **Review tab**, in the **Changes group**, click the **Track Changes arrow**, and then click **Accept/Reject Changes**. In the **Select Changes to Accept or Reject** dialog box, be sure the **When** check box is selected and that it indicates *Not yet reviewed*. Be sure the **Who** check box is selected, click its arrow, and then click **Everyone but Me**. The first date that was changed is surrounded by a border. Click **Accept**. The first change is accepted, and the second change is indicated. Click **Accept**, and then click **Accept All**.

7 **Save** your workbook and **Close** the workbook but leave Excel open. If necessary, display the **Excel Options** dialog box, and change the **User name** back to its original setting. If directed by your instructor to do so, submit your paper printout, your electronic image of your document that looks like a printed document, or your original Excel file. **Close** Excel.

END | You have completed Project 11E

Apply 11B skills from these Objectives:

4 Inspect a Workbook

5 Prepare a Final Workbook for Distribution

Mastering Excel | **Project 11F Instruments Distributed Workbook**

In the following Mastering Excel project, you will assist Stephen Brown, Associate Dean of Music, in distributing a workbook of musical instruments inventory to the music faculty at the college. Your completed worksheet will look similar to Figure 11.34.

PROJECT FILES

For Project 11F, you will need the following file:

e11F_Music

You will save your workbooks as:

Lastname_Firstname_11F_Music
Lastname_Firstname_11F_Music_Compatibility
Lastname_Firstname_11F_Music_Encrypted

PROJECT RESULTS

Musical Instruments

Instrument ID	Category	Instrument	Condition	Student ID
INST-1222	Woodwinds	Clarinet	Poor	
INST-1223	Brass	Trumpet	Excellent	STU-1012
INST-1224	Woodwinds	Saxophone	Good	STU-1013
INST-1225	Percussion	Snare Drum	Poor	STU-1033
INST-1226	Woodwinds	Clarinet	Good	STU-1025
INST-1227	Woodwinds	Clarinet	Poor	STU-1016
INST-1228	Percussion	Xylophone	Excellent	STU-1017
INST-1229	Woodwinds	Flute	Excellent	STU-1028
INST-1230	Woodwinds	Flute	Fair	STU-1019
INST-1231	Brass	Baritone	Poor	
INST-1232	Brass	Trumpet	Good	STU-1021
INST-1233	Brass	Trumpet	Good	STU-1024
INST-1234	Woodwinds	Saxophone	Fair	STU-1023
INST-1235	Woodwinds	Saxophone	Good	STU-1022
INST-1236	Percussion	Bass Drum	Good	STU-1017
INST-1237	Percussion	Snare Drum	Good	STU-1026
INST-1238	Brass	Trombone	Excellent	STU-1027
INST-1239	Brass	Trombone	Good	STU-1018
INST-1240	Woodwinds	Piccolo	Good	STU-1034
INST-1241	Percussion	Cymbals	Good	STU-1030
INST-1242	Brass	French Horn	Poor	
INST-1243	Brass	French Horn	Fair	STU-1032
INST-1244	Brass	Tuba	Good	STU-1014
INST-1245	Brass	Tuba	Poor	STU-1032
INST-1246	Woodwinds	Clarinet	Good	STU-1034
INST-1247	Brass	Baritone	Excellent	STU-1020
INST-1248	Percussion	Xylophone	Poor	
INST-1249	Brass	French Horn	Excellent	STU-1031
INST-1250	Brass	Trumpet	Good	

Lastname_Firstname_11F_Music_Encrypted

Excel 2016, Windows 10, Microsoft Corporation

FIGURE 11.34

(Project 11F Instruments Distributed Workbook continues on the next page)

Mastering Excel Project 11F Instruments Distributed Workbook (continued)

1 Start Excel. From your student files, open the file **e11F_Music**. **Save** the file in your **Excel Chapter 11** folder as **Lastname_Firstname_11F_Music** Check the workbook for accessibility and correct the three problems identified. Use the alt text **piano** and the sheet name **Instruments**

2 Run the **Document Inspector** and then return to the worksheet. Click cell **D6**, and notice the comment that displays. **Unhide** the *Music Instructors* worksheet to verify it exists and then hide the worksheet.

3 **Save** your workbook, and then run the **Document Inspector**. Remove the **Comments and Annotations** and **Hidden Worksheets**, identified by the document inspector. Insert a footer in the **left section** that includes the file name. Display the **document properties**. In the **Author** box, type your firstname and lastname, in the **Subject** box, type your course name and section #, and in the **Tags** box, type **musical instruments Save** your workbook.

4 With your **Lastname_Firstname_11F_Music** file open, **Save** the file in your **Excel Chapter 11** folder as **Lastname_Firstname_11F_Music_Encrypted** In the **Tags** box, type **musical instruments, encrypted** Encrypt the

workbook with the password **goseries** and then **Close** and reopen the workbook to verify that the password will open the file.

5 Mark the **Lastname_Firstname_11F_Music_Encrypted** file as final. **Close** the workbook.

6 From your student files, open the file **e11F_Music**. Check the workbook for compatibility. Display the **document properties**. In the **Author** box, type your firstname and lastname, in the **Subject** box, type your course name and section number and in the **Tags** box, type **musical instruments, compatibility**

7 Insert a footer in the **left section** that includes the file name. Save the file in your **Excel Chapter 11** folder as an **Excel 97-2003 Workbook** with the name **Lastname_Firstname_11F_Music_Compatibility** and then **Close** your workbook.

8 If directed by your instructor to do so, submit your paper printout, your electronic image of your document that looks like a printed document, or your original Excel file. **Close** Excel.

NOTE: If you are submitting your project in MyITLab as a grader project, submit your Lastname_Firstname_11F_Music_Encrypted file.

END | You have completed Project 11F

Mastering Excel Project 11G Sports Distributed Workbook

In the following Mastering Excel project, you will assist Eric Marks, Athletic Director, in distributing a workbook of sports equipment inventory to the sports coaches at the college. You will also create a shared workbook that the Athletics Department will use to review proposed salary changes. Your completed worksheets will look similar to Figure 11.35.

PROJECT FILES

For Project 11G, you will need the following file:

e11G_Salary

You will save your workbook as:

Lastname_Firstname_11G_Salary

PROJECT RESULTS

Salary Budget

Last Name	First Name	Present Grade	Present Salary	Anticipated Grade	Proposed Salary
Anderson	Nancy	17	$ 51,480	17	$ 53,000
Carlton	Elaine	18	56,100	18	57,222
Desprez	Jan	16	50,050	17	56,000
Hernandez	Jose	19	61,688	19	62,922
Mandala	Eduardo	17	51,700	17	52,734
Philips	Matt	17	53,900	17	54,978
Thomas	Doris	16	46,200	16	47,124
Wagner	John	18	57,255	18	58,500
			$ 428,373		$ 442,480

Lastname_Firstname_11G_Salary

Salary Budget

Last Name	First Name	Present Grade	Present Salary	Anticipated Grade	Proposed Salary
Applebee	Linda	20	$ 63,800	20	$ 65,076
Matthews	Chuck	19	62,150	20	63,393
McIntrye	Allison	17	51,700	17	52,734
Patel	Asad	18	54,010	18	56,000
Randolph	Thomas	20	63,800	20	65,076
Reid	James	16	47,300	17	49,000
Ricciardo	Geoff	19	58,575	19	59,747
Williams	George	19	59,180	19	60,364
Zelnik	Charles	18	53,570	18	54,000
			$ 514,085		$ 525,389

Lastname_Firstname_11G_Salary

FIGURE 11.35

Excel 2016, Windows 10, Microsoft Corporation

(Project 11G Sports Distributed Workbook continues on the next page)

Mastering Excel | Project 11G Sports Distributed Workbook (continued)

1 Start Excel. From your student files, open the file **e11G_Salary**. **Save** the file in your **Excel Chapter 11** folder as **Lastname_Firstname_11G_Salary** Group the sheets and insert a footer in the **left section** that includes the file name. Ungroup the worksheets.

2 Display the **Highlight Changes** dialog box. Select the **Track changes while editing** check box, and be sure **When** indicates *All*, and **Who** is selected and indicates *Everyone*. **Close** the file, and then open it again. Display the **Excel Options** dialog box. Make note of the current **User name**, and then change the **User name** to **Grace Johnson**

3 On the **Aquatics** worksheet make the following changes:

LAST NAME	ANTICIPATED GRADE	PROPOSED SALARY
Anderson		53000
Desprez	17	56000
Wagner		58500

4 **Save** the file and **Close** it. Reopen the file and change the **User name** to **Ken Saito** On the **Sports** worksheet make the following changes:

LAST NAME	ANTICIPATED GRADE	PROPOSED SALARY
Matthews		63000
Patel		56000
Reid	17	49000
Zelnik		54000

5 **Save** the file and **Close** it. Reopen the file and change the **User name** to **Dean Angelo** the Dean of Athletics, who will accept or reject the changes. Display the **Highlight Changes** dialog box, change **When** to **All**, and be sure **Who** is selected and displays **Everyone**.

6 Display the **Select Changes to Accept or Reject** dialog box and save if prompted. Review changes for **Everyone but Me**. Accept all changes except the change for *Matthews* in the Sports Department. After reviewing the changes, change Matthews's **Anticipated Grade** to **20** Turn off Sharing.

7 Run the **Document Inspector,** and **Remove All** document properties. If any comments display, remove the comments.

8 Run the **Accessibility Checker** and correct the error indicated. **Group** the worksheets, and then center horizontally. Display the **document properties**. In the **Author** box, type your firstname and lastname, in the **Subject** box, type your course name and section number, in the **Tags** box, type **salaries** and then **Save** the workbook.

9 **Ungroup** the worksheets, and then mark the workbook as final. **Close** the workbook. Display the **Excel Options** dialog box and change the **User name** back to the original user name.

10 If directed by your instructor to do so, submit your paper printout, your electronic image of your document that looks like a printed document, or your original Excel file. **Close** Excel.

> **END | You have completed Project 11G**

Apply a combination of the 11A and 11B skills.	GO! Fix It	Project 11H Fall Schedule	MyITLab
	GO! Make It	Project 11I Fall Sports	MyITLab
	GO! Solve It	Project 11J Weekend Classes	MyITLab
	GO! Solve It	Project 11K Scholarships	

PROJECT FILES

For Project 11K, you will need the following file:

e11K_Scholarships

You will save your workbook as:

Lastname_Firstname_11K_Scholarships

Open the file e11K_Scholarships and save it as **Lastname_Firstname_11K_Scholarships** Inspect the document and remove the hidden worksheet. Encrypt the workbook with the password **goseries** Insert the file name in the footer in the left section. Add appropriate information to the document properties including the tag **scholarships** Mark the workbook as Final. Submit as directed by your instructor.

Performance Level

Performance Criteria		Exemplary: You consistently applied the relevant skills	Proficient: You sometimes, but not always, applied the relevant skills	Developing: You rarely or never applied the relevant skills
	Inspect a Document	The document has been inspected for a hidden worksheet.	Not applicable.	The hidden worksheet was not removed from the document.
	Encrypt a Workbook	The document has been encrypted with goseries as the password.	Not applicable.	The document has not been encrypted with a password.
	Mark a Workbook as Final	The document has been Marked as Final.	Not applicable.	The document has not been Marked as Final.

END | You have completed Project 11K

OUTCOME-BASED ASSESSMENTS

RUBRIC

The following outcomes-based assessments are open-ended assessments. That is, there is no specific correct result; your result will depend on your approach to the information provided. Make Professional Quality your goal. Use the following scoring rubric to guide you in how to approach the problem and then to evaluate how well your approach solves the problem.

The *criteria*—Software Mastery, Content, Format and Layout, and Process—represent the knowledge and skills you have gained that you can apply to solving the problem. The *levels of performance*—Professional Quality, Approaching Professional Quality, or Needs Quality Improvements—help you and your instructor evaluate your result.

	Your completed project is of Professional Quality if you:	Your completed project is Approaching Professional Quality if you:	Your completed project Needs Quality Improvements if you:
1-Software Mastery	Choose and apply the most appropriate skills, tools, and features and identify efficient methods to solve the problem.	Choose and apply some appropriate skills, tools, and features, but not in the most efficient manner.	Choose inappropriate skills, tools, or features, or are inefficient in solving the problem.
2-Content	Construct a solution that is clear and well organized, contains content that is accurate, appropriate to the audience and purpose, and is complete. Provide a solution that contains no errors of spelling, grammar, or style.	Construct a solution in which some components are unclear, poorly organized, inconsistent, or incomplete. Misjudge the needs of the audience. Have some errors in spelling, grammar, or style, but the errors do not detract from comprehension.	Construct a solution that is unclear, incomplete, or poorly organized, contains some inaccurate or inappropriate content, and contains many errors of spelling, grammar, or style. Do not solve the problem.
3-Format and Layout	Format and arrange all elements to communicate information and ideas, clarify function, illustrate relationships, and indicate relative importance.	Apply appropriate format and layout features to some elements, but not others. Overuse features, causing minor distraction.	Apply format and layout that does not communicate information or ideas clearly. Do not use format and layout features to clarify function, illustrate relationships, or indicate relative importance. Use available features excessively, causing distraction.
4-Process	Use an organized approach that integrates planning, development, self-assessment, revision, and reflection.	Demonstrate an organized approach in some areas, but not others; or, use an insufficient process of organization throughout.	Do not use an organized approach to solve the problem.

OUTCOMES-BASED ASSESSMENTS

GO! Think | Project 11L Budget

PROJECT FILES

For Project 11L, you will need the following file:

e11L_Budget

You will save your workbook as:

Lastname_Firstname_11L_Budget
Lastname_Firstname_11L_Budget - Copy

Open the file e11L_Budget, and then save it in your **Excel Chapter 11** folder as **Lastname_Firstname_11L_Budget**

Group the worksheets, insert a footer, and in the left section, add the file name. Add appropriate information to the document properties including the tag **budget** Create a shared file and a copy of the workbook so that it can be completed by the various department chairs who need to do so. Open the original Lastname_Firstname_11L_Budget file. Write down the User name that displays in Excel Options to restore it later. Change the user name to **Melissa Dever, Nursing** Be sure the Nursing sheet tab is displayed. In column F, starting in cell F6, enter the budget figures that reflect a modest increase from the previous years. Save and Close the file.

Open the Lastname_Firstname_11L_Budget - Copy file. Change the User name to Richard Wyatt, Radiology. Click the Radiology sheet tab. In column F enter budget figures that reflect a modest increase from the previous years, and then Save and Close the file.

Open the Lastname_Firstname_11L_Budget file. Change the User name to **Dean Peale** so that you can review all the various changes for the Division Dean. Compare and merge the workbooks. Review the Nursing worksheet. Because the total budget and individual items seem reasonable, no changes are needed for the Nursing budget. Click the Radiology sheet tab. Because the total budget and individual items seem reasonable, no changes are needed for the Radiology budget. Accept all changes in the file and stop sharing the workbook.

Submit as directed by your instructor. Restore the original User name and remove the Compare and Merge Workbooks button from the Quick Access Toolbar.

END | You have completed Project 11L

GO! Think | Project 11M Purchase Orders   **MyITLab**

GO! | Project 11N Class Schedule   **MyITLab**

Appendix

MICROSOFT OFFICE SPECIALIST EXCEL 2016			
Obj Number	Objective text	GO! Activity	Page Number
1.0 Create and Manage Worksheets and Workbooks			
1.1	**Create Worksheets and Workbooks**		
1.1.1	create a workbook	1.01	4
1.1.2	import data from a delimited text file	10.04	604
1.1.3	add a worksheet to an existing workbook	2.30	160
1.1.4	copy and move a worksheet	2.34	163
1.2	**Navigate in Worksheets and Workbooks**		
1.2.1	search for data within a workbook	2.11	136
1.2.2	navigate to a named cell, range, or workbook element	5.03	319
1.2.3	insert and remove hyperlinks	5.09	329
1.3	**Format Worksheets and Workbooks**		
1.3.1	change worksheet tab color	2.21	149
1.3.2	rename a worksheet	2.21	149
1.3.3	change worksheet order	2.34	163
1.3.4	modify page setup	1.14, 1.07	17, 80
1.3.5	insert and delete columns or rows	1.25, 3.17	97, 214
1.3.6	change workbook themes	1.10, 5.05	73, 323
1.3.7	adjust row height and column width	1.26	98
1.3.8	insert headers and footers	1.14	80
1.4	**Customize Options and Views for Worksheets and Workbooks**		
1.4.1	hide or unhide worksheets	10.02	599
1.4.2	hide or unhide columns and rows	5.02, 10.02	318, 599
1.4.3	customize the Quick Access toolbar	OF 1.11, 9.05	26
1.4.4	change workbook views	5.07	326
1.4.5	change window views	2.13, 2.19, 5.04	138, 143, 320
1.4.6	modify document properties	1.15	81
1.4.7	change magnification by using zoom tools	2.18	143
1.4.8	display formulas	1.17	83
1.5	**Configure Worksheets and Workbooks for Distribution**		
1.5.1	set a print area	1.16	82
1.5.2	save workbooks in alternative file formats	5.11–5.13	332, 335, 336
1.5.3	print all or part of a workbook	1.15, 2.35	81, 165
1.5.4	set print scaling	1.17, 2.20	83, 144
1.5.5	display repeating row and column titles on multipage worksheets	2.20, 5.08	144, 328
1.5.6	inspect a workbook for hidden properties or personal information	11.13	666

1.5.7	inspect a workbook for accessibility issues	11.11	664
1.5.8	inspect a workbook for compatibility issues	11.12	665
2.0 Manage Data Cells and Ranges			
2.1	**Insert Data in Cells and Ranges**		
2.1.1	replace data	2.11	136
2.1.2	cut, copy, or paste data	2.24	154
2.1.3	paste data by using special paste options	2.24, 3.16	154, 211
2.1.4	fill cells by using Auto Fill	1.03	63
2.1.5	insert and delete cells	Online Supplemental	
2.2	**Format Cells and Ranges**		
2.2.1	merge cells	1.08	71
2.2.2	modify cell alignment and indentation	10.02	599
2.2.3	format cells by using Format Painter	3.14	209
2.2.4	wrap text within cells	1.26	98
2.2.5	apply number formats	1.09, 1.24	72, 96
2.2.6	apply cell formats	1.05	11
2.2.7	apply cell styles	1.08	71
2.3	**Summarize and Organize Data**		
2.3.1	insert sparklines	1.13, 2.33, 6.01	79, 162, 377
2.3.2	outline data	5.20	351
2.3.3	insert subtotals	5.20	351
2.3.4	apply conditional formatting	2.10	135
3.0 Create Tables			
3.1	**Create and Manage Tables**		
3.1.1	create an Excel table from a cell range	2.14	139
3.1.2	convert a table to a cell range	10.03	602
3.1.3	add or remove table rows and columns	10.03	602
3.2	**Manage Table Styles and Options**		
3.2.1	apply styles to tables	2.14	139
3.2.2	configure table style options	5.06	324
3.2.3	insert total rows	2.16	141
3.3	**Filter and Sort a Table**		
3.3.1	filter records	2.16, 5.16, 5.17	14, 343, 345
3.3.2	sort data by multiple columns	2.15, 5.14	140, 339
3.3.3	change sort order	2.15, 4.10	140, 267
3.3.4	remove duplicate records	10.05	606
4.0 Perform Operations with Formulas and Functions			
4.1	**Summarize Data by using Functions**		
4.1.1	insert references	1.22, 2.31	93, 161

4.1.2	perform calculations by using the SUM function	1.06, 2.03	68, 127
4.1.3	perform calculations by using MIN and MAX functions	2.05	130
4.1.4	perform calculations by using the COUNT function	Online Supplemental	
4.1.5	perform calculations by using the AVERAGE function	2.03	127
4.2	**Perform Conditional Operations by using Functions**		
4.2.1	perform logical operations by using the IF function	2.09	134
4.2.2	perform logical operations by using the SUMIF function	8.13	516
4.2.3	perform logical operations by using the AVERAGEIF function	Online Supplemental	
4.2.4	perform statistical operations by using the COUNTIF function	2.08	133
4.3	**Format and Modify Text by using Functions**		
4.3.1	format text by using RIGHT, LEFT, and MID functions	10.07	608
4.3.2	format text by using UPPER, LOWER, and PROPER functions	10.07	608
4.3.3	format text by using the CONCATENATE function	10.07	608
5.0 Create Charts and Objects			
5.1	**Create Charts**		
5.1.1	create a new chart	1.11, 3.02, 3.17, 6.02, 8.06	74, 193, 214, 378, 500
5.1.2	add additional data series	Online Supplemental	
5.1.3	switch between rows and columns in source data	1.11, 6.03	74, 382
5.1.4	analyze data by using Quick Analysis	1.04, 1.21, 6.01	65, 92, 377
5.2	**Format Charts**		
5.2.1	resize charts	8.06	500
5.2.2	add and modify chart elements	1.12, 3.03, 3.20, 6.05, 6.07, 6.10, 6.11, 8.03, 8.06	76, 194, 221, 384, 386, 388, 390, 495, 500
5.2.3	apply chart layouts and styles	1.12	76
5.2.4	move charts to a chart sheet	3.02, 6.02	193, 378
5.3	**Insert and Format Objects**		
5.3.1	insert text boxes and shapes	8.18	522
5.3.2	insert images	6.21	403
5.3.3	modify object properties	Online Supplemental	
5.3.4	add alternative text to objects for accessibility	11.11	664

Obj Number	Objective text	GO! Activity	Page Number
MICROSOFT OFFICE EXPERT EXCEL 2016			
1.0 Manage Workbook Options and Settings			
1.1	**Manage Workbooks**		
1.1.1	save a workbook as a template	6.23	406
1.1.2	copy macros between workbooks	Online Supplemental	
1.1.3	reference data in another workbook	Online Supplemental	
1.1.4	reference data by using structured references	Online Supplemental	
1.1.5	enable macros in a workbook	9.02	550
1.1.6	display hidden ribbon tabs	9.01	549
1.2	**Manage Workbook Review**		
1.2.1	restrict editing	6.24, 11.14	407, 668
1.2.2	protect a worksheet	6.24	407
1.2.3	configure formula calculation options	Online Supplemental	
1.2.4	protect workbook structure	6.24, 11.14	407, 668
1.2.5	manage workbook versions	Online Supplemental	
1.2.6	encrypt a workbook with a password	6.24	407
2.0 Apply Custom Data Formats and Layouts			
2.1	**Apply Custom Data Formats and Validation**		
2.1.1	create custom number formats	8.01	491
2.1.2	populate cells by using advanced Fill Series options	Online Supplemental	
2.1.3	configure data validation	4.12	272
2.2	**Apply Advanced Conditional Formatting and Filtering**		
2.2.1	create custom conditional formatting rules	2.10	
2.2.2	create conditional formatting rules that use formulas	10.13	620
2.2.3	manage conditional formatting rules	10.13	620
2.3	**Create and Modify Custom Workbook Elements**		
2.3.1	create custom color formats	Online Supplemental	
2.3.2	create and modify cell styles	Online Supplemental	
2.3.3	create and modify custom themes	Online Supplemental	
2.3.4	create and modify simple macros	9.04	552
2.3.5	insert and configure form controls	9.08	561

2.4	**Prepare a Workbook for Internationalization**		
2.4.1	display data in multiple international formats	Online Supplemental	
2.4.2	apply international currency formats	Online Supplemental	
2.4.3	manage multiple options for +Body and +Heading fonts	Online Supplemental	

3.0 Create Advanced Formulas			
3.1	**Apply Functions in Formulas**		
3.1.1	perform logical operations by using AND, OR, and NOT functions	8.16, 8.17	519, 521
3.1.2	perform logical operations by using nested functions	10.03	602
3.1.3	perform statistical operations by using SUMIFS, AVERAGEIFS, and COUNTIFS functions	8.14, 8.15, 8.18	517, 517, 522
3.2	**Look Up Data by using Functions**		
3.2.1	look up data by using the VLOOKUP function	4.10, 4.11	267, 269
3.2.2	look up data by using the HLOOKUP function	Online Supplemental	
3.2.3	look up data by using the MATCH function	Online Supplemental	
3.2.4	look up data by using the INDEX function	Online Supplemental	
3.3	**Apply Advanced Date and Time Functions**		
3.3.1	reference the date and time by using the NOW and TODAY functions	2.12	137
3.3.2	serialize numbers by using date and time functions	Online Supplemental	
3.4	**Perform Data Analysis and Business Intelligence**		
3.4.1	import, transform, combine, display, and connect to data	7.14	461
3.4.2	consolidate data	7.15	464
3.4.3	perform what-if analysis by using Goal Seek and Scenario Manager	4.02, 4.03, 8.10	250, 251, 511
3.4.4	use cube functions to get data out of the Excel data model	Online Supplemental	
3.4.5	calculate data by using financial functions	4.01	247
3.5	**Troubleshoot Formulas**		
3.5.1	trace precedence and dependence	4.13, 4.14, 4.15	275, 280, 282
3.5.2	monitor cells and formulas by using the Watch Window	4.18	286
3.5.3	validate formulas by using error checking rules	4.12, 4.16, 4.17	272, 283, 285
3.5.4	evaluate formulas	4.14	280
3.6	**Define Named Ranges and Objects**		
3.6.1	name cells	4.06	257
3.6.2	name data ranges	4.06, 5.19	257, 350

Glossary

3-D The shortened term for three-dimensional, which refers to an image that appears to have all three spatial dimensions—length, width, and depth.

Absolute cell reference A cell reference that refers to cells by their fixed position in a worksheet; an absolute cell reference remains the same when the formula is copied.

Accessibility Checker An Excel tool that finds any potential accessibility issues and creates a report so that you can resolve the issues to make your file easier for those with disabilities to use.

Accounting Number Format The Excel number format that applies a thousand comma separator where appropriate, inserts a fixed U.S. dollar sign aligned at the left edge of the cell, applies two decimal places, and leaves a small amount of space at the right edge of the cell to accommodate a parenthesis for negative numbers.

Active area The area of the worksheet that contains data or has contained data.

Active cell The cell, surrounded by a border, ready to receive data or be affected by the next Excel command.

ActiveX control A graphic object, such as a check box or button that you place on a form to display or enter data, perform an action, or make the form easier to read. When the person filling in the form clicks the ActiveX control, VBA code runs that automates a task or offers options.

Add-in Optional command or feature that is not immediately available; you must first install and/or activate it to use it.

Advanced filter A filter that can specify three or more criteria for a particular column, apply complex criteria to two or more columns, or specify computed criteria.

Alignment The placement of text or objects relative to the left and right margins.

Alignment guides Green lines that display when you move an object to assist in alignment.

Alternative text Text added to a picture or object that helps people using a screen reader understand what the object is.

Alt text Another name for alternative text.

Alt text Text used in documents and webpages to provide a text description of an image.

And comparison operator The comparison operator that requires each and every one of the comparison criteria to be true.

AND function A logical function that can be used to develop compound logical tests using up to 255 arguments. The function returns a result of TRUE if ALL of the conditions are met.

App A self-contained program usually designed for a single purpose and that runs on smartphones and other mobile devices.

Apps for Office A collection of downloadable apps that enable you to create and view information within Office programs, and that combine cloud services and web technologies within the user interface of Office.

Arguments The values that an Excel function uses to perform calculations or operations.

Arithmetic operators The symbols +, −, *, /, %, and ^ used to denote addition, subtraction (or negation), multiplication, division, percentage, and exponentiation in an Excel formula.

Arrange All The command that tiles all open program windows on the screen.

Ascending The term that refers to the arrangement of text that is sorted alphabetically from A to Z, numbers sorted from lowest to highest, or dates and times sorted from earliest to latest.

Associated PivotTable report The PivotTable in a workbook that is graphically represented in a PivotChart.

Auditing The process of examining a worksheet for errors in formulas.

AutoCalculate A feature that displays three calculations in the status bar by default—Average, Count, and Sum—when you select a range of numerical data.

AutoComplete A feature that speeds your typing and lessens the likelihood of errors; if the first few characters you type in a cell match an existing entry in the column, Excel fills in the remaining characters for you.

Auto Fill An Excel feature that generates and extends values into adjacent cells based on the values of selected cells.

AutoFilter menu A drop-down menu from which you can filter a column by a list of values, by a format, or by criteria.

AutoFit An Excel feature that adjusts the width of a column to fit the cell content of the widest cell in the column.

AutoSum A button that provides quick access to the SUM function.

AVERAGE function An Excel function that adds a group of values, and then divides the result by the number of values in the group.

AVERAGEIFS function A statistical function that enables you to specify multiple criteria when computing an average.

Axis A line that serves as a frame of reference for measurement and that borders the chart plot area.

Background image An image inserted in a worksheet that is behind, not in, the worksheet cells.

Backstage tabs The area along the left side of Backstage view with tabs to display screens with related groups of commands.

Backstage view A centralized space for file management tasks; for example, opening, saving, printing, publishing, or sharing a file. A navigation pane displays along the left side with tabs that group file-related tasks together.

Base The starting point when you divide the amount of increase by it to calculate the rate of increase.

Bevel A shape effect that uses shading and shadows to make the edges of a shape appear to be curved or angled.

Bookmark A command that identifies a word, section, or place in a document so that you can find it quickly without scrolling.

Break-even point The point at which a company starts to make a profit.

Category axis The area along the bottom of a chart that identifies the categories of data; also referred to as the x-axis.

Category labels The labels that display along the bottom of a chart to identify the categories of data; Excel uses the row titles as the category names.

Cell address Another name for a cell reference.

Cell content Anything typed into a cell.

Cell reference The identification of a specific cell by its intersecting column letter and row number.

Cell style A defined set of formatting characteristics, such as font, font size, font color, cell borders, and cell shading.

Cell The intersection of a column and a row.

Center alignment The alignment of text or objects that is centered horizontally between the left and right margin.

Certificate authority A commercial organization that issues digital certificates, keeps track of who is assigned to a certificate, signs certificates to verify their validity, and tracks which certificates are revoked or expired.

Change history Information that is maintained about changes made in past editing sessions.

Chart The graphic representation of data in a worksheet; data presented as a chart is usually easier to understand than a table of numbers.

Chart area The entire chart and all of its elements.

Chart elements Objects that make up a chart.

Chart Elements button A button that enables you to add, remove, or change chart elements such as the title, legend, gridlines, and data labels.

Chart Filters button A button that enables you to change which data displays in the chart.

Chart layout The combination of chart elements that can be displayed in a chart such as a title, legend, labels for the columns, and the table of charted cells.

Chart sheet A workbook sheet that contains only a chart.

Chart style The overall visual look of a chart in terms of its graphic effects, colors, and backgrounds; for example, you can have flat or beveled columns, colors that are solid or transparent, and backgrounds that are dark or light.

Chart Styles button A button that enables you to set a style and color scheme for your chart.

Chart Styles gallery A group of predesigned chart styles that you can apply to an Excel chart.

Chart types Various chart formats used in a way that is meaningful to the reader; common examples are column charts, pie charts, and line charts.

Check Accessibility A command that checks the document for content that people with disabilities might find difficult to read.

Check box A type of ActiveX control that the person filling in the form can select to indicate a choice.

Check Compatibility A command that searches your document for features that may not be supported by older versions of Office.

Clear Filter A button that removes a filter.

Clipboard A temporary storage area that holds text or graphics that you select and then cut or copy.

Cloud computing Applications and services that are accessed over the Internet, rather than accessing applications that are installed on your local computer.

Cloud storage Online storage of data so that you can access your data from different places and devices.

Collaborate To work with others as a team in an intellectual endeavor to complete a shared task or to achieve a shared goal.

Collaboration In Excel, the process of working jointly with others to review, comment on, and make necessary changes to a shared workbook.

Column A vertical group of cells in a worksheet.

Column chart A chart in which the data is arranged in columns and that is useful for showing data changes over a period of time or for illustrating comparisons among items

Column heading The letter that displays at the top of a vertical group of cells in a worksheet; beginning with the first letter of the alphabet, a unique letter or combination of letters identifies each column.

COLUMNS area An area to position fields that you want to display as columns in the PivotTable. Field names placed here become column titles, and the data is grouped in columns by these titles.

Comma delimited file A file type that saves the contents of the cells by placing commas between them and an end-of-paragraph mark at the end of each row; also referred to as a CSV (comma separated values) file.

Commands Instructions to a computer program that cause an action to be carried out.

Comma Style The Excel number format that inserts thousand comma separators where appropriate and applies two decimal places; Comma Style also leaves space at the right to accommodate a parenthesis when negative numbers are present.

Comparison operators Symbols that evaluate each value to determine if it is the same (=), greater than (>), less than (<), or in between a range of values as specified by the criteria.

Compatibility Checker An Excel tool that finds any potential compatibility issues that might cause a significant loss of functionality or a minor loss of fidelity in an earlier version of Excel, and creates a report so that you can resolve the issues.

Compatibility Mode Using a workbook in Excel 97-2003 file format (.xls) instead of the newer XML-based file format (.xlsx).

Compound criteria The use of two or more criteria on the same row— all conditions must be met for the records to be included in the results.

Compound filter A filter that uses more than one condition—and one that uses comparison operators.

Compressed file A file that has been reduced in size and thus takes up less storage space and can be transferred to other computers quickly.

CONCATENATE A text function used to join up to 255 strings of characters.

Conditional format A format that changes the appearance of a cell— for example, by adding cell shading or font color—based on a condition; if the condition is true, the cell is formatted based on that condition, and if the condition is false, the cell is not formatted.

Conditional formatting A format that changes the appearance of a cell—for example, by adding cell shading or font color—based on a condition; if the condition is true, the cell is formatted based on that condition, and if the condition is false, the cell is not formatted.

Constant value Numbers, text, dates, or times of day that you type into a cell.

Constraint cell In Solver, a cell that contains a value that limits or restricts the outcome.

Constraint In Solver, a condition or restriction that must be met.

Content app An app for Office that integrates web-based features as content within the body of a document.

Context-sensitive commands Commands that display on a shortcut menu that relate to the object or text that you right-clicked.

Context menus Menus that display commands and options relevant to the selected text or object; also called shortcut menus.

Context sensitive A command associated with the currently selected or active object; often activated by right-clicking a screen item.

Contextual tabs Tabs that are added to the ribbon automatically when a specific object, such as a picture, is selected, and that contain commands relevant to the selected object.

Copy A command that duplicates a selection and places it on the Clipboard.

COUNT function A statistical function that counts the number of cells in a range that contains numbers.

COUNTIF function A logical function that counts the cells that meet specific criteria in a specified range.

COUNTIF function A statistical function that counts the number of cells within a range that meet the given condition and that has two arguments— the range of cells to check and the criteria.

COUNTIFS function A logical function that counts the cells that meet specific criteria in multiple ranges.

Create from Selection A command by which you can name a cell range based on existing row or column titles.

Creative Commons A nonprofit organization that enables sharing and use of images and knowledge through free legal tools.

Criteria Conditions that you specify in a logical function.

Criteria Conditions that you specify in a logical function or filter.

Criteria range An area on your worksheet where you define the criteria for the filter, and that indicates how the displayed records are filtered.

CSV (comma separated values) file A file type in which the cells in each row are separated by commas and an end-of-paragraph mark at the end of each row; also referred to as a comma delimited file.

Custom filter A filter with which you can apply complex criteria to a single column.

Custom list A sort order that you can define.

Cut A command that removes a selection and places it on the Clipboard.

Cycle A category of SmartArt graphics that illustrates a continual process.

Data Facts about people, events, things, or ideas.

Data bar A cell format consisting of a shaded bar that provides a visual cue to the reader about the value of a cell relative to other cells; the length of the bar represents the value in the cell—a longer bar represents a higher value and a shorter bar represents a lower value.

Data connection A link to external data that automatically updates an Excel workbook from the original data whenever the original data source gets new information.

Data labels Labels that display the value, percentage, and/or category of each particular data point and can contain one or more of the choices listed—Series name, Category name, Value, or Percentage.

Data marker A column, bar, area, dot, pie slice, or other symbol in a chart that represents a single data point; related data points form a data series.

Data Model A method of incorporating data from multiple, related tables into an Excel worksheet.

Data point A value that originates in a worksheet cell and that is represented in a chart by a data marker.

Data series Related data points represented by data markers; each data series has a unique color or pattern represented in the chart legend.

Data table A range of cells that shows how changing certain values in your formulas affect the results of those formulas and that makes it easy to calculate multiple versions in one operation.

Data validation A technique by which you can control the type of data or the values that are entered into a cell by limiting the acceptable values to a defined list.

Database An organized collection of facts related to a specific topic or purpose.

DAVERAGE function A function that determines an average in a database that is limited by criteria set for one or more cells.

DCOUNT function A function that counts the number of occurrences of a specified condition in a database.

Decision variable In Solver, cell in which the value will change to achieve the desired results.

Default The term that refers to the current selection or setting that is automatically used by a computer program unless you specify otherwise.

Defined name A word or string of characters in Excel that represents a cell, a range of cells, a formula, or a constant value; also referred to as simply a name.

Delimited A text file in which the text is separated by commas or tabs.

Dependent cells Cells that contain formulas that refer to other cells.

Descending The term that refers to the arrangement of text that is sorted alphabetically from Z to A, numbers sorted from highest to lowest, or dates and times sorted from latest to earliest.

Deselect The action of canceling the selection of an object or block of text by clicking outside of the selection.

Design Mode An Excel feature in which you can add and modify ActiveX controls.

Desktop app A computer program that is installed on your PC and requires a computer operating system such as Microsoft Windows; also known as a desktop application.

Detail data The subtotaled rows that are totaled and summarized; typically adjacent to and either above or to the left of the summary data.

Detail sheet The worksheets that contain the details of the information summarized on a summary sheet.

Dialog Box Launcher A small icon that displays to the right of some group names on the ribbon and that opens a related dialog box or pane providing additional options and commands related to that group.

Digital certificate An electronic means of proving identity issued by a certificate authority.

Digital signature An electronic, encrypted, stamp of authentication. A means of proving identity and authenticity that ensures that a file originated from the signer and has not been changed.

Displayed value The data that displays in a cell.

Document Inspector An Excel feature that can find and remove hidden properties and personal information in a workbook.

Document properties Details about a file that describe or identify it, including the title, author name, subject, and keywords that identify the document's topic or contents; also known as metadata.

Drag The action of holding down the left mouse button while moving your mouse.

Drag and drop The action of moving a selection by dragging it to a new location.

DSUM function A function that sums a column of values in a database that is limited by criteria set for one or more cells.

Dual-axis chart A chart that has one series plotted on a secondary axis. Useful when comparing data series that use different scales or different types of measurements.

Edit The process of making changes to text or graphics in an Office file.

Ellipsis A set of three dots indicating incompleteness; an ellipsis following a command name indicates that a dialog box will display if you click the command.

Embed The action of inserting something created in one program into another program.

Embedded chart A chart that is inserted into the same worksheet that contains the data used to create the chart.

Encryption The process by which a file is encoded so that it cannot be opened without the proper password.

Enhanced ScreenTip A ScreenTip that displays more descriptive text than a normal ScreenTip.

Enterprise fund A municipal government fund that reports income and expenditures related to municipal services for which a fee is charged in exchange for goods or services.

Error Checking command A command that checks for common errors that occur in formulas.

Error value The result of a formula that Excel cannot evaluate correctly.

Event The action that causes a program or macro to run, such as clicking a button or a command or pressing a combination of keys.

Excel pointer An Excel window element with which you can display the location of the pointer.

Excel table A series of rows and columns that contains related data that is managed independently from the data in other rows and columns in the worksheet.

Expand Formula Bar button An Excel window element with which you can increase the height of the Formula Bar to display lengthy cell content.

Expand horizontal scroll bar button An Excel window element with which you can increase the width of the horizontal scroll bar.

Explode The action of pulling out one or more pie slices from a pie chart for emphasis.

Extensible Markup Language (XML) A language that structures data in text files so that it can be read by other systems, regardless of the hardware platform or operating system.

Extract The process of pulling out multiple sets of data for comparison purposes.

Extract area The location to which you copy records when extracting filtered rows.

Field A specific type of data such as name, employee number, or social security number that is stored in columns; or, a single piece of information for every record.

Field button A button on a PivotChart with an arrow to choose a filter, and thus change the data that is displayed in the chart.

Field names The column titles from source data that form the categories of data for a PivotTable.

Field section The upper portion of the PivotTable Fields pane containing the fields—column titles—from your source data; use this area to add fields to and remove fields from the PivotTable.

Fill The inside color of an object.

Fill handle The small square in the lower right corner of a selected cell.

Filter The process of displaying only a portion of the data based on matching a specific value to show only the data that meets the criteria that you specify.

Filtering A process in which only the rows that meet the criteria display; rows that do not meet the criteria are hidden.

Filtering button A button on a slicer used to select the item by which to filter.

Filtering controls The arrows that display in the column titles of Excel data when the data is converted to a table and than enable you to sort and filter the data.

FILTERS area An area in the lower portion of the PivotTable Fields pane to position fields by which you want to filter the PivotTable, enabling you to display a subset of data in the PivotTable report.

Financial functions Pre-built formulas that perform common business calculations such as calculating a loan payment on a vehicle or calculating how much to save each month to buy something; financial functions commonly involve a period of time such as months or years.

Find A command that locates and selects specific text or formatting.

Find and Replace A command that searches the cells in a worksheet—or in a selected range—for matches and then replaces each match with a replacement value of your choice.

Fixed expense Expense that remains the same each month regardless of the amount of activity.

Flash Fill An Excel feature that predicts how to alter data based upon the pattern you enter into the cell at the beginning of the column. The data must be in the adjacent column to use Flash Fill.

Font A set of characters with the same design and shape.

Font styles Formatting emphasis such as bold, italic, and underline.

Footer A reserved area for text or graphics that displays at the bottom of each page in a document.

Forecast A prediction of the future, often based on past performances.

Form An Excel worksheet or object containing fields and controls that enable a user to easily enter or edit data.

Form control A graphic object that does not require VBA code. A Form control is compatible with versions of Excel that do not support ActiveX.

Format Changing the appearance of cells and worksheet elements to make a worksheet attractive and easy to read.

Formatting The process of establishing the overall appearance of text, graphics, and pages in an Office file—for example, in a Word document.

Formatting marks Characters that display on the screen, but do not print, indicating where the Enter key, the Spacebar, and the Tab key were pressed; also called nonprinting characters.

Formula An equation that performs mathematical calculations on values in a worksheet.

Formula Auditing Tools and commands accessible from the Formulas tab that help you check your worksheet for errors.

Formula AutoComplete An Excel feature which, after typing an = (equal sign) and the beginning letter or letters of a function name, displays a list of function names that match the typed letter(s).

Formula Bar An element in the Excel window that displays the value or formula contained in the active cell; here you can also enter or edit values or formulas.

Freeze Panes A command that enables you to select one or more rows or columns and freeze (lock) them into place so that they remain on the screen while you scroll; the locked rows and columns become separate panes.

Function A predefined formula—a formula that Excel has already built for you—that performs calculations by using specific values in a particular order or structure.

Fund A sum of money set aside for a specific purpose.

Future value (Fv) The value at the end of the time period in an Excel function; the cash balance you want to attain after the last payment is made—usually zero for loans.

Gallery An Office feature that displays a list of potential results instead of just the command name.

General format The default format that Excel applies to numbers; this format has no specific characteristics—whatever you type in the cell will display, with the exception that trailing zeros to the right of a decimal point will not display.

General fund The term used to describe money set aside for the normal operating activities of a government entity such as a city.

Get External Data A group of commands that enables you to bring data from an Access database, from the Web, from a text file, or from an XML file into Excel without repeatedly copying the data.

Goal Seek One of Excel's What-If Analysis tools that provides a method to find a specific value for a cell by adjusting the value of one other cell—find the right input when you know the result you want.

Go To A command that moves to a specific cell or range of cells that you specify.

Go To Special A command that moves to cells that have special characteristics, for example, to cells that are blank or to cells that contain constants, as opposed to formulas.

Gradient fill A fill effect in which one color fades into another.

Gridlines Lines in the plot area that aid the eye in determining the plotted values.

Groups On the Office ribbon, the sets of related commands that you might need for a specific type of task.

Header A reserved area for text or graphics that displays at the top of each page in a document.

Hierarchy A category of SmartArt graphics used to create an organization chart or show a decision tree.

HLOOKUP An Excel function that looks up values that are displayed horizontally in a row.

Horizontal Category axis (x-axis) The area along the bottom of a chart that identifies the categories of data; also referred to as the x-axis.

HTML (Hypertext Markup Language) A language web browsers can interpret.

Hyperlink Text or graphics that, when clicked, take you to another location in the worksheet, to another file, or to a webpage on the Internet or on your organization's intranet.

Icon set A set of three, four, or five small graphic images that make your data visually easier to interpret.

IF function A function that uses a logical test to check whether a condition is met, and then returns one value if true, and another value if false.

Information Data that has been organized in a useful manner.

Info tab The tab in Backstage view that displays information about the current file.

Insertion point A blinking vertical line that indicates where text or graphics will be inserted.

Inspect Document A command that searches your document for hidden data or personal information that you might not want to share publicly.

Integer A whole number.

Interest The amount charged for the use of borrowed money.

Interval The number of cells to include in the average.

Intranet A network within an organization and that uses Internet technologies.

Keyboard shortcut A combination of two or more keyboard keys, used to perform a task that would otherwise require a mouse.

KeyTip The letter that displays on a command in the ribbon and that indicates the key you can press to activate the command when keyboard control of the Ribbon is activated.

Keywords Custom file properties in the form of words that you associate with a document to give an indication of the document's content; used to help find and organize files. Also called tags.

Labels Column and row headings that describe the values and help the reader understand the chart; or, another name for a text value, and which usually provides information about number values.

Landscape orientation A page orientation in which the paper is wider than it is tall.

Layout Options A button that displays when an object is selected and that has commands to choose how the object interacts with surrounding text.

Layout section The lower portion of the PivotTable Fields pane containing the four areas for layout; use this area to rearrange and reposition fields in the PivotTable.

LEFT A text function that returns the specified number of character from the beginning (left) of a string of characters.

Left alignment The cell format in which characters align at the left edge of the cell; this is the default for text entries and is an example of formatting information stored in a cell.

Legend A chart element that identifies the patterns or colors that are assigned to the categories in the chart.

Lettered column headings The area along the top edge of a worksheet that identifies each column with a unique letter or combination of letters.

Line chart A chart type that is useful to display trends over time; time displays along the bottom axis and the data point values are connected with a line.

List A series of rows that contains related data that you can group by adding subtotals.

Live Preview A technology that shows the result of applying an editing or formatting change as you point to possible results—before you actually apply it.

Location Any disk drive, folder, or other place in which you can store files and folders.

Locked [cells] In a protected worksheet, data cannot be inserted, modified, deleted, or formatted in these cells.

Logical functions A group of functions that test for specific conditions and that typically use conditional tests to determine whether specified conditions are true or false.

Logical test Any value or expression that can be evaluated as being true or false.

Lookup functions A group of Excel functions that look up a value in a defined range of cells located in another part of the workbook to find a corresponding value.

LOWER A text function that changes the case of the characters in a string, making all characters lowercase.

Macro An action or a set of actions with which you can automate tasks by grouping a series of commands into a single command.

Macro virus Unauthorized programming code in a macro that erases or damages files.

Mail app An app for Office that displays next to an Outlook item.

Major sort A term sometimes used to refer to the first sort level in the Sort dialog box.

Major unit The value in a chart's value axis that determines the spacing between tick marks and between the gridlines in the plot area.

Major unit value A number that determines the spacing between tick marks and between the gridlines in the plot area.

Mark as Final command Prevents additional changes to the document and disables typing, editing comments, and proofing marks.

Matrix A category of SmartArt graphics used to show how parts relate to a whole.

MAX function An Excel function that determines the largest value in a selected range of values.

MEDIAN function An Excel function that finds the middle value that has as many values above it in the group as are below it; it differs from AVERAGE in that the result is not affected as much by a single value that is greatly different from the others.

Merge & Center A command that joins selected cells in an Excel worksheet into one larger cell and centers the contents in the merged cell.

Metadata Details about a file that describe or identify it, including the title, author name, subject, and keywords that identify the document's topic or contents; also known as document properties.

Microsoft Access A database program used to manage database files.

MID A text function that extracts a series of characters from a text string given the location of the beginning character.

MIN function An Excel function that determines the smallest value in a selected range of values.

Mini toolbar A small toolbar containing frequently used formatting commands that displays as a result of selecting text or objects.

Module The place where the Visual Basic for Applications (VBA) programming code is stored.

Moving average A sequence of averages computed from parts of a data series.

MRU Acronym for most recently used, which refers to the state of some commands that retain the characteristic most recently applied; for example, the Font Color button retains the most recently used color until a new color is chosen.

Name A word or string of characters in Excel that represents a cell, a range of cells, a formula, or a constant value; also referred to as a defined name.

Name Box An element of the Excel window that displays the name of the selected cell, table, chart, or object.

Navigate The process of moving within a worksheet or workbook.

Nested function A function that is contained inside another function. The inner function is evaluated first and the result becomes the argument for the outer function.

Nonprinting characters Characters that display on the screen, but do not print, indicating where the Enter key, the Spacebar, and the Tab key were pressed; also called formatting marks.

Normal view A screen view that maximizes the number of cells visible on your screen and keeps the column letters and row numbers close to the columns and rows.

NOT function A logical function that takes only one argument and is used to test one condition. If the condition is true, the function returns the logical opposite false. If the condition is false, true is returned.

NOW function An Excel function that retrieves the date and time from your computer's calendar and clock and inserts the information into the selected cell.

Nper The abbreviation for number of time periods in various Excel functions.

Numbered row headings The area along the left edge of a worksheet that identifies each row with a unique number.

Number format A specific way in which Excel displays numbers in a cell.

Number values Constant values consisting of only numbers.

Object A text box, picture, table, or shape that you can select and then move and resize.

Objective cell In Solver, a cell that contains a formula for the results you are trying to determine.

Office 365 A version of Microsoft Office to which you subscribe for an annual fee.

Office Store A public marketplace that Microsoft hosts and regulates on Office.com.

One-variable Data table A data table that changes the value in only one cell.

OneDrive Microsoft's free cloud storage for anyone with a free Microsoft account.

Open dialog box A dialog box from which you can navigate to, and then open on your screen, an existing file that was created in that same program.

Operators The symbols with which you can specify the type of calculation you want to perform in an Excel formula.

Option button In a dialog box, a round button that enables you to make one choice among two or more options.

Options dialog box A dialog box within each Office application where you can select program settings and other options and preferences.

Or comparison operator The comparison operator that requires only one of the two comparison criteria that you specify to be true.

OR function A logical function that can be used to develop compound logical tests using up to 255 arguments. The function returns a value of TRUE if ANY of the conditions are met.

Order of operations The mathematical rules for performing multiple calculations within a formula.

Organization chart A type of graphic that is useful to depict reporting relationships within an organization.

Page Width A view that zooms the document so that the width of the page matches the width of the window. Find this command on the View tab, in the Zoom group.

Pane A portion of a worksheet window bounded by and separated from other portions by vertical and horizontal bars.

Paragraph symbol The symbol ¶ that represents the end of a paragraph.

Password An optional element of a template added to prevent someone from disabling a worksheet's protection.

Paste The action of placing cell contents that have been copied or moved to the Clipboard into another location.

Paste area The target destination for data that has been cut or copied using the Office Clipboard.

Paste Options gallery A gallery of buttons that provides a Live Preview of all the Paste options available in the current context.

PDF (Portable Document Format) A file format developed by Adobe Systems that creates a representation of electronic paper that displays your data on the screen as it would look when printed, but that cannot be easily changed.

PDF The acronym for Portable Document Format, which is a file format that creates an image that preserves the look of your file, but that cannot be easily changed; a popular format for sending documents electronically, because the document will display on most computers.

Percent for new value = base percent + percent of increase The formula for calculating a percentage by which a value increases by adding the base percentage—usually 100%—to the percent increase.

Percentage rate of increase The percent by which one number increases over another number.

Picture A category of SmartArt graphics that is used to display pictures in a diagram.

Picture element A point of light measured in dots per square inch on a screen; 64 pixels equals 8.43 characters, which is the average number of characters that will fit in a cell in an Excel worksheet using the default font.

Pie chart A chart that shows the relationship of each part to a whole.

PivotChart A graphical representation of the data in a PivotTable.

PivotTable An interactive Excel report that summarizes and analyzes large amounts of data.

PivotTable Fields pane A window that lists at the top, all of the fields—column titles—from the source data for use in the PivotTable and at the bottom, an area in which you can arrange the fields in the PivotTable.

Pixel The abbreviated name for a picture element.

Plot area The area bounded by the axes of a chart, including all the data series.

PMT function An Excel function that calculates the payment for a loan based on constant payments and a constant interest rate.

Point and click method The technique of constructing a formula by pointing to and then clicking cells; this method is convenient when the referenced cells are not adjacent to one another.

Pointer Any symbol that displays on your screen in response to moving your mouse.

Points A measurement of the size of a font; there are 72 points in an inch.

Portable Document Format A file format that creates an image that preserves the look of your file, but that cannot be easily changed; a popular format for sending documents electronically, because the document will display on most computers; also called a PDF.

Portrait orientation A page orientation in which the paper is taller than it is wide.

Precedent cells Cells that are referred to by a formula in another cell.

Present value (Pv) The total amount that a series of future payments is worth now; also known as the principal.

Primary key The field used to uniquely identify a record in an Access table.

Principal The total amount that a series of future payments is worth now; also known as the Present value (Pv).

Print Preview A view of a document as it will appear when you print it.

Print Titles An Excel command that enables you to specify rows and columns to repeat on each printed page.

Procedure A unit of computer code that performs an action.

Process A category of SmartArt graphics that is used to show steps in a process or timeline.

PROPER A text function that capitalizes the first letter of each word.

Properties The details about a file that describe or identify the file, including the title, author name, subject, and tags that identify the file's topic or contents. Also known as metadata.

Property A characteristic of an object that can be changed.

Protected View A security feature in Office 2016 that protects your computer from malicious files by opening them in a restricted environment until you enable them; you might encounter this feature if you open a file from an e-mail or download files from the Internet.

Protection A feature that prevents anyone from altering the formulas or changing other template components.

pt The abbreviation for point; for example, when referring to a font size.

Pyramid A category of SmartArt graphics that uses a series of pictures to show relationships.

Query A process of restricting records through the use of criteria conditions that will display records that will answer a question about the data.

Quick Access Toolbar In an Office program window, the small row of buttons in the upper left corner of the screen from which you can perform frequently used commands.

Quick Analysis Tool A tool that displays in the lower right corner of a selected range, with which you can analyze your data by using Excel tools such as charts, color-coding, and formulas.

Range Two or more selected cells on a worksheet that are adjacent or nonadjacent; because the range is treated as a single unit, you can make the same changes or combination of changes to more than one cell at a time.

Range finder An Excel feature that outlines cells in color to indicate which cells are used in a formula; useful for verifying which cells are referenced in a formula.

Rate In the Excel PMT function, the term used to indicate the interest rate for a loan.

Rate = amount of increase/base The mathematical formula to calculate a rate of increase.

Read-only A property assigned to a file that prevents the file from being modified or deleted; it indicates that you cannot save any changes to the displayed document unless you first save it with a new name.

Recommended Charts An Excel feature that displays a customized set of charts that, according to Excel's calculations, will best fit your data based on the range of data that you select.

Record All of the categories of data pertaining to one person, place, event, thing, or idea.

Record Macro A command that records your actions in Visual Basic for Applications (VBA).

Refresh The command to update a worksheet to reflect the new data.

Relationship An association between tables of data that share a common field; or, a category of SmartArt graphics that is used to illustrate connections.

Relative cell reference In a formula, the address of a cell based on the relative positions of the cell that contains the formula and the cell referred to in the formula.

RIGHT A text function that returns the specified number of characters from the end (right) of a string of characters.

Right-click The action of clicking the right mouse button one time.

Rotation handle A circle that displays on the top side of a selected object used to rotate the object up to 360 degrees.

Rounding A procedure in which you determine which digit at the right of the number will be the last digit displayed and then increase it by one if the next digit to its right is 5, 6, 7, 8, or 9.

Row A horizontal group of cells in a worksheet.

Row heading The numbers along the left side of an Excel worksheet that designate the row numbers.

ROWS area An area to position fields that you want to display as rows in the PivotTable. Field names placed here become row titles, and the data is grouped by these row titles.

Sans serif font A font design with no lines or extensions on the ends of characters.

Scale The range of numbers in the data series that controls the minimum, maximum, and incremental values on the value axis.

Scale to Fit Excel commands that enable you to stretch or shrink the width, height, or both of printed output to fit a maximum number of pages.

Scaling The group of commands by which you can reduce the horizontal and vertical size of the printed data by a percentage or by the number of pages that you specify.

Scenario A set of values that Excel saves and can substitute automatically in your worksheet.

Scenario Manager A what-if analysis tool that compares alternatives.

Scope The location within which a defined name is recognized without qualification—usually either to a specific worksheet or to the entire workbook.

Screen reader Software that enables visually impaired users to read text on a computer screen to understand the content of pictures.

ScreenTip A small box that that displays useful information when you perform various mouse actions such as pointing to screen elements or dragging.

Select All box A box in the upper left corner of the worksheet grid that, when clicked, selects all the cells in a worksheet.

Selecting Highlighting, by dragging with your mouse, areas of text or data or graphics, so that the selection can be edited, formatted, copied, or moved.

Self-signed A project signed with a certificate that you create yourself.

Series A group of things that come one after another in succession; for example, January, February, March, and so on.

Serif font A font design that includes small line extensions on the ends of the letters to guide the eye in reading from left to right.

Share button Opens the Share pane from which you can save your file to the cloud—your OneDrive—and then share it with others so you can collaborate.

Shared workbook A workbook set up to allow multiple users on a network to view and make changes to the workbook at the same time.

SharePoint Collaboration software with which people in an organization can set up team sites to share information, manage documents, and publish reports for others to see.

Sheet tab scrolling buttons Buttons to the left of the sheet tabs used to display Excel sheet tabs that are not in view; used when there are more sheet tabs than will display in the space provided.

Sheet tabs The labels along the lower border of the workbook window that identify each worksheet.

Shortcut menu A menu that displays commands and options relevant to the selected text or object; also called a context menu.

Show Formulas A command that displays the formula in each cell instead of the resulting value.

Signature line Specifies the individual who must sign the document.

Sizing handles Small squares or circles that indicate a picture or object is selected.

Slicer Easy-to-use filtering control with buttons that enable you to drill down through large amounts of data.

Slicer header The top of a slicer that indicates the category of the slicer items.

SmartArt graphic A visual representation of information and ideas.

Solver A what-if analysis tool with which you can find an optimal (maximum or minimum) value for a formula in one cell—referred to as the objective cell—subject to constraints, or limits, on the values of other formula cells on a worksheet.

Sort dialog box A dialog box in which you can sort data based on several criteria at once, and that enables a sort by more than one column or row.

Sort The process of arranging data in a specific order based on the value in each field.

Source data The data for a PivotTable, formatted in columns and rows, that can be located in an Excel worksheet or an external source.

Sparkline A tiny chart in the background of a cell that gives a visual trend summary alongside your data; makes a pattern more obvious.

Split The command that enables you to view separate parts of the same worksheet on your screen; splits the window into multiple resizable panes to view distant parts of the worksheet at one time.

Split button A button divided into two parts and in which clicking the main part of the button performs a command and clicking the arrow opens a menu with choices.

Spreadsheet Another name for a worksheet.

Standardization All forms created within the organization will have a uniform appearance; the data will always be organized in the same manner.

Statistical functions Excel functions, including the AVERAGE, MEDIAN, MIN, and MAX functions, which are useful to analyze a group of measurements.

Status bar The area along the lower edge of the Excel window that displays, on the left side, the current cell mode, page number, and worksheet information; on the right side, when numerical data is selected, common calculations such as Sum and Average display.

Style A group of formatting commands, such as font, font size, font color, paragraph alignment, and line spacing that can be applied to a paragraph with one command.

Sub Short for a sub procedure.

Sub procedure A unit of computer code that performs an action.

Subtotal command The command that totals several rows of related data together by automatically inserting subtotals and totals for the selected cells.

SUM function A predefined formula that adds all the numbers in a selected range of cells.

SUMIF function A logical function that contains one logic test—it will add values in a specified range that meet a certain conditions or criteria.

SUMIFS function A logical function that will add values in multiple ranges that meet multiple criteria.

Summary sheet A worksheet where totals from other worksheets are displayed and summarized.

Switch Row/Column A charting command to swap the data over the axis—data being charted on the vertical axis will move to the horizontal axis and vice versa.

Synchronization The process of updating computer files that are in two or more locations according to specific rules—also called syncing.

Syncing The process of updating computer files that are in two or more locations according to specific rules—also called synchronization.

Syntax The arrangement of the arguments in a function.

Tab delimited text file A file type in which cells are separated by tabs; this type of file can be readily exchanged with various database programs.

Table Data stored in a format of rows and columns.

Table array A defined range of cells, arranged in a column or a row, used in a VLOOKUP or HLOOKUP function.

Tabs (ribbon) On the Office ribbon, the name of each task-oriented activity area.

Tags Custom file properties in the form of words that you associate with a document to give an indication of the document's content; used to help find and organize files. Also called keywords.

Task pane app An app for Office that works side-by-side with an Office document by displaying a separate pane on the right side of the window.

Tell Me A search feature for Microsoft Office commands that you activate by typing what you are looking for in the Tell Me box.

Tell me more A prompt within a ScreenTip that opens the Office online Help system with explanations about how to perform the command referenced in the ScreenTip.

Template A special workbook that may include formatting, formulas, and other elements and is used as a pattern for creating other workbooks.

Text function A function that can be used to combine or separate data, change case, and apply formatting to a string of characters.

Text Pane A window that displays to the left of the SmartArt graphic, is populated with placeholder text, and is used to build a graphic by entering and editing text.

Text values Constant values consisting of only text, and which usually provide information about number values; also referred to as labels.

Theme A predesigned combination of colors, fonts, and effects that looks good together and is applied to an entire document by a single selection.

Tick mark labels Identifying information for a tick mark generated from the cells on the worksheet used to create the chart.

Tick marks The short lines that display on an axis at regular intervals.

Title bar The bar at the top edge of the program window that indicates the name of the current file and the program name.

Toggle button A button that can be turned on by clicking it once, and then turned off by clicking it again.

Toolbar In a folder window, a row of buttons with which you can perform common tasks, such as changing the view of your files and folders.

Trace Dependents command A command that displays arrows that indicate what cells are affected by the value of the currently selected cell.

Trace Error command A tool that helps locate and resolve an error by tracing the selected error value.

Trace Precedents command A command that displays arrows to indicate what cells affect the value of the cell that is selected.

Tracer arrow An indicator that shows the relationship between the active cell and its related cell.

Track Changes An Excel feature that logs details about workbook changes including insertions and deletions.

Transpose To switch the data in rows and columns.

Trendline A graphic representation of trends in a data series, such as a line sloping upward to represent increased sales over a period of months.

TRIM A text function that removes extra blank spaces from a string of characters.

Triple-click The action of clicking the left mouse button three times in rapid succession.

Trusted Documents A security feature in Office that remembers which files you have already enabled; you might encounter this feature if you open a file from an e-mail or download files from the Internet.

Two-variable Data table A data table that changes the values in two cells.

Type argument An optional argument in the PMT function that assumes that the payment will be made at the end of each time period.

Underlying formula The formula entered in a cell and visible only on the Formula Bar.

Underlying value The data that displays in the Formula Bar.

Unlocked [cells] Cells in a protected worksheet that may be filled in.

UPPER A text function that changes the case of the characters in a string, making all characters uppercase.

Validation list A list of values that are acceptable for a group of cells; only values on the list are valid and any value not on the list is considered invalid.

Value Another name for a constant value.

Value after increase = base x percent for new value The formula for calculating the value after an increase by multiplying the original value—the base—by the percent for new value (see the Percent for new value formula).

Value axis A numerical scale on the left side of a chart that shows the range of numbers for the data points; also referred to as the y-axis.

VALUES area An area to position fields that contain data that is summarized in a PivotTable or PivotChart. The data placed here is usually numeric or financial in nature and the data is summarized—summed. You can also perform other basic calculations such as finding the average, the minimum, or the maximum.

Variable cell In Solver, cell in which the value will change to achieve the desired results.

Variable expense Expense that varies depending on the amount of sales.

VBA The abbreviation for the Visual Basic for Applications programming language.

VBA construct An instruction that enables a macro to perform multiple operations on a single object.

Vertical Value axis (y-axis) A numerical scale on the left side of a chart that shows the range of numbers for the data points; also referred to as the y-axis.

Visual Basic Editor The window in which you can view and edit Visual Basic code.

Visual Basic for Applications The programming language used to write computer programs in the Microsoft Windows environment.

VLOOKUP An Excel function that looks up values that are displayed vertically in a column.

Volatile A term used to describe an Excel function that is subject to change each time the workbook is reopened; for example, the NOW function updates itself to the current date and time each time the workbook is opened.

Walls and floor The areas surrounding a 3-D chart that give dimension and boundaries to the chart.

Watch Window A window that displays the results of specified cells.

Watermark A faded image or text used as a background of a document

What-If Analysis The process of changing the values in cells to see how those changes affect the outcome of formulas in a worksheet.

Wildcard A character, for example the asterisk or question mark, used to search a field when you are uncertain of the exact value or when you want to widen the search to include more records.

Windows apps An app that runs on all Windows device families—including PCs, Windows phones, Windows tablets, and the Xbox gaming system.

WordArt An Office feature in Word, Excel, and PowerPoint that enables you to change normal text into decorative stylized text.

Workbook An Excel file that contains one or more worksheets.

Worksheet The primary document that you use in Excel to work with and store data, and which is formatted as a pattern of uniformly spaced horizontal and vertical lines.

Worksheet grid area A part of the Excel window that displays the columns and rows that intersect to form the worksheet's cells.

X-axis Another name for the horizontal (category) axis.

.xlsx file name extension The default file format used by Excel 2016 to save an Excel workbook.

XML Paper Specification A Microsoft file format that creates an image of your document and that opens in the XPS viewer.

XPS The acronym for XML Paper Specification—a Microsoft file format that creates an image of your document and that opens in the XPS viewer.

Y-axis Another name for the vertical (value) axis.

Zoom The action of increasing or decreasing the size of the viewing area on the screen.

Index